Sex, Power, & the Violent School Girl

Sibylle Artz

 Teachers College
Columbia University
New York and London

First published in Canada in 1998 by Trifolium Books.

Published in the United States of America in 1999 by Teachers College Press, 1234 Amsterdam Avenue, New York, NY 10027

Trifolium Books Inc. acknowledges with gratitude the generous support of the Government of Canada's Publishing Industry Development Program (BPIDP) in the production of this book.

Editing/Design/Desktop publishing: Francine Geraci
Cover photo: First Light

Library of Congress Cataloging-in-Publication Data

Artz, Sibylle, 1949–
    Sex, power, & the violent school girl / Sibylle Artz.
        p.   cm.
    Originally published: Toronto: Trifolium Books, 1998.
    Includes bibliographical references (p.) and index.
    ISBN 0-8077-3854-9 (pbk.)
    1. School violence—Canada—Case studies.   2. Violence in women—Canada—
Case studies.   3. Female juvenile delinquents—Canada—Case studies.   4. Female
juvenile deliquents—Social conditions—Canada.   I. Title.   II. Title: Sex, power and
the violent school girl.
LB3013.3.A78   1999
373. 15'8'0971—dc21   98-32007

ISBN 0-8077-3854-9   (paper)

Printed and bound in Canada

06   05   04   03   02   01   00   99   8   7   6   5   4   3   2   1

Contents

Dedication

This book is dedicated to my parents, Cornelia and Eric Artz, who showed me that it is possible to do the seemingly impossible and still find time to laugh.

Acknowledgments

This book could not have been written without the participation, expertise and goodwill of key people.

To those who participated in this study, I would like to express my heartfelt thanks. Had you not been as willing as you were to talk openly about your sometimes painful and difficult experiences, all those who read this book, and I, would never have been able to learn from the insights you so freely shared. I believe it takes a special kind of courage to give of oneself in the way that you have. I deeply respect and appreciate what you have done.

Next, I wish to acknowledge and thank my research colleague, Dr. Ted Riecken, for encouraging me to undertake this project and for contributing to it in so many ways through his ongoing work with, and his dedication to, the Youth Violence Project, our collaborative undertaking. Without Dr. Riecken, this book and the project that engendered it would not have been possible.

I wish to thank Francine Geraci, my editor, for her immense contribution to making this book a reality, and I wish to thank Grace Deutsch and Trudy Rising of Trifolium Books for never wavering and for bringing this book to publication.

Lastly, I want to say thank you to my partner, Stan Olsen, for his support and patience, and to Stephanie Olsen for her insightful comments.

Introduction

In recent years, in the Western industrialized world, much attention has been paid to youth violence and with it, the ever-increasing participation of school children in all forms of violence and aggression. To combat this growing problem, research and youth violence prevention programs have begun in Europe (e.g., Olweus, Block, & Radke-Yarrow, 1986; Tutt, 1988, 1991; Klicpera & Klicpera, 1993), Australia (Jenkins, 1994; Rigby, 1996), the United States (e.g., Boothe, Bradley, Flick, Keough, & Kirk, 1993), and Canada (Hamilton, 1993). In North America, youth violence and violence in schools have become the object of intense media attention: The topic has been widely discussed in newspapers, magazines, scholarly journals, and television and radio programs; it has also been the focus of academic and community conferences.

Educators and social scientists appear to agree that youth violence, particularly violence in schools, is on the rise at an unprecedented rate, and that this violence is more intense, vicious, and deadly than ever before. In an article entitled "The Violence at Your Door," which distills the findings of a 1993 U.S. national survey of school executives, Boothe et al. (1993) state that "violence has increased markedly in U.S. public schools in the last five years." In Canada, Hamilton (1993) draws on government- and teacher-compiled data to state categorically that

> few young people today have not experienced some form of violence, either first-hand or involving a friend. Bullying, sexual assault, and violent incidents involving children and teens are happening more and more frequently ... in big cities and small towns, in parks and shopping centers, in private and public schools.

These sources and others (e.g., Bibby & Posterski, 1992; Mathews, 1994; Cameron, deBruijne, Kennedy, & Morin, 1994) specifically mention an increase in *violence among school girls*. For example, Mathews, Ryan, and Banner (1994) found that girls had become more directly involved in assault or the use of weapons, either as individuals or in groups or gangs, with most attacks directed against other individual girls or groups of girls. In one school, female students self-reported that they were as likely as male students to rob another student, and more likely than male students to threaten or hurt someone with a weapon. In another school, older females (grade nine) were more likely than males to be perpetrators of most categories of violent offenses, with the exception of sexual violence. Finally, in Canada, murder charges were recently laid against juveniles — among them two 14-year-old girls who were charged with manslaughter — in connection with the slaying of a motorist who had apparently stopped his car to give them a ride.

The overall reported increase in youth violence has made this a hot topic. The involvement of females has made it even hotter.

Females and violence in schools

Hot topics usually generate much literature. When I undertook a search in this area, therefore, I was surprised to find very little. Much of the literature consisted of articles in academic journals that are not readily accessible to front-line workers, educators, parents, or indeed to the girls themselves. The vast majority of articles on school violence failed to address girls' violence, and the major trend on violence in general offered prescriptions without benefit of research.

Antiviolence programs, no matter how well meaning, stand scant chance of success if they do not apply to the individuals and groups they intend to affect. This is particularly true for girls: Little research has been done with respect to violent females because, for the most part, violence and delinquency are seen to be almost exclusively a male problem. As well, the handful of studies that do exist focus on Afro-American or Hispanic-American girls who are marginalized because of color or ethnicity, live in ghettos, and are either members of known youth gangs or heavily involved with the juvenile justice system.

The violent, non-gang, white girl and the violent white school girl who is not in juvenile detention have been virtually ignored. It is as if such girls do not exist — but in fact they do; and they are very much in the forefront of the rise in violence in schools, both as victims and as perpetrators. Nevertheless, most antiviolence programs ignore gender differences and base their interventions on theories derived from research on boys and men. This means that there is a marked lack of information upon which to base meaningful and effective violence prevention aimed at violent girls.

My involvement in the problem

I initially became interested in the topic of youth violence early in 1993, while working with teachers on the conflicts arising from differences in learning and teaching styles. I was struck by the number of times violence was brought into our discussions: Teachers described gang fighting, drug use, vigilantism, and extortion among students, along with an increase in intimidating behavior towards adults.

My response was to seek out more information on school-based violence. I also contacted my colleague, Dr. Ted Riecken. Together, we set out to research the nature and incidence of such violence in order to provide a realistic and concrete understanding of the extent of the problem. The result of our collaboration was an 11-page self-report questionnaire designed to tap into various aspects of students' experiences, which we administered to over 1,500 students aged 13 to 16, both male and female. The results appear in the *Survey of Student Life* (Artz & Riecken, 1994).

The second step in our inquiry involved my spending many days and weeks, for a period of one year, with six violent school girls, their parents, teachers, and counselors, in order to learn about the girls' lives and about how they make sense of their participation in violence. It is on this study that this book is based.

The third step, in which we are now deeply immersed, is the Youth Violence Project, which involves working at the community-based level with 16 schools on violence prevention from the ground up.

The purpose of this book

This book inquires into the life-worlds and practices of school girls who are involved in violence, but who are not involved with the juvenile justice system, nor are they members of a gang or a visible minority group. The girls chosen for this study range in age from 13 to 16 years, because this population shows the highest participation of girls in school-based violence.

This book has the following objectives:

- To provide a well-researched and well-articulated description of the life-worlds of violent school girls.

- To provide an understanding of where the violent school girl stands in relation to her nonviolent female peers and her violent and nonviolent male peers.

- To provide information that may be applied to the design and implementation of programs and interventions that have the power to reach violent girls and help them to stop participating in violence.

Chapter One presents an overview of past and current theories of crime and delinquency, in order to ground the reader in the ways in which the problem of girls' violence has thus far been understood.

Chapter Two, which draws mostly on the extensive data generated by the *Survey of Student Life* (Artz & Riecken, 1994), presents profiles of the adolescent school girl and her violent female peer and the adolescent school boy and his violent male peer, and discusses gender similarities and differences.

Drawing on case study material, Chapters Three through Eight explore the life-worlds of individual violent school girls. These chapters focus on the girls' descriptions of themselves, their families, their social activities, friends, and friendships; on their school activities and relationships with teachers, administrators, and counselors; and on their moral understanding of their own participation in violence.

Chapter Nine summarizes and analyzes the findings described in the preceding chapters, while Chapter Ten ties these findings to existing approaches to violence prevention, points out the gaps, makes suggestions for change, and outlines possibilities for working effectively with violent school girls.

Sibylle Artz
Associate Professor
School of Child & Youth Care
University of Victoria
Victoria, British Columbia, Canada

CHAPTER ONE

Exploring Theories of Female Crime and Delinquency

> Prior to the 1970s researchers treated females as marginal to the study of juvenile delinquency. Albert Cohen (1955), for example, well known for his study of male delinquent subcultures, paid only token attention to females, proposing that male delinquency was "versatile," while female delinquency was "specialized" and limited to "sexual crimes" (p. 144). He concluded that girls became delinquent because they were preoccupied with establishing sexual relationships with boys. (Berger, 1989, p. 375)

In order to ground the reader in theories of female crime and delinquency, a synopsis follows based on the literature reviews produced by Chesney-Lind and Koroki (1985), Ronald Berger (1989), and Chesney-Lind and Shelden (1992). These scholars have written succinct overviews of some 200 articles, reports, and books produced between 1985 and 1991. In summarizing their findings, I consulted other sources, notably Warren (1981) and Flowers (1990); but for the most part, this synopsis is guided by Chesney-Lind and her associates and by Berger.

Mainstream Theories of Crime and Delinquency

Early theorists in this area included Burgess (1928), who studied ecological patterns of crime and delinquency and the effects of social disorganization and deprivation on crime; Thrasher (1927), who studied juvenile gangs; and Shaw and McKay (1942), whose work further investigated the effects of social factors on crime and delinquency. These theorists demonstrated the powerful effects of social disorganization, class, and the breakdown of social conventions on crime and delinquency. Yet for the most part, they overlooked females and concentrated on the experiences of males.

Focusing on inner-city crime, these researchers showed that communities that are (a) largely populated by transitory, economically underprivileged people coming from similar ethnic backgrounds and (b) characterized by a collective inability to make provisions, solve problems, and maintain social control through the adequate use of organizations, groups, and individuals, invariably give rise to disproportionately high crime rates. The work of these researchers, who focused primarily on the socially derived motivational aspects of crime, was seminal for others, notably those who developed "strain" theories of delinquency and crime. These theories concentrate on the explanatory power of frustrated social opportunity and its relationship to crime.

STRAIN THEORIES OF CRIME AND DELINQUENCY

Building on Emile Durkheim's (1933) notion of *anomie*, described in Webster (1975) as "lawlessness: a state of society in which normative standards of conduct and belief are weak or lacking" (p. 47), and described by Chesney-Lind and Shelden (1992) as a "breakdown in moral ties, rules, customs, laws and the like that occurs in the wake of rapid social change" (p. 64), strain theorists beginning with Robert Merton (1938) developed theories that "explain juvenile delinquency as a response of adolescents to their lack of socially approved opportunities" (Flowers, 1990, p. 127).

Merton, focusing on males, noted that unequal opportunity and limited access to legitimate means for achieving culturally defined male success goals created "strain" or pressures that pushed some males into finding alternative means to achieve these desired ends. Merton postulated five alternative adaptive responses to anomie and strain: (a) becoming a *conformist*, which implied unquestioning acceptance of culturally defined success goals and means, with no guarantee of goal attainment; (b) becoming an *innovator*, which implied acceptance of commonly held success goals while replacing socially sanctioned means with deviant means; (c) becoming a *retreatist*, giving up and rejecting both goals and means; (d) becoming a *ritualist*, or blindly following the means while rejecting the goals, thus following rules only for rules' sake without attaining the goal; and (e) becoming a *rebel*, redefining success goals in one's own terms and inventing one's own means for attaining them (Chesney-Lind & Shelden, 1992; Flowers, 1990).

Other researchers have noted that the most common adaptive responses used by delinquents are *innovation*, expressed through illegal means such as theft, fraud, and robbery to achieve material gain; *retreatism*, the flight to drugs and alcohol as a means of escape from frustration; and *rebellion*, the rejection of conventional authority through aggressive and hostile behavior (Flowers, 1990).

Although Merton's theories may have had explanatory power for males, they do not hold for females, especially in the late 20th century. Given that many females now have success goals similar to those of men (Adler, 1975; Morris, 1987; Simon, 1975), and given also that women's opportunities are still far more limited than those of men (Faludi, 1991), it might be expected, according to Merton, that women would experience more strain than men, and would therefore commit more crime. Yet, this is clearly not the case: women still engage in crime at far lower levels of incidence than men.

Theories that followed on Merton's continued to explore the links between strain, social class and gender, and crime and delinquency. Among these are Albert Cohen's (1955) theories of delinquent subculture, which saw delinquency as a phenomenon brought about by the inability of lower-class[1] males to achieve recognition and success commensurate with the standards set by the dominant middle class.

Central to Cohen's thesis is the notion that problems of adjustment are different for males and females because each individual's behavior must first of all be in keeping with his or her identity as male or female. Thus, females must preserve their frail and dependent state in order to affirm themselves as feminine and as such, are not inclined towards crime and delinquency. Males, however, must preserve their independent and dominant state in order to affirm themselves as masculine, and thus, when thwarted, are more inclined to delinquency. For Cohen, delinquency is a male solution to a male problem:

> ... Both the respectable middle class pattern [for success, i.e., getting an education and success in the business world] and the delinquent response are characteristically *masculine*. Although they differ dramatically, to be sure, they have something in common. This common element is suggested by the words "achievement," "daring," "active mastery," "pursuit." Every one of these terms has, to be sure, a different twist of emphasis or direction when combined with the different values orientations of the respectable and the delinquent culture. ... In both cultures however, one measures his manhood by comparing his *performance*, whether it be in stealing, fighting, athletic contests, work or intellectual achievement, against those of his own sex. (Cohen, 1955, p. 139)

Cohen suggested that because lower-class males were for the most part blocked from ever achieving success as defined by the middle class, they instead inverted middle-class standards and developed a reactive and rebellious subculture. In redefining the rules for success in a way that made it attainable for them, they established themselves as "rogue males," "untrammeled in their masculinity" and therefore free from the domination of others (p. 140). Cohen described the values and standards of this subculture as "short run hedonism" that is "malicious, negativistic and non-utilitarian." Yet, he concluded: "However it may be condemned by others on moral grounds, [this behavior] has at least one virtue: it incontestably confirms, in the eyes of all concerned, [the rogue male's] essential masculinity" (Cohen, 1955, pp. 139–140).

Cohen's claim that a defense of masculinity is at the bottom of crime and delinquency leaves little room for the formation of an understanding of female crime and delinquency. This gap in applicability does not appear to have deterred others from continuing to build theory based exclusively upon male experience. Miller (1958) further explored conflict in class standards and values and argued, much as Cohen did, that a lower-class male focus on trouble, toughness, smartness, excitement, fate, and autonomy ultimately leads to engagement in delinquency and crime. He further suggested that this is often the outcome of males' tendency to seek the company of other males in street-corner groups, which become gangs. This, Miller argued, was the result of the absence of fathers in lower-class households and the inability of mothers to provide adequate male role models, thus forcing young males to learn male behavior from their peers.

Cloward and Ohlin (1960), also concentrating on males and delinquent gangs, elaborated on Miller's (1958) notions and argued that although lower-class males indeed had far less opportunity to achieve success through legitimate means and therefore experienced intense frustration, they still had ample access to illegitimate means (especially because of their propensity to congregate in gangs), which they frequently exercised. Like Miller, Cloward and Ohlin suggested that the underlying cause for delinquency could be found in the absence of males in the life-world of the lower-class adolescent. Lower-class males,

> engulfed by a feminine world and uncertain of their own identification ... protest against femininity ... in the form of robust aggressive behavior, and even malicious, irresponsible, and destructive acts. Such acts evoke maternal disapproval and thus come to stand for independence and masculinity to rebellious adolescents. (Cloward & Ohlin, 1960, p. 49; quoted in Chesney-Lind & Shelden, 1992, p. 67)

Quite apart from the fact that Miller (1958) and Cloward and Ohlin (1960) offer nothing to females — and in some ways, seem to hold females responsible for male deviance — they also overlook the fact that, despite the disproportionate representation of lower-class (or, more appropriately, working-class males in index crime statistics, the vast majority of working-class males are not before the courts for delinquency and crime. According to Flowers (1990), such theories have also been widely criticized for assuming that lower-class males automatically wish to adopt middle-class norms of material success and educational and occupational achievement, and for overlooking the fact that even those who become gang members for the most part eventually abandon their delinquent lifestyle and lead conventional adult lives.

Differential association theories of crime and delinquency
Noting that delinquents tend to gather in groups and gangs, and also that those who engage in delinquency appear to interact more with others who engage in crime than those who do not, Sutherland (1939) and others (Sutherland & Cressey, 1978) argued that deviant behavior, like other human behavior, is learned. Thus, close association with others who engage in such behavior provides opportunities to learn the techniques, motives, and values that facilitate criminal behavior. According to Flowers (1990), differential association theory suggests that

> the probability of delinquent behavior varies directly with the priority, frequency, duration, and intensity of a person's contacts with patterns of delinquent behavior, and inversely with their non deviant contacts. Interaction with anti-social elements tends to take place more often when an individual's perception of their circumstances is supportive to violations of the law. (p. 130)

Flowers expands on this by adding:

> ... the theory contends that delinquency is a social rather than anti-social behavioral pattern. Thus, if most of a juvenile's interaction is with people who frequently violate the law and who express beliefs that seek to justify their behavior, then the juvenile has a greater chance of becoming delinquent or criminal than one who interacts with persons who do not violate the law or disapprove of such violations. (p. 130)

Sutherland, while not confining himself to a study of the working class in that he included white-collar crime and professional theft in his work, did however focus only on males. Despite this, Sutherland's differential association theories hold some promise with regard to females, given that recent research indicates that females who have frequent contact with deviant females appear to engage in deviant behavior to a greater degree than those who do not (Giordano & Cernkovich, 1979). As pointed out by Giordano, Cernkovich, and Pugh (1986; see also Morash, 1986 and Singer & Levine, 1988), females who become involved in deviance and delinquency still participate at lower rates than males, but nevertheless

> adopt a set of attitudes in which they [see] delinquency as appropriate, possible, or desirable ... and a friendship style in which they ... encourage each other as a group to act on these orientations. (Giordano et al., 1986, p. 1,194; cited in Berger, 1989, p. 389)

Social control theories of crime and delinquency

Also promising — from the point of view of understanding female violence — are social control theories of crime and delinquency, which focus on the capacity of all human beings to engage in deviance and crime (although most researchers who conceptualized these theories still focused on males as research subjects). For social control theorists, crime and delinquency have less to do with motivation to deviate from the norm and more to do with the presence or absence of conditions (internal and external) that are favorable to breaking the law. Social control theorists explored personal control or inner containment of deviant urges grounded in a positive self-concept (Reiss, 1951; Reckless, 1961), effective family and other external social controls of deviance grounded in a positive social structure (Nye, 1958; Toby, 1957), and the absence or presence of a social bond (Hirschi, 1969). Both Chesney-Lind and Shelden (1992) and Flowers (1990) select Hirschi as the most influential of the social control theorists, largely because research has borne out his notion that individuals with strong bonds to social institutions (e.g., family and school) are more likely to have lower rates of crime and delinquency.

Hirschi (1969) suggested that the social bond — that which keeps one's deviance in check — is made up of four components: (a) *attachment*, largely emotional, to family, friends, peers, and institutions such as school; (b) *commitment,* or one's personal stake or investment in conformity based in what one would stand to lose if one did engage in crime and delinquency; (c) *involvement,* or one's participation in legitimately sanctioned activities such as school, work, and non-deviant forms of recreation; and (d) *belief,* or one's acceptance that socially sanctioned moral values provide the correct foundation upon which to build one's own standards. Hirschi (again, working exclusively with boys) found that attachment, commitment, and belief were the best predictors of delinquency or the lack of it, while involvement had a lesser effect (Chesney-Lind & Shelden, 1992).

Hirschi's (1969) notions that social bonds, and the social controls exerted by these bonds, had a direct effect on the level of an individual's participation in delinquency and crime generated much further research, including research on females. Jensen and Eve (1976) and Cernkovich and Giordano (1987) found that attachment to conventional others and a belief in the legitimacy of rules had predictive power for both male and female delinquency. Cernkovich and Giordano also found that lower rates of female delinquency could be partly explained by higher levels of parental supervision and intimate communication between parents and daughters.

Hagan, Simpson, and Gillis (1987) and Hagan (1988, 1990) took up the theory of social control and argued that social control or constraint varies across gender, with females experiencing more control especially in more traditional, patriarchal families. Hagan et al. define the "ideal-type patriarchal family" as including "a husband who is employed in an authority position and a wife who is not employed outside the home" (p. 791). They define the "ideal-type egalitarian family" as including a mother and father who are both employed in authority positions outside the home (p. 792). They also define single-parent households headed by women as "a special kind of egalitarian family" which, like other egalitarian households, experiences "freedom from male domination" (p. 793).

It is the contention of Hagan et al. (1987) that whenever males are dominant, as they most often are in the ideal-type patriarchal household, mothers are charged with the task of child-rearing as a result of a division of labor along gender lines. This leaves fathers in control of production (i.e., participation in the work force) and mothers in control of consumption, domestic labor, and the "day-to-day control of their children, especially their daughters" (p. 792). According to

Hagan et al., such families reproduce the gender divisions they model and enforce and allow much less risk-taking behavior in their daughters. As a result, these families produce lower deviance and delinquency rates for females than for males, while ideal-type egalitarian families (which allow more risk taking in their female members) produce higher delinquency rates for females, rates that tend to close the gender gap. Therefore, according to Hagan et al., the more traditional the family, the lower the female delinquency rate.

The argument of Hagan et al. (1987) rests upon two points: one which suggests that mothers who work outside the home (especially in positions of authority) constitute a move away from patriarchy towards a more egalitarian system, and a second which suggests that such a move towards egalitarianism is linked with higher delinquency rates in girls. Therefore, for Hagan et al., the greater the control of men over women and girls in families, the lower the risk for female adolescent deviance. When this is not the case, and adult women in families take up more equal power with males, or find themselves in the position of being single heads of households, girls in these families become more like boys and as a consequence also take more risks, including deviant risks.

In effect, Hagan et al. (1987) appear to suggest that working mothers contribute to higher delinquency in their daughters. But, as Chesney-Lind and Shelden point out,

> no evidence suggests that as women's labor force participation has increased, girls' delinquency has increased. Indeed, during the past decade [the 1980s], when women's labor force participation and the number of female-headed households soared, aggregate female delinquency measured both by self-report and official statistics either declined or remained stable (Ageton, 1983; Chilton & Datesman, 1987; Federal Bureau of Investigation, 1986). (Chesney-Lind & Shelden, 1992, pp. 96–97)

Thus, even if Hagan and his associates are correct in pointing out that gender and patriarchy are important in shaping both male and female behavior, their assumption that a mother working outside the home increases the risk of female delinquency does not appear to hold. This theory, like others that will be discussed below, is an example of backlash theories which, in effect, recommend that women maintain traditional gender roles because in the end, liberation — seen here as a move towards the masculine — carries too great a price.

LAbelING THEORIES

One final mainstream theoretical approach that may shed light on female crime and delinquency is labeling theory. Labeling theory is concerned primarily with the selective social construction of certain behaviors as criminal and delinquent rather than with original causes of behavior. Schur (1972) suggests that

> human behavior is deviant to the extent that it comes to be viewed as involving a personally discreditable departure from a group's normative expectation and it elicits interpersonal and collective reactions that serve to isolate, treat and correct or punish individuals engaged in such behavior. (p. 21)

Thus, deviance becomes the creation of those in society whom Becker (1963) called "moral entrepreneurs," that is, those who designate deviance through the creation of certain rules and standards which, when broken, constitute deviance. Deviance, then, is not characterized by certain behaviors, but is rather the consequence of assigning the label of deviance and its differential application.

This theory helps us to understand the social construction of certain behaviors as deviant for females although they are not designated as such for males. A prime example of this is the propensity of those who work in juvenile justice systems to characterize women and girls as deviant based upon the perception that they are engaged in promiscuous sexual behavior and to incarcerate them for status offenses (e.g., running away) and curfew violations because they are designated as "unmanageable" and "beyond control," a standard that is rarely applied to men and boys (Chesney-Lind & Shelden, 1992). Further, labeling theorists, unlike other mainstream theorists discussed thus far, did in fact include women in their theorizing. Schur (1984) extended his theories to women and argued that "women's powerlessness has resulted in an extensive array of labels being used against them to characterize them as deviant and to devalue and objectify the very condition of womanhood itself" (Chesney-Lind & Shelden, 1992, p. 70).

SUMMARY: MAINSTREAM THEORIES

Few mainstream sociological theories appear to have dealt with female crime and delinquency. Content with the assumption that crime and delinquency were masculine forms of behavior, and bolstered in that assumption by statistical evidence of the overwhelming participation of males in such behavior, the majority of theorists (who were themselves male) focused on males. Those who did address female participation in crime and delinquency still grounded most of their thinking in male experience.

A Brief History of Theories of Female Crime and Delinquency

As outlined above, most researchers treated females as marginal to the study of crime and delinquency prior to the 1970s. Interest in female crime and delinquency arose, in part at least, as the result of two forces: (a) the involvement of more women in scholarship and (b) the possibility that female crime and delinquency may be on the rise.[2] A careful reading of work focusing on females reveals that most research on female crime and delinquency has been geared towards answering the question, "Why do so *few* girls and women engage in crime and delinquency?" rather than, "*Why* do girls and women engage in crime and delinquency?" When females are considered, the focus is generally on the gender gap and the proportionally low participation of females, rather than on the conditions or motivations that move females towards crime and delinquency.

Three categories of theory have emerged from the literature:

- those that explain the gender gap in crime and delinquency as given in the *biological differences* between the sexes and explain female deviance in terms of biologically based sexual problems;

- those that explain the gender gap in crime and delinquency as derived from differences in *gender role socialization* and explain the kinds of deviance females do participate in as based on their gender roles; and

- those that accept that female deviance is on the rise relative to male deviance and explain this trend in terms of a *"masculinization" of women* brought on by women's liberation and the feminist movement.

All three categories explain female crime and delinquency as a move away from the feminine towards the masculine. Only Chesney-Lind and her colleagues (1985, 1992) call for a shift away from theories of delinquency that are uncritically grounded in male behavior. In place of such theories, Chesney-Lind et al. suggest a move towards a broader understanding of the lives of deviant girls and women.

Biologically based theories of female crime and delinquency

Early theories of female crime, like early theories of male crime, were strongly affected by social Darwinism. Biology was destiny, and criminal behavior was seen as the result of problems with evolution. Cesare Lombroso, working in 1895, explained all criminal elements in society as biological *throwbacks* resulting from an arrested evolutionary process. According to Lombroso, females were by their very nature less disposed to crime than males because (a) they had evolved less than males and were therefore naturally more childlike, sedentary, weak and passive, and thus not able to participate in challenging and independent activities like crime; (b) their primary functions were childbearing and caretaking, which made them unsuited to criminal activity; and (c) their underdeveloped intelligence, as well as their maternity, piety, and weakness, tempered their often jealous and vengeful natures and prevented them from behaving like criminals. Thus, Lombroso reasoned that if women did choose to become criminals, it was largely because they did not possess a maternal instinct and were most probably degenerate, unwomanly (read, masculine) throwbacks.

The belief that biology is destiny — along with the notion that men and women had natural roles and true natures — outlived Lombroso, although his work has long been, for the most part, discredited. Otto Pollack, working in the 1950s, and Cowie, Cowie, and Slater, working in the 1960s, wrote extensively about imbalances in women's physiology and sexuality as causes of female crime.

For Pollack (1950), the explanation for the consistently low rates of female crime (relative to male rates) lay in the fact that women were naturally more deceitful and secretive, and could therefore get away with far more than men could. He suggested that this ability to deceive has its origins in women's sexual passivity and their ability to conceal or feign sexual arousal — something that men cannot do. Therefore, women's ability to be deceitful, coupled with the various hormonal imbalances brought about by menstruation, menopause, and pregnancy, predisposed women towards criminality and at the same time provided them with the means to escape detection and responsibility for their actions.

As Chesney-Lind and her colleagues (1985, 1992) point out, the notion that biology is destiny lives on in more recent studies. For example, for Cowie, Cowie, and Slater (1968), differences in male and female delinquency were largely explained by anatomy. According to Cowie et al. (1968), two primary forces were responsible: (a) biological, somatic, and hormonal differences, which derived from chromosomal differences between the two sexes, and (b) the natural timidity and lack of enterprise found in females. If females did get involved in criminal activity, Cowie et al. attributed this to an excess of male chromosomes. Of interest here is the notion that what's good for the gander is not good for the goose.

Criminality in males has thus far been described in positive terms as the outcome of males' more advanced evolvement and greater honesty, coupled with their propensity to become involved in challenging and independent activities. However, when females engage in criminality, the tone becomes more negative. They are variously described as lacking in some capacity, especially so-called feminine capacities, such as the maternal instinct, or natural female passivity (which term is used pejoratively), and they are accused of the ultimate faux pas: an excess of male chromosomes, those very same chromosomes that lend strength of purpose to males.

The notion that biological factors exert a strong influence persists among some criminologists to the present day. Slade (1984) and Binder, Geis, and Bruce (1988) proposed premenstrual syndrome (PMS) as a cause for female criminality, although little evidence was brought to bear in support of this claim, and Wilson and Herrnstein (1985) repeated the argument that biological factors determine levels of aggression as well as differentials in male and female law breaking. Konopka (1966, 1983), who was one of the first researchers actually to study adolescent females in order to understand their life-worlds (and who broke more new ground by emphasizing the effects on female crime and delinquency of the changing cultural position of women and the sexual double standard), nonetheless concluded that girls and women were largely controlled by biology and sexuality. As Chesney-Lind and Shelden (1992) point out, Konopka, in noting that most girls come to the attention of the juvenile justice system because of sex-related behaviors, was convinced that "most female delinquency is either 'sexual' or 'relational' rather than 'criminal' in nature" (p. 61) and therefore requires help with sexual adjustment.

The assumption, made by so many researchers, that delinquency in juvenile females is largely sexual delinquency borne of sexual maladjustment, can be explained by the fact that in the United States, the ratio of arrests for prostitution is 50:1 for girls over boys (Chesney-Lind & Shelden, 1992, p. 8). Noteworthy as this arrest pattern may be, it may in fact reflect not girls' sexual deviance, but the American judicial system's preoccupation with girls' sexuality, a preoccupation that mirrors the preoccupation of the culture at large.

Gender role theories of female crime and delinquency

In contrast to and in protest against biologically based theories of crime, gender role theories of delinquency and crime emerged in the 1950s (Grosser, 1951) and have grown in strength and number to the present day (Balkan & Berger, 1979; Hagan et al., 1985, 1987; Hoffman-Bustamente, 1973; Morris, 1965). Given that males are socialized to be more active, aggressive, and independent and are rewarded for flaunting conventional behavior, while females are socialized to be more passive, caring, and dependent and are rewarded for engaging in conventional behavior (Berger, 1989; Gilligan, 1982; Hoffman-Bustamente, 1973), it is reasoned by gender role theorists that male/female differences in aggression and crime can be accounted for by differences in socialization.

The power of gender role theories lies in the clear differentiation that exists between the kinds of crime committed by men and those that are committed by women. Berger (1989) notes that "male juveniles have been consistently more likely than females to be arrested for every crime category (except running away and prostitution)" (p. 378). Citing Federal Bureau of Investigation data from 1987, he states that

> male juveniles accounted for 89% of all juvenile arrests for "index" violent crimes (i.e., murder, non-negligent manslaughter, forcible rape, robbery, aggravated assault) and 79% of all juvenile arrests for index property crimes (i.e., burglary, larceny-theft, motor vehicle theft, arson) as well as 91% of arrests for vandalism and 81% of arrests for disorderly conduct (FBI, 1988). (Berger, 1989, p. 377)

Chesney-Lind and Shelden tell a similar story using self-report data gathered in the United States by Cernkovich and Giordano (1979):

> Boys are more likely to report involvement in gang fighting, carrying a hidden weapon, strong-arming students and others, aggravated assault, hitting students, sexual assault [and sex for money]. Boys are also disproportionately involved in serious property crimes; they are much more likely to report involvement in thefts of more than $50. (Chesney-Lind & Shelden, 1992, pp. 16–17)

Again, males show dominance in all areas including trading sex for money, a delinquent behavior traditionally considered "feminine." Comparable data were reported by Figueria-McDonough, Barton, and Sarri (1981), who found significant gender differences in theft, vandalism, fraud, serious fighting, carrying weapons, and prostitution, with males reporting their involvement at ratios of between 3:1 and 6:1 over females.

With regard to official crime statistics, Hindelang, Hirschi, and Weis (1981) also reported stable, offense-specific, male/female differences in U.S. uniform crime reports from 1960 to 1976, with males showing a distinct dominance in burglary, weapons offenses, assault, robbery, and auto theft. Data on admissions to youth corrections facilities gathered in British Columbia (the Canadian province in which the study described in this book was conducted) between 1986 and 1993 show a similar trend.

Figures on the incidence of admission to custody (1986 to 1993) provided by the British Columbia Ministry of the Attorney General show that where youth in custody are concerned, males account for 94% of breaking and entering convictions, 81% of crimes against persons, 84.5% of property crimes, 76.7% of sex crimes, 68.5% of theft by fraud, 69.8% of theft under $1,000, and 89.6% of violent crime on average, over the seven-year period since the Young Offenders Act became law in Canada. Data provided by the Police Services Division, also of the British Columbia Ministry of the Attorney General, tell very much the same story: From 1986 to 1993, males were charged with 85.7% of murders, 82.6% of attempted murders, 96% of sexual assaults, 75% of all other forms of assault, 87% of robberies involving the use of weapons, 93% of breaking and entering, 91% of thefts of motor vehicles, and 68.5% of other thefts (including shoplifting).

Although the data reported here are by no means exhaustive, whether one turns to official crime reports or to self-report data for serious crimes, males clearly participate in significantly greater numbers than females. What must be noted as well is that while the population of adolescents in British Columbia increased at the rate of 6% during this period (1986 to 1993), the number of male youths charged with assault increased 118%, rising from 672 charges in 1986 to 1,468 charges in 1993, and the number of female youth charged increased by 250%, rising from 178 charges in 1986 to 624 charges in 1993. Thus, male young offenders are still in the forefront where assault is concerned, but female young offender participation rates are increasing more rapidly than those of males. In 1986, females accounted for 26% of all assault charges laid against youths in British Columbia. By 1993, this had risen to 42%. Although the seven-year average for assault by female youth in British Columbia still hovers at 25%, this figure masks what appears to be an alarming rise in the participation of female youth in all forms of assault other than sexual assault.

British Columbia is not the only province to record a rise in crime among young offenders, although as with all crime rates in Canada, it continues to lead the way. Data provided by Statistics Canada (Canadian Crime Statistics, 1995) show a similar trend across the country. From 1986 to 1993, the number of female youths charged with assault increased by 190%, rising from 1,728 charges in 1986 to 5,096 charges in 1993, and the number of male youths charged increased by 117%, rising from 7,547 charges in 1986 to 16,375 charges in 1993.

Reports from the United States also paint a grim picture. According to figures released by the U.S. Department of Justice on November 12, 1995, the number of juveniles arrested for weapons violations has more than doubled between 1985 and 1993. The rise in arrests for weapons offenses among juveniles is three times higher than that for adults for the same period. Newspapers report that in the United States, minors under the age of 18 now account for nearly 25% of arrests for violations of laws controlling deadly weapons ("Juvenile weapons arrests double," Globe & Mail, November 13, 1995).

Tom Gabor, a criminologist at the University of Ottawa, Ontario, who completed a national survey of school violence for the Solicitor General of Canada in 1994, concluded that school violence and armed students are on the increase and that females are now more often involved in violence than in the past ("Tremendous increase in violence among girls," Victoria Times Colonist, October 15, 1993). In view of such reports, it is not surprising that the media, school officials, and ordinary citizens are reporting an escalation in youth violence, particularly for female adolescents.

When theorists attempt to explain the gender gap in youth crime statistics, those who favor gender role theories often explain differences in male/female participation as an outcome of imposing higher moral expectations and greater social controls on girls and women. As Berger (1989) points out,

> family arrangements have kept females, in comparison to males, more cloistered, and females have been expected to provide support and nurturance to others. In the occupational world, these traditions have been reflected in and reinforced by "gender appropriate" occupations such as secretaries, waitresses, teachers, and social workers. As a result, girls have been more closely supervised by their parents than boys and have had less opportunity than boys have had to commit delinquent acts. They have been more likely to accept general moral standards, blame themselves for their problems, feel shame for their misconduct, be taught to avoid risks, fear social disapproval and be deterred by legal sanctions. (p. 377) (See also: Balkan & Berger, 1979; Giallombardo, 1980; Hagan, Gillis, & Simpson, 1985; Mawby, 1980; Morash, 1983; Morris, 1965; Richard & Tittle, 1981.)

Given the consistency of the gender gap in both official crime rates and self-report data, especially for more serious crimes, an understanding of socialization patterns and gender expectations may indeed contribute to an understanding of male/female differences in participation. However, it does not explain either the motivations for females to take up crime and delinquency, nor the engagement of females in so-called male crimes and delinquencies. Therefore, a reliance on socialization patterns and gender expectations "fails to explore motivation and intent as an integral part of female crime. ... While significant in its contribution ... role theory still provides only a limited perspective on female crime and behavior" (Chesney-Lind & Koroki, 1985, p. 7). Further, in bringing into focus the need to understand the differences in social experiences and their effect on behavior for males and females, gender role theories also provide a basis for the feminist backlash notion that a change in women's roles and the emancipation of women will ultimately lead to a greater participation of women in criminal activity.

"Masculinization" theories of female crime and delinquency

Freda Adler (1975) is generally credited with promoting the belief that a convergence of gender role expectations brought about by feminism and the women's movement in the late 1960s and 1970s has contributed significantly to a rise in female crime. Adler claimed that "the phenomenon of female criminality is but one wave in ... [the] rising tide of female assertiveness — a wave which has not yet crested and may even be seeking its level uncomfortably close to the high-water mark set by male violence" (quoted in Berger, 1989, p. 379). Basing her claims on largely unfounded notions that traditional attitudes towards women were rapidly changing and that women were indeed making substantial gains in all areas of the corporate world (Anderson, 1991; Faludi, 1991), Adler contended that

> in the same way that women are demanding equal opportunity in the fields of legitimate endeavor, a similar number of determined women are forcing their way into the world of major crimes ... as the position of women approximates the position of men, so does the frequency and type of their criminal activity. (Quoted in Chesney-Lind & Koroki, 1985, p. 9)

Adler's claims supported those of Simon (1975), who noted a rise in women's arrest rates for white-collar crimes (e.g., embezzlement and fraud) and attributed this to women's greater participation in the workforce.

Adler's (1975) claims created a continuing debate because they appeared to be supported by official arrest statistics for the period between 1960 and 1975, which showed dramatic increases in female crime, especially in non-traditional offenses for females. The primary objection to her thesis came from scholars who disputed her analysis of official crime statistics. Specifically, they argued that although percentage increases in non-traditional crimes for females (murder, aggravated assault, robbery) showed dramatic leaps, these increases were based on very small absolute numbers where even a small change in number could create a large change in percentage (Chesney-Lind, 1992; Miller, 1986).

As well, most increases in female crime were found in non-violent offenses. Simon (1975) found the greatest increases in such offenses as larceny, fraud, and check forgery; he argued that this was the direct result of the feminization of poverty brought on by the rise in single-family households headed by females. This was confirmed by Steffensmeir (1978) and Steffensmeir and Cobb (1981), who found major increases in female crime largely in shoplifting and check forgery, crimes that are consistent with traditional female roles.

Although they and others concurred that female violence for adults and juveniles had risen between 1960 and 1977, Steffensmeir and his associates found that male violence had also increased at an equal rate, thus preserving the gender gap. Steffensmeir's work itself sparked a further debate centering around interpretation of data and methods for calculating comparative changes in crime participation rates (see Berger, 1989).

This debate continues and is reflected in the current alarm about greater participation of females in violence in schools. At the present time, it does appear that both males and females are participating more in all forms of crime and delinquency, and that sex differences are narrowing somewhat, at least with regard to assault (Summary Statistics, British Columbia, 1994).

Although Adler (1975), Simon (1975), and others hold the emancipation of women responsible for an apparent narrowing of the gender gap in crime rates, a number of researchers have found evidence to the contrary. For example, James and Thornton (1980) found that attitudes towards feminism had little to do with the extent and kind of female participation in delinquent behavior. Cernkovich and Giordano (1979) found that positive attitudes towards feminism were not related to participation in delinquency. Rather, they found that feminist attitudes may *inhibit* delinquent behavior, and that more traditional attitudes towards the role of women were associated with increased delinquency. As Chesney-Lind and Shelden (1992) point out,

> serious research efforts to locate the dark side of the women's movement have almost without exception been unsuccessful. Careful analyses of existing data fail to support the notion that girls have been committing nontraditional (i.e., "masculine") crimes. It seems peculiar … that so many academics would be willing to consider a hypothesis that assumed improving girls' and women's economic conditions would lead to an increase in female crime when almost all the existing criminological literature stresses the role played by discrimination and poverty (and unemployment and underemployment) in the creation of crime. Because rectification of these social injustices has been put forward as a major solution to crime, it is more than curious that in the case of women's crime, the reverse was argued with such ease and received such wide public acceptance. (pp. 77–78)

Despite this, the notion that feminism is responsible for a rise in female delinquency and crime persists, especially in the popular press. Claims such as those made by McGovern (1995) that "prodded by feminism, today's teenage girls embrace antisocial behavior" underline the popular notion that somehow feminism is contributing to a decline in social values (p. 28). As McGovern sees it, "the rate of cultural degeneration seems to be accelerating" because of "new masculinized attitudes [that] permeate girls' attitudes" (p. 29).

Despite the fact that "masculinization" theories of female crime and delinquency have been shown to be inadequate, the "persistent theme ... that masculinity, of one sort or another, is at the core of [female] delinquency" (Chesney-Lind & Shelden, 1992) nevertheless appears to be central to all sociological theories of crime. In every case, female experience is measured against that of males, and theories about female delinquency are constructed out of already existing theories premised upon male experience.

The Implications

If "all theories of delinquency are built around the lives and experiences of males, whose development, behavior, and options are radically different from those of females" (Chesney-Lind & Shelden, 1992, p. 80), how then are we to understand the deviant girl, particularly the violent girl, in her own right?

Chesney-Lind and Shelden suggest turning to the girls themselves and beginning the search for an understanding of female deviance with their personal accounts. They call for a qualitative exploration of the lives of deviant girls by pointing out that much insight into male delinquency grew from the willingness of male researchers to spend large amounts of time interacting with delinquent boys. They note that researchers such as Frederick Thrasher (1927) and Clifford Shaw (1930, 1938) generated volumes of information on the lives of the boys they studied, sometimes devoting an entire book either to one boy or to a small group of boys. Chesney-Lind and Shelden point out that other researchers relied heavily on the work of Thrasher and Shaw, and lament the fact that much of delinquency research on girls, including their own, has taken a quantified view — one that seeks to understand delinquency in terms of sociological and psychological variables and factors, rather than in terms of the essential features of delinquent action as a lived experience. Such a view does not provide the same qualitative basis for understanding that has been granted to theorists of male delinquency.

It appears, therefore, that if we are to understand delinquent girls, we must first of all understand the circumstances of their lives. Few such studies exist. Chesney-Lind and Koroki (1985) interviewed female delinquents in custody in Hawaii. Chesney-Lind and Shelden (1992) mention three others: Bottcher (1986), who interviewed girls in California training schools; Arnold (1990), who conducted a retrospective study of black women's reflections upon turning to criminal behavior in New York; and Gilfu (1988), who studied adult female offenders in Massachusetts. Two of these studies involved talking to women about what it had been like to be deviant girls; they did not involve adolescent females. Locating research that focuses on the life-worlds of delinquent girls, especially those not yet involved with the justice system, proved to be difficult. Where violent school girls were concerned, no such study could be found.

Four independent researchers were located who had produced a total of eight studies, each of which explored the lives of girls who were gang members (Brown 1977; Campbell, 1984, 1986, 1987; Horowitz, 1983, 1986, 1987; Klein, 1971). These studies do not focus directly on girls' violence, but do deal with girls' accounts of their own experience. As such, they contribute to the qualitative basis for the kind of understanding that Chesney-Lind and Shelden call for. However, all these researchers confine themselves to the lived experiences of girls who are struggling at the sociocultural and socioeconomic margins and who are American, mostly black or Hispanic, or — in the case of Chesney-Lind and Koroki's (1985) study — members of a racially mixed Hawaiian group. White school girls have so far not been included, thus leaving the mistaken impression that they have little involvement with violence.

The girls in Chesney-Lind and Koroki's (1985) study were interviewed about a number of dimensions of their lives. They reported coming from extremely troubled homes, in which they experienced divorce, abandonment, death of a parent, problems with stepparents, alcoholism, and frequent moves. They reported feeling lonely and isolated both from peers and family; they also reported feeling suicidal and in some cases, made suicide attempts. All had experienced violence and physical abuse, and six of the ten had experienced sexual abuse. School life was problematic, although only two actually reported not liking school. Despite their school difficulties, they all expected to graduate from high school, and six of the ten wanted to go to college. Their notions of gender were for the most part stereotypical, and their gender role expectations for the future were traditional. Most of the girls were experienced users of drugs and alcohol, and most had been involved in deviant behavior for some time before they were arrested and put into detention. Typically, they reported deliberately adopting a "bad girl" image because this afforded them status, excitement, and a sense of pride. Finding themselves unable to make it in the role of "good" girl, they found a new lease on life in the role of "bad" girl. Here, at least, was a release from boredom — even a chance to shine.

Chesney-Lind and Koroki (1985) point to poverty, severe family problems, and physical and sexual abuse as factors that thrust the girls in their study into difficulties in school and into behavioral patterns that eventually brought them into the juvenile justice system. They also highlight the girls' traditional notions of sex and gender as a contributing factor, in that their participants

> typically hope to escape from their present situation by marriage to men who, like their fathers, stepfathers, and brothers abuse them. Wedded to traditional and rigid sex roles, these girls see no other way out, and their fantasies, while enabling them to deal with the loneliness of the present, guarantee nothing but another generation of "bad" girls in the future. (p. iv)

Chesney-Lind and Shelden (1992), reflecting further upon the Hawaiian study, suggest that for these girls, delinquency was an adaptive move, a way of coping with otherwise dismal life-worlds. When all that one can expect at home is abuse, then running away, truancy, and even trading sex for money, food, or shelter become survival strategies. Chesney-Lind and Shelden (1992) point out that girls, particularly working-class (and especially poor) girls from dysfunctional families[3] (i.e., families characterized by marital discord, violence, and the abuse and neglect of children), are disadvantaged early in life by entrenched stereotypical notions of gender, limited educational prospects, the constraints of the sexual double standard, and by the emotional and psychological impact of physical and sexual abuse.

Campbell (1984, 1991), who studied black and Hispanic girls in New York City, found that her subjects participated in gangs primarily because they were attempting to escape violent and dysfunctional families and the resulting emotional isolation. Typically, they had experienced severe parental alcohol and drug misuse, family disintegration through marital discord or the alcohol- or drug-related death of a parent, and extreme poverty. Added to these factors were the ever-present difficulties they experienced as young women of color. When they joined gangs, they wanted somewhere to belong: a community that would afford them safety, continuity, loyalty, and unconditional acceptance. As well, the support of a gang held out the promise (if not the reality) of improved financial status, albeit through illegal means.

As gang members, these girls engaged in violence as a means of survival and as a way of proving their worth to other members. They participated also because violence was accepted and expected. Typically, they fought for one of two reasons: (a) to settle disputes over boys and (b) to enhance their reputations as "tough girls." Being known as "tough" meant that other girls (and also some boys) would fear them and show them respect. This gave them a sense of worth and power. As one girl in Campbell's (1991) study put it:

> It's true — you feel proud when you see a girl that you fucked up. Her face is all scratched or she got a black eye, you say, "Damn, I beat the shit out of that girl you know." And it makes you feel stronger, then you want to fight more and more ... .(p. 263)

All the studies suggest that the subjects' marginality facilitates their participation in a delinquent and/or gang life — and the violence that accompanies it. Missing in the literature are studies that seek to understand the life-worlds and practices of non-marginalized, violent, working-class and middle-class girls — girls who are not found in youth custody and who are not part of an identifiable gang.

Bridging the Gap

The fact that the literature does not as yet address the participation of non-marginalized girls in violent and aggressive behavior helped my colleagues and me to choose the focus of our work. Together we undertook to follow the three-pronged approach outlined in the introduction to this book: We began our study by taking a statistical baseline of students' perceptions of and experiences with violence, and we quite deliberately included questions on a range of their life factors in order to allow us to interpret our findings more fully with respect to violence.

Following this, I undertook a qualitative study that inquired into the life-worlds and practices of school girls who were involved in violence, but who were neither involved with the juvenile justice system nor members of a gang. I sought to answer a number of questions:

- Who are the young women who engage in violence? Where do they come from, and how do they find one another?

- How do they arrange their activities, make decisions, carry out their acts of aggression?

- How do they explain their actions to themselves, to one another, and to others who might oppose them?

- What kinds of home lives do these girls have? What are their families, parents, siblings, grandparents like?

- What stories might the girls tell me? What stories might their parents tell me?

- Who interacts with the girls at school? Whom do they know, and who knows them?

- What forces are at work at home, at school, and in the community that serve to suggest to these young women that aggression and violence are a legitimate means to an end?

- How do these girls make sense of their participation in violence? How do they perceive violence in others and in general?

My main purpose in pursuing these questions was to formulate an understanding of the girls' participation in violence. It is my belief that we do the things we do because we have made sense of ourselves and the world along particular lines and are therefore impelled to act in certain ways. I view action in Michael Novak's (1978) terms, that is, as "a declaration of faith: one cannot act without implicitly imagining the shape of the world, the significance of one's own role, the place at which the struggle is effectively joined" (p. 45). Thus, I concluded that if I wanted to understand violence among teenage school girls, I needed to approach them in ways that would allow me to discover all I could about their "declarations of faith." I needed to learn how they lived their lives and how they made sense of their actions.

Upon completing the analysis of our baseline data and the qualitative study of the *Life Worlds and Practices of Violent School Girls* (Artz, 1995), we became involved in the current phase of the Youth Violence Project: A Community-Based Violence Prevention Project. This phase is a collaborative, community-based initiative designed to address the problem of youth violence in a Vancouver Island school district. It involves teachers, counselors, parents, and students, as well as representatives from health care and social service agencies. It consists of 13 individual antiviolence initiatives that have been developed by school-based health teams located in each of the local school communities for whom these initiatives are intended. Although there are 13 initiatives, these in some cases extend to more than one school; thus, they involve a total of 16 school communities. The school-based health teams include the participation of over 60 parents, 118 students, 60 educators, and 20 local agency workers (some of whom participate on more than one health team). The overall project serves over 5,400 students, their families, educators, and community members. It is intended to educate and train students and community members in a preventative approach to violence that includes helping individuals change their behavior and acquire and master skills that will enable them to act differently in circumstances that previously would have called forth violent responses.

This project will provide us with much needed information about violence prevention. The research dimensions of the project focus on the evaluation of the effectiveness of the various initiatives, using a model of participant-based program evaluation. Because the writing of this book and the implementation and evaluation of the prevention initiatives are concurrent, it is possible to report here only preliminary findings. Nevertheless, much has already been learned about programs and interventions that speak to violent girls.

NOTES

1. "Lower class" refers to a socioeconomic status (SES) category where "lower" means "lower income and status." "Working class" generally refers to the connection between social class and work — in this case, blue-collar work. The distinction between the two terms comes down

to money. "Lower class" always means "having lower socioeconomic levels of income," whereas "working class" refers to the kind of work an individual does regardless of income, as physical or skilled labor is often highly paid.

2. This possibility solidified into a reality in the 1990s, as the statistics presented on pages 13–15 show.

3. Although most of the literature surveyed here focuses on a sociological understanding of female crime and delinquency, it is clear from the material provided by Chesney-Lind and her associates (1985, 1994) and by Campbell (1991) that dysfunctional families are strongly implicated in the deviance and delinquency of their daughters.

Flowers (1990, pp. 133–139), in his overview of the literature on juvenile offenders, states that "many experts believe that it is the inter-actants of family life that is the greatest predictor of adolescent delin-quency" (p. 133). In examining the familial correlates of delinquent behavior, Flowers (1990) cites over 40 studies and notes that child abuse (especially sexual abuse) and physical violence are strongly asso-ciated with deviance and delinquency for both males and females. According to Flowers, numerous studies have shown that sexual abuse is strongly linked with prostitution and sex crimes. He also notes that many studies have shown that violent adolescents have often witnessed brutality in their families and experienced it at the hands of their par-ents or other family members. Such abuse is not only strongly linked to extra-familial violence; it is also linked to intra-familial violence, in that children who have been physically and sexually abused also tend to abuse their parents more than children who have not been abused.

Other familial correlates of delinquent behavior also listed by Flowers are: lax or inconsistent discipline and harsh discipline; lack of parental affection; absence of the kind of parenting that promotes con-structive interpersonal communication and encourages the develop-ment of normative values and prosocial behavior and of academic and professional skills; the "broken home factor," in which one or both par-ents are absent through death, desertion, separation, or divorce; and family dissension, where families have remained intact but are charac-terized by a climate of conflict and discord. With regard to this last cor-relate, Flowers suggests that "there is indication that intact families beset by conflict and turmoil are more significant in delinquency for-mation than broken home families" (p. 139). Finally, Flowers includes intergenerational cycles of violence and abuse grounded in "a lifestyle of neglect that comes from sharing and passing on of family misfor-tunes" as the context in which the familial correlates he itemizes have their anchor (p. 135).

CHAPTER TWO

Profiles of the Protagonists

> More kids from middle to upper middle income backgrounds are committing violent assaults on their own peer group or on the adult group or the teaching staff than they used to. (Auty, Dempsey, Duggan, Lowery, West, & Wiseman, 1993, p. 5)

> Violence: a use of physical force so as to damage or injure ... an abusive use of force ... . (*The New Lexicon Webster's Encyclopedic Dictionary of the English Language*, 1988, p. 1,099)

> Assault: a vigorous armed attack ... a violent critical attack ... an unlawful threat to use force against another person (*The New Lexicon Webster's Encyclopedic Dictionary of the English Language*, 1988, p. 56).

This chapter draws on the findings of the *Survey of Student Life* (Artz & Riecken, 1994) in order to provide profiles of students who report that they engage in violence in schools. In creating these profiles we, like all other researchers, were faced with the task of defining our terms. We had to ask ourselves the following questions:

- What did we mean when we described someone as violent?
- How would we delineate between violent and non-violent youth?
- Given that our study had a broader basis than violence alone, what else did we want to investigate in relation to violence?

How we answered these questions is explained in the section that follows.

Defining Violence and Creating Comparison Groups

Embedded within the *Survey of Student Life* (Artz & Riecken, 1994) was a question consisting of 13 variables that tapped into rule-breaking and deviant or violent behavior. This question has previously been used by Gordon Barnes (1991), a noted Canadian researcher in the fields of family violence, addictions, and substance abuse, in his *Northern Family Life Survey*. Barnes adapted his questionnaire from an earlier one developed by American researcher Richard Jessor (1977), director of the Institute of Behavioral Science and director of the MacArthur Foundation Research Program on Youth at Risk.

Using Barnes's question meant we did not have to re-invent the wheel; it also meant that we were working with a measure that had been previously tested and that lent credibility to our findings. This question investigated such behaviors as smoking without parents' permission, lying about one's whereabouts, various degrees of skipping classes or school, and various levels of stealing, damaging property, violence, and carrying weapons.

Of the 13 variables investigated, the one that spoke most directly to violence reads, "During the past year, how often have you beaten up another kid?," thus defining violence ("beating up another kid"). Students responded by circling the number corresponding to one of four choices: (1) "Never," (2) "Once or twice," (3) "Several times," or (4) "Very often." For purposes of analysis, students' answers were dichotomized into "Never" and "Once or More." These groups were termed "nonhitters" and "hitters," respectively. This dichotomy was deemed to represent the clearest and most natural distinction between the two groups, and was used for both males and females in the creation of the profiles of the protagonists.

Of the 1,466 students who provided an answer to the variable that separated hitters from nonhitters, *51.9% of the males* (i.e., 396 of 763) *and 20.9% of the females* (i.e., 147 of 703) *answered that in the past year, they had beaten up another kid once or twice.* This means that 37% of our sample identified their involvement in physical violence in the past year. Further, the male:female ratios for self-reported participation in violence found in previous research (Hindelang, Hirschi, & Weis, 1981; Berger, 1989) have typically been on the order of 3:1 to 4:1, whereas we are reporting a male:female ratio of slightly under 2.5:1. Given the magnitude of the response rates, the seriousness of violence in schools is not to be underestimated, nor is the participation of girls.

The Overall Picture: Gender-Based Comparisons of Nonhitting and Hitting Students

In order to discover how those who reported beating up another student differed from those who reported that they had not done this, we created four groups: nonhitting females, nonhitting males, hitting females, and hitting males. We tabulated their answers to all other questions in the *Survey of Student Life*, and then compared outcomes for all the groups we created. A chi-square analysis of our data showed that: (a) there were *more differences* between males and females who *had not beaten* up another student in the past year (56/168) than there were between males and females who had beaten up another student in the past year (31/168); and (b) there were *more differences between males* who had and had not beaten up another student (52/168) than there were between females who had and had not beaten up another student in the past year (30/168).

Thus, males and females who do not engage in violence appear to be more distinguishable along gender lines than males and females who engage in violence; males who engage in violence are more readily distinguishable from males who do not; and females who engage in violence, despite showing some similarities with their male counterparts, are still more like girls who don't engage in violence than they are like boys.

To facilitate an overview of the comparisons generated by our database, we have presented our findings using the following categories:

- Relationships and Social Attitudes.
- Personal and Social Concerns.
- Support Systems.
- Sources of Enjoyment and Sources of Concern.[1]
- Experience of Abuse and Victimization (Physical and Sexual).
- Participation in Deviant Behavior.

RelATioNships aNd SociAL ATTiTudEs

In this category, participants were asked to provide information about their perspectives on and experiences with family, peer groups, schools and teachers, interpersonal values, moral judgments, and self-concept.

FAMily

Eighty-four point four percent of students surveyed were living in two-parent households. The overall breakdown of living arrangements was: 64.5% were living with both biological parents, 11.9% were living with mother and stepfather, 3.8% were living with mother and a common-law partner, 2.8% were living with father and stepmother, 1.4%

were living with father and a common-law partner, 13% were living with mother only, and 2.6% were living with father only.

Most participants' parents were employed, and few were experiencing the deprivation of poverty. As well, the majority of parents were educated at the high school graduation level or better. (See Tables A-1 and A-2 in Appendix I for a breakdown of parental occupation/education for the sample as a whole.)

Neither males nor females who hit reported any significant differences in family configuration, living arrangements, parental employment, or parental education from those reported by males and females overall. Familial differences were, however, found in family dynamics. (See Tables A-3a and A-3b in Appendix I.)

Hitting females and hitting males reported placing significantly less importance upon family life than either nonhitting females or nonhitting males. Hitting females also reported that enjoyment of their mothers was less applicable to them than all other groups, and that they feared being physically abused at home, and were physically abused at home, at significantly greater rates than those reported by all other groups. As well, hitting females smoked without their parents' permission more than all other groups. However, nonhitting females also smoked more often without parental permission than nonhitting males, and at the same rates reported by hitting males.

A similar pattern emerged with regard to lying about one's whereabouts. Hitting females lied more often than nonhitting females and nonhitting males, while nonhitting females lied more often than nonhitting males. Hitting females and hitting males reported lying at about the same rates (i.e., their rates, while numerically different, were not statistically different). Thus, on average, females reported smoking more and lying more than males. Finally, hitting females and hitting males reported the same rates for staying out all night without parents' permission and for deliberately ruining an item of parents' property after an argument, rates that were significantly higher than those reported by nonhitting females and nonhitting males, who reported the same significantly lower rates.

PEER GROUPS

In the survey, students were asked if they were members of a number of groups including school clubs, youth clubs, sports teams, religious organizations, and specific street groups ("Bangers," "Rappers," or

"Skates"). The only significant differences that emerged with regard to group affiliation and participation centered around self-reported group membership and the differential importance participants placed upon their involvement in dating, party-going, and negative experiences with sex. We found that both hitting males and hitting females reported being members of either the Bangers or Rappers at far higher rates than nonhitting males and nonhitting females. When Skates were also considered, we found that 68.8% of hitting females' and 53.5% of hitting males' group membership could be accounted for. (See Table A-4 in Appendix I.)

The following brief descriptions will help the reader understand those street groups in which hitting participants claimed membership.

Rappers. Rappers are people who listen to rap music, which has its origins in reggae and American inner-city, black-ghetto street music. Rap involves rhyming and dancing; its main appeal is its tribal rhythms. Rap is "cool" in the style of black America; rap is also angry. Rap endorses gangs, crime, machismo, and misogyny, as well as freedom from white dominant-group oppression. Being a Rapper means acquiring an instant style: baggy clothes, designer sneakers, and brand-name (and sports-team affiliated) jackets, shirts, and pants. For most adolescents, being a Rapper has more to do with fashion and style than it does with espousing the sentiments expressed in the lyrics of rap music.

Though the main draw with rap is beat and image, Rappers do take a position with regard to violence. Mostly, their message is, "I'm tougher than you." This holds true for both males and females. In the final analysis, a Rapper is loath to back down and must guard his or her reputation for toughness by exhibiting a willingness to fight, especially if "dissed"; that is, if one perceives that he or she is being treated with disrespect.

Bangers. Bangers are people who particularly like heavy metal music. Their favorite bands include Guns 'N Roses, Alice In Chains, and Metallica. Heavy metal music is largely blue-collar and antiestablishment in its origins. Often the music expresses angst, anger, and rage, and sometimes the focus is on a self-absorbed examination of substance abuse. Bangers' values are expressed in their music, and their heroes are heavy metal musicians.

Both male and female Bangers wear T-shirts and tight jeans emblazoned with the names of their favorite music groups. Banger males usually grow their hair long, and females may dye their hair blond. Females often carry large purses or bags in order to carry alcohol and drugs for boys. Bangers believe in male dominance; females "look after" (read, serve and look up to) males. Banger girls, like Rapper girls, are tough, particularly when it comes to beating off competition from other girls vis-à-vis their boyfriends.

Skates. Skates, or Skaters, are people whose focus is predominantly on the activity of skateboarding and somewhat less on style and music, although they also have a clothing style and music preferences. Skates enjoy thrash, punk, and hip-hop music, and tend to dress in anything they can find, although their preference in sneakers and skateboarding equipment is expensive and brand-name driven. The look they try to achieve is unmistakable: oversize T-shirts, shorts, and pants; long underwear worn under shorts; toques and sometimes baseball hats worn backwards; strategic holes, tears, and cut-off cuffs, sleeves, and pant legs.

Skates are less concerned with toughness and anger than Rappers. In an altercation, they usually take the defensive. They see themselves as outcasts, often in conflict with authority because their skateboarding is rarely welcome. There are many fewer Skater girls than boys, largely because skateboarding appeals more to boys, but also because most adult involvement with the sport is commercially driven and encourages competition and product endorsement aimed very specifically at males. Occasionally, a girl does join a group of Skaters, and in one or two larger urban centers, it's possible to find groups of female Skates. These girls sometimes call themselves "Betties" and congregate in all-female groups. More often, if a girl is a Skate, she became one through her connection with a Skater boy.

Finally, in connection with their self-reported high level of group affiliation, both hitting males and hitting females placed significantly greater importance on belonging to a group or gang, and having the right clothes to fit their group or gang, than did nonhitting males and nonhitting females. (See Table A-5 in Appendix I.)

One final difference reported by those who had beaten up another kid and those who had not was the enjoyment they received from parties: 50.1% of male hitters reported receiving "a great deal of enjoyment" vs. 34.1% for male nonhitters, while 60.0% of female hitters reported receiving "a great deal of enjoyment" from parties, vs. 41.7% for female nonhitters.

School and teachers

Respondents to the *Survey of Student Life* (Artz & Riecken, 1994) were asked how much enjoyment they received from school; whether they agreed that, overall, their teachers were genuinely interested in them; whether they were afraid they would be attacked at school; whether they had ever stayed away from school because they were afraid; if they had ever been attacked on their way to or from school; how often they had damaged school property in the past year; and whether, compared with elementary school, life was safer, less safe, or about the same.

Females hitters and nonhitters and male nonhitters reported the same level of enjoyment from school (75.6% reported receiving at least some enjoyment from school, although all agreed that out of 23 possible items, school ranked lowest as a source of enjoyment). Male hitters also ranked school lowest as a source of enjoyment, and did so at a level (57.8%) that was significantly lower than either nonhitting males or hitting and nonhitting females.

Neither female nor male hitters reported significant differences with regard to any of the following:

- being afraid to go to school because they might be physically attacked (19.6% of all students said they were afraid).

- staying away from school because they were afraid (7.6% of all students said they had stayed away).

- finding life at junior high school safer, less safe, or about the same as life in elementary school (48.9% of all students said it was less safe, while 38.4% said it was about the same).

- agreeing that their teachers were genuinely interested in them (57.6% of all students did not agree).

However, both female and male hitters reported significantly higher levels of damaging school property than their nonhitting peers. They also reported acting up in school if they didn't like their teachers to a significantly greater degree than their nonhitting counterparts. (See Table A-6 in Appendix I.)

Interpersonal social values

A gender-based comparison of the endorsement of selected interpersonal dynamics and social values (friendship, being loved, concern for others, respect for others, forgiveness, honesty, politeness, generosity, and being respected) revealed that where these dynamics and values are concerned, the between-group differences (females to males) are more striking than the within-group differences (males to males and females to females). (See Tables A-7, A-8, and A-9 in Appendix I.)

Nonhitting females endorsed all the relational dynamics and social values listed at significantly higher levels than nonhitting males. However, when nonhitting females were compared with hitting females, the only value that was differentially endorsed by hitting females was honesty. This finding must be interpreted with caution, however, because the difference only approaches significance; that is, given that the level required to claim statistical significance ($p <$ .0001) is almost achieved, we may only speculate that this difference can be attributed to something other than chance.

In contrast to the findings that emerged with regard to females, a comparison of nonhitting and hitting males did yield some differences with regard to self-reported endorsement of interpersonal social values. According to the data provided, respect for others, forgiveness, honesty, politeness, and generosity are *less important* to hitting males than they are to nonhitting males.

An overview of the self-report data provided by the survey respondents showed that females, whether they are nonhitting or hitting, place more importance on all the interpersonal social values explored, but they (like the males) *place more importance on how they themselves are treated than on how they treat others* (e.g., friendship, being loved, and being respected). For females, the only significant difference that distinguishes one group from another in this sample is the differential value placed on honesty when nonhitting and hitting girls are compared.

For males, some interpersonal values do seem to help in distinguishing males who hit from those who do not. It appears that among males, the endorsement of respect for others, forgiveness, honesty, politeness, and generosity seems to contribute to an inhibition against beating up other kids.

The male/female differences in interpersonal social values reported here are similar to those reported by Bibby and Posterski (1992), who tapped into some of these same values and also found that females had a greater commitment to interpersonal values than males did. In view of this, Bibby and Posterski (1992) sounded a warning note: They suggested that "a major trend characterizing life for young people today is the devaluing of personal ideals" (p. 141). The data provided by the participants in this study suggest exactly what Bibby and Posterski (1992) predicted when they wrote:

> Young women in the 90s are … far more likely than males to place a very high value on interpersonal traits, including … honesty, concern for others … politeness and generosity… . The current low proportion, less than one in two, of young males who highly value such interpersonal traits is enough to make one wonder about the confidence people can have in their dealings with these emerging young men. When honesty is downplayed, along with concern and courtesy, the implications for social life are a bit scary. (p. 142)

This statement has implications that cannot be ignored. Social scientists must develop a different understanding of females with regard to the impact of subscribing to interpersonal values, especially because the girls in our study reported participating in violence despite endorsing interpersonal values. For my colleague and me, these findings raised the question: If, for girls, hitting is largely unconnected to differences in interpersonal social values, what, then, helps us to distinguish female hitters from female nonhitters? The answer became clear when we examined survey participants' moral judgments.

Moral Judgments
Participants were presented with the following statements in order to gauge their endorsement of the problematic behaviors described:

- If someone has something you really want, it's OK to make them give it to you.
- It's OK to punch or hit someone when you're having an argument.
- Fighting is a good way to defend your friends.
- It's OK to use threats to get what you want.
- If I don't like my teacher, it's OK to act up in school.
- It's OK to damage buildings and property as a way of getting even.
- Right or wrong is a matter of personal opinion.
- The use of marijuana should be legalized.

Responses to these statements provided us with insight into participants' moral judgments with regard to aggressive and violent behaviors and produced significant gender differences, as well as significant differences between nonhitting and hitting females and nonhitting and hitting males. (See Table A-10 in Appendix I.)

Male nonhitters, despite reporting that they had not beaten up another kid in the past year, still endorsed making someone give them something if they really wanted it, punching or hitting someone during an argument, fighting to defend friends, using threats, acting up in school if they didn't like their teacher, and damaging buildings and property as a way of getting even, at a significantly higher level than nonhitting females. It is especially noteworthy that 32% of nonhitting males agreed with the statement that "fighting is a good way to defend your friends," and 21.2% agreed with the statement that "it's OK to punch or hit someone when you're having an argument."

Significant differences emerged between nonhitting and hitting females and between nonhitting and hitting males. (See Tables A-11 and A-12 in Appendix I.) Hitters, whether male or female, endorsed violence to a significantly greater degree than their nonviolent counterparts. However, further examination of the data showed that despite these differences between hitters and nonhitters (whether male or female), such differences were not found when female hitters were compared with male nonhitters (see Table A-13 in Appendix I) and when female hitters were compared with male hitters (see Table A-14 in Appendix I).

Female hitters endorse five of the eight problems presented to a greater degree than male nonhitters (punching and hitting during an argument, using threats, acting up in school, right or wrong as a matter of personal opinion, and legalization of marijuana. Thus, female hitters differed significantly not only from their nonhitting female counterparts, but also from nonhitting males. Further, female hitters appear to have most in common with male hitters in that the only significant difference that distinguished female hitters from male hitters was the higher level of fighting in defense of friends reported by male hitters.

To summarize: For females especially, endorsement of moral judgments that sanction aggression and violence clearly distinguishes females who engage in violence from those who do not. This endorsement also distinguishes hitting females from nonhitting males. At the same time, where hitting females are concerned, interpersonal social values appear to play little or no role in providing a barrier to violence. This is different for males. With males (as with females), moral judgments play a key role in distinguishing those who hit others from those who do not, but (unlike females) interpersonal values also play an important role.

Self-concept

Because many educators and parents believe that negative behavior is connected to poor self-concept, we asked four questions that required students to describe themselves according to a four-point scale, where 1 = "Not very well at all," 2 = "Not very well," 3 = "Fairly well," and 4 = "Very well." Most students answered 3 = "Fairly well," or 4 = "Very well." (See Table A-15 in Appendix I.) However, males, whether hitters or nonhitters, reported significantly higher levels of agreement with the positive self-concept statements than females, whether they were hitters or nonhitters. Further, when students' scores for all four questions were summed, and means or averages were calculated and compared, three of the four items in the self-concept scale yielded statistically significant gender differences. Overall, males reported perceiving themselves as "good-looking" more often than females did; they also saw themselves as being able to "do most things well" and having "lots of confidence" to a significantly greater degree than females. This difference was not altered by membership in the hitter or nonhitter groups, thus suggesting that participation in violence is not particularly connected to self-concept as we conceptualized it in our survey. (See Table A-16 in Appendix I.)

Personal and social concerns

Respondents to the survey were asked to assess the seriousness of 16 social problems or issues facing Canadians today, identified first by Bibby and Posterski (1992): AIDS, child abuse, racial discrimination, teenage suicide, violence against women, the environment, the unequal treatment of women, violence in schools, drug abuse, alcohol abuse, youth gangs, native–white relations, the economy, global awareness, spirituality, and one's cultural group or heritage. What was notable in the responses was that most of the significant differences reported distinguished between males and females overall rather than between hitters and nonhitters. (See Table A-17 in Appendix I.) Females consistently reported higher levels of social concern than males in all areas, whether they were nonhitters or hitters.

For females, when comparing hitters and nonhitters, only three significant differences emerged. Hitting females reported higher levels of concern about the unequal treatment of women, and lower levels of concern with regard to violence in schools and global awareness, than did nonhitting females.

For males, four significant differences emerged. Nonhitting males reported higher levels of concern with regard to violence in schools, drug abuse, alcohol abuse, and youth gangs than hitting males, although these levels of concern were still lower than those reported by nonhitting females.

Also relevant to this category were those questions that asked survey respondents to comment on their ambitions, their monetary concerns, and certain aspects of their quality of life.

With regard to ambition, only one statistically significant difference emerged: Male hitters reported receiving more enjoyment from working than female hitters. (See Table A-18 in Appendix I.) They also reported enjoying working slightly, though not significantly, more than female and male nonhitters. Interestingly, although hitting males seemed to like having jobs, they (along with hitting females) appeared to place somewhat less (though not significantly less) importance upon working hard. Also, hitting males and hitting females reported having slightly (though not significantly) less confidence that "anyone who works hard will rise to the top." As well, given the percentage of students who responded that they experience "a great deal" of pressure to do well in school, hitting males and hitting females reported experiencing slightly (though not significantly) more pressure. Finally, it also appeared, from the percentage of students who reported that never having enough time bothers them "a great deal," that nonhitting males seemed less (though not significantly less) bothered by this than nonhitting females or hitting males and hitting females.

Questions related to students' monetary concerns revealed that fewer than half of all respondents worked during the school year. (See Table A-19 in Appendix I.) Of those who reported working, hitting boys reported having jobs most often, although they were not employed at statistically significant higher rates than others. Nonhitting males reported working fewer hours than hitting males and nonhitting or hitting females, although the number of hours they worked was not significantly lower than the rest. A significantly greater number of hitting males reported earning more than seven dollars an hour (the minimum wage in British Columbia) than either nonhitting males, hitting females, or nonhitting females, although a significant number of hitting females also reported earning more than seven dollars an hour when compared with nonhitting females. Finally, with regard to receiving an allowance, well over half of all respondents reported receiving one, with hitting females and hitting males reporting that they received the highest levels of allowance. Overall, hitters, whether male or female, reported having more money than nonhitters. Hitting males reported having the most money, although they also reported being significantly more bothered by a lack of money than did members of the other groups.

The quality-of-life questions asked students to state the importance of having a comfortable life, intelligence, humor, and good looks. Their answers showed that all groups (hitters and nonhitters, males and females) placed the same relative importance on these four variables, although male nonhitters seemed to place slightly more importance upon having a comfortable life and intelligence, while male hitters seemed to place slightly more importance on their looks. (See Table A-20 in Appendix I.) None of these slight differences proved to be statistically significant.

Support Systems

We asked respondents to answer a number of questions that identified to whom they would turn for help with specific problems. We also asked them two global questions, one which focused broadly on people and places to whom they could go for help, and one which asked how bothered they were at not being understood by their parents.

In answer to the first global question: "There are places and people I can go to if I need help" ("Strongly disagree," "Disagree," "Agree, "Strongly agree"), well over 80% of all students agreed that there were such people and places. At 92.2%, female nonhitters reported the highest levels of agreement with the statement, "There are places and people I can go to for help." Male nonhitters were next at 87.8%, then females hitters at 84.7%, followed by male hitters at 81.8%. Although some small differences in percentages were reported by these groups, *none of these differences are statistically significant.* This means that these are not actual differences, but merely artifacts of chance.

With regard to the second question, "How much does not being understood by your parents bother you?" ("A great deal," Quite a bit," "Some," "Little or none"), 47.9% of female hitters, 37.8% of male hitters, 37.7% of female nonhitters, and 25.5% of male nonhitters reported being bothered by not being understood by their parents "a great deal." Again, despite the fact that these numbers suggest real differences among groups, these are not statistically significant and must therefore be put down to chance.

Outlined below are the eight questions that probed some of the specifics regarding students' support systems. The data are reported here to allow the reader to see what the participants in the survey told us about their support systems, but have not been analyzed for statistically significant differences in the same way as the rest of the data reported here. This is because of the complexity of these comparisons. (See Tables A-21 to A-28 in Appendix I for raw-score data.)

1. Who are you most likely to turn to concerning spending money?
Overall, survey participants' responses indicated that most students (about 50% of nonhitting males and females and about 40% of hitting males and females) would turn to their parents.

2. Who are you most likely to turn to concerning relationships?
Overall, survey participants' responses indicated that most students would turn to their friends in this situation. Nonhitting females and hitting females indicate the highest levels of turning to friends (80.6% and 77.3%, respectively). Nonhitting males and hitting males also reported turning mostly to their friends for help with relationships, although they do this at somewhat lower rates than females. Further, nonhitting males report the lowest levels of turning to friends (59.6%), while at the same time reporting the highest levels of turning to no one (25.42%).

3. Who are you most likely to turn to concerning sex?
Hitting males and nonhitting females reported that they would turn to their friends at about the same rates (46.2% and 49.3%, respectively). Hitting females reported a higher rate (59.4%) of turning to friends; nonhitting males, however, reported a noticeably lower rate (34.2%)

than the other three groups. As well, as in question 2, nonhitting males, while reporting the lowest rates of turning to friends, also reported the highest rates of turning to no one (47.4%).

4. Who are you most likely to turn to concerning having fun?
Most survey participants, male or female, reported that they were most likely to turn to friends for fun. Females, especially hitting females, chose their friends over the other possibilities offered at rates that were about 10% higher than those for males. While all respondents gave low response rates when it came to choosing parents, hitting females chose parents at the lowest rate of all (0.7%). As well, respondents reported turning to no one at higher rates than those they reported for turning to parents. This is especially noticeable for males, who reported that they would turn to no one at the rate of about 14%, while their rates for turning to parents were about 4% to 5%.

5. Who are you most likely to turn to concerning right and wrong?
Nonhitting males and females reported turning most often to their parents (49.7% and 48.6%, respectively). Hitting males and females also report turning to their parents, but at lower rates (36% and 32.6%, respectively), with hitting females preferring friends over parents (38%). Nonhitting and hitting males report turning to no one at slightly higher rates than they report turning to friends (27.3% no one vs. 18.2% friends, for nonhitting males; and 29.6% no one vs. 25.8% friends, for hitting males).

6. Who are you most likely to turn to concerning school?
Nonhitting males and nonhitting females reported turning to their parents at higher rates than they reported turning to others (53.5% and 51.6%, respectively). Hitting males and females also reported turning to their parents more than to others, but their rates for doing this were lower than those of their nonhitting counterparts (39.1% and 37.5%, respectively). Further, hitting females reported turning to friends at almost the same rates that they reported turning to parents (36.0% vs. 37.5%). As well, although males' rates (both hitters and nonhitters) indicated that after parents, they would turn to friends, they also reported that they would turn to no one at nearly the same rates at which they reported turning to friends (16.8% vs. 18.8% for nonhitters, and 20.7% vs. 24.7% for hitters). School counselors were

chosen by some students as a source of help; but with the exception of hitting females, these rates were lower than those reported for turning to no one.

7. Who are you most likely to turn to concerning careers?
Most nonhitting males (65.7%) and females (60.0%) reported that they would turn to their parents. Hitting males followed suit, but at somewhat lower rates (52.0%), while hitting females once again reported the lowest rate of turning to their parents for help (44.9%). Respondents' second highest rates, with regard to whom to turn to, were those reported for turning to no one. For hitting males and non-hitting males, these were 24.4% and 16.4%, respectively, while for nonhitting females, the rate was 17.3%. Hitting females reported turning to friends at a slightly higher rate (21.0%) than they reported turning to no one (19.6%). With the exception of hitting females, who reported turning to school counselors at the rate of 10.9%, few students reported turning to school counselors for help with careers.

8. Who would you turn to concerning a major problem?
According to participants' self-reports, females (hitters and nonhitters alike) turned more to their friends than to their parents (48.0% and 51.2%, respectively). Nonhitting males turned more to their parents (52.9%), as did hitting males (37.9%), although they reported turning to friends almost as often as they did to parents (34.6%).

Overall, parents and friends were the two social support groups most respondents turned to most often. However, it is noteworthy that in the absence of turning to parents or friends, survey participants chose the category "no one" as their third option.

SOURCES of ENJOYMENT and SOURCES of CONCERN

SOURCES of ENJOYMENT
We provided survey participants with 23 items intended to gauge their enjoyment from a variety of sources. These items were originally compiled by Bibby and Posterski (1992) as factors common to teenage life. We asked respondents to assess each item on a four-point scale: (4) "A great deal," (3) "Quite a bit," (2) "Some," and (1) "Little or none."

The items were then ranked in descending order according to the mean (overall average) score for enjoyment that respondents reported deriving from each. (See Table 2-1.)

According to Table 2-1, all respondents identified their friends as the number one source of enjoyment. High enjoyment ratings were also given to items generally associated with the adolescent subculture (e.g., music, parties, boyfriends/girlfriends and dates, sports, television, VCRs). In comparison, lower enjoyment ratings were accorded to various family members. As well, although friends were ranked number one by all respondents, females reported deriving significantly more enjoyment from their friends than males did. Also, although music was ranked number three overall, females reported significantly more enjoyment from music than males did. Lastly, although reading was ranked last by all respondents, females still reported deriving significantly more enjoyment from reading than males did. Conversely, males reported deriving significantly more enjoyment from sports, television, and VCRs than females did.

Despite these gender differences, males and females generated very similar rankings for most of the items. Further, those rankings that distinguished between hitters and nonhitters were few in number. Female and male hitters reported receiving significantly more enjoyment from parties and stereos than female and male nonhitters did. Also, male hitters reported receiving significantly more enjoyment from dating and from girlfriends than male nonhitters did. Finally, the reader should note that the difference between the highest- and lowest-ranked item was only 1.4 points. This suggests a cautious interpretation of the rankings, and indicates that all respondents derived at least some enjoyment from all the items offered.

SOURCES OF CONCERN

Survey participants were asked to rate how often they were bothered by various problems. The 12 problems were rated on a four-point scale from "little or none" to "a great deal." Table 2-2 (page 44) provides a ranking, in descending order, of the average level of "bothersomeness" elicited by each problem.

The adolescents in this sample tend to be bothered by all these problems to some degree. The most bothersome problems were the adolescents' perceptions of lack of time and money. To a lesser degree, the respondents were bothered by the uncertainty of what to do after

Table 2-1

Self-reported rating of enjoyment that adolescents receive from various sources and activities (N=1,479)

Mean	Rank	Variable
3.550	1	Friends**
3.281	2	Car
3.277	3	Music**
3.273	4	*Girlfriend/Boyfriend*
3.260	5	Own room
3.220	**6**	**Stereo**
3.140	**7**	**Parties**
3.030	8	*Dates*
3.000	9	Being part of a group of kids/teens
2.980	10	Sports*
2.940	11	Pet
2.750	12	Mother
2.700	13	Television*
2.670	14	VCR
2.640	15	Father
2.540	16	Job
2.530	17	Grandparents
2.470	18	Self
2.400	19	City/Town you live in
2.330	20	Adult friend
2.224	21	Brothers and sisters
2.223	22	Reading**
2.140	23	School

Means are on a scale of 1 to 4, where:
1 = Little or no enjoyment   3= Quite a bit of enjoyment
2 = Some enjoyment   4 = A lot of enjoyment

* Denotes a gender difference ($p < .0001$), with males reporting more enjoyment.
** Denotes a gender difference ($p < .0001$), with females reporting more enjoyment.
Bold type denotes more enjoyment ($p < .0001$) for all hitters, male and female.
Italic type denotes more enjoyment ($p < .0001$) for hitting males.

graduation, and not having things to do. Adolescents were the least bothered by the fear of being attacked or beaten up, and by pressure to engage in sex.

As indicated in Table 2-2, three gender differences emerged in the respondents' ratings of bothersome problems. Females tended to report that they were more bothered by lack of parental understanding than

Table 2-2
Ratings of how often participants reported being bothered by various problems

Mean	Rank	Variable
2.958	1	Never seem to have enough time
2.828	2	Lack of money
2.788	3	Not understood by parents**
2.729	4	Pressure to do well in school
2.569	5	The way you look**
2.502	6	Losing friends**
2.462	7	What to do after finishing school
2.374	8	Not having things to do
2.181	9	*Not having a place to hang out*
2.146	10	Not having a girlfriend/boyfriend
1.180	11	Fear of being attacked or beaten up
1.630	12	*Pressure to engage in sex*

Means are on a scale of 1 to 4, where:
1 = Little or no bother   3 = Quite a bit of bother
2 = Some bother   4 = A lot of bother

**Denotes a gender difference ($p < .0001$), with females reporting being more bothered.
Italic type denotes a greater level of bother ($p < .0001$) reported by hitting males.

were males. Females were also more frequently bothered by the way they looked. In addition, females were significantly more bothered by the loss of friends. Also, hitting males reported that they felt significantly more bothered than nonhitting males and all females by not having a place to hang out and by feeling pressured to engage in sex.

Experience of Abuse and Victimization

All researchers who have inquired into violent behavior have noted that those who engage in violence are also victimized more often that those who do not engage in violence. We therefore asked survey participants to provide us with information about their experiences of victimization and abuse. We also asked them to answer questions about their perceptions and fears with regard to being victimized and abused.

Our findings followed the same patterns as those established by previous researchers in that hitters, both male and female, reported significantly greater rates of victimization and abuse. (See Flowers, 1990 and Chesney-Lind & Shelden, 1992 for in-depth discussions.)

Fear of being victimized or abused

Survey participants were asked to respond to seven questions about their fears of being victimized and/or abused. Of these seven questions, four yielded significant differences among groups. All significant differences reported are significant at $p < .0001$ (chi-square). Each of the seven questions is discussed in turn. (See Tables A-29 to A-40 in Appendix I.)

1. How often does the fear of being attacked or beaten up bother you?
According to all respondents (hitters and nonhitters), 20% to 25% of students are bothered by a general fear of being attacked or beaten up.

2. Are you afraid of being physically attacked at school?
As with question 1, no significant differences were found to distinguish among groups. Overall, roughly 20% of students reported feeling afraid that they might be attacked at school.

3. Are you afraid of being beaten up by a gang of kids?
Although there was some variation among groups in the number of respondents who answered "yes" to this question, this variation is not statistically significant, and is therefore a chance-based rather than a systematic variation. Thus, overall, approximately 20% of respondents reported being afraid of being beaten up by a gang of kids.

4. Have you ever stayed away from school because you were afraid?
Nonhitting males reported the lowest levels of this behavior. When their responses are compared with those of nonhitting and hitting females, the differences are statistically significant. This is not the case when a comparison is made between nonhitting and hitting males. At the same time, when comparing all females with hitting males, their rates of staying away from school were not statistically different. Thus, we may infer that nonhitting males stay away from school least often, and that females and hitting males stay way from school about 10% to 12% of the time.

5. Are you afraid that you might be physically abused at home?
As noted earlier in this chapter, nearly 20% of hitting females reported that they were afraid of being physically abused at home. This stands out in stark contrast to the level of fear reported by nonhitting

females (6.6%) and both nonhitting and hitting males (3.3% and 4.9%, respectively). The level of fear of being physically abused at home reported by hitting females is significantly higher than that reported by those in all other categories.

6. *Are you afraid that you might be sexually assaulted?*
Females (whether hitters or nonhitters) reported significantly higher levels of fear that they might be sexually assaulted. Hitting females reported the highest levels of fear (37.2%), levels that were significantly higher than those of nonhitting females (28.0%). Although some males reported fearing sexual assault, the vast majority (over 92%) reported having no such fear.

7. *Are you afraid that you might be talked into having sex with your boyfriend/girlfriend against your will?*
Females (both nonhitters and hitters) reported more fear than males of being talked into having sex against their will. Hitting females reported the highest levels of fear (33.4%). These were significantly higher than those reported by nonhitting females (14.3%), nonhitting males (2.8%), and hitting males (8.2%). As well, when compared with the level of fear reported by nonhitting males, the level of fear reported by all females (nonhitting and hitting) was significantly greater. However, the level of fear reported by nonhitting females was not significantly greater than that reported by hitting males; here, the level of fear was approximately the same, statistically speaking. Thus, nonhitting males appear to have the least fear with regard to being talked into sex against their will, while hitting females have the most fear, although the level of fear reported by nonhitting females is also substantial.

Experience of being victimized or abused
As well as asking about their fears, we had survey participants respond to five questions that explored their actual experiences of victimization and abuse. Each of these questions yielded significant differences among the four groups. All significant differences reported are significant at $p < .0001$ (chi-square).

1. *Have you ever been the victim of a gang of kids?*
Students' responses show two statistically significant differences, that between nonhitting females (4.1%) and hitting males (14.9%) and

that between nonhitting males (6.0%) and hitting males (14.9%). A comparison between hitting males and hitting females yielded no significant difference. Nor is there a significant difference between nonhitting males and nonhitting females. Thus, overall, nonhitters (whether female or male) experience the least amount of victimization at the hands of gangs of kids, while hitters (whether male or female) experience the most.

2. *Have you ever been attacked on your way to or from school?*
Significant differences were reported between hitting males (18.9%) and hitting females (5.4%), and between hitting males (18.9%) and nonhitting females (3.6%). Although the absolute values provided show a numerical difference between hitting males and nonhitting males, this difference is not statistically significant. Thus, overall, hitting males reported experiencing the highest rates of victimization on the way to or from school.

3. *Have you ever been physically abused at home?*
As noted earlier in this chapter, hitting females (19.9%) reported significantly higher rates of physical abuse at home than nonhitting females, nonhitting males, and hitting males. Also significant is the difference reported between hitting males (9.6%) and nonhitting males (3.0%). Nonhitting males (3.0%) and nonhitting females (6.3%) reported experiencing levels of abuse that are quite similar (i.e., they are not significantly different). Thus, of the four groups, hitting females reported the highest rates by far of victimization in the home, although hitting males also reported higher rates, at least in relation to their nonhitting male counterparts.

4. *Have you ever been sexually abused?*
Hitting females (23.5%) reported significantly higher rates of sexual abuse than nonhitting females (11.2%), nonhitting males (0.8%), and hitting males (4.5%). However, nonhitting females also reported significantly higher levels of sexual abuse than nonhitting males and hitting males. Overall, females reported greater rates of sexual abuse than males. Of the total number of participants, 96 females (13.6%) and 21 males (3%) reported that they had been sexually abused. According to the data provided by our respondents, females experienced sexual abuse at a ratio of 4.5:1 when compared with males.

5. *Have you ever been talked into having sex with your boyfriend/girlfriend against your will?*

Hitting females (13.7%) reported the highest levels of being talked into sex against their will. Their rates of experiencing this were significantly greater than those reported by nonhitting females (7.3%), nonhitting males (2.8%), and hitting males (7.1%). Hitting males and nonhitting females reported virtually the same rates of having been talked into having sex against their will. Nonhitting males reported the lowest levels of this of all the respondents. Where sexual abuse and forced sex is concerned, hitting females appeared to fare worst of all, while nonhitting males fared best.

Participation in Deviant Behavior

Beyond participating in violence (i.e., beating up another kid), students in the survey were asked to report on their involvement in a number of rule-breaking, deviant, and delinquent behaviors, as well as the misuse or illegal use of substances. These are summarized in Tables A-41a and A-41b (rule breaking, deviant/delinquent behaviors) and Table A-41c (misuse or illegal use of substances) in Appendix I.

Rule Breaking, deviant and delinquent behaviors

As noted earlier in this chapter, hitting females reported smoking without their parents' permission at significantly greater rates (38.4%) than nonhitting females (20.4%) and all males. As well, hitting females also reported lying, staying out all night without parents' permission, skipping classes or school, and stealing small items that didn't belong to them at significantly higher rates than nonhitting males and females, but not hitting males. Nonhitting females, while reporting lower rates of engagement in the six listed behaviors than hitting females, still reported higher levels of engagement in two of these — smoking without parents' permission and lying — than nonhitting males, who reported the lowest levels of all groups for these two behaviors. Hitting males reported higher levels of all six behaviors than nonhitting males, and statistically the same rates of behavior as hitting females, for staying out all night without parents' permission, skipping classes, skipping school, and stealing small items that didn't belong to them.

For the six behaviors listed in Table A-41b in Appendix I

(purposefully ruining parents' property after an argument, damaging others' property just for fun, taking something from a store without paying for it, breaking into a place just to look around, purposefully damaging school property, and carrying a weapon), hitting females reported significantly higher rates for all behaviors than nonhitting females and nonhitting males. Nonhitting females and males reported no statistically significant differences for any of the six behaviors listed. Hitting males, however, while also reporting significantly higher rates than nonhitting males and nonhitting females for all six behaviors, also reported significantly higher rates than hitting females for three of these: damaging others' property just for fun, breaking into a place just to look around, and carrying a weapon.

Misuse and illegal use of substances

As previously noted in this chapter, hitting females reported the highest rates (56.5%) of smoking cigarettes of all groups, while nonhitting males reported the lowest rates (9.9%). Nonhitting males also reported significantly lower rates of use of over-the-counter drugs (6.3%) than all other groups. With regard to the use of over-the-counter drugs, nonhitting females (10.6%), hitting females (15%), and hitting males (10.7%) reported similar rates which, when compared with those of nonhitting males, were all significantly higher. Hitting females also reported higher rates of drinking alcohol (26.9%), smoking marijuana (26.5%), and using other illegal drugs (17.9%) than both nonhitting females and nonhitting males. With respect to these last three behaviors, hitting females and hitting males reported virtually the same rates of misuse and illegal use. As well, nonhitting females and nonhitting males reported the same rates of use of these substances, rates that were significantly lower than those of their hitting counterparts. Finally, both nonhitting females and hitting females reported stopping themselves from eating (misuse of food as a substance) at rates that were significantly higher (10.9% and 13.8%, respectively) than those of either nonhitting or hitting males (1.7% and 3.3%, respectively). (See Table A-41c in Appendix I.)

The overall pattern that emerged from participants' self-reports suggests that with regard to rule-breaking, deviance, delinquency, and substance misuse, those who engage in beating up other people have far more in common with one another than they do with members of their own sex who do not engage in beating up other people. Hitters, whether female or male, reported statistically the same rates of behavior for 12 of the 18 behaviors listed.

A further pattern that emerged suggests that, overall, nonhitting males were least involved in rule-breaking, deviance, delinquency, and substance misuse, at least insofar as our survey was able to determine. Of the 18 surveyed behaviors, nonhitting males reported significantly lower rates than all others for four, and the same significantly lower rates as nonhitting females for 13 of the remaining 14 behaviors. They shared only one similarity in behavior with their hitting male counterparts: a significantly lower rate of misusing food. Their hitting male counterparts, however, outranked even hitting females on three of the 18 behaviors: damaging property, breaking and entering, and carrying weapons. Still, according to these data, similarity outweighs difference where hitters are concerned.

Who Is the Violent School Girl?

Having collected all the foregoing data, we next asked ourselves:

- Who is the violent school girl? How can we distinguish her from the nonviolent school girl?
- How does the violent school girl compare with the nonviolent school boy?
- How is the violent school girl similar to and different from the violent school boy?

The violent school girl: Similarities and differences

According to our data, the violent school girl comes from a family that at least superficially resembles the families of her nonviolent and violent counterparts, both male and female. In other words, differences in family configuration and living arrangements (two parents, including common-law and stepparents, or single parent), parental occupation, and parental education did not distinguish the violent school girl from the other groups considered.

Family dynamics did, however, provide a basis for identifying the violent school girl. She reported placing significantly less importance on family life than the nonviolent school girl did, although the level of importance she accorded the family was not statistically different from that reported by nonviolent and violent school boys. She also reported that enjoyment of her mother was significantly less applicable to her than did all other groups. Further, she feared being physically abused at home, and had been thus abused at a significantly greater rate than all other groups. As well, she smoked without parents' permission more than all other groups; lied to her parents more often than nonviolent school girls and nonviolent school boys (but at the same rate reported by violent school boys); stayed out all night and deliberately damaged her parents' property more than both nonviolent girls and nonviolent boys (and at the same rate as violent boys).

Belonging to a group or a gang such as the Rappers or Bangers was of great importance to both violent females and violent males, as was having the right clothes to fit in with the group or gang, and receiving enjoyment from parties. Where peer affiliation is concerned, the line of demarcation between groups did not run along gender lines, but rather along the violent/nonviolent distinction: that is, regardless of sex, those who engaged in violence reported more similarities than those who reported being nonviolent.

This violent/nonviolent distinction continued with regard to school: Violent students, whether female or male, reported significantly greater levels of acting up in school if they did not like their teachers, and significantly higher levels of damaging school property than their nonviolent counterparts.

The gender line was, however, clearly drawn with regard to interpersonal values and self-concept. Females, whether they were violent or nonviolent, reported that they saw themselves as less attractive, less capable, and less confident than the males (violent or nonviolent) reported themselves. At the same time, females, whether they were violent or nonviolent, reported a significantly higher rate of endorsement of friendship, being loved, concern for others, respect for others, forgiveness, honesty, politeness, generosity, and being respected, than males (violent or nonviolent). When violent school girls were compared with nonviolent girls, the only value that they endorsed at what approached a significantly lower level was honesty, which they endorsed at almost the same level as nonviolent school boys, a level significantly higher than that of violent boys.

The gender gap did not prevail where moral judgments were concerned. Although nonviolent school girls endorsed aggressive, violent, and illegal behavior at significantly lower rates than nonviolent and violent school boys, this was not the case with violent girls. Their rates of endorsement for such behavior were significantly higher than those reported by nonviolent girls. With regard to punching, using threats, acting up in school, the legalization of marijuana, and the notion that right and wrong is a matter of personal opinion, violent school girls' rates of endorsement were significantly higher than those reported by nonviolent school boys, and not significantly different from those reported by violent boys. Violent school girls differed from violent school boys on only one variable: fighting to defend one's friends, which violent boys endorsed at significantly higher rates than all other groups.

The gender gap did, however, prevail with regard to social and personal concerns. Here females, whether they were violent or nonviolent, consistently reported significantly higher levels of concern for all issues: AIDS, child abuse, racial discrimination, teenage suicide, violence against women, the environment, the unequal treatment of women, violence in schools, drug abuse, youth gangs, and native-white relations. In fact, violent girls reported higher levels of concern than all groups, including nonviolent girls, for the unequal treatment of women and for violence in schools. This pattern shifted only where alcohol abuse was concerned: Here, violent school girls and violent school boys reported the same levels of concern, levels that were significantly lower than those reported by both nonviolent girls and nonviolent boys.

Violent school girls and violent school boys also reported making more money than their nonviolent counterparts. Although violent boys reported earning higher hourly wages than members of all the other groups, violent girls reported higher wages than nonviolent girls and nonviolent boys. As well, violent school girls, along with violent school boys, reported significantly higher levels of allowance than nonviolent girls or boys, who reported very similar and lower levels of allowance.

With regard to sources of enjoyment, gender again prevailed, although for the most part, both sexes ranked the surveyed sources of enjoyment in the same order. Females, whether violent or nonviolent, placed more importance upon friends, music, and reading than males did; males, whether violent or nonviolent, placed more importance upon sports and television than females did. Although violent males placed more importance upon girlfriends and dating than all other groups, and violent females and males placed more value upon parties and their stereos than both nonviolent females and nonviolent males, violent students reported similarities with regard to only two out of 23 items, thus suggesting that gender determined preferences more often than involvement in violence did.

This pattern continued with regard to problems that were a source of bother to survey participants. On the whole, all participants ranked sources of bother in the same order, although females (violent and nonviolent) ranked not being understood by their parents, concerns about the way they looked, and losing friends as more bothersome than males (violent or nonviolent) did. Violent males ranked not having a place to hang out and experiencing pressure to engage in sex as more bothersome than all the other groups ranked these two items.

No significant gender or group differences were reported with regard to survey participants' sources of support. In general, all participants (violent and nonviolent) turned to their parents with concerns about money, right and wrong, school, careers, and major problems, and to their friends with regard to concerns about relationships, sex, and fun.

With regard to fears of victimization and abuse, two gender difference emerged: Females (violent and nonviolent) feared sexual assault and being talked into having sex against their will at significantly greater rates than males (violent and nonviolent). Violent school girls reported both these fears at rates that were significantly higher than those reported by all males, and significantly higher than those reported by nonviolent females. Otherwise, participants reported the same rates of fear of general attack, attack on the way to school, and being beaten by a gang. Violent school girls, nonviolent girls, and violent boys also reported the same rates for staying away from school because of fear, rates that were all significantly higher than those reported by nonviolent school boys.

Gender differences again emerged with regard to experiences with victimization. Females (violent and nonviolent) reported significantly higher rates of sexual abuse and being talked into sex against their will than males (violent and nonviolent). Further, as with levels of fear of these two experiences, violent females reported significantly higher rates of experience with victimization than those reported by non-violent females.

Self-reports about other forms of victimization yielded some interesting connections. Violent school girls were victimized by gangs of kids as often as violent school boys were, although violent boys were more often attacked on their way to and from school. As well, violent girls were more often physically abused at home than any other group, including violent boys. Thus, violent girls reported more victimization in the form of physical abuse, sexual abuse, and attack by a gang of peers.

Finally, with regard to rule-breaking, deviance, and delinquency, the violent school girl was hard to distinguish from her violent male peers. She reported engaging in smoking without permission, lying to her parents, staying out all night without permission, skipping classes or school, stealing small items that didn't belong to her, stealing from stores, ruining her parents' property after an argument, and damaging school property at rates that were the same as those reported by violent school boys, rates that were significantly higher than those reported by both nonviolent boys and nonviolent girls. Violent school girls also reported breaking into places just to look around, damaging property just for fun, and carrying a weapon significantly more often than nonviolent girls and nonviolent boys, although these rates were not as high as those reported by violent boys. Further, violent school girls reported smoking more than members of all other groups, drinking alcohol, smoking marijuana, and using other illegal drugs significantly more often than nonviolent girls and nonviolent boys, and at the same rates reported by violent boys. Both violent and nonviolent girls stopped themselves from eating significantly more often than either violent or nonviolent boys.

Summary: The Violent School Girl

According to our data, in many respects, the violent school girl looks much like the violent school boy: She misuses drugs and alcohol; engages in rule-breaking, deviance, and delinquency; endorses aggression. She enjoys similar pastimes, and she is affiliated with the same social groups.

She differs from the violent school boy in several key areas: She places greater importance on interpersonal values, and she is more concerned about social issues. She places more importance on friendship than both violent and nonviolent school boys do, and (like the violent school boy) she considers family of less importance than her nonviolent counterparts do. She places the least value of all the groups on her connection with her mother.

What stands out most clearly about the violent school girl is her greater fear of abuse, and actual experience of physical and sexual abuse, than all others who participated in the survey.

Moving Beyond Statistics

In the chapters that follow, the life-world and practices of the violent school girl are more clearly outlined and examined through case study accounts. These provide strong corroboration for the portrait of the violent school girl drawn with data from the *Survey of Student Life* (Artz & Riecken, 1994). They also provide insight into the perspectives that violent school girls bring to bear upon their own and others' behavior, and help the reader to understand that the girls' participation in violence is integral to a view of life in which violence makes sense.

Constructing an ethnography

My objective in using the case study approach was an ethnographic one: I was primarily concerned with understanding the lived experience of these girls. Ethnography, an approach to the study of human group life first used by anthropologists, has been variously defined as "written representation of culture[2] (or selected aspects of a culture)" (Van Maanen, 1988, p. 1), the inscription of social discourse (Geertz, 1973), the analytic description or reconstruction of cultural scenes and groups (Goetz & LeCompte, 1984), and "a type of writing, putting things to paper" (Geertz, 1988, p. 1) that addresses cultural questions through fieldwork or direct personal involvement with the subjects of one's study. According to Wolcott (1975),

> the term ethnography belongs to anthropology; ethnography provides the basic descriptive data on which cultural anthropology is founded. An ethnography is literally an anthropologist's picture of the way of life of some interacting human group. (p. 112)

Within the field of qualitative social research, ethnography is used not only by anthropologists, but also by sociologists (Dietz, Prus, & Shaffir, 1994), psychologists (Osborne, 1994), and educators (Wolcott, 1975). The focus of ethnographic research is, as Wolcott says, "the way of life of some interacting human group," whether that is a group living at a great distance or one that gathers down the street or next door.

Constructing an ethnography entails the gathering and interpretation of multiple kinds and forms of information concerning the group to be studied. This process is undertaken not at arm's length, but in the field. Ethnographers are participant-observers in the processes they study. They live and work among their subjects in order to understand how and why they behave as they do. Ethnographers use their own first-hand personal experiences with the study group to produce descriptive accounts that accurately reflect the characteristics and perceptions of that group. According to Wolcott (1975), an ethnographic account can be judged adequate if a person reading it

> could subsequently behave appropriately as a member of the society or social group about which he has been reading, or more modestly, whether he can anticipate and interpret what occurs in the group as appropriately as its own members. (p. 112)

Within the parameters of working towards a faithful documentation of the patterns and forms of the study group, the ethnographer enjoys what Wolcott describes as the freedom to "muddle about" and pursue hunches as she or he sees fit. Ethnographers discover patterns and problems. They do not test their data against predetermined hypotheses under the constraints of the experimental method, nor do they enter their inquiry with anything more than the foreknowledge gained from their previous experience as a guideline for action and interpretation.

Thus, for my study, I wanted to learn about "the ways in which [violent school girls] accomplish their activities on a day-to-day, moment-to-moment basis" with a view towards understanding "how [they] make sense of the situations they encounter in their daily routines and how they deal with these situations on an ongoing basis" (Dietz, Prus, & Shaffir, 1994, p. 2). Central to an understanding of violent school girls' meaning-making processes was an understanding of their "symbolic interactions." That is, I wanted to understand their violent behavior in terms of their internalization of the culturally produced sign systems generated and interpreted by their particular group or subculture.

The meaning of meaning
Blumer (1969), who coined the term "symbolic interactionism,"

suggested that the meaning we find in objects and experiences is neither intrinsic to those things, nor is it the product of accumulated psychological attributes brought to those experiences by the meaning maker. Instead, meaning is perspective-dependent. This means that we cannot expect to find only one meaning and one interpretation for each object in the sense that a chair is only and always a chair, a house is only and always a house, and a mother is only and always a woman. The perspective of the seer can transform a chair into a lion-tamer's training tool, the house into a valuable piece of real estate, and the mother into an agent that originates, engenders, or masterminds (as in, "necessity is the mother of invention").

Further, meaning is more than mere "psychical accretion brought to things by the person for whom the thing has meaning," that is, more than simply the "expression of constituent elements of a person's psyche, mind or psychological organization [that comes from] ... such things as sensations, feelings, ideas, memories, motives and attitudes" (Blumer, 1969, p. 4). In symbolic interactionism, meanings arise "in the process of interaction between people ... [and thus] as social products, as creations that are formed in and through the defining activities of people as they interact" (Blumer, 1969, pp. 4–5).

Thus described, meaning-making involves interactive interpretation. Interpretation, according to Blumer, requires two distinct steps. The first involves the human actor in communication with herself: She indicates to herself the objects towards which she is acting and the meanings that these have for her. The second step requires that she interprets and applies these meanings in the light of her situation and her actions.

Blumer (1969) emphasizes that the process of interaction with self is not merely premised on the interplay of the actor's psychological elements, but involves instead the internalizing of a social process which is the basis for the actor's communication with herself.

Social processes and participant-observation

In order to learn about the meaning-making processes of the violent school girls who participated in this study, I set out to understand the social processes in which they were immersed by becoming a participant-observer in their world. Participant-observation is described by Spradley (1979) as a research strategy that actively involves the researcher in the life-worlds of her participants in order to gain first-hand knowledge of their lived experience. Thus, the researcher becomes not merely an observer, but also an actor and an informant in the research process. The rationale for participant-observation is that

> it offers to those who are able and willing to assume the role of another in a more comprehensive sense, a unique and instructive form of data. ... Since it typically puts researchers in close, sustained contact with others, participant-observation generates further opportunities to gain insight into the viewpoints and practices of the other ... . (Prus, 1994, p. 21)

It is acknowledged that participant-observation is by definition a subjective approach to data gathering that places certain restrictions upon the interpretation of data. For example, a researcher would not seek to generalize from her data; rather, she would underscore the fact that her findings are personal and descriptive rather than empirical and analytic.[3] It is also acknowledged that the insights gained from first-hand experience allow a unique understanding of the phenomenon under study, moving the researcher beyond a search for psychological and sociological determinants of behavior into knowledge about

> the process of self-interaction through which the individual handles his world and constructs his action [and] the vital process of interpretation in which the individual notes and assesses what is presented to him and through which he maps out lines of overt behavior... . (Blumer, 1969, p. 15)

As the central thrust of my inquiry was to form an understanding of how adolescent school girls engaged in violence and made sense of this engagement, I believed that participant-observation would be a helpful and useful research methodology because it would bring me closer to the girls' lived experiences and to the lived experiences of others in their life-worlds.

My bAckgRoundd in the community

My status as a participant-observer in this inquiry was anchored in my four years of consulting with and training teachers and administrators in the school district in which I did my research.

I had worked with over 100 teachers (about 20 of whom were either principals, vice-principals, or board office personnel) in a series of workshops, each of which consisted of seven sessions spread over a period of three to four months. In these workshops, I helped teachers deal with their day-to-day problems in managing their most difficult students, and therefore had some understanding of the violence and aggression that they were encountering in their classrooms and schoolyards. The relationships I developed during this period lent me the credibility to be allowed to engage in the present inquiry; they also provided me with a basis from which to approach students, parents, and youth workers in the district. Further, as I visited the schools where I conducted my workshops, I began to develop an intuitive feel for the school-based life-world of my research participants, as I had the opportunity to see them in classrooms, on playgrounds, and on their way to and from school.

I also had other long-term participatory experience in this community. Having made my home there from 1975 until 1984, I knew it to be multifaceted and multidimensional. In part, it is a bedroom community that sprawls over a wide hinterland housing the people who work in the offices, shops, and businesses in the city. It is also an industrial community in which one finds small manufacturing businesses, heavy equipment yards, and unkempt strip malls interspersed with gas stations and doughnut shops. In some parts there is great affluence: architecturally designed homes housing well-paid professionals who prefer a quasi-rural lifestyle. In other parts one finds ramshackle buildings and rundown housing mixed with subsidized townhouse complexes occupied to a large extent by welfare recipients and the working poor. There are rural lanes, horse farms, and well-groomed subdivisions overlooking the ocean. There are also heavily traveled routes that pass by rusty car hulks and empty dump trucks parked in front of half-finished houses guarded by German shepherds on chains. Members from all social classes live together here, but the predominant flavor of the community is working class. It is a community that is always in the making, where enterprising developers continue to carve subdivisions out of forests and mountainsides. It is also a community that contains pockets of history reaching back to the earliest incursions of white settlements.

While living in this community, I was also employed there as a youth worker from 1981 to 1987. I still have collegial relationships with agency workers and the police which keep me current with local issues. I taught life skills to adult students at a local high school in 1988, and this experience gave me the opportunity to take part in some of the everyday life of a school.

Further, while living in this community, I fostered four special-care foster children (all girls aged 11 to 16) whose behavioral problems included acting out at school and (in two cases) participation in violence. This gave me first-hand parental experience in dealing with behavioral difficulties, hostility, aggression, and violence.

When I began this study, I made my status as researcher clear to all concerned. I was introduced to all participants as a researcher, and my role as researcher and theirs as voluntary informants in the research process were clearly outlined in the consent forms that were signed by the girls, their parents, and all adult participants. I also stated clearly to all involved that I entered into the research process in the spirit of understanding how it was that girls engaged in violence, and with the participants' help, hoped to apply that knowledge; that is, I viewed participants as partners who had much to contribute to the research process.

The study

I gained access to the study participants in a variety of ways:

- Because it was known within the school district and the community that I was engaged in local research on youth violence, and because teachers and administrators saw it as useful for the district, I was given the opportunity to conduct a series of teachers' professional-development day workshops in which the focus was violence in schools. At these workshops, teachers and parents were invited to describe and discuss their first-hand experiences with violence in schools, thus providing me with descriptive data about the phenomenon. In all, three such workshops were conducted, in which over 50 people participated.

- My colleague, Ted Riecken, and I were invited to present a forum on youth violence to a parents' network, which we conducted as a workshop, again inviting parents to share their personal experiences. Two parent-network staff, four youth workers, and 12 parents attended the forum; all contributed their experiences and helped me to round out my description of the phenomenon of youth violence.

- As a result of these contacts in the community, several teachers, administrators, and parents volunteered to become further involved in the study by agreeing to be interviewed and by facilitating contact with their children or their students.

- The contacts that were made through these connections led to research relationships with six adolescent girls who had personal involvement with violence, and who became the key informants[4] in this study.

The key informants

Six key informants — all of whom had been involved in violent altercations — were identified by school and community agency counselors, by their classmates, and by the girls themselves, and agreed to participate in this inquiry. Five of the six were referred by their school counselors; one I approached myself. The names and any overtly identifying characteristics of all participants have been altered in order to preserve anonymity.

INFORMANT 1: Sally. Sally, who volunteered for the study because she saw herself as a victim of violence, was 13 years old and in grade eight. She was known to the students in her school and to her teachers as a "tough" girl who intimidated both male and female classmates. Just before the interviews, she had been severely beaten by Marilee (Informant 2) and Marilee's best friend, Sarah. Since her beating, Sally had stopped attending school and was being schooled at home via correspondence. Since the age of six, Sally has been living with her mother and stepfather. She also has frequent contact with her father and his second wife of six years and their five-year-old daughter, Sally's half-sister. All four parents work, the women in offices, and the men at blue-collar jobs.

INFORMANT 2: Marilee. Marilee (Sally's assailant) agreed to be part of the study at my request because she, like Sally, wanted to contribute her input as a self-described victim of violence. She was 16 and, like Sally, had given up attending school and was being educated at home via correspondence since sustaining a beating by a group of her fellow school girls two years previously. Marilee lives with her mother and father, who have been married for nearly 26 years. She has an older sister who is away at college. Both Marilee's parents work, her mother in an office, her father as a dispatcher for a taxi company.

Informant 3: Molly. Molly initially volunteered to participate in the study because, like Sally and Marilee, she had been beaten by a student at her school. Molly was no stranger to violence: She was known to use threats and intimidation and, on occasion, pushing, shoving, and banging into other people to let them know that she was in charge. She has an older brother who also has a reputation for toughness, and whom she relies upon to back her up if need be. Molly was 14 and in grade eight at the time of this study. She lives with her parents and three brothers (one older, two younger) in a small house in a modest part of the community. Molly's mother works in an office; her father is a carpenter. They have been married for 22 years.

Informant 4: Mary. Mary came to the study with the toughest of reputations because of her nearly constant involvement with fighting and other difficulties in school. She volunteered to participate because she had been attacked by another girl and now wanted to "do something about violence." Mary was 15 years old at the time of this study. She lives at home with her mother, father, and older brother, who (like Molly's brother) has a reputation for violence. Mary's father is a self-employed skilled tradesperson; her mother works in an office.

Informant 5: Linda. Linda volunteered for the study because, like Mary, she wanted "to do something about violence." She had been suspended from school on two occasions for fighting with Jenny (Informant 6), yet she saw her own involvement in violence as the result of victimization by Jenny. Linda was nearly 16 at the time of the study. Linda's parents have been married for 20 years. Her mother works as a clerk, her father as a mechanic.

Informant 6: Jenny. Jenny volunteered to participate in the study because she also saw herself as victimized by other girls, as well as by boys. Yet, previous to our interviews, Jenny had instigated three fights, each of which attracted large crowds of spectators (over 70 to 100 youths, and in one case over 300). Jenny is well known to other students in her school as a fighter (although Mary, who has known her since grade two, called her an "amateur"). Jenny was 14 and in grade eight at the time of this study. She lives with her parents and younger sister. Jenny's parents have been married for 16 years. Her mother manages a restaurant; her father works as a groundskeeper.

Over the course of just 15 months (from July 1993 to October 1994), I spent over 100 hours with the six key informants, approximately 15 hours with their parents, 50 hours with their educators, counselors, and law enforcement officers, and countless hours in their community observing everyday life.

Three of the key informants (Molly, Mary, and Linda) were friends, and often met with me as a group as well as individually. Also, Marilee knew Sally (and had helped her best friend Sarah beat Sally up); Molly, Mary, and Linda were well acquainted with Jenny, who attended school with them. These three disliked Jenny intensely and believed she deserved to be beaten, especially in view of Linda's having been suspended from school for hitting Jenny. Finally, Mary was close friends with Cathy, who had severely beaten Molly, a beating both Mary and Linda had witnessed.

The conversations I had with the key informants covered many aspects of their lives: their involvement in violence; their views of their parents, siblings, and other family members; their sense of self; their experiences of being female; their notions of friends and friendship; the social activities they pursue; their perspectives on their educators and their own educational performance; their ideas about right and wrong, and the origins of their moral stance.

All those involved in the study, including the informants who had participated in violence, saw themselves as contributors to an understanding of violence that would move us collectively closer to finding ways to prevent it. In that sense, we had a common purpose.

My discussions with the key informants and others who are part of their lives yielded over 1,400 pages of tape transcriptions and field notes. These pages became the basis for the next six chapters, which present the personal stories of each of the participants, and for Chapter Nine, which outlines my understanding of these young women. Chapter Ten, which concludes this book, outlines my suggestions for violence prevention and intervention.

Notes

1. The first four categories listed here, and the questions relating to them, were devised by Bibby and Posterski (1992) and are included with permission

2. "Culture" is a term that has been variously defined. Geertz (1973) lists

11 different definitions generated by noted anthropologist Clyde Kluckholm, as well as two more general descriptors used by other anthropologists; he also outlines his own. Accordingly, culture has been taken to mean: (1) "the total way of life of a people"; (2) "the social legacy the individual acquires from his group"; (3) "a way of thinking, feeling, and believing"; (4) "an abstraction from behavior"; (5) "a theory on the part of the anthropologist about the way in which a group of people in fact behave"; (6) a "storehouse of pooled learning"; (7) "a set of standardized orientations to recurrent problems"; (8) "learned behavior"; (9) "a mechanism for the normative regulation of behavior"; (10) "a set of techniques for adjusting both to the external environment and to other men"; (11) "a precipitate of history"; (12) a "sieve"; and (13) a "matrix." Geertz himself defines culture as a semiotic concept and notes that he believes, along with Max Weber, that "man is essentially an animal suspended in webs of significance he himself has spun." He therefore sees the analysis of culture "not as an experimental science in search of law but an interpretative one in search of meaning" (pp. 4–5). In this study, I will not use the term "culture" other than in the above references to definitions of ethnography. Instead, I will speak directly about behavior and meaning.

3. "Empirical and analytic" are terms assigned by Ted Aoki (1987) to the epistemological orientation that approaches understanding "in terms of informational knowledge (data, facts, generalizations, cause and effect laws, concepts, theories)" and attempts to link cause and effect through hypothetic-deductive reasoning. According to Aoki, the main focus of this orientation is prediction and control. Other researchers (Lather, 1991; Osborne, 1994) refer to this orientation as positivist and logical-empirical, and connect it, as does Aoki, to the practices of traditional natural science.

4. "Key informants" are those participants in an inquiry whose role it is to initiate and inform the researcher with regard to the phenomenon under study. It is their role to teach and to explain, to uncover and to demystify the processes that contribute to the creation and construction of the life-worlds and experiences in which they participate as "natives" (Spradley, 1979).

CHAPTER THREE

Sally's Story

The Daisy Chain

The daisy chain fits together as one,
Like a man and a woman they have lots of fun.
As the years go by they come apart and wither away
And there's no longer a sweet scent of love.
Hate takes over and it drives them both insane.
Hate take over and it drives them both insane.
Four years go by and they've both remarried,
But the love inside for each other still blossoms
Like the day the daisy chain was made,
Like the day the daisy chain was made.
(*Song written by Sally*)

Family dynamics

Sally has two families. She lives with her mother and stepfather, but she also has frequent contact with her father, stepmother, and their daughter, Sally's five-year-old half-sister.

Sally's parents split up when she was six years old and have been living with their new partners for over six years each. Sally's mother married her new partner; Sally's father lives common-law. As Sally sees it, her parents are better off with their present spouses; while they were together, they fought constantly, and both were unhappy.

At first, Sally was quite angry with both her parents for separating. She was angry with her mother for driving her father away, and with her father for leaving. But by the time she was eight, she had come to terms with what had happened. Things "fell into place," she said; she herself was now "fine" with regard to her parents' divorce.

Sally regards the family that consists of herself, her mother, and stepfather as an "all right family that has its bad times." The ups and downs center around how well she and her stepfather get along. During the "bad times," they fight and shout at each other, call each other names, and swear, sometimes loudly enough that neighbors have called the police.

According to Sally, the bad times happen because her stepfather "is not like a father unless he has to be." Instead, he "acts like a brother":

He listens to her music, talks the way Sally and her friends do (using such expressions as "dude"), and relates to everything she does much as she and her friends do. This leads to a kind of rivalry which Sally describes as "constantly fighting like brother and sister." Sally explains her stepfather's behavior as arising from the fact that he is nine years younger than Sally's mother, and that at 30 years of age, he still likes to "act like a kid." This situation creates problems for Sally because, as she puts it, "I do need him to act like a parent."

When Sally and her stepfather quarrel, Sally's mother "makes us talk about our problems instead of just yelling at each other … [She] gets really mad at us if we don't." Her mother also acts as an intermediary, approaching daughter and husband in turn to suggest better ways for them to relate to each other in the interests of domestic peace.

With regard to her other family, Sally hates her stepmother; during her visits there she prefers to spend time only with her father and half-sister, whom she feels able to control. Sally's hate for her stepmother stems from feeling continually criticized by her. Further, her stepmother has stated that Sally will not be included in her forthcoming wedding to Sally's father, because she wants no reminders there of his previous marriage. This exclusion leaves Sally feeling alone and angry.

Sally's general sense of her home life with her mother and stepfather is that "things are okay because mostly I'm never there." She finds her parents' rules fairly flexible — for example, curfews are negotiated to accommodate her activities. Sally compares her situation favorably with that of some of her friends, who "want to kill their parents" because they have too many rules. Most of Sally's closest friends have parents who have been divorced, and most think that family life is depressing.

Sally's MOTHER

I learned more about the dynamics of Sally's family from her mother, whom I also interviewed. Sally's mother's main concern when I spoke to her was to break her own co-dependent patterns of interaction with those around her. That is, she wanted to stop controlling others by caring for them too much, and by trying to make them feel good. She had joined a co-dependents' group which she attends weekly, and which she says helps her. Yet, when it comes to Sally and Sally's stepfather, she continues to play the part of peacemaker. Often, this places her in a parental role in relationship to her husband.[1]

Sally's mother experiences further confusion with regard to co-dependency when she tries to take an authoritative or directive stance with Sally. For example, on the day of Sally's beating (when Sally was set up by her friend Adel to be beaten by Sarah and Marilee), her mother was reluctant to allow Sally to go to the store with Adel. However, she let her daughter go just so that she herself would "not act like a co-dependent." That is, she overruled her strongly suspicious hunch about Adel, and her own better judgment, because she did not wish to make Sally's decisions for her in the manner of a "co-dependent" mother.

In hindsight, she reflects that she might have questioned Adel, or encouraged Sally to do so, or refused permission, or diverted the girls' attention to keep them at home. Now, although she feels guilty for not acting on her hunch, she tries to suppress her negative feelings and thoughts about Sally's continuing friendship with Adel, because she does not want to influence or alienate Sally.

Sally's mother struggled with her co-dependency also when dealing with the police who investigated Sally's assault. On the one hand, she wanted the police to make Sally's case a priority and take action; on the other hand, she did not want to be "pushy." Thus, she forced herself to be patient with the police to the point that she found herself making excuses for them, in spite of feeling frustrated and angry with them for not returning her phone calls.

Sally's mother seems uncertain about what messages she should give to those around her: Should she be direct and clearly state her thoughts and feelings? Should she temper her message with understanding? Should she compromise without ever stating her ideas? This debate takes place only in Sally's mother's mind; those around her hear only messages so modified that they don't always grasp them.

Sally talked of her mother in generally positive terms but also described her as "co-dependent because she's always looking after other people" (a description that eerily echoes her mother's own description of herself). After the beating, Sally related, her mother followed through with the police and with the school, and obtained trauma counseling for Sally.

Sally's schooling

In the aftermath of the beating, Sally regressed, behaving in ways one might expect of a much younger child: She took to staying at home, dressed in flannel pajamas and a bathrobe; she sat in her mother's lap on the couch and would not let her mother out of her sight, even to go to the bathroom or have a shower.

Although Sally said her mother wanted her to face her fears and return to school, her mother herself expressed caution with regard to this. She had debated with both her husband and the police, and recalled fighting for the middle ground between Sally's father, who introduced the idea of correspondence schooling (and made arrangements with Sally to do this without first consulting Sally's mother), and Sally's stepfather, who had tried correspondence schooling himself and felt that Sally would do better to return to school immediately. In fact, Sally's mother had arranged with the school counselor for Sally to return gradually, with counseling support — but her idea somehow got lost in the flurry of family opinions.

A further debate regarding her return to school involved Sally and her stepmother, who warned that Sally would lose all her friends if she didn't go back. Sally disagreed, and set out to prove her stepmother wrong. She evidently didn't hear her mother's idea of a gradual return because the more immediate message — from her father as well as her stepmother — seemed to be, "go back to school at once."

In the end, the adults, who could not reach agreement among themselves, turned the decision over to Sally, who decided to stay home and do her lessons by correspondence.

Sally plans to stay with this arrangement until she enters grade 11. She is presently more successful at her school work than she was while attending school.

Peer relationships

Like most of the young people she knows, Sally looks to friends rather than family for feelings of connectedness, belonging, and protection. She and many of her friends are enthralled with the notion of gangs, which they seem to spend much time discussing.

Sally often spoke to me of her connections with gangs, particularly a gang called the "Bloods." Early in our conversations, she revealed that prior to being beaten up by Sarah and Marilee, she had cultivated a tough attitude and projected a threatening image. In fact, she felt it was ironic that she had been beaten, as she saw herself as "usually the tougher person who'd be like the one that people would have to back down against."

Conversations with Sally's fellow students revealed that this was not a spurious claim. However, both Sally and Adel (the "best friend" who helped lure Sally to the corner store where she was beaten up) also had reputations for toughness among their fellows, especially the younger ones. In fact, Sally's friendship with Adel was to some extent premised on toughness. As Sally described Adel's participation in her beating: "That's the kind of friendship we have, she wanted to see me get pushed around, and I would love to see her pushed around too."

Sally assured me that she isn't afraid of being beaten up again because "I have like tons of friends in gangs, and I'm not even scared." Although she briefly mentioned her injuries (which were considerable), and then discussed laying charges against Sarah, she was emphatic that she was unmoved because she felt protected by her affiliation with gang members.

When Sally talked about gangs, she became animated and excited. I followed her lead and asked her to tell me more about her connections with these gangs. She offered a detailed description of her notions of local gang life and her connections with people who carry guns and can arrange to kill people. For Sally, a gang is a group of people who

> go around killing people that bug them. Like the toughest guys and the toughest girls get together and then just form a gang and they go down and get guns and stuff.

When I asked whether these gangs actually killed people, Sally informed me that this

> depends. Okay, if they were to fight, they'd give the other gang the option, and if they wanted to use guns then they'd have gun fights and if they wanted to have fist fights, then they would do it. But they let them have the option. Like if I was to go to one of my friends and say, "Can you go and kill this person for me?" they would say, "How do you want them killed? When do you want it done?" and then they'd go and do it like a hit man.

Certainly, in Sally's eyes, these people are tough, but they are also "friendly people that would come up and talk to you," thus making it possible for Sally to get to know them. As she explained:

> There's a whole bunch of girls that I know that are in gangs, and they're pretty

nice, it's just staying off their bad side, 'cause they can do serious damage to you.

When I asked what might provoke girls in a gang to do serious damage to Sally or any other girl, she replied:

> Anything. Like, okay, if you go to the club where they all hang out — and say you thought one of the guy Bloods was good-looking and you went up and started talking to him, if a girl Blood just didn't like the way you looked or didn't know why you were talking to her boyfriend, like you just wanted to ask him for a cigarette or something — that can provoke them, or if you were to call them names or give them a dirty look. Like, you just gotta be really careful around them, 'cause they could beat you up just for the way you look, or if they want your shoes, or if they don't like the shirt you're wearing or something.

Despite the personal risk involved, knowing people in gangs seemed very important to Sally. She told me rather proudly, "Did you hear about the drive-by shooting downtown, those two guys that did the drive-by shooting? Those were my friends."[2] Finally, she identified herself as a gang member in her own right:

> I'm in a Skate gang — the Blue Snakes. Blue Snakes are not as extreme as Green Iguanas because we don't tattoo ourselves. I'm the only girl. It's rare to have girls as Skates ... .

When I asked her what it was like to be a Blue Snake, she answered:

> It's perfect being a Skate because you, you've got your skateboard. That's something to do. You've got your skateboard, that also counts as weapon. And — there's not, like, but Skates don't get hassled a lot.

I asked her to explain to me how a skateboard could be used as a weapon and learned that

> you pick it up and hit people. People only do this if they were gonna, like gonna get mugged or something. Usually, like, they yell, like they just kind of like, "Leave me alone!" I don't know, like my friend Allan, he used his skateboard to fight someone — a whole bunch of Rappers came up to him, stole his Walkman, stole his skateboard and he grabbed it back and hit them. So then they ran off, but they took his Walkman. Rappers and Skates fight each other. It's like Rappers think they're too good for Skates because that's all we hear on

the news now is Rappers this and rap this and everything and Skaters, we are just calm and keep to ourselves. WE don't do anything. We like, our pastime is skateboarding. That's not hurting anybody.

When Sally talked about her connection with Skates and skateboarding, she premised her identity not on the individually oriented "I" but on the plural "we," and she had clear ideas about who constituted the "we" with whom she identified. As a Skate she is part of a group who pursue a certain activity. Skateboarding involves learning to do certain tricks, participating in skate-offs, and wearing certain clothes such as Airwalks, Doc Martens, and second-hand clothes bought at thrift stores. She was also clear that Skates are further distinguished by not being Rappers. For Sally, Rappers are people whose

pastime is going around beating people up, fighting, everything. ... The Rappers, they go out and buy like, sixty dollar jeans. We go to Value Village and get ours for like five dollars. I mean there, there's like, that's what Skates are. They [Rappers] wear, they have baggy jeans, but we cut ours off at the bottom so it goes like straight down and they're pretty short, and then we wear like a big, big, big, oversized striped T-shirt, a toque, and there we go. They, they have to wear like a name brand hat, a name — like a labeled shirt, cross-colored jeans, like or whatever kind of shoes they're wearing now, and then start talking like the Rappers, start listening to their music and then they're slowly, slowly classified as one. And us, we go down to the thrift stores and — there we go. Rappers like to pick on Skates, nobody picks on Rappers.

To grasp the distinction between Skates and Rappers, I not only listened carefully to Sally, but also discussed this with other young people. I learned that Skates and Rappers do indeed have very different orientations, which are recognizable through differences in clothing styles and tastes in music (as outlined in Chapter Two). As Sally explained to me: Skates, Bangers, and Rappers all know one another; and Bangers are not as threatening to Skates as Rappers because

like, there's no what's it called like, fighting, there's no fighting between the Bangers and the Skates. It's the Rappers, 'cause they like brand names and everything.

Sally appeared to feel strongly connected to her identity as a Skate, and traced her membership in a Skate gang back to her elementary school friendship with a boy who had initiated her into the world of skateboarding. Both the friendship and the affiliation to the sport have endured for a number of years, despite the fact that Sally has moved away from the neighborhood in which her Skater friend lives.

When I asked why she thought young people join gangs or groups such as the ones she described, she explained:

> Like, I think that people who go into one of those gangs, it's like they don't have a good family life, so they're using the gang as a family. Like, okay, well, if I'm in this gang, then the gang members are going to treat me like I'm there and they're gonna do this for me ... so it's like having the comfort of like being somewhere where they belong, where like people are paying attention to you ... .

According to Sally, some young women will go to great lengths to achieve a sense of belonging. They will submit to having sex with as many as 12 young men, hand-picked for them by the existing gang members, and/or endure being beaten without flinching for a specified number of minutes (where the beating consists of being kicked in the stomach, kicked in the head, and punched in the face) by the toughest girl in the gang. All this is considered the price of admission. Although Sally had never encountered such treatment herself, she seemed convinced that such things did take place.

For Sally, gang or group membership implied "being treated like I'm there," getting attention, and having a family. In our conversations, Sally gave me a great deal of information about her family, and several factors stand out in connection with "being treated like I'm there." During our second meeting, when I asked how things were going at home, she responded, "Fine, I'm never there." But when we talked about what Sally liked and wanted most from her family and from people in general, she revealed that she liked being listened to and getting attention. In other words, although she didn't spend much time with her family, she actually wanted their time and attention. Sally expressed all this clearly and simply: "I like it when people look at me ... I like attention ... I like people to recognize what I do and give me attention for it ... ."

Sally does a number of things to get attention. She dyes her hair using unusual colors: greens, purples, odd shades of red. She tries out many different hairstyles, all of them deliberately "weird" and "original." She wears clothes that she describes as "weird," just like her hair, and in social settings she subscribes to behaviors that she hopes will make people notice her. When I first met with her, she had dyed her hair auburn, but unfortunately this was not bringing her the response from her parents that she was looking for:

> My dad didn't even notice, like he hasn't said anything and I've had it in for two weeks … . When I got home, my mom, she's like, "Get out of here." … I got in the house and she said, "Get out of my sight and don't come back until that's washed out."

Aside from getting attention from her parents, Sally likes to get reactions from other people, anyone who will look, anyone who will react:

> I wear like a really nice dress, that doesn't like, it's got like little tiny straps and then I'll wear a different patterned shirt and like, hifi socks that are striped. Then I'll wear my big Doc boots and I'll put my hair all in these weird positions and do little braids and everything and then when they [my parents] walk with me they go, "She's not with us, we don't know her," but I do it because I like it when people look at me, but I kind of like the glances, but not the stares — Then I feel different … . It's cool because there's no one else that's dressed like me … and people just look at me and some of them go, "Oh neat," and some of them go, "Oh my gosh," you know, but it's up to them. I like it. I like the attention … . And yes, I'd like to be on stage.

Music groups: The Beastie Boys (and beastie girls)

With regard to being on stage, Sally had much invested in someday being a performer. She and two of her friends have dreams of becoming musicians, performers just like their idols, the Beastie Boys, a punk music trio from New York. Sally was wearing a Beastie Boys T-shirt while telling me about her strong identification with these musicians:

> So, I'll play the bass and we're all going to be singers, we don't want to fight over who sings … . And Beverley is going to play drums and Lorraine's going to play electric guitar. … We're going to be just like the Beastie Boys, like I'm wearing this T-shirt here because MCA, he's my favorite, and he plays the bass, and Mike D., this is of course Beverley's favorite and he plays the drums, and King Ad-Rock, this is of course Lorraine's favorite and he plays the electric guitar, so we're a kind of like girl Beastie Boys kind of thing … . We want to be unique like that. We want to have a kind of weird sound that no one else has.

Rolling Stone Magazine describes the Beastie Boys as a band that offers a sly blending of the styles ... . *Ill Communication* [one of their albums] fuses jazz-laced hip-hop, crabby 1980-style punk thrash, aggressive, groove-heavy rap and the kind of infectiously sleazy instrumentals that can be heard playing in porn movies just after someone says, "Hey, you're not the regular cabana boy." (Mundy, 1994)

The Beastie Boys, whose dress style blends everything from thrift store finds to the latest in Skater gear (all of it several sizes too large), also blend language into word-association free-for-alls reminiscent of Joyce's *Finnegans Wake*. Thus, a Beastie Boy might describe another band he admires as, "Fly, fresh, dope and phat, they are ultimately the shit" (*Rolling Stone*, August 11, 1994) or perhaps respond to a reporter's question about whether or not he owns and uses exercise equipment with, "I have a uh, John Holmes penis pull. I have a basketball, a brand new Voit black streetball basketball. It's the best basketball I ever owned" (Mack, 1994). The group has become what Mundy (1994) terms "a leading cult" with an "original posture as cartoonish beer-swilling assholes" who are now considered "musical innovators, cultural pioneers and the kind of upstanding citizens [read, successful businessmen] that deserve to kick back and dig their bad selves" (p. 48).

Millions of young people like Sally and her friends identify with the Beastie Boys. Millions emulate their style of dress, their hair (which features wild colors and oddly angled razor cuts), their style of talking and their attitudes. For some, the identification goes beyond style and extends to life experiences.

Like Sally, Ad-Rock Horovitz's parents divorced when he was young (aged three), and he went to live with his mother. Like Sally, he discovered skateboarding early and still pursues this activity. Like Sally and her friends, who began to use marijuana, magic mushrooms, and acid (LSD) in grade six, and who have no trouble obtaining drugs and alcohol whenever they want, drugs and alcohol are part of Ad-Rock's everyday life and have been since at least grade four, when he first got caught for smoking pot. Ad-Rock's mother, whom he describes as "the coolest person ever" because she ran a hip thrift shop in New York City's West Village and liked to go to see rock bands and stumble down streets singing and laughing, died from alcoholism when he was in his teens.

Also like Sally, Ad-Rock is no stranger to violence. In a single year, he was charged with assault twice: once for throwing a full beer can at a female fan, and once for assaulting a television camera man who was trying to film him at a time when he did not wish to be filmed. The first charge was eventually dropped; the second brought him 200 hours of community work.

The other Beastie Boys, MCA Yauch and Mike D. Diamond (who lost his father at the age of 16), share Ad-Rock's history of early initiation into drug and alcohol misuse. And while all three grew up on New York's affluent upper west side among wealthy families, attended expensive liberal private schools, and were exposed to New York's intellectual and artistic elite, all three chose public acting out as a way of making their mark in the world. Credited with inventing the epidemic fad of ripping off hood ornaments from expensive European cars and the wearing of one's baseball cap back to front; known for being young, drunken, and bad, and for prancing about in clothes meant to shock, the Beastie Boys (all now well past the age of 30) have made a life's work of never growing up, at least in public. Instead, they have become trend setters whose greatest preoccupation is themselves, followed by sex, drugs, alcohol, and violence — as the lyrics from their songs demonstrate:

From "The New Style":
Father of many — married to none
And in case you're unaware I carry a gun
Stepped into the party — the place was overpacked
Saw the kid that dissed my honey and shot him in the back
I had to get a beeper because my phone is tapped
You better keep your mouth shut 'cause I'm feeling fully strapped
I got money in the bank — I can still get high
That's why your girlfriend thinks that I'm so fly
I've got money and juice — twin sisters in my bed
Their father had envy so I shot him in the head
If I played guitar I'd be Jimmy Page
The girlies I like are underage (check it!)
Girls with boyfriends are the kind I like
I'll steal your honey like I stole your bike
Your father — he's jealous 'cause I'm making that green
I've got the girlies' numbers from the places I have been[3]

From "No Sleep 'Til Brooklyn":
Another place — another train
Another bottle in the brain

Another girl — another fight
Another drive all night
Our manager's crazy — he always smokes dust
He's got his own room at the back of the bus
Tour 'round the world — you rock around the clock
Plane to hotel — girls on the jock
We're thrashing hotels like it's going out of style
Getting paid along the way 'cause it's worth your while
Four on the floor — Ad-Rock's out the door
MCA's in the back because he's skeezin' with some whore
We've got a safe in the trunk with money in a stack
With dice in the front and Brooklyn's in the back.[4]

Sally and her friends want to be girl Beastie Boys when they grow up, and in the meantime they are practicing for the role. For Sally, this includes overcoming shyness in order to be able to become a performer. Thus, she must change the way she behaves in social settings and must take risks that could get her into trouble:

> Like, I'm really shy, but it's like if you get up there and act like an idiot people don't think you're shy, so even if I am shy, I can't do that ... . If you don't act shy, people don't treat like you're shy, so I'm crazy now ... . Like I'm totally over my shyness and everything, and last weekend, when we were downtown, I got Beverley's boyfriend in trouble. He's a Rapper, and he was really bugging me, so I go up to these big, big Rapper guys that look like they're real tough and I go, "See that guy over there? Well he thinks you're an idiot and he wants to fight with you." So he goes over and he's like, "What are you saying?" and he's like, "Nothing, I'm sure I didn't say nothing," and I'm just embarrassing myself going up to everyone and saying, "I think you're cool," and — everyone's like, "Stop it, stop it," and it was so much fun.

Practicing also includes doing drugs and believing that in her school of several hundred students "only about 12 kids don't smoke drugs and drop acid and they're all chess players." It means being a Skate and trying to be "original and different and like nobody else," while carefully emulating a music group that is the focal point for many other adolescents. It means wanting to live in a loft in New York City like the Beastie Boys did when they started out. It means talking the way the Beastie Boys talk, that is, juxtaposing insults with unusual word-associations meant to shock, amuse, and sometimes baffle the listener. It means talking about using drugs as if it were just something everyone did. Sally talks about getting drugs as if this were the most common of everyday experiences:

Uhm, there's about seven dealers at our school, you walk up to them and you say, "Can I get a gram or a hit?" And they say, "Okay," and you give them the money, and they give you the drugs, and you walk away. Or if they don't have any on them they say, "I can get it to you at lunch." They skip their class, their first class before lunch, and they go over to the high school and get it off a dealer at the high school and then come back to school.

Sally's assumption is simply that this is how it's done, and "we" (meaning everybody except maybe the odd chess player) all do it.

When I asked why the street groups she had described to me organized their identities around the music they listened to, Sally stated that for her, there was a direct connection between the music one listened to and the way one acted: "It's like the total biggest influence." When kids talk about what it is that makes them a Rapper or a Skate,

they're like, well, the music. It's just neat and it draws you to it and I like, I like to listen to it, I'm like, "Oh ya."

Further, Sally offered an explanation for why Rappers in particular are violent:

'Cause everyone's like, like it's like gangster music and everyone's like, "Oh ya, I gotta be tough. I gotta go kill people," like that and stuff ... . 'Cause the lyrics in the rap music, it's like, "Ya, go out and kill your mom and then get the money and then go kill your dad" ... . And then they say things like they're going to, they're going to get their gang after them and stuff ... . Like, the reason why the kids wanna kill 'em is 'cause they have rules.

When I probed further into the actuality of such killings, Sally became vague but assured me that if someone wanted to get someone killed, it could be arranged. When I asked more questions as to the lives of kids whom she knows to engage in violence on a regular basis, she replied:

They're like always, they always need to either be drunk or like smoked up, and they always like have to be like doing something — like breaking into cars, houses, stuff like that.

In Sally's estimation, what lies beneath these behaviors is "a bad family life" and not enough personal attention, which together drives kids to seek out the connectedness and feeling of belonging found in groups and gangs. As a Rapper, a Banger or, in Sally's case, a Skate, a kid can be "somebody" with a ready-made and recognizable identity that is broadcast to others through music, dress, and the activities endemic to their group.

Sally expanded on the notion of a "bad family life" when she talked about her friends' families. With the exception of Lorraine, most of Sally's friends have experienced family break-ups that, like Sally's parents' break-up, followed several years of quarreling and fighting. But even Lorraine had not escaped experiencing difficulties at home and a "bad family life." As Sally described it, Lorraine was deeply unhappy with her family:

> Lorraine's parents are still together, and that's why she's so depressed. She hates her mother and she hates her father and wishes they would get divorced … . Her mother won't let her go and won't accept the fact that she's getting older and her dad's never there … . He goes away for months at a time to work, and she gets depressed … . She loves being depressed. She couldn't be happy, like her brother is such a goody goody, and she's just the opposite, and her mother's always going, "Why can't you be like Jim?" and people say, "You're Jim's little sister." That's like her name. Whenever she writes me a note she signs it "Jim's little sister," and she's really depressing. She's like so depressing, she makes Beverley and me want to cry whenever she goes on one of her depressing modes. She just sits there and her room's so dark, like a prisoner in jail … . She says, "Too many people are happy, what's there to be happy about? Trees are being cut down and people are dying. Who cares?" But she's really smart like me, and me and her are exactly alike, except I'm crazy and she's depressing.

It seems that only when the three girls get together and work at being "beastie girls" does Lorraine achieve some relief from her depression. When she engages with the other two in song writing, she begins to brighten up a little.

Growing up Female
As Sally and I talked, besides being struck by the emotional abandonment she described, I also noticed that the sources from which she drew most of her inspiration and her identity were male and even degrading to women.

When I asked whether she wanted to be like any women she knew, Sally named four women. One was the 17-year-old daughter of a friend of her mother's whom she admires because "she's the nicest person and she's got a weight problem and she doesn't care," but whose real attraction is that she has a "gorgeous" brother. The second was Madonna, the world-famous pop-music sex idol. Sally's reason for looking up to Madonna is that "she can do anything she wants and not care what anybody thinks about her." (As well as being a lionized sex symbol, Madonna is a former battered wife whose marriage to Sean Penn — a Hollywood actor known for his tough, bad-boy image — floundered because Penn beat her during fits of drunken rage.)

The next woman she named was Marilyn Monroe, about whom she didn't have much to say except that she was dead. (As most people over 30 know, Marilyn Monroe died because she took an overdose of antidepressants combined with alcohol. Idolized by millions, romantically linked to John F. Kennedy, a veteran of four marriages and a survivor of sexual abuse in her younger years, Marilyn Monroe was never able to find peace.)

The last woman Sally named was Naomi Campbell, whom she described as "like a runway supermodel" whom she liked primarily because "she's got like a neat accent and she's really pretty."

Three of the four women Sally named are sex objects, highly paid and much adored for their bodies, their faces, and the images of narrowly defined female desirability that they project into the public mind in the service of the multibillion-dollar entertainment and fashion industries. At least two of them, Madonna and Marilyn Monroe, have suffered publicly for being the sex symbols their audiences pay them to be.

The very idols Sally chose (other than the daughter of her mother's friend) presented her with difficulties in being a girl. For her, the images provided for girls and women by the entertainment and fashion industries create expectations which all females must fulfill. Thus, Sally believes that most boys and a lot of other girls think that all young women must be "like Cindy Crawford, a supermodel, she's like underweight, like a perfect body, so pretty, like everything." And although Sally stated she didn't think she personally needed to conform to this image, she was well aware of it and constantly fighting against it.

In part, Sally finds refuge from the pressure to be thin and perfect by being the only girl in her Skate group. But here she faces a different kind of pressure and a different kind of discrimination. Here the boys tell her, "You, you gotta learn how to skate better, come on, you gotta alley a little bit higher." Although it's clear that she is welcome in the group largely because one of the good Skaters is her friend, she is not really contending as a Skate, who can enter skate-offs and find sponsorship through one of the local skate equipment suppliers, because she is a girl.

Because little encouragement is extended to girls to engage in skating for its own sake, there are few really good female Skaters to be found, especially in Sally's community. Therefore, Sally must often fight against the accusation that she is merely a "poser," someone who carries around a skateboard but can't really skate. As well, she faces harassment from other girls who accost her when they see her with a skateboard and yell out, "Oh yeah, what are you trying to be, a guy or something?" Often, such remarks provoke an aggressive reaction from Sally; and it is mostly under such circumstances that she has threatened other girls and faced them down.

The gender-based discrimination that Sally experiences with regard to her body and her participation in skateboarding reaches into other areas of her life as well. She gave me the following two examples. The first has to do with being prevented from taking part in an activity; the second has to do with being subjected to abuse as a result of the still deeply entrenched sexual double standard:

> A lot of Skater guys, they go snowboarding and then girls that want to go snowboarding, they get dumped on, and the guys go, "Stick to the ski slopes," you know, do the girls' thing and stuff. My friend Lorraine, her boyfriend's this big-time snowboarder, she wants to try it, but every time she asks her brother, her brother's like, "Don't, Lorraine, don't," he like tells her, "You're just going to get mocked and stuff," so she says, "Okay," and she just goes skiing.
>
> ***
>
> Uhm, it's like girls can be called sluts if they have sex, but guys are rewarded. If a girl's to go and do it with 50 guys, then they're called a slut or something, but if a guy's going to do it with 50 girls then like, it's "Right on!" ... Like, guys get rewarded and girls get beat up or pushed around or talked about, like rumors or something. I think it's really dumb because they're both doing the same thing.

Sally gave me a first-hand example of being the victim of the double standard she so abhors:

> My last boyfriend was a big-time Rapper and he was such a jerk, you can't explain it. There's something about him, I can't stand him now, I'd like to see

him die … . He called my friend a slut, and I do not like that name, slut is a word I hate, and he wouldn't stop calling her that and I told him to stop it … and he wouldn't let up with calling her that … . And there was a lot of stuff that he did that was, I don't know, low, like he set up his friend, who's a virgin and hated it, with Adel so she'd sleep with him, but somebody else told her it was a set-up so she said, "Okay, fine, you're dumped," but he still kept calling her a slut. And he well, used me, like we finally had sex and then as soon as that was over he's like, "Bye" … . And like, I'm so mad at myself for like actually letting him. We weren't going out for that long and stuff. I got so mad at myself for letting somebody do that to me, so, I don't know, I hate him so!

The fact that girls get "beat up or pushed around" and construed as "sluts" for showing an interest in sex led us back to discussing violence, because Sally's beating occurred under just such circumstances. Marilee, Sarah, and their friends had decided that Sally was a "slut" for showing interest in Sarah's boyfriend. The designation "slut" made Sally fair game for a beating, according to the rules as understood by Sally and by the girls in her social circle. (This insult is hurled at girls by other girls far more often than it is by boys, although boys also use it.)

Sally thinks the sexual double standard is "stupid" and says that she "just calls guys sluts too if they're going to call me and my friends that." But she also plays into the double standard by believing that being called a slut is "the biggest insult" — one that must be addressed, a direct attack worthy of an aggressive response:

> Like, it'd be people taking me on, and then if someone was to pick on me, I'd turn around and do it right back. It's like this girl called Adel and me sluts, so I got really mad and I said, "You, you don't go around talking like that … and I'm like, "Who are you, like who are you to judge us?" and everything, and she's like, "Well I can if I want," so I pushed her and I said, "I don't wanna ever hear you calling anybody a slut, you can call them any other name, but like that one is just degrading." And she's like, "Fine!" So I just like pushed her again and walked away.

Thus, girls — even those who know that designating another girl a slut is simply buying into a "stupid" double standard — take such name calling seriously; they push each other around and beat each other up over it.

Despite her personal rejection of these standards, Sally knows them well. She knows also that these standards govern rules which, in the end, must be followed. As she explained earlier to me, if you were out somewhere and say you thought one of the [girls' boyfriends] was good-looking and you went up and started talking to him, if [she] didn't like the way you looked or didn't know why you were talking to her boyfriend, ... [she could] do serious damage to you.

Thus, when Sally showed an interest in Sarah's boyfriend and consequently got beaten up by Sarah and Marilee, she fell victim to the very double standard that she hates. It is a double standard that operates on many levels in Sally's life.

This became clear to me when Sally described how she likes to spend time with her little sister. Other than practicing to become a girl Beastie Boy, and being a Skate, Sally very much enjoys playing with Barbie dolls — not only with her little sister, but also with her friends, the same girls who want to be female Beastie Boys. Every afternoon,

> I do my school work and after, I play Barbies with my sister, and it's okay, as long as I get to be in charge of the game, and I love to put on Barbie's wedding dress and play them getting married ... . I have tons of Barbies myself and I keep them. I've got so much furniture. I've got three cars and a bathroom set and all this stuff so, and I'm not going to give it to my sister because when I have kids I want it. It's okay, sometimes I get sick of it because I take so long to get set up, like I have to have the house perfect and everything. Like I'm a perfectionist. I get it from my mom. After I'm set up, that takes an hour and then I only have half an hour to play with her because I leave at four-thirty ... . And I tell my friends that I play with Barbies and they go "Yeah, you're cool," some of them.
>
> Sibylle: How many of your friends do that?
> Sally: Lorraine, Beverley. Beverley is so crazy, she needs to go, she's like psycho, she loves Barbies, loves making them do things ... .

After our discussion, I read and reread the transcripts. I was reminded of the work of A.N. Leontyev (1981), a Russian psychologist who worked with and expanded on L.S. Vygotsky's theories on the development of self and mind. Leontyev suggests that, because it provides an arena in which children practice entering into an active relationship with self and others, play makes a strong contribution to the development of mind, self, and world. Within the serious practice (praxis) that is play, children try out and formulate their identities, and their understanding of how the world works. Given this, I considered what Barbie dolls might offer Sally.

Barbie dolls offer a version of womanliness premised on largely unattainable and very narrow standards of body image. They suggest that women ought to be long-limbed and thin, small-hipped and narrow-waisted, and above all else, large-breasted. They suggest that a woman's hair must be thick, long, and wavy, and preferably blond. They also suggest that women are and should be primarily preoccupied with how they look, with what they wear, and with their material possessions, particularly those that are useful to their domestic life. Barbie's primary focus is her wardrobe.

Barbie first appeared on the market in March 1959, as the embodiment of the perfect American teenage fashion model. According to a pamphlet enclosed in the package of the 35th anniversary reissue of the original Barbie, this doll was created by Ruth Handler, who describes Barbie (in an open letter to those who acquire the reissued doll) as "a role model for girls for over three decades ... [because] she allows girls from all around the world to live out their dreams and fantasies in spite of a real world that may seem too big" (manufacturer's pamphlet, Mattel toys, 1995).

The roles that Barbie offers — through her nearly 30 different guises — involve sunbathing, exercising, preparing for gala evenings on the town, singing in rock bands, dancing, and dressing glamorously in sexually alluring costumes. Some Barbies do seem to work for a living, but these are hard to find. I was able to locate one doctor Barbie, dressed in a white coat, a short skirt, and tight sweater, sporting a stethoscope and weighing a baby. She was also blond, buxom, and wearing a great deal of make-up on her "oh so coy ... delicately painted face" (manufacturer's pamphlet, Mattel Toys, 1995).

Since 1959, little has changed with regard to Barbie's underlying message about women's bodies and women's focal points. Barbie is still "a perfect blend of innocence and glamour, right down to ... her pretty pink polished fingertips," engaged primarily in achieving a "perfect look" (manufacturer's pamphlet, Mattel Toys, 1995). Over the years, Barbie has acquired a larger wardrobe and a greater range of accessories. She has acquired Ken as a playmate, as well as a house, a camper, and cars; but the underlying premise — that the ideal woman looks like a *Playboy Magazine* centerfold — has not altered.

For Sally, being like Barbie reinforces the notion of having to be thin and extends to getting married, playing the wedding game over and over again to perfectionist standards. Sally knows she should be thinner. She's clear that what is expected of a girl in the 1990s is "to be like Cindy Crawford," a thin and (according to Sally) "annoying" example of what "guys and other girls think girls should be like." She also knows that even though she wants to be a girl Beastie Boy and identifies herself as a Skate, the ultimate achievement for a woman is a wedding. Young women like Sally still understand (as did the women of my generation and generations of women before us) that no matter how else we occupy ourselves in the meantime, the greatest, most important goal is getting married. It is a goal that we can hope to achieve only by emulating, as closely as we can, the female templates provided for us by models like Cindy Crawford and that enduring symbol of ideal womanhood, Barbie.

Sally has "got the message" loud and clear. When I asked what she wanted to be when she grew up, she answered, "a model and a musician." And Sally is not alone.

School

As Sally and I talked, I wondered how education fit into her life in the midst of all these other largely negative influences. I asked Sally about her experiences at school, and what they meant to her.

For Sally, school — when she did go there — was primarily a place to meet with other young people, and only secondarily a place where she went to receive an education. Mostly, she didn't go:

> Like I'd go to school, to get Adel, and then leave. So, we'd like walk, we'd have to walk to my house or her house, which takes about an hour, and like the principal kept calling our parents, and my mom just said that she knows that I don't like school, but she wants me to know that for her, school is a big deal, so she told me that I had to go.

When I asked her what school was like, Sally replied:

> Mmm … I got a B in math once when I was in junior high. Everything else I failed, 'cause I was walking around and watching television.

When I probed further so that I could understand what she found difficult about school, Sally explained:

> I don't like having people at school. Like, I like to keep to myself, unless, unless my friends from downtown, 'cause they're my loyal friends. And, I don't know, there's just no one there I like. 'Cause at school, you've always got

someone around you. You go to class with your friends and you get five-minute breaks with your friends, and then you get lunch. I just like being by myself ... .

Further discussion led us back to drugs and violence. According to Sally, school is where "fights happen almost every day" and where people are mean to one another. School is where Sally had to act tough. School is where she learned about drugs and sexual harassment. School is where she had a reputation to uphold, and where she made friends whom she defended when others called them sluts. School is where, in academic terms, she mostly failed. Sally hated school.

By contrast, Sally "loved" working on her correspondence courses at her father's house under his supervision:

Easy, I got an A in French. Then I got an E in French and I need to get tutoring, then I got a C+ in Science and I'm getting B's and A's in English and like, B's and A's in Math, and I haven't done any Guidance and Socials, I haven't sent anything in yet, but everything else is real easy, and it's better than school. It's like I can do whatever I want for as long as I want. It's just better than school. I don't like school ... . I'm going to stay on correspondence 'til grade 11.

In the end, the social demands of school were too much of a distraction for Sally; friends and drugs and sexual harassment and violence drove her out. She is far happier at home.

Each day Sally spends time with her father and sister and rides back and forth to the city with her mother. Each day she plays Barbies, and on weekends she meets her Skater friends and skates; or she gets together with Beverley and Lorraine and writes songs and practices being a girl Beastie Boy. When she wants excitement, she and the girl Beastie Boys go downtown, hang out with other kids, and create some diversion for themselves:

I just get this big bolt of energy and, okay, I'm in this hyper mood and when I get hyper, I am just like, if you don't want to be embarrassed, walk totally away from me because I'll just go up and talk to everyone. Like, "I think you're cool, but you need a haircut," like I'm so critical, it's really funny. And Beverley is exactly the same way only she's not so — she wouldn't go and do it, she mocks everybody behind their back, but I'm the person that goes up and says it. "You know what my friend just said about you?" and she goes, "You're an idiot," and stuff, and like, people just laugh, and we do it to have fun, for something to do ... .

Ultimately, Sally loves to do anything that will earn her some attention and a sense of belonging. She will dye her hair a multitude of colors and dress herself in weird and wonderful clothes. She will make friends with gang members. She will go to church socials with new acquaintances and sing religious songs on Friday nights when she has nothing else to do. She will take drugs and get into fights. She will go with her stepfather to the mall and pretend he's her older brother, and with her mother to Tupperware parties. And — although her mother "dragged" her there at first — she will go to see a counselor. Going for counseling is something that Sally really loves because it's

> uhm, really good, it's time … a time to talk. (*Short laugh*) So you can talk about, like, all your problems and they can give you advice and stuff. 'Cause at first I said, "Well I won't go." And then when I met her [the counselor] and everything I'm like, "Okay. This isn't that bad." And now it's like, my mom has an hour-and-a-half appointment and she comes out to the car and I'll still be talking to my counselor, like we'll have a two-hour session. And my mom's like, "What kept you guys so long?" Tomorrow I'm going to bring in coffee and we're going to sit there and talk as long as we want … .

This is where I left Sally: seeing her counselor on a weekly basis, and staying away from school.

NOTES

1. The wife's assumption of a parental role with respect to her husband also features in other key informants' families. See, for example, "Mary's Story" (Chapter Six).
2. This information fits the facts. There was a drive-by shooting near a downtown park in which two youths from Sally's neighborhood drove by in a car and shot another youth in the leg. This shooting took place on November 22, 1993 and was reported in the *Victoria Times Colonist* on November 24, 1993.
3. Lyrics by M. Diamond, R. Rubin, A. Yauch and The King; music by R. Rubin and The King. Copyright © 1986 by Def Jam Music Inc. (ASCAP)/Brooklyn Dust Music (ASCAP). All rights reserved.
4. Lyrics by M. Diamond, A. Yauch, and The King; music by R. Rubin, A. Yauch, and The King. Copyright © 1986 by Def Jam Music Inc. (ASCAP)/Brooklyn Dust Music (ASCAP). All rights reserved.

CHAPTER FOUR

MARILEE'S STORY

One time when my dad was drinking he kicked me out of the house, he hit me a couple of times, so I left that night and went to a friend's house. My dad regrets it, and he says he wouldn't do it again. He hit my mom too. He had her down on her knees right by the coffee table and he had her arm behind her back and he threatened to break it an' stuff and then she screamed. And I came down the stairs and she told me to phone the cops. So my dad left, and now they're back together and he's in counseling and it's better, but I'll never forgive him. Like inside, I'll never, ever forgive him, but I'll forgive him enough to keep my love for him and stuff. (*Excerpt from taped interview with Marilee*)

Family dynamics

Although Marilee described her family as basically good, there was much in what she told me that pointed to deep-seated and long-standing difficulties. Her parents have been together for nearly 26 years during which they have had many mini separations, short periods of time when one parent or the other left the family in order to cool off after a fight.

Fights occur frequently (as they did in Marilee's father's family when he was growing up). Everyone participates: Fights take place between mother and father, father and daughters, mother and daughters, or between the sisters. These altercations begin over small things and escalate into major confrontations. As Marilee described it:

All our fights start over stupid things, just little stupid things, and they always seem to happen on vacation or something like that. 'Cause Christmas time we'd always get in a fight, and the family would split up. My dad would go somewhere for a couple of days before Christmas, them come back. My sister and I got in a big huge fight on Valentine's Day, and I ran away ... .

The Valentine's Day fight was over who could wear a particular pair of shoes. Running away as a way of dealing with this fight was actually sanctioned or perhaps even suggested by Marilee's mother, who told her, "Okay, you can get out of the house, you know," and drove her to the house of a friend who had agreed to take her in.

According to Marilee, when her father is involved in the fighting he is usually drinking and listening to country music and feeling angry.

Furthermore, drinking together as a family and getting drunk is very much a part of any holiday and the celebration of birthdays and anniversaries. Marilee's parents purchase the alcohol for Marilee, her sister, and their friends, and sanction their drinking at home under their supervision. The trouble seems to be that the parents themselves drink right along with everyone else and set limits neither on their own nor on others' drinking.

As Marilee describes it, both parents "used to like to really party and stuff," but have lately cut back because "they figure they're getting too old for it." Drinking is still, however, Marilee's father's chosen form of recreation. It is his ritual to drink with the boys at the local bar every Friday, and while according to Marilee, he has cut back somewhat on the amount he drinks during the week, he "has to" drink on Fridays because he "needs his time to have fun," especially since his best drinking buddy has just "dropped dead" at age 50.

Most conflict in the family seems to be characterized by an "either/or" approach, that is, "either you do what I want you to do or I'll let you have it." "Letting you have it" begins with screaming, yelling and name calling, escalates to threats and, on occasion, physical violence, and usually ends in someone being told to "get out" or choosing to leave as a way of punishing his or her opponent.

People often leave, but they always come back. Ultimatums are frequently held over the heads of family members who are seen to be in the wrong. For example, at the time I spoke to her, Marilee's father was seen to be in the wrong because of hitting his wife. He was therefore given the ultimatum to "never do it again" or he's had it, "because he knows that if he makes one more mistake, he's gone!"

Marilee herself has a similar ultimatum hanging over her, although hers is not about her conduct during fights, but rather about her commitment to school. She knows that she has only one choice: "either do [schooling by] correspondence or get out." Marilee made it clear to me that she is no stranger to conflict and violence in her home.

Marilee's mother

As Marilee told me her story, I kept flashing back to my conversations with her mother, whom I had met when she addressed a parent network forum on youth violence which I attended.

Marilee's mother had expressed astonishment and dismay with regard to her daughter's involvement with violence. She talked at length about how shocked she was to learn of Marilee's participation in the beating of Sally.

In searching for an explanation, she and the other parents who participated in the forum focused on their children's peers as the culprits who had persuaded them to engage in violence. No one mentioned family violence. Everyone saw it as a "kids' problem" brought on by the need for status, which could be gained through intimidation of others.

Each parent in turn elaborated on this thesis, telling the others how their own children had never been violent and never experienced violence before they changed "180 degrees" when they "hit puberty" and started to hang around with their present friends. Several parents stated emphatically that since they had never even spanked their kids, there could be no connection between their children's violent behavior and anything they had experienced at home.

Marilee's mother said not a word about her husband, about the conflict in her family, about the violence each family member had both witnessed and experienced at the hands of other family members, and about the many times she or her husband had left the family temporarily because of fighting. She did not mention that her husband was currently in counseling under threat of being expelled from the family home if he stepped out of line. Instead, she talked about Marilee's need for anger management and about her own efforts to persuade Marilee to accept counseling. For Marilee's mother, and for the other parents who participated in this forum, youth violence is somehow derived from the state of being adolescent.

Marilee offered a different explanation. She saw her own violence as directly connected to her experiences with her family and to her deeply felt anger.

Peer relationships

Marilee agreed to talk to me only once because she was afraid of being labeled a "narc" (informer) by her peers for telling me what she knew about violence. Nevertheless, she was willing to enter into a lengthy discussion about many aspects of herself and her life.

Besides family, we talked about what most occupied Marilee, namely, "trying to become the person I'm supposed to be." When I asked who that person was, she answered: "Just the person I am right now, the person who doesn't do drugs."

It seemed that, since grade eight (Marilee was now completing grade ten by correspondence), she had not been the person she was "supposed" to be because she had become involved with "the scummy people," those who were "druggies and just didn't care," those who "did whatever they wanted."

As a self-described "scummy" person, Marilee had enjoyed herself by "basically living on the edge every second you were there." When I asked what living on the edge meant, I learned it meant defying one's parents primarily by taking drugs. When I asked what had induced her to become involved with drugs and "scummy" people, she told me:

> I met Rosie, a friend of mine, and she kind of, I never knew she was hangin' around with them, and I got pulled into them, and it just seemed like a good idea at the time. (*Laughs*) "Cause it was fun. It was exciting — rebelling against your parents, just being in control.

When I probed to find out why she was no longer "there," Marilee explained that her change of heart had occurred as a result of a "mishap" — that is, a narrowly averted beating at the hands of the very people she found so exciting to be around.

It seems that because she was a newcomer to this crowd, Marilee was also a target for suspicion. Thus, when a rumor circulated that the local police knew the members of this "scummy" crowd were smoking dope and had a list of their names, Marilee was targeted as a "narc" and singled out for a beating by some 40 people. She was to receive the beating at the hands of a number of girls who were threatening to "bash her face in."

These girls (whom Marilee had hitherto regarded as her friends) organized the beating, which was to take place just outside the same junior high school that Sally attended. The boys, who were also involved in targeting Marilee, were to be spectators. Their role was to watch and not to speak to Marilee, who was to receive her punishment at the hands of the girls.

Marilee avoided the beating by calling her mother and pleading with her to come to the school with her car and take Marilee home and out of harm's way.

She has been at home ever since. Like Sally, Marilee refuses to return to school, and is receiving the balance of her education by correspondence.

Goals and aspirations

While staying home and working on her correspondence course, Marilee began to consider what it meant to become the person she was "supposed" to be. When I spoke with her some two years after her threatened beating, she appeared to have reached some clarity about this.

At first, Marilee talked about herself in positive terms, and outlined her plans for the future: She would be a person who would not allow violence in her home. Her children would not experience the terror and the pain of being beaten or of watching their parents engage in violent quarrels, as she herself had.

Unlike her mother, Marilee would follow through on avoiding violence in her family, even if it meant divorcing her husband. She would not smoke in front of her children so that they would not pick up the habit from her, as she had picked it up from watching parents of friends smoke. She would marry as soon as she finished school.

Before that, perhaps when her boyfriend moved out of his family home and found an apartment, she would move in with him. She would "get out" (of her family home), get a job, "just a normal regular job, something to afford my car and my apartment, maybe pet grooming or daycare."

She would have children, a little boy and girl, for whom she had already picked names that her boyfriend also liked. She would build on her present situation:

> Everything's so good right now. You know, I've got a boyfriend, and he loves me, I love him, and my parents are fine. You know my sister's doing fine, and I've got my learner's [license]. You know I've finally turned 16, you know, so, and I've finally found friends and I finally realize that I don't have to find friends or boyfriends that everyone's gonna agree with. 'Cause I used to try and find, you know, find popular guys, good lookin' guys, but now, you know, Danny, and like all my friends, Rick and Tim and them, people think they're losers, other people consider them the losers. So they say, "Oh gross, don't hang out with them!" And it's like, "Excuse me, they're my friends, you know, they treat me good," and I'm tired of trying to find people that all my other friends are happy with. So I'll just be friends with who I'm friends with, and I'm fine.

Anger

As we talked and I tried to learn more about what "fine" looked like in the everyday sense, it turned out that things with Marilee were really not all that fine. In fact, most of the time, she struggles with feelings of anger, fear, insecurity, and grief. Despite her hopes of a rosy and secure future premised on marriage and children, she also suffers daily in a private world where the threat of violence is never very far away.

Marilee explained that violence occurs because kids have "attitudes." Citing herself and her friend Tanya as examples, she told me that

> most of my friends' parents hit them. It's like Tanya and her mom, it just happens. It's just like the kid has an attitude, and the parent gets fed up. I mean my mom told me, you know, from time to time, she wants to just punch me in the face. You know it's understandable why she does that. You know, I mean I can admit it, I get an attitude, it's just, you get an attitude … .

For Marilee, the feeling of anger is far more familiar than feeling "fine." As she describes it, everyday life is

> just like the commercials that are on now, the one uh, with the girl from "Sisters" on there, where she was saying how uhm, she was saying how kids look up to their mom and dad. You know, "Let's dress like mom, let's shave like dad." Uhm, and then they watch mom and dad yell and fight, you know and it's true enough. Kids grow up with violence, and — so I'm violent, and I'm a very angry person … . I can get very angry, and just, I don't always know why. Somehow, I mean something, just a little thing, triggers me off, and I'll just be like all angry. You know, I've grown up a very angry person … I'm that angry that I will deck someone, I'm just scared of the day that I end up punching a person when I shouldn't, 'cause I get so angry, I get so excited. I get angry and my adrenaline pumps up and I'm just like, "Ya, let's do it!" you know.

Thus, Marilee — in a condition that she describes as "pumped with anger" — had "decked" someone when she helped Sarah beat up Sally. Yet, she did not consider her involvement in that fight to be problematic. Indeed, she felt perfectly justified in pushing, shoving, and choking Sally and holding her for Sarah to beat up, because in her mind, Sally "deserved" such treatment for showing an interest in Sarah's boyfriend. Further, Marilee acknowledged that she hadn't actually hauled off and punched Sally although she wanted to, because she was afraid that if she did her parents would find out, and she wouldn't be able to get her learner's license.

Anger is a constant for Marilee. She is angry with her father for bringing violence into the home. Although she talked about things being "fine" with her sister, they often engage in what she describes as "huge fights over stupid little things." (For the moment there was peace between the sisters, likely because they were living several provinces apart.) On occasion, she is angry with Danny, her boyfriend, and fights with him just as she fights with her sister:

> It's like, somethin' little he'll say, I'll just start yelling at him, and then he'll start yelling back at me, and he'll start bringing somethin' else into it, and then I'll bring somethin' else into that and it's just like a big fight. Bang! and then it's like, "See ya!"

She also gets angry with her friends, the same friends she is so happy to have found, the "losers" whom she defends to other people and whom she describes as treating her "good." On the Saturday before I interviewed her, Marilee had become involved in a violent altercation with some of these very people:

> Me and my boyfriend, we were down at Seven-Eleven, and it was with the people that I was friends with at the time. Then, they just went against me so I got angry at them. So we were dr… I was drunk. Down at Seven-Eleven. I was fingering Rick and, you know, I was saying "Fuck you, man! Na na na … " You know, stuff like that. And, just to joke around and Rick's was like, "'Kay let's go." I'm like "'Kay." 'Cause I was the only one saying it to him. You know, so, uhm, Danny took me and we walked, and then I got mad at Rick and I started walking ahead of them, for some reason, I don't know. So then, Mike and them drove by in the van and Danny's like "Fuck you!" and Rick hangs out the window and goes "What?," and Danny said "I said go fuck yourself!" So they stopped, and Mike come out. I just — try and stop Mike I'm like, "Don't touch him! Don't touch him!" Like, I'm "Don't touch my goddamn boyfriend!" He's like, "Oh, screw you!" So then he walks and I'm trying to stop Rick at the same time and I just turned around, and I just saw them fighting. I just walked off. I left. I was in tears. I was crying. I knew where I was going. I was gonna go straight to Tanya's but I just kept walking past Tanya's. I was just scared that I was gonna, you know, they're gonna come after me. The cops were gonna come up behind me saying "Danny's in — going to the hospital." "Danny's laying dead on the road." You know, "Danny's going to jail." You know, it's just, stuff was going through my head. I thought it was my fault. But Danny said it wasn't 'cause if he hadn't yelled anything out to them they wouldn't have stopped. 'Cause they were going right by us. But, I just thought it was stupid. So Sarah thinks that uh, Danny should charge Mike for it. 'Cause Mike's the one who started it.

Friendships with other girls

Marilee also gets angry with her girlfriends, even those she describes as her "best" friends — girls like Sarah, with whom she beat up Sally.

In the week before our interview, Marilee had decided "not to bother" with Sarah; she was angry with her for criticizing the amount of time Marilee spent with Danny. They had resumed speaking only because Sarah had gossip to share about the Saturday night Seven-Eleven fight, most particularly about Danny and the other boys, which Marilee wanted to hear.

Marilee's friendships with girls are tenuous and often premised on alliances against other girls, who are seen as "competition" for boys. For Marilee and her friends, boys are central to their sense of self-worth, largely because they have been abandoned physically or emotionally by their fathers. This was Marilee's explanation for Sarah's need to beat up Sally:

> It's her dad, I don't know what happened to him, but Sarah, I think, gets her anger from him. I can't remember the whole story, but I think her dad just basically left her, and so when guys leave Sarah, she can't handle it, because her dad did it to her. And when she was going out with Chris, she had an obsession with Mike, you know, she was fooling around with Mike when she was going out with Chris. And she just used to have an obsession with two guys all the time. And if one would try and leave her she would say, "Oh well, I'll be with you," to the other guy. So she gets lots of anger and depression from that, and so I think the fact that she might have thought that Chris might have left her, just because something could go wrong and Sally could have said something that Chris believed, or something like that, and Sarah got mad, right? Sally might try to take Chris away from her, and he was Sarah's, and nobody could touch Chris. Sarah could touch somebody else, but nobody could touch Chris.

As Marilee described it, she and other girls constantly look one another over in order to assess how much "competition" they might represent. As a consequence, she rarely forms alliances with those she views as giving her too much "competition." But with Sarah, she had made an exception:

> Sarah's very pretty. She's the only friend of mine that I have competition with, 'cause all my other friends I have no competition with, but she's the only one that I do … .

Violence, responsibility, and fear

Although she was one of the aggressors in their altercation, Marilee is still angry with Sally. She called Sally a bitch the last time she saw her because

> she had the snarkiest look on her face when we saw her the other day. It was like just two days ago, and I had the perfect chance just to go and punch her, but I go to my friend, I go, "Well let's just jerk her around and follow her … ."

As far as Marilee is concerned, Sally caused her own beating, and Sally is still in the wrong. Just after Sally's beating, Sarah, Marilee, and their boyfriends went to McDonald's and had something to eat. Except for making a few remarks such as, "Oh, that bitch broke my nail!" and "Oh, that bitch got blood on my sweater!" they didn't give Sally much thought. Their thoughts and feelings were focused on themselves.

The strongest emotion Marilee recalled feeling after the fight was justification. Marilee felt certain that she was right to help Sarah beat up Sally because

> I don't know how strong Sally is, and I don't know what she could have done to Sarah, so I basically saved Sarah if Sally had done damage to her.

Justification shifted to fear — another of Marilee's recurring emotions — when, during the course of their meal, a policeman walked into McDonald's. Marilee experienced a strong reaction, with her heart going "boom":

> 'Cause I, I think that's what scares me the most, is seeing the cop afterwards. It's like, he's gonna come up to me and say, "Hey, you're comin' with me," you know, it's just quite scary.

The policeman merely came over briefly and said hello to Marilee and her friends, bought his coffee, and left.

What Marilee had found so frightening about this encounter was the possibility of punishment: If she were caught, she might not be allowed to get her driver's license. She wasn't remorseful about what she had done; she was unconcerned about the effects of the beating on Sally's physical and emotional health. She demonstrated no empathy for Sally.

Indeed, during the fight, Sally's fear and Sally's blood served only to feed Marilee's aggression because she saw these as further wrongdoing on Sally's part. When Sally tried to escape, Marilee saw this as an act of defiance against Sarah. This prompted her to grab Sally, swing her around to face Sarah, and yell, "You stand there until she's done with you!" When Sally's blood spurted onto Sarah's sweater, the girls saw this as all the more reason to beat her up.

Fear of punishment was the sole factor that prevented Marilee from taking a more active role in Sally's beating:

> If there was no punishment at the time that Sarah was beating up Sally, I mean if there was nothing about going to Juvey [the local juvenile detention center], ... nothing about getting busted for it, I would have just killed her right there. Not like literally killed her, but I would have punched her as well.

Sarah, on the other hand, was not inhibited by fears of punishment. According to Marilee, Sarah's strongest reaction after the fight was a feeling of pride: "'Oh ya, wicked! I beat somebody up.' And [Sarah] got all this attention for it from everyone."

Marilee also got a lot of attention because of her involvement, attention she tried very hard to divert because

> that got me scared at the time, because everybody's thinkin' that I did it, so I'm thinkin' the word's gonna get around and then finally a parent was gonna get hold of the cops and say that I was the one who did it.

Interestingly, word did get around almost immediately to Marilee's mother, who did nothing. She talked with Marilee about the fight, asked her questions about what happened, but did not hold Marilee responsible (even though she had most of the details, which she later relayed to me). Ultimately, Marilee told me, her mother's only response was to suggest to Marilee that

> the only way I can fight is with her permission, if they've got me backed into a corner and I have no way out. You know if I have to fight that person to get myself out of there, then that's what I have to do.

For Marilee, the imperative to fight depends on how angry and how scared she is. It also depends on her commitment to what is, for her, an inviolable rule: that she must hate those whom her friends hate, and fight for her friends when called upon to do so.

Indeed, the need to fight for her friends further fuels Marilee's fear. As a consequence of her involvement with other girls and boys who fight, Marilee fears that she will be attacked or jumped from behind. This fear keeps her tied to "safe" parts of her neighborhood and prevents her from going to school. It also keeps her from going downtown, an area that she believes is rife with the threat of violence.

It is not only downtown that frightens Marilee; it is the whole world, which for Marilee is an altogether horrid place:

> I don't like the world right now, I think it's a piece of shit. It's filled with drugs and guns. I mean it's the guns that bother me. Because those kids, the ones that were by that park and the one that got shot, those were my friends [a claim that Sally also made]. All of them were my friends, the one guy that got shot in the leg was my friend and the guy that shot him was my friend too. So it was, I was involved with that.

It would seem, from Marilee's point of view, that guns are easy enough to get. The friend who was the shooter in the incident alluded to above sold his stereo and used the money to buy the gun through the illegal underground market. Marilee and her boyfriend have access to guns through the boyfriend's father, who takes them both into the countryside to shoot rifles. One of her closest girlfriend's mothers has a handgun which she keeps loaded and ready to hand because "her and Daniella's dad are getting divorced right now and her mom's so mad at her dad that she's ready to shoot him." Marilee herself (although she states emphatically that she hates guns and would never have one in the house or use one) also remarks that she would nevertheless use one if "like, I had to use one, like there was no other choice." Thus, Marilee lives with the ever-present threat of violence and death.

Death is already a very real part of Marilee's life. Two weeks before our interview, she lost two friends. One 14-year-old was killed when a 16-year-old he was driving with lost control of a sports car he had persuaded a salesman to let him test drive. The 16-year-old had just passed his driver's test and was inexperienced with fast cars. He attempted to negotiate a sharp curve in the road near his house at high speed, wrapped the demonstrator around a telephone pole, and killed his passenger.

The other friend, a 14-year-old girl, died of leukemia. As well, in the past year, Marilee's sister's boyfriend's best friend committed suicide by pulling his car into the family garage, attaching a hose to the exhaust system, and gassing himself. Marilee's explanation was:

Uhm, he was really screwed up mentally. Like not screwed up, screwed up, but he did a lot of drugs. And he didn't handle life. And people just thought of him as a party person, like, "Hey, there's party Chris." People never thought about Chris.

After telling me this story, Marilee noticed the time and abruptly ended our interview, because her boyfriend was coming over. I thanked her for allowing me to talk with her. As I sat on the steps by the door tying up my shoelaces, she said: "So, do you ever talk to girls about rape and molesting and that kind of thing?" I replied, "Well, sometimes they tell me about it when we're talking together; is there something you'd like to say to me about that?" She replied:

> Well, only that when I was three I was molested by a baby sitter who put his fingers inside me, but just that, and when I was 14 and on summer vacation and visiting some friends, a 20-year-old guy got me drunk and raped me, and my mother knows and my counselor knows, and I still wake up every morning angry about it and hurt by it and wondering whether I should charge him.

On that note, Marilee left me standing in her driveway, got into her boyfriend's truck, and drove away.

CHAPTER FIVE

Molly's Story

My older brother molested me, he abused me up to about a year and a half ago, and I have these feelings, these flashbacks, it's like I can feel it happening all over again. When it happened, my mother didn't really believe me at first, but then my older brother went to live with my grandparents for six months and we all went for counseling, even him. And we talked a lot about what happened to my [younger] brother ... when he was little, when he got really sick, and the whole family got disrupted. We talked about this stuff [sexual abuse] too, but I don't like to bring it up because I get this feeling like they think I'm lying and everything, and then especially when it did everything to the family, I just don't want to talk about it. It's taken me forever to feel comfortable around my parents. With your parents, they love you so much and in your brother's case, they love him so much and they don't want to believe that he could do that to their daughter. They just want to try and block it out of their minds, they think it will just go away. My parents didn't really believe me until about uh, two weeks after I told them, I tried committing suicide by slitting my wrists and I tried taking an overdose of pills and all that, and that's when they finally believed me, and that really hurt. (*Excerpt from taped interview with Molly*)

Molly volunteered to participate in this study because she had been beaten by a schoolmate, Cathy. This was not, however, her first encounter with violence. Molly was well known at school for her threatening and aggressive behavior; she often pushed and shoved other students to let them know who was in charge. The school counselor, who introduced me to four of the six key informants in this study, seemed most concerned about Molly.

Family dynamics

Both Molly and her mother assured me that theirs was a "loving and close family" in which people really care about one another. But what does "loving and close" mean?

For Molly, close became too close, especially where her older brother was concerned. "Loving" requires clarification. Does "loving" mean you swallow your own experience and keep your mouth shut because you don't want trouble? Does it mean that, when you go for counseling to deal with sexual abuse in your family, you allow your brother's experience to become more important than your own so that you can put it all behind you and he can come home?

Two events stand out for Molly with regard to her family: The first, a traumatic illness involving Molly's second youngest brother, happened 10 years ago. The second event is her long-standing sexual abuse at the hands of her older brother, which began when she was about eight (and he was 10) and continued for nearly four years. In Molly's family lore, the first event explains the second, and the second event, according to Molly, has been subsumed by the first.

I pieced together my understanding of Molly's family climate from both Molly's and her mother's remarks. Molly's family is one in which "everyone feels everyone else's feelings," that is, Mother gauges the state of the family through the state of her own feelings. Thus, "if they're fine, chances are Mom's okay; if they're in distress, Mom is."

Family is also the source of their closest friendships. Parents and kids are intensely involved in one another's lives. Father and sons engage in physical combat, but that's "only natural." People yell and scream when they're angry, but that "happens in every family." Women make demands by yelling, but men hold sway. The family closes ranks against outsiders. Doors are left open, including doors to bedrooms; and Molly (despite advice from counselors given directly to her mother) still does not have a lock on her bedroom door.

Molly's family's central organizing story — the one they tell when they wish to illustrate the kind of family theirs is — was told to me as follows: While Molly's mother was pregnant with her fourth child, the third child, a boy, had a life-threatening episode as the result of being given a food substance to which he was allergic by an unwitting family member. This required major medical intervention, including an airlift from the small community in which they lived. The event caused much upset and turmoil, but the family pulled together and supported one another through it all.

This story is still central to the family's saga, even 10 years after the fact. It is the story they tell to show how everyone helped out, how everyone can forgive, how important it is to consider the second youngest brother's special food needs, and how this family can make it through anything.

This event also became central to the family's counseling experience in the wake of Molly's sexual abuse by her older brother. Somehow, the focus shifted from Molly's abuse to the early life trauma caused by her younger brother's near death, and the family's constant need for vigilance on his behalf. Somehow, this became the reason why the older brother molested his sister. Somehow, this became the reason why no one noticed.

Molly's MOTHER

When Molly's mother told me the family story, she didn't even mention her oldest son's sexual abuse of her daughter, although she knew that I had been told about it. Even when I provided openings in our conversation, Molly's mother side-stepped this issue.

It may indeed be true that Molly's family is close and tries to support its members. But it is also true that much that happens is denied, concealed, or overlooked, and that conflict arises frequently.

Molly's mother's acknowledges that her oldest son has often been in trouble. And while he and Molly participate in sports and play on school teams and work at part-time jobs, they also fight and get kicked out of school. Molly's father dominates the family (using physical force with the boys, angry silence and bad moods with his wife and daughter), and Molly's mother, while vocal in her opinions, ultimately defers to her husband.

I believe that if I had relied only upon Molly's mother to give me insight into her family and Molly's participation in violence, I would have heard only that kids get involved in violence because, as she explained to me,

> everybody starts to buck for their rank. It starts in grade six, when well, we're 11 years old and we're starting to develop and we're starting to look to who we're gonna be and some kids (like Molly) do very well, she's on every committee, she does extremely well in sports activities, she was "Miss Popularity" and all that. And those that aren't at that stage can either turn around and shoot you down to make themselves look better or to pull you down to their level. And then it's like, "I hate her," and she doesn't know how to handle it ... and it all grows out of a kind of teenage rivalry ... .

Molly's EXPERIENCE of violENCE

Molly's own version of herself and her involvement with violence was quite different from the analysis offered by her mother. At the time of our conversations, Molly was meeting with me in the context of a group that also included two other key informants, Mary (Chapter Six) and Linda (Chapter Seven). In these discussions, Molly was always the least vocal participant, who sometimes needed a little assistance from me to be heard. There were, however, two topics to which

Molly returned time and time again: that of having been beaten, and that of having been sexually abused.

At our first group meeting, I invited Molly to speak before the others because at that time, her beating at the hands of Mary's friend Cathy was still fresh and I wanted to give her the opportunity to say whatever was on her mind. She declined to say much until well into the first hour of our conversation. At that point, encouraged by promises of confidentiality, Molly began to describe her experience of having been beaten while 30 or 40 students stood by and watched.

She began by outlining the history of her interactions with Cathy. Like Sally, Molly made the mistake of showing interest in a boy who was already considered someone else's boyfriend, in this case Cathy's. The competition with Cathy for male attention began in September, right at the beginning of Molly's grade eight year, and culminated in a vicious beating the following January:

> It was like right in September, right, in my TAG[1] group, there was this guy I was talking to and Cathy came over and talked to us too. So later I told Jessica that Cathy was a real bitch. So Jessica told Cathy at lunch that I'd said she was a bitch, so I like, kinda apologized, like a lot, but she kept mouthing me off and she kept pushing me in the hallway wanting to fight, but that time a whole bunch of people stopped her. But another time, we were by the side of the school and there was this big rumor going around that I said that two guys molested me at a party or whatever and all that, and she walks up to me and goes, "What happened?" and I said, "Nothing fucking happened," and she goes, "Bullcrap!" and then she punched me and goes, "Hit me back!" and I was going to hit her, but then I wanted to get her in crap with the principal so I didn't hit her back. I know it's not good to rat on people, but I was mad. And then, like last week, I was talking about some guy that Cathy likes, and so a couple of days ago when I was walking home from school by the store, Cathy saw me and wanted me to fight her in front of a whole bunch of people, and she wouldn't stop, and started hitting me and she kept hitting me until Mr. Robertson came along in his car and made her stop and brought me home.

When I asked how she made sense of this event, Molly attributed Cathy's behavior to Cathy's hatred of her and her desire to "get" her:

> It's like, I don't know, the first time, you know like I don't know where it came from, but I did call her a bitch, but then there were a lot of other things that people told me that I said, that I didn't and I apologized to her like crazy and everything, and then after that she said like, "Okay," and everything, but then I heard that she just didn't like me like no matter what and if she could think

of a reason she'd use it against me. And so after a lot of incidents like pushing and calling me names, she just, I think that was like her chance by the store, and she took it.

When I asked whether Molly herself would beat up a schoolmate just because she disliked her, Mary jumped in and stated that while she probably would not do that, she might like to. When I asked what would stop her, Mary explained:

> It's because I've got morals which I got from my mom, and there's certain rules, like, if they're older than me, if they're bigger than me, I would fight them, but if they're younger than me and smaller than me, there's no way that I would. I couldn't, I couldn't unless they were sitting there and just taunting me. If someone taunts me, then I get mad, and it's like it takes a lot to get me mad enough to fight. I don't like seeing it in myself, and I don't like being around it. And so when, if, and like if they taunt me and I get mad at them, there's no way in hell I'm gonna put up with it.

I turned again to Molly to ask for her perspective. She informed me that she had no real morals to speak of. Those she did have had come from her mother, and had mostly to do with sex because

> … my mom didn't really have any morals until, uhm, like my brother had this big accident, and then I think after that she started to have all kinds of morals that she didn't show before, that she didn't really talk about. After that, everything came out, and after that she's like always letting us know how she's feeling. Like now she says, she sits me down and she goes, "You think sex is a game," and stuff, and she gives me this big lecture … . But when it comes to fighting, like if I get really mad, like with Jenny [another key informant; Chapter Eight] last night, I just felt like belting her 'cause she just kept coming up to me and bugging me and then saying she was sorry that she'd challenged me to a fight and "I hope we can be friends" and then following me around, and I was going, "Take a hike, Jenny, I'm not going to hit you or anything, but if you keep following me around, I'm going to fuckin' belt you."

Molly's remarks led to further discussions about fighting and how girls became embroiled in physical battles with each other. Again, Mary leaped in with her explanation before Molly had a chance to speak:

> I don't know, I have this feeling, it's like instinct … . If someone does something wrong to you, there's a certain extent where you're gonna put up with it, and when that, when you stop putting up with it, that's when you get mad. And, and I usually give them another chance after I get mad, like if they make

me mad, okay, okay, I'll let it boil for awhile. And if they piss me off again, then they're just gonna have to deal with it ... .

When Mary finished her explanation, both Molly and Linda agreed that they fought physically with others whenever someone "made them mad." Thus, Molly wanted to "fuckin' belt" Jenny because Jenny was making her mad by following her around. Both Mary and Linda recalled several instances when they felt perfectly justified in hauling off and smashing someone because they were angry. Again, Mary supplied the words for all three:

> I hate being angry, 'cause it gets me in a bad mood. So I get rid of that anger and I take it out on something or someone, it gets rid of it.

That seemed clear enough to me, even though I could not agree with the sentiments expressed. What I still had trouble understanding was why those who were not angry and had no personal involvement in the fight would stand by and watch while someone else were being beaten. Here, Mary was again the quickest to supply the answer:

> Well, if there's a fight, everybody in the school just basically goes to watch it because it's different, entertainment sort of, a lot of people want to see somebody get their butt kicked in real life. It's kind of like TV, but only it's real life, and that's entertainment kind of, except if you're the one being beaten up.

When I still had trouble understanding how people could watch without intervening when someone was clearly being as badly hurt as Molly had been, Molly went on to tell me that,

> ... the crowd was yelling to Cathy, "C'mon, hit her!" It wasn't the girls, it was the guys who did it, 'cause they want to see girls fight. It gets them pumped. It gets them excited, not in the physical, in the sexual ... . Like this guy I was walking with when Cathy saw me said to me, "That's the chick who wants to beat you up," and then he waved at her and she started saying all these things to me and he just took off, and I felt like shit, but I'm fine now ... .

GROWING UP FEMALE
Molly's reference to girls fighting as entertainment for boys that "got them excited, not in the physical, [but] in the sexual" sense of the word prompted me to ask what it was like to be a girl in this day and age. This time, Molly was the first to speak, and what she said was unquestioningly echoed by Linda and Mary. As Molly put it:

The guys here degrade you, they try to do that all the time. Like at the beginning of the year, there was like quite a bit of us that in my class, wore body suits and stuff and the guys would sit there staring at you, and you'd go, "What are you lookin' at?" and then they'd start saying all these things to you, stuff that made you feel really low. It was sort of sleazy, they'd say things like, "Oh, close your legs," like and "You smell like a fish," or whatever, and "Watch it, flies are comin' in," and "Flies are attacking," and "You smell like tuna."

When I asked how the girls made sense of the boys' behavior, they told me, "Oh, [the boys] think [such talk] is cool," and "It's their hormones and stuff."

Molly then spoke of feeling a great deal of pressure from boys, and also from certain girlfriends, to engage in sex:

I've noticed that there is pressure, like I've had people try to pressure me. Like more the pressure is from your boyfriend, or it's like from friends who are like, "Have you got laid yet?" And this is from the friends of the boyfriend, or it could be your friends. It's like with your friends, they sort of like when they're, when you're talking about it and you get into a conversation, they sort of get the hint that you have been or you haven't been by how you talk about it, but the guys, they're just like, "Oh, you're still a virgin," and they block their eyes and stuff. But if the guys do it, they're like big studs and stuff, and we're sluts. Like if they do it, they can be doin' it like many times and they think people consider them studs, and when we do it, we're sluts. Like, they dump you if you don't have sex with them, but when you break up with them and they've taken your virginity or whatever, he, he, he calls you a slut .... Guys, I think guys perceive us to be playing hard to get, and they perceive themselves as trying hard to get it constantly, and if we're just, if you're not playing hard to get then they think you're a slut.

I then asked whether the girls saw this as a double standard — one rule for the boys and one rule for the girls. They seemed confused by this question and required further explanation. After I gave it, to my great astonishment they told me that they didn't think it was a double standard; rather, "that's the way guys are."

It seemed to me that these girls had accepted the notion that they were sexual objects, an impression that was confirmed by the women they identified as female role models. Like Sally, they all chose Madonna as their number one favorite, followed by Marilyn Monroe and Cindy Crawford. They saw these women as role models because they had the power to "do whatever they want," that is, to direct their own lives.

While the girls admired this independence, they failed to see that any power these women had was directly related to their desirability as sexual objects. Thus, their power is male-dependent and male-controlled. But all the girls saw was that these women were wanted and worshiped because they were sexually desirable. Given that they had bought into the misconception that women's power is derived mainly from their sexual currency, the girls saw no way out, and endured harassment and abuse because "that's just the way it is."

Sexual harassment and abuse

At the end of one of our meetings, I had an opportunity to witness sexual harassment in action. This incident took place as Molly, Linda, and I were getting into my car so that I could drive them home. A group of boys were lined up at the top of some steps near the school entrance, apparently the better to ogle the girls as they went by. One boy called out, "Hey Melissa, nice bazongas [breasts]! You're doing a great job, keep growing them just like that." When I asked him to account for himself, he replied that he was "just a bad boy, I guess," and laughed while a chorus of admiring louts applauded.

Both Molly's and Linda's perception of this incident was that "that's just how it is; you put up with it because if you don't, it just gets worse." They told me that they didn't like such encounters and "really hated macho guys," but that "you gotta expect guys to be pigheaded; it's the way they are."

Our discussions about the difficulties of being young women in the late 20th century were not confined to talking about sexual harassment. Molly (and, it turned out, Linda) had both experienced sexual abuse before reaching puberty; Mary had experienced date rape. Molly had alluded to her sexual abuse in our first meeting when she referred to her mother's sense of "morals" vis-à-vis her older brother's "big accident." This "accident" later turned out to be his sexual abuse of her.

The girls' stories emerged in the context of a single discussion of sexual harassment generally, and what it means to be a young woman in the 1990s. The conversation ended with three disclosures of sexual abuse.

As suggested at the beginning of this chapter, Molly's parents had some difficulty accepting that Molly's brother had abused her; it took her suicide attempt for them to believe her. The fact of Molly's abuse came to be subsumed by the previous family trauma involving the youngest child's brush with death. This event focused both parents' attention on the younger boy, perhaps at the expense of their oldest son, who later acted out his need for attention by molesting his sister (or so the story goes).

That story had yet another dimension, one that was not immediately clear to me: namely, that Molly's mother also explained her son's abuse of his sister as an "accident." Further, this "accident" was caused not only by the boy's need for attention, but also (at least in part) by Molly's interest in sex as a game. As Molly explained:

> It all happened like that last year, like I was driving with her in the car and I told her about like what happened, and she was like, "Oh yeah," and she gave me a lecture on it and she said, "Well, did your brother do any of that to you?" and I felt so low, I felt so crummy. She was going back to work early. It was like the first time I told her what my brother did to me, and she gave me a lecture. She goes, "Did he have sex with you then?" It was really stupid. It was like she ended up giving me a lecture on sex for me to know what it is, and she said, "You think sex is a game." ... Like, I hate it when we're driving in the car and I mention something to my mom, and she goes, "Well, I don't need to give you this lecture, because you got it after everything your brother did to you," and then she starts giving me the lecture all over again. ... Then after that, after my brother's big accident [i.e. his sexual abuse of Molly], she had all these morals, these morals that she never had before, all to do with sex.

Disclosing her sexual abuse to her parents did not bring Molly much comfort, nor did engaging in a brief period of family counseling. Molly had found this experience embarrassing and wanted all discussion with family to end as quickly as possible. At the time of her disclosure to me, she was still a long way from resolving these issues, and apparently in need of more help. When I offered to facilitate this by finding her a counselor through a local agency, she rejected the idea. She knew that because of her age, her parents would have to be informed that she was receiving help, and she was unwilling to participate in anything that would put the subject of her sexual abuse back on the table. She said she did not wish to hurt her family.

But Molly had more to say on the subject of sex. Her experiences of sexual abuse did not end with being molested by her brother. About two months before our first meeting, she had been to a party where she and most of the other adolescents who attended got drunk.[2] At the time, Molly was taking medication to ease the pain of an injury sustained in gym class. In the course of the evening, she mixed pain killers with alcohol:

... I took 10 extra strength Tylenols and I just chugged back a bottle of rum and Coke and had a reaction, like I was really out of it, and I was like all over these guys. Like, people said I was acting like the biggest slut, but I didn't know what was going on. I was like really out of it, and I fell asleep in this chair, and everybody said that all these people were doing all this stuff to me, like these two guys were sitting at the party doing stuff to me ... .

This incident would fuel Cathy's justification, some weeks later, for challenging Molly to a fight. In Cathy's mind, Molly was a slut who deserved a beating.

School, sex, and violence

For Molly, Linda, and Mary, sex and female sexuality is fraught with difficulties. It has involved sexual harassment, sexual abuse, and date rape, as well as violence at the hands of other females just like themselves.

But the difficulties did not end there. They arose again in their sex education class, when the girls were presented with material on childbirth that frightened and disgusted them. What follows is a composite of all three girls' perceptions of sex education and childbirth:

We got this video all day yesterday, and one of the guys in the class passed out. It was so gross. I've never seen it in my life and I was just horrified. I'm never gonna have kids, it scared me big. It looked so painful. And the interviewer is sitting there and [the woman he was talking to] she goes, "I was pregnant," like she was talking about how the doctor put his things in to make the hole bigger and all this, and it hurt, but she didn't care, 'cause it would be for her own good and all this, 'cause he got some kind of gel and all this, but I would never do that. I think it's gross and scary, and it looks like it would hurt ... .

The lady giving birth just looked a mess, and I don't, I wouldn't want, like if I was a man, I don't know if I'd wanna be attracted to her anymore ... .

The labor that we watched, it lasted for something like 10 hours, and the lady would like, she'd go and have a shower and she was, while she was giving birth. And the girls in the class are just sittin' there going "ahh," and, and then as soon as she gave birth, and after, all that stuff came out after the baby, just as the bell rang and we just got up and "Uhm, gotta go." ... And I wouldn't want to do it, I wouldn't want to have a baby.

At the end of this lesson, the students had been left hanging. There had been no discussion, no time for debriefing, no time to deal with their feelings of fear and disgust.

In the end, for these young women, sex is for the most part a fright-ening, painful, and embarrassing fact of life, something that happens almost inevitably; it is certainly not viewed as a possible source of joy or pleasure. Mostly, sex is associated with confusion and a sense of alienation and humiliation.

Talking about sex education led to a discussion of the girls' experi-ences of being educated, of going to school and working with teachers.

Molly's experience of school mostly involved living down her older brother's reputation as a trouble-maker and struggling with the feeling that she was being "stereotyped," that is, categorized as being just like him. Of the eight teachers she had encountered in her first year in junior high, she picked only two that she liked and respected. She found she could like and respect a teacher, and work hard in class, if the teacher was

> laid back and understanding, and I can have some kind of relationship with them. Like most teachers don't remember what it's like to be a kid or what-ever. I don't think we're supposed to be angels, but they want us to be angels. … If I like a teacher, I work harder in his class, and I get better marks if I like the teacher … .

When I inquired about marks, Molly described herself as a "C+, B student, but I'm not working to the max. If I wanted to I could get A's, but that would take work." For Molly, school wasn't so much about going to classes; rather, it was about navigating her complex social world. This included networking among friends and acquaintances, gossiping, defending her reputation, and finally, engaging in violence.

At the time of our meetings, Molly was spending much time out of class talking with the school counselor. She was also spending a great deal of time in class (and during her breaks) discussing other people and busying herself with the details of her own and others' private lives. At one point, all her teachers met in order to develop a strategy for dealing with Molly. It was decided that she would no longer be given permission to leave classes to go for counseling.

Molly's mother was consulted and she agreed with this approach. She believed that stopping counseling would somehow normalize Molly's behavior and help her get back on track. Molly's school coun-selor thought otherwise, but her opinion was overruled. In the coun-selor's estimation, much of Molly's behavior stemmed from unresolved issues relating to her sexual abuse, and to the aftermath of having been beaten. Without extensive therapy, the counselor believed, Molly would continue to experience difficulties, both at school and at home. Events proved her to be correct.

Molly returned to school a few days after being beaten by Cathy, and spent several weeks being treated as something of a sensation. She also became a target for attention from Jenny (Chapter Eight), who wanted to challenge Molly to a fight. Jenny thought it would enhance her own reputation if she were able to beat up a celebrity like Molly.

Molly didn't engage in fighting Jenny, but she did let it be known that if Jenny didn't leave her alone, she would beat her up with help from Mary and Linda. Jenny backed down, apologized, and then dogged Molly for days, trying to make friends. This infuriated Molly, who threatened to "belt" her.

Not only was Molly annoyed and frustrated at being dogged by Jenny; further, Jenny's behavior and Molly's lack of retaliation would eventually call Molly's social position into question, because Jenny was "hacking her down." The social rules that operate among these girls demanded that Molly stick up for herself. As they explained to me:

> If someone is hacking you down, they're making you look like an idiot, 'cause like, people look at you and mock you and they're thinking, "Oh, that person must be an idiot now." If you let somebody hack you down, and you don't do something about it and other people are watching you, they're going to think you're a goof, so you have to do it. You have to do it because you get angry and because you have to teach them a lesson.

Molly's problem with Jenny was solved for a time because Mary and Linda came to her aid. All three girls issued threats against Jenny. This brought action from Jenny's parents, who came to the school Christmas dance with the express purpose of keeping an eye on Linda, Mary, and Molly. At one point during the evening, Jenny's mother actually walked by Linda and gave her a push. This drew the girls' wrath, although they refrained from retaliating. What irked them most was their sense that Jenny's mother wasn't behaving as she should:

> Jenny's mother was being an immature little bitch. When you're an adult, you're supposed to be an adult, you're not supposed to be pushing around teenagers, I mean it's over and done with. You shouldn't be doing that. She was setting a bad example for her daughter ... .

After the Christmas dance episode, Mary and Linda rallied around Molly for some time. Mary, who had witnessed Cathy's beating of Molly, even offered to testify for the crown at Cathy's upcoming trial. And then Molly blew it all.

One day during a lull in one of her classes, Molly took it upon herself to tell four friends the details of Linda's sexual abuse, details that Linda had disclosed in our group meetings under strictest confidentiality. This information was passed along from person to person until Linda came to hear of it.

Molly was once again in danger of being beaten up, this time by Linda and Mary. But Linda and Mary thought better of it. Because of our discussions, they had begun to question violence as a means to an end. And although they felt justified about wanting to beat up Molly, they had also begun to entertain the notion that there were other ways to deal with problems.

This was a new and difficult way of thinking for these girls. Instead of ambushing Molly, they made an appointment with the school counselor, who arranged a meeting among the three. It was Mary and Linda's intention to confront Molly and give her an opportunity to account for herself. They also invited me to come to speak with them about what had happened.

Molly came to the meeting, but avoided even the smallest step towards taking responsibility for her actions. She excused herself by saying that she just couldn't hold in the things she knew about Linda anymore; the stress was such that she just had to tell someone. She had trouble apologizing to Linda, and sought instead to blame her actions on the situation.

Later, Molly lied to her mother and said that she had been scapegoated by the other two girls. She told her brother that she was being threatened, and he escorted her to and from school for several weeks. Her brother complained that he was receiving death threats by telephone, and Molly told her parents and her friends that these were coming from Mary. (The threats were real enough; they came not from Mary, however, but from an acquaintance of hers who took it upon himself to threaten Molly's brother.)

Fortunately, the school counselor intervened and gave Molly's mother the facts. Molly's mother had trouble acknowledging what her daughter had done, and instead put her behavior down to "school girl hysteria." She characterized Molly's indiscretion as an "accident" — a slip of the tongue.

Linda and Mary were shocked, hurt, and angered by Molly's behavior, but by this time they were committed to trying a non-violent approach. They met with the school counselor three more times, and I joined them once more.

We discussed the girls' feelings and continued to meet until Linda felt she had resolved the incident in a way that she could live with. They decided to exclude Molly from all their activities, school and social. They expressed the wish to continue meeting with me as a twosome. Further, they demanded an apology from Molly and a contract that she would stay away from them in the hallways and on the school grounds.

Molly complied with Mary and Linda's requests. She withdrew from contact with me, even though I offered to meet with her on her own. She made plans to change school districts in the coming year, and she stayed away from the counseling area for some time.

I saw Molly once more. She was getting into a car with her basketball teammates. She made eye contact with me but said nothing, and that's the last I saw of her.

Notes

1. TAG refers to Teacher Advisor Group, a mixed-grade group that students enter in their first year of junior high and in which they continue until graduation. The rationale is to offer students a chance to see, on a daily basis, at least one teacher in the capacity of advisor rather than classroom teacher. This personal relationship is intended to provide support and guidance. The idea behind having mixed grades in the same group is to broaden the students' social contacts. This is the ideal; the reality is not always so genial.
2. Molly started drinking alcohol in grade seven, at the age of 13. She began smoking cigarettes in grade eight. At the time of our meetings, she was also beginning to experiment with marijuana. All these substances were freely available to her through older friends. Molly's understanding of alcohol use is limited. When she drinks, she tends to drink large quantities. She said that the weekend before one of our meetings, she had drunk "a bottle of rum with Coke, but I've never drank it straight, and I can't drink whiskey unless it's mixed."

CHAPTER SIX

MARY'S STORY

Yeah, well, my dad's punched me a couple of times, and we've gotten into fist fights actually quite a few times. Usually that happens when there are other people around like my mom, but one time it happened when my mother wasn't around, then my brother jumped in and pulled him off me and started beating him up. And one time that I remember, this happened when I was about eight or nine years old, and this is just horrifying to me, but I want to talk about it. I remember my brother was locked in his room [as punishment for a misdemeanor] and my dad punched a hole through the door and then went into my brother's room and got on top of him and started hitting him and my mom grabbed a mirror, about the size of that calendar there [approximately 12" by 16"], and she grabbed it and had to smash it over my dad's head to make him stop. And I was just sitting in the kitchen just hollerin'. I didn't know what was going on. I was about ready to call the police. I was scared and I still get scared. (*Excerpt from taped interview with Mary*)

Family dynamics

Mary's family is characterized by violent behavior on all fronts. All family members engage in violence inside and outside the home. Mary's older brother often fights with other boys, and with Mary as well. Mary's father, a streetfighter since his youth, has lately begun to push around those young people whom he considers threatening to his children. Mary's mother admits to punching a postal worker in the nose during a recent postal strike.

Just before I began this study, Mary's father had an affair with Mary's mother's best friend while she was renting a room in their house. When Mary's mother discovered them in bed together, she was deeply upset, yet permitted her friend to remain. Tension in the household mounted until Mary's parents joined forces against the friend. They pushed her around, threatened her with violence, ordered her out of the house, and finally threw all her belongings from an upstairs window while Mary and her brother watched. Mary has been unable to forgive her father for his behavior, and cannot understand her mother's continued acceptance of him.

Mary's father is central to the in-home violence. When he fights physically with one of his children, either his wife or the other sibling may intervene to the point of counter-attacking him. Violent altercations take place in this family roughly once every three or four weeks.

At other times, everyone "tiptoes around in order not to upset Dad," but some minor irritation eventually escalates into physical combat between father and children. Mother then "reams Dad out" once again and "makes him smarten up," and the cycle begins anew. Father never hits Mother.

In spite of this climate of conflict, Mary's family expressed strong feelings of mutual affection and closeness. In particular, Mary spoke of loving her mother and loving yet hating her father; she also described her brother as her "best friend," one of the few people she felt she could rely on.

Mary's mother

Similarly, Mary's mother referred to her husband as her "best friend," and expressed her love for him very clearly. In our interviews, Mary's mother showed her feelings easily: She cried when things upset or moved her and showed a range of emotions from anger to joy, which she made no effort to conceal. As she described herself:

> I get emotional very easily; I'll cry in cartoons if they're sad ... And I'm stubborn; ... I won't back down, and I stand up for myself and demand the respect I deserve.

When I asked about standing up for herself, Mary's mother said she has to do this every day, especially with her husband, who strongly believes in traditional gender roles. That is, he demands that his wife take on all the domestic chores and cater to his feelings. If his wife is not available, he expects his daughter to jump into the breach.

While I talked with Mary's mother, her husband "hovered." Although we held our interview in the dining room of their home, well removed from the kitchen where Mary's father was working, Mary's father seemed to find it necessary to pass by the dining room frequently and look through the closed French doors. He also went up and down the stairs by the dining room a number of times. Once, he came bursting through the doors with a portable telephone in hand, insisting that the only plug that would work for the phone was in the dining room. At another point, he saw his wife crying, so he came into the room to comfort her and to question me. In reassuring his wife, he hugged her and brought her Kleenex, and told me with much feeling that he needed to know she was okay. As I observed these interactions, I was reminded of the kinds of behaviors that young children exhibit when their mother is talking with another adult or is engaged in an activity that takes her focus off the children.

When I asked Mary's mother what factors she thought might contribute to girls' violence, she suggested it was because "girls have always been repressed": Perhaps they were "ripping each other's faces off" because they were "frustrated that things are not equal." Other than that, she had "no idea where they get their ideas" and had no further insights into girls and violence.

Mary's Father

During my discussions with Mary and her mother, I learned that Mary's father left home when he was 15 years old because of continuing conflicts with his own father. (Mary's paternal grandfather is a life-long alcoholic who is not "allowed" to drink in his son's house, and chooses to make his visits to his son in a mobile home so that he can drink.)

After he left home, Mary's father lived on the street, taking shelter under a bridge. He worked as a janitor and then in the building trades, and saved enough money to buy a house by the time he was 19 years old. Mary's parents met when her father was 17 and her mother 15. They married four years later, and soon after had two children two years apart. According to Mary's mother, her husband has made it a daily crusade to be the center of her attention. She describes him as having

> a very controlling personality … . [Almost every day] I have to keep telling him he can't have complete control of everything … .

Mary describes her father as a "power-tripper" and an "asshole … who's got to have everything his way." Her feelings about him are strongly mixed:

> I love him for being my dad and I love him for all the things he has done for me, but I hate him for the things he's done to me and the family.

Mixed emotions were often apparent when Mary talked about her father. She recounted the good times she'd had with him, such as going skiing with him and her brother. At other times she was full of rage and hurt, such as when he declined her offer of help with his construction projects, or criticized her work, or refused to help her with chores, expecting instead that she serve him.

Mary discussed her continuing gender-related battles with her father with the same frustration, sadness, anger, and determination that I heard her mother express. Mary described it as follows:

> I think he should do more around the house. ... Half the stuff around this house is from him. I mean all this shit right here, all those papers there are his. ... Normally he's got a mess all over this table, like old statements and estimates and stuff. The computer room upstairs is a mess because he's just a slob and he walks into the house with his big work boots on and tracks dirt everywhere and it pisses me off ... and when I say, "Take your damn boots off your feet for the last time!" he goes, "I'm doing business, so get out of here."

On one occasion, I overheard a heated exchange between father and daughter that I found instructive. While I was visiting with Mary at her home, her father phoned. His truck had broken down, he was unable to pick up his wife and son from work, and he wanted Mary to find them and tell them what had happened. He also wanted Mary to tell her brother to find a ride home, then get in the family's second car which was parked in the driveway, and drive to where his father was in order to bring him home.

Mary lost her temper. She was angry with her father for being at a pub and calling from there to ask her to take care of his business. She told him to leave the pub, take a bus home, take the second car, and pick up the rest of the family himself. In fact, Mary's father appeared to have no idea how to find the bus. He preferred spending $20 to take a taxi if no one could pick him up. Mary got out a bus schedule and very carefully, albeit loudly and angrily, gave him detailed instructions for getting the bus home. When Mary's father simply refused to take a bus, she swore at him and told him how irresponsible he was.

I was struck by the role reversal that I was witnessing. To me, Mary sounded like an angry, out-of-control parent, while her father sounded like a lost and difficult child who did not want to take responsibility for his own actions. The language that flew back and forth was also instructive. Words like "fuck," "bitch," and "asshole" were used freely and frequently. After the exchange, Mary was visibly agitated, and talked at length about her father.

The family situation had not always been so volatile and difficult, she said, but much had changed in recent years. From the time she was "a little kid" until she turned 12 four years ago, her relationship with her father had been relatively happy. That year, however, her father had a number of anxiety attacks, which he attributed to stress over his children (particularly his son, who had begun stealing) and his work. He eventually took time off work and began taking Prozac (an antidepressant). The family saw a counselor, but Mary and her brother refused to cooperate, largely because they were angry with their father for blaming them for his emotional state. In any case, the approaches learned in counseling (such as family meetings) seemed to work best when the counselor was present, and less well when the family was on its own. Left to themselves, Mary's family returned to their old patterns of attack, blame, and defensiveness. Mary gave the following example of her father's behavior:

> Well, every time he got sick or something went wrong with him it was me and my brother's fault. … If he gets stressed out about something, it's usually because me and my brother were fighting, or we were fighting with him, or he was frustrated at us because we were being stupid or something like that. Like he'd pulled a muscle. He tore a muscle and he was having muscle spasms underneath his ribs when he was hooking up a trailer to our car so we could go motorbike riding, me and my dad and my brother. Because we used to motorbike all the time. And any way, he was hooking up the trailer for us to do that and [he pulled a muscle and had a muscle spasm] and he was on his back for about two weeks and he blamed it on us because he said we weren't helping enough.

When Mary's father blames Mary and her brother for his difficulties, Mary worries that her father may be right, that she or her brother may indeed be at fault. When I asked what she tells herself after her father has blamed her for something, she answered:

> I don't know … me and my brother both see it like it was something that we did wrong … Because he's fine with my mom. They get along great. She's the only reason why he hasn't left. All the times he's threatened to leave was because of me and my brother.

For Mary, the change in her father and in their relationship is "like he died or something, because it's not him anymore." And when she is not angry with him for being "such a jerk," she is deeply saddened by the absence of the father she once knew, whom she describes as someone who "would never do anything to hurt anybody … . He'd do anything he could to make us happy, and now he does anything possible to make us sad."

Mary's home has become a battleground. The battles are not constant; they are interspersed with good times. But she has learned to expect them — inside and outside the home.

School

For Mary, school was always problematic. Bullied as a child because of her weight and stereotyped (like Molly) as a "tough kid" because of her older brother, Mary soon found school to be a battleground not unlike home.

As with everything, Mary has strong opinions about school and her teachers. She believes that the teachers who "stereotype" her do so because of a particular vice-principal who

> will pick me and my friends out of a crowd and blame everything on us ... just for something to do, because we're his pet peeve. ... When I told him I didn't like being stereotyped, he told me if I didn't like it, then stop hanging around with my friends. Like we hang around at the corner, and he and the counselor told me I was with the wrong crowd. Not all the corner people are bad, like a lot of them have a good head on their shoulders ... . We like to hang out at the corner and I don't think we're different from anybody else, except for the fact we smoke. And some of the people out there do drugs and drink on weekends, but then again, I, the people in the school do drugs too. I mean you don't have to smoke to do drugs ... .

Being singled out and judged in this way made Mary angry and convinced her that the vice-principal was unfair in his approach to her and others like her. This was confirmed on two more occasions, which she described at length and with great feeling:

> I remember one time I was just totally mad at someone. ... These guys at the corner were kicking around a squirrel, and I went to the [vice-principal's] office and I was totally choked, like I was just furious. I wanted to beat the crap out of the guys for doing this and I poured my pop over these guys' heads and I told the vice-principal what happened and he said, "Well, you're at fault, you insulted those guys by pouring pop over their heads." And I'm going, "Oh my god, what an asshole!" I just wanted to totally deck him. I was sitting there going like this (*demonstrates*): my fists were clenched, I was so mad. ... I told my mom about it, and she gave me permission to give him the third degree on the last day of school, right after my last exam.

> I remember last year, I was so mad. Like because I had Mr. Jackson, it was the second year in a row, and he didn't like me because of my brother ... and I just

couldn't stand him. And it was getting to the end of the year and he just, we, he tried so hard with me but there's no, like, he treated us like children and I hated him. I'd do my work and I was getting good grades like B's and stuff and, Mr. Jackson, one day, we were, we were doin' our work and I was, Roberta was helping me because I was absent the day before. I finished all my work from the day before plus the work of that day. And he said that I was talking to Roberta and, uhm, he's like, and he goes, he's just checkin' everybody's work so to see if they can be dismissed, and I go, "I've done all my work," and he, he glanced at it and he looked away and he goes, "No you haven't, it's not all there," and I hadn't been able to flip over the page and I'd try, like, for about a half an hour I tried to tell him that I've done my work but it's all finished because I was finished five minutes before the end of class, and I was talking to Roberta because we were finished. And he was just like, and he, he said, "You have a detention," and I go, "Whatever!" and I just, I didn't want, I didn't want to swear and I didn't want to get totally choked so I sat there and he said, "You haven't done any work," and I go, "You haven't checked, I've done all my work," and he wouldn't check again. And he refused to. And so I said, "This is bull!" and I walked out of the classroom, and he's going, "Mary, get back here!" and I go, "Whatever!" and I kept walking. And then I went out for lunch and then next class was like, that was a Friday and the next class was on the next Tuesday, and I went into class and he's like he, he goes, "Hey, Mary, can you, can you come here for a sec?" and he called me up to his desk, and everybody's watching eh, and he goes, he has a big sheet and it's a behavior sheet, and it says "Mary talks constantly, Mary never, uhm, brings her books to class," which I always did, I, I tried hard. Well, I did talk, but only when I knew I could finish my work. And, "Mary, Mary, Mary obstructs the class," and all these different things and he'd circled the ones that I did, and I looked at him and I go, "You're full of shit!" and I slammed the paper down on his desk and he goes, "Get to the office!" and I go, and I go, "You're a waste of my time," and I kept on walking and I, I went, and I fff … . And then I walked. And I walked down to the office and then the vice-principal called me into the office and he goes, uhm, "What did you say to Mr., Mr. Johnson?" And I go, I told him, "You're full of shit," and he said, "Okay, pack your books up, you're out of here for four days." He didn't ask me why I said it, he didn't give me any chance to explain myself, and I was just, "This is bullshit." And my dad went in with me the, the next day, my dad is uhm, he's a businessman, so he knows how to conduct meetings, he, the vice-principal sat down, Mr. Johnson sat down, I sat down and my dad stood there and took a stand with his arms crossed. He wouldn't sit down, and the vice-principal says, "Would you like to have a seat?" and he said, "No," 'cause my dad likes to look down on people, especially the vice-principal, 'cause he doesn't like him. Uhm, and, he's, he's like, my dad's standing there going, "Well, you, you have no right to, uhm, to, like, limit my daughter's education just for an outburst in class which is caused by the teacher," and the vice-principal said, "No. She said the words. It came out of her lips. She has no excuse." And that was it. I mean, I, we tried. And he was gonna give me, something like, he didn't tell me that I was suspended when he said, "Go home," and he's just, he was a total, utter asshole over the whole deal. ... If you ask me, he's the most disgusting, disliked guy. He disrespects most every student in the school and he, he uhm, stereotypes the people who I want to hang out with.

Ultimately, what matters most to Mary, where teachers and school vice-principals are concerned, is respect. Mary defines respect as being listened to, being treated fairly, not being lied to, being treated with consideration, and being liked by the teacher. Whenever she did not encounter respect from teachers, she disliked them and engaged in battles with them that went on for years at a time. When I asked what it meant not to have respect, she responded:

> It's when they look down on us. Like, uhm, as a teacher sitting there and they're like, "I'm Mr. or Mrs. Whatever, and you are my student and you're a thing and you are supposed to learn." ... Like, school is for learning, but you can't learn from that. You can't learn if you're frustrated, you can't learn if you're upset. And when the teacher gets you upset, it's just like, "Go to hell!" ... When the teacher gets me upset I feel like hell inside and I can't learn. It's like Mr. Gray, He said something to me, we were just starting a test, and it was the first test of the year, right, and I asked him, "Well, does spelling count?" And he said, "Of course, are you stupid?" and he started putting me down, and I looked up and just gave him the dirtiest look, I go, "You are the biggest goof I've ever met in my entire life," and I went down and I wrote the test out, right, and I did, I failed the test 'cause I was so mad. I ended up breaking my pencil. And I wrote on the top before, like, just before I'd start yelling at him. I wrote on the top of my test, "You respect me and I'll respect you. Until then, I won't."

For Mary, being respected and liked by her teachers is vitally important. For one thing, this gives her incentive to work harder, even if she has difficulty with the subject matter. Mary described herself as an average student with marks ranging from C to C+, who occasionally gets D's in those classes which are taught by teachers whom she describes as "iffy." Despite her sometimes belligerent stance, Mary believes that teachers deserve respect, provided they show respect for their students:

> I don't know, I think you have to respect teachers, you know, if you get in their classes. I know that there's some I don't like, so I kinda act up or whatever, but I also got teachers I respect, so I'm good in their classes.

For Mary — as for Molly (Chapter Five) and Linda (Chapter Seven) — the lines are clearly drawn: If students don't like a teacher, he or she becomes fair game for acting-out, which includes a range of behaviors from talking in class to hurling insults, books, or other objects:

> One time I got kicked out of class for doing something I wasn't supposed to be doing, and he goes, "Get out," and I'm like, "You're wearing a hearing aid buddy, so you can't hear me whispering, right?" And he's like, "Just get out." And I'm like, "I wasn't talking," and he's like, "I heard you," and I go, "You, you have to wear a hearing aid, so how can you possibly have heard me?" And then he kicked me out and the next day the exact same thing happened. It was like a replay, so I just picked up my books and threw them at him (*laughs*) and I said, "Screw you!" and I walked out. Then the vice-principal had to teach me math for the rest of the term ... . So when I get treated like that, I get mad, and when I get mad, I get the person back.

For Mary, being angry is sufficient justification for any kind of acting-out or violent behavior. At the time of our meetings, she firmly believed that she owed it to herself to discharge her anger at anyone who provoked her — in effect, that she must punish people for making her angry because if she didn't, she did harm to herself. Thus, lashing out both verbally and physically was acceptable to Mary:

> It lets you get in the last word, and it also gets your anger out at the same time, like you sort of go, "Ahh ... It's over with."

POWER IMBALANCES AND VIOLENCE

Conditions that demanded a violent response from Mary generally involved some kind of power imbalance: an older, bigger person picking on a younger, smaller person; a teacher picking on a student; a parent picking on a child; anyone hurting an animal. Mary hates such "power-tripping." For her, the ultimate power-tripper is her school vice-principal, closely followed by her father:

> [The school vice-principal] is real power-tripper, and I hate power-trippers... . But you know, if there's somebody you really hate and they're in higher authority than you, you can't really say anything, and I can't do that, so the hatred just built and built ... .

When she sees her father power-tripping, she usually takes him on — as, indeed, she does with anyone whom she believes is abusing their power over others. With fellow students, she also wades in:

My friend Cathy was going to beat up Sylvia Rivers, and I stepped in front of her and said, "Don't you touch her, she's my friend." And she goes, "Well, she called me a bitch," and I go, "I don't care if she called you a bitch, she's a hell of a lot smaller than you, and you're not touching her because if you do, I'll kick you back." And she's like, "Fine!" and she walked away. And then she tried to — as soon as I came out of the school and was walking over there and everybody's going, "There's a fight, there's a fight," and I said, "Who's fighting?" and they said, Cathy and Sylvia Rivers." And I'm like, "What the hell?!" So I run over there and jumped right in front of Cathy and I'm going, "What the hell is going on here?" And Cathy started telling me, "She's being a total bitch to me," and I just like stopped her. She would have had to fight me, so she didn't … .

Mary's intervention on Sylvia's behalf was also a move to help Cathy. At the time of our meetings, Mary was deeply concerned about Cathy, whom she saw as needing not just help with self-control, but help with the conditions of her life. Cathy lives with her mother, well known in the community as a "biker's moll." She is a heavy drinker and former drug addict who causes Cathy great concern. Cathy's stepfather, who lives in another city, is "not allowed" in Cathy's mother's house because he "treated Cathy like shit." Cathy's mother "threw him out" for beating up Cathy. He also beat up Cathy's mother.

According to Mary, "you have to tiptoe around this man much like you have to around my father, only he's much worse, he gets mad easier." Mary's reaction to Cathy's situation is to try to act as a counselor to her. She gives Cathy advice, and on many more occasions than the one described above, has tried to prevent Cathy from engaging in fights.

Mary also plays this role with other students, and is frequently called upon to act as a mediator. She even encouraged Molly to press charges against Cathy because Cathy "needs to be taught a lesson." Mary can always be drawn into a fight if she sees her engagement as one that upholds her stand against an imbalance of power.

Mary's well-publicized fight with a schoolmate, Andrea, also involved her in a power imbalance, in that Andrea was older and bigger than Mary. Mary thus felt perfectly justified in beating Andrea up:

I didn't start it. She's like 17, 18 and she's like six foot one and 200 pounds. All's I did was call a girl a bitch, and she got her older friends, 17-, 18-, 19-year-olds to come after me, and Andrea was one of them. She cursed at me, and I just laughed in her face. And she did it again the next night, and I laughed in her face again, and her friends wanted me to fight her, but I wouldn't because she was on drugs, and I don't fight people on drugs, 'cause … it doesn't hurt them as much and they can't feel things, so they don't know when they're hurt. But they kept spreading rumors about me, saying I was going to fight them all, so they showed up one night to fight me and they started swearin' at me, and I just laughed in their faces, I thought they were pathetic. And then Andrea grabbed me by the hair and started pulling me away from the lights into the dark, so I started to fight back. I kicked her in the stomach and pulled her coat over her head and won the fight. I caused her internal bleeding because she was on some kind of acid, and her stomach lining was really sensitive, only I didn't know that 'til later.

Mary has lived and breathed conflict for so long that she finds herself engaged in it wherever she goes. She takes on causes. She defends small animals against would-be torturers. She takes on teachers she believes are "acting like assholes." She stops older, bigger people from beating up younger, smaller people, and when pushed or insulted, she stands up for herself immediately.

HierArchies And violeNce

Paradoxically, along with Mary's finely tuned appreciation for power imbalances, she also appreciates hierarchies and her place in them. While she abhors others "looking down" on her and rebels against anyone who suggests that she bow to their authority, she also dislikes it intensely when those whom she considers beneath her don't stay in their places. In Mary's eyes, such behavior calls for immediate redress. This is most apparent when younger girls from lower grades try to step out of line. For example, Mary was quite angry with Jenny (Chapter Eight) because

> she walks around acting like King Shit because she can fight, and you're not King Shit until you're in grade 10. While you're in grade eight, you're a nobody.

In Mary's eyes, Jenny is "a cocky little bitch" who has brought problems on herself not only because she doesn't know her place, but because she shows signs of being what Mary hates most — a power-tripper:

> I've had my run-ins with her. She's sort of a power tripper too. I mean, I can see when the grade 10s leave, Jenny will be the queen of the school, like sort of putting herself in a position of power, I don't know.

At this point, Mary shared a bit of insight into the behavior she most hated in Jenny:

> I think one reason why I haven't gotten really mad at her yet, is because she reminds me of me when I was in grade eight. I didn't fight like that, but I mouthed people off. I was really cocky. ... When you're in grade eight, everybody tries to set up their own reputation. ... That's why the grade eight boys are usually the cocky ones, because they want to set up a class-clown-type, cool-person reputation. And then there's the people in grade eight who are always trying to fit in somewhere because they haven't really got into a big school yet. They're like in a big sea and they're little fish instead of big fish, so they're trying to get a position where they're comfortable and sometimes they find the wrong position that they're in, like Jenny. I mean she's gotten so many people mad at her. She thinks that it's cool, and you have to mouth off a lot of people and get into a lot of fights to be cool.

It was around the notion of "cool" that Mary saw herself as different from Jenny. Mary did not enter into fights with people because she wanted to be cool, but only to redress perceived imbalances of power, to keep those who should be in their places in those places, and most importantly, to discharge her anger. In her mind, older and more mature and more righteous people like herself entered into fights because they were angry about an injustice, and that made a big difference.

Gender equity and violence

Mary had one further reason for engaging in confrontations and fights: equality with the males in her life. Mary believes that in order to achieve equality, she must prove to men (particularly her father) that she can handle herself:

> There's more equality now between girls and guys. And the guys think that if we're going to have equality, then we gotta be equal with them ... . We were having this discussion in English class, and the guys think that girls are wimps because whenever they get in a fight they don't just duke it out, they just cry and about a month later they finally talk to each other, and then they cry again and they get all sappy and they're friends. Or they hate each other one day, and the next day they're friends. Guys are just like, "All we do is duke it out and then go for a beer."

Equality makes good sense to Mary, especially in view of her daily quest to get her father to acknowledge her, to help her with the chores, or even to take his shoes off when she has washed the floor. It also makes sense in view of Mary's mother's battles for equality with her husband. However, neither Molly nor Linda agreed with this explanation.

Linda believed that girls fight because "in some ways we're trying to be equal and in other ways, we're just doing what we want." Molly suggested that "I think it's more just kinda the image I want — like, don't mess with me!"

But — as our meetings revealed to me — the bottom line for Mary wasn't really equality; it was getting rid of her anger, an anger fueled by anything she perceived as unjust and unfair. With the view in mind that she wanted to be prepared to take on any physically threatening challenges, Mary had been taking karate lessons for some time, as had her mother and brother. Mary is truly proud that she can handle herself physically.

DATE RAPE

Indeed, much of Mary's talk focused on her ability to take people on, to take charge and be in control. Yet, despite her readiness to fight for herself and for those who are weaker, Mary did not fight on the night she was date-raped.

Mary's rape happened a year before she took part in this study, when for six months, owing to her continuing disagreements with her father, she took refuge at her grandmother's house. Mary rarely dates, but at that time she was "hanging around" with a 28-year-old man who supplied her with drugs and alcohol and drove her around in his car. On the night of her rape, she was completely confused:

> ... We were seeing each other for about, I guess a week or two weeks or whatever. I didn't want to have sex with him, but I never really told him that, because I was basically pissed out of my tree[1] and I didn't want to tell him because I, I felt really insecure because like I, I, it doesn't, I don't get very many chances to go out with people ... so I wasn't prepared, I wasn't like, I, I wasn't expecting it at all, and I just did it anyways. But I didn't want to and so ever since, I've just like — I broke up with him after. But I've like, you know, I didn't want to and I can't believe I did that.

The experience left Mary with lasting questions about herself because she blames herself for what happened. This sense of guilt and shame was further complicated by the reactions of her mother and grandmother, who found out about the rape by reading Mary's diary:

When my mom … found out about this, this guy, she found out from my Gramma, … and my Gramma read my diary, 'cause I left it there, but actually, 'cause you know I was like, "I don't mind," and it was underneath my bed and she read everything and that's when I was like heavily into drugs and I was heavily into alcohol … . And my mom said to me, she said, "You," she started crying and then she told me that my Gramma, she said, "My mom invaded my trust by doing that when I was little [reading her diary]. I would have never done it to you, but she showed me the pages and I regret looking at them." She goes, "I'm not disappointed in you. I know everybody goes through it, and I just want you to know I'm there for you." But I didn't talk to my Gramma for about a year after that, even though she'd hound me, for that invading of trust.

Thus, in the aftermath, Mary's rape was sidelined. Instead, the issue had become betrayal of trust through the reading of her diary. Yet, the damaging betrayal of trust that is rape was never broached by Mary's mother and grandmother. It was buried along with all further references to Mary's construal of sexuality.

However, in our group meetings, Mary, Linda, Molly, and I talked a great deal about sex and sexuality, largely because the girls said talking made them feel better. The girls summed up sex in one word: "gross." They struggled with mixed feelings about whether or not they wanted to engage in sex, and had harsh things to say about girls who were sexually active.

For the most part, when these girls did engage in sex, they were usually drinking alcohol in large quantities. By the time they came to the point of intercourse, they were drunk and feeling ill from too much alcohol, and were not in control of their bodily functions. In the aftermath of taking part in sex under such conditions, they felt disgusted with themselves and with their partners. Similarly, whenever they heard of others engaging in sex, they felt righteously angry — particularly with the girls involved. They later used their knowledge and their anger as a justification to harass, threaten, and beat such girls.

Alcohol and drug use

Alcohol and drug use plays a large part in the girls' participation in sex and, on occasion, in violence. For Mary (as for Molly), alcohol use is synonymous with alcohol misuse. When they drink, these girls rarely stop at one or two drinks. Mary has been drunk to the point of being ill so many times that there are certain kinds of alcohol that she cannot even smell because she begins to feel sick:

Me and my friend shared a mickey of tequila shooters where you get the lemons and salt and water. ... That was harsh, we were on our butts soon, flat out. My cousins [who were with Mary and her friend in the family trailer, drinking on their own while their parents got drunk with Mary's parents up at the house], they were like mad at me, though, the next morning. They didn't tell my parents, and they were like, "We're cleaning up all your throw-up!" — there was throw-up from one end of the trailer to the other, it was so bad. And they're like, "We were thinking of getting your stomach pumped, 'cause you were starting to throw up blood and all that." And I can't even smell hard liquor any more. I can drink beer or coolers ... .

Sometimes when Mary gets drunk she "feels like punching people." Because of this, she prefers to drink only with those whom she feels she can trust. She gave an example of an experience she had while drinking around people whom she couldn't trust:

One of my friends, one of my ex — well he's never been my friend, we hang around the same crowd, his name is Grant. He is the most violent drunk I've ever met in my life. He was just brutal. He'd throw around his friends and beat the crap out of them when he was drunk. ... He was pissed one night, and I was drunk ... and we were all down at Taylor Lake and Grant's throwing around [my friend] Brent, just beating him up. I threw Grant off Brent and I go, "Don't you fucking touch him!" and I freaked out on Grant — he wanted to hit me, and Brent's like, "You hit this person, and I'll kill ya, literally." And Brent's not a violent drunk, like he'll run around and he'll fall and laugh 'cause he's falling ... and he'll tell you, "I'm a happy drunk, unless I'm pukin'." ...

After telling this story, Mary expressed a preference for drugs over alcohol, because

when you're smoking dope, you just break out laughing, you don't feel like punching people because it's just too hard. It takes too much ... . You're mellow ... . You just want to sit there and trip out on everybody ... . It's even good for school work. When I used to get stoned all the time last year, I remember, I used to sit in class and do my work because I didn't want the teacher to catch me, and this year I'm getting failing marks 'cause I'm not doing my work 'cause I'm never stoned.

Marijuana was not the only drug Mary used. In the past year, she had also used LSD regularly. She had a less favorable opinion of this drug because she had seen people "freaked out" while "doing acid." In her opinion, "people that are violent when they're on drugs are usually on acid or coke or something like that." She saw this as reason to stop using such drugs. But Mary had a further reason for quitting:

I used to use acid myself, and I quit completely because it was the type of drug, if you like it, you like it and if you don't you don't, and I liked it, and I quit because I liked it. ... It's not an addictive drug, but if you like it you want to do it again. And if you want it, you'll do it again and again. And okay, it got to the point where I was almost critically insane, like clinically, 'cause after a certain point of doing so much you can be clinically insane or — and I was just like, "There's no way!" ... I didn't want to be like Jeanette LeBlanc last year, who did acid so much that I like noticed a big change in her attitude — Like she got weird. She wore weird clothes and she was kind of a "low-life" and she was different. She, like, they get less brain cells; they lose their values. She got violent. She picked on smaller people.

In the end, despite her preference for marijuana and acid, Mary picked alcohol as her substance of choice because it didn't make her "weird," it was easy to get, and if she stayed home or near home to drink, her parents would give her permission to do so.

Mary's parents seem to make the abuse of alcohol relatively easy. They also seem to have encouraged Mary's use of tobacco. Mary has been smoking since age 10, as has her brother, who gave her her first cigarette. Everyone in Mary's home smokes, and her parents frequently pay her with cigarettes to do chores. Alternatively, they give her cash for extra chores so that she can buy her own cigarettes.

Much of Mary's social time revolves around cigarettes, alcohol, and drugs. She is a "corner person," that is, a smoker who hangs around the intersection nearest her school. This puts her in touch with other smokers, who on occasion also smoke marijuana both in and out if school, drop acid, and use cocaine when they can get it. On weekends especially, they drink large quantities of alcohol.

Mary pointed out that not all kids who smoke cigarettes automatically progress to drug and alcohol use and misuse. But the fact remains that their chances of coming into contact with kids who do are greater when they gather with other smokers at the corner.

For Mary, substance misuse is a part of life: All social occasions involve this. She spends much of her time hanging around spots where other kids congregate to "party." Near her house, there are several such haunts — an ocean beach, a lakefront, a wilderness trail — where young people regularly gather to drink and smoke. Partying when parents are away is also a favorite pastime:

When my parents went away this time it was really great, because we had a whole lot, we had about 20 to 30 people, we had an all-night party. Nothing got broken, nothing got stolen. There were no problems at all. Like, the music wasn't loud, 'cause we have renters. ... Like, everybody helped us to clean up the pizza boxes and everything. It worked because I managed it, my brother didn't. He had all his friends over, and I, I was the one with the authority. I was the one who was, you know, looking after things and making sure nothing was going out of hand with his friends, that there was no fights or anything and he, he went to bed actually, and I, I stayed up until the next morning, then went to bed about one the next day.

Friendships

For Mary, such parties are wonderful times: times to spend in close company with others, times when she can shine, when she can be in charge and ensure that things run smoothly. Mary likes to have control in social situations. She likes to keep order and see that her form of justice prevails.

With both her male and her female friends, Mary likes to engage in sports such as riding and biking. She likes to compete and she likes to win. She also plays the role of peacebroker, protector/enforcer, and leader/guardian — roles that she backs up with physical threats when the friends she is trying to help step out of line:

With her friend Cathy:
Cathy's not tough. She's got this butch layout, but she's not tough, 'cause when we were best friends, I'd start wrestling with her on the trampoline or something in my front yard, and I'd hit her lighter than I'd hit my other friends and we were just joking around, we were just play fighting, and Cathy'd go, "Ow, that hurts," and it's just like, I didn't even swing hard. She doesn't know how to hit properly, she'd go something like this (*shows twisted arm*) when you're supposed to keep a straight fist and you should follow through like that (*demonstrates*). But now she's hanging out with this chick Eileen, she's wears these spiked rings, and ever since Cathy started hanging around with her, she thinks she's tough, and her and Eileen will go around looking for fights and ... I just want to beat the crap out of Eileen and get her out of the picture so that Cathy can straighten up ... .

With Jenny, when Jenny provoked Linda:
I was in the mall, and Jenny was there and I go, "Jenny, come here," and she broke down in tears. She was crying and she comes up to me and she goes, "I did not call you a bitch," and I go, "I'm talking to you right now, I never said I was gonna kick your ass, but other people said I was gonna kick your ass. I'm gonna ream you out right now, 'cause I'm pissed off at you. I'm gonna give you a second chance. You think you're King Shit of this school, you're not King Shit, me and Linda and all the other grade 10s are King Shit. ... Don't mess

with us, 'cause we stick together, we're friends." And I go, "If you're not one of our friends and you piss us off, we stick together and we'll gang up on you." And she said, "Well, why haven't you, then?" And I go, "You know, you really got a mouth on your face, you know," and she goes, "Oh?" And I freaked out and I just started yelling at her again, and then I went on for another 15 minutes. I really know how to talk when I'm mad. ... But she doesn't know when to quit. There's a point when you stop scowling at someone and calling them a bitch, like after they ream you out and threaten to beat the crap out of you, you should stop. Most people would stop, but Jenny doesn't.

Similarly, Mary persuaded her parents to allow her best friend Brent (who had moved out of province with his father, yet missed his friends and wanted to return) to come and live with them as a boarder. She organized the social life of her friends Tanya and Faye, and kept them involved in activities that she herself enjoyed pursuing. She takes control of her father's bad behavior. She supports her mother and acts as her confidante. She is defender and comrade-in-arms with her brother in the battle against their father.

In each of these relationships, Mary has definite expectations with regard to how her allies should behave. When they do not, she becomes first disappointed and hurt, then furiously angry.

When Brent moved back to town and struck up a relationship with Faye that sometimes excluded Mary, she was devastated and began to take exception to many of Brent's habits (drinking, misusing drugs, skipping school) that she had previously overlooked. (Eventually, she persuaded her parents to send him back to his family.) When Tanya disagreed with Mary's judgments about other people, Mary became frustrated and angry and wanted to beat Tanya up. When Faye became involved with Brent, Mary felt deserted and betrayed and stopped being friends with her. When her father "steps out of line," she "reams him out and gives him the third degree." When her mother is unavailable, she feels angry and abandoned. When her brother became mentally ill, she became irritated with the amount of time and attention he was receiving, then angry with her parents and her brother for failing to give her the attention she herself felt she needed.

Mostly, Mary believes that she benefits those whom she cares about. She acts as she does because she wants her friends to like her and spend time with her. She wants her brother to be healthy and happy so that she can continue to be his comrade. She wants her father to be easy-going and to acknowledge her contributions to the family.

She wants her mother to be less preoccupied with her father. And she wants other people to see her as a friendly person, someone who likes to have fun.

Abandonment and Loneliness

In the end, Mary feels like an "outcasted little person," very much alone, somehow deprived of what she needs and what she feels she is entitled to.

For example, although she cooks the family's dinner, she frequently finds reasons not to eat with them in order to avoid the arguments that regularly occur at the table. Thus, she finds herself alone at a time when she might actually like some company. When she struggles with her chores or school work, she often seeks help from her parents or brother, but can rarely pin them down long enough to assist her.

> When I get home, well, I automatically stoke up the stove. That takes me about 15 minutes … . Then when the house gets warmer, I sit down for about half an hour, then it's about 5:30, and then I get going outside and do the animals. I have to feed the chickens, do their water. if it's cold, I bring them water from the house because the pipes freeze and stuff. Sometimes I have to take the horse out of the barn. I usually have to tidy the kitchen before my mom gets home, and then I have to come in and cook the dinner … .

The day before one of our interviews, Mary had actually received help from her mother and, after some urging, from her father:

> I've been sick the last couple of nights and I haven't done anything. Like yesterday I just helped my mom make dinner, … and I didn't really do anything other than that. I've just been totally zonked. … I was tired, I was grumpy and I was sick, and I was sitting in the family room, and my dad — when he's sick, he expects everybody to drop everything to do something for him. And I asked him to run to the store to get me some cough medicine, and he was sitting down watching TV … and he said, "Ho, ho, give me a minute, you won't even let me sit down, raw, raw, raw." And I just freaked on him and I said, "Look, you asshole, you expect me to do everything when you're sick, and you won't even get off your lazy ass and go to the store to get me some cough syrup. Well, I'll tell you something, next time you're sick, I'm not going to do jack shit for you and you're gonna learn from that, 'cause then you're gonna have to get off your lazy ass and do something yourself!" And so he got up and went and got it for me, and that really fixed him for about two hours after that.

When I asked her where she learned to talk to people (especially her father!) in this manner, she was quick to answer: "Probably my dad; that's the way he talks to me all the time." In fact, every interaction between Mary and her father that I overheard rang exactly as described above.

Mary still holds out the hope that one day she will no longer feel lonely and abandoned in her own home, that her father will see the light and straighten himself out — preferably with direction from Mary — and that she can hang onto her dream of a family that is held together by love:

> I love my dad ... but I just don't like him. When I was a little girl, me and my dad were best friends, and now he doesn't even talk to me. [*Sobbing*] I don't know who he is any more ... Me and my brother both see it like it was something that we did wrong .... All of this just makes me feel shitty about myself.

Ultimately, what Mary seeks is recognition and love, especially from her father, with whom she has built a pattern of interaction that neither of them seems able to break. When Mary talks about this, she first becomes angry and strident about "fixing" her father. Then she becomes quiet and sad and small, filling the room with a palpable loneliness mixed with the deepest sorrow.

NOTES

1. Mary has been drinking alcohol since about age 10, when she began sneaking drinks from the adults' glasses at her parents' parties. Both Mary's parents consume quite a bit of alcohol and combine most social events with heavy drinking. Mary appears to follow her parents' pattern of drinking. She does not like to travel far to parties because, after steady drinking, she does not wish to have to struggle to get home. Two examples of her drinking style:

> Last New Year's, I drank a bottle of Crown Royal whiskey straight — I chugged it back ... just kept going and going and going and there was just about one inch left out of the whole bottle and I was just like, "Oh this is fun, Happy New Year's!" — but after like a half an hour, I was in the bathroom throwing up. ... And about three or four weeks ago, I got drunk with some friends; we had a beach party and I drank two-thirds of a bottle of rye, another half of a two-liter [bottle], and I drank four maximum lights ... .

CHAPTER SEVEN

Linda's Story

My dad just doesn't trust me with guys, he thinks they'll just use me. One time when I got suspended from school for fighting, he said to me, "What do you think you are, a biker bitch? Why don't you go out and get filled up by the titties and done up by the ass and stuff." ... It goes back to when I was younger, when uhm, I was uhm, molested for four years, by like a friend of the family, and my parents didn't believe me. Like I remember, I was like in grade three and they had this good feelings, good touches and bad touches program, and I told my teacher and she, like, told my principal and then my principal called my parents and my parents woke me up and I was in grade three, grade two or three, and they're like, "Well, what did he do to you?" uhm and I didn't, just, I didn't, I was scared to answer them so they like, "Did he do this, did he do that?" and I'm like, "Well ya," and they go, "Okay, well, we don't think he'd really do anything like that." And he kept coming over after that. He was my baby-sitter, and my parents kept having him over for dinner, and I remember one time when I was sitting at the table and there he was, this guy, he was just 17 and he used to help my dad build his car and stuff. And I remember sittin' at the table and I was just like, I felt embarrassed to be there in front of him, and I remember he had this headband on and I was just staring and my dad took me in the next room and told me I'd better stop acting rude and stuff. And later my dad made me watch a TV program on kids who, uhm, say they've been molested but have lied, and I just can't talk to my parents about sex or anything. (*Excerpt from taped interview with Linda*)

Family dynamics

Linda's description of her family focused primarily around her father's domination of her mother, her sister, and herself. Linda talked about her father often, and brought him up within the first 10 minutes of our first meeting with Mary and Molly (see "Molly's Story," Chapter Five). Like Mary, she describes herself as being unable to get along with her father because "he has to prove his authority all the time." Linda experiences her father as a man who doesn't listen to her, because "he never listens to anyone." This, according to Linda, makes him "like most guys, because guys never listen anyway."

Rather than listen, Linda's father "gives ultimatums and gets the belt." Not only does he use a belt; he also uses a martial arts exercise tool made up of two wooden batons joined by a chain, with which he hits his daughters across the legs. On occasion, being hit in this way has left the girls with bruises. In assessing her father's behavior, Linda suggested that he does what he does because she has a bad temper and therefore "I kind of like deserve what I get."

As well as using physical abuse, Linda's father makes frequent use of put-downs, lectures, and punitive gestures to straighten out his wife and daughters. For example, he wants his wife, a woman described by Linda as "all sweet and cute and quiet" and who manages her husband by "holding everything in until it hurts her," to change into a more outgoing person. To force her to do this, he has for the past three years refused to wear his wedding ring, because his wife is not behaving as he wants her to.

Linda seemed deeply troubled by her father's treatment of her mother, and expressed the wish that her mother would speak out more often:

> I don't want my mom to sit back and like hold everything in 'cause she'll just explode. And just like, I think it's better when she let's it out, 'cause it makes me feel better too. Like then she's like, not hurting herself. ... And when she wouldn't stick up for her rights, I don't know, we'd have some problems, like my mom and me, 'cause like, I'd just, I get mad at her and stuff, 'cause she wouldn't spend any time with me. And like it was my dad that told me about sex, 'cause she won't even talk about it, and I want her to talk about it 'cause when mothers talk to you it's comforting, and I can't talk to my mother about anything personal whatsoever. Some of my friends go home and ask their parents a question, and I don't want to ask my parents, and my friends are like, "Well, doesn't this girl have a mom?" Like, I just don't feel comfortable. Like, she doesn't feel comfortable talking about it, then it makes me feel uncomfortable talking to her.

Linda spends much of her time at home both craving contact with her parents and very carefully avoiding it. Although she wants desperately to be able to talk to her parents, particularly her mother, the risks are too great. Her father has often encouraged her to talk to him about "anything," but on the few occasions that she has actually approached him, he has greeted her openness with verbal and physical abuse. Her mother has never issued an invitation to talk, and has mostly kept her mouth tightly shut with regard to her private feelings on any subject. She has, however, joined her husband in denouncing Linda.

Not surprisingly, Linda spends as much time as possible by herself. This angers her parents, who believe she is being rude and secretive. In some ways, Linda's parents' perceptions that she has a secret life are accurate. According to Linda, they "don't have a clue" what she really does, and she does in fact take a number of precautions to keep her life completely separate from theirs.

Her chief allies in maintaining this secrecy are her best friend, a girl who has been suspended a number of times from school for fighting, and her best friend's mother. This mother "covers" for Linda by lying to Linda's parents about her whereabouts. She also occasionally joins Linda and her own daughter at parties with other adolescents and allows them to drink and use drugs in her presence. When Linda is out with her friends on weekends, she often drinks a great deal. Unlike her friend and her friend's mother, she doesn't engage in much sexual experimentation. She is too overcome with revulsion and often frightened by flashbacks from her own sexual abuse to allow herself much pleasure in sex.

School

Linda described herself as having a short temper and needing to prove that she has authority. By way of illustration, she talked extensively about school, where her main focus was engaging in fights with fellow students and power struggles with the vice-principal and some of her teachers.

She described the students she fights with as "cocky, little obnoxious kids who mouth you off and are trying to be cool and fit in, but they look like idiots." She described the vice-principal as someone who told her that she would be a "nobody" and who, just like her father, won't let anybody talk and won't listen.

Linda understood that she had an "anger problem" which manifested in her interactions with those who displeased her. Chief among those was her schoolmate Jenny (Chapter Eight), with whom she had several altercations. One of these culminated in Linda's suspension from school for backhanding Jenny across the face after Jenny told her to "kiss my god-damned ass."

Within the first half hour of our meeting, Linda had touched upon her propensity for anger, struggling with authority figures, and fighting with fellow students. These were her recurring themes; they came up in every meeting I had with her.

Anger and violence

Linda described herself as being capable of anger that can explode into violent rage. She also felt she had a deep capacity to hate. For Linda anger, rage, and hate come into play especially when she is confronted by someone she deems is treating her with disrespect. Jenny and the vice-principal have been most instrumental in triggering Linda's rage:

> I just got a lot of hatred for some people. ... When I don't like somebody, say if somebody goes around, especially if they're, it really bothers me, 'cause it's that respect thing. If they're younger and they're calling me a bitch, I'll go up to them and confront them ... and I'll say, "Look! Don't call me a bitch unless you're looking for a fight. Because I never did anything to you, so don't worry about it. You've got a problem here and you'll have even more of a problem if you keep your attitude up!" And like people, the crowd might see me, I can't really like, see myself when I'm doing it, I just know I got a lot of hatred. But when people like, see me they're like, "Calm down." I mean it's like they had a bet going with me that I can't go two days without saying a negative thing and all that, and I couldn't. ... And there's one person [Jenny], and it just kinda happened after she mouthed me off, I was just like totally freaked with her and now I just want to slam her head into something. I wanna shoot her with a gun or something. I wanna kill her. ... If I could I get away with it I'd kill her. I wouldn't necessarily kill her, but I'd get her good. I just want to teach her a lesson. I'd beat the crap out of her. She's pissed me off so badly, I just want to give her two black eyes. Then I'd be fine. I'd have gotten the last word in.

The vice-principal once triggered her rage by a telephone call he made to her home. The call was made after Linda took part in an incident in a school hallway in which one of her closest friends tripped a male student "by accident." The student reported this "accident" to the vice-principal, and later informed Linda and her friend that the vice-principal had told him he could press charges. To Linda, this was proof that the vice-principal was "out to get people," specifically herself and her friends.

Her anger grew when later that same day, the vice-principal called her at home to discuss her behavior with her. She was not home at the time, but her mother relayed the call to the home of the "best friend," whom Linda was then visiting. The call was received by Linda's friend's mother, who handed her the phone with the remark, "It's that asshole of the year!" This remark only served to solidify Linda's sense of having been wronged. By the time she took the phone, Linda was very angry, mostly because she found it intrusive and strange that she would be called first at home, then at a friend's home. When the vice-principal told her that he was calling because he wanted to discuss his impression of her and to let her know that several younger students had complained to him about her, Linda flew into a rage:

He didn't necessarily have to go and call me, he could have told me at the office. [When he called] I was so mad at the time, I was so mad. It just ruined my evening. I was just like, "Oh my god, I can't believe this! When I find out who did that [complained to the vice-principal] I'm going to kill them!" I was so mad!

This anger permeates Linda's life even when she actually knows better or has some understanding of an opponent's position. For example, even though she herself was picked on and bullied when she was younger, she finds herself picking on and bullying those students in her school who are picked on by others. Her reason for this is simple: "I've just got a lot of hatred."

The anger also emerges in her interactions with teachers, particularly those she has identified as "trying to be like your enemy." In Linda's mind, such teachers place themselves "above" their students and appear to convey dislike. With such a teacher, Linda goes out of her way to create disorder and distraction:

Miss Sangster, she doesn't like us. She just doesn't like anybody. She thinks that she's better than you. She struts around and points her finger. She, she's rude. The other day I walked out of her class 'cause I turned around and like, everybody was talking, and she doesn't like me, so I turned around like, I just turned around and laughed and she sent me to the back of the room. ... She's got no right to do that. She's very negative, she's got no right!

In an attempt to "get her teacher back," Linda purposefully set her up the next time she attended her class. She complained that she had a headache and asked her teacher for a Tylenol, knowing full well that her teacher could not comply because teachers cannot dispense medication to students. Linda repeated her request until a classmate offered to run across the street to her own home to get a pill for Linda. Miss Sangster refused the student permission. Linda then challenged her: "So this is the way you care for your students!" and was subsequently sent to the office.

At the office, she encountered her math teacher, who asked if she was being mouthy again, and her English teacher, with whom she had so far had a reasonably good relationship. The English teacher remarked that he "had now seen the other side" of Linda. This incident left Linda feeling angry and humiliated, but also fully justified in her behavior. Every aspect of it confirmed how wrong and bad teachers could be. Nothing that happened prompted her to revisit her own behavior because, in her mind, she was fully justified in everything that she did.

Unlike Mary, who prefers the direct-assault approach to teachers and anyone else who gets in her way, Linda chooses to undermine and undercut those teachers whom she dislikes. She saves direct attacks for fellow students, usually those who are younger and in a lower grade than herself. However, one of the four incidents she was involved in over one three-month period included an altercation between herself and the "best" friend who had "accidentally" tripped the male student in the hall. This friend was suspended for five days for fighting with a female student, as Linda was for hitting Jenny.

When Linda engages in a direct attack on another student, she usually feels justified because she does this only when she feels provoked. Provocation, for Linda, is being called names, either behind her back or to her face; this is enough to get her going. Here is how she described a typical incident:

> So I had this miff with a girl, actually a couple of days ago, and she, she ended up calling me a bitch and she would talk about me behind my back, and she's got a carrot stuck up her rear so far that she, it's true (*laughter*), she walks standing straight. No one likes her. That's just how bad she is. And she, she, you know, like, I gave her the chance in the first place, like I was friends with her and then she messed it up by calling me a bitch, like, in front of everybody. And I said, "Did you call me a bitch?" And it makes me so mad, especially when they're younger. My parents have always said, "Just walk away from it," but when other people walk away, I just get so mad, 'cause I think, "Oh, they're not gonna listen to me," so I just want to pound the crap out of them. So I wanted to beat the crap out of her. And I told her, and Mary told her too, that I could hit her. I mean I can take her, I mean I could just slam her down on the ground and that would be it. She's just a weakling, and she uses her snootiness to look down on people, and I don't like it. People like her shouldn't do that.

With Jenny, Linda was even more harsh:

> I told her she was in my face, she was calling me names and everything, like on the third day of school … and she's like giving me dirty looks and I'm like, whatever, okay, and then a couple of days later, I'm walking out and I hear this, "Fucking slut," and I turn around and say, "What the hell is that for?" and we kinda get in an argument and then I walked away. The next day it's, "There goes the bitch," and I'm, like, this is a grade eight talking to a grade 10.

And then at the dance she pushed me and I go, "Nice fucking outfit!" and then she went and told the vice-principal and then about a week went by and like I hadn't talked to her or anything and I was standing in the hall talking to my friend and I hear, "Kiss my ass!" so I said, "Say it to my face!" and so she did and then it was just like a reflex and I just went like that (*demonstrates a backhand smack*) and I backhanded her. I should have punched her. She pissed me off so badly.

For Linda, such provocation justified her own behavior of smacking Jenny across the face.

When we arrived at this point in the discussion, I told Linda (and Mary and Molly, who were also present) that I could understand her anger with Jenny but had a great deal of difficulty accepting that she or anyone could resort to a smack across the face merely because of being angry. She explained it to me this way:

Well, we've got to, because the teachers don't really help you, and there's not anything you can do to get them [people like Jenny] back. I mean if you go to a teacher, they don't really do anything. They just say, "Oh well, she's in grade eight, you should be able to handle it yourself. And it's just like, well, what can I do, I'm not allowed to hit her? And if you do hit her, it's like you get the message to her, "Don't mess with me again," basically, and you've got to get her back, 'cause we're older and they make us look like idiots by sitting and mouthing us off. And I definitely want to do it because I want to get her back.

Linda believed she had further justification for "getting Jenny back":

Jenny's a little liar. I even told her that. There is no way I'll ever resolve anything with her, and there's no way I'll ever be friends with her. ... She's a slut, she wears clothes that don't fit her, and we have every right to call her a slut. No offense [to me, the interviewer], but she's a slut. She slept with people at the beginning of the year, and then she was denying it, she's got a screw loose — and anyway, she really pisses me off right now because since she got in this one fight, she thinks she can beat up anybody. And that's, like, just so annoying. She fought that other chick just because she wanted to, she really didn't have any reason. ... Now she's running around saying that I couldn't fight worth a shit and that she's going to beat me up at the store and she's going to flatten me and stuff. And she goes to the elementary school where my sister goes and threatens grade sixes ... . And then she started giving my sister lip, so I turn around to her and I go, "Don't you even think about my sister, you don't even look at her, don't even walk by her!" I go, "Don't even think of her!"

Linda had no doubts at all that Jenny deserved a beating. In the final analysis, she had no doubts about what should happen whenever she was provoked. The rule was simple: When provoked, get them back! Neither Mary nor Molly offered a dissenting voice here. For all three, the choice was clear:

> You have to do it because if you don't you'll get angry, and that's just the way it is when you're a teenager. You don't really care if you get in trouble or whatever, There's not much maturity, I guess. And anyway, the trouble part isn't when you're hitting someone, because at least then you're not sittin' there fumin' anymore, the trouble part comes after that.

Drug and alcohol use

At this point in our conversation, the discussion moved from violence to the use of drugs. For Linda, drugs (marijuana and LSD) were a thing of the past, a past that began a few short weeks before our interviews. For the moment at least, Linda had "quit doing dope" because she had had enough for now. Having smoked pot nearly every day in grades eight and nine, and in the first two months of grade 10, she thought she would leave it alone. She offered no explanation for this decision other than to agree with Mary that maybe smoking dope and doing drugs such as LSD could become psychologically addictive, and might therefore pose problems. Linda had an image of a former friend in mind when she spoke about smoking dope:

> Melody, do you remember Melody, she smoked pot and she did acid, and she got really weird, like she'd dress weird and she did so much dope, like it made her violent sometimes, even when she wasn't violent, and she didn't really like people, I don't know … .

While Linda may have put marijuana and LSD aside, she had not done the same with alcohol. Like Molly and Mary, Linda drank regularly, especially on weekends, and she drank to get drunk. Linda had discovered alcohol when she was seven years old:

> When I was seven, I went to a wedding and me and my friends sat under a table drinking. It was like they [Linda's parents] didn't know, they were all up having a great time, and we just sat there drinking out of these little glasses. I got really out of it, and I was throwing up and they were all like, "Food poisoning!" Parents are so naive, like they couldn't imagine their seven-year-old daughter getting drunk, you know … .

SEXUAL ABUSE

Linda, Molly, and Mary also talked about sex and morals. For Linda, what stood out was the extent to which she had been subjected to sexual abuse, and the clarity with which she could discuss her experiences of it. After disclosing her abuse (see "Molly's Story," Chapter Five), Linda described what it has been like for her to live with this experience:

> I just kept pushing it back and back and I, I even forgot about it. Like, that might sound weird, but uhm, uhm, I, I, I forgot it for a lot of years, and then last year it started coming back and I'd like seclude myself from my family, I'd just sit in my room. And, uhm, my parents would get mad like, 'cause I was, like I wasn't spending time with the family. And uhm, and then they'd, I just, I kept, I had like dreams, and this feeling that I kept having of how I felt like all the time that that happened. But now it gets more, I like get it more often. I, it's hard to, like, there's two different feelings, like one that like, if I hold something it will feel gross, and I like, just like, I let go of it. ... Like, it could be anything I'm holding onto, like I could be pulling my covers over me, and I just get grossed out like. ... And then there's this one [the other feeling] where it's in my head and I can hear something, but it's like a feeling but it's also what I'm hearing, and every time I hear it, I like kinda get — it's like something, something is being said to me and every time I hear it comes in more clearer, sort of. It's weird, I and uhm, now but, it's like I noticed like, over the years it's not like before when it was just a blur, now it's like I can almost hear what it says, but I can't. ... It's in my head ... and uhm it, it only like, it only, I can only have like, maybe not even five seconds to figure out what it is because once it goes away, then I just forget what it was like until it happens again, then it's like, "Oh ya." And then right after it happens it's like, I can't remember what it was like, but it's a voice ... .

Linda has experienced a number of difficulties in the aftermath of her abuse. As well as what she described above, she has experienced nightmares, flashbacks, and feelings of distrust for those around her:

> I'm not used to putting down on myself, but this made me really put down on myself. So when I put down on myself, I go into deep depression at home, and I won't talk to anybody and when I come to school I put on a fake smile and nobody can tell. And it's just like really stressful for me and for my friends when I tell them, and that's why I have a hard time. ... I just get really sensitive and a lot of people just, they don't know exactly why and it really hurts me more when my dad gets mad.

Linda's loneliness is poignantly clear. So far, only lying and "putting on a fake smile" has made it possible to cope with her parents.

As we continued to talk, Linda revealed more of the dimensions of the abuse she had been subjected to:

It's weird, 'cause I, last year I thought, "Well, I can handle this myself, right?" Like I'm going, "I don't need counseling for this." Like, I, in a way I sort of think that, but it just bugs me that not knowing what I'm feeling, and I certainly can't talk to my parents about anything. And my mom just kinda looks at me as if I was lying, so does my dad. And I remember, he [the abuser] used to get me and this little boy that lived down the road to do things with him, and he'd sit and watch … uh, he'd like, he'd get me and him [the boy from down the road] to do something and we'd have to like do the same back to him [the abuser]. Uhm, I remember one time like I was only young, I was about five 'cause I was still in play school, I remember. And we were in the back of this car and we thought it was normal. Like we didn't think there was anything wrong, and I just feel so embarrassed. … We, like I, we did just like normal people would have sex. That's sort of what happened, and my mom walked in and I was grounded for two weeks, I remember that. I was grounded, and I just feel so uncomfortable around my parents now. … Another thing that really bugs me, uhm, like shortly after that was done, they, we — I didn't have many friends when I was little 'cause we lived in a small town and like — but, uhm, we had this tree house that we used to play on where, and we'd always play house and uhm, this guy would like always play house with us and stuff, and he, he like told us that the kids, the parents have to do such and such to the kids, that sort of thing. So, like, we're like playing the role, and then, me and this other boy, like we had to uhm, do stuff to him [the abuser] and, uhm, we had to do the same to this other little boy. Like, he got us to do it to another kid, like we molested him … . Nobody wants to feel as bad as I do. … I've always thought I was a bad person … .

I asked Linda if she had ever had any help with her feelings as a result of being abused. In fact, she had approached the school-based child and family counselor for help, but was not at all happy with the outcome of this intervention:

[I don't want help] 'cause I remember, the family worker tried to go to Social Services[1] and then go to the cops and all that, and I was like really mad at her for that. I didn't, like it was done, over with, and I just wanted to, like, leave it at that, and just like, live with this sort of thing. Like, inside I kinda felt like when I found out that now these other people knew, it was like, well, I wonder — were they talking about me when they were discussing my business? … It, it's never like, she's [the family worker] never gone through with it, it's like I was so mad I wouldn't even come out and talk to her or like do anything. It just made me feel worse, and I didn't, like, I couldn't concentrate in school … .

Yet, Linda wished to speak of her sexual abuse almost every time we met. Talking about it seemed to help her feel better.

At the end of every meeting, before we parted, I asked each participant how she was feeling and what effect, if any, having told her story to the group had on her. Linda (and Molly and Mary, for that matter) replied each time that talking helped a great deal. For these girls, having the opportunity to talk — and most of all, to be listened to — was vitally important. As Linda put it:

> Ever since we started doing this, I kinda got everything out, so I kinda feel fine. ... I've learned a lot from it too, just sort of things that you know you have it, but you never recognized it before. Like it sort of brings you from the top [surface] to the inside. Like before [we met as a group], I thought it'd be spooky, that's basically what I thought, and I don't know, now I think you guys are totally smart, and when Mary and I went to the dance together and all those people were, like, interested and they're, like, it couldn't be [that we're actually doing something together], and they're like, Mary looks so nice and I'm like ... I feel a whole lot better. ... I feel better every time I talk about it.

In fact, talking about how she felt about her abuse prompted Linda to raise the issue one more time with her father:

> Remember when I told you guys about how my parents didn't believe and stuff [about being sexually abused]. Well, it was weird, 'cause about two weeks ago we were arguing and I've always had resentment towards my dad and he was like, "Why do you always treat me that way?" and stuff like that, and it took about two hours, but we kinda got down to it. And he asked me why I never go to him to talk to him. And I said, "'Cause I don't trust you," and he said "Why?" and I said, Because I don't." And he goes, "Why?" and I go, "Because you don't believe a thing I say." And he's like, "What, what, what?" getting all mad at me, and then I told him and he was like, "Well?" and I felt so ashamed about telling him, but he believed me this time. Then he said, he goes, "Yeah, well, all he did was show you his private parts and make you touch them." And I was like, "Well, that's not all," and I didn't want to tell him anything else, but he was like, "We, I can't believe that we didn't believe you, but it's just like you were a little kid at the time and we just thought you were getting ideas from something or whatever." He's like, "I'm sorry we didn't believe you," and then he was trying to make up, going, "Are you okay, blah, blah, blah?" They [both parents] were crying. ... But I wish now that I didn't tell them because they treat me like a kid. ... My dad's calling me his buddy, and then saying, "Oh, I better not call you that, 'cause that was the guy's [the abuser's] name," and he makes a big deal about it. ... It's like I wish I hadn't told him, I don't feel comfortable. ... And I told him that I went to counseling, and he

was like, "Well, it's water under the bridge, you shouldn't let it get you," and he told me to quit seeing a counselor ... .

Thus, while Linda did eventually feel better because now she was at least believed by her parents, she still felt uncomfortable and uneasy with their intimate knowledge of her sexuality. As well, she felt unsure what to do with those feelings. Her parents frowned upon counseling, since it involved seeking help outside the family. Further, Linda still had a great deal of unresolved anger over how the school-based social worker had dealt with her request for help. When I suggested a different counselor, one who would make herself available merely to talk and to listen, Linda, Mary, and Molly all declined because

> we just don't want to tell our parents about this, and we've kind of resolved this in our families and we don't want to go to Social Services again, 'cause I've [Linda] already had it happen twice [meaning the social worker had contacted her family on two occasions]. And if that's any of the things [we have to do], I'm totally against it, 'cause that worker tried to press charges against him, and I'm like, well ... . She called my parents the day after I told her and she questioned my parents about everything. My parents said it was true, and that's when it got brought up again, and she, like, went to Social Services and all that was really ahhh ... . And I was so mad at her 'cause I didn't even want to bring it up and she went to the police and stuff ... .

What Linda wanted was to be able to talk freely about her sexual abuse without anyone but herself taking action. She wanted to be heard, and she wanted to hear what had happened to other people. She expressly did not want me or anyone else to proceed upon the information she had shared. Most of all, she did not want her parents involved in what for her was a deeply painful and embarrassing experience.

Given that she had already talked with another counselor who had satisfied the requirements of the law about sexual abuse disclosure (i.e., by alerting Social Services and the police), I was able to do as Linda wished. I listened, as did the other two members of our small group. This seemed to help.

It helped until Molly broke her commitment to the group's confidentiality. One day, during an interlude in one of her classes, Molly told some fellow students about Linda's sexual abuse (see "Molly's Story," Chapter Five), despite her own first-hand experience with the shame and embarrassment of having others know.

Even with the continuing support of the school counselor and myself, this latest betrayal sent Linda a clear message: There is no really safe place anywhere. And while Linda continued to meet with Mary and me after Molly's betrayal, I believe the experience of being violated yet again only served to confirm for Linda that the world is a hostile place.

NOTES

1. Any adult who hears a disclosure of sexual abuse from a youth under the age of 19 is obliged by law to report this to a ministry social worker.

CHAPTER EIGHT

JENNY'S STORY

We're a very close family, and they always back me up whenever I want them to. And I stand up for my sister. I learned to stand up for myself from my uncle. He didn't have the same problems like I did with kids picking on him, but he did get called out for a fight and he beat the guy up and broke his nose, so he tells me how to box because he had to take boxing when he was younger. So he showed me, he said, "You've got to do this," and he'd push me over, and he's always play fighting. He always says, "Don't let anybody push you around." So he pushes me and I push him back. He's bigger than me, and he showed me how to defend myself. So did my grandfather. He's got eight guns. He told me, "Don't let anybody push you around," too, and so did my grandmother. My grandparents don't like it when I get pushed around, and my parents don't either. When another kid tied to push me around at the mall my dad went over and said "You better watch it," and started yelling at her. And my grandfather wanted to run over these girls that wanted to beat me up. I've seen him when he's mad. He throws things and breaks them. Like, if he's got a glass he'll just throw it up and like smash it on a table. He's been in fights like at weddings like with some of my cousins, when they were all drunk. And my dad, he's been in lots of fights, like, when he lived on the streets. He sort of lived on the streets and at home, because his parents were alcoholics and they died. His mom died when he was 13 or 14, and his dad when I was five, but they were alcoholics so they beat him, so he didn't live at home and he couldn't go to school. He doesn't hit people anymore though, he doesn't believe in it unless it's another guy. But when he gets mad he calls me horrible names and that makes me mad and it makes me cry. And when I'm mad I punch, I'm so used to punching I punch everything. I punch my sister, and when I'm mad at school, I punch the lockers, but it doesn't hurt. (*Excerpt from taped interview with Jenny*)

Family dynamics

Jenny's family, like Molly's, is "close," not just emotionally, but geographically: Jenny's parents, her sister, her grandmother and grandfather, and her maternal uncle all live together in two houses set about 100 feet apart on a piece of country property. Mother and grandmother work together, and the family spends most of its social and recreational time together.

This family togetherness has some limits, which are dictated by rigid family rules. For example, several of Jenny's mother's siblings and their children are excluded from all family activities because Jenny's grandparents strongly disapprove of their lifestyle (they live on social assistance). These relatives are not spoken to and are never invited to family gatherings; should they appear, they are fair game for a beating.

Family exclusion also extends to Jenny's father's brothers, mostly because of minor infractions, such as not returning tools that they have borrowed. At the time of my meeting with Jenny, one such brother-to-brother fight had evolved into a court battle and a family rift that caused Jenny to "hate" her cousins and not speak to them at school.

"Closeness" is also withheld from other members of Jenny's extended family, specifically Jenny's father's son, who was born to a woman he had a relationship with before he became involved with Jenny's mother some 16 years ago. Jenny's father had never acknowledged this son, who was now 18 years old; the boy had often been trouble with the law and was currently in jail.

In this family, "closeness" also entailed a high degree of emotional reactivity to one another's actions. For example, when Jenny became involved with a boy who did not meet with the family's approval, her parents and grandparents became very angry with her, and demanded that she stop seeing him. Jenny, however, was adamant about not giving her boyfriend up, and frequently lied about being with him. This conflict escalated into a six-week-long battle during which family members yelled and screamed at one another. Jenny's father frequently referred to her as a "bitch," a "tramp," and a "whore." In the midst of it all, Jenny's mother became ill with migraines and stomach pains, symptoms similar to those she had experienced when she had stomach cancer nine years earlier. Jenny's grandmother told Jenny she was the cause of her mother's illness, because she was the source of her mother's stress.

Jenny then became the center of a family storm in which everyone came down hard on her for upsetting her mother. Finally, Jenny's father told her, "If you can't live by my rules, you can't live here at all!" and kicked her out of the house. Her mother then began to cry and asked Jenny if she really wanted to leave the family. Jenny retorted: "If you can't stand my fighting with you, why don't you just sign me over to a group home!" Jenny's mother then pleaded with her to stay.

Jenny's father relented, and she was allowed to remain. Promises of better behavior were then extracted from her. Jenny made these promises willingly enough, but continued to lie about her whereabouts and to see her boyfriend (until he broke up with her because he found a girl he liked better).

In general, conflicts in Jenny's family quickly become extremely emotionally charged. When any two people clash, all the others choose sides:

> When we get mad in my family, we just yell and scream. So if I get mad at my sister and I push her, she'll yell at me and I'll get back at her. Then I'll go to my room and turn on the music. I hate my sister, and my mom gets mad at me. … If my mom gets mad she'll hit me in the back of the head, and she tells me to ignore my sister but I can't. She comes right up to me and yells in my face and I get mad, so I hit her or push her, and it happens every day. … We don't get along because we're totally different people. Like, I take after my dad and she takes after my mom. My dad wants everybody to like him. He gets 30 people in a room and he talks to everybody, and I do the same thing. I like people to like me, and I don't like people hating me. And my mom, she's got a bad temper, and my sister does. So if I do something wrong, my mom will get mad and my dad will get mad at her, so I don't get grounded. But if my dad gets mad at my sister, then my mom yells at my dad.

Taking sides is a common practice and, during extended periods of family conflict, hate and anger prevail between opposing sides. However, if any member is attacked by someone from outside the family, this hate is temporarily suspended, and the family closes ranks. Thus, while Jenny "hates" her sister, she nevertheless threatens any of her sister's schoolmates who give her trouble. At the time when Jenny was threatened with expulsion from the household, her parents nevertheless attended a school Christmas dance in order to "keep an eye on" her schoolmate Linda (Chapter Seven), who had been suspended for hitting Jenny but had returned to school in time to attend the dance.

I found Linda's description of Jenny's parents' behavior illustrative of the family's style:

> Jenny got her mom and dad to go to the dance because she said we [Linda, Mary, and Molly] were going to beat her up or something, and her mom came up to me and pushed me. It happened when Jenny was pointing me out to her mom and all that and she was walking one way and I was walking the other way and she just kinda of pushed me. And her dad's a total asshole. He's like at the dance the whole time. He's like eyeing us all and all that, he's just an idiot.

The family's style, and their stance towards those whom they consider adversaries, is perhaps best summed up by the bumper sticker displayed on the family camper: *A boss is like a diaper: full of shit and always on your ass.*

Jenny's mother

Jenny's mother is baffled by what she describes as a "180 degree" personality change in her daughter, who until junior high had been a quiet and "perfect" child who didn't require much attention. Jenny's mother appears not to grasp the connection between her family's aggressive and combative stance and Jenny's involvement in fighting outside the home. She described her own and her husband's involvement in Jenny's outside conflicts very matter-of-factly as "talking to" people. She cannot fathom how Jenny may have learned to fight, because in her mind, nothing that happens at home could possibly be connected to Jenny's behavior at school and on the street.

Jenny's mother thinks Jenny's aggression springs from (a) her moving from elementary school to junior secondary school, with a consequent change in friends, and (b) the fact that "nowadays, girls compete to be equal because you don't have to be a wallflower, you sort of have to do what the boys do to be accepted as an equal."

For Jenny's mother, Jenny's new friends (male and female) provided the central influence in Jenny's progression to violence, because many of them came from homes that were in constant turmoil, where children and parents battle frequently and strife is commonplace. She could not see, however, that her own home was not all that different. Rather, she considered it a place where people care about one another, a factor she saw as being absent in the homes of Jenny's friends.

Interestingly enough, Mary — who attended grade school with Jenny and had known her and her relatives for seven years — had no difficulty in seeing a connection between Jenny's behavior and that of Jenny's family. She recounted frequently seeing them in the midst of some altercation or other, either in the schoolyard, on the street, or in the mall. Jenny's mother, however, like Molly's, can see only her family's closeness.

Self-image

Unlike her mother, Jenny herself likes her "180 degree" personality reversal. She feels her life has changed for the better since she began to engage in fights, and often spoke to me about her involvement in, and her attachment to, fighting. Being known as a fighter had become a vitally important part of her self-image.

Jenny knew she had a great deal invested in acting "tough" and being seen by others as a force to be reckoned with. At 5'3" and weighing about 107 pounds, she described herself to me this way:

> Kids are scared of me, because I can look really tough, especially when I'm mad. It's because I'm built big. My parents even say that. I've got big shoulders compared to my mom, and when I'm big, everyone tells me, "You're going to be scary," and I stand up and I look down on them and I always give them a dirty look, and everyone's sure I'm going to get them. And if I get mad, I don't yell, I get mad and I hit.

When I asked Jenny what she thought about herself when she behaved in this manner she answered, "I don't think I like myself. I don't think I'm pretty, and I think I'm fat." She then disclosed that hating herself and being hated by others hearkened back to earlier experiences of being bullied and scapegoated in school, and to her eventual evolution into a fighter, a "tough girl" with an image to protect.

When Jenny started school years ago she was "shy and quiet, and the teacher didn't think I understood well, so I was put back into grade two." From what Jenny and her mother both told me, Jenny was so quiet that her teachers were concerned that she might be developmentally delayed. Jenny had her first experiences with being bullied shortly after being held back a grade. She was picked on and ridiculed by her fellow students, first for being slow, and as time went on, also for being fat. This continued for several years until, in grade five, Jenny decided to take action:

> ... I stood up for myself. I was getting tired of being pushed around by everybody saying I was fat and I didn't like that ... . In grade six, I was so tired of being told I was so fat, I started going on a diet. ... I went right down to 80 pounds, I didn't eat for two weeks. ... I won't do that again, I felt terrible, but in a way I felt good because I was getting thinner and I had to get new clothes. But then I got so sick [Jenny developed shingles at age 13], so I just watch what I eat now.

Since that time, Jenny has worked hard to stay thin and to cultivate her reputation as a fighter who will take on all comers.

Dieting and being thin brought Jenny immediate attention from many people:

> I didn't eat and I got sick ... and my doctor, he was just telling me that I shouldn't do that because you can get sick and you can die, so I started eating

again. ... I can't eat cookies or cake, I get sick, I think because I'm not used to eating sugar now — or chocolate. ... Sometimes I skip breakfast, and I don't really eat lunch. I eat very little for supper ... I watch my weight all the time. I weigh myself every day, but sometimes I don't look. ... Nobody ever thinks I'm fat. Everybody tells me to eat. They all tell me to eat, like my best friend. She was over the other night and I'll give her a cookie, but I won't eat any. Then she'll get mad until I at least have one. My friends want me to eat, because sometimes I go the whole day without eating. ... My mom doesn't like it. That's why I started eating, because she got upset. She told the doctor and phoned the school to make sure I ate my lunch. She kept me home a couple of days and told me to eat. ... The doctor phones once in a while to see how I am. ... There was a time when I got shingles. He said that I was run down from not eating. My doctor said it was strange for a 13-year-old girl to have it. ... I got it when I wasn't eating and I'd go out and then I went to a concert and I didn't have anything to eat ... and I collapsed a couple of times at the concert. I had like lots of money to buy food, but I'd already bought a T-shirt instead, so my friends bought me something to drink ... .

Thus, while Jenny has suffered from not eating, she has also received a great deal of caring attention — something she did not get when she was a "perfect," shy, and very quiet kid.

Fighting also has brought Jenny a number of rewards: Almost as soon as she began to stand up for herself, the amount of bullying and ridicule she was subjected to declined, and her fellow students began to see her in different light. Some saw her as someone to turn to when they needed protection. Others saw her as someone who could provide them with entertainment, because she could so easily be goaded into fighting. Overall, Jenny was no longer alone, and rarely without some form of attention.

In the end, Jenny's "rep" provides her with a far better role to play than the one she was originally assigned by those who bullied her. In fact, Jenny's investment in fighting has become so central to her sense of self that it is now "just something I do," and something she would find extremely difficult to stop:

I could only stop fighting if I get arrested, 'cause I haven't got arrested yet, and if I was taken out of school or put in an alternative [school], then I'd try to stop, or if it's hurting my parents really bad. I'd stop if I really got into trouble for it. Like, I would never stab anybody because I don't believe in using weapons [except rings in lieu of knuckle dusters], but I don't know, if I really got in trouble because I really hurt them, like if I broke their nose and I was getting charged for that or I hit them first and I got arrested for it, then I'd try not to fight because I wouldn't want that to happen again because I don't really like getting in trouble with the police. But I can't stop myself, because it's just because everybody I know is so used to me fighting that, "Oh, this person's bugging me," and half my friends can't take care of themselves and I say, "Fine, I'll take care of it." And I guess too, if like, I got beaten up really bad, I'd definitely learn to walk away — beaten up like in the hospital beaten up. Like if I get a black eye or a broken nose, that wouldn't stop me, because that can happen to anybody. But mostly there's no other way I can think of [to stop] 'cause everybody, everybody, like I've got people at both [junior and secondary] schools knowing me as a fighter, and it would be just kind of awkward like, "Now there's going to be a fight, do you want to go?" I'll probably go. I'd still go 'cause everybody's just used to me going, "Yeah, sure, I'll go," and I'll be the first one there. And all my friends, a lot of people said, "Well, if you want to stop, go ahead. Like we're not going to stop being your friend or anything," but in a way, I might lose a couple of my friends, and a lot of people won't like me after a while, and I like having a lot of friends.

Peer relationships

Friends are the most important thing in Jenny's life, especially in view of her years of suffering as a friendless scapegoat. Peer relationships are usually important to adolescents (Bibby & Posterski, 1992; Artz & Riecken, 1994). But with Jenny, there is an added level of intensity to how firmly she grasps onto her friendships, largely because she never again wants to be bullied and alone:

Right now, my friends — I don't really think my family's not important — but I'd rather spend most of my time with my friends because my family is so boring and right now my friends are the most important thing.

However, some of Jenny's friendships are difficult and fraught with contradictions, as friends turn into enemies and then back again into friends:

Janet Williams, she was my friend and we were enemies first and she didn't like my friends, so she'd always get me into trouble. Like, there was a new girl who came and we said this and that about each other and we got mad at each other, so we hated each other for two years and then the new girl left, and we found out what she did, that she said things about each other to us, so we apologized for everything, so we were friends, but then she didn't like that I liked Todd, and she didn't like my clothes, so she called me out, and that's how we had a big fight [which was watched by over 100 spectators].

In order to keep the attention of her friends and maintain her image as a fighter and defender, Jenny engages in fights more or less constantly. (If she hasn't had a fight for some time, she will systematically work her way through the people she knows, or knows about, until she finds someone she can provoke into fighting.) She also diets continually so that she will never again be fat. And she spends as much money as possible on clothes.

Jenny is primarily interested in forming friendships with boys. Her greatest source of joy is the knowledge that she can attract positive attention from males. She attributes this directly to having lost weight. As a child, however, her tormentors were mostly boys:

> It started in about grade three, all the boys used to pick on me. They used to go around calling me fat and ugly. … It bothered me, and after a while, even my good friends started doing that, so I couldn't take it anymore. So I started pushing them or yell back and they stopped bugging me. It didn't matter how big they were … .

Things are different now, and although Jenny still believes that she is "fat and ugly" and still hates herself, she feels good when she is getting attention from boys. Her best day of the year was her first day of junior high school: On that day, she got 15 phone calls from 15 different boys. At times like that, Jenny likes herself at least momentarily because

> it's really important to have a guy ask you out. I thought it was neat [when they all called me]. And I like myself when all the guys I hang out with don't think I'm fat and ugly. They like me, and my friend, she doesn't really get that many boyfriends because of her weight. She doesn't like if she's around me and I get a guy asking me out, and a couple of hours later someone else asked me out. … I feel good about myself, I have a boyfriend.

Dynamics of violence

While Jenny enjoys having a boyfriend and tries hard never to be without one, she also likes having other male friends. On occasion, she will fight with males as well as with females. When Jenny fights with males, her reasons for fighting are different from those she gives for fighting with females.

With females, Jenny engages in fights for male attention. These fights are usually triggered by a dispute about who has the right to look at or talk to a particular boy, or who has the right to wear a particular style or article of clothing — clothing that is meant to attract boys.

Jenny will also try to provoke fights with girls whose attitudes she doesn't like. She will fight girls who appear to threaten her friends. In the last analysis, she will fight anyone (male or female) with a reputation for being tough, in order to uphold and increase her own reputation as a fighter. Here is how Jenny described a fight with a female opponent:

> I got in a fight with a girl at school because she didn't like the way I wear my clothes. It got started when, umm, I was going out with this boy from another school, and she was mad, she liked him and she didn't like the fact I was going out with him so she picked on me about my clothes and my attitude and I just kept ignoring her 'til the point where she called a fight. She said. "You probably are scared to have a fight," so I went [to the place where the fight had been called] but I wasn't scared [just] 'cause she's in grade nine, but she was [scared]. I found out where she was hiding and I said, "If you want to fight," I said, "Come on, let's go!" Okay, so well, we ended up fighting and we haven't seen each other since. … She pulled my hair and slapped my face, and I punched her in the face. I cut her right by the eye [with my rings] and I scratched her and she backed off and left. … There were about 50 people watching.

With male opponents, the dynamics are somewhat different. Jenny will engage in fights with males either because of derogatory (usually sexual) comments they have made about Jenny or her friends, or because they have challenged her for intimidating or hurting their girl-friends. The dynamics also involve a desire on Jenny's part to be considered equal to males.

Jenny's fight with Marty was typical of her fights with males. Marty had shown an interest in Jenny, but she rejected him. This made him angry, and he began to express a dislike for her. At the same time, he also found another girlfriend. When Jenny and another friend began phoning Marty, his new girlfriend objected. Jenny and her friend replied that they could call anyone they wanted to. This angered Marty, who told some of Jenny's friends: "Yeah, I'll get Jenny, and I'll jump her from behind and I'll stab her!" (As Jenny understood it: "He was going to kill me with a knife, a machete.") This prompted Jenny to enlist several friends, male and female, to set up Marty by inviting him to the movies with the express understanding that Jenny would not be there. Of course she was there, along with two male friends, who began to beat up Marty for her:

> First Jim [her boyfriend] started punching Marty in the face, Jim and Ted did. Then Derek Holmes came and said, "What's going on?" and they told Derek

that Marty wanted to beat me up, so Derek took Marty and slammed his head into a wall. And then he started punching him, and then Marty's dad came around the corner to pick up Marty, so he got in the truck, and then his dad said, "You want to fight? All of you come down to the house!" So at the time when I got there, there was about 75 kids there on my side, but only about 20 of us went down to the house because people couldn't stay because they were getting picked up. ... So 20 of us went down, and Marty wouldn't come out of the house until I got off the property, because I went right up to the door and said, "Come on outside! You wanted to fight!" and he says, "I ain't coming out till Jenny's off the property!" So I got dragged off by Jim and Matt and Andy. They had to drag me off because I was really mad. And then Marty came outside and it was going to be a one-on-one fight with Derek, and like Derek didn't even know about it till that night, so they started fighting. Derek was fighting because he was afraid I'd really get hurt and because it wasn't right for a girl to fight a guy, he didn't think. And I'm like, "I want to get in there!" ... because it wasn't fair that Derek was doing it for me. But then it stopped and the dad, he was there, yelling at me, and I was yelling and screaming, "Yeah, well, your oldest son tried running me over, he tried hitting me with his car!" — But he didn't hit me because I got pulled out of the way by Carey Henderson. ... I fell, but I was okay... And then I was yelling and Derek and Marty stopped and Marty yelled, "Come on, you wanted to hit me, so hit me!" And he spat in my face. I got really mad. I took off my coat, I had a leather coat, and dropped it and grabbed him by his hair and he turned around and hit me ... so I punched him in the face. I cut him and then he got mad and he sort of punched me in the face ... and Derek was busy talking to the dad and yelling at the dad. The dad was telling us, "Leave! The fight's over!" But then I sort of attacked his son and then the dad came over, and I tripped and fell. Marty pushed me into his brother's car and I dented the door with my shoulder and my head, so I had big bruises. Jim came and he's yelling, "Get off her, get off her!" He's kicking Marty, trying to get him away, and Derek came over to try and get Marty away from me. Marty's dad came over and took Derek and punched him in the jaw and held him on the ground and so Marty jumped off me and I got up and walked away, and he started kicking Derek in the face. So the dad let go, and Derek was like, "Oh my jaw, oh my jaw!" He thought he broke it, and we all took off and the dad got in his truck and started it, so he thought he was going to chase us. And we all took off and he got out of his truck, so we all went back and then the police showed up and took down all our names ... .

That ended the fight for the time being, but it continued the following day:

The next day like, when I was walking with my friend down the road, he [Marty's dad] saw me and I'm like, "Whatever!" and I gave him a dirty look and he drove by so he stopped just like dead in the middle of the road, turned around and started chasing me. I'm running down the road towards the mall and Jim and about 15 guys I know from school came around the corner and I'm screaming. They came over and got all around me. The dad pulled in the parking lot and was yelling at me, so they're all yelling at him and he went to leave and he stopped and came out because this boy, Carey Henderson, was yelling at him. He came out and just started strangling Carey. He picked him up and strangled him and put him down and then like left. And then we left and the dad followed us for the rest of the day. ... And then I went home, and I felt really bad because I don't know what the dad was going to do because he's so mental, so I told my parents and they got mad, but then we were going to press charges but we didn't because I would have got in the most trouble if anybody pressed charges because it was because of me. But so then everything cooled down after that ... .

When I asked Jenny how she felt about all this, she had a great deal to say:

I was mad for Derek because of what happened to him, and if he didn't know [about Marty wanting to stab me] it would never have happened. ... And I felt bad in the fight because I wanted to fight Marty. I wanted to fight him to see if he would hit me or not, because if he did and hurt me, I had 19 other people behind me. They would have all jumped in. ... They were all trying to hold me back because I was really wanting to get in. I didn't even think about anything, I was just so mad. After a while, I didn't even know where I was, I was so mad. ... I didn't want Derek fighting, I wanted to do it. But Derek did fight, so I gave him hugs for that. I was hugging him because his jaw was all sore and he got bit. Marty bit him, so we were trying to make him laugh, and then after a while, he got so mad and he just wanted to fight again. ... I was so mad, I wasn't scared [even though] Marty told everyone he has a gun. ... He really has a gun because he lives with his dad and his older brother and they don't have a mom. So his dad has a gun for hunting. So Marty has a gun and he was gonna use it on me if he saw me going down the road. I heard he was gonna, but I didn't think he would because he knows if he did anything he wouldn't live. And he's not gonna use it anymore because I talked to the dad, and the dad didn't know anything about it. He thought it just started that Friday night. And I told him, "Your effing son this and your son that, he was going to use his gun on me and he was going to stab me and hit me." And he's going, "Yeah, well, I gave him permission to hit you, but I promise he will not use any weapons on you." I said, "Well just make sure of that, because if he uses any weapons on me, you'll have weapons used on you." My dad would use weapons on him, he was really mad. My grandfather's a hunter. He has eight guns. So if like, I got shot, my grandfather would.

Jenny felt emphatically that, all in all, fighting was a good thing:

I like fighting. It's exciting. I like the power of being able to beat up people. Like, if I fight them, and I'm winning, I feel good about myself, and I think of myself as tough. … I'm not scared of anybody, so that feels good. My friends are scared of a lot of people, and I go, "Oh yeah, but I'm not scared of them." Some of my friends, like this one girl from the other junior high school, admire me. … It's getting on my nerves because she phones me 15 times a night, it's boring. … She admires me because like, if someone's picking on her, I said, "Well, tell them I'll have a talk with them." And I did, and she told all her friends and they're all scared of me now and they don't even know me. (*Chuckle*) All these people in grade eight at that junior high are scared of me, they don't even know me, and they're scared of me. It makes me feel powerful.

In fact, Jenny has come to like this feeling of power so well that she finds fights wherever she can: in her own school, at the other junior high school in the district, and even in the elementary school her sister attends. On occasion, Jenny threatens and bullies students in grades five and six.

When I suggested that her behavior sounded quite a bit like that of those who had once bullied her, she assured me that what she was doing was different. In her mind, she was keeping order and threatening only those who appeared to be intimidating or otherwise irritating to her friends. To Jenny, this meant she was doing the right thing.

GANGS

Jenny revealed that she was interested in knowing people in gangs. Like Sally (Chapter Three), she was enamored of the "Bloods" because

like, they're always there for you. … Like, I watched this show "Geraldo." There's like six of them, girls that belong to gangs and mom says, "You admire them, don't you?" I go, "Yeah, I do." Like, they're always there for you, like if you need something. … They're tough. They're all pretty, too. Everybody's scared of them. … I like it when people are scared of me. It just makes me feel good. I feel like, "Oh, finally someone's scared of me."

Jenny believed that if she were to join a gang, she would be forever safe from attack. Then, she would not only have herself to depend upon, she would have the gang. The attraction was not so much the gang itself, but rather the safety she thought the gang would provide. However, Jenny was clear that if joining a gang meant either upsetting or losing her friends, she would forgo seeking out a gang to join.

I asked about her attraction to the six gang girls displayed on the talk show she had seen. I wondered if Jenny wanted to be like them. Her answer was illuminating:

> I admired them, but I didn't really like them … because they were bad, and they were all dumb. There was this one girl, she was 13. I'm older than her and she looked like she was 17 and … it seemed like she could only say three words, "Fuck you, you're a fucking bitch," like three or four words, and she couldn't say anything else. And none of them were in school. But this one girl, I admire out of them all because she was getting out of the gang. She's got a baby. She's 15 and her boyfriend is in the gang as well. He's leaving and they're in school so they can get a job. It's like I want an education. I want a good job, I just don't know what I want to be … .

Goals and aspirations
Although friends, fighting, and being tough and powerful were most important to Jenny, she also placed some value upon school. She stated that she didn't think that she would drop out of school before completing grade 12, despite the fact that she dislikes school. But Jenny's main focus with regard to the future is not on further training or education; it is on getting married:

> I wanted to be an airline stewardess, but that changed. I don't want to do that because I love traveling, but I got to thinking that if I have to travel, I can't have a husband and kids. I plan to have a husband and have kids and get a job, a good paying job. … I want to get married when I'm 20 and have two kids, a boy and a girl, and I plan to stay with all my friends that I have now. … I don't want to go to university. I don't like school that much, I wouldn't be able to take it. … Some teachers told me I could be a cop because I've already experienced everything so I'd understand, but I don't like police at all. … I won't be able to be a teacher … , it's just I don't like kids, 'cause like I have a bad temper sometimes, but I can be a counselor, 'cause of this fighting and everything, I'll be able to help other kids that's fighting. … I'd probably be against it later on, but right now, I like it … .

Thus, although Jenny envisions a very traditional future, for the moment, fighting and its associated perquisites take precedence over anything else.

Death
Along with her interest in gangs and fighting, Jenny also has a fascination for death. When I asked about the violence associated with most gangs, she told me that violence wasn't an issue:

[It] doesn't bother me, like my mother thinks there's something wrong with me 'cause I'm so into death. I'm very much into death. When we're moving into my grandma's house, she goes, "What color do you want your room?" I go, "Black, what other color?" She goes, "Fine." So I got black walls, carpet, absolutely everything I own is black. I'm getting rid of all my stuff that's not black. I sit and draw crosses that are black and I draw so that they're bleeding. Like I sit in class and I write about death. Once in a while, I'll have the devil's star. I don't worship the devil, but like, I like believing in the devil more than I believe in God because there's something evil, I don't know. ... I know about this stuff because I read a book called *Michelle Remembers* [a psychiatrist's account of ritual abuse], and it was all about the devil and what really got me is my uncle's ex-girlfriend lived in the house where all this stuff happened to [Michelle] when she was five. ... I like knowing what happened. ... I didn't like [the people who abused Michelle] but I like the devil himself. ... I don't know. ... What I don't like about it is if you get possessed, like I watched *The Exorcist* and I go, "Oh my god, I don't want to be possessed by the devil!" I don't know, I just admire death. ... I like the devil. He's evil. He's powerful. He likes killing people. I don't like killing people, but I like death.

When I asked Jenny to tell me what it was about death that interested her, she replied:

It's hard to say, I like it, it's just black, black and someone being dead. You know, like watching TV, like I like horror movies. Sometimes I like the way people die in the movies, like in *The Exorcist*, when she got possessed, she was able to throw people out the windows, so that's what she did. ... It's just I like the devil and evil. ... I don't like God. I don't go to church. It's boring. ... If I was possessed I could sit here and this glass would explode. And I can make just anything happen. Like I admire that. ... I like death and the color black, but I don't like watching "live" someone who is really dying. I cry when someone in my family dies ... .

I was somewhat relieved to hear that Jenny did not want to see an actual death, but I probed further to assure myself that her fascination did not carry with it a plan to harm either herself or someone else. Jenny was clear that she did not want to kill anyone. She was also clear that she herself did not want to die, but she had considered suicide:

I don't want to go, it makes me sad, but I did. Like, I don't know, like I thought about ways I could and I know that if I ever wanted to I know how to do it. But I don't like pain. I wouldn't be able to stab myself or like shoot myself, I wouldn't be able to stand the pain. I was thinking about doing that last year. My friend and I were sitting and talking about ways that we could kill ourselves. Like she was really into it. She still is. She's like one of those people who, "Oh yeah, I'll slit my wrist and my throat." I'm like, Oh, I wouldn't be able to stand the pain. ... She's weird. She's unhappy. She doesn't like herself. ... She's overweight. ... She thinks she's ugly because she's fat. She doesn't really like herself, and she has weird ways of doing things.

Ways of belonging

Jenny's reflections on death and suicide prompted me to check again to see how she felt about herself. Again, she told me that she was ugly and fat, but that she felt good about herself for now because she has a boyfriend and is getting a great deal of attention from boys. When I asked Jenny about how she felt about being a girl, she replied,

> It's hard, just because everybody's fighting, so like if you don't fight, you're going to get beaten up. Like we [girls] can't do most things. ... I can't box because only guys are allowed to. ... There's so many things you have to do, like watch who you are. If you're not a fighter, and there's a gang, and they don't like you, you can get hurt, so you have to watch your back. Like, I have to watch my back all the time. ... It's hard too because everybody wants to have friends and wants to be cool and if you're not, if you're some sort of geek [it's hard]. And right now, I'm not considered as a geek. If you're not a geek, you can have hundreds of friends, but you have to do a lot to keep them ... .

When I asked Jenny what things she "has to do" to keep friends, she gave as examples the fact that she drinks alcohol to the point of throwing up, and aspires to the current fashion of body piercing and tattooing. Her best friend wants to have her eyebrow, belly button, and nose pierced, while Jenny wants to begin with having only her belly button pierced. Part of the girls' attraction to body piercing is that doing this would be a direct rebellion against their mothers, and there-fore a statement of autonomy and power.

Similarly, both girls wanted to get a tattoo. Jenny envisioned "a black panther that's walking on my shoulder; since I like black, it's going to be black." When I asked Jenny where she got the idea for this tattoo, she told me,

> My dad. He's got a black panther and an eagle, and I admire my dad. He's like, I don't know. ... Like he's very tough. He's not a wimp. If someone's bugging me, he'll go and beat him up.

Thus, getting a tattoo not only signals kinship with her friend; it also signals a connection to her father and to his image of toughness.

In order to identify with a group she can call her own, Jenny calls herself a "Rapper." She embraces rap music and Rapper fashions, as well as the concomitant values of antagonism and hostility towards outsiders. For Jenny, being a Rapper means hanging out primarily with boys, wearing baggy clothes, and listening to music that Jenny describes as

> heavy, with lots of swearing, and some of them say bad things about girls and women like they should be told when they should have a baby and stuff, but some of them don't, and I always listen to that. ... Women are equal. ... I think that women being equal is fair. I don't think it's fair that they can't do certain things. Like I don't think it's fair, there's this boxing club that I'm supposed to join, but they won't let me in because I'm a girl ... . [When they said I couldn't join] I was mad. My uncle's friends with the guy [who runs the boxing club], so he's gonna come out to my house every night... . I'm gonna learn to box ... .

REflECTiNq oN violENCE

Throughout our conversations, Jenny returned again and again to the importance of being able to fight, and seemed unable to see fighting in anything but a positive light. At one point we were discussing this while sitting in the food court of a local mall. Sitting near us was a man with a five- or six-year-old boy. They were laughing and talking, and appeared to be enjoying each other's company. I pointed them out to Jenny just after she had finished telling me about yet another fight she had been in that had made her feel "good" because she won, and because the other person had sustained worse injuries than she had.

I asked Jenny what she saw when she looked at the man and boy sitting at the next table. She saw them as a father and son who were out having a good time together. I asked her next what it might be like if the boy were to be beaten up by someone and had to go home to his father with his face all beaten and bruised, and then I asked how she thought the father might feel upon seeing his son in that state. Suddenly, Jenny dropped her face into her hands. She ran both hands over her face and into her hair, and groaned. Then she looked at me and said:

> Don't ask me to think about that. If you ask me to think about that, I'll have to stop what I'm doing, and I don't want to stop what I'm doing.

Jenny, at the time of our meetings, was unprepared to stop fighting of her own volition.

The last time I saw Jenny she was at her home. She had been suspended from school for participating in two fights in one day. The "main event," a planned battle with a girl who was sometimes her "good" friend, was called by both girls as a way of deciding which of the two had the right to wear certain clothes and go out with a certain boy.

This fight was held in front of a crowd of over 300 students. It was broken up by the principal of Jenny's school with assistance from a male counselor. The two men had driven to the fight as soon as they heard what was going on, and put an end to it as quickly as they could.

The "warm-up" before the main event took place as Jenny made her way to the fight. As she walked along the road to the corner store that was the designated "arena," a car pulled up and another girl, also a rival for the attention of a boy, jumped out and attacked Jenny from behind. Jenny managed to best her and continued on her way in order to fight the agreed-upon battle.

Both Jenny and her opponents were battered and bruised. No charges were laid because it was difficult to decide who was the victim and who was the assailant. Jenny was proud of herself, but she was grounded. Her mother took time off work and stayed home to supervise Jenny. She also went to Jenny's school and returned with a stack of books and homework. When Jenny was finished, she went back for more.

Jenny's mother had decided to take action. She intended to do everything in her power to prevent Jenny from participating in any more fights, and was receiving backing from the school. I gave Jenny and her mother the name of a violence counselor at a local social services agency, along with that of a youth group leader who works with young people who, like Jenny, are moving rapidly towards involvement with the juvenile justice system.

When I left them, Jenny and her mother were making phone calls to the people I suggested. Eventually, Jenny joined the youth group and saw the counselor. While she may still value fighting and toughness, she has not been engaged in a major physical battle since that time.

CHAPTER NINE

Making Sense

> [Young] women, the focus of this [work], develop into social beings in the following sequence. Initially copying other's gestures, the infant girl progresses through play and game stages until she forms a *mind* with the rational ability to understand symbolic gestures. This mind allows her to become an object to herself with the capacity to make moral judgments and decisions on courses of action. Each woman develops in this way a *self* that is reflective and capable of viewing actions from both her own point of view and that of *others*. She is historically located in the community through this learning process, called socialization. (Mead, 1934, cited in Deegan, 1987)

In this chapter, I summarize the key informants' perspectives on themselves and their worlds. I also offer my own analysis of their experience, and outline what I have come to understand about violent girls as a result of this study.

Family Dynamics of the Key Informants

Larson, Goltz, and Hobart state that "Whatever the form, and wherever it is found, the family is the primary source of meaningful relationships from birth to death" (p. 3). The authors offer three basic assumptions that speak to the depth and endurance of familial experience:

1. The family is primarily responsible for the reproduction and nurturant care of children.
2. The family is primarily responsible for the establishment of an individual's social identity, social role and social status.
3. The family is the primary source of intimacy and need fulfillment for the individual throughout the life span. (pp. 3–6)

If we accept these assumptions, the family is the primary matrix for the internalization of social processes, in that the family mediates and interprets the larger social context to its members, particularly its children. The internalization of social processes (noted by Vygotsky, 1978, and Blumer, 1969) is, of course, not limited to the family. But in looking to the family, one may uncover the core social and interpersonal processes by which individuals draw meaning and create a foundation for their perspectives of self, others, and the world.

Through the *Survey of Student Life* (Artz & Riecken, 1994), my colleague and I learned that we could expect violent school girls to live in two-parent families at very much the same rates as non-violent school girls, and that their parents were likely to have about the same level of education and occupation. These findings were borne out by the six key informants, all of whom lived in two-parent families in which both parents worked, and for whom material poverty was not a factor. We also learned that we could expect violent school girls to place less importance on family life than non-violent girls, and that enjoyment of their mothers was less applicable to them than to other students. After hearing my informants' stories, I was able to understand some of the reasons why violent girls may have responded in this way.

In the course of our discussions, my six key informants frequently talked about family. Within the first five minutes of meeting with Molly, Mary, and Linda, they had brought parents, brothers, and sisters into the discussion. Throughout our time together, these girls continued to ponder their own actions and feelings in the light of their experiences with their families. Sally, Marilee, and Jenny also mentioned family members each time we met to talk. Many times, the girls used their parents' behaviors and viewpoints as reference points for their own. Although each girl had her own unique family story to tell, all six had in common an experience of family that included strife and disruption, deep pain and sorrow.

Often, after meeting with the six girls and their parents, I would drive home in a state of grief. At times I was overwhelmed by the conditions of the lives these girls were revealing to me. Despite my 18 years of front-line child and youth care work, and my four years of working with adult women survivors of abuse, and despite the fact that I know well that children are used and abused by their family members and others on a daily basis, the raw immediacy of the stories I was hearing hit me hard.

There was something in the matter-of-fact way in which they recounted their experiences that particularly bothered me, for while they did not shy away from expressing their anger and frustration, they also took it for granted that this is simply the way life is. Basically, they saw their own families as "okay," although they saw the families of others who lived similar lives as "bad." Both the girls and their parents appeared to be looking through a glass darkly and not seeing their own reflections.

The parents

The mothers seemed unable to make the connection between life as lived within the family and their daughters' involvement in violence. They welcomed me into their homes, gave freely of their time, made me cups of coffee, met me for lunch, attended parent forums, chatted with me on the telephone, and told me details about their private lives that in some cases, they had not shared with anyone else. They wanted to help me to "do something" about youth violence, and I believe they were sincere in that desire. They were committed to the project, as were their daughters, but what they seemed unable to do was to look inward for the answers.

Perhaps the greatest source of my grief was that I saw families in deep trouble, families with multiple and serious problems, who were constructing life worlds and ways of dealing with life that transmitted to their daughters ways of being and doing that did not and could not serve them well. And while these families were engaging in this sad and sorry game of "pass it on," they were also looking around for someone to blame and punish for youth violence. The Young Offenders Act, the Ministry of Social Services, the schools, adolescence itself and hormones, other families — all were candidates for the role of chief culprit. And while they looked elsewhere, I looked to them, not so much as culprits, but as the place to start the work. And as I looked to them, I wondered where one could begin.

My answer to myself was, "Begin at the beginning." The beginning, as I saw it, was the parents' families of origin. In this respect, I have data from Marilee, Mary, and Jenny that are quite similar. They each have fathers who come from families who threw them out at an early age after subjecting them to physical abuse and other effects of parental alcoholism. These three men spent time living on the streets, surviving by dint of hard physical labor and the willingness to use their fists. They got married early in life, around the age of 20 or 21, to women as young as themselves or younger. The women they married (or who married them) also share similar backgrounds.

Two of these women (Mary's and Jenny's mothers) understood that they themselves had been silenced and undervalued as they grew up. Mary's mother describes her father, an educated man with a PhD, as a domineering individual who gave her very clear messages about the unimportance of women and women's ideas and who, to this day, believes that women should be led by the men they are there to serve.

Mary's mother articulated her experiences:

> When it came to getting a college or a university education, my dad just said things like, "You can't" and "Girls can't do this" and messages like, "Look after your man"-type messages instead of "Look after yourself"-type messages.... . And I had a hard time talking because I was always scared of people judging me and giving me a hard time. I guess my parents are very judgmental people. You know, whatever you say, you get judged on, instead of being okay.

Jenny's mother described herself as feeling unhappy and invisible as she grew up:

> I was the one daughter, middle child, with an older brother and a younger brother. And my parents were geared towards sports, men's sports, hunting, and I'm not. I didn't really have much to contribute to any conversation. My brothers and my dad, they worked the same type of job, so they had all those things in common. So when I was growing up, I always felt I had nothing to contribute, so I didn't need to say anything. I didn't need to be in the same room ... . I always felt out of place because I'm different; I think I'm different from my family.

The silencing and devaluing at the hands of, and in the name of, men that these women describe is not unlike Linda's account of her mother's experience: "holding everything in until it hurts her" in order to avoid her husband's wrath. It also ties in with Sally's mother's struggle with what she calls her co-dependency, that is, her well-ingrained habit of putting others' (particularly men's) feelings and needs before her own, and her propensity to arrange her life and that of her family to satisfy the demands of her partner (witness her battle with her husband and ex-husband over Sally's school plans). Consistent with the survey findings cited in Chapter Two, namely, that violent girls reported the highest levels of concern about the unequal treatment of women, the key informants were worried about their mothers.

The fathers in each of these families behave in ways that destroy family harmony. Sally's stepfather enters into a sibling rivalry with her out of which come shouting matches that cause the neighbors to call the police. Marilee's father drinks, gets angry, and hits his wife and daughters. Molly's father uses physical force to control his sons, and his sons live out the dominance message in a number of ways, including sexual abuse. Mary's father regularly physically abuses his children. Linda's father rules his household with intimidation and physical abuse. Jenny's grandfather and uncle engage in physical violence, while her father models intimidation in his approach to Jenny's rivals in the community.

In some cases, the mothers fight back. Mary's mother engages in daily battles with her husband over her rights and the rights of her children. Sometimes she uses physical force to restrain her husband's violence; sometimes she uses it to make her point outside the family. Jenny's mother is no longer silent, and where her husband and her daughters are concerned, expresses her views loudly and clearly, as do Molly's and Marilee's mothers. Jenny's mother also engages in verbal battles and even pushing-and-shoving matches with Jenny's friends. Sally's mother does what she can to "make" her husband and her daughter fight less. Sometimes she accomplishes this by yelling and screaming at them. And while the mothers may yell and scream, the effect of this is only momentary, especially where their husbands are concerned. With their husbands, the mothers of the key informants appear to be committed to fighting the same battles over and over again. Linda's mother still maintains a guarded silence, and has been willing to do this for many years.

All these couples, with the exception of Sally's parents, have been married for between 16 and 26 years. All profess a strong commitment to marriage and family, for while Sally's mother and father have been divorced, they have each sought out other partners with whom they intend to remain. When I discussed this with the mothers, they let me know that they were proud of having stayed married for so many years. They interpreted the fact that they had not divorced as a strong indicator that their families were good families. In fact, several mothers told me that they were mystified by their daughter's behavior because after all, mom and dad were still together.

Typically, these women act as both wife and mother to their husbands. In the role of wife, they remain subordinate even while attempting to fight for equality because, despite their considerable efforts, nothing really changes. In the role of mother-to-their-husbands, they admonish and lecture and attempt to teach, they make rules and give ultimatums, and they punish. They also demand that their children behave in ways that won't upset their oldest "man-child." For while they fight for equality on the one hand, they help to maintain their subordinate positions on the other, by assuming responsibility for the family's climate of feeling, specifically the emotional states of their husbands.

Sally's mother's struggle with her "co-dependency" is a good example of this. Although she fights to get free of mothering her husband by managing his emotional world for him, she is unable to understand her own experiences without reference to her "co-dependent" label. Thus encumbered, she is unsure of just how to respond to the inequities around her. Each move she makes must be second-guessed in the light of her "co-dependent" problems: whether to counsel her daughter, even when she intuitively senses trouble on the horizon; whether to entreat her husband and daughter to avoid antagonizing each other; whether to hold the police accountable for following through on the charges laid against her daughter's assailant. Everything she does is colored by the possibility that she may be doing it solely because she is "co-dependent." Thus, wavering and inaction keep her tied to precisely the behavior she is working so hard to change.

THE MEANING OF INTIMACY

Despite the obvious tension and conflict apparent in all these families, both the mothers of the key informants and their daughters believe they have good families because all family members are "close." In the course of our interviews, I came to recognize that, in the life-worlds of the key informants, being "close" means being deeply emotionally enmeshed, especially in a destructive way. That is, the more family members felt one another's feelings, took on one another's battles, engaged in knowing one another's business, told one another what to do, and attempted to exert control over one another's behavior, the "closer" they were.

In these families, one mark of "closeness" is knowing something about a family member that no one else knows. Thus, to share a secret, or to know the latest family gossip and to team up in an effort to control another's life, makes two people "close." Further, being "close" is often equated with having the right to place demands or expectations on one another. For example, when Mary described herself as close to her brother, she meant she had special privileges with regard to him that gave her first call on his time and attention; in other words, she owned a part of him.

Closeness also extends to exerting strong influence over others' mental, physical, and emotional states. Thus, Jenny's parents and grandparents believe that Jenny made her mother physically ill; Mary's father believes that his children are responsible for his stress, and sees them as the cause of injuries that he suffers while doing things for them; and Molly's mother measures her family's emotional health according to the state of her own feelings. Finally, being close in these families does *not* mean understanding and accepting family members on their own terms, while making an effort to respect and value their unique contributions. Closeness does *not* extend to attempting to understand why people do what they do. Instead, it means that one expects other people to be as much like oneself as possible.

In fact, the state of being close (which is really the state of being the-same-as) is strongly connected to the state of being right and good. Individual differences are not applauded; they are seen as threats to connectedness and goodness. When differences exist, closeness is withheld; family members are rejected, ejected, and excluded, sometimes for many years. A refined individuation of self and other is largely absent here. Closeness is not based in an understanding of individual differences, nor is it based on an acceptance of the kind of mutual independence that ultimately leads to secure notions of relatedness and the possibility of truly loving others for themselves. Instead, it is based on rigid notions of self and others that demand conformity.

Conflict and its resolution

Often, violation of the expectations that arise out of closeness lead to conflict. Conflict very quickly becomes vehement and ugly, and frequently includes physical as well as emotional violence, largely because the perspective in which righteous action is grounded is one that endorses the use of power over others and construes others as the source and cause of one's feelings.

Power in these families is anchored in two things: (a) physical might, and (b) the right to determine and enforce rigidly held rules (and one's own point of view). This right is usually tied to one's role in the family. Roles are hierarchically arranged with fathers at the top, mothers a distant second, and children at the bottom, in descending order according to age.

Fathers can delegate disciplinary duties within the household to mothers, which is the case in both Jenny's and Sally's families. So, for example, when Jenny's mother struggles with Jenny, she engages on the following grounds: (a) because she believes that when she is frustrated with Jenny it is because of something Jenny has done to her (emotional enmeshment); and (b) because she sees it as her job to enforce the household rules, which Jenny is violating. These rules are largely premised on absolute and hierarchical notions of power, such as: "I'm your mother; therefore you do what I say," or, "as long as you're under my roof, I'll call the shots." Therefore, if Jenny does not uphold the rules (behavior that always somehow hurts or offends the rule maker), Jenny is wrong and bad, and deserves to be punished.

In Jenny's family, given the personalizing of all offenses, punishment involves personal rejection which, in its ultimate form, means getting thrown out — out of the house or, in some cases, out of the family. Mary's father proceeds in a similar fashion. If his children displease him, he sees them as the source of his frustration and anger and believes himself to be perfectly justified in yelling at them and pushing them around or beating them if they dare to answer back. When his anger reaches its pinnacle, he threatens to desert his family, or to eject the designated offender, as he did his son. If Molly's mother feels angry or frustrated, she takes this as a signal that something is wrong in the family and goes looking for the source of her frustration among her children. In Marilee's family, the rules are well known: One either upholds them or gets out. Linda's father takes for himself the right to decide what is right and wrong and who deserves punishment, and enforces his views with the aid of belts and sticks. Sally's stepfather yells and screams to make his point. Sally's mother, while somewhat milder than the rest, uses her anger to make her family members behave. All this enforcement involves the use of rough and foul language. People call one another assholes, jerks, and idiots. Girls and women are whores and sluts. Family members tell one another that they are stupid and worthless. The general tone created by the use of such crude language is punitive and judgmental in the extreme.

When conflict arises, resolution is achieved by first establishing the identity of the offender. The offender is relatively easy to find; she is usually the one who has broken the rules and "made" the offended person feel frustrated and angry. When the identity of the culprit has been established, she is then judged and blamed, and held responsible for the offended person's feelings and those of anyone else who has taken the offended person's part. This makes the offender fair game for punishment at the hands of the offended person and his or her allies.

Punishment involves calling the offender names, screaming at her, and (if the offended person is not yet satisfied) pushing the offender around or punching her. The type of punishment and its duration is decided upon by the offended person, and is directly tied to that individual's personal sense of satisfaction. When the offended person is satisfied that punishment has been carried out, order has been restored, and the problem is — for the moment — resolved.

The use of physical and emotional violence is justified on instrumental grounds: Violence is used as a means to stop or control those who are upsetting the person who applies it. Nothing has changed, however, because source and problem have been collapsed into one. The source of the problematic behavior has been punished, but the problem itself (usually a behavior) has not been addressed. No new approaches or strategies have been discussed, negotiated, or modeled. No distinction is made between person and behavior. The message being delivered loudly and clearly is that the offender behaves badly because she *is* bad.

This person-based badness makes the offender deserving of punishment which is specifically aimed at her personhood, that is, punishment that is purposefully designed to hurt and degrade the offender. Acts are overlooked because the focus is on actors. Behavioral alternatives are not considered, because only differences in states of feeling are entertained. Thus, people are not asked to consider different courses of action; they are asked to *be* different people. In the end, people don't really change what they do; they just get better at hiding it and, most of all, at hiding themselves.

Messages conveyed

What, then, do these families offer their daughters as a base for forming interpretations of self and world? What has been conveyed to these girls about men and women, power, relationships, attachment, feelings, conflict, rules, punishment, and most of all, themselves?

They have seen that men are far more important and more powerful than women, and that men's importance is not connected to the contributions they make to the greater good. Rather, it is bound up in their being stronger and more forceful than women. Thus, they have seen that power resides for the most part in physical force, that right is tied to might, and that rules have their source in those who have the power to impose them.

Where relationships are concerned, they have seen that pride is taken in the duration of relationships rather than in their quality, and that relationships are based upon roles rather than the development of mutual understanding. Thus, one stays married simply because one is a wife; one loves one's child simply because she is one's daughter. In this way, these girls have seen their parents partake of relationships that last for many years, yet bring with them continuous cycles of abuse and pain, and in which role-bound behavior never shifts. They have seen that being "close" means having no personal boundaries, that closeness demands sameness and does not tolerate deviation from the narrow confines of being like the person to whom one is close. Further, this closeness also demands the ability to anticipate the needs and wants of others and the ability to feel another's feelings.

They have seen that feelings are caused by forces outside themselves and arise because of what others do; thus, feelings must be controlled through controlling others. They have seen that conflict arises out of creating destructive feelings in others, feelings for which the offending person is solely responsible, and which justify the offended person's wrath. They have seen that when wrath has been aroused, punishment must follow, a punishment that is administered in a fit of rage and is designed to maximize the pain of the offending person.

As indicated by the self-report data generated by the *Survey of Student Life* (Artz & Riecken, 1994), violent girls reported the highest rates of fear of, and experience with, physical abuse. Physical and emotional abuse were certainly facts of life for the key informants. All had been beaten at home, and had witnessed the beating of other family members. The implicit message conveyed to them here is that when someone behaves badly, it is because he or she is bad.

This sense of badness is intensified by the shared language of these interactions. The message that speaks to the badness of the offender is delivered with tones of voice and gestures that underline the worthlessness of the offender, while the labels and judgments that are being hurled at her make clear exactly how she is being construed. "Look what you've done to your mother, you fucking little whore!" leaves little room for doubt.

How are these interactions translated into notions of self and world?

Experiences of Self

Each of the key informants left me with a unique impression of how she saw herself. Sally presented herself as a "Skate," a member of a recognizable street group, and as an individual enamored with being "weird, original, and different," someone who loves attention and enjoys provoking shocked reactions in other people. Marilee presented herself as one very much involved in trying to be "the person she is supposed to be," someone who plans to break the cycle of family violence through creating a traditional and harmonious, "white-picket fence" future for herself. Molly described herself mostly as confused and stressed by her experiences with abuse. Mary saw herself as the champion of just causes and defender of the underdog, a person who takes charge and takes people on. Linda saw herself as struggling to overcome her experiences with sexual abuse. Jenny presented herself as a person who loves to fight and is intrigued by death.

Although each girl's self-image was unique, each of the six had a great deal in common with the other five, whether they happened to be opponents or allies. Each had come forward as a participant in the study first of all because she had identified herself as a victim of female-to-female violence. After some discussion, each participant also emerged as a perpetrator, an individual as experienced with threatening, intimidating, and beating others as she was with being attacked. The key informants' self-reports with regard to participation in violence and victimization fit with the data generated by the *Survey of Student Life* (Artz & Riecken, 1994) in that they, like the violent girls who participated in the survey, were both perpetrators and victims.

ANGER

As a group, the key informants presented themselves as tough and street-wise, knowledgeable about and connected with most aspects of youth violence in their community, and willing to take on those who dared to question their carefully crafted images of power. They also shared a deeply felt anger which at times turned into rage, even hate; and they shared a painful sense of loneliness and abandonment.

As the girls discussed their anger, I saw a strong connection with the physical and emotional abuse they suffered at home, and in Jenny's case, also with the bullying and degradation she experienced while in elementary school. I also saw a strong connection with the sexual abuse that five of the six suffered at the hands of someone they knew and trusted. Their loneliness and abandonment — exemplified through Sally's and Jenny's search for connectedness and belonging in groups like the Skates and the Rappers, Mary's notion of herself as "an outcasted little person," Linda's isolation from her family, Molly's unfulfilled need to be safe and understood in her own home, and Marilee's view of the world as a "piece of shit" — seem to be tied, in large part, to the same experiences that engender the key informants' anger. Having been violated physically, emotionally, and in some cases also sexually, the key informants seemed to have little hope that they could trust even those closest to them.

Fear

Even when the girls thought that they could depend upon their families (as Jenny did when she expressed the belief that her father and grandfather would protect and defend her, or take retaliatory action if someone hurt her), they seemed unable to let their guard down for any length of time. Her family's support did not exempt Jenny from feeling that she must always "watch her back," and from hoping to find refuge in a local gang.

The notion of having to "watch one's back" was one that also affected the other informants: Marilee feared leaving her own neighborhood to go downtown or to school; she feared being exposed as a "narc" because she had talked to me. Similar fear showed itself in Mary's offensive and belligerent approach to adult authority figures. It also came out in the generally defensive way in which all six girls positioned themselves in relation to those around them.

Self-worth

Despite describing themselves as tough and powerful, the key informants also saw themselves as lacking worth in their own eyes and in the eyes of others.

Jenny described herself as "fat and ugly"; Marilee felt herself to be one of the "scummy" people who aligned herself with "losers." Linda, in the aftermath of her sexual abuse, thought of herself as a "bad person," bad-tempered and deserving of the abuse she received at the hands of her father. Mary felt she was not liked by her teachers and was stereotyped as a "bad kid" by the vice-principal of her school. Though she sometimes felt responsible for her father's problems, she was also keenly aware that he considered her less important and less able because she is a girl.

Sally, in her persona as a Skate, saw herself as a member of a group of outcasts, people who are generally singled out by others, especially

Rappers, as targets for aggression. She also felt ignored by her parents and rejected and disliked by her stepmother. Molly, who struggled with the designation of "slut" after being sexually abused while drunk at a party, described herself as having no morals and as being somehow hurtful to her family because she disclosed that she had been sexually abused by her brother.

Although the *Survey of Student Life* (Artz & Riecken, 1994) indicated that self-concept was not necessarily connected to participation in violence, the descriptions of self offered by the key informants left no doubt that their self-concept was tied to a sense of worthlessness.

This sense of worthlessness became even more clear when they talked about their bodies. In describing how they believed they should look, the key informants endorsed the standard for beauty identified and questioned by Wolf (1990) as a "mass disseminated physical ideal" which holds up the "gaunt youthful model" as the example of what all women must embody in order to have personal and social worth (pp. 11–12). Each girl saw herself through the eyes of those who might be looking at her and judged herself according to that mass disseminated ideal.

None of the key informants believed that she measured up. Instead, each believed that she was constantly in competition with other girls and, most of all, with the examples of ideal womanhood created by the entertainment and fashion industries. All the informants felt great pressure to be "thin and perfect."

The general acceptance that girls should be thin was indicated in the *Survey of Student Life* (Artz & Riecken, 1994) by the significant number of girls who reported stopping themselves from eating. Sally put it most clearly when she said that in her world, most boys and many girls believe that all young women should look like supermodel Cindy Crawford, "who is underweight, and has like a perfect body." Jenny, in describing her struggle with being bullied for being fat and her subsequent refusal to eat, made clear how difficult and painful nonconformity to socially sanctioned standards of female beauty can be. Marilee was so focused on competition from other females that she deliberately chose friends whom she considered not competitive, that is, not as attractive as herself.

All the key informants looked to males for acceptance and confirmation of their worth. For Jenny and Marilee, confirmation came from having a boyfriend. Jenny, in particular, placed a great deal of importance upon being sought after by boys, and was happy with herself only when receiving attention from males. Sally's confirmation of worth came from being accepted by male Skaters as more than a mere "poser." For Mary and Linda, confirmation was very much tied to acknowledgment from their fathers, something that they experienced only rarely. Molly's confirmation of worth came from being protected by her older brother — the same person who abused her.

Goals and aspirations

The desire for acceptance and acknowledgment from males is also revealed in the key informants' plans for the future. Their aspirations are very traditional: They want to get married and raise children, even though they have strong fears (even revulsion) with respect to pregnancy and childbirth. They have no career plans and no goals or plans for further education beyond finishing high school. They want to get jobs that are merely jobs — that is, a way of making money, seen as a means to achieve their central goal of marriage. Marilee and Jenny are so certain of marriage and children that they have made choices with these goals in mind, and thus, behave in very male-focused ways.

Growing up female

Overall, despite their desire and their efforts, positive acknowledgment from males is not a common experience for the key informants. Mostly, they see themselves as being discriminated against because of being female.

Sally spoke of being excluded from certain aspects of skateboarding and snowboarding because of being female. Jenny lamented being barred from boxing for the same reason. Mary talked about not being considered an able helper in her father's construction business, despite having demonstrated both skill and reliability, merely because she was female. She also talked of her extended workday serving her father and her brother and attending to all the domestic chores, including the care of the family's animals. Mary, Marilee, and Linda also described being emotionally and physically abused by their fathers. In general, in each of the key informants' households, the orientation is not one of equality and respect for women, but rather, the opposite.

Consistent with the significantly high levels of reported sexual abuse among violent girls generated by the *Survey of Student Life* (Artz & Riecken, 1994), all six key informants have received sexually abusive messages and sexually harassing or abusive treatment from males that "made them feel low." The degradation they experienced as part of being female was graphically illustrated by the examples they gave of sexual harassment at school (see Chapter Five, "Molly's Story"). Everyday life for them meant running a gauntlet of staring eyes, groping hands, and derogatory comments about their bodies. Although they despised such treatment, they saw it as an integral and inevitable part of being female. Similarly, they saw the males' behavior as so much a part of being male that they explained it (to themselves and to me) as being caused by hormones — physical urges beyond the control of the offensive boys.

As the key informants see it, there is nothing particularly positive about being female. A girl has to be vigilant about staying thin; she is restricted with regard to the kinds of activities she can undertake; she is less respected and less important than a boy. She is routinely subjected to sexual discrimination and harassment. If she attempts to take the initiative or experiment sexually, she is a "slut" and deserves a beating. If a woman has children, she faces a great deal of pain, and if her husband is present to see the "mess," she risks losing him because, through pregnancy and childbirth, her body becomes unattractive.

Role models

The notion that women achieve their greatest importance when they command attention from males was elaborated in the key informants' choice of role models. Sally, Marilee, Molly, Linda, and Jenny all named Madonna as their number one female idol. The reason they each gave was best expressed by Sally: "She can do anything she wants and not care what anybody thinks of her."

Yet, Madonna's power and freedom rest on her ability to capitalize on the sexual double standard. She derives her position primarily from displaying herself sexually, from "holding onto the sustained mass patriarchal gaze for as long as she can keep the public's attention" (hooks, 1994, p. 12). Far from being a symbol of female power and creativity, Madonna has played into exactly those images and values that serve to underline women's roles as sexual objects. She has become a major link in what hooks (1994) describes as "the marketing chain that exploits representations of sexuality and the body for profit, a chain which focuses on images that were once taboo," a chain aimed directly at those conventional consumers of pornography, men (pp. 14–15).

The role that Madonna offers to women is that of the classic whore. The joke is in her name, though I doubt that the girls who participated in this study understood this. They see her as powerful because she can get away with behavior that they can't. If they acted like her, someone — probably a group of girls — would beat them up. They see her as being able outdo all other women and attract the desiring gaze of millions of men, with no one to beat her at her game.

I feel my key informants missed the point here, because they failed to recognize Madonna's extreme dependence. They also missed the significance of her violent marriage to Sean Penn. Further, they missed the ignorance, and the danger and hate for females in Madonna's statement about male violence against women: "I think for the most part if women are in an abusive relationship and they know it and if they stay in it they must be digging it" (hooks, 1994, p. 17). Far from offering women freedom and power, Madonna offers them the most standard form of enslavement that exists for women.

Of the six key informants, only Mary did not completely accept all of the above. She believed that "sluts" deserved to be beaten; she accepted that males could and would treat females in demeaning ways. But she did not want to be like Madonna. She had given up on being thin and sexy and on attracting male attention through conforming to what, for her, were standards of beauty that were impossible to achieve. Instead, she concentrated on getting her father's attention through proving to him that she was as good as any male. She focused on correcting her father's behavior and making him over into the kind of man to whom she could relate. She saw nothing intrinsically useful or valuable in being female. She found value in emulating males, and described herself proudly as a tomboy. She did not understand that being one of the boys offers girls no autonomous value at all.

Oppressed group behavior and horizontal violence

In according women and girls so little intrinsic value, and particularly in selecting as targets for female-to-female violence girls whom they see as having lost all worth (because they appear to be sexually accessible), the key informants seem to be exhibiting what Roberts (1983; after Friere, 1971) calls "oppressed group behavior." Such behavior is premised upon an "attitude of adhesion to the oppressor" (Friere, 1971, p. 30), which demands that those who suffer at the hands of the dominant group turn upon members of their own kind whenever they behave in ways that are deemed unacceptable to the dominant group.

Because all standards and roles are prescribed by the dominant group, the subordinate group's greatest hope lies in achieving dominant-group standards and fully enacting the roles assigned to them. At the same time, another possibility is held out to the subordinate group: If their members could but emulate the dominant group well enough, they might be offered acceptance by it; perhaps even membership in it. (This is the approach Mary has taken.)

In the world in general, and in the life-worlds of the key informants in particular, males are the dominant, women the subordinate group. Further, as members of a subgroup of girls who come from homes where women are given even less value than usual, these six girls and others like them are yet more vulnerable to the internalization of oppressed group behavior. It is not surprising that they think of girls and women as they do. In accepting without question that girls and women must submit themselves to the needs and expectations of boys and men, the key informants make manifest the values that permeate their lives and engage in behavior that is characteristic of oppressed groups. Specifically, in the hope of gaining a measure of power, they engage in "horizontal violence" — that is, they beat each other up.

Roberts (1983) shows that such behavior does nothing more than support the status quo. Noting that leaders of powerless groups are generally controlling, coercive, and rigid, and that members of oppressed groups often spend most of their aggressive energy in hurting one another, Roberts (1983) suggests that such horizontal violence is a safe way to release tension: The threat posed by members of one's own group is never as great as that posed by the dominant group. When aggression is directed at members of the dominant group, little changes. Subordinate-group members can never fully assimilate, since they will always be members of the group to which they were, by definition, originally assigned.

Obviously, a girl or woman can never be a boy or a man, no matter how much she assumes the characteristics of males. In fact, too much emulation puts a girl or woman in danger of losing any kind of group membership and with it, any chance of belonging. Too much emulation leads to marginalization, the inability to belong either to one's group of origin (because one has assimilated so many characteristics of the dominant group) or to the dominant group (because of one's origins). Thus relegated to the fringes, a marginalized person has nowhere to go except to those who are similarly marginalized (Roberts, 1983). It is no accident that the six key informants are so well known to one another.

Friends and Friendship

The low value the six key informants placed upon women and girls also came through, in part, as they discussed their friends and their notions of friendship. Although all seemed to place importance upon friendship and all believed they should fight to defend their friends (another finding of the *Survey of Student Life* [Artz & Riecken, 1994]), their friendships with other girls were tenuous relationships that tended to shift over time. In some cases, these were alliances made on the basis of having a common female enemy rather than a genuine bond based on care and trust.

Each girl described a relationship with a "best friend" that involved ambivalence and conflict. Sally described her friendship with Adel, who betrayed her, as a close friendship, but one that involved loving to see each other get pushed around. Although Marilee considered that her friendship with Sarah required her to help Sarah beat up Sally, she also saw it as a relationship she didn't really want to bother with, one that she continued largely because Sarah was a good source of information about boys. In Mary's friendship with Cathy (the girl who beat up Molly), she saw herself as the one who prevented Cathy from descending further into violence, yet she herself was prepared to use violence against Cathy. Mary was also prepared to use violence against Tanya, her closest female friend. In Jenny's friendships, girls shifted from being enemies to friends and back again as they competed for male attention. This theme was mirrored in Marilee's friendships with girls.

During the time I spent meeting with Molly, Linda, and Mary as a group, I witnessed some of these shifts in allegiance. When Molly, despite swearing an oath of confidentiality to Linda and Mary, broke that oath and disclosed Linda's history of sexual abuse to others, she sacrificed Linda to her own immediate need for attention. Linda and Mary then banded together with Molly as their common enemy. Later, when Linda excluded Mary from a social outing, Mary became angry and was Linda's enemy for a time.

Mary was also "best friends" with Faye and Brent, yet cut her ties with both when they became friends with each other. While Mary was struggling with the changes in these dynamics, she phoned me several times to discuss her feelings of anger and loneliness. She wrestled with the question of whether she should beat up Faye, finally deciding against this, largely because I insisted that beating someone up was not a viable method for resolving a dispute. She, in turn, made it clear to me that refraining from violence, at least in this case, carried a high price for her: It meant that she would have to forego the cathartic experience of unleashing her anger against her friend and "letting her have what she deserved." Consistent with the notion that connections with boys are of greater value than connections with girls, Mary ultimately placed more importance on her friendship with Brent. Although she cut her ties with him as she did with Faye, it was the loss of her friendship with Brent that Mary mourned.

Sally's friendships with Beverley and Lorraine (the other two "beastie girls") were not as subject to the shifts in alliance that characterized most of the key informants' relationships. What struck me about this group of friends, however, was the underlying sense of isolation, especially from family, that brought these three together. In seeking one another out, and in seeking out groups like the Skates, the Rappers, and the Bloods, Sally and her friends seemed to be looking for somewhere to belong.

What the key informants sought from their affiliation with a group was attention and a sense that they had worth in other people's eyes, a feeling of safety, an identity, and a surrogate family. Further, they were willing to put themselves at considerable risk in order to achieve this.

Social Activities

The groups the key informants sought out engage in risky and potentially harmful behaviors. Drugs and alcohol are regularly misused, violence is a pastime as well as a means to an end, sex is largely akin to sexual abuse, and danger is glamorized.

The six key informants and their friends gather at corner stores, Seven-Eleven convenience markets, fast-food restaurants, shopping malls, and school yards. The main attraction of these public venues is other people and the possibility of excitement, any kind of excitement.

In imitating the Beastie Boys, Sally and her friends regularly take chances. They engage strangers on street corners in order to try to provoke some kind of action or reaction. Sally's romantic notions about gangs as safe havens and gang members as friendly people make her vulnerable to being drawn into activities that involve harm to herself and others. The same is true of Jenny, who referred to gangs with the same enthrallment that Sally did. Marilee is similarly attracted to people who participate in deviant and criminal activities, such as the "friend" who committed a drive-by shooting. These girls seemed to value the notoriety that they believed rubbed off on them as a consequence of knowing someone "really bad."

The *Survey of Student Life* (Artz & Riecken, 1994) indicated that violent school girls and boys considered parties of great importance, and parties were indeed very important to all the key informants. Mary's idea of a "really good time" was an all-night party at which 20 to 30 young people got together to drink and do drugs without interruption. At such parties (which happen almost every weekend at houses where the parents are away, or at the beach, or in some other place chosen for its remoteness from adults), "accidents" happen. People drink so much that they become violently ill, and in some cases, incur alcoholic poisoning. Sexual intercourse takes place in a way that leaves no participant free of the taint of having taken part, voluntarily or otherwise, in a degrading act. People drive cars while "under the influence," harming or killing themselves and others.

The adults involved in the key informants' lives have provided ample modeling of such behavior in that they themselves engage in just such activities. They sometimes provide not only the example but, as in Marilee's and Mary's cases, also the means, by purchasing alcohol for their children. Each of the girls had her first encounter with drunken behavior in her own family.

In all these social interactions one finds an ever-present undercurrent of violence. In fact, violence that seems poised to erupt at any moment is sometimes the focus of social engagement. Thus, fights don't only happen; they are arranged. Factions are formed, audiences gather, violence is orchestrated. As Mary pointed out, fighting is "entertainment sort of, a lot of people want to see somebody get their butt kicked in real life. It's kind of like TV."

Fighting between girls carries added entertainment value; it is, as Molly pointed out, not only physically, but also sexually exciting for the boys. According to Molly (and Mary, Linda, and Jenny, who concurred), boys like to watch girls fight because "it gets them pumped. It gets them excited, not in the physical, in the sexual." Thus — given the key informants' internalized attitudes of adhesion to the oppressor, their propensity for horizontal violence, and their need for attention from males — these girls fight to oblige their confreres.

The Rules of Violence

Besides its entertainment value, the key informants made it clear that for them, violence is not chiefly a matter of lashing out in the heat of the moment. Instead, it is a rule-bound and purposeful activity engaged in to redress the intolerable imbalances they perceive in their largely hierarchical social world. An imbalance usually arises when the rules, which form a kind of code of conduct, have been broken.

For example, when a grade eight girl "mouths off" a grade nine or ten girl, a lower-grade, lower-status girl has attempted to behave in a manner acceptable only for someone with higher status in a higher grade. That is, she is acting "cocky" when she should be subordinate, and thus, may rate a beating. Or, one girl may decide it is her right (usually because she is older or stronger or tougher or prettier or better established) to forbid others to wear certain kinds of clothing, yet another girl may wear those clothes anyway, either in defiance or out of sheer ignorance. In this case, the offending girl should "know better," and is now at risk for attack. Or, a girl has entered territory that is not her turf but is the turf of another girl (perhaps a "gang" girl); she looks the other over (or worse yet, looks at the girl's boyfriend) in a manner that is deemed provocative. Or, a girl has talked to other girls about her interest in a boy already designated as another's boyfriend; she may now be called a "slut" and may receive a beating from her peers.

Some rules, if broken, are sufficient in and of themselves to be construed as provocation to violence. Others need to be broken several times, or in combination, before they constitute cause for retribution. For example, mouthing off an older girl might not be enough cause for an immediate fight, but it will start the meter ticking in the countdown to provocation. Eyeing the wrong boy could start a fight (especially if the offender is dressed in a way that meets with the disapproval of the girl who has claimed the boy being eyed), but then again, it might merit only a strongly worded warning. Provocation, while definitely a rule-bound construct, is also governed to some degree by personal perception and mood (e.g., Mary gave Jenny a second chance, while Linda did not). However, talking about being interested in someone else's boyfriend is a clear violation of the code, an infraction almost certain to lead to the designation of "slut." This insult, in turn, rates highest on the list of possible provocations, and demands immediate redress.

If the rules are broken, girls will set upon each other, usually one-on-one, but often with help from a best friend, who is bound by further aspects of the code to lend such assistance. Others (sometimes as many as 300) will look on without attempting to stop the fight. Spectators too are bound by the code, which dictates their behavior be passive — to the point that few witnesses ever "snitch." The combatants will beat each other mercilessly until one, most often the one who has "brought the beating on herself" by breaking the code, is black and blue with bruises and bloody with cuts, usually to her face. The bruises are simply part of the action; the cuts are deliberate, put there by rings worn expressly as weapons. In the eyes of the assailants, no wrong has been done. Why not? Because (as all the girls I spoke with told me at one point or another) "I never hit anyone unless I have to," and "I only hit people who deserve it." For them, the beatings they dole out are punishment, and the punishment only fits the crime.

Shifting responsibility
This notion that hitting and beating one's chosen victim is the "right thing to do" bears further examination. At various times during our conversations, each of the six key informants told me she was against violence. All participated in the study because they saw themselves as contributors to violence prevention. But all of them also felt completely justified in beating those girls whom they had beaten. Further, in every case, the perpetrator found ways to shift the responsibility for the beating onto the person whom she was beating. None of the key informants found her way to feeling empathy for her victim. As each girl saw it, she was meting out just punishment, "doing the right thing."

In shifting the moral and causal responsibility for their violent action from themselves to their victims, the key informants appeared to recreate their parents' ways of making sense of their own punitive and violent behavior. When lashing out against, berating, and physically beating their daughters, these parents regularly blamed the girls for creating the feelings and behaviors that the parents exhibited. Using the premise "look what you made me do" as justification, the parents (and the key informants themselves) locate the source of their own violence in those whom they attack, and thereby excuse themselves from responsibility for their actions.

In constructing others as deserving of punishment, the key informants always believe that their own actions are both just and inevitable (i.e., determined by their victims). True to symbolic interactionist notions that people "act towards each other and toward things in terms of the meanings that these ... have for them, and these perspectives are the basis for their reality" (Prus, 1994, p. 19), the key informants beat their victims because of the meanings they impute to their victims' behaviors.

This way of making sense of aggressive and violent behavior is reminiscent of Katz's (1988) analysis of the dynamics between interrogator and interrogee in a war zone. Interrogators routinely escalate the amount of physical assault and torture that they visit upon interrogees in the name of "having to" keep up the pressure in order to achieve their goal of procuring the required information. Beginning with the premise that the captured interrogee is undoubtedly somehow connected to the enemy, the interrogator moves forward on what Katz calls the "paths of determinism," which demand that he fulfill his obligation to extract the necessary intelligence. Citing the "Americal Rule" (sic) employed by the U.S. military in Vietnam as an example ("If he wasn't a Vietcong then, he sure as hell is one now"), Katz (1988, p. 6) notes:

> At the start, interrogators were often unsure of the political sympathies of the interrogee, but in the end it did not matter. Either the interrogee was a Vietcong sympathizer or, if not, the eminently dispassionate reasoning went, he was likely to turn hostile after being slapped unjustly. In either case, it was reasonable after a while to consider his failure to cooperate as being motivated by malevolence. At that point, the interrogee's hostility is blocking the progress of the interrogation and thus is provocative: the *interrogee* is giving the *interrogator* a hard time!

Marilee, in making sense of her involvement in beating Sally, used just such a rationale. Citing the determinants that Sally had (a) expressed an interest in Sarah's boyfriend, (b) apparently called

Sarah a "slut" behind her back, and (c) in the course of attempting to resist being beaten, broken one of Marilee's nails and bled onto Sarah's sweater, Marilee construed Sally's behavior as the cause of what followed.

Indeed, each of the key informants, in describing her involvement in physical violence against others, expunged herself of responsibility in the name of being forced to respond as she had because of her victim's behavior. This construction of the victim as the original assailant clearly recalls the reasoning used by the informants' parents when attacking them.

Noticeably absent in this way of viewing victims is the "different voice" — the voice of a morality of care and response to others — described by Gilligan (1983) in her work on the moral development of women and girls. Gilligan and her colleagues (Gilligan, Ward, & Taylor, 1988; Gilligan, Lyons, & Hanmer, 1990; Brown & Gilligan, 1992) have conducted research with students at the Emma Willard School, an independent high school for girls in Boston, from 1981 to 1984, and the Laurel School, an independent coeducational high school in Cleveland, from 1985 to 1989. They have consistently found that adolescent girls are strongly motivated by relational concerns and by a desire to help others — even, on occasion, at the expense of self. Although Gilligan and her colleagues have never made the claim that all girls approach life in this way, they have stated that girls, more than boys, demonstrate the inclination to avoid conflict and understand moral problems in the light of a commitment to the preservation of relationships. They found little evidence of victim blaming and the displacing of moral responsibility from assailant to victim in the way that Katz (1988) and the key informants describe it.

Victim blaming as a phenomenon was not, however, identified by Katz (1988); it was previously recorded and explored by psychologists focusing on moral development. Arbuthnot (1992) points out that nearly all the studies examining moral reasoning of delinquents (male and female) that he reviewed give examples of shifting moral and causal responsibility from assailant to victim in just the manner displayed by the key informants in this study. Basing his analysis on Kohlberg (1969, 1984), Arbuthnot suggests that such moral reasoning is limited and indicative of Stage 1 and Stage 2 (of a possible six stages) of Kohlberg's Stages of Sociomoral Reasoning. These stages are described by Kohlberg as "preconventional" (Colby & Kohlberg, 1987,

p. 18) and circumscribed by a social perspective that is both self-centered and self-serving.

In Kohlberg's terms, in Stage 1 of moral development, an individual exhibits a "heteronomous morality [one that is subject to external controls] which equates right behavior with concrete rules backed by power and punishment" (Arbuthnot, 1992, p. 286). In Stage 2, an individual takes an individualistic utilitarian approach, in which "right behavior is that which serves one's own interests," and one is "aware of others' needs in an elementary fashion, but not of others' rights" (Arbuthnot, 1992, p. 286). Thus, fairness is "strict, rigid, [and] concrete," and "reciprocal agreements are pragmatic" (Arbuthnot, 1992, p. 286).

According to Kohlberg and Colby (1987), one can expect to find a clear relationship between age and stage of moral judgment. For example, one typically finds Stage 1 and Stage 2 moral reasoning at or around age 10. At age 13 to 14, there is usually evidence of a move from Stage 2 to Stage 3, with a concomitant perspectival shift to a "conventional" level of moral reasoning. This implies that the individual is now able to see beyond his or her own immediate needs or desires to the good of the group and, later, the good of society (Colby & Kohlberg, 1987, p. 18). In Stage 3, an individual exhibits the need to be a good person, the desire to care for others, and a belief in the Golden Rule. If such reasoning is not found by the age of 13 or 14, the individual is said to exhibit a developmental delay (Arbuthnot, 1992; Colby & Kohlberg, 1987).

In light of the above, the question then arises: Are we to take the key informants' behavior as the outcome of a symbolic interaction in which they have pursued the "good" by constructing as necessary, though undesirable, the use of violence against someone who has violated or threatened group norms? Or, are we are to take their behavior as the outcome of delayed moral development? The answer to this question is beyond the scope of this study; it is posed as groundwork for further research.

Porter (1991) provides some direction for such an undertaking. She suggests that, by construing moral decisions as the outcomes of underlying developmentally driven cognitive structures, systems such as Kohlberg's fail to take into account both the agency of persons as self-interpreting beings and the personal context of moral dilemmas. It is Porter's contention that if one is to understand moral judgment, one must first of all understand the interpretative, contextual basis of that judgment. To that end, one must engage the interpretative self of those involved and work from there. If one were to engage another person's interpretative self with the notion in mind that this individual suffers from a developmental delay and must therefore be stimulated to mature along appropriate lines, one may foreclose the kind of dialogue that can promote understanding — and with it, change.

Further Dimensions of Violence

Along with the shifting of moral and causal responsibility for their violent actions from themselves to their victims, the key informants share one other similarity with the interrogators described by Katz (1988): They are drawn further into violence by the sensual dimensions of participating in violent behavior.

As Katz (1988) describes it, assailants appear to experience first of all an imperative to attack their victims based on construing the victim as the cause of the aggressor's displeasure. This engenders a heightened sense of excitement and passion, along with a seductive compulsion to engage in violence until that passion is spent. According to Katz, the emotions that seem to be most potent in fueling the assailant's moral righteousness are frustration, humiliation, shame, hurt, and anger, all of which call forth a need to redress a perceived imbalance of power (Katz, 1988, pp. 4–11).

In justifying their involvement in violence, the key informants singled out these same emotions. For them, humiliation especially — that is, being seen to be put down, threatened, or otherwise undercut, either through word or deed — called forth their anger and their need to retaliate. Thus engaged, the assailant's emotions and sensations serve to heighten the conviction that the assailant must act.

In describing what it felt like to engage in violence, the key informants talked about excitement, adrenaline rushes, and the feeling of "getting pumped." They described the anger and rage they felt towards their victims, and the sense of well-being and power they experienced when they had beaten someone up. They mentioned the importance of discharging their anger against the victim who had, after all, caused that anger in the first place.

The emotional quality of their violent interactions can be further understood through attending to the key informants' language.

Describing one's victims as "sluts," "total bitches," "cocky little bitches," "assholes," or "jerks" suggests a unilateral construction of one's opponents as detestable and worthy only of contempt. As I have said elsewhere (Artz, 1994), the words we use are the windows to the worlds in which we live. That is, the words that we choose in order to describe our experience reveal how we have interpreted that experience. This is not a new notion, but one that has been considered and explored by others.[1]

If we listen to the language of the key informants, we can hear echoes of life worlds that are harsh and mean and crude. As Marilee said, "the world is a piece of shit"; or, as Linda and Mary believe, it is a place where one is forlorn and lonely, "outcasted"; and where, as Jenny says, "you've gotta watch your back." This is a graphic indictment of a life-world in which violence and abuse are part of the fabric of everyday life.

Violence in Schools

Schools are sites for everyday violence. Much of the violence in which the key informants were involved took place in school corridors, school yards, on the way to and from school, in front of the corner stores, and in the shopping malls closest to the schools. While schools and school districts don't cause violence, they do provide the ground for the social networks that support it: They draw together all the young people of a certain age in a given area and demand that they operate within a certain set of rules, in a certain building, under the guidance and supervision of a relatively small number of adults.

With few exceptions, most people between the ages of five and 18 go to school. In the province of British Columbia, where this study was undertaken, one cannot legally leave school before the age of 15, and school boards are obliged to provide all students within their jurisdiction with educational programming until they attain that age.

The key informants most often met their victims, and were themselves selected by others as targets, while they were at school. Yet, students alone are not responsible for all school conflict. Educators, administrators, and support staff each make their own contributions to the overall climate, which is on occasion hostile. It may further be argued that structural aspects of the education system, such as graduated grades and the investment of authority and power in educators and administrators (i.e., the older and stronger) over students (i.e., the younger and weaker), become — along with examples set by rigid and controlling parents — models for the rule-bound and hierarchical system the students themselves set up in order to control one another. Within the forced confinement of a school building, human dramas are enacted that necessarily involve rubbing up against other people in ways that are not always optimal or pleasant. Invariably, conflict arises; and when it does, violence is sometimes the result.

In the *Survey of Student Life* (Artz & Riecken, 1994), 28.2% of students (males and females) reported that they agreed with the statement, "If I don't like my teacher, it's okay to act up in school." High-deviant girls, and girls who identified themselves as having beaten up another kid at least once in the past year, reported subscribing to this notion with an agreement rate of 41.9%, while girls who were not in the high-deviant/violent group reported an agreement rate of 11.9%.

The key informants in this study believed that actions from school personnel or other students demanded aggressive and violent reactions whenever they (a) showed the key informants a lack of respect, (b) subjected them to a loss of status or power, or (c) perpetrated an injustice against them. Whether these reactions were directed against their teachers and school administrators or against fellow students is immaterial. For the key informants, violence is not necessarily desirable, but it is necessary. When they resort to it, it is because they perceive that they must.

In the last chapter of this book, I offer some suggestions on how schools may help to change this perception.

NOTES

1.   For example, the philosopher Wilhelm von Humboldt (1767–1835) wrote that, because of the mutual dependency of thought and word, language is not so much a means of representing the truth that has already been ascertained, as it is a means of discovering the truth not previously known (cited in Edwards, 1967, p. 74).

CHAPTER TEN

What Is to Be Done?

What would the ideal program for girls include? There are no easy answers to this particularly since the literature evaluating programs is quite lean, and especially so in regard to programs for girls. Further, a fair number of components of model programs rely on family-strengthening strategies; these need to be reviewed with care, given the gendered nature of family life and girls' special problems within families. (Chesney-Lind & Shelden, 1992, p. 198)

Readers may be disappointed if they expect to learn of many innovative, effective programs. Many evaluations of particular approaches do not deal with gender issues and frequently the evaluated programs do not even serve girls. (Chesney-Lind & Shelden, 1992, p. 183)

What the Key Informants Want

Like the participants in the *Survey of Student Life* (Artz & Riecken, 1994), the key informants of this study place a high value on being respected and liked, and on belonging. They want their parents and their teachers to listen to them and to treat them as if they have value and importance. They want their friends to do the same, and they want their peers — that is, those with whom they interact at school and in their social milieu — to give them what they believe is their due. This means that younger students should defer to older students, and no one should behave as Jenny does, that is, be "mouthy and cocky and try to act like King Shit," especially if she is "merely" a grade eight student in the presence of grade tens. For the key informants, hierarchies make sense, and given their internalized oppression, this comes as no surprise.

Being heard and being acknowledged seem to take precedence over just about everything else. Over and over, the key informants emphasized the importance of being heard and of receiving respect and attention. Positive attention is best, but negative attention is better than no attention at all.

Status, too, is important. It can be achieved through acquiring a "tough rep" as surely as it can through more conventional means, such as good grades and participation on school teams. Notoriety has its attractions; at least it ensures being known.

Being feared, or knowing people who are feared, also has its uses to the key informants. It offers a sense of security, however false. As Sally said after her beating: "I have like tons of friends in gangs and I'm not even scared."

When I asked how girls should be dealt with vis-à-vis their participation in violence, Mary (acting as a spokesperson for violent girls during a two-day community think tank on youth violence) said:

> Girls who get into trouble probably have some sort of self-confidence problems, and they need to figure out who they are, like by going to counseling. And, like, I think they should get community work, not just community hours. They should do something which is working within the community, doing something constructive instead of just sweeping grounds or whatever, something they can learn from instead of the punishment-type thing, something they might want to carry on after it's all done... .
>
> And their parents need counseling, their fathers need help, they're like the main source of the problem, and their mothers need something like a "Speak Out" group, a group where you get together with a bunch of people and learn to tell your feelings and thoughts and things instead of just being in a corner and being quiet. The mothers need to learn to be their own person and not be ordered around by their husband or being pushed around by their husband. If they're not being pushed around then they can get out of the situations they're in ... .
>
> And the victims need help, they need to get their self-conscious built, or their self-esteem built, because most people don't try to steal other people's boyfriends and go around calling people sluts and whatnot. There's gotta be something wrong there. Seems to me that those people are doing things the wrong way, trying to get on top in a negative way, and then they get pounded on. When you're a teenager you're in kind of a conflict position where you have to keep your own position and not let people put you down.

On the subject of violence prevention and intervention, Mary offered several suggestions:

1. With regard to the large number of students who choose to be spectators when there is a fight:

> Watching fights is just a normal occurrence. I mean if there's a fight happening, then everyone goes, "Oh, oh, I wanna see it." It's sort of like an entertainment-type thing 'cause they're bored 'cause there's nothing else to do, and it's not like it's an everyday occurrence. So there's some people where they're just like going, "I wanna be there," kind of thing. I remember last year they tried to suspend people who were viewing fights, and there ended up being so many people around the fights that they couldn't suspend everybody so — I think if

they sorta prepared people or like suggest and say, "Look, it's not right," and teach it in schools or family life skills, or life skills in grade eight, or something in grade nine or ten — You could get a teacher, you could stop it... .

2. *With regard to suspensions:*

... If you suspend someone, they should give them an in-school suspension and get them to work like with the victims, not just their victims, but other victims, so they can see how victims are feeling, and how the victims' families are feeling. In-schools [suspensions] work better than regular suspensions, I mean I was suspended for being mouthy with my teacher and I went to the beach every day. Got a nice suntan for a week ... .

3. *With regard to treatment of victims:*

... [Usually] the victim doesn't wanna go back to school. But I think if they got her together [with the girl who beat her up] the day it happened or the day after or whatever, when she's feeling better and she wants to come, if there's an environment where she knows she's safe, then she can come to school and talk it out with the other girl, and she can say her thoughts and feelings and how she's been hurt, not only physically, but other ways ... and the other girl [the one who beat her up] can say her thoughts and feelings and how she's been hurt ... .

4. *With regard to the use of counselors:*

The counselors' area is kind of a safe place, and it's used, but not with people like — With friends and stuff, you can talk it out, but with people who aren't really your friends, and you just don't like 'em, and say someone wants to beat them up, they're not gonna talk it out, they're gonna go ahead and do it and then talk about it after, 'cause there's no real connection that can get them in there, unless the person that's gonna get beat up comes in and says, "Look, this person, I've heard threats that she was gonna beat me up" — they often know it's gonna happen to them — so you can get them down and ask them why ... . But you gotta watch it, 'cause when you're angry, you don't wanna work it out ... . But I think there needs to be a lot of talking done, people need to talk to each other.

To summarize: Mary says that for her, violence among adolescent females needs to be understood as a problem that has its beginnings in families where parents need help along with their children, where fathers are violent and "push around" mothers who "need to learn to be their own persons," and girls lack self-confidence and "don't know who they are." According to Mary, adolescent female violence also needs to be understood as a problem that involves both perpetrators and victims — victims who have the same kinds of problems with self-confidence that perpetrators have; victims and perpetrators who need to be able to talk to one another in a climate of safety, begin to understand one another's feelings and thoughts, and thereby begin to develop the empathy and connectedness that make the resolution of problems possible.

For Mary, connectedness seems to play a key role, because from her perspective, girls are more willing to talk with those whom they can consider "friends and stuff" — that is, with those whom they know and hold in some regard. But anger management is also key here, because when anger sets in, it overrules the girls' willingness to talk, even with friends. Therefore, something is needed that helps girls deal with anger, so that talking and listening can take place.

As well, Mary believes that teachers and counselors have a major role to play in the prevention of violence. Mary suggests that teachers and counselors, and the skills they teach and the rules they make with regard to what is right and wrong, will have some impact on students' behavior.

Mary's comments ring a hopeful note. If troubled and particularly violent girls nevertheless still have faith in teachers and counselors, this suggests that teachers and counselors who are trained in violence prevention could be instrumental in reducing violence among adolescent girls.

In part, this faith in the power of teachers and counselors may have something to do with the hierarchical universe in which Mary and the other key informants live. Since they believe that being older equates with having more power and a concomitantly greater share of respect, they may be willing to give certain adults, especially those who don't abuse their power, the authority to stop fights and to create rules for what is right and what is wrong.

For Mary and for the other key informants, those counselors who have listened and paid attention to the feelings and thoughts of their clients have been role models for constructive problem solving. It is to these people that Mary and the other girls have turned in seeking alternatives for violence.

It was my experience that being listened to and being treated with respect (i.e., being treated as if what one has to say is important) meant so much that none of the key informants engaged in violence while she was involved in this research project. Instead of resorting to violence, they called me or their counselor to discuss alternatives. Even when the alternatives did not appear to be as satisfying as "belting" someone, to my knowledge, the girls refrained from resorting to violence because they knew that their counselors and I did not hold with it as a way of settling conflict. On reflection, I find this to be significant, because it suggests that there may be a great deal of value in the relationships that the counselors and I built with the six key informants with a view to preventing their further engagement in violence.

Emerging Patterns

In contemplating all that I have heard and seen in the course of this study, what stands out for me are the apparently clear patterns in the key informants' lives that have prepared them for involvement in violence:

- All come from families with many generations of experience with violence, alcohol misuse, and a generalized dysfunction that has left them with a less than helpful way of constructing self and world.

- All have internalized notions of being female that assign low general worth to women, hold that women achieve their greatest importance when they command the attention of males, and support the entrenchment of the sexual double standard. They have learned to accept the objectification of women and support the monitoring of women's sexuality; thus, they monitor one another's sexual activities closely, and judge any girl or woman harshly if she shows signs of engaging in "unsanctioned" sex (i.e., sex that is not legitimated through a long-term relationship; also flirting, or other kinds of sexually based interaction, especially with males who are already spoken for).

- In their immediate families, and in their social circle, the key informants have been exposed to no forms of conflict resolution other than those that settle disputes through threat, intimidation, and violence. They have internalized a way of perceiving those who displease them that shifts moral and causal responsibility for their own displeasure onto those with whom they are displeased, and thus makes lashing out and punitive action justifiable.

- As well, as is always the case with oppressed groups, the key informants have accepted their own and others' subordination to hierarchies built upon power and domination to such a degree that they become extremely incensed with those of their own kind whom they consider below them on the ladder, who dare to buck the system. They do, of course, buck the system themselves, especially with adult authority figures, but only when in their eyes, these people displease or otherwise stymie them, thus provoking retaliation.

- Finally, given their extensive personal experiences with emotional, physical, and sexual abuse, they are quick to anger, and quick to assume that others "have it in for them." Yet, they are also strangely blind to risk and danger, probably because the terrain is so familiar. The known seldom appears dangerous.

When the key informants engage in violence — which they do most often with girls just like themselves — they enact all that they have come to take as given and exhibit a classic form of oppressed group behavior (as discussed in Chapter Nine). At some level, some of the girls (e.g., Mary and, to a lesser extent, Jenny) realize they are doing this, but changing is difficult. It means giving up the only form of status and power that they understand.

Where to Go From Here?

Violence prevention and gender issues

Programs that focus on the treatment of delinquency, like most theories of delinquency, rarely deal with gender issues (Chesney-Lind & Shelden, 1992; Gordon, 1988). Most programs that serve females derive from programs originally designed for males.

Programs specifically concerned with violence prevention are typically gender neutral. That is, they operate on the assumption that "one size fits all" and that no special consideration need be given to male–female differences when examining participation in and diversion from violence.

Gender neutrality, or gender blindness, also prevails in school-based violence prevention. An inventory of some 50 violence prevention programs (including school-based programs) offered in the community in which this study was done showed that only seven (five adult-focused, and two child- and youth-focused programs) concerned themselves with violence against females (Orom, 1995). Only one of the seven offered any additional programming specifically designed for violent females.

In Canada, as elsewhere, school systems attempt to address the issue of youth violence through both policy and curriculum initiatives. Often, the first line of defense against violence is the development of strict discipline policies, codes of student conduct, and structured consequences for offenders, including temporary suspension and even expulsion. For the most part, violence prevention curricula have as their goal the development of a variety of pro-social attitudes, skills, and knowledge intended to help students resolve conflict in peaceful and non-violent ways. Rarely do such programs address gender differences in youth involvement in violence.

As Ted Riecken and I surmised elsewhere (Artz & Riecken, 1994), this gender blindness can perhaps be explained by the fact that the forerunners of such curricula are to be found in the character-education movements first seen in the United States early in the 20th century, and later in the moral-education and values-education movements of the 1970s in Canada and the United States (Leming, 1993). Such programs typically do not concern themselves with gender. In a review of the literature on character education, Leming observes that to date, there is little empirical evidence to indicate that such programs, whether policy or curricular, are effective in changing student behavior. Leming (1993) notes:

> With the caveat that the present research base is small, disparate, and inconsistent, we can offer the following observations:
> • Didactic methods alone — codes, pledges, teacher exhortation and the like — are unlikely to have any significant or lasting effect on character.
> • The development of students' capacity to reason about questions of moral conduct does not result in a related change in conduct. Apparently, one cannot reason one's way to virtuous conduct.
> • Character educators should not expect character formation to be easy. Schools that expect easily achieved and dramatic effects will be disappointed. (p. 69)

Lockwood (1993) offers a further critique of such programs and also questions the assumption that changes in behavior will arise from systematic teaching of values and morals alone. Leming's (1993) and Lockwood's (1993) observations are troubling, particularly in light of two recent studies that suggest antiviolence curricula have the opposite effect from what was expected.

In a study done by the Department of Evaluation of the Saginaw Michigan Public School Board (1991), a district-wide school safety project was evaluated in its third year of operation. Objectives for the project were: (a) the employment and training of home-school liaison officers, (b) establishment of an advisory council, (c) development and implementation of school-based initiatives, and (d) reductions in violence and vandalism. It was found that by the third year of the program, reports of criminal or delinquent acts had *increased* by 47%.

A similar study (Madak & Bravi, 1992) conducted in Canada examined the effects of the Second Step Curriculum, a popular antiviolence program developed in Seattle, Washington, and used extensively in schools in Western Canada. Madak and Bravi (1992) found that the total number of behavioral incidents *increased* during the second year of the project.

The two studies raise questions about the efficacy of such programs when they appear to be associated with an increase in the very behaviors they are designed to reduce. Madak and Bravi (1992) hypothesize that the increase in behavioral incidents noted in their study may be the result of teachers being "hyper-vigilant" in reporting such behavior as a result of being exposed to the program. It is difficult to assess the validity of this hypothesis, although it should be noted that a similar explanation (i.e., hypersensitivity) is sometimes offered for the large statistical increase in reported youth crime (Frank, 1994).

Evidence from research studies that call into question the effectiveness of such character development and violence prevention programs indicates that one of the reasons such programs fail is their inability to recognize the complexity of the issue of violence among young people. Leming (1993) writes that "character develops within a social web or environment. The nature of that environment, the messages it sends to individuals, and the behaviors it encourages and discourages are important factors to consider in character education" (p. 69). Lockwood (1993) comments that "at minimum, some mix of psychological, situational, and sociological variables are involved in determining behavior" (p. 73). Gender and its effects upon persons and groups must be included for consideration in this mix of variables.

Complex roots of female violence

Clearly, the problem of youth violence, both male and female, is bigger than the school systems which, up to now, have been the main agencies responsible for trying to address and modify the behavior of young people. Youth violence is a complex social issue that is borne of multiple origins.

Data from this study point directly to family dysfunction, abuse, and neglect as part of the grounding that prepares school girls for participation in violence. I have found what many others[1] before me have found, in setting themselves the goal of understanding the lives of violent children.

Although the participants in the *Survey of Student Life* (Artz & Riecken, 1994) were mostly white, and the six key informants of this study were all white and comparatively more affluent and privileged than the participants in Campbell's (1984, 1991) studies, Chesney-Lind and Koroki's (1985) study, and Chesney-Lind and Shelden's (1992) overview of girls' delinquency and juvenile justice, the lived experiences of my key informants are similar to those of the participants in the other studies.

The families of the six key informants are characterized by the same kinds of problems with alcohol misuse, marital discord, and family violence encountered by the participants in the above-mentioned studies. Despite their mothers' claims of family unity as evidenced by enduring marriages and professions of "closeness" to other family members, the key informants' experiences with family are largely negative. The social bond that is premised upon attachment, seen by Hirschi (1969) to contribute to the containment of delinquency (see Chapter One), is not operative here. Instead, the key informants report experiencing a kind of enmeshment with family members that violates their personal boundaries and leaves them in a state of emotional abandonment.

The key informants' families are battlegrounds organized along traditional lines. Men rule over women, who are charged with the care and control of the children. On the surface, these families, while they are not "ideal patriarchal" families because the fathers are blue-collar workers and the mothers also work, are nonetheless similar (by virtue of their traditional organization) to those described by Hagan (1987) as the kinds of families that generally have lower rates of female delinquency. That is not the case here, however.

Although males are dominant and the women take care of the children, these families are producing girls who are violent. In these families, dominance is synonymous with petty tyranny and the negation of women. The gender divisions that are modeled and reinforced serve to produce internalized oppression and appear to contribute to the horizontal violence exhibited by the key informants. Further, these families also model a way of interpreting others' behavior that supports the shifting of moral and causal responsibility for one's actions onto those same others.

In suggesting that the internalization of victim blaming is central to the final step towards violence, I join Katz (1988) in pointing out that sociological and psychological factors alone are insufficient for an understanding of why some people engage in violence. If we are to work effectively, both at understanding how violence happens and at creating interventions that serve to prevent violence and its rationalization, I believe we must take into account how people make sense of their violent behavior beyond the psychosocial factors that give context to their experience.

After all, not all people who have been abused become abusers (Gelles & Straus, 1988). Thus, more must be at work than past experience alone. So far, an understanding is missing from the literature of how girls make sense of and rationalize their behavior. Such an analysis would move beyond the confines of moral-developmental and character education. I believe that there is much to be learned from exploring this area further.

In concluding that sexual abuse and sexual harassment play an important role with regard to the key informants' low sense of self-worth and negative views of other girls and women, I have raised issues previously suggested by Chesney-Lind and Koroki (1985) and Chesney-Lind and Shelden (1992). I take this line of inquiry one step further by suggesting that the key informants, and others like them, may extend their negative view of females by making moral judgments about their predominantly female victims. That is, they have drawn the conclusion that girls and women deserve to be beaten for certain behaviors (those judged as unacceptable according to a rigid reading of the sexual double standard), and thus exhibit horizontal violence and other oppressed group behaviors. Here, too, is an area for future inquiry into female violence, particularly in the light of attempts to understand it as the dark side of feminism (Adler, 1975; McGovern, 1995).

In my view, the judgments of women exhibited by the key informants do not arise because these girls are becoming more emancipated. Rather, this arises because within their life-worlds, they still apply narrow notions of male-focused behavior as the standard for what is right and good for women. If I am correct, this insight may be significant for preventing the perpetuation of violence across generations, especially female-to-female violence: Any such interventions must emphasize the valuing of women not in male terms, but as individuals who have worth in and of themselves as women.

Violence prevention in schools

Gelles and Straus (1988), in their exhaustive study on the causes and consequences of abuse in the American family, suggest that "sexual inequality is a prime cause of family violence" and that "eliminating sexism can prevent violence in the home" (p. 203). Evidence provided by the key informants of this study suggests that sexual inequality also has a major role to play in the violence participated in by adolescent school girls outside their homes. By extension, eliminating sexism may contribute substantially to preventing violence among these girls. Violence prevention programming aimed at adolescent school girls should focus on violence against women and should not assume that it is only males who act violently towards females.

The participants in this study (and others) have spoken eloquently about their experiences with abuse and their resulting anger and emotional pain. This suggests that any violence prevention programming we envision — including programs aimed at adolescent school girls — should include an abuse-survivor recovery component that addresses the female experience in positive and strength-giving ways.

Finally, in view of the loneliness and abandonment described by the key informants, and which has been linked by other researchers to deviance, delinquency, and violence (Hirschi, 1969; Jensen & Eve, 1976; Cernkovich & Giordano, 1987), we must find the means to help young women participate in our social institutions in ways that are important and relevant to them. That is, we must enable them to experience respect, affirmation, and connectedness. If we do not, they will pay every price asked of them in order to matter to someone, regardless of how destructive the relationship. And we, as a society, will pay the cost of their demise.

Keeping Violent Girls in Mind

Chesney-Lind and Shelden (1992) suggest that if we are to serve delinquent girls with regard to programming, we must always keep in mind their special needs vis-à-vis their experiences with sexual objectification and brutalization. I believe this applies to violence prevention programming in schools, as well. In all that we do, we must count gender in.

Evidence from several U.S. studies indicates that intervention in early childhood has a significant impact in reducing antisocial and criminal behavior later in life (Hechinger, 1994). Often, such programs involve both parents and children, and offer parents the chance to develop constructive, non-violent child-rearing skills. The goal of such programs is the development of healthy and stable parent–child relationships that lay the foundations for children's future interactions with peers and society. Given the findings of the present study, effective parent education for preventing violence must also include education and training in gender equity.

Some programs in violence prevention include not only parents, but other community members as well. MacDougall (1993) writes:

> A growing number of successful violence prevention/safe school initiatives throughout Canada share a common feature. They are products of partnerships. Pooling experience, skills, talent, and expertise better utilizes resources. Marrying previously fragmented groups towards a goal of reducing violence increases benefits to children, youth and families. Partnerships include educators, parents, students, police, government officials, artists, social service and mental health workers and others.

In Canada, an example of such partnerships is to be found in a program created by the Wellington Board of Education in Guelph, Ontario. In 1990, in response to growing community concerns about youth violence, the Wellington Board brought together representatives from education, police, social services, the Crown Attorney's Office, and parents. The mandate of this group is to develop and maintain cooperative strategies to reduce youth violence.

The Family Violence Prevention Project of the Community Child Abuse Council of Hamilton-Wentworth in Ontario is a similar collaborative effort. This project involves over 25 organizations and agencies representing school boards, social service agencies, health care providers, and government (MacDougall, 1993).

Given the small number of evaluations that have targeted violence intervention projects, more research is clearly needed. It appears, though, that the most successful programs are more broadly based in approach and, through collaboration, take into account contextual, environmental, familial, social, and gendered dimensions of violence — and do so at an early age.

Crime statistics in North America indicate that violence among young people, and especially young women, is on the rise. School systems have also noted this increase. Thus, it cannot be disputed that violence intervention and prevention are currently among our most pressing issues. Further, it makes sense, given the critical role that schools play in the socialization of young people, that schools should be the sites to begin the campaign against violence.

Teachers recognize the importance of sexism in school violence. In a survey on violence in schools (Macolmson, 1994), about one half of the teachers who participated said they believe that sexism plays a role in instigating violence at school. If school-based violence prevention programs are to be successful, they must move beyond merely transmitting violence-related curricula to students and must be grounded in the following principles:

- Early intervention. Waiting until young people reach adolescence before providing intervention compounds the problem.

- Involvement of students, parents, and community agency personnel with educators in the development of program initiatives and curricula that are meaningful to those for whom they are intended.

- Collaboration among students, parents, community-based agencies, and other community members in the implementation of co-developed programs and curricula.

- Continuous monitoring and evaluation of the implementation process in order to verify that programs are, in fact, achieving their purpose.

- A focus on gender and inequity. Questions of gender can no longer be ignored or subsumed into more general questions. Violence, sex, and gender must be studied, understood, and dealt with together.

All the current work of the Youth Violence Project focuses on gender. Thus far, it is clear that the gender differences identified in the self-report data of Phase I (described in Chapter Two) persist. In a related study (Artz & Blais, 1995), a number of resources designed to educate teens about sexual harassment and date rape were explored (see Appendix II). These resources provide useful information about male-to-female violence and make important points about gender equity, but do not address female-to-female violence.

Programs and materials that seek to prevent male violence against females are of paramount importance, especially because the majority of females will almost certainly encounter such violence at some point in their lives (Statistics Canada, 1993). It must now be recognized that most female-to-female violence is also a form of sexual harassment, given that it is so often perpetrated as a means of keeping female sexuality under control. It must therefore be included in any kind of programming that seeks to deal with sexual harassment.

The two kinds of violence against women, male-to-female and female-to-female, have their origins in the same belief systems. These hold that females are inferior to males and are, in the last analysis, sexual objects. Such beliefs are still deeply rooted in many aspects of our culture, and are especially visible and audible in media aimed at young people. The images of girls and women that predominate on television, in the movies and particularly in rock music and the videos that promote it, are overwhelmingly sexist and misogynist. Violence prevention programming must take into account the systemic ways in which girls and women are sexually misused and exploited, and must help both females and males find constructive ways to understand and relate to females.

Given the dominance of the male-focused perspective of females, it is no surprise that most girls grow up seeing themselves through the eyes of males. In families that devalue women, it takes little for girls to progress from a negative vision of women to overt violence against them. A thorough understanding of gender is thus central to any understanding of female violence, and integral to all violence prevention programming in the future.

Notes

1. See Flowers, 1990, for an overview.

References

Adler, F. (1975). *Sisters in crime*. New York: McGraw-Hill.

Ageton, S. (1983). The dynamics of female delinquency, 1976–1980. *Criminology, 21*, 555–584.

Anderson, D. (1991). *The unfinished revolution: The status of women in twelve countries*. Toronto: Doubleday.

Aoki, T. (1987). *Toward understanding curriculum orientations*. Unpublished manuscript.

Arbuthnot, J. (1992). Sociomoral reasoning in behavior-disordered adolescents. In J. McCord & R. Tremblay (Eds.), *Preventing antisocial behavior*. New York: The Guilford Press.

Artz, S. (1994). *Feeling as away of knowing: A practical guide to working with emotional experience*. Toronto: Trifolium Books.

Artz, S., & Blais, M. (1995). *An evaluation of an awareness and violence prevention project directed at sexual harassment, abuse and date rape among teens*. Unpublished report to sponsor, Victoria, BC: British Columbia Ministry of Education, Gender Equity Branch.

Artz, S., & Riecken, T. (1994). The survey of student life. In *A study of violence among adolescent female students in a suburban school district*. Unpublished report, British Columbia Ministry of Education, Education Research Unit.

Ashbury, H. (1928). *The gangs of New York*. New York: Alfred Knopf.

Attacks on trendy teenagers not just kid's stuff. (1993, March 21). *Victoria Times Colonist*.

Atwater, E. (1992). *Adolescence*. Englewood Cliffs, NJ: Prentice Hall.

Auty, S., Dempsey, M., Duggan, S., Lowery, G., West, G., & Wiseman, D. (1993). A dialogue on the nature and extent of the problem. In G. West (Ed)., Violence in the schools, schooling in violence. *Orbit, 24* (1), 1–5.

Ayto, J. (1990). *Bloomsbury dictionary of word origins*. London, UK: Bloomsbury Publishing.

Balkan, S., & Berger, R. (1979). The changing nature of female delinquency. In C. Knopp (Ed.), *Becoming female: Perspectives on development*. New York: Plenum.

Beaten at playground, boy, 11, wins at chess. (1993, April 13). *Victoria Times Colonist*.

Becker, H. (1963). *Outsiders: Studies in sociology and deviance*. New York: Macmillan.

Belenky, M., Clinchy, B., Goldberger, N., & Tarule, J. (1986). *Womens' ways of knowing: The development of self, voice and mind*. New York: Basic Books.

Berger, R. (1989). Female delinquency in the emancipation era: A review of the literature. *Sex Roles, 21* (5/6), 375–399.

Bibby, R., & Posterski, D. (1992). *Teen trends*. Toronto: Stoddart.

Binder, A., Geis, G., & Bruce, D. (1988). *Juvenile delinquency: Historical, cultural, legal perspectives*. New York: Macmillan.

Blumer, H. (1969). *Symbolic interactionism: Perspective and method*. Englewood Cliffs, NJ: Prentice Hall.

Boothe, J., Bradley, L., Flick, M., Keough, K., & Kirk, S. (1993, February). The violence at your door. *The Executive Educator*, 16–21.

Brenauer, J., & Rasmussen, D. (Eds.). (1984). *The final Foucault*. Cambridge: MIT Press.

Brenner, M., Brown. J., & Canter, D. (Eds.). (1985). *The research interview: Uses and approaches*. Orlando, FL: Academic Press.

Brown, L., & Gilligan, C. (1992). *Meeting at the crossroads*. New York: Ballantine Books.

Brown, W.K. (1977). Black female gangs in Philadelphia. *International Journal of Offender Therapy and Comparative Criminology, 21* (3), 221–228.

Burbank, V.K. (1987). Female aggression in cross-cultural perspective. *Behavior Science Research, 21* (1–4), 70–100.

Burgess, E.W. (1928). The growth of the city. In R.E. Park, E. Burgess, & R.D. McKenzie (Eds.), *The city*. Chicago: University of Chicago Press.

Cameron, E., deBruijne, L., Kennedy, K., & Morin, J. (1994). *British Columbia Teachers' Federation task force on violence in schools: Final report*. Vancouver, BC: BCTF.

Campbell, A. (1984, 1991). *The girls in the gang*. (2nd ed.) New York: Basil Blackwell.

Campbell, A. (1986). Self-report by fighting females. *British Journal of Criminology, 26*, 28–46.

Campbell, A. (1987). *Self-definition by rejection: The case of gang girls*.

Canadian Crime Statistics (1995). Catalogue #85-205. Ottawa, ON: Statistics Canada.

Canadian Review of Sociology and Anthropology, 27, 137–156.

Cernkovich, S., & Giordano, P. (1979). A comparative analysis of male and female delinquency. *Sociological Quarterly, 20*, 131–145.

Cernkovich, S., & Giordano, P. (1987). Family relationships and delinquency. *Criminology, 25*, 295–321.

Charon, J. (1979). *Symbolic interactionism: An introduction, an integration*. Englewood Cliffs, NJ: Prentice Hall.

Chesney-Lind, M., & Koroki, J. (1985). *Everything just going down the drain: Interviews with female delinquents in Hawaii*. Hawaii: University of Hawaii Youth Development & Research Center report.

Chesney-Lind, M., & Shelden, R. (1992). *Girls' delinquency and juvenile justice*. Pacific Grove, CA: Brooks/Cole.

Chilton, R., & Datesman, S. (1987). *Gender, race and crime: An analysis of urban arrest trends, 1960–1980*. Paper presented at the annual meeting of the American Sociological Association.

Cloward, R., & Ohlin, L. (1960). *Delinquency and opportunity*. New York: Free Press.

Cohen, A. (1955). *Delinquent boys: The culture of the gang*. New York: Free Press.

Colby, A., & Kohlberg, L. (1987). *The measurement of moral development: Theoretical foundations and research validation*. (vol. 1). Cambridge: Cambridge University Press.

Cole, M., John-Steiner, V., Scribner, S., & Souberman, E. (1978). *L.S. Vygotsky — Mind in society: The development of higher psychological processes*. Cambridge: Harvard University Press.

Cormier, L., & Hackney, H. (1993). *The professional counselor: A process guide to helping*. Boston: Allyn & Bacon.

Cowie, J., Cowie, V., & Slater, E. (1968). *Delinquency in girls*. London, UK: Heinemann.

Deegan, M. (1987). Symbolic interactionism and the study of women: An introduction. In M. Deegan & M. Hill (Eds.), *Women and symbolic interactionism*. Boston: Allyn & Unwin.

Denboer, R. (1994). *CRD demographic atlas*. (1994). Victoria, BC: Capital Regional District.

Dietz, M., Pruz, R., & Shaffir, W. (1994). *Doing everyday life: Ethnography as human lived experience*. Toronto: Copp Clark Longman.

Durkheim, E. (1933). *The division of labor in society*. (G. Simpson, trans.) New York: Free Press.

Edwards (Ed.). (1967). Von Humboldt. *The encyclopedia of philosophy*. New York: Collier MacMillan.

Evans, E.D., & Warren-Sohlenberg, L. (1988). Patterns of analysis of adolescent behavior towards parents. *Journal of Adolescent Research, 3* (2), 201–206.

Faludi, S. (1991). *Backlash: The undeclared war against American women.* New York: Anchor/Doubleday.

Federal Bureau of Investigation. (1988, July). *Crime in the United States, 1987.* Washington, DC: U.S. Government Printing Office.

Figueria-McDonough, J., Barton, W., & Sarri, R. (1981). Normal deviance: Gender similarities in adolescent subcultures. In M. Warren (Ed.), *Comparing male and female offenders.* Newbury Park, CA: Sage.

Flowers, R. (1990). *The adolescent criminal: An examination of today's juvenile offender.* Jefferson, NC: McFarland & Company.

Fowler, H. (1965). *A dictionary of modern English usage.* New York: Oxford University Press.

Fox Keller, E. (1990). Gender and science. In J. McCarl Nielsen (Ed.), *Feminist research methods: Exemplary readings in the social sciences.* San Francisco: Westview Press.

Frank, F. (1994). Violent youth crime. In *Canadian social trends: A Canadian studies reader.* (vol. 2). Toronto: Thompson Educational Publishing.

Friere, P. (1971, 1984). *Pedagogy of the oppressed.* New York: Continuum.

Geertz, C. (1973). *The interpretation of cultures.* New York: Basic Books.

Geertz, C. (1988). *Works and lives: The anthropologist as author.* Stanford: Stanford University Press.

Gelles, R., & Straus, M. (1988). *Intimate violence: The definitive study of the causes and consequences of abuse in the American family.* New York: Simon & Schuster.

Giallombardo, R. (1980). Female delinquency. In D. Shichor & D. Kelly. (Eds.), *Critical issues in juvenile delinquency.* Lexington, MA: Lexington Books.

Gilligan, C. (1982). *In a different voice: Psychological theory and women's development.* Cambridge: Harvard University Press.

Gilligan, C., Lyons, N., & Hanmer, T. (Eds.). (1990). *Making connections: The relational world of adolescent girls at Emma Willard School.* Cambridge: Harvard University Press.

Gilligan, C., Ward, J., & Taylor, J., with Bardige, B. (1988). *Mapping the moral domain.* Cambridge: Harvard University Press.

Giordano, P., & Cernkovich, S. (1979). On complicating the relationship between liberation and delinquency. *Social Problems, 26,* 467–481.

Giordano, P., Cernkovich, S., & Pugh, M. (1986). Friendships and delinquency. *American Journal of Sociology, 91*, 1170–1202.

Goetz, J.P., & LeCompte, M.D., (1984). *Ethnography and qualitative design in educational research*. Montreal: Academic Press.

Gordon, L. (1988). *Heroes in their own lives*. New York: Viking.

Grosser, G. (1951). *Juvenile delinquency and contemporary American sex roles*. Unpublished doctoral dissertation, Harvard University.

Habermas, J. (1971). *Theory and practice*. Boston: Beacon Press.

Hagan, J. (1988). *Structural criminology*. New Brunswick: Polity Press.

Hagan, J. (1990). The structure of gender and deviance: A power-control theory of vulnerability to crime and the search for deviant role exits. *Canadian Review of Sociology and Anthropology, 27* (2), 137–156.

Hagan, J., Gillis, A., & Simpson, J (1985). The class structure of delinquency: Toward a power-control theory of common delinquent behavior. *American Journal of Sociology, 90*, 1151–1178.

Hagan, J., Simpson, J., & Gillis, A. (1987). Class in the household: A power-control theory of gender and delinquency. *American Journal of Sociology, 92*, 788–816.

Hamilton, J. (1993). *It's a jungle out there. In Leading the way to violence free schools*. Conference handbook, British Columbia School Trustees Association/British Columbia Teachers' Federation Conference. Vancouver, BC: BCSTA.

Hancock, E. (1989). *The girl within*. New York: Fawcett Columbine.

Hechinger, F. (1994) Saving youth from violence. *Carnegie Quarterly, 33* (1), 1–15.

Hindelang, J., Hirschi, T., & Weis, J. (1981). *Measuring delinquency*. Newbury Park, CA: Sage.

Hirschi, T. (1969). *Causes of delinquency*. Berkeley: University of California Press.

Hoffman-Bustamente, D. (1973). The nature of female criminality. *Issues in Criminality, 8* (Fall), 117–136.

hooks, b. (1994). *Outlaw culture: Resisting representations*. New York: Routledge.

Hopper, C.B., & Moore, J., (1990). Women in outlaw motorcycle gangs. *Journal of Contemporary Ethnography, 18* (4), 363–387.

Horowitz, R. (1983). *Honor and the American dream*. New Brunswick, NJ: Rutgers University Press.

Horowitz, R. (1986). Remaining an outsider: Membership as a threat to research rapport. *Urban Life, 14*, 238–251.

Horowitz, R. (1987). Community tolerance of gang violence. *Social Problems, 34*, 437–450.

Jagger, A., & Bordo, S. (1990). *Gender/body/knowledge: Feminist reconstructions of being and knowing.* New Brunswick, NJ: Rutgers University Press.

James, J., & Thornton, W. (1980). Women's liberation and the female delinquent. *Journal of Research in Crime and Delinquency, 17*, 230–244.

Jenkins, J. (1994). *Resolve I: Resolving violence through education, an anti-violence curriculum for senior secondary students.* Campbelltown, NSW: University of Western Sydney, Macarthur.

Jensen, G., & Eve, R. (1976). Sex differences in delinquency. *Criminology, 13*, 427–448.

Juvenile weapons arrests double. (1995, November 13). *The Globe & Mail.*

Katz, J. (1988) *Seductions of crime: Moral and sensual attractions of doing evil.* New York: Basic Books.

Kelly, D. (1993) *Deviant behavior: A text-reader in the sociology of deviance.* New York: St. Martin's Press.

Klicpera C., & Klicpera B. (1996). Die situation von "Tatern" und "Opfern," agresiver handlung in der schule. *Praxis der Kinderpsychologie und Kinderpsychiatre, 45*, 2–9.

Kirby, S., & McKenna, K. (1989). *Experience, research, social change: Methods from the margins.* Toronto: Garamond Press.

Klein, M. (1971). *Street gangs and street workers.* Englewood Cliffs, NJ: Prentice Hall.

Kohlberg, L. (1969). Stage and sequence: The cognitive developmental approach to socialization. In D. Goslin (Ed.), *Handbook of socialization theory and research.* Chicago: Rand McNally.

Kohlberg, L. (1984). *Essays on moral development: The psychology of moral development.* (vol. 2). San Francisco: Harper & Row.

Konopka, G. (1966). *The adolescent girl in conflict.* Englewood Cliffs, NJ: Prentice Hall.

Konopka, G. (1983). *Young girls: A portrait of adolescence.* New York: Hayworth Press.

Kostash, M. (1987). *No kidding: Inside the world of teenage girls.* Toronto: McClelland & Stewart.

Larson, Goltz, & Hobart (1994). *Families in Canada: Social context, continuities and changes.* Toronto: Prentice Hall Canada.

Lather, P. (1991). *Getting smart: Feminist research and pedagogy within the postmodern*. New York: Routledge.

Leading the way to violence free schools. Conference handbook, British Columbia School Trustees Association/British Columbia Teachers' Federation Conference. Vancouver, BC: BCSTA.

Leming, J. (1993). Synthesis of research: In search of effective character education. *Educational Leadership, 51* (3), 63–71.

Leontyev, A. (1981). *Problems of the development of mind*. Moscow: Progress Publishers.

Lockwood, A. (1993). A letter to character educators. *Educational Leadership, 51* (3), 72–75.

Lombroso, C., & Ferrero, W. (1895). *The female offender*. New York: Philosophical Library.

MacDougall, J. (1993). *Violence in the schools: Programs and policies for prevention. A report from the Canadian Education Association*. Toronto: CEA.

McGovern, C. (1995). You've come a long way, baby. *Alberta Report, 1* (33), 24–27.

Mack, B. (1994). Mission impossible. *Grand Royale* magazine, a division of Grand Royale Entertainment, available on the Internet through the Beastie Boys home page: http://www.nando.net.music/gm/BeastieBoys/../BeastieBoys/press

Madak, P., & Bravi, G. (1992). *Second step: A violence prevention curriculum in a western Canadian elementary school. An evaluation*. ERIC Document No. ED 350 542.

Mahoney, M. (1991). *Human change processes: The scientific foundations of psychotherapy*. New York: Basic Books.

Malcolmson, J. (1994). *Violence in schools: An overview of findings from the "Teaching in the 90's Survey."* Vancouver, BC: British Columbia Teachers' Federation.

Mathews, F. (1994). *Youth gangs on youth gangs*. Ottawa: Solicitor General Canada.

Mawby, R. (1980). Sex crimes: Results of a self-report study. *British Journal of Sociology, 31*, 526–543.

Mead, M. (1934). *Kinship in the Admiralty Islands*. New York: American Museum of Natural History.

Merton, R. (1938). Social structure and anomie. *American Sociological Review, 3*, 672–682.

Miller, E. (1986). *Street women: The illegal work of underclass women.* Philadelphia: Temple University Press.

Miller, W. (1958). Lower class culture as a generating milieu of gang delinquency. *Journal of Social Issues, 14,* 5–19.

Mishler, E. (1986). *Research interviewing.* Cambridge: Harvard University Press.

Morash, M. (1986). An explanation of juvenile delinquency: The integration of moral reasoning theory and sociological knowledge. In W.S. Laufer & J.M. Day (Eds.), *Personality theory, moral development, and criminal behavior.* Lexington, MA: Lexington Books.

Morris, A. (1987). *Women, crime and criminal justice.* New York: Basil Blackwell.

Morris, R. (1965). Attitudes towards delinquency by delinquents, nondelinquents and their friends. *British Journal of Criminology, 5,* 249–265.

Mundy, C. (1994). Where the wild things are. *Rolling Stone,* Issue 688, pp. 45–53 and 73–74.

Novak, M. (1978). *Ascent of the mountain, flight of the dove: An invitation to religious studies.* New York: Harper & Row.

Nye, F. (1958) *Family relationships and delinquent behavior.* New York: Wiley.

Olweus, D., Block, J., & Radke-Yarro, M. (1986). *Development of antisocial and prosocial behavior: Research, theories, and issues.* Orlando, FL: Academic Press.

Orom, C. (1995). *Violence prevention in the community: A report and inventory of prevention initiatives in the community of Victoria.* Victoria, BC: Community Social Planning Council.

Osborne, J. (1994). Some similarities and differences among phenomenological and other methods of psychological qualitative research. *Canadian Psychology, 35* (2), 167–189.

Pecukonis, E.V. (1990). A cognitive/affective empathy training program as a function of ego development in aggressive adolescent females. *Adolescence, 25* (97), 59–76.

Police Management Information System Summary Statistics, 1977–1991. Victoria, BC: Queen's Printer.

Pollack, O. (1950). *The criminality of women.* New York: Barnes.

Porter, E.J. (1991). *Women and moral identity.* North Sidney, Australia: Allen & Unwin.

Prus, R. (1994). Approaching the study of human group: Symbolic interaction and ethnographic inquiry. In M. Dietz, R. Pruz, & W. Shaffir

(Eds.), *Doing everyday life: Ethnography as human lived experience*. Toronto: Copp Clark Longman.

Rabinow, P. (Ed.). (1984). *The Foucault reader*. New York: Pantheon.

Reckless, W. (1961). *The crime problem* (3rd ed.). New York: Appleton-Century-Crofts.

Reiss, A. (1951). Delinquency as the failure of personal social controls. *American Sociological Review, 16*, 196–207.

Richards, P., & Tittle, C. (1981). Gender and perceived chance of arrest. *Social Forces, 59*, 1182–1199.

Rigby, K. (1996). *Bullying in schools and what to do about it*. Melbourne: The Australian Council for Educational Research.

Roberts, S. (1983, July). Oppressed group behavior: Implications for nursing. *Advances in Nursing Science*, 22–30.

Rogers, C. (1957). The necessary and sufficient conditions for therapeutic personality change. *Journal of Consulting Psychology, 21*, 95–103.

Ryan, C., Mathews, F., & Banner, J. (1993). *Student perceptions of violence*. Toronto: Central Toronto Youth Services.

Saginaw Public Schools. (1991). *School safety project: Product evaluation, 1990–1991*. Saginaw Public Schools, Department of Evaluation Services. ERIC Document Number, ED 343 267.

Schur, E. (1972). *Labeling deviant behavior*. New York: Harper & Row.

Schur, E. (1984). *Labeling women deviant*. New York: Random House.

Shaw, C. (1930). *The jack roller*. Chicago: University of Chicago Press.

Shaw, C., & McKay, H. (1931). *Social factors in juvenile delinquency*. Chicago: University of Chicago Press.

Shaw, C., & McKay, H. (1942). *Juvenile delinquency in urban areas*. Chicago: University of Chicago Press.

Short, J. (1968). *Gang delinquency and delinquent subcultures*. Chicago: University of Chicago Press.

Simon, R. (1975). *Women and crime*. Lexington, MA: Lexington Books.

Singer, S., & Levine, M. (1933). Power-control theory, gender and delinquency: A partial with additional evidence on the effects of peers. *Criminology 26*, 627–647.

Slade, P. (1984). Premenstrual emotional changes in normal women: Fact or fiction? *Journal of Psychosomatic Research, 28*, 1–7.

Spradley, J. (1979). *The ethnographic interview*. New York: Holt, Reinhardt & Winston.

Statistics Canada (1993). *Violence against women survey: Survey highlights.* Ottawa: Author.

Steffensmeir, D. (1978). Crime and the contemporary American woman: An analysis of changing levels of female property crime, 1960–1975. *Social Forces, 57,* 566–584.

Steffensmeir, D., & Cobb, M. (1981). Sex difference in urban patterns, 1934–1979. *Social Problems, 29,* 37–50.

Steffensmeir, D.J., Steffensmeir, R.H., & Rosenthal, A.S. (1979). Trends in female violence. *Sociological Focus, 12* (3), 217–227.

Summary Statistics: Police Crime, 1985–1994 (1995). Vancouver, BC: Police Services Division, Ministry of the Attorney General.

Sutherland, E. (1939). *Principles of criminology.* Philadelphia: Lippincott.

Sutherland, E., & Cressey, D. (1978). *Criminology* (10th ed.). Philadelphia: Lippincott.

Teen beating suspects remanded. (1993, April 13). *Victoria Times Colonist.*

Thrasher, F. (1927). *The gang: A study of 1,313 gangs in Chicago.* Chicago: University of Chicago Press.

Toby, J. (1957). Social disorganization and stake in conformity: Complementary factors in predatory behavior in hoodlums. *Journal of Criminal Law, Criminology and Police Service, 48,* 12–17.

"Tremendous" increase in violence among girls. (1993, October 15). *Victoria Times Colonist.*

Tutt, N. (1991). The future of the juvenile justice system. In Jungen-Tas, Boendermaker, & van der Laan (Eds.), *The future of the juvenile justice system* (pp. 107–129). Acco Leuven: Netherlands.

Tutt, N. (1988). Report to the European Council of Ministers, Council of Europe of the Expert Committee on Juvenile Crime. Council of Europe, the Hague, Netherlands.

Van Maanen, J. (1988). *Tales from the field.* Chicago: University of Chicago Press.

van Manen, M. (1977). Linking ways of knowing with ways of being practical. *Curriculum Inquiry, 6* (3), 205–228.

Warren, M. (Ed.). (1981). *Comparing female and male offenders.* Beverly Hills: Sage.

Wilson, J., & Herrnstein, R. (1985). *Crime and human nature.* New York: Simon & Schuster.

Wilson, S. (1977). The use of ethnographic techniques in educational research. *Review of Educational Research, 47* (1), 245–265.

Wolcott, H. (1975). Criteria for an ethnographic approach in research in schools. *Human Organization, 34* (2), 111–127.

Wolf, N. (1991). *The beauty myth*. Toronto: Vintage Books.

Appendix I
Tables of Survey Results

Table A-1
Parental occupation by percentage reported

Parent	Professional	Managerial	Clerical	Service	Manual	Military	Self-Employed
Mother (n=833)	21.1%	5.5%	31.6%	30.0%	7.6%	1.2%	3%
Father (n=1,084)	12.7%	8.7%	3.5%	25.6%	32.0%	12.5%	5%

Table A-2
Parental education by percentage reported[†]

Parent	Less Than High School	High School	Trade or Business School	University Degree	Graduate Degree
Mother (n=1,086)	13.1%	44.6%	13.0%	20.3%	9.1%
Father (n=1,002)	16.9%	37.0%	17.2%	17.3%	11.7%

[†] In interpreting these data, it is important to keep in mind that these percentages are based on students' knowledge of their parents' occupation and education. This knowledge may be less than completely accurate, since over 30% of students indicated that they did not know the level of their parents' education. However, these figures do correspond to those provided in local census data.

Table A-3a
Familial differences for males and females

Family Dynamics	Nonhitting Females (n=556)	Hitting Females (n=147)	Nonhitting Males (n=367)	Hitting Males (n=396)
Family life is "very important"	46.4%	**35.4%*** less when compared with non-hitting females and nonhitting males	42.5%	33.8%
Enjoyment from mother not applicable	1.3%	**9.5%*** more nonapplicable when compared with all other groups	2.5%	3.5%
Afraid of being physically abused at home	6.5% Yes	**18.4%*** Yes more often when compared with all other groups	4.8% Yes	3.3% Yes
Have been physically abused at home	6.3% Yes	**19.7%*** Yes more often when compared with all other groups	3.0% Yes	9.6% Yes

*Significant at $p < .0001$, chi-square

Table A-3b
Familial differences for males and females

Family Dynamics	Nonhitting Females (n=556)	Hitting Females (n=147)	Nonhitting Males (n=367)	Hitting Males (n=396)
Smoked without parents' permission	46.4% Never	29.3%* Never less often when compared with all other groups	66.2% Never	41.4%* Never less often when compared with nonhitting male
Lied about where they had been or whom they were with	29.7% Never (in the past year)	11.6%* Never (in the past year) less often when compared with nonhitting females and nonhitting males	43.1% Never (in the past year)	18.2%* Never (in the past year) less often when compared with nonhitting femal and nonhitting males
Stayed out all night without parents' permission	68.7% Never (in the past year)	36.1%* Never (in the past year) less often when compared with nonhitting females and nonhitting males	69.8% Never (in the past year)	35.9%* Never (in the past year) less often when compared with nonhitting femal and nonhitting males
Deliberately ruined something their parents valued after an argument	89.4% Never (in the past year)	70.1%* Never (in the past year) less often when compared with nonhitting females and nonhitting males	91.0% Never (in the past year)	72.2%* Never (in the past year) less often when compared with nonhitting femal and nonhitting males

*Significant at $p < .0001$, chi-square

Table A-4
Group membership of survey participants, percentage indicating affiliation

Relationships and Group Membership	Nonhitting Females (n=556)	Hitting Females (n=147)	Nonhitting Males (n=367)	Hitting Males (n=396)
Rappers	13.5%	31.3%* when compared with nonhitting females and non-hitting males	10.9%	24.2%* when compared with nonhitting females and non-hitting males
Bangers	11.5%	29.3%* when compared with nonhitting females and non-hitting males	9.5%	24.2%* when compared with nonhitting females and non-hitting males
Skates	5.2%	8.2%	4.6%	5.1%
Total % claiming group membership in Rappers, Bangers, and Skates	30.2%	68.8* when compared with nonhitting females and non-hitting males	25.0%	53.5%* when compared with nonhitting females and non-hitting males

*Significant at $p < .0001$, chi-square

Table A-5
Self-reported importance of belonging to a group or gang and having the right clothes (percentage reporting "very important")

Important Peer Group Dimension	Nonhitting Females (n=556)	Hitting Females (n=147)	Nonhitting Males (n=367)	Hitting Males (n=396)
Belonging to a group or gang	20.4%	38.5%* when compared with nonhitting females and non-hitting males	18.3%	37.0%* when compared with nonhitting females and non hitting males
Having the right clothes to fit your group or gang	26.2%	41.8%* when compared with nonhitting females and non-hitting males	24.0%	30.1%* when compared with nonhitting females and non hitting males

* Significant at $p < .0001$, chi-square

Table A-6
Self-reported levels of damaging school property and endorsing acting-out against teachers

Behavior and Attitude	Nonhitting Females (n=556)	Hitting Females (n=147)	Nonhitting Males (n=367)	Hitting Males (n=396)
Damaged school property at least once or twice in the past year	12.4%	32.0%* when compared with nonhitting females and non-hitting males	18.7%	42.6%* when compared with nonhitting females and non-hitting males
Endorsed "If I don't like my teacher, it's OK to act up in school"	13.1%	27.2%* when compared with nonhitting females and non-hitting males	15.1%	33.3%* when compared with nonhitting females and non-hitting males

* Significant at $p < .0001$, chi-square

Table A-7
Self-reported interpersonal values comparison for nonhitting females and males

Interpersonal Values (rated as "very important")	Nonhitting Females (n=556)	Nonhitting Males (n=367)
Friendship	91.9%	76.6%*
Being loved	77.3%	53.1%*
Concern for others	69.4%	40.6%*
Respect for others	66.9%	49.6%*
Forgiveness	66.2%	40.9%*
Honesty	64.2%	46.3%*
Politeness	42.1%	33.5%*
Generosity	41.2%	28.3%*
Being respected	71.0%	55.3%*

* Significant at $p < .0001$, chi-square

Table A-8
Self-reported interpersonal values comparison for females

Interpersonal Values (rated as "very important")	Nonhitting Females (n=556)	Hitting Females (n=147)
Friendship	91.9%	91.2%
Being loved	77.3%	74.1%
Concern for others	69.4%	68.0%
Respect for others	66.9%	61.2%
Forgiveness	66.2%	55.8%
Honesty	64.2%	49.7%*
Politeness	42.1%	34.0%
Generosity	41.2%	30.6%
Being respected	71.0%	66.7%

* Significant at $p < .001$, chi-square, but *not* at $p < .0001$

Table A-9
Self-reported interpersonal values comparison for males

Interpersonal Values (rated as "very important")	Nonhitting Males (n=367)	Hitting Males (n=396)
Friendship	76.6%	69.9%
Being loved	53.1%	46.7%
Concern for others	40.6%	35.1%
Respect for others	49.6%	36.9%*
Forgiveness	40.9%	33.6%*
Honesty	46.3%	31.1%*
Politeness	33.5%	21.0%*
Generosity	28.3%	21.2%*
Being respected	55.3%	50.0%

*Significant at p <.0001, chi-square

Table A-10
Self-reported moral judgment comparison for nonhitting females and males (percentage indicating agreement)

Moral Judgment	Nonhitting Females (n=556)	Nonhitting Males (n=367)
If someone has something you really want, it's OK to make them give it to you	4.1%	12.8%*
It's OK to punch or hit someone when you're having an argument	8.3%	20.7%*
Fighting is a good way to defend your friends	14.0%	31.4%*
It's OK to use threats to get what you want	6.1%	10.7%*
If I don't like my teacher, it's OK to act up in school	13.1%	15.1%*
It's OK to damage buildings and property as a way of getting even	3.4%	7.9%*
Right or wrong is a matter of personal opinion	83.7%	80.7%
The use of marijuana should be legalized	51.5%	43.5%

*Significant at p <.0001, chi-square

Table A-11
Self-reported moral judgment comparison for females (percentage indicating "agree" and "strongly agree")

Moral Judgment	Nonhitting Females (n=556)	Hitting Females (n=147)
If someone has something you really want, it's OK to make them give it to you	4.1%	16.3%*
It's OK to punch or hit someone when you're having an argument	8.3%	36.0%*
Fighting is a good way to defend your friends	14.0%	42.2%*
It's OK to use threats to get what you want	6.1%	22.5%*
If I don't like my teacher, it's OK to act up in school	13.1%	27.2%*
It's OK to damage buildings and property as a way of getting even	3.4%	11.6%*
Right or wrong is a matter of personal opinion	83.7%	92.3%*
The use of marijuana should be legalized	51.5%	66.0%*

*Significant at $p < .0001$, chi-square

Table A-12
Self-reported moral judgment comparison for males (percentage indicating "agree" and "strongly agree")

Moral Judgment	Nonhitting Males (n=367)	Hitting Males (n=396)
If someone has something you really want, it's OK to make them give it to you	12.8%	26.8%*
It's OK to punch or hit someone when you're having an argument	20.7%	50.1%*
Fighting is a good way to defend your friends	31.4%	63.4%*
It's OK to use threats to get what you want	10.7%	31.0%*
If I don't like my teacher, it's OK to act up in school	15.1%	33.3%*
It's OK to damage buildings and property as a way of getting even	7.9%	24.0%*
Right or wrong is a matter of personal opinion	80.7%	86.1%
The use of marijuana should be legalized	43.5%	66.5%*

*Significant at $p < .0001$, chi-square

Table A-13

Self-reported moral judgment comparison for hitting females and nonhitting males (percentage indicating "agree" and "strongly agree")

Moral Judgment	Hitting Females (n=147)	Nonhitting Males (n=367)
If someone has something you really want, it's OK to make them give it to you	16.3%	12.8%
It's OK to punch or hit someone when you're having an argument	36.0%*	20.7%
Fighting is a good way to defend your friends	42.2%	31.4%
It's OK to use threats to get what you want	22.5%*	10.7%
If I don't like my teacher, it's OK to act up in school	27.2%*	15.1%
It's OK to damage buildings and property as a way of getting even	11.6%	7.9%
Right or wrong is a matter of personal opinion	92.3%*	80.7%
The use of marijuana should be legalized	66.0%*	43.5%*

*Significant at $p < .0001$, chi-square

Table A-14
Self-reported moral judgment comparison for hitting females and males (percentage indicating "agree" and "strongly agree")

Moral Judgment	Hitting Females (n=147)	Hitting Males (n=396)
If someone has something you really want, it's OK to make them give it to you	16.3%	26.8%
It's OK to punch or hit someone when you're having an argument	36.0%	50.1%
Fighting is a good way to defend your friends	42.2%	63.4%*
It's OK to use threats to get what you want	22.5%	31.0%
If I don't like my teacher, it's OK to act up in school	27.2%	33.3%
It's OK to damage buildings and property as a way of getting even	11.6%	24.0%
Right or wrong is a matter of personal opinion	92.3%	86.1%
The use of marijuana should be legalized	66.0%	66.5%

*Significant at $p < .0001$, chi-square

Table A-15
PARTICIPANTS' SELF-ASSESSMENT ON QUESTIONS OF SELF-CONCEPT (PERCENTAGE ANSWERING THAT THIS STATEMENT DESCRIBED THEM "FAIRLY WELL" OR BETTER)

Self-Concept Questions	Nonhitting Females (n=556)	Hitting Females (n=147)	Nonhitting Males (n=367)	Hitting Males (n=396)
I am well liked	94.6%	97.3%	91.0%	90.9%
I am good-looking	67.3%	72.1%	76.3%	78.3%
I can do most things well	80.0%	73.5%	91.5%* when compared with all females	89.3%* when compared with all females
I have lots of confidence	69.5%	66.0%	81.7%* when compared with all females	82.6%* when compared with all females

*Significant at $p < .0001$, chi-square

Table A-16
RATINGS OF SELF-CONCEPT, MEAN SCORE COMPARISONS FOR MALES AND FEMALES

Self-Concept Questions	Females (n=703)	Males (n=763)
I am well liked	3.20	3.14
I am good-looking	2.79	2.90*
I can do most things well	2.97	3.19*
I have lots of confidence	2.79	3.12*

*Significant at $p < .0001$, chi-square

Table A-17
Gender comparisons of personal and social concerns (percentage reporting "very serious" or "very important")

Social and Personal Concerns	Nonhitting Females (n=556)	Hitting Females (n=147)	Nonhitting Males (n=367)	Hitting Males (n=396)
AIDS	87.6%*	85.2%*	72.9%	75.9%
Child abuse	80.7%*	84.5%*	57.5%	60.9%
Racial discrimination	71.0%*	71.7%*	54.9%	50.1%
Teenage suicide	70.8%*	70.5%*	48.7%	47.1%
Violence against women	67.7%*	67.1%*	46.1%	46.4%
The environment	67.1%*	67.6%*	58.0%	56.2%
The unequal treatment of women	55.6%*	67.8%**	31.4%	35.8%
Violence in schools	52.8%*	37.1%†	46.0%††	37.8%
Drug abuse	64.1%††	52.1%††	59.2%††	48.2%
Alcohol abuse	59.8%*	48.6%	53.5%††	42.9%
Youth gangs	50.3%*	47.8%*	41.9%††	37.1%
Native–white relations	34.9%*	38.2%*	24.6%	26.5%
The economy	38.5%	32.5%	43.4%	38.1%
Global awareness	33.0%*	16.0%†	22.0%	17.7%
Spirituality	29.0%*	23.5%	19.3%	18.9%
Cultural group or heritage	15.5%	13.5%	12.8%	12.2%

* Significant at p <.0001, chi-square. All significant differences apply to an overall comparison with males
** This significant difference applies to a comparison with nonhitting females and all males
† This significant difference applies to a comparison with nonhitting females
†† This significant difference applies to a comparison with hitting males

Table A-18
Participants' responses to questions relating to ambition (percentage reporting "a great deal" or "very important")

Ambition Questions	Nonhitting Females (n=556)	Hitting Females (n=147)	Nonhitting Males (n=367)	Hitting Males (n=396)
How much enjoyment do you receive from your job?	(n/a=54.0%) 18.8%	(n/a=58.5%) 14.8%	(n/a=55.3%) 18.3%	(n/a=43.2%) **26.7%*** significant difference when compared with hitting females
How important is working hard?	43.5%	35.9%	44.38%	34.85%
How important is success in what you do?	64.3%	59.2%	68.6%	61.4%
How much does pressure to do well in school bother you?	22.9%	31.5%	25.1%	31.5%
How much does never having enough time bother you?	35.0%	36.3%	29.5%	40.3%
How much does the question of what you are going to do when you finish school bother you?	21.3%	23.1%	20.1%	33.1%
Do you agree or disagree that anyone who works hard will rise to the top?	84.6% Agree	72.2% Agree	85.2% Agree	78.7% Agree

* Significant at $p < .0001$, chi-square

Table A-19
PARTICIPANTS' RESPONSES TO QUESTIONS RELATING TO MONEY

Monetary Questions	Nonhitting Females (n=556)	Hitting Females (n=147)	Nonhitting Males (n=367)	Hitting Males (n=396)
Do you have a job during the school year?	38.4% Yes	42.0% Yes	35.6% Yes	47.23% Yes
How many hours per week do you work?	20.03% 10 hrs. or more	29.6% 10 hrs. or more	23.5% 10 hrs. or more	33.5% 10 hrs. or more
What is your hourly wage? (% reporting $7/hour or more)	12.68%	**26.7%*** significant when compared with hitting females	41.22%	**50.0%*** significant when compared with a females and non-hitting males
Do you receive a weekly allowance?	55.3% Yes	66.2% Yes	58.0% Yes	60.9% Yes
What is your weekly allowance? (% reporting over $25)	5.6%	**17.7%*** significant when compared with nonhitting females and non-hitting males	6.22%	**13.2%*** significant when compared with nonhitting female and nonhitting males
How much does the lack of money bother you? (% reporting "a great deal")	29.5%	33.8%	31.2%	**45.7%*** significant when compared with nonhitting males and females and hitting females

* Significant at $p < .0001$, chi-square

Table A-20
Participants' responses to four quality-of-life questions (percentage reporting "very important")

Quality-of-Life Questions	Nonhitting Females (n=556)	Hitting Females (n=147)	Nonhitting Males (n=367)	Hitting Males (n=396)
How important is a comfortable life to you?	62.0%	54.9%	69.2%	55.7%
How important is intelligence to you?	40.7%	42.4%	50.6%	41.4%
How important is humor to you?	64.5%	61.9%	64.5%	60.9%
How important are your looks to you?	28.8%	33.3%	35.7%	45.9%

Table A-21
Participants' responses to social support network questions

To Whom Will You Turn Re: Money?	Nonhitting Females (n=556)	Hitting Females (n=147)	Nonhitting Males (n=367)	Hitting Males (n=396)
Parents	52.2%	40.0%	50.4%	44.2%
Friends	25.9%	35.7%	22.6%	25.6%
School counselor	0.0%	0.0%	0.3%	0.3%
Minister or priest	0.0%	0.0%	0.3%	0.3%
Adult friend	0.4%	2.1%	0.8%	1.4%
No one	18.3%	20.2%	25.1%	27.5%
Other	2.3%	1.4%	0.6%	0.8%

Table A-22
Participants' responses to social support network questions (cont'd)

To Whom Will You Turn Re: Relationships?	Nonhitting Females (n=556)	Hitting Females (n=147)	Nonhitting Males (n=367)	Hitting Males (n=396)
Parents	7.7%	10.6%	11.3%	7.9%
Friends	80.6%	77.3%	59.6%	67.3%
School counselor	0.9%	0.0%	0.9%	0.5%
Minister or priest	0.2%	0.0%	0.3%	0.8%
Adult friend	1.1%	1.4%	1.7%	2.1%
No one	7.9%	9.2%	25.4%	19.5%
Other	1.5%	1.4%	0.8%	1.9%

Table A-23
Participants' responses to social support network questions (cont'd)

To Whom Will You Turn Re: Sex?	Nonhitting Females (n=556)	Hitting Females (n=147)	Nonhitting Males (n=367)	Hitting Males (n=396)
Parents	14.7%	11.2%	12.3%	11.4%
Friends	49.3%	59.4%	34.2%	46.2%
School counselor	1.9%	0.7%	0.9%	1.3%
Minister or priest	0.6%	0.0%	1.2%	1.1%
Adult friend	1.6%	2.8%	1.5%	2.1%
No one	28.6%	25.2%	47.4%	35.1%
Other	3.3%	0.7%	2.6%	2.9%

Table A-24
PARTICIPANTS' RESPONSES TO SOCIAL SUPPORT NETWORK QUESTIONS (CONT'D)

To Whom Will You Turn Re: Fun?	Nonhitting Females (n=556)	Hitting Females (n=147)	Nonhitting Males (n=367)	Hitting Males (n=396)
Parents	4.1%	0.7%	5.4%	4.3%
Friends	88.0%	90.7%	78.1%	78.1%
School counselor	0.0%	0.7%	0.0%	0.3%
Minister or priest	0.0%	0.0%	0.6%	0.8%
Adult friend	0.0%	0.0%	0.3%	1.6%
No one	7.1%	7.1%	14.2%	14.4%
Other	0.7%	0.7%	0.8%	0.5%

Table A-25
PARTICIPANTS' RESPONSES TO SOCIAL SUPPORT NETWORK QUESTIONS (CONT'D)

To Whom Will You Turn Re: Right and Wrong?	Nonhitting Females (n=556)	Hitting Females (n=147)	Nonhitting Males (n=367)	Hitting Males (n=396)
Parents	48.6%	32.6%	49.7%	36.0%
Friends	30.6%	38.0%	18.2%	25.8%
School counselor	1.4%	2.9%	1.1%	2.3%
Minister or priest	0.2%	0.7%	0.9%	0.8%
Adult friend	2.5%	3.7%	1.7%	2.3%
No one	14.0%	19.7%	27.3%	29.6%
Other	2.7%	2.2%	1.1%	1.9%

Table A-26
PARTICIPANTS' RESPONSES TO SOCIAL SUPPORT NETWORK QUESTIONS (CONT'D)

To Whom Will You Turn Re: School?	Nonhitting Females (n=556)	Hitting Females (n=147)	Nonhitting Males (n=367)	Hitting Males (n=396)
Parents	51.6%	37.5%	53.5%	39.1%
Friends	27.7%	36.0%	18.8%	24.7%
School counselor	7.6%	13.2%	8.4%	10.4%
Minister or priest	0.0%	0.0%	0.6%	1.1%
Adult friend	1.9%	2.2%	0.3%	2.9%
No one	8.7%	10.3%	16.8%	20.7%
Other	2.1%	0.7%	1.7%	1.1%

Table A-27
PARTICIPANTS' RESPONSES TO SOCIAL SUPPORT NETWORK QUESTIONS (CONT'D)

To Whom Will You Turn Re: Careers?	Nonhitting Females (n=556)	Hitting Females (n=147)	Nonhitting Males (n=367)	Hitting Males (n=396)
Parents	60.0%	44.9%	65.7%	52.0%
Friends	13.2%	21.0%	10.6%	12.6%
School counselor	5.3%	10.9%	2.1%	4.8%
Minister or priest	0.0%	0.7%	0.9%	1.1%
Adult friend	1.2%	1.5%	2.4%	4.0%
No one	17.3%	19.6%	16.4%	24.4%
Other	2.2%	1.5%	1.8%	1.1%

Table A-28
PARTICIPANTS' RESPONSES TO SOCIAL SUPPORT NETWORK QUESTIONS (CONT'd)

To Whom Will You Turn Re: A Major Problem?	Nonhitting Females (n=556)	Hitting Females (n=147)	Nonhitting Males (n=367)	Hitting Males (n=396)
Parents	32.1%	27.2%	52.9%	37.9%
Friends	48.0%	51.2%	26.4%	34.6%
School counselor	5.7%	5.6%	2.4%	4.5%
Minister or priest	0.2%	6.4%	1.2%	1.1%
Adult friend	3.7%	4.8%	1.2%	5.1%
No one	5.3%	4.8%	13.2%	14.3%
Other	5.1%	4.8%	2.7%	2.5%

Table A-29
LEVEL OF BEING BOTHERED BY FEAR OF ATTACK

How often does the fear of being attacked or beaten up bother you?	Nonhitting Females (n=556)	Hitting Females (n=147)	Nonhitting Males (n=367)	Hitting Males (n=396)
A great deal or quite a bit	25.8%	20.6%	18.4%	20.4%
Little or none	74.2%	79.4%	81.6%	79.6%

Table A-30
PERCENTAGE OF PARTICIPANTS FEARING ATTACK AT SCHOOL

Are you afraid of being physically attacked at school?	Nonhitting Females (n=556)	Hitting Females (n=147)	Nonhitting Males (n=367)	Hitting Males (n=396)
Yes	17.6%	17.4%	19.8%	20.6%
No	82.4%	82.6%	80.2%	79.4%

Table A-31
PERCENTAGE OF PARTICIPANTS FEARING BEING BEATEN BY A GANG OF KIDS

Are you afraid you might be beaten up by a gang of kids?	Nonhitting Females (n=556)	Hitting Females (n=147)	Nonhitting Males (n=367)	Hitting Males (n=396)
Yes	21.2%	16.6%	25.1%	21.5%
No	78.8%	83.4%	74.9%	78.5%

Table A-32
PERCENTAGE OF PARTICIPANTS STAYING AWAY FROM SCHOOL BECAUSE OF FEAR

Have you ever stayed away from school because you were afraid?	Nonhitting Females (n=556)	Hitting Females (n=147)	Nonhitting Males (n=367)	Hitting Males (n=396)
Yes	12.5%	12.9%	5.8%	9.2%
No	87.5%	87.1%	94.2%	90.8%

Table A-33
PERCENTAGE OF PARTICIPANTS FEARING PHYSICAL ABUSE AT HOME

Are you afraid you might be physically abused at home?	Nonhitting Females (n=556)	Hitting Females (n=147)	Nonhitting Males (n=367)	Hitting Males (n=396)
Yes	6.6%	18.5%*	3.3%	4.9%
No	93.4%	81.5%	96.7%	95.1%

* Significant at $p < .0001$, chi-square

Table A-34
PERCENTAGE OF PARTICIPANTS FEARING SEXUAL ASSAULT

Are you afraid you might be sexually assaulted?	Nonhitting Females (n=556)	Hitting Females (n=147)	Nonhitting Males (n=367)	Hitting Males (n=396)
Yes	28.0% when compared with all males	37.2%* when compared with all males and nonhitting females	4.1%	7.7%
No	72.0% when compared with all males	62.8%* when compared with all males and nonhitting females	95.9%	92.3%

* Significant at $p <.0001$, chi-square

Table A-35
PERCENTAGE OF PARTICIPANTS FEARING SEX AGAINST THEIR WILL

Are you afraid you might be talked into having sex with your boy/girl-friend against your will?	Nonhitting Females (n=556)	Hitting Females (n=147)	Nonhitting Males (n=367)	Hitting Males (n=396)
Yes	14.3% when compared with all males	22.4% when compared with all males and nonhitting females	2.8%	8.2%
No	85.7% when compared with all males	67.6% when compared with all males and nonhitting females	97.2%	91.8%

* Significant at $p <.0001$, chi-square

Table A-36
Percentage of participants who have been victimized by a gang of kids

Have you ever been a victim of a gang of kids?	Nonhitting Females (n=556)	Hitting Females (n=147)	Nonhitting Males (n=367)	Hitting Males (n=396)
Yes	4.1%	10.2%	6.0%	14.9%* when compared with nonhitting males and female
No	95.9%	89.8%	94.0%	85.1%* when compared with nonhitting males and female

* Significant at p <.0001, chi-square

Table A-37
Percentage of participants who have been attacked while going to or from school

Have you ever been attacked on your way to or from school?	Nonhitting Females (n=556)	Hitting Females (n=147)	Nonhitting Males (n=367)	Hitting Males (n=396)
Yes	3.6%*	5.4%*	10.2%	18.9%*
No	95.9%*	89.8%*	94.0%	85.1%*

* Significant at p <.0001, chi-square

Table A-38
Percentage of participants who have been physically abused at home

Have you ever been physically abused at home?	Nonhitting Females (n=556)	Hitting Females (n=147)	Nonhitting Males (n=367)	Hitting Males (n=396)
Yes	6.3%	19.9%*	3.0%	9.6%
No	93.7%	80.1%*	97.0%	90.4%

* Significant at p <.0001, chi-square

Table A-39
PERCENTAGE of participants who have been sexually abused

Have you ever been sexually abused?	Nonhitting Females (n=556)	Hitting Females (n=147)	Nonhitting Males (n=367)	Hitting Males (n=396)
Yes	11.2%*	**23.5%***	0.8%*	4.5%*
No	88.8%*	**76.5%***	99.2%*	95.5%*

* Significant at p <.0001, chi-square

Table A-40
PERCENTAGE of participants who have been talked into sex against their will

Have you ever been talked into having sex with your boy/girlfriend against your will?	Nonhitting Females (n=556)	Hitting Females (n=147)	Nonhitting Males (n=367)	Hitting Males (n=396)
Yes	7.3%	**13.7%***	2.8%	7.1%
No	92.7%	**86.3%***	97.2%	92.9%

* Significant at p <.0001, chi-square

Table A-41a
Participants involved in rule-breaking, deviant, and delinquent behaviors (percentage reporting "very often") (all differences significant at $p < .0001$, chi-square)

Behavior	Nonhitting Females (n=556)	Hitting Females (n=147)	Nonhitting Males (n=367)	Hitting Males (n=396)
Smoke without parents' permission	20.4% significantly higher than nonhitting males	38.4% significantly higher than nonhitting males and females	6.8% significantly lower than all other groups	27.6% significantly higher than nonhitting males
Lie to parents	12.6% significantly higher than nonhitting males	31.5% significantly higher than nonhitting males and females	4.7% significantly lower than all other groups	23.5% significantly higher than nonhitting males and females
Stay out all night without parents' permission	1.6%	8.9% significantly higher than nonhitting males and females	2.5%	15.2% significantly higher than nonhitting males and females
Skip classes	4.9%	17.7% significantly higher than nonhitting males and females	3.8%	16.4% significantly higher than nonhitting males and females
Skip school	4.0%	17.7% significantly higher than nonhitting males and females	3.6%	15.8% significantly higher than nonhitting males and females
Steal little things that don't belong to you	2.7%	12.9% significantly higher than nonhitting males and females	2.7%	14.9% significantly higher than nonhitting males and females

Table A-41b
Participants involved in rule-breaking, deviant, and delinquent behaviors (percentage reporting "very often") (all differences significant at $p < .0001$, chi-square)

Behavior	Nonhitting Females (n=556)	Hitting Females (n=147)	Nonhitting Males (n=367)	Hitting Males (n=396)
Deliberately ruin parents' property after an argument (1–2x/year or more)	10.6%	**29.9%** significantly higher than nonhitting males and females	9.0%	**28.8%** significantly higher than nonhitting males and females
Damage others' property for fun	0.5%	**3.4%** significantly higher than nonhitting males and females	1.6%	**10.4%** significantly higher than nonhitting males and females and hitting females
Take something from a store without paying	1.6%	**8.9%** significantly higher than nonhitting males and females	2.2%	**13.9%** significantly higher than nonhitting males and females
Break into a place to look around	0.2%	**4.8%** significantly higher than nonhitting males and females	0.0%	**9.6%** significantly higher than nonhitting males and females and hitting females
Purposefully damage school property	0.5%	**2.1%** significantly higher than nonhitting males and females	0.8%	**5.8%** significantly higher than nonhitting males and females
Carry a weapon	0.9%	**6.2%** significantly higher than nonhitting males and females	2.2%	**16.9%** significantly higher than nonhitting males and females and hitting females

Table A-41c
Participants involved in rule-breaking, deviant, and delinquent behaviors (percentage reporting "very often") (all differences significant at $p < .0001$, chi-square)

Behavior	Nonhitting Females (n=556)	Hitting Females (n=147)	Nonhitting Males (n=367)	Hitting Males (n=396)
Smoke weekly or more	**29.1%** significant when compared with nonhitting males	**56.5%** significant when compared with nonhitting males and females and hitting males	**9.9%** significantly lower than all other groups	**32.2%** significant when compared with nonhitting male
Drink alcohol weekly or more	11.3%	**26.9%** significantly higher than nonhitting males and females	8.5%	**27.0%** significantly higher than nonhitting males and female
Smoke marijuana weekly or more	10.5%	**26.5%** significantly higher than nonhitting males and females	8.8%	**27.2%** significantly higher than nonhitting males and female
Use other illegal drugs weekly or more	3.5%	**17.9%** significantly higher than nonhitting males and females	3.3%	**15.8%** significantly higher than nonhitting males and female
Use over-the-counter drugs weekly or more	10.6%	15.0%	**6.3%** significantly lower than all other groups	10.7%
Stop oneself from eating in order to lose weight weekly or more	**10.9%** significantly higher than nonhitting and hitting males	**13.8%** significantly higher than nonhitting and hitting males	1.7%	3.3%

Appendix II
Resource List*

Pamphlets
Dating Violence Prevention (March 1993)
Child Abuse Prevention Program for Adolescents
The Canadian Red Cross Society, B.C./Yukon Division

Working Together to Understand and Stop Sexual Harassment (1992)
Stop Sexual Harassment
King County Sexual Assault Resource Center
P.O. Box 300
Renton, WA 98057

Surviving Sexual Assault: Stress and Relaxation (1991)
King County Sexual Assault Resource Center
P.O. Box 300
Renton, WA 98057

The Abuse Began Just After We Started Going Out:
  What Young Women Should Know About Abuse by their Boyfriends
Battered Women's Support Services
P.O. Box 1098, Postal Station A
United Way Affiliated Agency
Vancouver, B.C. V6C 2T1

Booklets
Just A Kiss: A Photo Novella About Dating Violence (1993)
Battered Women's Support Services
P.O. Box 1098, Postal Station A
Vancouver, B.C. V6C 2T1

Today's Talk About Sexual Abuse: A Booklet for Teens
Project 1993–94 (© 1994)
Victoria Women's Sexual Assault Centre

* This resource list was developed by Monica Blais, MA.

Manuals

Healthy Attitudes, Healthy Relationships: Men Working to
  End Men's Violence Against Women
by Kathleen Folliot, Kimberley Morrison, and Michael Kaufmann
Prepared by White Ribbon Campaign
Activities for Classrooms and Schools
CAW/TCA Canada
The White Ribbon Campaign
220 Yonge Street, Suite 104
Toronto, ON M5E 2H1

Flirting or Hurting: A Teacher's Guide on Student-to-Student
  Sexual Harassment in Schools (Gr. 6–12) (1994)
by Nan Stein and Lisa Sjostrom
NEA Professional Library Publication
National Education Association
Washington, DC

Dating Violence Prevention: Overview and Response, Part III (1993)
by Judi Fairholm, RN, BScN
The Canadian Red Cross, B.C./Yukon Division

So What's It To Me: Activity Guide Sexual Assault Information for Guys
by Gayle M. Stringer and Deanne Rants-Rodriguez (1987)
King County Rape Relief
1025 S. Third
Renton, WA 98055

Accompanying Booklet — *So What's It To Me: Activity Guide Sexual Assault*
Information for Guys (1989)

Top Secret: A Discussion Guide
by Billy Jo Flerchinger and Jennifer J. Fay (1985)
Network Publications
Santa Cruz King County Rape Relief

Accompanying Booklet — *Top Secret: A Discussion Guide* (1982)
King County Sexual Assault Resource Center
P.O. Box 300
Renton, WA 98057

Sexual Harassment and Teens: A Program for Positive Change
by Susan Strauss and Pamela Espeland (1992)
Free Spirit Publishing
Minneapolis, MN

Dating Violence: A Discussion Guide on Violence in Young People's Relationships
by Debra J. Lewis (1994)
Battered Women's Support Services
P.O. Box 1098, Postal Station A
Vancouver, B.C. V6C 2T1

Books

No Is Not Enough: Helping Teenagers Avoid Sexual Assault
by C. Adams, Jennifer Fay, and Jan Loreen (1990)
Martin Import Publishers
San Luis Obispo, CA

Videos

When Dating Turns Dangerous
Sunburst Communications (1995)
Pleasantville, NY

Other Resources

Viraj — Programme de prévention de la violence dans les relations amoureuses des jeunes
(1) Animation classe
(2) Session de perfectionnement
(3) Guide de participation à la session de perfectionnement
Gouvernement du Québec
Ministère de l'Éducation
Québec, 1993

*Responding to Sexual Assault in Schools — Towards Zero Tolerance:
   A Discussion Paper*
by Catherine Stewart (1992)
Catherine Stewart & Associates

Index

The HOLLYWOOD BOOK OF LOVE

AN IRREVERENT GUIDE TO THE FILMS THAT RAISED OUR ROMANTIC EXPECTATIONS

James Robert Parish

Contemporary Books

Chicago   New York   San Francisco   Lisbon   London   Madrid   Mexico City
Milan   New Delhi   San Juan   Seoul   Singapore   Sydney   Toronto

Library of Congress Cataloging-in-Publication Data

Parish, James Robert.
　　　The Hollywood book of love : an irreverent guide to the films that raised our
　romantic expectations / James Robert Parish.
　　　　　　p.　　cm.
　　　Includes bibliographical references and index.
　　　ISBN 0-07-140280-2 (acid-free paper)
　　　1. Love in motion pictures.　　2. Motion pictures—United States.　　I. Title.

　PN1995.9.L6P37　　2003
　791.43'6543—dc21　　　　　　　　　　　　　　　　2003046009

1 2 3 4 5 6 7 8 9 0　AGM/AGM　2 1 0 9 8 7 6 5 4 3

ISBN 0-07-140280-2

McGraw-Hill books are available at special quantity discounts to use as premiums and
sales promotions, or for use in corporate training programs. For more information, please
write to the Director of Special Sales, Professional Publishing, McGraw-Hill, Two Penn
Plaza, New York, NY 10121-2298. Or contact your local bookstore.

This book is printed on acid-free paper.

For those in love—then, now, and later

Contents

Acknowledgments

With appreciation to the following for their kind assistance:

Academy of Motion Picture Arts and Sciences: Margaret Herrick Library, Mark R. Akey, Larry Billman (Academy of Dance on Film), Billy Rose Theater Collection of the New York Public Library at Lincoln Center, John Cocchi, Ernest Cunningham (research associate), Mimi Day, Echo Book Shop, Alex Gildzen, Bill Givens, Pierre Guinle, Harry Haun, JC Archives, Matthew Kennedy, Jane Klain (Museum of Television and Radio— New York), Alvin H. Marill, Lee Mattson, Doug McClelland, Jim Meyer, Eric Monder, Albert L. Ortega (Albert L. Ortega Photos), Michael R. Pitts, Diane Pons, Barry Rivadue, Brad Schreiber, Arleen Schwartz, Nat Segaloff, André Soares, Les Spindle, Sam Staggs, Allan Taylor (editorial consultant and copy editor), Bryan Taylor, Vincent Terrace, Gerry Waggett, Steven Whitney, Don Wigal.

Special thanks to my literary agent, Stuart Bernstein, and to my editor, Matthew Carnicelli.

Introduction

"That's your problem. You don't want to be in love. You want to be loved in a movie."

Sleepless in Seattle (1993)

For years I've repeatedly heard the expression "I don't hear bells" when someone is discussing a fresh relationship and wondering whether or not the newly met couple share that magical emotional chemistry. On the surface, this remark refers to the potential of church wedding bells chiming in the future for the twosome. However, at the heart of this frequently used phrase—and one understood by most people—is that the thrilling romantic sparks between the duo are (sad, to say) missing. In short, the love level between the pair does not match the degree of romantic excitement that we have seen played out over and over again on movie screens. Thus, in our not-so-humble judgments, this actual encounter does not meet the fabricated romantic standards established for us in the movies. The duo is *not* a genuine love couple. End of case.

As youngsters, many of us watched movies and wondered when all the mush (i.e., the kissing between hero and heroine) would stop and the story would finally get back to the good stuff—the action, the special effects, the slapstick comedy, or whatever. But even then, in our "innocence," we were taking in what we saw and heard onscreen about romance. In such scenes of affection, the slickly edited visuals along with the mood-heightening background music combine to set a standard for "real" love—or, at least, what Hollywood is teaching us *should* happen when the romantic sparks are genuinely there.

Of course, most of us, even as children, sense that we might never look as physically great as the couple romancing on the big screen: they with their too-perfect hairstyles, ultrasmooth complexions, and expertly tailored clothes. As youngsters, we also suspect that the characters' great love dialogue may not be that spontaneous but the product of professional writers. But even with all that in mind, we, as the audience, are vicariously experiencing the romantic activity as the characters play it out. If such film footage really grabs our attention (and let's leave XXX-rated porno footage for another discussion), the line separating performers from movie roles blurs, making the actors and characters nearly interchangeable. We understand that this is the picture-perfect, best version of what life is supposed to be like, and if it can happen to screen characters, it can (and should!) happen to us in reality.

By the time we reach adolescence and are (at long last) searching for/making our own love connections, the majority of us have already been well indoctrinated by the movies as to what qualifies for an A grade in a romantic and/or sexual situation. By now, we expect sparks to fly (or, as in 1955's *To Catch a Thief* with Cary Grant and Grace Kelly, fireworks to magically explode) when we meet that oh-my-God special person. When we talk with our love target in actual life, our brains are often "hearing" how, for example, Humphrey Bogart spoke to Ingrid Bergman in 1942's *Casablanca* or the tone of Leonardo DiCaprio's love chatter with Kate Winslet in 1997's *Titanic*. Then too, we can see in our mind's eye how a kiss should really be accomplished—according to Ryan O'Neal and Ali McGraw in *Love Story* (1970) or Tom Hanks and Meg Ryan in *You've Got Mail* (1998). In short, we've been brainwashed by Hollywood on matters of love, romance, and sex—and we, more or less, expect our actual experiences to follow suit. (When they don't match up to these unrealistic expectations, we're disappointed, frustrated, and, sometimes, mad as hell.)

All of this is what prompted me to write *The Hollywood Book of Love*. I wanted to suggest how, over the twentieth century and into the new millennium, Hollywood movies have established romantic standards, both subtle and blatant. These guidelines, to one degree or another, affect us as we embark on a new love situation. In actuality, our real-life encounter might lead to only a one-night stand or to a platonic friendship, or it could progress to marriage and "living happily ever after." However the situation with the new person may work out, we somehow expect— thanks to Tinseltown propaganda—that, if it is the genuine thing, there must be dramatic music pulsating in the background, artistic lighting casting flattering shadows across our faces, and the correct interplay of sexy glances and sparkling conversation in order for everything to be romantically perfect. As our hearts thump madly, we'll know that this is really it (and not a heart attack) because we have found true love—Hollywood style.

In the following chapters, I cover different situations in a romance (from startup to breakup) from representative Hollywood movies, providing factual illustrations as well as my personal observations. Because customs and interests differ so widely from country to country, I have focused exclusively on American-made feature films.

A fascinating by-product drawn from preparing this work is realizing anew just how much movie ad teasers can distort the actuality of a plot's premise by wooing moviegoers with seductive catchphrases referencing love and romance. For example, the World War II drama *Air Force* (1943) was promoted with "The name of their love was Mary Ann." Left unsaid was that *Mary Ann* was actually the name of an American bomber plane and the love referred to was the crew's affection for their sturdy craft. Or a really serious-minded picture like *Angelo, My Love* (1983) could be positioned as a comedic romance by the ad folks' choosing an isolated line of dialogue from the film to become its identifying tag line: "Elizabeth, if you don't love me no more, I'm moving to Cincinnati."

Sometimes the crafty ad makers engineer a film's ad slogan that is bound to amuse the more sophisticated who grasp the intended double meaning (e.g., for the melodrama 1963's *All the Way Home*, the tag line announces: "Love is not a thing that grows only in the dark!"). On other occasions, the teaser coyly plays with the *L* word (e.g., 1997's *Fools Rush In*: "What if finding the love of your life meant changing the life that you loved?"). Another frequently used tack by product pushers is to make the picture's come-on ad line be a "romantic" command (e.g., 2000's *Bounce*: "This October, fall in love with fate"). Finally, there are those movie tag words about romance that defy planet Earth logic but, nevertheless, are used anyway (e.g., 1958's *The Black Orchid*: "More than a story of love . . . a story of life!").

Just as viewing Hollywood-made movies affects—often warps—our expectations in a real-world romantic situation, so do the stars we watch repeatedly on the screen. For example, when celebrities such as Jennifer Lopez or Ben Affleck make personal statements to the media about the quality of love or what marriage means to them, we absorb it on one level or another. We subconsciously add such information to our ever-expanding data bank of facts on the all-important topic of romance and sex.

Then too, when we see video clips on a TV tabloid news show or photos in a supermarket publication showing a film notable's lavish or unusual wedding, these often-extravagant images and descriptions register with us and are on tap for future comparisons to nuptials in our own lives. As such, this book contains several sidebars dealing with the show business famous discussing love, romance, marriage, and so forth. With these intriguing examples I am suggesting that, even knowing that these personalities are operating in a rarefied atmosphere, we "mere folks" create expectations by which we judge our own lives in such matters as duration and frequency of marriages.

In reading *The Hollywood Book of Love*, it's useful to keep in mind the caliber of Tinseltown movers and shakers who ultimately fashion what we see onscreen and, in turn, what we come to anticipate as essential in a "real" romance. As such, I am reminded of a writer friend who, a few years ago, was summoned to a TV network conference. It seemed the honchos were stalled creatively in their approach to a planned miniseries and wanted fresh input. The scripter met with a young network executive who excitedly described that this miniseries was to be a real "event" that might run for six or even eight hours of evening programming. When the writer asked the exec what the project was about, the big shot answered—framing the word as a picture with his hands—"Relationships!"

After moments of dead silence, the scripter inquired, "You mean between men and women?" Following another long pause, the exec suddenly smiled, as if a great thought had just hit him, and he said, "Say, that could be a big part of it."

1

Young Love

When people undergo their first romances, a new uncharted world of emotions opens up to them, flooding their minds with feelings and experiences that remain with them for the remainder of their lives. No matter what type or intensity of love relationships they enjoy thereafter, never again will they deal with such a range of passions so innocently, so naïvely, and so honestly.

Down through the ages, young love—with all its joys, excitement, and bewilderment—has been celebrated by poets, playwrights, and novelists. Their writings provide us with a reflection of how cultures in different eras and various parts of the world have thought about, dealt with, and reacted to this important coming of age in which adolescents reach toward maturity by exploring and experiencing feelings of love, passion, and lust for other individuals.

The movies are another art form that have recorded the rituals of first/early love throughout the twentieth century and right up to today. Whether it be a 1910s silent entry

with Mary Pickford, a late 1930s offering with Deanna Durbin, 1980's *Little Darlings* with Tatum O'Neal, or a 2002 release such as *Tuck Everlasting*, Hollywood has been there to capture all elements of blossoming first love. Sometimes one has to dig beneath the surface of a seemingly childish screen entry such as Sandra Dee's *Gidget* (1959) to appreciate how the establishment at that time—the conformist Eisenhower era—was slowly and begrudgingly giving way to an uncharted new moral climate in which individuality of thought/ expression and adventurousness in social activities were fast replacing the public's adherence to formerly strict social guidelines.

For film audiences—particularly for adolescents—of any given generation, often these Tinseltown movies about young love provide an educational guidepost of how (supposedly) more hip and experienced contemporaries are dealing with all the ramifications of first romance. Who would have imagined that Hayley Mills in the 1960s, Molly Ringwald in the 1980s, or Freddie

Prinze Jr. in much more recent times would be role models for many moviegoers about to experience (or already have done so) the joys and pain—and sometimes embarrassment—of young love.

Love Finds Andy Hardy

Metro-Goldwyn-Mayer, 1938, black-and-white, 90 minutes
Director: George B. Seitz
Cast: Lewis Stone, Mickey Rooney, Judy Garland, Ann Rutherford, and Lana Turner

*F*ive-foot, three-inch Rooney, who would win a special Academy Award for his performance in *Boys Town* (1938) and would soon become the box-office king of American movies, owed a good deal of his increasing popularity to his ongoing series of Andy Hardy movies. Set in the fictional city of Carvel, U.S.A., these pleasing entries—there would be sixteen in all—focus on the emotional growing pains of a "typical" American teenager, whose maturing interest in the opposite sex far outweighs his attention to high school academics. In his picture-perfect small-town life, he constantly gets into predicaments and emotional tangles that require his father (Stone), a local judge, to step in and have a heart-to-heart talk with his momentarily confused son. With such a lecture over, father, son, and the audience breathe a collective sigh of relief, for they

Mickey Rooney, the star of *Love Finds Andy Hardy* (1938).   Courtesy of JC Archives

know that the young hero is now back—for the time being—on the approved path to adulthood. (Would that teenage problems of the heart, the wallet, or whatever could be solved so easily in real life.)

Having put a deposit on a prized jalopy, Rooney needs to come up with the balance he owes by month's end. To earn the needed amount, Mickey agrees to escort a pal's flirtatious girlfriend (Turner) around town while the friend is away visiting relatives. The plan is that chaperone Rooney will keep her away from the clutches of other young Carvel men. Because of the attention Rooney is paying to shapely Lana, his steady girl (Rutherford) becomes jealous and refuses to go to the Christmas dance with him. Enterprising Mickey turns to adolescent Garland, in town to visit her grandmother, to be his replacement date at the big country club dance. Having long idolized Mickey, she willingly agrees to be his savior. Later, Judy, a Miss Fix-It who appreciates how much he cares for Ann, brings the two teenagers back together. With the universe put right, Garland returns to New York.

Although the movie reveals the lusty and crass sides of the young hero, the script carefully twists everything to make the narrative end on a positive note. Despite Rooney's having manipulated Garland to save him from the humiliation of not having a date for the

dance, she accepts all too sweetly her current fate as a mere matchmaker for beloved Rooney. Says a bubbly Garland of her knight in "shining" armor, "I'm going to write Andy Hardy pages in my scrapbook and read it for five years. For one night I was grown up. So you see, now I know how wonderful life will be when I'm sixteen." Poor girl, get a life!

Blue Denim

Twentieth Century-Fox, 1959, black-and-white, 89 minutes
Director: Philip Dunne
Cast: Carol Lynley, Brandon de Wilde, Macdonald Carey, Marsha Hunt, and Warren Berlinger

Blue Denim, based on a Broadway play, was promoted with the tag line: "The lost innocence . . . the rude awakening to what they had done. . . ." This tale of troubled young love reflected America's—and Hollywood's—realization that the desire in the United States after World War II to return to normalcy and conformity was increasingly wishful thinking. More and more, adolescents were experimenting with drink (and drugs) and jumping into adult romantic and/or sexual relationships with or without their parents' knowledge and/or permission.

Two sensitive teenagers (de Wilde and Lynley) share the commonality of having difficulty communicating with their parents.

Mickey the Romeo

The talented, diminutive **Mickey Rooney (b. 1920)** was renowned for his women-chasing behavior. Reportedly having lost his virginity at age ten, he has married eight times, including being wed to rising sex siren **Ava Gardner (1922–1990)** for a year in the early 1940s. Brash, impetuous Mickey has often spoken out on the subject of women and marriage:

- "I had money in my jeans. If I wanted to get laid, I just went out and got laid, with no romantic illusions."

- "I am the only man who has a marriage license made out 'To Whom It May Concern.'"

The lonesome, attractive duo quickly falls in love, and soon Carol confesses to Brandon that she is pregnant. Confused as to how to best handle the traumatic situation, the duo makes an unsuccessful attempt to get married but can't because they are underage and lack parental permission. When neither young person can find the courage to confide the truth to their parents, de Wilde learns of an abortionist through a pal (Berlinger). He forges a check from his father's account and rushes off with Lynley to the quack's organization. Meanwhile, the couple's parents learn the facts and reach the abortionist's workplace before the procedure is done. It is decided that the twosome will go live in another city and that Carol will have their child.

Despite the picture's too-simplistic presentation, the alienated youths get the moviemakers' sympathy. On the other hand, the baffled, frustrated parents are seen as one-dimensional obstacles to the teen leads' dealing successfully with the many emotional problems of their maturing during first love.

The Real Gidget

A year after making *Gidget*, **Sandra Dee (b. 1942)** married the six-year-older singer/ actor Bobby Darin (who had previously dated singer Connie Francis). A year later, Sandra and Bobby's son was born. By 1967 the couple had divorced. Only years later did the actress confide publicly that her seemingly Cinderella life had actually been a nightmare. Suffering from childhood abuse and being a victim of an eating disorder, she had a most troubled marriage with Darin who she said, "woke up one morning and didn't want to be married anymore." Dee never remarried. Over the years, as she unsuccessfully tried to revive her once-thriving acting career, she became involved in a cycle of substance abuse and treatment.

Gidget

Columbia, 1959, color, 95 minutes
Director: Paul Wendkos
Cast: Sandra Dee, James Darren, Cliff Robertson, Arthur O'Connell, and Tom Laughlin

Thanks to this confection, the world came to know that "gidget" is a nick- name for a girl midget. Blond, pert Dee plays the bubbly teenager whose greatest desire is to mature physically and stack up favorably against the bikini babes the guys all want. At the time, Sandra was fast becoming the chief role model for millions of adolescent girls who thought her picture perfect.

On a summer "manhunt" at a Malibu beach with slightly older girls, sixteen-year-old Sandra wins the attention of handsome surfer Darren—the prize catch—when she accidentally almost drowns. She also meets the older Robertson, a former Air Force pilot, who has become a beach bum. Excited by the new lifestyle, she persuades James and his pals to teach her the art of surfing. Before long she's become the group's mascot. By summer's end she's fallen in love with Darren, but he seems to prefer another beach "bunny." To make her dreamboat jealous, she persuades Cliff to take her to a remote beach house and tries to convince him to make love to her. He politely rejects her advances, but their being together is enough to shake Darren into realizing he cares a lot for Dee. Before he returns to college, he gives Sandra his fraternity pin. As for Robertson, because of Dee's continued faith in him, he decides to return to being a pilot.

Sandra Dee and Cliff Robertson discuss the reality of their "romance" in *Gidget* (1959).

Courtesy of JC Archives

One might ask, why see this blissfully contrived fare that has little to do with reality (either in the late 1950s or today)? Because, to quote Gidget herself, "Honest to goodness, it's the absolute ultimate!"

Cooley High

American International, 1975, color, 107 minutes
Director: Michael Schultz
Cast: Glynn Turman, Lawrence Hilton-Jacobs, Garrett Morris, Cynthia Davis, and Corin Rogers

*P*romoted as a black *American Graffiti* (1973), this superior picture with a sterling cast got lost in the shuffle of black action pictures that engulfed Hollywood at the time.

In 1964 Chicago, Hilton-Jacobs, girl-crazy Turman, and Rogers skip high school one day. They visit the local zoo, play basketball, and try to connect with several girls they meet along the way. Although he loves another (Christine Jones), Turman flirts with snobby Davis. Later the group takes a joy ride in a stolen car and barely misses being corralled by pursuing police. Glynn and Cynthia make love, and she makes sure that sweet Jones learns of the activity. Later, Glynn and some of his car thief buddies are captured by the cops. However, Turman's teacher (Morris) puts in a good word for the student, and he and Hilton-Jacobs are let go. The others are prosecuted by the law, leading some of the defendants' pals to believe that Glynn and Lawrence are traitors. Later, after Hilton-Jacobs is found beaten to death, Turman attends his friend's funeral. Standing away from the others, he reads a farewell poem to his pal.

Based on autobiographical reminiscences by the film's screenwriter (Eric Monte), *Cooley High* has become a cult favorite over the years. It captures the flavor of the period well, in particular by its use of Motown Records hits of the 1960s. Director Schultz effectively handles his cast as the story moves from the comic to the serious and reveals how these teens deal with a wide range of adolescent experiences.

Glynn Turman and Lawrence Hilton-Jacobs as high school classmates and best friends in *Cooley High* (1975). Courtesy of Echo Book Shop

Fast Times at Ridgemont High

Universal, 1982, color, 92 minutes
Director: Amy Heckerling
Cast: Sean Penn, Jennifer Jason Leigh, Judge Reinhold, Robert Romanus, and Phoebe Cates

*B*ased on Cameron Crowe's book/screenplay, this trendsetting feature rambunctiously (and to a large degree, honestly) follows the lives and loves of students from Southern California's Ridgemont High, most of whom have part-time jobs at the local mall. For many viewers, the most vibrant images from this comedy involve stoned-out surfing dude Penn who'd rather smoke grass than pay attention to the likes of disciplinarian teacher Ray Walston. However, Sean is but one of the ensemble of young adults who are profiled in this offering (which includes an impressive cast of fledgling actors such as Nicolas Cage and Forest Whitaker).

Trimming some of its more blatant sexuality to change its rating from X to R, the picture traces Leigh's odyssey as she desperately seeks to shed her virginity and get on with life. While shy Brian Backer, who does duty as a movie usher, hankers to build a relationship with her, it is fast-talking, concert-ticket scalper Romanus who scores with willing Jennifer Jason. This leads to Leigh's pregnancy and to Backer's angrily confronting Romanus when the latter does not provide his needed share of funds for her abortion. Later, Brian and Jennifer start a relationship in earnest. At the same time, Leigh's frequently agitated brother (Reinhold), a fast-food chef who fantasizes over classmate Cates, stops a robbery at a mall shop. As for strung-out Sean, taskmaster teacher Walston relents and allows him to attend the big school dance.

With a regimen of sex, drugs, and rock 'n' roll, it's a wonder any of these "students" ever graduate high school, let alone survive the academic year. Thankfully, they have their mall work experience to add to their resumes.

Pretty in Pink

Paramount, 1986, color, 96 minutes
Director: Howard Deutch
Cast: Molly Ringwald, Harry Dean Stanton, Jon Cryer, Annie Potts, Andrew McCarthy, and James Spader

*C*an love between a rich man and a girl from a blue-collar family work? *Pretty in Pink* deals with that timeless question.

Ringwald, who comes from a low-income part of Chicago, meets well-to-do McCarthy at a record shop where her girlfriend Potts is the manager. Molly is intrigued with this rich guy, which makes her childhood friend (Cryer) feel jealous. Andrew invites Molly to a party hosted by his arrogant preppie pal (Spader), and she quickly feels out of place among these snooty "richies." Later at a club, it is McCarthy who feels awkward, a situation heightened when Jon kisses Annie to arouse Molly's jealousy.

Despite their differences and tentativeness toward each other, Andrew asks her to the senior prom. However, snobbish Spader soon convinces him that the invitation is a bad decision. As a result, McCarthy ignores Molly. She eventually confronts him on the matter and is unhappy with his ambivalent response. Convinced she is batting out of her league—especially coming from a broken home where her father (Stanton) is floundering since his wife left him—she chooses to attend the big dance alone. After constructing a new outfit out of two old pink dresses, she arrives at the dance. There Cryer magically appears and leads her onto the dance floor. McCarthy interrupts their dance to tell Molly "I love you, always." Egged on by Jon, Ringwald follows Andrew as he departs the building. In his car, the couple embrace. Meanwhile, a neat girl in pink asks Cryer to dance and they glide off together.

Molly Ringwald as an insecure student before she becomes *Pretty in Pink* (1986).
Courtesy of JC Archives

If you think the upbeat ending of *Pretty in Pink* seems contrived, you get five bonus points for your final exam in film history 101. The movie's original script concludes with Ringwald and Cryer dancing together at the prom. In this version, because she cannot surmount her social status and leap into the rich class inhabited by McCarthy and his blue-blooded crowd, she and McCarthy are destined not to have a future together.

Before Sunrise

Columbia, 1995, color, 100 minutes
Director: Richard Linklater
Cast: Ethan Hawke, Julie Delpy, Andrea Eckert, Hanno Pöschi, and Erni Mangold

The burning question of this Generation X love story is, "Can the greatest romance of your life last only one night?" If you look like Hawke and Delpy, the answer is a decided yes.

On a train between Budapest and Vienna, American tourist Ethan chats with pretty French student Julie. Hawke convinces Delpy to get off the train with him in Austria so they can spend the day together. (He is catching a plane back to America the next morning.) As the duo moves about Vienna, they each learn more about the other. At sunset they are riding a Ferris wheel at the local amusement park and share a kiss.

Later that night at a nightclub, and especially thereafter at a café where they undertake a role-playing game (i.e., pretending to phone a best friend and discussing their new love), they become more intimate. Delpy tells him that because they plan never to meet again, she will not have sex with him. Dawn breaks, and they agree to meet in Vienna in six months. Ethan takes the bus to the airport, while Julie boards a train for France.

With its limited number of main characters, *Before Sunrise* soon evolves into a talkathon between its two personable leads. Often their dialogue rings pretentious (He: "I know happy couples . . . but I think they lie to each other." She: "I have this awful paranoid thought that feminism was mostly invented by men so that they could like, fool around a little more.") Occasionally—and then the often-somber love story turns spontaneous and joyful—the coleads engage in short, staccato dialogue that rings far truer:

She: "You know what I want?"
He: "What?"
She: "To be kissed."
He: "Well, I can do that."

If You Say So, Uma

Married to **Ethan Hawke (b. 1970)** since 1998, with whom she has two children, actress **Uma Thurman (b. 1970)** once observed, "When you're in a relationship, it's better to be with somebody who has an affair than with somebody who doesn't flush the toilet."

As *Before Sunrise* instructs us, be bold, be aggressive, and quickly get to the point in your romantic chatter with your significant other. So what if the other person walks away from you while you're still talking. Maybe he or she just needs space to consider your proposition.

10 Things I Hate About You

Buena Vista, 1999, color, 97 minutes
Director: Gil Junger
Cast: Heath Ledger, Julia Stiles, Joseph Gordon-Levitt, Larisa Oleynik, and Andrew Keegan

A modern riff on William Shakespeare's late-sixteenth-century comedy *The Taming of the Shrew*, this teen love entry has more bite and substance than the rash of similar films being churned out by such movie personalities as Freddie Prinze Jr.

A newcomer (Gordon-Levitt) to a Seattle, Washington, high school sets his eyes on pretty Oleynik. But alas, the lass is not allowed to date by her exasperated accountant father (Larry Miller) until her man-avoiding, shrewish sister Stiles changes her unsocial ways. With the financial help of Keegan—who also wants to step out with Larisa—Joseph persuades surly Ledger to take out Stiles. As the contrived courtship gets under way, Julia proves a difficult sort to tame, but soon she becomes intrigued with the persistent Heath. Meanwhile, Oleynik can't decide between Gordon-Levitt and Keegan until her sister confides that she had lost her virginity to Andrew and thereafter he ignored her. With Larisa and Joseph now a couple, Stiles lets Ledger know that she cares for him. True love has triumphed once again.

Playing on the Shakespearean text, the update is more substantial than the usual fluff, and it gives Stiles ample opportunity to play the young heroine reluctantly falling in love with the man she tells herself is just another Mr. Wrong. (At one point she informs Ledger, "I hate the way I don't hate you.") One element of the bard's play that is toned way down for modern tastes is the heavy dose of male chauvinism that permeated the original stage work.

40 Days and 40 Nights

Miramax, 2002, color, 95 minutes
Director: Michael Lehmann
Cast: Josh Hartnett, Shannyn Sossamon, Vinessa Shaw, Paulo Costanzo, and Maggie Gyllenhaal

*C*ostanzo tells his roommate (Hartnett), "You can't do it. You can't. . . . I'm just saying that no man can do it. It goes against nature. The male was biologically designed to spread his seed. . . ." What is this hue and cry about? It seems Josh, a website designer in San Francisco, has been dumped by his girlfriend (Shaw) and sinks into a funk. Afraid that, when he recuperates emotionally, he will leap

Josh Hartnett plays a man of great sexual fortitude in *40 Days and 40 Nights* (2002).
Photo by Albert L. Ortega

into a new love connection for all the wrong reasons, he gives up sex for Lent (hence the film's title).

Having maneuvered this high-concept plot setup, the moviemakers next (naturally!) have their hero encounter an enticing young woman (Sossamon). The two meet at the local Laundromat and develop a platonic relationship that turns romantic. However, Josh does not tell her about his vow of abstinence. Shannyn eventually learns of Hartnett's situation and that his office coworkers have a pool to see when he will break his promise.

This Year's Heartthrob

According to six-foot, three-inch bachelor **Josh Hartnett (b. 1978),** Hollywood's reigning young cinema hunk:

- "I've had my heart broken, and it's not fun. But I'd rather have my heart broken than break someone else's heart."

- "It's hard for me to work closely with a girl and not completely fall in love with her as a person."

She is, at first, upset, but then she decides to be "friends" with him. Their complex relationship turns sour when Josh's ex-girl has a change of heart and seeks to reunite with him. When he refuses to patch things up, Vinessa vengefully seduces him in his sleep and makes sure that her rival learns of the deed. This is the final straw for Sossamon. However, a few days after Lent ends, she and Hartnett run into each other at the laundry, and their romance is back on the hot track.

Now, if you can buy into this harmless but far-fetched concoction, you really need to stop watching TV's *Everwood* so much and get out more often into the real world.

Because most of the teen love fantasies turned out by Hollywood are typically scripted by twenty-somethings and older, we moviegoers get only a distillation of what the current crop of adolescents are doing and saying in actuality to make their romantic dreams come true. Care to predict how Hollywood a few decades hence will be visualizing the good old days of those much more innocent 2000s?

2

Love Down Through the Ages

Since the dawn of humanity, men and women have been preoccupied with love and sex. In this regard, individuals' emotional and sexual priorities have remained basically the same over thousands of years. However, as cultures around the world developed distinctive rituals and traditions, their customs and viewpoints varied greatly on how to express romance and how to deal with the emotion of love. In days of old, for example, a primitive caveman might bang his beloved over the head with a club and drag her by her hair back to his cave. That was considered proper etiquette then. But such primal courtship behavior would have caused a major furor in Roman or Elizabethan times or in twenty-first-century America. On the other hand, is there much real difference between natives in seventeenth-century darkest Africa performing a tribal mating dance around the campfire versus the gyrations of hip-hop dancers in a hot new joint in today's New York City?

As the fledgling motion picture industry developed in the early 1900s, moviemakers quickly appreciated that a conventional love story could be greatly enhanced if it were set in a past (or future) era in which the costumes, habits, and viewpoints were thus put into great contrast to contemporary times. They knew such dressed-up presentations would provide novelty value for filmgoers who could learn from, feel superior to, or even be in awe of the ways things were done in different societies throughout history. (And, a film made in 1934 about ancient Egypt would have a far different approach and look than one made in 1963 about the same locale and time period. This would occur not only because more accurate information is constantly being uncovered regarding the past but also because each generation of society, as it changes its habits, laws, and popular culture, reinterprets past times through the eyes of its own era.)

Another virtue of setting a screen love story in bygone times is that, often, in those historical periods the expression of love was far more grandiose, was much more highly romantic, and more frequently involved life and death situations (such as the man rushing off to do battle in the latest war or young lovers caught up in a deadly family feud). Generally, peoples of the past were not only more gallant in behavior (and flowery in prose) but they also abided by very strict lifestyle rules within their societies. To flout the established social rules of one's country in past eras was a brazen, often deadly thing to undertake. To go against the norm for the sake of a loved one was a grand gesture that really stood out and would lend itself to heightened moments of oncamera passion. In contrast, in today's far more liberal, flexible, and individual-dominated world, there are fewer story lines that will capture for the big screen a couple making dramatic sacrifices to make their love relationship possible. Today, for example, if a man gives up watching *Monday Night Football* on TV to accompany his girlfriend to a museum lecture or to a symphony concert, many consider that to be a supreme sacrifice. In the same mode, when was the last time you ripped off your jacket and threw it to the ground to cover a puddle so your female companion could walk with dry footwear?

♥   ♥   ♥   ♥   ♥

A Tale of Two Cities

Metro-Goldwyn-Mayer, 1935, black-and-white, 128 minutes
Director: Jack Conway
Cast: Ronald Colman, Elizabeth Allan, Edna May Oliver, Blanche Yurka, and Basil Rathbone

There had been many screen adaptations of Charles Dickens's novel (1859) before and after this entry, but this is the definitive presentation. Not only is it sumptuously mounted (although filmed in black-and-white) but also its first-rate cast comfortably handles the period dialogue, costumes, and manner with authority and flair. Most of all, this exciting tale of love, sacrifice, and death during the French Revolution benefits from the presence of swashbuckling movie favorite Colman. With his dashing figure, his fine, British-accented speaking voice, and those expressive, darting eyes, he is well up to his tasks. As such, his performance has the ring of truth and idealistic nobility that work in tandem with Allan as his lady love.

On the eve of the French Revolution in the late eighteenth century, the cruel marquis (Rathbone) is indifferent when his carriage runs over a little boy in the crowded streets. The angered peasants vow that Basil must pay with his life, which he does. Before long the tumultuous uprising is going full tilt, with French aristocrats (good and bad) being guillotined in horrifyingly large numbers. Mean-

Donald Woods and Ronald Colman play characters whose lives intertwine in the French Revolution drama *A Tale of Two Cities* (1935).   Courtesy of JC Archives

while, back in England, barrister Colman is in love with a beautiful French lady (Allan), but she, instead, marries a nobleman (Donald Woods) from her homeland. Donald, a relative of the late Rathbone, is soon tricked by the revolutionists into returning to France, where he is quickly imprisoned. Back in England, a frightened Elizabeth confides her husband's plight to Colman. Tired of his own unpromising life in which alcohol has become his balm, Colman volunteers to venture

across the English Channel to save Woods. He manages to sneak into the French jail and substitute himself for Donald, the latter being whisked to safety by friends. Soon Ronald faces his destiny with great dignity. As he ascends the scaffold to meet his end under the blade, he says, "It's a far, far better thing that I do than I have ever done. It's a far, far better rest I go to than I have ever known."

Most guys nowadays think life has come to an end if they nick their face while shaving and see a droplet of blood. So think long and hard before you wish you were back in time a few centuries and falling head over heels in love with a fair damsel whose heart belongs to another. Remember the lessons of anatomy 101: it's kinda hard to function in any activity when your skull is detached from your body.

The Plainsman

Paramount, 1936, black-and-white,
115 minutes
Director: Cecil B. DeMille
Cast: Gary Cooper, Jean Arthur, James Ellison, Charles Bickford, and Porter Hall

This sagebrush epic was promoted as being about "the hardest boiled pair of lovers who ever rode the plains . . . a glorious romance set against the whole flaming pageant of the Old West." In reality, fiction ruled the day with this fabrication of authentic historical figures and actual events. For example, the real-life Calamity Jane was a smelly drunk who would never win a beauty contest. In contrast, Arthur's tomboy version of the nineteenth-century sharpshooter was much glamorized physically and boasted a wisecracking personality that could turn flirtatious when in the company of her beloved (i.e., Cooper's Wild Bill Hickok).

Set in the post–Civil War period, the action occurs in the Midwest where the villainous Bickford is selling rifles to Native American warriors. At one point in the fighting between the cavalry troops and the Cheyenne, Arthur and Cooper fall into the hands of the tribesmen. The two are tortured and threatened with death unless they reveal the whereabouts of Buffalo Bill Cody (Ellison), who has been making life so troublesome for the warrior braves. Before the saga concludes, George Armstrong Custer and his regiment have been massacred at the Battle of Little Bighorn with other U.S. troops vowing revenge. Later, Gary is shot in the back by a desperado. As he lies dying, Jean kisses him, saying, "That's one kiss you won't wipe off."

A Man's Man

At six feet, two inches, strapping, handsome **Gary Cooper (1901–1961)** was quite a ladies' man during his many decades in Hollywood. Both before and after his marriage to socialite Veronica Balfe in 1933, he had many love affairs. His most tempestuous relationship was with actress **Lupe Velez (1908–1944)** in the late 1920s. The Mexican Spitfire, as she was known, was barely five feet tall, but the svelte dynamo kept Gary in a constant state of physical terror when he wasn't satisfying her insatiable sexual appetite. She thought nothing of punching and scratching him in their many tiffs. One time when he was slinking out of town to recover from his emotionally exhausting time with her, the jealous miss learned of his imminent departure. She rushed to the railroad station, and when she spotted her "beloved" boarding the train, she took a shot at him, barely missing the "ah shucks" screen hero.

Historical accuracy and political correctness aside, *The Plainsman* is rousing entertainment with the rugged lovers playfully bickering between moments of facing great danger or demonstrating real bravery. Its entertaining presentation almost makes you ready to jump on the nearest saddled horse and seek similar great adventures in the dangerous terrain—always, of course, with a potential love interest at your side. But keep levelheaded—they were treacherous times then.

The Adventures of Robin Hood

Warner Bros., 1938, color, 104 minutes
Directors: Michael Curtiz and William Keighley
Cast: Errol Flynn, Olivia de Havilland, Basil Rathbone, Claude Rains, and Patric Knowles

Swordplay, romancing, carousing, good triumphing over evil—they are a few of the key ingredients in this rousing, nonstop cinema adventure. What makes it a classic is the combination of the brilliant Technicolor photography (then a rarity), the fast pacing, the rich Erich Wolfgang Korngold soundtrack, and, most of all, the stellar cast. Among the onscreen ensemble are the love team of swashbuckling Flynn and spirited de Havilland, the sinister Rathbone (in actuality a far better fencer than Flynn), Rains, and a sup-

Errol's Way

Errol Flynn (1909–1959) cut a wide path through Hollywood during his three decades in the film colony and enjoyed a reputation as a heavy-duty ladies' man and drinker. He married three times and had numerous affairs, several of which were with underage girls. Despite his legendary status as an aggressive seducer, he claimed once, "Before I got to Hollywood, I had gone along on the assumption that it was the role of the male to pursue the female. I discovered that women know far more about seduction than men. Maybe it was the air around Hollywood, the competition among women to get places. It made some of them wild."

porting cast of Merry Men (including Alan Hale's Little John and Eugene Pallette's Friar Tuck), who are based in Sherwood Forest and help their leader to rob the rich and give to the poor.

Adding to the fun of this historical adventure set at the time of England's King Richard the Lionhearted and the Crusades is the lively dialogue. For example, at one point, Olivia says archly to the man she will soon come to love, "Why, you speak treason!" To which Errol replies—tongue in cheek, "Fluently." At the finale when the dastardly characters have been properly dispatched, a grateful King (Ian Hunter) knights Errol for his many good deeds. The monarch then tells his new nobleman, "My first command to you, Lord Earl, is to take in marriage the hand of the Lady Marian. . . . What say you to that, Baron of Locksley?" This leads a very pleased Flynn to respond mischievously, "May I obey all your commands with equal pleasure, sire!"

Such behavior and action on the screen seems so natural and unassuming. It's the stuff to make imaginative filmgoers dream of being in Robin and Maid Marian's shoes and romping through the countryside. Enjoy your fantasy, but don't overlook the fact that most public parks close at dusk. Moreover, the law has a very dim view of suspicious characters lurking in trees who make a habit of jumping down on travelers passing through the forest and relieving them of their worldly goods.

Gone with the Wind

Metro-Goldwyn-Mayer, 1939, color,
231 minutes
Director: Victor Fleming
Cast: Clark Gable, Vivien Leigh, Olivia de Havilland, Leslie Howard, and Hattie McDaniel

*M*argaret Mitchell's historical bestseller (1936) told of "a civilization gone with the wind." It romanticized the mid-nineteenth-century South in which surface gallantry, quaint customs, and a dreamy sense of daily life were far more important to the parade of superficial characters and the intricate plot than the thousands of suffering slaves at the mercy of their masters below the Mason-Dixon line. Even in its depiction of the bloody Civil War, the sweeping story focused more on the plight of the self-centered heroine, Scarlett O'Hara (Leigh), and her inner circle than on the outnumbered, poorly equipped, and militarily outmaneuvered Confederate soldiers who were dying in droves for Old Glory.

By now, nearly everyone can recite from memory most details of this screen offering, especially the misadventures of headstrong Leigh as she loses refined Howard to overly sweet de Havilland. Thereafter, Vivien initiates a love-hate relationship with a Southern rogue (Gable) that eventually leads to marriage, their having a child (who dies in a horse-riding accident), and his eventually leaving his spoiled wife. Vivien is now left to contemplate her unpromising future, bucking herself up with thoughts that "Tomorrow is another day" and surely things will seem better then. Ha!

Regarded as one of Hollywood's greatest screen achievements, *Gone with the Wind* won nine Academy Awards, including one for McDaniel (playing Mammy) as Best Supporting Actress (the first African American talent to win an Oscar). Her role as Mammy, as well as the screen parts (as servants) played by the other black performers conformed to 1930s skewed viewpoints about white power and discrimination against blacks.

Other distorted elements of *Gone with the Wind* include the glorified presentation of the gracious way of life that disappeared when the South admitted defeat and surrendered in 1865. Whether it be the oversized perfor-

mances of the ruffian carpetbaggers, the pret-
tified squalor of life in shantytown, or fearless
Gable surviving a wagonload of obstacles in
the story, nothing gives the reader the real feel
of what life was like then or how actual people would (re)act in such extreme situations.
Audiences—then and now—seeking surface
glamour, romance, and excitement never seem
fazed by these fairy-tale distortions. For them
it is part of the epic's charm and attraction.

But the next time you watch this mammoth feature, don't be shy in these proactive
days. When Leigh vows, "As God is my witness, I'll never go hungry again," shout out
that you have a box of power nutrition bars
you'd gladly share with her. When smug
blockade runner Gable remarks to willful
Vivien, "I've always thought a good lashing
with a buggy whip would benefit you
immensely," pull out your cell phone and dial
911. Physical abuse, you know, is against
the law.

Biblical seduction à la Hollywood as Hedy Lamarr
uses her wiles on Victor Mature in *Samson and
Delilah* (1949).   Courtesy of JC Archives

Samson and Delilah

Paramount, 1949, color, 130 minutes
Director: Cecil B. DeMille
Cast: Hedy Lamarr, Victor Mature,
George Sanders, Angela Lansbury, and
Henry Wilcoxon

*I*f it's in the Bible it must be so. Well, the
story of Samson and Delilah is in the
Book of Judges (Old Testament). However,

what emerges on the screen is pure escapism
as only master showman DeMille could con-
ceive for this three-ring celluloid circus. It's
hard to accept Hollywood good-timers
Mature and Lamarr in their key assignments,
and game Britisher Lansbury is a bit of a
stretch as Hedy's mantrap of a sister. Then
there is the business of muscle-bound Victor
battling a fierce lion. Because he refused to

tussle with a real-life beast (whether the actual animal used had a mouthful of teeth or not), a stuntman found work substituting for the star. (In close-ups, Mature did manly combat with a stuffed lion skin.)

But the cap to this colorful, pretentious, sexist nonsense (disguised as a legitimate Biblical story) is the hero's solo struggle against a huge number of very angry Philistines. His weapons of choice are his bare fists and the jawbone of an ass. Talk about an asinine situation! Later, Mature gets that fateful haircut from vengeful Lamarr (whom the hero once rejected in a moment of pique), which sends his life spiraling into a tailspin. Didn't the boy have a clue that this gorgeous dame was not a licensed barber?

By the way, it is only rumor that Siegfried and Roy are abandoning their Las Vegas lair long enough to costar in a TV miniseries remake of *Samson and Delilah*.

Timeless Dialogue

Any DeMillean screen epic has its share of extravagant text that the cast must speak with earnestness and enthusiasm. *Samson and Delilah* is no exception:

Lamarr: "If you crush the life out of me, I'd kiss you with my dying breath."
Mature: "[After he slays the lion, a sexually aroused Hedy is panting for her he-man. He shoves her away saying,] One cat at a time."

Ivanhoe

Metro Goldwyn Mayer, 1952, color, 106 minutes
Director: Richard Thorpe
Cast: Robert Taylor, Elizabeth Taylor, Joan Fontaine, George Sanders, and Emlyn Williams

Since its publication in 1820, millions have read Sir Walter Scott's famous novel of life and strife in twelfth-century England. This lavish movie adaptation is visually splendid as it re-creates the times of King Richard the Lionhearted when the king is captured following one of the Holy Crusades and Saxon knight Robert Taylor searches the Continent for the vanished ruler. He discovers the monarch is being held hostage in Austria. Robert immediately returns to England to raise the necessary ransom money to free the ruler. This leads the chivalrous nobleman into a deadly struggle with two Saxon-hating Norman knights (including Sanders) who are extremely loyal to the king's traitorous brother (Guy Rolfe).

But even a gallant knight deserves rest and relaxation. In his travels and fund-raising within *Ivanhoe*, Robert Taylor meets two lovely women. One is the beautiful Lady Rowena (Fontaine), the aristocratic ward of his father (Finlay Curie). The other, more buxom and even more enticing, is Rebecca (Elizabeth Taylor), the daughter of a Jewish moneylender (Felix Aylmer). Elizabeth or Joan? Joan or Elizabeth? It's a true dilemma that happens only to a Hollywood star—*not* to you or me!

Between the splendid high action on the fields of battle, the impressive storming of a castle, and a special guest appearance by none other than Robin Hood and his forest rangers, this is an exciting screen adventure. However, the plot always gets back to poor Robert deciding between Elizabeth and Joan or Joan and Elizabeth. What's a guy to do?

For the record, Liz Taylor was never fond of this film project, always referring to it as that "big medieval western."

Knights of the Round Table

Metro-Goldwyn-Mayer, 1953, color,
115 minutes
Director: Richard Thorpe
Cast: Robert Taylor, Ava Gardner, Mel Ferrer, Anne Crawford, and Stanley Baker

Using some of the talent and crew that had made the hit *Ivanhoe* (1952), this British-shot film was MGM's first experience with shooting a feature in CinemaScope, the trendsetting wide-screen process. The handsome cast—which mixed American and British actors—was everything the later *Camelot* (1967) should have been but wasn't.

Based on Sir Thomas Malory's *Le Morte D'Arthur* (1483), this well-known narrative is set at the court of King Arthur (Ferrer), where his sensual wife (Gardner) is making

eyes at her armor-clad heartthrob (Taylor) and is willing to give up everything to be with this medieval stud. To make the pageantry more miraculous, there's Merlin (Felix Aylmer) the magician who weaves his spells and does his magic act for one and all. Before the visually stunning adventure concludes, Ferrer has fallen in battle, Taylor has revenged the king by murdering the dastardly Baker, and luscious Ava has been ordered, "Get thee to a convent."

With all the courtly manners, bloody battles, and romantic intrigue in *Knights of the Round Table*, one might feel, at times, that one was trolling the corridors of the West Wing of the White House watching King Bill and Queen Hillary as in their days of old.

Too Busy for Each Other

At the time of making *Knights of the Round Table*, **Robert Taylor (1911–1969)** had recently divorced his superstar wife, actress Barbara Stanwyck, and was involved with German-born actress Ursula Thiess, whom he wed in 1954. As for colead **Ava Gardner (1922–1990)**, she was then in the process of marrying crooner/actor Frank Sinatra and, for a change, was too preoccupied to dally on the set with any romantic intrigue or to lose her famous temper on the soundstage. (Ava is the one famous for saying, "If people making a movie didn't keep kissing, they'd be at each other's throats.")

Richard Burton and Elizabeth Taylor as two of history's most passionate lovers in *Cleopatra* (1963).
Courtesy of Echo Book Shop

Cleopatra

Twentieth Century-Fox, 1963, color,
243 minutes
Director: Joseph L. Mankiewicz
Cast: Elizabeth Taylor, Richard Burton,
Rex Harrison, Hume Cronyn, and
Roddy McDowall

*T*he ads for this epic of ancient Egypt insist this is, "The motion picture the world has been waiting for!" And well it was.

For many months prior to its New York City premiere in June 1963, filmgoers around the globe were being spoon-fed delectable morsels of gossip concerning the latest wrinkles in the ongoing Taylor-Burton scandal. In the course of their unbridled affair during the protracted making of *Cleopatra*, each star had shocked the public by leaving his/her mate to wallow in adulterous happiness with each other. Meanwhile, the struggling film studio backing this picture was sinking under the financial weight of the trouble-plagued project, which included a change of directors and several cast members, the near death of Taylor from pneumonia, the substitution of Rome for London as the base of filming operation, and many more indulgences than usual provided to the trio of highly pampered lead players (which included Harrison).

If you can visualize Liz cruising down the Nile River in a luxuriant barge, making a spectacular entry into Rome on an intricate gold litter supported by muscled bearers, and all the while wearing more eye makeup than Tammy Faye Bakker, you have a brief hint of the magnitude and historical "accuracy" of this leaden feature. Not that director Mankiewicz didn't create noble dialogue for his characters to mouth, but when delivered it sounded so ponderous, especially when spoken by whiny Taylor and sullen Burton. (For example, using her best MGM manner, Liz uttered such immortal lines as, "Time is never reasonable. Time is our enemy, Caesar.")

Perhaps it is fitting that taking a leaf from history, this bloated rendition of Cleopatra's *True Hollywood Story* should conclude with Taylor's queen dying from a self-inflicted bite of an asp on her ample bosom.

This hugely expensive feature went down in the annals of show business history not because of its artistic merits but rather for the long list of creative elements it failed to achieve—and at such a high cost. Did this soggy spectacle—especially with its *Romeo and Juliet*-like finale—have any impact on overly impressionable moviegoers? Well, it has been recorded that the black market price for venomous asps temporarily rose by a few dollars.

Doctor Zhivago

Metro-Goldwyn-Mayer, 1965, color,
197 minutes
Director: David Lean
Cast: Omar Sharif, Geraldine Chaplin, Julie Christie, Rod Steiger, and Alec Guinness

A sleigh ride on the snowy Soviet tundra . . . a lilting love melody dedicated to Lara . . . two extremely handsome costars (Sharif and Christie) . . . and the backdrop of the Russian Revolution (1917–1921). All this rolled into one gorgeously filmed adaptation

Geraldine Chaplin and Omar Sharif in the Russian-set *Doctor Zhivago* (1965). Courtesy of JC Archives

The Possibilities

The most memorable movies about tragic romance are full of "what-ifs"—situations that might have changed the course of the lovers' lives. In *Doctor Zhivago,* the wistful, ill-fated couple—each married to or involved with another every time they encounter over the years—compare their might-have-beens:

He: "Wouldn't it have been lovely if we'd met before?"
She: "Before we did? Yes."
She: "We'd have gotten married, had a house and children. If we'd had children . . . would you like a boy or girl?"
He: "I think we may go mad if we think about all that."
She: "I shall always think about it."

of Boris Pasternak's highly political 1958 novel.

Most of the action takes place in flashback in Russia during World War I and the great revolution. A young doctor (Sharif) falls in love with a beautiful nurse (Christie), but each is attached to another person. As time passes and the tumult within the country grows, both keep returning to one another, all the while sensing that fate will never allow their love to flourish peacefully. Both Omar, for his (rebellious) poetry, and Julie, for her association with Sharif and her marital ties to a bandit general (Tom Courtenay), suffer at the hands of the new regime. Years later, when a middle-aged Omar is traveling to

work, he spots Julie. As he rushes from the streetcar to catch up with her, he collapses on the street. As for Christie, she is soon arrested by the regime, and her last years are spent in a government labor camp. Returning to the present, Sharif's half-brother (Guinness), now a Russian general, locates Omar and Julie's love child, although the young woman (Rita Tushingham) knows nothing of her origins.

The cruelty of lost love is so deliciously served up in this film that it is tempting to wish—God forbid—to suffer the pangs the hero and heroine endure in *Doctor Zhivago.* OK, so wintertime sleigh rides are wonderful, but what do you do when the snow melts?

Shakespeare in Love

Miramax, 1998, color, 122 minutes
Director: John Madden
Cast: Gwyneth Paltrow, Joseph Fiennes, Colin Firth, Geoffrey Rush, Judi Dench, and Ben Affleck

Winner of five Academy Awards (including Best Picture) and six additional Oscar nominations, this humorous but exceedingly romantic excursion neatly blends the sensibilities of late-sixteenth-century England with a premillennium point of view. In this comedy of love among the middle and upper classes, an ambitious young William Shakespeare (Fiennes) is experiencing writer's block. Fortuitously, the frustrated artist encounters a radiant Lady (Paltrow). She proves to be his muse, inspiring him to write *Romeo and Juliet.*

En route, good Queen Bess (Dench) is a bystander to the madcap love affair, and the heroine must masquerade as a man. However, as the bard would say, all's well that ends well.

Watching this modern interpretation—with its mixture of high and low comedy—of the life and times of the great Elizabethan playwright makes one *almost* (but not quite) hanker to watch a real Shakespearean production. Anyone for Leonardo DiCaprio's *Romeo and Juliet* (1996)?

Still undecided if you want to experience love contemporary-style or use the handy time machine to see if the grass was really greener in a different century, say, during the time of the American Revolution? Here's a thought: rent Mel Brooks's *History of the World—Part One* (1981). He and his stock company seemed to have had a lot of fun traipsing through Imperial Rome and other historical eras. But a word to the wise: if you jump back in time, you might miss a lot of household conveniences not yet invented. Life without satellite TV? No way!

3

From Two Different Worlds

*T*he old adage insists that opposite types of individuals attract, and this is frequently proved out when it comes to matters of the heart. Big or little differences between people sometimes add that special novelty (and spice) to their situation and stimulate the sparks that lead to a love connection, whether the budding romance lasts for the short or long run.

She is tall and he is short. The man is young while the woman is older. The heroine is an upper-class elitist while the hero proudly boasts a blue-collar working-class background. These are but a few of the many dissimilarities that may emotionally attract one person to another. (Please see Chapter 7 for a discussion of interracial romances.) Often, once the couple gets beyond physical appearances and becomes acquainted with each other's inner qualities, such initial surface dissimilarities no longer play much of a role in their situation.

Also factoring into the emotional equation is the effect this coming together of a disparate couple has on those around them. For example, when family, friends, or acquaintances register positive support for this blending of contrary kinds of individuals, it provides a comforting affirmation of the relationship. On the other hand, when those observing this oddly matched new couple voice concerns or stronger negative feelings, it often has just the opposite effect than intended. Sometimes this criticism unites the duo into a strong bond of "us against the world"—which makes the situation all the more challenging, exciting, and, for some participants, deliciously romantic.

Then too, there are the situations in which the potential lovebirds take an instant dislike to one another, letting these dissimilarities rule their initial reaction to the other person. Eventually, they realize that they adore the other person just for these differences. Hollywood particularly likes this type of situation because it fulfills one of the key ingredients needed for a successful and exciting screenplay: c-o-n-f-l-i-c-t.

Alice Adams

RKO, 1935, black-and-white, 99 minutes
Director: George Stevens
Cast: Katharine Hepburn, Fred MacMurray, Fred Stone, Evelyn Venable, and Frank Albertson

*I*t was near-perfect casting to team Hepburn and MacMurray in this sparkling screen adaptation of Booth Tarkington's novel (1921). Each star already had an established public image that matched their new screen characters: she being a snobbish intellectual who lives in a rarefied, self-absorbed world; he being a man of the people who appreciates life's simpler pleasures and is immediately suspicious of anyone who puts on airs. A twist to this ideal assignment of roles is that here Hepburn's heroine is from a struggling middle-class household, while MacMurray is the well-bred stranger to town who has impeccable social connections.

In a small Midwestern town Katharine, the daughter of an ailing business clerk (Stone), dreams of one day being accepted into the fancy social set headed by local debutante Venable. When Evelyn's cousin, Fred, comes to town, Hepburn is immediately intrigued by him but worries that she has no chance with this potential suitor because of her family's precarious social position. Hoping to impress MacMurray, she invites him to a formal dinner at the homestead. All her grandiose attempts to make the situation appear elegant fall apart disastrously. (This

How to Seem What You Are Not

Alice Adams offers several useful illustrations of how to gild the lily in your social life:

- When purchasing a corsage to wear to a fancy party that Mr. Right might be attending, don't tell the florist you're having cash flow problems. Instead, select the cheapest posies, explaining, "You see, when one goes to lots of parties, it is so difficult to find something new and original, something no one else would think of wearing."

- You've invited the new man in your life to meet your parents. When he arrives, be sure to defensively explain away the plainness of it all. "Here's the foolish little house where I live. It is a queer little place, but you know my father is so attached to it that my family has just about given up hope to get him to build a real house farther up."

segment of the picture is one of the true classics of Hollywood's Golden Age.) She is convinced that she will never see her gentleman caller again. However, a family crisis forces her to step away from her dream world and solve a potential financial disaster for her dad. To her amazement, Fred has not disappeared from the premises but had been taking the evening air on the front porch. Impressed by Hepburn's sensible and sensitive handling of matters, he embraces her tenderly. To which the heroine replies, "Gee whiz."

Although by now many of the class distinctions that separated Hepburn's world from that of her social "betters" have disappeared or certainly blurred, the gambit of social climbing (whatever the destination) is still very much with us. In real life, would the heroine's parents have put up with this pretentious and affected offspring who is ashamed of her honest, well-intentioned family? While it might have spoiled the film's premise, wouldn't it have been wonderful to behold if the story's gentle dad put his foot down and scolded his daughter for her uppity, dreamy ways that make her look so foolish to others?

Woman of the Year

Metro-Goldwyn-Mayer, 1942, black-and-white, 112 minutes
Director: George Stevens
Cast: Spencer Tracy, Katharine Hepburn, Fay Bainter, Reginald Owen, and William Bendix

*H*aving won an Academy Award (for 1933's *Morning Glory*) and then been labeled "box-office poison" by film exhibitors later in the same decade, Hepburn staged a brilliant comeback with *The Philadelphia Story* (1940). Her follow-up feature was *Woman of the Year*, the first of nine entries she made

with the married Tracy, who became her unofficial offcamera companion for the next twenty-five years.

Can a sophisticated international affairs columnist (Hepburn) and a rugged sportswriter (Tracy) turn their initial incompatibility into a successful marriage? What do you think? This is Hollywood we are talking about!

The Right Size and Other Matters

- While headstrong **Katharine Hepburn (b. 1907)** suggested to studio officials that she and Tracy be teamed for *Woman of the Year*, she nevertheless had some reservations about the pairing. She wondered if at five feet, seven inches she wasn't "a bit tall" for **Spencer Tracy (1900–1967)**, who was only three and one-half inches taller than she. The film's producer, Joseph L. Mankiewicz, turned to her and said, "Don't worry. He'll cut you down to size."

- As filming on the picture got under way, Katharine delicately broached the subject to Spencer as to which of them would receive top billing onscreen. He gave Hepburn one of his patented squints and reminded her that this was not a case of lifeboats where women and children came first. End of discussion.

The self-made, rowdy Spencer and the stylish Katharine (the daughter of a diplomat) both work for the same New York newspaper but have never met. When she remarks publicly that baseball should be banned for the duration of World War II, the two square off for a battle of wits in their respective columns. After the duo is finally introduced and start conversing, Tracy is immediately drawn to Hepburn. They soon marry, much to the amazement of their friends. However, their home life becomes a war zone, for each has a dramatically different view of the responsibilities of matrimony. Later, she finds great irony when, on the day she is chosen Woman of the Year, she begins to understand her "failings" (remember, this was made in pre–women's liberation times) as a proper wife. Further on, when her dad (Minor Watson) reweds, Katharine pays full attention to the wedding vows. It gives her new perceptions on life, and now she fully intends to make a success of her union with Tracy.

Love Is in the Air

A smart moviegoer can generally tell when two polar opposites onscreen are soon going to be whispering sweet nothings to one another. Sometimes it becomes instantly clear in the dialogue, as when he says about the leading lady: "I understand that she doesn't like to talk to anyone who hasn't signed a nonaggression pact."

Rarely has Hollywood handled the battle of the sexes so smartly as in *Woman of the Year*. However, considering the many progressive changes regarding sexual equality in the several decades since this romantic comedy was made, imagine how this story line would play out in the twenty-first century when terms like *male chauvinism* and the *weaker sex* have become dirty words.

Sunset Boulevard

Paramount, 1950, black-and-white,
110 minutes
Director: Billy Wilder
Cast: Gloria Swanson, William Holden, Erich Von Stroheim, Nancy Olson, and Fred Clark

Horror story? Love tale? Murder caper? *Sunset Boulevard* is all of these and more. It still resonates with contemporary audiences because it is so well constructed and acted. Besides being a biting condemnation of the Hollywood custom of spitting out its celebrities after they have fueled the system, it is also a weird account of Tinseltown romance where opportunists and the desperately needy cohabit in a precarious balance. In this ambiance of flashy materialism and destructive artistic insecurities, a Norma Desmond and Joe Gillis were bound to collide and destroy one another.

Told in flashback, down-and-out scriptwriter Holden encounters Swanson, a reclusive silent screen queen, when he hides his car in her garage to escape pursuing repossession agents. The egomaniacal Gloria, delusional

Two Sides of the Coin

In this bizarre film noir love tale, both Swanson and Holden's characters operate according to different value systems. He's the cynical screenwriter who describes his practical entanglement with the demanding movie legend as: "You know, older woman who is well-to-do and younger man who is not doing well." In contrast, self-deluded, middle-aged Gloria, who thinks of herself as still extremely desirable and professionally powerful, reasons to her restless kept man: "No one ever leaves a star. That's what makes one a star."

William Holden as the gigolo and Gloria Swanson as his mad keeper in *Sunset Boulevard* (1950).

Courtesy of JC Archives

about making a movie comeback, invites William to be her houseguest and help her with her *Salome* script. Soon he becomes her paid but reluctant lover. Observing the situation is her tight-lipped valet who was once her director and much more. When her comeback does not materialize and a bored Holden announces he is leaving, Swanson becomes insane with murderous rage. It ends with William dead and Gloria being taken into police custody.

What this film teaches us is that dating a demanding individual twice your age, who also lives several eras in the past, doesn't bode well for a healthy relationship. If you really want to mingle with celebrities, why not go to a taping of TV's *Hollywood Squares*. It'd be a lot safer.

Born Yesterday

Columbia, 1950, black-and-white,
103 minutes
Director: George Cukor
Cast: Judy Holliday, Broderick Crawford,
William Holden, Howard St. John, and
Frank Otto

"*I* am stupid and I like it. I got everything I
want. I got two fur coats. . . . I tell you
what I would like. I'd like to learn to talk
good." So says the dumb blond central figure
(Holliday) of this uproarious comedy. Before
long the ex-chorine, freshly arrived in Washington, D.C., with gruff Crawford, an
unscrupulous junk dealer, is proving an
embarrassment to her protector. He must
mingle with the town's powerful and rich to
keep his crooked schemes running smoothly,
and Judy is proving to be a social embarrassment. Broderick hires idealistic newspaper-
man Holden to give the broad some instant
class. Used to being appreciated for her body
and her easy virtue, she asks William, "Are
you one of these talkers or would you be
interested in a little action?"

Before long—surprise, surprise—Holliday
and Holden have hit it off, he coming to
appreciate her untapped inner qualities and
she responding to his kindness and respect. In
the process, brassy Judy becomes more
sophisticated and views her keeper with new
eyes: "You eat terrible. You got no manners.
That's another thing—picking your teeth.
You're just not couth!" Realizing that he

should have been more careful about what he
asked for, Crawford is miserable that his dame
has outgrown him. He asks, "Do you think
we could find someone to make her dumb
again?"

Holliday won an Academy Award for her
gem of a performance, but in today's actual
nation's capital, would she have fared so well
rubbing elbows with the big shots of the current administration? You can plead the Fifth
Amendment on that one.

The Music Man

Warner Bros., 1962, color, 151 minutes
Director: Morton DaCosta
Cast: Robert Preston, Shirley Jones, Buddy
Hackett, Hermione Gingold, and Paul Ford

A great 1950s Broadway musical, the show
translated well to screen, even with the
distracting presence of such oddball personalities as Hackett and Gingold, who are probably the very last individuals one would expect
to encounter in River City, Iowa, circa 1912.

At the heart of this joyful song-and-dance
fest is a most unlikely duo: a glib con man, in
town selling the locals on musical instruments
and uniforms for their children to form a
marching band, and the Midwestern town's
stern librarian/music teacher who makes no
time for love in her life. A trio of the picture's
songs ("Being in Love," "Till There Was
You," and "Goodnight, My Someone")

reflect the growing romance between this cheating salesman and his prim miss, the latter needing to be goaded into reaching out for romantic happiness.

Would any computer-dating service have paired Harold Hill and Marian Paroo as likely compatible dates? But then in all the times you might have seen this movie, have you actually counted "Seventy-Six Trombones" and their players marching down Main Street?

Harold and Maude

Paramount, 1971, color, 95 minutes
Director: Hal Ashby
Cast: Ruth Gordon, Bud Cort, Vivian Pickles, Cyril Cusack, and Charles Tyner

Can a young man in his early twenties find happiness with a woman old enough to be his great-grandmother? (No, I'm *not* kidding.) The answer, according to *Harold and Maude*, is yes. Its strange love match is at the heart of this cult classic, a witty satire on false values and conventionality as well as a vote of endorsement for senior citizens who remain vibrant, optimistic individualists right up to the end. So what, insists this offbeat comedy, if the two central characters are at the opposite ends of the age spectrum.

A very depressed Cort lives with his wealthy, widowed mother (Pickles) who is so preoccupied with her superficial life that she has no quality time for him. He fakes hanging

A Companion Worth Having

Regardless of other people's negative feelings, if you find a potential mate who has an upbeat personality that complements your psyche, don't let that individual get away. How do you know if that unique person is for you? Well, she might be if she says things like this:

- "Everybody should be able to make some music. That's the cosmic dance."

- "Greet the dawn with a breath of fire."

- "[For fun] I like to watch things grow."

- "A lot of people enjoy being dead, but they are not dead, they're just backing away from life."

- "It's fun not to be *too* moral. You cheat yourself out of too much life."

- [When you tell this special person you love her] "Go and love some more."

himself and pretends to set himself on fire, but nothing jars her dormant maternal instincts. Eccentric to a fault, Bud's sole pleasure is driving his vintage hearse to strangers' funerals and participating in the services. On two consecutive outings he meets seventy-nine-year-old Gordon. She is so youthful of heart and optimistic of spirit that he is soon drawn into her orbit. (When he compliments Ruth on her jubilant way with people, she answers, "Well, they're my specie.")

Together they go on madcap rides in vehicles she's "borrowed," dine on fresh ginger pie, and become close. As she shares confidences with him, he comes out of his shell and decides this is the first woman he loves. They sleep together, and he proposes marriage to her. However, after an eightieth-birthday celebration in which she says good-bye to her friends, she takes a lethal dose of sleeping pills. A shocked Cort is about to drive his beloved hearse over the cliff but, at the last minute, jumps out. Remembering Ruth's sage advice, he begins strumming his banjo as he dances up a hill, committed to the spirit of life.

Crazy as the premise sounds and daffy as the pair is, one almost wants to believe these individuals are meant for each other. Thankfully, none of the other characters in the picture offer the typical clichés mouthed in such April-December hookups, such as, "When you're fifty Harold, Maude will be one hundred and ten," or "But what about having children?"

The Way We Were

Columbia, 1973, color, 118 minutes
Director: Sydney Pollack
Cast: Barbra Streisand, Robert Redford, Bradford Dillman, Lois Chiles, and Patrick O'Neal

The title song from this elaborate Streisand showcase won an Academy Award and has become a romantic standard. The pic-

Love North of the Border

Between marriages to actor Elliott Gould in the 1960s and to actor James Brolin in the late 1990s, **Barbra Streisand (b. 1942)** had a string of high-profile romances that included actors Omar Sharif, Warren Beatty, Kris Kristofferson, Ryan O'Neal, and Don Johnson. Breaking out of the show business rut, she began dating Canadian Prime Minister Pierre Trudeau not long after her 1971 divorce from Gould. La Diva really thought this relationship was going places and might include her becoming Canada's First Lady: "I'd have to learn how to speak French. . . . I would only do movies made in Canada. I had it all figured out." But, alas, the twosome fizzled and Barbra remained Hollywood-bound.

ture's narrative revolves around two unlikely mates: she a vocal, Jewish radical with a very ethnic look; he the ultimate handsome WASP, a genteel literary sort who wants to sail calmly through life. In true movie fashion, the two meet briefly on the New York college campus in the 1930s then reunite during World War II when he is a serviceman and she, now working in radio, lures him home (but he passes out dead drunk). More time elapses, and he becomes a published novelist. Thinking they are now finally on the same wavelength, they begin a romance, which astounds his snobbish friends. Nevertheless, the couple weds and moves to Hollywood so he can adapt his book to the screen. They have a plush lifestyle, but the Red Scare that washes through Tinseltown in the late 1940s divides them. He finds comfort with an ex-girlfriend (Chiles), and the marrieds finally split. Years later, Redford (now a TV writer) and Streisand (who has remarried and is still an activist) chance upon each other in New York City. In their momentary reunion, they realize they each still love the other but that their beliefs and lifestyles are worlds apart.

This is the ultimate fantasy trip with a sex-reversal twist. Here we have a Jewish miss who craves the good-looking gentile blond. For nearly two hours of screen time she convinces herself that she is attracted to his "brainpower" and "integrity," only to discover what she knew all along: she had been projecting qualities on him that were not there in order to rationalize her lust for this hunk from another culture.

Robert Redford and Barbra Streisand play opposites who attract one another romantically in *The Way We Were* (1973). Courtesy of Echo Book Shop

Manhattan

United Artists, 1979, color, 96 minutes
Director: Woody Allen
Cast: Woody Allen, Diane Keaton,
Michael Murphy, Mariel Hemingway, and
Meryl Streep

*A*lthough Allen's *Annie Hall* (1977) claimed four Academy Awards, *Manhattan* is, for many, a more mature and satisfying Woody project in which the characters, including the New York City backdrop, are dimensional and compelling.

Divorced from his first wife (Streep), a now-out lesbian, Allen is a TV writer who wants to move on to more serious creative pursuits. A card-carrying neurotic, he finds amusement and distraction with seventeen-year-old Hemingway. But he is too hung up on his phobias and perpetual angst to enjoy this free-spirited teen. Always searching for the next emotional fix in life, he meets the new girlfriend (Keaton) of a married friend

(Murphy). At first Woody is put off by Diane's phony surface charm, which is the pose she thinks people want from her. When he gets to know the real Keaton, Allen is entranced and they begin an affair. However, he soon realizes that she still loves Murphy and that the latter really cares for her but

Two New Yorkers (Diane Keaton and Woody Allen) share space and romance in *Manhattan* (1979).
Courtesy of JC Archives

What Are the Odds?

Talk about yin and yang, the two lovers (Allen and Keaton) in *Manhattan* are universes apart in their life approaches. She is impulsive, exuberant, and prone to exaggeration. He is meditative, cynical, and an emotional minimalist who punctuates his conversations with sarcasm. Their *Manhattan* interchanges should have been an immediate clue to each of them that they are *not* meant for one other:

Keaton: "[Discussing her ex-husband] I was tired of submerging my identity to a very brilliant, dominating man. He's a genius."
Allen: "Oh, really. He was a genius. Helen's a genius and Dennis's a genius. You know a lot of geniuses. . . . You should meet some stupid people once in a while. . . . You could learn something."

Or:

Keaton: "I'm honest, what do ya want? I say what's on my mind and, if you can't take it, well then f**k off."
Allen: "And I like the way you express yourself too. . . . It's pithy yet degenerate. You get many dates?"

needs a push to leave his loveless marriage. As for Allen, he regrets having rejected Mariel in favor of Diane. Hoping to repair that damaged relationship, he rushes to Hemingway's apartment building only to find that she is leaving for six months of study abroad. She promises that when she returns they can resume their relationship. Too full of self-doubts to believe her, he voices his many fears. As she rushes into a taxi, she tells him, "You have to have a little faith in people."

Would a beautiful young woman with creativity and smarts fall in love with a plain-looking nebbish twice her age? I guess if you are directing, writing, and starring in the picture, any of your whims are possible—at least on the big screen.

Dirty Dancing

Vestron, 1987, color, 97 minutes
Director: Emile Ardolino
Cast: Jennifer Grey, Patrick Swayze, Jerry Orbach, Cynthia Rhodes, and Jack Weston

A trio of highly romantic dance musicals peppered the 1980s: *Flashdance* (1983), *Footloose* (1984), and *Dirty Dancing*. The latter features a most dubious oncamera love match: a sheltered teenage Jewish girl who tangles with a street-smart gentile whose ambitions are fixated on sex and hot dancing. Like the unlikely onscreen romance, this sleeper picture proved successful. The smash-hit movie won both an Oscar and a Golden Globe for its appealing theme song: "(I've Had) The Time of My Life."

It's the year 1963 and a middle-class doctor (Orbach) has brought his family for their annual summer vacation at a Jewish resort in the Catskills. Grey, called "Baby," is her

As Cynthia Rhodes (left) watches, Jennifer Grey and Patrick Swayze find romance on the dance floor in *Dirty Dancing* (1987).   Courtesy of JC Archives

father's favorite and is overly pampered. However, she's to enter college in the fall and plans to pursue her activism full throttle. Jumping the gun in becoming independent, she avoids the hotel's usual activities. She quickly is drawn to Swayze, a handsome young employee noted for his prowess on the dance floor and in the bedroom. Jennifer becomes part of the workers' social circle, soon sharing their enthusiasm for "dirty dancing." In short order, she and Patrick become lovers. When his dance partner/coworker (Rhodes) becomes ill, Swayze recruits Grey to take her place in an exhibi-

tion event at another local hotel. The finale finds Patrick cleared of charges of stealing valuables from the guests. Meanwhile, he defies the disbelieving resort owner (Weston) at the facility's end-of-season show with a display of dirty dancing that features Jennifer and the rest of their gang. Summer over, there are intimations that the young lovers may reunite in the near future.

Suggestion: how about a quick trip to Arthur Murray's Dance Studio before you book your next Club Med vacation. If *Dirty Dancing* is to be believed, it could be your ticket to mucho social success.

Kate & Leopold

Buena Vista, 2001, color, 118 minutes
Director: James Mangold
Cast: Meg Ryan, Hugh Jackman, Liev Schreiber, Breckin Meyer, and Natasha Lyonne

"*A*re you for real?" she wants to know. He replies, "I believe so." But what is real when he's from 1876 thrown into a time warp and she is a suspicious, modern-day New Yorker? As such, this explains the film's tag line: "If they lived in the same century they'd be perfect for each other." How perfect can you be when you're from eras separated by 130 years?! But this being a Hollywood vehicle for Ryan, we know that dreamy romantic love is the film's thrust and that somehow the plot will bring the two opposites into close harmony.

The movie's premise is far-fetched but engagingly handled by the charismatic Jackman. He plays an impoverished English duke, a bachelor who has just relocated to New York City in the 1870s. His uncle is in the

Hugh Jackman plays a nineteenth-century Britisher who slips through a time warp and finds love with Meg Ryan in present-day New York City in *Kate & Leopold* (2001).   Photo by Albert L. Ortega

The Cynical Way

Ryan's skepticism in *Kate & Leopold* is not one of her character's most endearing qualities, but it provides the needed plotline conflict before she has a romantic change of heart. At the film's start she is downbeat on the subject of love:

Ryan: "I'm not very good with men."
Jackman: "Perhaps you haven't found the right one."
Ryan: "Maybe that whole love thing is just a grown-up version of Santa Claus, just a myth we've been fed since childhood."

Ah, come on Meg, where's your holiday spirit?

process of marrying him off to any interested rich woman, when Hugh gets into a struggle with a photograph-taking stranger. They end on the Brooklyn Bridge and soon fall into the East River and into a void. Jackman awakes in present-day Manhattan where the stranger (Schreiber), a time-travel specialist, befriends him. While staying at Liev's apartment Hugh meets his downstairs neighbor, market researcher Ryan, who happens to be Schreiber's ex-girlfriend.

Meg is initially put off by Hugh's very formal manners and period outfits. Suspicious of his charm, sincerity, and ignorance of contemporary matters, she labels him a flake. Before long, however, her wariness turns to affection and love. When Liev convinces Jackman he must return through the time portal to the 1870s, Hugh reluctantly leaves his love behind. But she cannot bear life without him and slips through the time crack to be by his side. Once they are reunited, he proposes marriage and she accepts. She has fulfilled her destiny.

Now, if Ryan is living happily back in the nineteenth century, who's that look-alike we've been watching in *Sleepless in Seattle* (1993) and *You've Got Mail* (1998)?

Such Hollywood productions as these should give anyone hope that their perfect mate is out there somewhere, even among the most seemingly unlikely candidates. And if the already discussed pictures don't point up that where love is concerned (1) great opposites often attract, and (2) in movies *anything* is possible, then I remind you of another cinema example. It's that classic story of beauty and the beast, better known to some as *King Kong* (1933), in which a lonely monster ape and a petite lady with a mighty loud scream get pretty intimate onscreen.

4

Love Letters in the Sand

There is something magical about beaches that has lured people to the shores since the dawn of mankind. (This may be because, as some anthropologists have long suggested, primitive life on planet Earth might well have started in the oceans.) In more recent centuries, shorelines, with their cooling breezes, have enticed work-weary adults seeking to escape from steamy cities in the summertime. As for youngsters, hot sparkling sand and rippling waves represent a perfect setting for innocent fun and games.

For teenagers and the young-adult crowd, the beach has developed its own special associations (including beer, wine coolers, and cookouts). Besides providing sunbathing, swimming, waterskiing, surfing, and so forth, the waterside also especially represents for this age group romance (and sex) in an atmosphere where adult responsibilities, concerns, and stricter mores seem to evaporate. Where better than the beach for a man to show off his physique or a woman to display her feminine curves in bathing attire that leaves little

to the imagination? In such a conducive outdoor setting, the opposite sexes can show off in front of one another in ways that might cause the older crowd to blush with embarrassment (or envy!).

Hollywood has long used beach locales to give variety—and spice!—to its movie product. Back in the 1910s, filmmaker Mack Sennett paraded his famous bathing beauties through many silent, short comedies that highlighted the scantily clad (by that day's standards) array of shapely young actresses. One of the great selling points of *Hula* (1927) was to exhibit the plump but quite provocative figure of Clara Bow (the "It" Girl) in a Hawaiian setting that had her swaying enticingly on the tropical sands wearing a revealing hula skirt ensemble. By the 1930s it had become standard Tinseltown practice for the studios to create beachside and aquatic scenarios to show off the impressive physical forms of their more appealing contract players/stars. Think, for example, Tarzan (Johnny Weissmuller) and Jane (Maureen O'Sullivan) romping in the water in *Tarzan, the Ape Man* (1932) and several of its sequels, or the Busby Berkeley chorines performing the elaborate geometric "By a Waterfall" number in *Footlight Parade* (1933). In the early 1940s, MGM, noting the recent great success of Billy Rose's Aquacade at the World's Fair in New York, hired ace swimmer Esther Williams. After her terrific success in *Bathing Beauty* (1944), she spent the next years submerged in a studio tank doing oncamera her precision routines that showcased her enticing figure and winning smile for enthusiastic filmgoers. By then, there was just no turning back.

Song of the Islands

Twentieth Century-Fox, 1942, color,
75 minutes
Director: Walter Lang
Cast: Betty Grable, Victor Mature, Jack Oakie, Thomas Mitchell, and Hilo Hattie

*W*orld War II was in full swing and already blond movie star Betty Grable was becoming the American GIs' favorite pinup girl. What better lush backdrop (courtesy of process camera work and studio sets) to show off her famous figure than a tropical paradise such as Hawaii where one's outfits are typically flimsy and revealing? Not to be unfair to female moviegoers, hunky Victor Mature—whom Grable was then dating offcamera—was cast as her leading man. Promoted in

That Grable Figure!

Weighing 112 pounds, five-foot, three-and-a-half-inch, blond, blue-eyed **Betty Grable (1916–1973)** was a joyous sight to behold. At the peak of her box-office fame in the 1940s, her impressive stats included a 34-23-35 figure. Her famed legs were insured for one million dollars with Lloyds of London. (For the record, she had a seven-and-a-half-inch ankle, twelve-inch calf, and an eighteen-and-a-half-inch thigh and wore a size-five shoe.)

Hollywood as "the Sweater Boy" (because such garb flattered his expansive, muscled physique), Mature effectively complemented Betty's tremendous sex appeal. As a result, they turned this musical romp—filmed not in the usual black-and-white cinematography of the day but in gorgeous Technicolor—into a titillating romp as the predictable battle of the sexes unfolded onscreen.

On a tiny Hawaiian island, an Irish beachcomber (Mitchell) welcomes back his daughter (Grable) who's been away at school for three years. At the celebratory luau where she performs for the guests, she encounters a handsome playboy (Mature) whose father's cattle ranch takes up much of the quaint isle. Mistakenly thinking her to be a native, he pursues her romantically. When he discovers her true identity, there are complications. It seems his dad wants to acquire Mitchell's harborside land, while the latter wants to keep it as a shelter for the natives. Eventually the battling parents reach an understanding, while their offspring reconcile in a romantic clinch and wedding bells are definitely in the air.

Frequently sporting a fetching grass skirt, in the course of *Song of the Islands* Betty leads a native hula dance and helps to deliver such tunes as "O'Brien Has Gone Hawaiian," "Down on Ami, Ami, Oni, Oni Isle," and "Sing Me a Song of the Island." With the constant focus on the costars' physical allure and their obvious sexual chemistry, filmgoers immediately get the message. A tropical isle plus sparkling sands and shimmering waters, with a big dash of sun-drenched days and moonlit nights, can only add up to steamy fun in the sun. The only fly in the ointment: how many filmgoers look anywhere near as good as Grable and Mature do?

From Here to Eternity

Columbia, 1953, black-and-white,
118 minutes
Director: Fred Zinnemann
Cast: Burt Lancaster, Montgomery Clift, Deborah Kerr, Donna Reed, and Frank Sinatra

*B*ased on the hugely successful James Jones novel (1951), this powerful picture boasted a strong cast—for many of its lead players, the film provided career-shaping roles. The box-office hit won a whopping eight Academy Awards. Ironically, however, the most enduring vision from this classic World War II drama is a turgid love scene that lasts for but a few minutes of screen time. On a more specific level, in the annals of Hollywood never had a romantic scene played out at a beach had such an enduring impact on filmgoers. In retrospect, it ranks as one of the most memorable screen clinches ever. It set the erotic standard for moviemaking that has yet to be equaled, even with later decades' far more explicit oncamera sexual interplay.

In *From Here to Eternity*, Clift extended his reputation for portraying sensitive, brooding souls, while Reed altered her pure screen image by playing a prostitute (with a heart of gold, of course). Sinatra, emerging from a singing/acting career free fall, made an amazing Oscar-achieving comeback as the free-spirited Italian American private who dies from a beating administered by a sadistic sergeant (Ernest Borgnine). But it was the erotic chemistry between burly Lancaster, as the sergeant who thinks too much, and Kerr (a replacement for the earlier announced Joan Crawford), as the army captain's unchaste wife stuck in a loveless marriage with a cruel, adulterous husband (Phillip Ober), that really stirred audiences' imaginations.

As the narrative—set on Honolulu before, during, and after the Japanese sneak attack on Pearl Harbor in late 1941—builds, one of the several plot threads involves Lancaster's growing romance with the promiscuous Kerr. As he discovers that her loose behavior is a reaction to her hellish life with a sadistic spouse, Burt's lust turns to love and Deborah responds in kind. The literal climax of their torrid

In *From Here to Eternity* (1953), Burt Lancaster and Deborah Kerr share great passion in the surf.
Courtesy of JC Archives

affair occurs on a lonely stretch of Honolulu beach as the couple's rendezvous turns into a highly passionate embrace. As their bodies— she wearing a relatively demure one-piece black bathing suit/skirt and he dark boxer trunks—blend together on the shoreline, the tide is coming in. While they hug and kiss with increasing ardor, the waves increasingly splash against their intertwined bodies. By the scene's fadeout, it is clear from the symbolic wave crashing that the overheated couple is in the throes of consummating its mounting passion.

Once having seen this famous love scene, it is almost impossible for anyone with a healthy (albeit superheated) imagination to lie out at the beach and not picture him- or herself reenacting this milestone movie moment. So, are you ready? OK. Lights! Camera! Action! Splish-splash!

Boy on a Dolphin

Twentieth Century-Fox, 1957, color,
111 minutes
Director: Jean Negulesco
Cast: Alan Ladd, Clifton Webb, Sophia
Loren, Laurence Naismith, and Jorge
Mistral

*E*ager to entice filmgoers back into the the-
aters who were now glued to watching
free TV fare at home, moviemakers waged a
battle against the rival medium by using big-
screen processes and color (TV was still
largely viewed in most homes on black-and-
white sets) and by searching the world for
new exotic locales as actual backdrops for
movies. With *Boy on a Dolphin* they succeeded magnificently in two impressive ways:
(1) presenting the wonders of Greece (ranging from the world-famous Parthenon and
Acropolis to the breathtakingly beautiful outdoor backdrops of Greek islands) and (2)
highlighting the splendors of voluptuous
Sophia Loren, here making her American
film debut.

Audiences had recently been treated to the
eye-filling allure of enticing Jane Russell—in
form-fitting bathing suits—in *Underwater!*
(1955), but nothing there equaled the sight of
Italy's magnificent export Loren scampering
through this scenic travelogue with a flimsy
story. In many sequences she is outfitted in
lightweight peasant garb (often with much of
her skirt hiked up to her impressive thighs
and the fabric tucked casually into her waist
belt). Her most noteworthy visual—often

repeated in the picture—is to emerge from
sponge diving (or later treasure diving) with
her drenched, filmy blouse clinging to her
hugely impressive chest. In an era before wet
T-shirt contests became a cliché, such sights of
Sophia's buxom figure made her hot box
office and the envy of most every woman
who ever donned bathing attire hoping to
attract a man.

While sponge diving near the isle of Hydra
with her boyfriend (Mistral), Loren cuts her
leg on an old sunken treasure. Before swimming back to the surface, she glimpses a gold-
covered statue of a boy atop a dolphin. Her
discovery leads her to Athens, where both the
head of the American Archaeological Foun-

Camera Illusion

Physically, Italian export **Sophia Loren (b. 1934)**
and veteran Hollywood star **Alan Ladd
(1913–1964)** were a most unlikely screen team.
Tinseltown insiders joked that he was twice her
age and half her height as he was twenty-one
years her senior and nearly five inches shorter
than the statuesque Italian actress. To create a
more harmonious visual matching onscreen,
whenever the two strolled together oncamera in
shoreline scenes, a trench was dug for Loren to
walk in. Thus, the couple seemed more even in
height. Because of Ladd's shortness, the two
could not properly perform a love clinch standing together, so they had to sprawl on the sand,
putting their mouths in reasonable proximity to
one another.

dation (Ladd) and an unscrupulous art collector (Webb) compete to have her help in gaining control of the much-prized sunken statue. By the finale, acerbic, wealthy Webb has been outfoxed, and the retrieved priceless relic has been turned over to the Greek government. As for Sophia, she has discovered that Mistral is a double-crossing lout and that restrained, well-intentioned Ladd is really the only man for her. Ego-crushed Webb is left to whimper on his plush yacht.

Once again movies reinforce the idea that sand, sun, and surf are the perfect recipe for spurring on the libidos of the lead characters to mutual sexual gratification, after the sanction of matrimony it is hoped (this, after all, was still the relatively prudish Eisenhower era). This particular feature also prompted a lot of red-blooded young male filmgoers to take up snorkeling, hoping that, as in *Boy on a Dolphin*, while diving for sponges and pretty shells, they might somehow get to tangle with a Sophia look-alike. Good luck!

A Summer Place

Warner Bros., 1959, color, 130 minutes
Director: Delmer Daves
Cast: Richard Egan, Dorothy McGuire, Sandra Dee, Arthur Kennedy, and Troy Donahue

The Percy Faith Orchestra's hit rendition of Max Steiner's theme song for this movie rose to number one on the music charts in early 1960, where it remained for two months and has since become an enduring love melody instantly recognizable around the globe. The movie itself, a dumbing down of Sloan Wilson's well-received 1950s novel, was, nevertheless, a carefully concocted amalgam of love, lust, and scandal. It depicts parallel titillating tales that encompass two generations, thus ensuring heightened audience appeal for different age groups of moviegoers.

At one point in this glossy soap opera, Egan's rags-to-riches character spits at his calculating, frigid wife (Constance Ford), "Must you suffocate every natural instinct in our daughter [Dee] too? . . . Must you label young lovemaking cheap and wanton? . . . Must you persist in making sex a filthy word?" If Ford is speechless at this tongue-lashing, later Dee, their obedient but petulant offspring, seems equally perplexed by the subject of sex. At one juncture she asks her sexually charged but caring precollege boyfriend (played with a perpetual pout by handsome Donahue) about his romantic past. Aroused by the stud at her side, but still at a chaste age, she inquires, "Have you been bad with girls?" Relieved to learn that he is a virgin also, Sandra pursues their romance, which leads to her eventually becoming pregnant, leaving boarding school, and hastily marrying Troy. Meanwhile, her father and Donahue's mother (McGuire), who were lovers years ago, have now divorced their rebound mates and wed one another. Who said life can't be truly complicated?

Much of *A Summer Place* is set on the New England coast (although making use of

Carmel, California, locales for its seaside scenes), and a great deal of the activity takes place at the oceanside summer resort operated by McGuire, her drunken blueblood husband (Kennedy), and their son (Donahue). Before long, the two blond young coleads are rushing off to the beach to explore one another emotionally and physically. Later, they are almost lost at sea when their sailboat is caught in a storm, and still further along in the tale, they make love on the deserted beach. By the film's finale, the young married couple has returned to the now-deserted Pine Island Inn for their honeymoon and to face the future together.

With its relatively frank and quite daring (for the times) sexual situations, *A Summer Place* set new boundaries for provocative, erotic drama among the younger set experiencing first love. It was so successfully fabricated that the movie made every hot-blooded emerging adult convinced that deserted sand dunes and beach coves were (and are) the perfect setting for life's big romance, with or without the strains of a lush theme song pulsating magically in the background.

Troy Donahue and Sandra Dee as the young lovers of *A Summer Place* (1959).

Courtesy of Echo Book Shop

Where the Boys Are

Metro-Goldwyn-Mayer, 1960, color,
99 minutes
Director: Henry Levin
Cast: Dolores Hart, George Hamilton, Paula Prentiss, Jim Hutton, Yvette Mimieux, and Connie Francis

*C*hronicling college students' annual Easter pilgrimage to Fort Lauderdale, Florida, might seem grist for a forgettable slapdash movie. However, this picture has several pluses as it examines the sex-and-fun rituals of the campus set as they abandon reason—let alone propriety—in their often-futile pursuit of instant gratification on the Sunshine State's beaches and in its swimming pools and overcrowded motel rooms during raucous spring break. The screen ensemble includes singing sensation Francis, who belts out the film's hit title tune, Hamilton as the well-tanned Brown University playboy (complete with yacht) romancing smitten Hart (the actress who later became a real-life nun), and a new movie team featuring the comedy interchanges of eccentric Hutton and acerbic Prentiss.

What made this daffy excursion so effective in its day was its loopy excesses (which included a bizarre swimming tank sequence, snappy patter as the prim coeds fend off their horny dates, and the pluckiness of the game guys determined to score with one girl or another) and the fact that, despite its adult themes, it was all a glossy, intentionally naïve Hollywood confection that would offend few viewers. The only character to run afoul of the story line's innocence is Mimieux, a pretty blonde insistent on snaring (at any cost) an Ivy League boyfriend. In a wacky melodramatic moment she gets into a bad situation with two unprincipled college guys, ending up wandering on the highway in a daze and being injured in a car accident. (It leads to the film's classic line in which her character, upon reawakening in the hospital from her mishap,

sighs dramatically and says of her unscrupulous date, "He wasn't even a Yalie.")

So, a word to the wise: before you head to Florida to celebrate that wild rite of spring, promise yourself *not* to have impossible love expectations for your cherished days in the sun. You have fifty-one other weeks of the year to satisfy your libido and find meaningful love (even, God forbid, if it's not with an Ivy League grad).

Mr. Hobbs Takes a Vacation

Twentieth Century-Fox, 1962, color,
115 minutes
Director: Henry Koster
Cast: James Stewart, Maureen O'Hara, Fabian, John Saxon, and Marie Wilson

As Hollywood of the early 1960s increasingly turned its attention to stories featuring young leads, this comedy proved a refreshing throwback to such earlier comedies as *Mr. Blandings Builds His Dream House* (1948, Cary Grant and Myrna Loy). This entry reveals that life, love, and complications during a beachside vacation are not the special province of teens and twenty-somethings only but also can involve the mature set.

St. Louis banker Stewart is disgruntled to learn that his well-meaning but extremely independent wife (O'Hara) has engineered a summer holiday at the shore in a rambling Victorian Gothic home that will accommo-

If anything, *Mr. Hobbs Takes a Vacation* points out that love at any age can be problematic and full of dangerous detours. It also suggests that the romantic lure of the beach can magnetize people other than the young. Then too, if you expect to have a long, wonderful marriage, an orderly household, children who learn to appreciate you, and never a dull moment, it will help the odds tremendously to have the likes of a whimsical Jimmy Stewart or a beautiful, fiery Maureen O'Hara as your mate. Is that asking *too* much?

Maureen O'Hara and James Stewart have an amazing family holiday in *Mr. Hobbs Takes a Vacation* (1962). Courtesy of JC Archives

date their large brood, including two married daughters and their families. Before long, harassed Stewart is not only at odds with the abode's malfunctioning equipment (including a defective water pump) but also finds that he is no better than his wife at repairing domestic riffs among the younger set or helping their two remaining young offspring adjust to adolescence. Between getting lost in the fog aboard a small sailing boat with his boy, accidentally walking in on a curvaceous houseguest (Wilson) taking a shower, and finding sufficient free time to be responsive to his own attractive wife and their mutual needs, Stewart is rightly exhausted by summer's end. To his dismay (but eventual amusement), he discovers that his spouse has already rented the same "lucky" home for the next beachside summer.

Beach Party

American International, 1963, color,
104 minutes
Director: William Asher
Cast: Bob Cummings, Dorothy Malone, Frankie Avalon, Annette Funicello, and Harvey Lembeck

When this relatively low-budget fabrication debuted in summer 1963, *Variety* offered the backhanded compliment that it "has the kind of direct, simple-minded cheeriness which should prove well nigh irresistible to those teenagers who have no desire to escape the emptiness of their lives. Thus it should swing at the box office."

Little did anyone realize at the time that this harmless, somewhat satirical picture would set the formula for several highly popular follow-ups and imitations in the coming years (remember 1964's *Ride the Wild Surf* and 1965's *For Those Who Think Young*?). Moreover, it created an enduring image for moviegoers of the (innocent) shenanigans that involve the young crowd at the beach. In later decades, when lifestyles became far more fast-moving, many of the movie's fans who were now middle-aged and thought contemporary times were more grim than game found great nostalgia in looking back at the innocent times depicted in *Beach Party* and its successors. They hungered for the relatively harmless mores presented in such 1960s screen offerings. For those looking back on that period through rose-tinted glasses, these simplistic (musical) romps with Annette and Frankie were about clean-cut romantic fun in the sand and were what movies were and still should be about; they were something to expound about to the new generation. That's how effectively the film industry brainwashed the American public!

Summer has arrived and Frankie and Annette—who are going together—rush to the Malibu shoreline. Funicello rhapsodizes, "You and me, honey, all alone. . . . It's like we're married. . . . There's nothing like the beach in the morning . . . so quiet . . . so mysterious." But her fantasies are soon shattered. While they and their pals are hanging out at the beach, there's a square—and somewhat horny—anthropologist (Cummings) observing the quaint social rituals of the teens. In addition, for comedy relief, there's a pesky motorcycle gang led by a dumb jokester (Lembeck) in leather. Before the film's end, several surfing tunes by Dick Dale and the Del Tones are performed and the kids emerge victorious over the cycle set. Most of all, Frankie and Annette realize that, despite their petty jealousies and distractions, they truly love one another. Right on, dude!

Rockin' Frankie and Annette

Frankie Avalon (b. 1939) and **Annette Funicello (b. 1942)** costarred several times together on the screen following their *Beach Party* success. Their joint entries included *Bikini Beach* (1964), *Pajama Party* (1964), *Muscle Beach Party* (1964), *Beach Blanket Bingo* (1965), *How to Stuff a Wild Bikini* (1965), *Fireball 500* (1965), *Back to the Beach* (1987), and *A Dream Is a Wish Your Heart Makes: The Annette Funicello Story* (1995 TV movie).

Lifeguard

Paramount, 1976, color, 96 minutes
Director: Daniel Petrie
Cast: Sam Elliott, Anne Archer, Stephen Young, Parker Stevenson, and Kathleen Quinlan

Promoted with the tag line, "Every girl's summer dream," this feature was an unheralded precursor to TV's *Baywatch* (1989–2001) and, in fact, shared a cast member (Stevenson). Unfortunately, this movie was overlooked by most filmgoers at the time.

However, once seen, its message and ambiance stick with the viewer.

Now in his midthirties, Elliott is the low key career lifeguard at Southern California beaches who has seen and done it all over the years. He's had his fair portion of sexual fun and games, thanks to his good looks and his presence in a job that makes him immediately glamorous to beach bunnies. He's also had his emotional rewards in saving endangered swimmers, as well as marshalling order amidst the rowdy, randy, and ridiculous on and off the shore. As the veteran guard, he passes on his work knowledge and tricks of the dating trade to his underlings (Parker et al.). However, attendance at his fifteenth high school reunion causes him to undergo a midlife crisis. Should he listen to a classmate (Young) who wants him to get into sports car sales or stick it out for a few more seasons on beach duty?

Far more than David Hasselhoff in the later *Baywatch* television series, the often-underrated Elliott was quite effective and sturdy in *Lifeguard* as the beach god who proves to be most mortal in his needs and desires. For many viewers over the years this feature has reawakened—if but temporarily—urges to abandon a dull, high-pressure nine-to-five desk job and head off to the surf and sun and that pedestal of authority and admiration—the high-platformed lifeguard watch station. However, before you impetuously resign your job, don't forget to check yourself out in a full-length mirror. How good will you look in your new uniform—a revealing bathing suit?

The Blue Lagoon

Columbia, 1980, color, 104 minutes
Director: Randal Kleiser
Cast: Brooke Shields, Christopher Atkins, Leo McKern, William Daniels, Eva Josephson, and Glenn Kohan

*U*nlike the tasteful, leisurely paced, British-made screen original of 1949 (featuring Jean Simmons and Donald Houston), the R-rated remake verges on exploitative (softcore) pornography. As such, the movie, with its shapely leads and appealing location filming in Fiji and Jamaica, drew in the anticipated large share of younger moviegoers and made a sizable profit on its $4.5 million budget.

En route to San Francisco during Victorian times, a schooner catches fire. Josephson and another young passenger (Kohan) are cast adrift in a lifeboat with the ship's cook (McKern). They reach shore where they pitch camp and learn from the cantankerous elder the rudiments of survival against Mother Nature and the natives (who are based on another part of the lush isle). Years pass and, by now, McKern has died, leaving the teens (now played by Atkins and Shields) to await, hopefully, their eventual rescue. With their hormones in superhigh gear, they explore lovemaking, which leaves both of them puzzled when Shields becomes pregnant (and flabbergasted at how to deal with the situation thereafter). After she gives birth to a baby boy the couple visit their first home on the island. En route, their dinghy drifts out to

Brooke Shields and Christopher Atkins as the romantic castaways in *The Blue Lagoon* (1980). Courtesy of JC Archives

isle and frolicking on the shore and in the water with an equally attractive partner. However, the striking images of the barely clad Atkins and Shields became memorable icons of the sexually aware 1980s. In 1991, the PG-13-rated *Return to the Blue Lagoon* was foisted onto the public. Featuring Brian Krause and Milla Jovovich, this latest cinematic excursion to the good old lagoon was a bomb.

sea. Eventually they are rescued by a schooner that has Shields's aged father (Daniels) aboard.

Relying on the expected tropical island adventures familiar to those who have read and/or seen a screen adaptation of *The Adventures of Robinson Crusoe* or *Swiss Family Robinson*, this feature also borrows a leaf from the old Esther Williams movie musicals. As such it devotes a good deal of time trailing the scantily clad lead figures as they cavort in and beneath the waters of the blue lagoon and get to "know" each other much better ashore. For many, the tantalizing erotic visuals of the good-looking duo eventually coupling compensate for the stilted dialogue and performances as well as the coy handling of such plot points as natural childbirth, breastfeeding, and so forth.

This crass, almost exploitative, screen trek sends distinctly mixed messages about the virtues and vices of camping out on a remote

Message in a Bottle

Warner Bros., 1999, color, 132 minutes
Director: Luis Mandoki
Cast: Kevin Costner, Robin Wright Penn, Paul Newman, John Savage, and Illeana Douglas

As the new millennium approached, Hollywood still believed there was box-office mileage to be gained in depicting onscreen love on the shoreline. However, in its bid for audience favor, this elaborate entry frequently ignored the key ingredients needed to win audience favor: a young(ish) cast, surmountable plot problems for the characters to overcome, ongoing sexual tension between the two leads, and, most of all, a happy ending to the narrative.

Visiting the shoreline, Penn comes across a bottle in the sand with a passionate love letter inside that is addressed to Catherine and signed "G." Greatly intrigued by the note, she returns to her researcher's job at a Chicago newspaper where coworkers help the divorcée track down its author. He turns out to be a reclusive sailboat builder (Costner) on the East Coast (along the Carolinas) whose wife died in childbirth two years earlier. Already in fantasy love with this brooding stranger, Penn visits Costner's hometown to research a follow-up to the sad story. Without explaining what brought her to town, she starts a budding relationship with him that is later consummated when he visits the Windy City. He leaves in anger, however, when he discovers the reality behind their contrived meeting. Later, Robin effects a semireconciliation. Thereafter, before the couple can be reunited on a full-time basis, he sails out to sea to dispatch another letter in a bottle to his deceased wife. On the trek, he drowns while rescuing a capsized family. At the funeral, his understanding father (Newman) consoles the heartbroken Penn by showing her his son's final note to his late wife—a letter of good-bye in which he informs Catherine of his new love.

Viewers are supposed to respond to Costner's screen character in this movie far more positively than they do. After all, he is cast as an extremely sensitive, romantic lead figure, one with a love of nature (especially the sea, and walking along the deserted shoreline). Above all he is depicted as believing in the politically correct things people nowadays claim to admire, such as ecology and nonpollution. Then too, his "hero" is a craftsman who works artistically with his hands. Moreover, and this was geared to appeal to female moviegoers, even after his spouse's untimely death he does not forget her. He remains convinced that he can communicate with her by sending messages via the ocean they both loved so much. But all these plotline virtues cannot overcome the star's constricted performance, which is frequently as dull as the film's drab color composition and the entry's symbol-laden cinematography.

The failings of this well-intentioned but bloated tearjerker to one side, learn something from what you have watched. Always keep a spare wine bottle in readiness. You never know when the Internet will be down and you will have that irresistible urge to send a very special someone that urgent message of love. Oh yes, it'll help if you both live adjacent to connecting waterways.

Are They for Real with Such Sappy Dialogue?

One of the downsides of *Message in a Bottle* is the often less-than-sterling dialogue provided for this big-budget tearjerker:

She: "Have you lived here your entire life?"
He: "Not yet."

Or:

He: "I don't want to lose you."
She: "Then don't."

As we've discovered herein, there's a lot to learn from Hollywood's many excursions to the world of sand and surf. Sure, many of the screen offerings have been contrived and too fanciful. However, they reflect that sense of freedom and joy we all would like to (but don't necessarily do) experience when we walk across the hot sand, feel the water's coolness, and stake out our temporary turf in the sun.

While thanks to the brainwashing of the movies our optimism for scoring with sex and romance beachside runs high, try to be real. Don't expect the impossible, and be careful. If you attempt lovemaking in the rolling surf, you could end up with a lungful of salt water and no rescue squad in shouting distance. Also, when last checked, the odds of a gorgeous mermaid emerging from the ocean deep to make your life beautiful à la *Splash!* (1984) are mighty slim. Finally, if you bring an electric guitar with you to the shore to accompany the likes of Frankie and Annette in a few ditties, don't forget the battery power pack. Extension cords, electricity, and water just don't mix.

5

Sailing Aboard the Love Boats

With today's emphasis on speed and economy, the stately, massive transatlantic ocean liners of past decades have been replaced as the transportation of choice by the more efficient jet planes. Those luxury vessels that survived bygone times have long since been converted into cruise ships, joining the array of new vessels built around the world for just such recreational purposes.

Long before TV's *The Love Boat* (1977–1986) confirmed the point for a new generation, Hollywood theatrical features were exploring and exploiting the romantic magic and excitement that could occur on the high seas (e.g., 1934's *Transatlantic Merry-Go-Round* with Jack Benny and Nancy Carroll, 1948's *Luxury Liner* with George Brent and Jane Powell, 1962's *Bon Voyage!* with Fred MacMurray and Jane Wyman). As these and other Tinseltown movies repeatedly portray, there is something refreshingly exhilarating about being on the oceans isolated from the daily concerns of onshore life. Once aboard, travelers enter a special new world where their tiniest whims are catered to by an obliging

crew and where they can share personal confidences with fellow passengers. On the other hand, because there is little chance of being discovered in one's deceptions, an imaginative individual can invent a fresh background for him- or herself and revel in the novelty and freedom of interacting with strangers aboard as an entirely "new" person (e.g., Kay Francis and George Brent in 1932's *One Way Passage*, Bette Davis in 1942's *Now, Voyager*).

With movies (and later TV) insisting for so many years that an ocean trek can (and will!) provide interested parties with a romantic fling (or better yet, for some, the start of a long-term relationship), travelers have come to have (sub)conscious expectations involving their oceangoing journeys. No matter the reality of their personal situation, they are convinced that, before the vessel docks at its destination, they will have embraced grand passion or, at the very least, a quickie love/sex connection. Unfortunately, the reality for most such passengers is that their most unforgettable moments on the trek probably will involve overindulging at midnight buffets, winning a shuffleboard championship, or, worse yet, enduring a sudden, unpleasant bout with seasickness.

One Way Passage

Warner Bros., 1932, black-and-white,
69 minutes
Director: Tay Garnett
Cast: William Powell, Kay Francis, Aline MacMahon, Frank McHugh, and Warren Hymer

On the high seas, reality can be most anything you make it—according to this compact celluloid romance that won an Oscar for Best Original Story. It also offers every requisite ingredient for a highly effective tearjerker: star-crossed lovers, tragic secrets, and a mystical love that is so strong it can surmount earthly bounds.

Powell and Francis meet briefly at a Hong Kong bar and there is instant attraction, but because of prior obligations, they soon part. Later, they reconnect while aboard a San Francisco–bound ship where their romance quickly builds. But there is much each does not know about the other. Pretty, sophisticated Kay, who seems the picture of health, is actually suffering from a terminal disease and has only a short time to live. As for dapper William, he has escaped from San Quentin prison after being convicted of a murder charge. Just after first meeting Kay, he had been captured by a policeman (Hymer) long

on his trail. Thereafter, on the California-bound ship Powell had saved the cop from drowning and, in appreciation, the law enforcer has now removed the convict's handcuffs so he can lead a "normal" life while aboard.

When the vessel stops over at Honolulu, Kay plans a shore excursion. Her lover, thanks to the assistance of two con artist cronies (MacMahon and McHugh) who happen to be on the ship, eludes his policeman shadow, and he accompanies Francis ashore. After they spend the day together, and just as he is about to reveal the truth about himself and tell her of his escape plan, she collapses with fatigue. To save her life and at the peril of his own, he carries her back to the ship. Once aboard, Hymer places him in strict custody. Before the ship docks in San Francisco, Kay learns the truth about William but pretends to him that nothing is amiss. The two doomed souls agree to meet on New Year's Eve at a club in Caliente, although both know they cannot make the rendezvous. The big holiday night arrives, and at the Caliente club a bartender is perplexed when he hears a noise, turns around, and finds the shattered remains of two crossed drink glasses—just as Powell and

The Second Time Around

When Warner Bros. remade the highly successful *One Way Passage* as 1940's *'Til We Meet Again* starring Merle Oberon and George Brent, Frank McHugh repeated his comedic role as a convivial con artist.

Lawman Warren Hymer interrupts the sophisticated shipboard romance of William Powell and Kay Francis in *One Way Passage* (1932). Courtesy of JC Archives

Francis had been accustomed to crossing their glasses when toasting one another in life.

The Big Broadcast of 1938

Paramount, 1938, black-and-white,
97 minutes
Director: Mitchell Leisen
Cast: W. C. Fields, Martha Raye, Dorothy Lamour, Shirley Ross, and Bob Hope

Who would ever guess that such a wacky, episodic comedy with a plot that defies logic and a cast of such disparate funsters—including Hope in his feature film debut—could contain such sparkling romantic interludes. But such is the case with this glossy musical excursion.

Radio announcer Hope, fleeing from missed alimony payments to his three ex-wives, boards the SS *Gigantic* as it prepares to leave New York Harbor and race another passenger ship to Cherbourg, France. With accident-prone, eccentric Fields and his loud-mouthed, clumsy daughter (Raye) aboard the *Gigantic*, mayhem reigns supreme, allowing the rival vessel to temporarily pull ahead in the transatlantic race. Meanwhile, love is blossoming among several passengers on the *Gigantic*. For example, flippant Hope is distracted from pursuing his relationship with Lamour (who quickly turns her attention to a handsome inventor) by one (Ross) of his former spouses. By the time the liner reaches France—just ahead of the *Colossal*—Hope and Ross have rekindled their former romance, and Dorothy is now free to be with her new man.

The sane highlights of this madcap entertainment are largely provided by the sparring, reminiscing, and romancing of Hope and Ross. In one of the picture's quieter moments, as the moonlight shimmers on the ocean's waves, the duo sings "Thanks for the Memory," a saucy but tender tribute to the couple's once-passionate domesticity. Watching this interlude as "Ski Nose" Bob and pert Shirley harmonize in wistful nostalgia, one is convinced that if this could happen for Hope (or Ross), it could easily happen to one of us. Ah, if only we could sing like them. . . .

A Memorable Love Song

"Thanks for the Memory," by Ralph Rainger and Leo Robin, won the Academy Award as Best Song of 1938. The whimsical, catchy tune became Hope's theme song, although, thereafter, when he sang the number, he generally omitted the song's risqué section, which referenced the pajamas he never wore to bed during his and his wife's passionate first months together.

The Sea Hawk

Warner Bros., 1940, black-and-white, 127 minutes
Director: Michael Curtiz
Cast: Errol Flynn, Brenda Marshall, Claude Rains, Donald Crisp, and Flora Robson

A galley boarded and conquered by pirate forces may not seem to be the perfect setting for the start of a grand romance, but *The Sea Hawk* proves mightily to the contrary. It offers Flynn at his seafaring, swashbuckling best in a rousing tale of high adventure, dastardly duplicity, and chivalrous lovemaking.

In the sixteenth century, when Spain and England are at great odds with one another, the Spanish ambassador (Rains) sails to England with his niece (Marshall). En route, their vessel is attacked by a British privateer (Flynn) and his boisterous followers. Initially, there is intense antagonism between boastful (yet chivalrous) Errol and prideful Brenda, but the two later meet in England in the gardens at the court of Queen Elizabeth (Robson) and realize their love for one another. Later, gallant Flynn sails to Panama to confiscate the plunder of Spanish treasure hunters to restock the Queen's treasury, only to have his plans thwarted by the conniving Rains. Thereafter, Errol makes his way back to British soil in time to warn Her Majesty about the Spanish armada's pending attack on England. For his continued gallantry and bravery, the monarch knights him. Now he and his lady love are happily reunited.

Such rousing cinema adventure, boasting a mix of exciting action and romantic interludes, left audiences wishing—maybe just for a few harmless hours—that they could slip back in the pages of time. There, in the safety and comfort of their imagination, they could dispatch an enemy with an expert thrust and win the undying love of a fair lady with a quick smile and a few chivalrous gestures. What a dream, my matey.

Week-End in Havana

Twentieth Century-Fox, 1941, color,
80 minutes
Director: Walter Lang
Cast: Alice Faye, Carmen Miranda, John Payne, Cesar Romero, and Cobina Wright Jr.

*U*sually what *happens* during a ship's cruise, not what does *not* happen aboard, is the starting point for a typical Hollywood romantic confection. However, not in the case of this sparkling musical starring the studio's resident blond songbird (Faye) and featuring the lot's latest novelty star, the Brazilian Bombshell (Miranda).

When a cruise ship bound for Havana runs afoul of the elements off the shore of Florida, the line's owner dispatches his vice president (Payne) to run damage control. Of all the passengers, only one, a Manhattan shop girl (Faye), refuses to sign a lawsuit waiver in exchange for a ticket to a later cruise. Because this is her only vacation time and she has saved for years for this trip, she demands to be immediately taken to Havana to fulfill the

ship's obligations. She is accompanied by the executive who soon finds he much prefers Alice's company to that of his socialite fiancée (Wright Jr.). Before long, however, Cobina is manipulating to steer John away from his growing attraction to Alice. But her deceit backfires and, by the end of the colorful weekend in Cuba, Faye and Payne are happily planning their future together. As for the peppery local club singer (Miranda) and her fortune hunter/manager/boyfriend (Romero), who were part of the weekend's whirl of activities, they realize they deserve each other.

Thus, in *Love Boat* style, everyone in the *Week-End in Havana* plot line lives happily ever after. But think about it. For most of us a vacation on the high seas is just that— merely a pleasant break from everyday actuality. If you're expecting that grand shipboard romance to happen according to your every little fantasy and to find that your life will be immediately wonderful thereafter, you probably need a major reality check.

Now, Voyager

Warner Bros., 1942, black-and-white,
118 minutes
Director: Irving Rapper
Cast: Bette Davis, Paul Henreid, Claude Rains, Gladys Cooper, and Bonita Granville

*B*y the time this slick melodrama was released, the United States was engulfed in World War II. Military duty abroad, death in battle, and all the effects of wartime had already separated many families and loved ones. It led to romantic/sexual abstinence—either temporarily or permanently—for many at home and on the battlefront. Thus this teary Davis excursion with its huge dollops of self-sacrifice and martyrdom fits in perfectly with the sensibilities of the time. And, the spark that sets this much-cherished love story into motion occurs aboard a cruise ship.

As a result of years of emotional abuse from her unloving, dictatorial mother (Cooper), a thirty-something, dowdy Boston spinster (Davis) is on the verge of a nervous breakdown. She recovers at Cascade, a Vermont sanitarium, where its chief psychiatrist/founder (Rains) advises the still-repressed society matron to spread her wings and sail forth into the world. After an extensive makeover, she takes a long cruise. Aboard ship

Two for the Price of One

One of the famous gambits in *Now, Voyager*—which surely would never gain favor with the U.S. Surgeon General—occurs when Henreid seductively lights two cigarettes in his mouth and, in a romantic gesture, hands one to the pleased **Bette Davis (1908–1989)**. This bit of business, long referenced by many sources as having originated in this screen weeper, actually dates back to 1932's *The Rich Are Always with Us* when **George Brent (1904–1979)** accomplished the same provocative gesture. In that drama, Brent's then wife, **Ruth Chatterton (1893–1961)**, played the lead role, while a young Davis had only a subordinate part.

Hollywood Words of Wisdom for Those into Self-Sacrifice and Junior-Level Martyrdom

- "To take, sometimes is a way to give, if two people love each other."

- On apologizing for crying in front of a lover: "[These are] only tears of gratitude . . . an old maid's gratitude for the crumbs offered . . . no one ever called me darling before."

- Analyzing the degree of mutual passion: "Do what you will. Ignore it. Neglect it. Starve it. It's stronger than both of us together."

- On being asked if one is happy in this new love: "Oh, Jerry. Let's don't ask for the moon, we have the stars."

she meets a handsome passenger (Henreid), who is also traveling alone. They spend time together and eventually share confidences. She learns that he is unhappily married, but because of their two daughters he won't leave the domestic situation. By the time the now lovers part, they resolve that they must not see each other again. Back in Boston, the revitalized heroine becomes engaged to an eligible widower (John Loder) but soon breaks the engagement when she realizes that she stills love Henreid. This breakup angers controlling Cooper, who dies of a heart attack.

Guilt-ridden Bette returns to Cascade, where she encounters Henreid's younger daughter (Janis Wilson), now a troubled patient at the facility. The two bond, and Davis eventually takes the recovering girl back to live with her in Boston. Paul comes to visit, and Bette advises him that Rains has said she may keep the youngster only if Davis and Henreid agree not to reignite their affair. He reluctantly agrees but still feels guilty for having imposed so much on her life. To the contrary, Davis says, he and Wilson have helped her establish a constructive future.

Romance on the High Seas

Warner Bros., 1948, color, 102 minutes
Director: Michael Curtiz
Cast: Jack Carson, Janis Paige, Don DeFore, Doris Day, and Oscar Levant

*P*opular band and radio songstress Day made her feature film debut in this entertaining shipboard musical. She plays a struggling singer and the kind of down-to-earth gal who says "Natch" and "I could eat a cow," and refers to a ship as a "tub." But it's just as well that her pert character lacks sophistication, for the script teams her with Carson, who is playing his patented good-natured lug, this time in the guise of a private investigator.

Paige, thinking that her spouse (DeFore) of three years is having affairs, hires out-of-work vocalist Day to take her place on a luxury cruise to South America. Janis plans to stay behind and spy on her potentially erring

Janis Paige introduces songstress Doris Day to a club audience in *Romance on the High Seas* (1948). Courtesy of JC Archives

mate. In the meantime, Don grows suspicious of Janis and hires Carson to trail his wife on the vacation jaunt. Aboard the plush liner, Doris's alias as the married society matron leads her into romantic complications with Jack as well as with her pianist boyfriend (Levant), who has caught up with her on one of the ship's stopovers. Nonetheless, to borrow from Shakespeare, all's well that ends well: DeFore and Paige reaffirm their love, Carson and Day are jubilantly reunited, and, as for dour-faced Levant, he's left to amuse himself with his keyboard dexterity and smart remarks. Whew!

Once again here the movies are setting our expectations far too high. Unless you are as pert and pretty as Day and can sing to boot, don't expect that Mr. Right will be the first person you encounter on the ship's main deck or that all the complications of such a romance will evaporate in time for a happy finale. Remember, the title of one of the romantic ballads Doris sings in the film is "It's Magic," *not* "It's Reality."

The African Queen

Columbia, 1951, color, 105 minutes
Director: John Huston
Cast: Humphrey Bogart, Katharine Hepburn, Robert Morley, Theodore Bikel, and Peter Bull

*O*ne of the true classics of American cinema, this feature was ranked number two on the American Film Institute's 1998 list of top 100 movies. Its unlikely star duo (Bogart

An unlikely romance springs up between a missionary spinster (Katharine Hepburn) and a boozing tramp steamer captain (Humphrey Bogart) in *The African Queen* (1951).   Courtesy of JC Archives

and Hepburn) were both Oscar-nominated, with him winning an Academy Award. This film showed that romance can befall even the most improbably matched characters: she a prim middle-aged spinster; he a gin-guzzling, grizzly skipper of a decrepit river launch. The bulk of their offbeat romance occurs on his thirty-foot boat as they navigate a river attempting to escape from the Germans in German East Africa in the mid-1910s.

When a missionary (Morley) dies from the shock of a German attack on local villagers at the outbreak of World War I, his old-maid sister agrees to accompany besotted Bogart into the backwaters where she hopes to sit out the war. As they navigate along the channels—braving the elements, gunfire from a German fort, and so forth—these two opposing souls gain respect and then love for one another. They hit upon the idea of making their way to a lake in Central Africa where a German gunboat is preventing the British from making inroads in the area. Humphrey fashions makeshift torpedoes, which he ties to the front of the *African Queen*. Before they reach their destination, their boat capsizes in a storm. The Germans rescue them and soon sentence them to hang and then grant their request to be married before they die. Just before their execution is to occur, the German vessel runs into the partly submerged remnant of the *African Queen* and explodes. The jubilant couple swims happily to shore.

Above and beyond its intriguing story line and unique characters, *The African Queen* puts forward the idea that love, adventure, and carrying out one's goals successfully—on sea or on land—are not the strict domain of the young, beautiful, and fortunate. Moreover, this well-crafted feature suggests that romance and fulfillment can happen to anyone—even in the uncharted waters of the Dark Continent in the midst of a war.

Gentlemen Prefer Blondes

Twentieth Century-Fox, 1953, color,
91 minutes
Director: Howard Hawks
Cast: Jane Russell, Marilyn Monroe, Charles Coburn, Elliott Reid, and Tommy Noonan

For any enterprising individuals with a mercenary taste for the better things in life, this humorous, eye-filling musical offers a road map of how an ocean voyage aboard a plush vessel can create a sea of rich opportunities. Of course, everything would be easier for most of us if we boasted even a small percentage of the animal magnetism and sex appeal displayed by the two female lead characters.

In the 1920s, two curvaceous gold-digging showgirls, one brunette (Russell), one blond (Monroe), embark on the luxurious *Ile de France*. Their transatlantic destination is Paris, where Marilyn is scheduled to wed wealthy Noonan. Aboard the liner rambunctious Jane tumbles romantically for Reid, not knowing at first that he is a detective hired by Monroe's prospective father-in-law to check out her worthiness to marry his son. Meanwhile, ditzy, delightful Marilyn focuses much of her shipboard attention on an aged wealthy Britisher (Coburn) who owns a lucrative diamond mine. Ensuing complications find the blond chorine accused of stealing a diamond tiara that belongs to Coburn's wife. Through courtroom maneuvering and a lot of wacky happenings, both women end up marrying the men of their choice.

With the mission completed and case closed, the heroines concede that, perhaps, after all, true love and *not* diamonds are a girl's best friend. Folks, take that lesson to heart.

An Affair to Remember

Twentieth Century-Fox, 1957, color, 115 minutes
Director: Leo McCarey
Cast: Cary Grant, Deborah Kerr, Richard Denning, Neva Patterson, and Cathleen Nesbitt

*M*ost women (of any generation) adore this romantic cream puff; most men are baffled why female viewers are so enamored of a love tale that leaves them weeping at the finale no matter how many times they've seen it.

En route from Europe to New York on a transatlantic liner, Kerr, who has a rich fiancé awaiting her in New York, meets notorious playboy Grant who is planning to wed a well-

A Good Story Never Fades Away

In 1939, Charles Boyer and Irene Dunne starred in *Love Affair*. The successful romantic drama was remade by its director, Leo McCarey, as 1957's *An Affair to Remember*. In 1994, it was done yet again as *Love Affair*, this time with Warren Beatty and his offcamera wife Annette Bening in the leads and Katharine Hepburn as Beatty's aunt. Meanwhile, 1993's *Sleepless in Seattle*, starring Tom Hanks and Meg Ryan, weaved a good many film clips from *An Affair to Remember*—and a humorous discussion of its key plot points—into its own story line.

heeled heiress (Patterson). A shipboard romance springs up between Cary and Deborah, a union as bubbly and delightful as the sparkling pink champagne they frequently consume. Declaring their mutual love, they agree to break with their intendeds and devote the next six months to proving that they can fend for themselves. Then they will meet atop the Empire State Building on a particular day at a certain hour. Grant becomes a portrait artist while Kerr functions as a café songstress. On the appointed day, she is crippled in an auto accident as she rushes to meet her lover. Not knowing the circumstances, he's heartbroken at her not showing up. Months later he reencounters Deborah and soon learns of her tragedy and that she has since been struggling to sustain herself as a music teacher. The two embrace and plan their future together.

How many men have the easygoing charm of handsome, debonair Grant? Equally so, how many women can match the dignity and quiet English beauty of redheaded Kerr? And whom can we hire to write witty dialogue? No clue? Well, there's always the option of applying to be a contestant on TV's *Blind Date*.

Deborah Kerr (left) is introduced to Cary Grant's grandmother (Cathleen Nesbitt) in *An Affair to Remember* (1957). Courtesy of JC Archives

An Unforgettable Love Song

The film's theme song, "An Affair to Remember (Our Love Affair)," by Harold Adamson, Leo McCarey, and Harry Warren was Oscar-nominated as Best Song of 1957. It became a hit on the pop charts, especially in the rendition sung by Vic Damone. Many years later, when Kerr was a guest on Mike Douglas's TV talk show, Damone made a surprise appearance, singing the perennially favorite love song for the actress. She was so overwhelmed with emotion by the experience that she promptly broke into tears.

Titanic

Paramount/Twentieth Century-Fox, 1997, color, 193 minutes
Director: James Cameron
Cast: Leonardo DiCaprio, Kate Winslet, Billy Zane, Kathy Bates, and Gloria Stuart

*E*verything about *Titanic* is oversized, just as was the actual luxury liner that, in 1912, collided with an iceberg and sunk, with hundreds of its passengers and crew perishing. Made at the humongous sum of $200 million, "Cameron's Folly"—as its detractors regarded this mammoth screen epic before its release—went on to gross more than $601 million in just domestic distribution and win eleven

Academy Awards. At the heart of this sweeping saga of an ocean tragedy is a highly romantic love story, as old-fashioned as the movie's period decor, yet amazingly compelling to contemporary audiences. *Titanic* is, perhaps, the grandest love story on the high seas ever to be filmed.

The narrative focuses on an impoverished young American artist (DiCaprio) who wins a steerage passage ticket on the maiden voyage of the *Titanic*. Also aboard the gigantic vessel is a pretty miss (Winslet) traveling in first class with her wealthy, snobbish fiancé (Zane) and her prim mother (Frances Fisher). One evening, Leonardo prevents a distraught Kate from nearly throwing herself overboard. Before long, the two have fallen madly in love, a situation that soon comes to Zane's attention. Meanwhile, Winslet has the young artist sketch her in the nude, and, later, the two make love in a sedan in storage. Not long thereafter, the giant ship collides with an iceberg in the North Atlantic. Despite the panic, Winslet and DiCaprio remain together. When the liner splits in half and sinks, the two lovers are tossed into the freezing ocean. He puts his beloved on nearby driftwood that will hold only one, while he is forced to remain in the icy water doing his best to keep her atop of the wood. By the time she is rescued he has frozen to death. Kate lives for many decades thereafter—but never forgets her long lost love.

With its elaborate production values (including intricate and hugely effective special effects), *Titanic* dwarfs previous screen versions of the great seafaring tragedy. Yet the heart of the film is the great love between

Leonardo DiCaprio gained box-office clout by playing the ill-fated young lover in *Titanic* (1997). Photo by Albert L. Ortega

two individuals who overcome their social differences with their heated passion. Few romances in real life could dare to play out and survive against such grand surroundings, tragedy, and extreme human responses (from high-minded courage to base cowardice) to a disaster of this magnitude.

So, the next time you board a vessel (of any size), rather than scanning the crowd of passengers with a set of heart-shaped binoculars, remember, it's more important to check where your life preserver is stored, what the dinner menu options are, and what time the late show in the nightclub starts. If love is meant to find you on the high seas, it will. Don't push fate. It can push back.

6

Love South of the Mason-Dixon Line

Since long before the Civil War, and certainly during it and even now, numerous decades after it, there has been a cultural, political, and financial tug-of-war between the American South and the rest of the United States. At times it has seemed that the territory south of the Mason-Dixon line was a part of a different world, one caught up in "alien" social traditions, cultural philosophies, and political principles far different from those of the remainder of the United States.

It took a century after the emancipation of the slaves and the end of the Civil War in the 1860s for civil rights legislation and changing public viewpoints on integration to help African Americans to gain their first rights in the South. The long-held attitude of whites versus blacks that was so much a part of the Old South—and fought for by the Confederates during the War Between the States—was at the heart of much of the conflict between these contrasting American cultures.

That said, Tinseltown has long played on the dissimilarities between North and South in film productions whether set in bygone centuries or in today's world. (Once the making of talkie pictures became part of Hollywood's technology in the late 1920s, the use of sound allowed for highlighting Southern accents of all types, which indicated how "foreign" these Southerners were in contrast to their Northern neighbors.)

As such, setting a love story in the "quaint" South always allowed Hollywood to infuse a romantic tale with a special flavor, utilizing distinctive local atmosphere (scenery, architecture, garments, the drawling accent, and so forth) to make the production seem far fresher and more unique than if the same narrative had been set up North, out West, or in the Midwest.

(For the record, in this chapter's discussion, the Lone Star State of Texas is not included as it has its own set of traditions, egos, and oil industry–based economics that separate it significantly from "the South.")

The Cabin in the Cotton

Warner Bros., 1932, black-and-white,
79 minutes
Director: Michael Curtiz
Cast: Richard Barthelmess, Dorothy
Jordan, Bette Davis, Henry B. Walthall, and
Berton Churchill

As part of its cycle of social injustice exposé movies (e.g., 1932's *I Am a Fugitive from a Chain Gang*), Warner Bros. turned out this tract on the dire plight of cotton pickers (also known as "peckerwoods" or tenants) in the Deep South during the Depression era. The oppressed workers live in dismal shacks, similar to the shantytown dwellings elsewhere in the country (especially in factory towns of the Northeast). These peckerwoods are made up of uneducated poor whites and blacks, both groups controlled in every facet of their lives by the local landowner. So mean is their daily existence and so bleak is their future that they are, in many ways, no better off than the slaves of the pre–Civil War South.

The deplorable lifestyle of these downtrodden tenants forms the backdrop for the story's love triangle. The "young" hero (played by thirty-six-year-old Barthelmess) wants to make something of his life and help to elevate his family's lifestyle. He avoids the backbreaking work of picking cotton to attend school. There he proves to be bright, which wins him the attention of Davis, the spoiled daughter of the local land baron (Churchill). Bette doesn't like Richard just for his mind—she is also turned on by his

good looks and by the fact that he is so different from the men she has met so far in life. Meanwhile, earnest Barthelmess continues his friendship with Jordan, the offspring of a long line of cotton pickers. She lacks education, social grace, and ambition, but she deeply loves Richard.

Having set her eyes on the hero, Bette uses her wiles and the luxuries of her lifestyle to tempt innocent Richard who, by now, is clerk/manager of her father's tenant store. She flaunts herself in front of him, hoping to lure him into bed. But sexually naïve Barthelmess has other weightier problems to consider. He has discovered that while the tenants have long robbed cotton from the planters to survive, landowners such as Churchill manipulate the account books to cheat their workers. Being a movie of social protest, the script has Richard siding with his own kind.

In the picture's big moment of truth, he must choose between teary, loving Jordan and saucer-eyed, seductive Davis. Being a man of the land, he picks Dorothy, leaving Davis the loser. (Interestingly, at the finale, an ambiguous smile crosses Bette's face. It could be the look of a good-sport loser or could suggest that this iron-willed miss still intends one day to get this man for herself.)

The moral of this story: stick to synthetic fabrics, or, if you must have cotton, think cotton candy.

Jezebel

Warner Bros., 1938, black-and-white, 104 minutes
Director: William Wyler
Cast: Bette Davis, Henry Fonda, George Brent, Margaret Lindsay, and Fay Bainter

*O*n the cusp of becoming Hollywood's reigning empress of screen drama, Davis won her second Oscar for her stellar performance in *Jezebel* as the Southern vixen redeemed by noble love.

Set in 1850s New Orleans, it showcases Davis as a strong-willed daughter of the Old South: pretty, demanding, and totally clueless about the needs of others. She and banker Fonda (a progressive sort with financial and cultural ties to the more progressive North) keep getting engaged but never married. The problem is her irascible nature, which finally leads him to break off their relationship and go North. During the many months he is away, a crestfallen Bette hits an emotional bottom and rethinks her role as a member of the "weaker" sex. She vows to be compliant to Henry's every wish when he returns to claim her—and she is sure he will. Her broken spirit is jolted when Fonda arrives in town with a Yankee wife (Lindsay) in tow. Bette's fiery spirit rises to the challenge of proving to her love that a Southern belle is much more appropriate for him than his Northern bride. It becomes a battle of wills between two cultures, with the flinty Margaret holding an ace card—she is Fonda's legal mate, and he is too honorable to break that vow, no matter how much Davis entices him.

While a miniature Civil War is playing out between Davis and Lindsay, an epidemic of yellow fever is spreading through New Orleans. The panicked city institutes martial order: the corpses of the fever dead are burned, and their contaminated homes are dynamited. Those who contract the deadly

Get Me Brent

Very debonair leading man **George Brent (1904–1979)** was one of **Bette Davis's (1908–1989)** favorite leading men because he was handsome, compliant, and never a scene stealer. They made eleven features together ranging from 1932's *So Big!* to 1942's *In This Our Lives* and including *The Old Maid* and *Dark Victory* (both 1939). Over the years he married five times, including unions to movie stars Ruth Chatterton and Ann Sheridan. However, during the late 1930s and early 1940s he found time to conduct an on-again, off-again love affair with four-time married Bette.

Bette Davis is a flirtatious Southern belle working her captivating spell on staunch George Brent in the pre–Civil War drama *Jezebel* (1938).   Courtesy of JC Archives

plague but are still somehow alive are shipped to die (or, unlikely, to recover) at a nearby island, the home of a leper colony. Fonda contracts yellow jack and is in a bad way. He is about to be sent to the dreaded isle of isolation. Having already beaten Lindsay to the punch by being on hand to nurse him initially, Bette begs her rival to allow her the great privilege of accompanying Henry to the island. In a fury of passion and reason she explains why she, as a Southerner familiar with local customs and the ways of its folk, is much better equipped to fight harder than Margaret to keep their man alive. After lying to Lindsay that yes, Henry loves only his wife, Bette is allowed to go on her dangerous mission of mercy (and to probably meet her own death).

If your romantic fancy is decency, nobility, and self-sacrifice, nothing tops the finale of

Jezebel as the medical wagon piled with plague-ridden victims (including Fonda) heads off into the night. Bette sits in the cart, shoulders erect, head held high, bravely facing the future—happy, at last, to be reunited with her beloved in this unique relationship.

For any love masochists out there, I have bad news. In the past 150 years, New Orleans has cleaned up its act and is *no* longer prone to outbreaks of yellow fever.

A Streetcar Named Desire

Warner Bros., 1951, black-and-white,
125 minutes
Director: Elia Kazan
Cast: Vivien Leigh, Marlon Brando, Kim Hunter, Karl Malden, and Rudy Bond

They say that the only type of person prouder than a Southern aristocrat is a former Southern aristocrat. Such is the case with the pathetic Blanche Dubois, the lead character in this searing drama based on Tennessee Williams's 1947 Broadway hit. To star

with Brando, Hunter, Malden, and others who had been in the landmark theater original, Britisher Leigh was chosen. Not only had she won an Oscar for playing another Southerner (Scarlett O'Hara in 1939's *Gone with the Wind*), but she had already appeared on the London Stage in *A Streetcar Named Desire*. (Leigh would win her second Academy Award for portraying Blanche Dubois.)

Blanche's well-known line, "I've always depended on the kindness of strangers," takes on new meaning as her life story unfolds oncamera. It recounts that this faded Dixie rose, whose husband committed suicide years earlier, has squandered the family estate because of bad business decisions. As her life disintegrated, she distracted herself with a series of brief affairs with men passing through her small town. Now in full disgrace, she has left there to visit her younger sister (Hunter). The latter is married to crude but highly sexual Brando. Their small apartment in the Elysian Fields part of the French Quarter in New Orleans is cramped already, with barely room to hold their forthcoming child, let alone the demanding, emotionally disturbed Leigh.

There are few similarities between the two sisters, and the posturing Vivien is aghast that Kim could marry such an uncivilized man. Hunter, however, is so much in love with her primitive mate that she refuses to side with Leigh. Meanwhile, the friction generating between Vivien and Marlon escalates. Eventually, frustrated by his wife's unavailability for sex and having been drawn to this once-refined lady from the start, Brando rapes Leigh. This trauma sends the disturbed lady

Baby Doll

Warner Bros., 1956, black-and-white,
114 minutes
Director: Elia Kazan
Cast: Karl Malden, Carroll Baker,
Eli Wallach, Mildred Dunnock, and Lonny
Chapman

Several of those responsible for 1951's *A Streetcar Named Desire* reunited for this erotic entry scripted by Tennessee Williams from his earlier Broadway play *27 Wagons Full of Cotton*. This screen drama was so provocative and lewd (by the morality standards of the era) that *Time* magazine labeled it: "just possibly the dirtiest American picture ever

over the edge into madness. She must be sent away to a mental institution. Horrified by what has happened, Hunter, now a new mother, angrily tells Brando: "Don't you ever, ever touch me again!" With that she takes her baby and rushes upstairs to a friend's apartment.

In the midst of Leigh's descent into insanity and her pathetic attempt to find a safe port with Brando's poker-playing pal Malden, much is detailed about the passionate love between the genteel (but pliable) Hunter and the brutish Brando. Even with all their compatibility problems, it is, at times, a love relationship that can make a viewer envious—at least briefly. But hey, if you must go the route of Kim in this flick, warn your man (1) shouting at you is unnecessary as you have perfectly good hearing, and (2) your name is *not* Stella.

Carroll Baker as the heroine on the verge of womanhood in *Baby Doll* (1956).
Courtesy of JC Archives

legally exhibited." (When released, the National Legion of Decency condemned the picture, although the film industry's production code administration had OK'd it as adult entertainment.)

In Mississippi, a redneck (Malden) who operates a cotton gin is married to the much younger (and quite infantile) Baker. Worried about the competition of a Sicilian (Wallach) in the cotton business, Karl steals onto the man's property and incinerates his equipment. Suspicious that Malden was the culprit, Eli comes to the man's run-down premises to learn what he can. So that he can spend the day with the virginal Baby Doll (as Carroll is called), who may accidentally tell him what he needs to know about the arson, Wallach sends Malden off on a wild-goose chase regarding potential business. Immediately Eli begins stalking the immature teenage girl, curious to know if she has kept to her promise (known by all the locals) that she will not have sex with her husband until she reaches her twenties. An elaborate, erotic, and very twisted seduction gets under way. Malden returns home and flies into a jealous rage, intending to shoot the visitor. Baker calls the police, and Karl is carted away. The wily Wallach promises Baker he will return the next day, which is her twentieth birthday.

Kinky and raw, *Baby Doll* is more erotic for what it suggests and the heat generated between the characters than for anything explicitly told. For some male moviegoers, Baker's screen character was an enticing vision worthy of the chase. But, truly, is a sex symbol really that sexy if she (at nearly twenty) still sucks her thumb, sleeps in a crib with a teddy bear, and spends her days gliding on the porch swing? Talk about your love *child*.

Tammy and the Bachelor

Universal, 1957, color, 89 minutes
Director: Joseph Pevney
Cast: Debbie Reynolds, Leslie Nielsen, Walter Brennan, Mala Powers, and Sidney Blackmer

*O*ne of the surprise hits of its film season, this feature spawned several movie sequels, a TV series, and a hit song ("Tammy"). The

Author! Author!

Three times married and divorced, **Debbie Reynolds's (b. 1932)** most famous union was to singer **Eddie Fisher (b. 1928)**. When he left her and their children in 1958 so he could wed movie queen **Elizabeth Taylor (b. 1932)**, the country was shocked. Reynolds wrote her first autobiography (*Debbie: My Life*) in 1988. It presented her account of the Fisher-Taylor affair and other aspects of her busy life to date. About penning the memoir Debbie said, "Writing my book was reliving a nightmare. Many times when I was writing, I would break into tears just recalling the agony I went through."

syrupy sweet picture asks the riveting question: can a simple girl from the bayou country down South find happiness with a sophisticated bachelor (blessedly, also a Southerner) whose once-wealthy family has had a run of bad luck? The answer, of course, is a resounding yes!

Reynolds lives with her colorful granddad (Brennan) on a shanty boat in the bayou. One day a plane crashes nearby. They rescue the pilot (Nielsen) and nurse him back to health. Leslie eventually returns to his family's once-proud plantation home, hoping somehow to restore their fortune. Meanwhile, Walter is arrested for moonshine activity. Before going to jail he orders Debbie to go stay with Leslie and his family. Her arrival is a mixed blessing as some (especially Nielsen's sophisticated fiancée Powers) find her too fresh-faced and countrified.

With spunky Reynolds to encourage him, Nielsen raises an experimental strain of sturdy tomatoes and the future seems bright. However, a sudden hailstorm wipes out the crop, and our hero is crushed. It's all too much for Debbie, who hightails it back to her shanty

Debbie Reynolds, the backwoods teenager, nurses Leslie Nielsen as Walter Brennan (right) looks on in *Tammy and the Bachelor* (1957).   Courtesy of JC Archives

boat. Before long Leslie realizes what he could be losing. He rushes to her side to announce that, despite their age and other differences, he loves her.

Doesn't husband searching Tammy-style seem the way to go?

Cat on a Hot Tin Roof

Metro-Goldwyn-Mayer, 1958, color,
108 minutes
Director: Richard Brooks
Cast: Elizabeth Taylor, Paul Newman, Burl Ives, Jack Carson, and Judith Anderson

*B*ased on yet another Tennessee Williams Broadway drama (1955) about steamy sex in the languid South, *Cat on a Hot Tin Roof* is a distillation of the original play because the homosexuality of Newman's character has been greatly downplayed (almost buried) in the timid movie adaptation (due to fear of the industry's self-censorship administration). Thus the real reason behind the man's heavy drinking and career inertia is cut out of the film version. Instead it is suggested that the hero's gorgeous wife has had an affair with Paul's best friend and that the latter has since committed suicide in remorse. OK, let's accept the magnolia blossom–drenched movie on its own terms.

The overbearing patriarch (Ives) of this contemporary Southern clan is Big Daddy, and he's just returned from an Eastern medical clinic. He thinks he is in good health, but his evah-lovin' wife (Anderson), Big Mama,

A Grieving Star

During the filming of *Cat on a Hot Tin Roof*, producer Mike Todd, the husband of **Elizabeth Taylor (b. 1932)**, was killed in a plane crash on March 22, 1958. After three weeks of mourning, Liz returned to the soundstage and completed her demanding assignment. Before long, one of those comforting her most off the soundstage was singer **Eddie Fisher (b. 1928)**, then wed to actress **Debbie Reynolds (b. 1932)**. (The couple had been close friends with Todd and Taylor.) In February 1959, Eddie and Debbie divorced; three months later, Fisher wed Taylor (who had converted to Judaism to please her fourth husband).

knows the truth: the man is dying of cancer. As Paul and Elizabeth battle it out verbally in their bedroom, Ives's other son (Carson) shows up at the family mansion with his wife (Madeleine Sherwood) and their five brats. Both Jack and Madeleine are grasping souls intent on winning over Big Daddy and becoming the prime beneficiaries in his will. Eventually, Burl learns his fate. After adjusting to the news, he badgers his favorite son (Paul) into again facing life. With that settled, Newman and Taylor resume their once-happy marriage with the suggestion that they plan to make lots of babies.

Rarely has the Tinseltown screen paired two such attractive stars, each at the peak of his or her physical appeal. Several sequences feature the gorgeous Taylor parading about in a formfitting slip as she seeks to renew her

Paul Newman is the recipient of Elizabeth Taylor's lusty advances in *Cat on a Hot Tin Roof* (1958).
Courtesy of JC Archives

hubby's sexual interest in her. The more he resists, the more she tries, and the more male moviegoers wish they could be in the male lead's shoes. Conversely, the challenge of a pretty female trying to rewin the affections of her handsome husband is something female viewers can appreciate and/or envy.

Everything ends happily ever after, so this movie suggests. However, do you want to take odds, given the nature of these two wild-card characters?

Coal Miner's Daughter

Universal, 1980, color, 125 minutes
Director: Michael Apted
Cast: Sissy Spacek, Tommy Lee Jones, Levon Helm, Phyllis Boyens, and Beverly D'Angelo

*E*ven with Hollywood prettifying the story to a degree and the clichés that abound in the last third of the picture, this screen drama (based on Loretta Lynn's autobiography) remains an entertaining story of the rise of one of country music's most famous female performers. Spacek, who did her own singing in the movie, won a Best Actress Oscar for her compelling performance.

The Southern influence is felt throughout this picture, from the singer's birth in Butcher Hollow, Kentucky, to her marriage at age thirteen to Jones, a World War II veteran. Within six years she has four children, and her simplistic husband—always fearful he will be dragged back into having to work in the deadly coal mines—encourages her to take her at-home singing of self-written songs to a professional level. This leads to her performing successfully at the Grand Ole Opry and being encouraged in her work by established genre star Patsy Cline (D'Angelo). As Sissy's career expands, there is a growing rift between her more sophisticated needs and Jones's hope that she will stay the same simple country girl. Following the death of her good friend Beverly and her own emotional collapse, Spacek returns to the stage, ready again to tackle her career. Meanwhile, she and her family reunite to face the future together.

For a change, a screen musical about a famed performer does not make the rise to stardom seem a simple task to accomplish, especially when the future celebrity is an old-fashioned, shy girl from a tiny hamlet. With that in mind, are you still ready to tackle Nashville? We can't promise you that a Tommy Lee Jones type will be waiting in the wings to cheer you on.

Two Moon Junction

Lorimar, 1988, color, 105 minutes
Director: Zalman King
Cast: Sherilyn Fenn, Richard Tyson, Louise Fletcher, Burl Ives, and Kristy McNichol

*T*his is highly erotic, sometimes laughably badly directed and acted, soft-core pornography in the guise of a real story. It boasts a cast that ranges from folk balladeer/actor Ives to Hervé Villechaize (TV's *Fantasy Island*) and, for good measure, Millie Perkins (the star of 1959's *The Diary of Anne Frank*) and McNichol (of TV's *Empty Nest*). It's one of those brooding Southern dramas (set in "the Crossroads of Destiny & Desire") that is filled with gothic overlays, steamy love scenes, and the scent of magnolia blossoms hanging in the sultry air.

The eldest daughter (Fenn) of a well-bred Alabama family is scheduled to wed a proper blueblood (Martin Hewitt). However, one night she visits a carnival in town and—pow!—everything changes. There she happens across a studly amusement ride attendant (Tyson) with whom she almost immediately has sex. Later they fight over his drinking and unruly behavior and again have sex. She returns to Martin, but, thereafter, rescues her lover from a scrape and they have sex once again. Tyson then vanishes. The night before her wedding, he returns just in time to couple with Sherilyn. Despite all of this, Fenn and Hewitt marry. During the very proper ceremony, Richard gets into a fight with one

Sherilyn Fenn and Richard Tyson share a wanton moment in the Southern-set *Two Moon Junction* (1988).   Courtesy of JC Archives

of the sheriff's men but escapes arrest. Time passes. Tyson, now a dishwasher, returns to his motel room and heads to the shower. Who should be waiting for him, but . . .

Want more of the same? You're in luck. In 1994 came *Return to Two Moon Junction*.

Something to Talk About

Warner Bros., 1995, color, 105 minutes
Director: Lasse Hallstrom
Cast: Julia Roberts, Dennis Quaid, Robert Duvall, Gena Rowlands, and Kyra Sedgwick

Very much a picture endorsing women's liberation and sexual equality, this slick Roberts vehicle was scripted by Callie Khouri (who wrote 1991's classic *Thelma & Louise*). A tract urging females to follow their personal dreams—both to career and romance—the picture wavers between being a romantic tale and a straight drama.

As in *Steel Magnolias* (1989), Roberts is a true daughter of the South. Here, she moves back to the family's horse ranch when she discovers that her husband (Quaid) has been cheating on her. What to do? Her parents (Rowlands and Duvall) urge her to return to Dennis, all in the name of reason and respectability. Her friends are shocked and/or titillated that Miss Perfect has reached a bump in life's road. Only her spunky sister (Sedgwick) actively takes her side and urges her to become her own person.

While an uncertain Julia debates her status with her charming, handsome mate, Gena is coping with the recent discovery of infidelity in her own marriage. Now it's two generations of women who must confront their futures and face up to what part their failing to take charge of their own lives (temporarily) played in damaging their unions.

By the finale, Julia is following her heart and is studying to become a veterinarian. The story ends cutely with her and Dennis on their "first" date, exploring the reality of a new future together.

If you think talking, analyzing, pondering, and talking some more with your love mate is the only way to express yourself, remember that the Kyra Sedgwick character in this film has a more physical response to the situation. When she sees Quaid after learning that he betrayed her sister, Sedgwick kicks him in the groin. When a stunned Julia asks why she did that, Kyra shoots back, "Consider it a blow for your dignity." All rightee. . . .

Sweet Home Alabama

Buena Vista, 2002, color, 108 minutes
Director: Andy Tennant
Cast: Reese Witherspoon, Josh Lucas, Patrick Dempsey, Candice Bergen, and Mary Kay Place

*F*or a change in a contemporary comedy, the New York characters are *not* putting down Los Angeles. Instead, they target quaint Southerners—especially those living in the movie-fabricated town of Pigeon Creek, Alabama. It's one of those folksy little (non-existent) burgs where the rich and poor mingle, the men love their huntin', and the women good-naturedly (or not) remain domestic slaves. Witherspoon's heroine is that rare bird who flew the coop. She rushed up North where, in a few years, she became an in-vogue fashion designer and snared as her fiancé the dapper son (Dempsey) of the mayor (Bergen) of the Big Apple. He has just proposed marriage.

The fly in the heroine's ointment is that when she hastily abandoned her impoverished past, she failed to get a divorce from her childhood love (Lucas). Now, freshly back on her home turf, she uses charm, bluster, and her fame to push him to sign those divorce papers. But, being the proud dude he is, he refuses in ever-so-manly (and charming) ways. By the time he admits defeat and is willing to end their in absentia union, she has—surprise, surprise—changed her mind.

Why does the spunky heroine ditch Patrick and all the fame awaiting her up North? She's had a chance to reexamine her values. It dawns on her that, despite the culture gap between herself and the locals (especially her too-down-to-earth parents), she—bless her heart—respects and loves them all dearly. She wants to be part of the old gang of friends once more. (We won't linger over her gaffe when she accidentally outs one of her best pals from the old days.)

Witherspoon, the heir apparent to Meg Ryan as the spunky leading lady of romantic comedies, makes an enviable heroine—one who has life by the tail. Her vulnerability is her past. But the scriptwriters really stack the deck when they deal with the hero. He's

Taxi, Anyone?

Blond, beautiful **Candice Bergen (b. 1946)**, who gained her greatest show business fame as the star of TV's *Murphy Brown* (1988–1998), has done her fair share of onscreen love scenes. Commenting on the mechanics of such sequences, she has noted, "Suddenly, you wind up in bed with a guy on top of you that you wouldn't want to share a cab with."

everything a sensible girl should want. After all, during his wife's long absence, he's grown up. Unknown to her until the finale, he's made something of himself (having opened a glass-blowing factory and a trendy new restaurant).

What more could a girl want? Oh, I don't know. How about reality in any part of her life?

What more could a guy want? Perhaps an inner radar that warns him off this condescending female who repeatedly shows signs of being a shrew in the making.

Having dipped into Hollywood's version of romance—Southern style—in which the average onscreen family ranges from eccentric to depraved to backwoods quaint, it amazes me that the South hasn't petitioned to again secede from the Union. Then the South could make its own movies about peculiar Northerners and their strange customs that adversely affect any and every love relationship they start.

7

Stick to Your Own Kind... or Not

In One Million B.C. (1940), a screen saga of prehistoric times, two contrasting tribes live in proximity to one another and eventually put aside their differences to fight off flesh-eating dinosaurs and other common obstacles. A goodly portion of this celluloid entry about the Stone Age is devoted to the blossoming love between Victor Mature (of the Rock People) and Carole Landis (of the Shell People) and how, despite their different backgrounds, they unite.

But by 1940 Hollywood already had a long history of movies dealing with romantic attraction between members of different races. For example, there were such landmark entries as *Broken Blossoms* (1919), set in London's Limehouse district, in which a Chinese man (Richard Barthelmess) falls desperately in love with a badly abused Caucasian girl (Lillian Gish). There was also *The Vanishing American* (1925) in which a Navajo tribesman (Richard Dix), while helping his people cope with abuse from the white majority, falls in love with a pretty Caucasian schoolteacher (Lois Wilson). Such pictures highlighted the rampant bigotry in the United States (and elsewhere) that kept interracial romances a legally and/or socially forbidden activity. These entries showcased onscreen lovers risking punishment—even death—to pursue their love despite racial barriers. Adding ethnicity to these love stories gave them further grist and poignancy because the hero and heroine were combating such odds.

Over the decades, as laws and social customs diminished some bigotry toward ethnic minorities and more interracial romances occurred in real life, Tinseltown films increasingly explored how individuals of contrasting cultural backgrounds overcame great prejudices to be with their special person of another culture. Even in today's more politically correct times, this topic is a frequent element in Hollywood movies.

Love Is a Many Splendored Thing

Twentieth Century-Fox, 1955, color,
102 minutes
Director: Henry King
Cast: William Holden, Jennifer Jones,
Torin Thatcher, Isobel Elsom, and
Murray Matheson

This movie is best remembered for its spectacular on-location cinematography and for its Oscar-winning theme song. However, especially for its time, it was a daring depiction of "forbidden" love between a Caucasian and a Eurasian. Based on a semiautobiographical fiction by Han Suyin, it tells of a widowed doctor (Jones) of mixed blood who falls desperately in love with a cynical, married American war correspondent (Holden) in 1950s Hong Kong.

Jennifer Jones as the Eurasian doctor in love with an American war correspondent (William Holden) in *Love Is a Many Splendored Thing* (1955).
Courtesy of JC Archives

The Price of Fame

By the time **Jennifer Jones (b. 1919)** divorced actor husband **Robert Walker (1918–1951)** in 1945 she had already won a Best Actress Academy Award for *The Song of Bernadette* (1943). By then she was heavily involved in a romance with married film producer David O. Selznick who was devoting the bulk of his professional efforts to furthering her acting career. The couple wed in 1949. Following his death in 1965, she wed industrialist Norman Simon in 1971, a marriage that ended with his passing in 1993.

"I'm Eurasian. The word itself seems to suggest a certain moral laxity in the minds of some people." If Jennifer tells William (and the audience) once in this picture, she reminds him repeatedly that they come from two different worlds ("You're not Eurasian. Your pride and sense of dignity are not involved") and that their relationship will never be accepted by either ethnic community. The fact that Holden is currently married is an issue but *not* the key one in this well-orchestrated tearjerker.

Making the maudlin tale even more of a weeper, our hero dies on the Korean battlefront. But not to worry—Jennifer rushes to the couple's favorite hill overlooking the harbor and thinks back to the romantic times they shared. Cinching the film's special-love-is-eternal message, the soundtrack swells with yet another rendition of the title song, while

Holden—in voice-over—reads the posthumous letter he wrote his beloved before going on his fatal wartime trek: "We have not missed, you and I—we have not missed that many splendored thing." With this the film ends on its dreamy note of deliciously terminated love.

Jones looks fetching in her Asian outfits, and her special makeup does suggest a mixed-blooded background, but wouldn't the film have been that much better if Hollywood had dared to use a real Eurasian in the part. As for Holden, popular as he was with filmgoers, by now he'd developed that dissipated, sour look that gave his screen vehicles an unintended jaded veneer.

West Side Story

United Artists, 1961, color, 153 minutes
Director: Robert Wise
Cast: Natalie Wood, Richard Beymer, Russ Tamblyn, Rita Moreno, and George Chakiris

Despite its rich score, this adaptation of the hit 1950s Broadway musical is quite dated in its simplistic presentation of New York City street gangs and their daily fights over local turf. Much acclaimed in its era (it won ten Oscars), the movie is an update of Shakespeare's *Romeo and Juliet.*

On the plus side in this feature, as the Anglo Jets (led by Tamblyn) and the Puerto Rican Sharks (headed by Chakiris) battle for supremacy, the love story takes center stage. In the limelight are Wood and Beymer, the star-crossed lovers of conflicting ethnic backgrounds, determined, at all cost, to enjoy their budding romance. In a moving duet ("Somewhere"), Natalie and Richard sing of a place where prejudice does not exist and interracial sweethearts can thrive in peace. But happiness is denied them, for Beymer is killed by a member of George's gang for having fatally knifed their leader in revenge for his (Chakiris) having murdered Tamblyn in a skirmish. At the finale, Wood's accusations shock the members of the two opposing gangs into realizing what they have done, and they join together in carrying Beymer's body from the playground. There is hope that peace may reign in the turf yet.

Like such earlier screen musicals as *The King and I* (1955) and *South Pacific* (1958)—also

Broadway based—*West Side Story* revels in its presentation of romance stymied by ethnic intolerance. This theme gave these tales of unlucky courtship social relevance and made audiences feel politically correct for empathizing with these unfortunate victims of racial bigotry.

If only Wood and Beymer and some of the other cast members had been real singers and not had their songs dubbed. Also, I kept wondering how often Natalie's makeup (to make her look more swarthy) left telltale smudges on costumes and caused scenes to be reshot.

Trouble brews between racial groups in *West Side Story* (1961). Seen here are Natalie Wood, George Chakiris, and Richard Beymer.   Courtesy of JC Archives

Rosalind Russell as a Brooklyn Jewish widow and
Alec Guinness as a Japanese businessman become
better acquainted in *A Majority of One* (1961).
Courtesy of JC Archives

A Majority of One

Warner Bros., 1961, color, 156 minutes
Director: Mervyn LeRoy
Cast: Rosalind Russell, Alec Guinness, Ray
Danton, Madlyn Rhue, and Mae Questel

*J*ust as love is not reserved exclusively for
the young, neither is prejudice. Here we
have a romance between middle-aged individuals who come from very opposing her-
itages. To make the story's preachy message
more palatable, it is enveloped within a
warmhearted comedy.

A Jewish Brooklyn widow (Russell),
whose son was killed by the Japanese during
World War II, reluctantly agrees to join her
daughter (Rhue) and son–in–law (Danton) on
a boat trip to Japan where he is negotiating a
major trade agreement with the Asians. En
route, she meets Guinness, a Japanese man
whose family perished in the war. Their
growing friendship makes Ray suspicious
because Alec is a member of the trade committee involved with Danton's mission.

Once in Japan, it is Russell who must convince tradition-bound Guinness to forgive Ray's accidental gaffe, which insulted the businessman and halted the trade meetings. Before leaving for the United States, Rosalind rejects Alec's marriage offer, not because of Madlyn and Ray's objections, but because she believes that she and her suitor are still too much caught up in their past grief. Months later, Guinness comes to New York as a United Nations delegate and renews his courtship of Russell. This time she is agreeable to his romantic intentions.

Russell fumbles badly in her attempts to replicate the warm Jewish matron characterization that came so naturally to Gertrude Berg, who had played the lead on Broadway. Britisher Guinness fares equally poorly in his impersonation of the Japanese gentleman. He is so focused on trying to seem Asian that he forgets to give any emotional shading to his performance. On a scale of one to four, this entry gets only one sushi star.

Diamond Head

Columbia, 1963, color, 107 minutes
Director: Guy Green
Cast: Charlton Heston, Yvette Mimieux, George Chakiris, France Nuyen, James Darren, and Aline MacMahon

*B*ased on a 1960 novel by Peter Gilman, this potboiler (with glorious cinematography and a handsome cast) is unsubtle soap opera that seems almost laughably naïve when viewed today. However, in its time, *Diamond Head* was touted as a major studio's "daring" study of a mixed-blood romance between a Caucasian and a Hawaiian.

Heston is the hard-nosed, bigoted patriarch of his family and ruler of the clan's pineapple plantations based on the Hawaiian island of Kauai. When he learns that his younger sister (Mimieux) is having a secret relationship with a full-blooded Hawaiian (Darren), he is furious. (Meanwhile, hypocritical Charlton is carrying on a not-so-secret affair with Hawaiian Nuyen.) Later, after James is accidentally killed saving Heston's life, an angered Yvette relocates to Honolulu, where she finds refuge with Darren's half-caste brother (Chakiris). Before this turgid drama concludes, France dies giving birth to Charlton's illegitimate son, and Yvette and George have become a permanent couple. Whew!

In this poorly fabricated sudser—in which *none* of the lead Hawaiian characters are played by native-born players—the racial bigotry issues are resolved in a simple-minded fashion to reach a "happy" finale. If only matters of the heart and emotions could be so easily worked out in real life. But then, when you cast the movies' Moses (from 1956's *The Ten Commandments*) in the pivotal part, anything is most certainly possible. So unless you have special powers to part a sea and lead a huge group through a desert expanse, I suggest you refrain from interfering in others' lives, especially when your motivations are based on unreasonable biases.

Guess Who's Coming to Dinner

Columbia, 1967, color, 108 minutes
Director: Stanley Kramer
Cast: Spencer Tracy, Sidney Poitier,
Katharine Hepburn, Katharine Houghton,
and Cecil Kellaway

When this love story with its emphatic social-consciousness theme was released, the United States was engulfed in civil rights unrest and debates over civil rights legislation, which made the picture seem very timely. Advanced as a politically correct, daring

Sidney Poitier and Katharine Houghton exchange confidences in *Guess Who's Coming to Dinner* (1967). Courtesy of JC Archives

movie, the picture was the ninth and final screen teaming of Tracy and Hepburn. (Two weeks after the project wrapped, Spencer died of a heart attack.)

Young Houghton returns to San Francisco from a Hawaiian holiday accompanied by the man (Poitier) she has fallen in love with there. He is thirty-seven, bright, and a dedicated research scientist. The one fly in the ointment—from some people's viewpoint— is that she's white and he's black. Sidney informs Spencer and Katharine Hepburn that, unless they approve of the union, he will not marry their daughter. This puts the well-established couple's idealistic, progressive beliefs to a crucial test. While the parents are debating the pros and cons of the situation, their friends have no problem in quickly registering their disapproval of such a mixed union. Matters aren't made any easier when Sidney's parents (Beah Richards and Roy E. Glenn Sr.) arrive from Los Angeles and are themselves split in their opinion of whether their son should wed his new girlfriend. Eventually, everyone concludes that Poitier and Houghton must decide for themselves what is best. With that they all adjourn for a family dinner.

One of the chief problems with this well-intentioned exercise was how much it stacked the decks. For example, not only is Sidney's character well educated, he is brilliant. He is not merely a dedicated researcher but a great humanitarian working for the World Health Organization. So what is there not to like about this handsome, congenial man who is bringing much more to the marriage table

The Food of Love

An interviewer once asked **Katharine Hepburn (b. 1907)** about her long-term offcamera relationship with **Spencer Tracy (1900–1967)**. The reporter posed the question, "If Tracy was a baked potato, what was she?" The very forthright Katharine replied, "I'm a dessert. Ice cream with chocolate sauce."

than is his intended bride? Then too, isn't it wonderfully convenient that the elders decide to leave the weighty decision to the ones actually involved, thus sparing the screenplay from having to present major figures as unmitigated bigots.

Portnoy's Complaint

Warner Bros., 1972, color, 101 minutes
Director: Ernest Lehman
Cast: Richard Benjamin, Karen Black, Lee Grant, Jack Somack, and Jeannie Berlin

Philip Roth's popular novel *Portnoy's Complaint* (1969) deals with the complexity of modern American Jewish life. Overwhelmed by his castrating mother (Grant) and unsupported by his henpecked father (Somack), the highly neurotic hero (Benjamin) asks his psychiatrist: "Am I being unreasonable, Doctor? I mean, this is my life,

my only life, and I'm still living in the middle of a Jewish joke—and it isn't a joke."

Successful in his career but emotionally unhappy, Richard equates his overly controlled existence with Judaism at large. In reaction, he seeks release with an uninhibited gentile woman (Black) whom he nicknames "Monkey." Knowing that his mother will disapprove of her makes his girlfriend all the more interesting. But there is no pleasing the phobic Benjamin who decides that Karen is *too* kooky, and he drops her. Later, while visiting Israel to rediscover his ethnic roots, he is rejected when he attempts to seduce an Israeli (Jill Clayburgh). At an emotional crossroads, put-upon Portnoy understands he must reevaluate all aspects of his unsatisfactory life.

A few years earlier, Hollywood would not have dared to make such a picture because of the Jewishness of the story. When released, several Jewish groups complained about the unfavorable light in which *Portnoy's Complaint* depicted Jewish mothers; others were disturbed by the narrative's interfaith relationship seeming to make eligible Jewish women appear undesirable.

Such problems this smarmy hero has! Can anyone undo the damage done by his suffocating formative years? As played by Benjamin—who specialized in such screen roles—the more pressing question is do we *really* care? Much more appealing are the two major love interests in this cinema exercise. Both reject him not because he is Jewish but for much sounder reasons—he is a manipulative prig who finds his only real sexual satis-

Offcamera Continuity

A former child performer, actor **Richard Benjamin (b. 1938)** is far less fickle in real life than he has been in his screen roles, which usually typecast him as a supercilious yuppie for whom no woman is ultimately satisfactory. Since 1961, Richard has been married to actress **Paula Prentiss (b. 1939)** with whom he costarred in, among other projects, the 1967–1968 TV sitcom *He & She*.

faction in constantly pleasuring himself. Didn't his mommy warn him about the dangers of such activities?

Dances with Wolves

Orion, 1990, color, 183 minutes
Director: Kevin Costner
Cast: Kevin Costner, Mary McDonnell, Graham Greene, Rodney A. Grant, and Floyd "Red Crow" Westerman

*F*illed with feel-good moments and a political correctness agenda, *Dances with Wolves* did much to make moviegoers more aware of—and sympathetic to—the rich history of Native Americans and their centuries of exploitation during America's westward expansion. Mammoth in length, this emotional saga won several Oscars and cleaned up at the box office.

A Yankee lieutenant (Costner), an accidental Civil War hero, requests to be posted on the western frontier and ends up in the sparsely populated South Dakota territory. In his isolation he makes friends with a wolf. He later comes to know a Native American horse thief (Grant) as well as a woman (McDonnell), the latter a white woman rescued years earlier by the Sioux from warring Pawnee. As time passes, Kevin assimilates into the tribal culture, romances Mary, and increasingly views life from a nonwhite point of view. Eventually, circumstances force him to leave the tribe, and he reluctantly heads westward accompanied by McDonnell.

In the rush to endorse this breakthrough ethnic drama, many viewers at the time of release overlooked the fact that in the story line the Native Americans are treated as unlucky souls who are rescued by the great white man. (The "rescue" proves useful for the pioneers/troops but much less fortunate for the Native Americans.) Then too, the romance between the white soldier and the widowed woman is really not interracial because both are Caucasians, although circumstances have put them into a love situation where they are fighting the establishment in order to continue their relationship.

On the other hand, *Dances with Wolves* gave work to many Native American talents, the Lakota Sioux's dialogue presented onscreen is delivered in their native language (with English subtitles used), and the end results show the close attention paid to the details of daily life among the Sioux in the nineteenth-century American West.

Jungle Fever

Universal, 1991, color, 132 minutes
Director: Spike Lee
Cast: Wesley Snipes, Annabella Sciorra,
Spike Lee, Ossie Davis, and Ruby Dee

This explosive feature makes no attempt at being subtle. Its thesis is that the lust between races is surface deep and is inspired primarily by the novelty of trying something different. Whether or not one accepts Lee's message is a personal matter. However, the increasingly adept filmmaker makes effective use of his name cast. A standout is Halle Berry as a drug-addicted prostitute.

Snipes, a rising African American architect in New York City, is married and has a family. Nevertheless, he begins an affair with office temp worker Sciorra, an Italian American. When his wife (Lonette McKee) learns of the betrayal, she bars him from their house. Meanwhile, Annabella's father (Anthony Quinn), now knowing of her fling, fixes her up with a local Italian boy (John Turturro), but the latter is more interested in a black woman he knows. Eventually, Annabella and Wesley's romance runs its course, the duo

exhausted from coping with the repercussions among family and friends. Snipes attempts to reconcile with his wife.

With its controversial subject matter, one might have expected a lot more focus to be on the dynamics of the amorous relationship between the coleads. However, Lee devotes much more of the screen narrative to the reactions of the couple's inner circle (which includes Spike wearing his acting hat) to this mingling of two races.

Lee Says

A few years before making *Jungle Fever*, movie director **Spike Lee (b. 1957)** told an interviewer, "I don't want to imply racism, but black sexuality makes people uncomfortable."

Snow Falling on Cedars

Universal, 1999, color, 126 minutes
Director: Scott Hicks
Cast: Ethan Hawke, Youki Kudoh, Rick Yune, Max von Sydow, and James Cromwell

In the early 1950s, newsman Hawke (who lost an arm in World War II) covers a local murder trial in a small fishing village on San Piedro Island (north of Puget Sound). It develops that the Japanese American (Yune) on trial for killing another fisherman (Eric Thal) is married to Kudoh. The latter had once been Ethan's high school sweetheart, but they had gone their separate ways because of the pressures of racial discrimination. When her family was interned in a wartime detention camp during the anti-Japanese hysteria, they had pressured her to wed Rick, someone of their own background.

As the courtroom proceedings unfold, the journalist recalls events with his once love.

Ethan Hawke plays a journalist whose interracial romance comes back to haunt him in *Snow Falling on Cedars* (1999).   Photo by Albert L. Ortega

from what is not said onscreen how these long-ago lovers really feel about each other now.

Crazy/Beautiful

Buena Vista, 2001, color, 99 minutes
Director: John Stockwell
Cast: Kirsten Dunst, Jay Hernandez, Lucinda Jenney, Taryn Manning, and Bruce Davison

This movie suggests, "When it's real. When it's right. Don't let anything stand in your way." OK, let's go with that.

In a reversal of ethnic stereotypes, Hispanic American Hernandez from East Los Angeles is the high-achieving, grade-A pupil (intent on attending the Naval Academy) involved with a confused upscale Caucasian

Meanwhile, he uncovers evidence that the victim, having tumbled to his death aboard his boat, was most likely the victim of an accident caused by a passing freighter. The newfound information is turned over to the judge and works in the defendant's favor.

While this multilayered drama wants to be a soulful study (the ad slogan reads, "First loves last. Forever") Hawke is too neutral in his acting, usually turning a blank-faced look to the cameras. In this beautifully lensed drama, we wait in vain for the ex-lovers to show emotional sparks in the present, but none are forthcoming. We can only imagine

Father-Daughter Talk

Sometimes a character deeply in love spills out hurtful truths but can't see the forest for the trees. In *Crazy/Beautiful*, mixed-up Dunst confronts her father (Davison) with, "How could you tell the only person in the world that I love, that I care about so much, to stay away from me? Do you think that the only thing I'll ever do to someone is screw them up? That I'm not worth loving?"

Is that a rhetorical question . . . or what?

(Dunst), a trouble-prone photography student at the same high school. After he spends a night cruising around his neighborhood with Kirsten, his mother scolds him for wasting time with this outsider. When Jay meets Dunst's father (Davison), he is amazed to learn that he is the congressman from whom he needs sponsorship for the Academy. Bruce

promises to help Hernandez achieve his goal on condition that he stop seeing the man's daughter. The twist is that the politician is *not* being bigoted but responsible in his demand—he fears his offspring (who has suicidal tendencies) will mess up Jay's career plans. In a happily-ever-after finale, the young leads reaffirm their love and give each other encouragement for the future—together. With Davison's support, Hernandez gets accepted to the Academy. Meanwhile, troubled Dunst vows to change for the better.

I hope it did not take you the movie's full running time to discover that the title refers to Dunst and Hernandez's characters: she = crazy, he = beautiful.

I don't know about you, but I'm ready now for a definitive epic on the great unfulfilled love between the daughter of a Phoenician shipbuilder and the son of a New Zealand sponge diver. Picture the drama . . . the pageantry . . . the romance!

The Opposite Sex

Former child star **Kirsten Dunst (b. 1982)** had her first screen kiss (from Brad Pitt) in *Interview with a Vampire* (1994). On the subject of dating, she has said,

- "Boys frustrate me. I hate all their indirect messages; I hate game playing. Do you like me or don't you? Just tell me so I can get over you."

- "Why would I cry over a boy? I would never waste my tears on a boy. Why waste your tears on someone who makes you cry?"

8

Drifters on the Prowl

Many people are born, grow up, and spend their entire lives in one locale, tied to the place by daily responsibilities, relationships, jobs, or just plain inertia. Such folks really venture out of their home turf only for business trips, vacations, or family emergencies. As such, everything in their immediate environment—including loved ones, friends, local attractions, and even the beauty of mother nature—eventually becomes overly familiar, often to the point of being taken for granted. For some individuals, this type of sameness gives needed consistency to their lives.

In contrast, there are others who crave the sight of a fresh face, the feel of a new situation, or a new response to an unfamiliar landscape to provide their lives with renewed zest. However, for one reason or another (including lack of funds or poor health) they can't break free to explore new turfs and enjoy novel experiences. The result is envy of those who have the opportunity to hit the open road and really see the country. When such a traveler shows up in their town, these stay-at-home types often look upon the stranger *not* with suspicion or fear but with enthusiasm and curiosity.

One type of casual visitor to town is the drifter, the man who calls no place home nor any person a neighbor. The more jaded observer might classify such a wanderer as a hobo, a homeless person, or a vagrant. On the other hand, the more optimistic (and/or romantic-minded) spectator might well attribute glamour, excitement, and laudable self-sufficiency to such wayfarers. They are intrigued by—and soon even admire and respect—these seemingly carefree strangers who migrate from place to place and seemingly always end up on their feet—or at least, so goes the premise in many American-made film features.

Four Daughters

Warner Bros., 1938, black-and-white,
90 minutes
Director: Michael Curtiz
Cast: Claude Rains, May Robson,
Priscilla Lane, Lola Lane, Rosemary Lane,
Gale Page, and John Garfield

*I*n the late 1930s, as America's primary focus shifted from the Great Depression to its pending involvement in World War II, class structure, lifestyles, and manners were altering tremendously. Life was moving from conformity to mainstream social standards to the flexibility of unrestricted individuality. This societal transformation was reflected in movies of the times. One of the earliest examples of the new breed of individualist on the screen was depicted in *Four Daughters*. In the process this picture introduced a fresh variation of the screen (anti)hero: the charismatic stranger who had a big chip on his shoulder (which was frequently caused by the mushrooming adverse effects of the Depression).

Such a cynical role fit ex–New Yorker Garfield like a glove, and here, in his first sizable screen assignment (which made him a star), he set the ground rules for such parts. The impact of his performance convinced many moviegoers that the next best thing to winning the lottery was meeting a tough-talking newcomer to town, a sarcastic but charismatic stranger who dangles a cigarette from his mouth, has an eye for the interesting available girls thereabouts, and, if asked nicely, might treat you to a recitation of the injustices he's experienced since birth.

A widowed musician (Rains) with four daughters (the Lanes, Page) invites an affable young composer (Jeffrey Lynn) to board at their home. He wins everyone's heart, including the love of Priscilla. Meanwhile, Lynn brings a talented young arranger (Garfield) to town to help him with a new composition. The scornful, tight-lipped newcomer finds himself falling in love with Priscilla, and that gives him a new lease on life. Later, he is crushed to learn that she and Lynn plan to marry. However, the bride-to-be discovers that her beloved older sister (Page) secretly loves Jeffrey. Out of respect for her sibling, Priscilla breaks off the wedding plans. Instead, she runs off with Garfield and they marry. A year later, when Priscilla and her husband return to town to visit her clan for the Christmas holidays, she learns that her sacrifice over Lynn was for naught (Page has instead wed a hometown suitor). Angered at himself for having spoiled Priscilla's chance for true happiness, Garfield deliberately crashes his car during a snowstorm and dies. The path is now open for Lane and Lynn to be reunited.

Having created a sensation with his role in *Four Daughters*, Garfield was rushed into many more screen outings as the cynical, embittered, but quite sensitive soul. His part always called for his character to be on the move (sometimes on the run from the law), on the make, and the first to explain through clenched jaws to everyone within hearing distance that life has given him a raw deal.

With this type of mug now popular with moviegoers, the clean-cut hero was no longer the only choice either in film scenarios or in real life. Suddenly, being a responsible man who was thoughtful and true was no longer fashionable. Good guys even finished last now! The topsy-turvy social situation didn't end with Garfield, for he was the forerunner of later generations of antiheroes, including Montgomery Clift, Marlon Brando, James Dean, and George Clooney.

Fallen Angel

Twentieth Century-Fox, 1945, black-and-white, 98 minutes
Director: Otto Preminger
Cast: Alice Faye, Dana Andrews, Linda Darnell, Charles Bickford, and Anne Revere

*M*urder and intrigue in a small Northern California coastal community form the basis of this hard-boiled film noir excursion, which reunited the director and costar (Andrews) of the prior year's big-screen hit *Laura*. At the heart of this cynical caper is a down-and-out stranger (Andrews) stranded in the town. His biggest (and only) assets are his good looks, his glib charm, and a winning smile (which hides a heart of stone). As the tale unfolds, his greed and duplicity are matched by the actions of some of the venal locals he encounters.

Thrown off a San Francisco–bound bus for not having the fare, Dana makes the best of the situation in the overgrown village in which he is forced to stay. After earning money for helping to promote a phony medium's show, Andrews remains in town because he's already attracted to a shapely, gorgeous waitress (Darnell) at the local café. She's the mercenary sort, which quickly inspires him to suggest that he'll con another local, the lonely Faye (who has already developed a crush on him), into marrying him. Once he controls her financial assets, he'll divorce her, leaving him in a position to go off with Linda. The nuptials take place, but the next day Darnell is found murdered. A retired New York cop (Bickford) is asked by local authorities to help with the investigation. One of the chief suspects is Andrews. Through it all, Faye remains faithful to her spouse, and her belief in him leads Dana to prove that he is not the killer. By the finale Andrews is promising his loyal wife that he is on the path to reformation.

The moral of this downbeat, well-executed tale? Cook meals at home. It will definitely keep you out of trouble.

The Postman Always Rings Twice

Metro-Goldwyn-Mayer, 1946, black-and-white, 113 minutes
Director: Tay Garnett
Cast: Lana Turner, John Garfield, Cecil Kellaway, Hume Cronyn, and Leon Ames

Sometimes, according to Hollywood, the appealing drifter newly arrived to town is not the instigator of the chaos that occurs but

Real-Life Femme Fatale

Oncamera the 110-pound Turner, with her 35-23-35-inch figure, was a stunner. Offcamera the beauty was wed eight times (twice to the same man). Her first husband was popular bandleader Artie Shaw. Their 1940 marriage ended in divorce the next year. In 1942, Lana wed restaurateur Stephen Crane (who became the father of her only child, Cheryl). The couple was united by the same official in Las Vegas who had officiated at her first union. When she arrived for the new nuptials, the judge greeted the movie star with: "Welcome back, Lana!"

merely a weak pawn in the hands of a more vicious local character. Nevertheless, it is his charming (at least to some) presence and ready availability to join into mischief that lead to an explosive, deadly situation onscreen.

Based on a steamy James M. Cain novel (1934), the die is cast in *The Postman Always Rings Twice* when a hitchhiker (Garfield) stops at a roadside café in a small California coastal town. He is immediately beguiled by a luscious woman (Turner) at the diner. The only fly in the ointment is that she's already married to the restaurant's elderly proprietor (Kellaway). No problem. John is hired on to work there, and in short order Lana is insisting the only way they can be happy together is to murder her husband and make it seem an accident. Once the crime is accomplished,

Unsuspecting Cecil Kellaway is about to be done in by John Garfield while a nervous Lana Turner looks on in *The Postman Always Rings Twice* (1946).   Courtesy of JC Archives

the police cannot prove it was homicide and the ill-fated couple is free to wed. However, by now, each mate is suspicious of the other, and their marriage nearly falls apart. Ironically, just as they reconcile, Turner dies in an auto accident. This time the law brings the husband to trial, and he is found guilty of murder and sentenced to die in the electric chair.

In this film, Garfield once again exhibited his patented tough-but-vulnerable-guy charisma that women moviegoers found so appealing. Probably if asked exactly what drew them to such a negative character—beyond his potential in the bedroom—they'd have a hard time rationalizing their attraction to this corrupt loser. After all, here was a vagabond who was always looking for the quick angle, the least amount of responsibility, and the fastest way to make it to easy street. For most real-life guys, it would take a lot of ignoring of one's basic nature and upbringing to get down to the moral/ethical level of this celluloid figure. And then, that person would most likely feel so lousy (and guilty) about his new phony Garfield-like bad self, that he'd mess up every chance for those short-term advantages that fate tossed his way. It would become a lose-lose situation.

Picnic

Columbia, 1955, color, 115 minutes
Director: Joshua Logan
Cast: William Holden, Rosalind Russell, Kim Novak, Betty Field, and Susan Strasberg

For some viewers, *Grease* (1978), *Footloose* (1984), or *Dirty Dancing* (1987) is the ultimate, but for others there's nothing to equal

Local town beauty Kim Novak and glib drifter William Holden express their budding romance in *Picnic* (1955).
Courtesy of JC Archives

the erotic feel of the Labor Day picnic dance scene in this classic movie. It puts into sensuous play the mating of the drifter (Holden) and the Midwestern small-town beauty (Novak)—opposites who spark an animal attraction in one another—leading to a wish-fulfillment finale.

Down on his luck, Holden arrives in the burg having stolen a ride on a freight train. His initial plan is to look up an old college chum (Cliff Robertson) whose father is the richest man in the area and from whom he hopes to get a cushy job. However, once William meets Cliff's fiancée, the detached young Kim, it's love at first sight. Like many of the other locals, she is immediately drawn to his good looks, his devil-may-care attitude, his captivating smile, and his manly swagger. He is that unpredictable fella who is always living life on the edge, quickly winning attention with his good manners, bravado, and virility and the promise of a magically wonderful, unconventional future. Later, William gets into a fight with Cliff and beats him up, forcing the drifter to run from the law. Even then the usually sensible, low-key Kim remains mesmerized by this stranger. Her attraction is so strong that she quickly packs a few belongings and rushes to catch a bus, planning to meet up with the stud who has hopped a passing freight train.

As the camera pans back for a long shot of the bus pulling out of the Kansas town and heading in the same direction as the train, the music (featuring the hit theme song "Moonglow") swells and the title card "The End" appears on the screen. But hey, hot sex fantasies to one side, picture the couple's *real* future—something those moviegoers, beguiled by this volatile character or by his real-life counterparts, hate (or refuse) to do. Will this antihero settle down to a job, and, if so, what kind of a position can he get with his shaky work history and his past problems with the law? How long before responsibilities weigh him down and the sound of a locomotive's horn in the night gives him the notion of an easy way out—leaving his mate (and, perhaps, children) for further adventures on the high rail and low road?

The Long, Hot Summer

Twentieth Century-Fox, 1958, color,
115 minutes
Director: Martin Ritt
Cast: Paul Newman, Joanne Woodward, Anthony Franciosa, Orson Welles, Lee Remick, and Angela Lansbury

On a hot summer's day, Mississippian Newman arrives in Frenchman's Creek only a few steps ahead of his bad reputation. (Like his late dad, he is reputed to be a hot-tempered man who settles scores by barn burning.) The sleepy Southern town is ruled by widower Welles, a man disappointed in his weakling son (Franciosa) and frustrated that his schoolteacher daughter (Woodward) has been dating a wealthy neighbor's son for six years and still has not set a marriage date. There is immediate physical chemistry between Paul and Joanne, but she is too spirited to give in emotionally to this "big stud horse." However, Orson brings Joanne and Paul together at every possible occasion. Soon Newman is in charge of Welles's town store and is proving to be a real go-getter. Later, Newman is almost run out of town when he is blamed for the burning of Orson's barn (a deed actually committed by Welles's jealous son), but the truth is made known. After Paul

Joanne Woodward makes her feelings known to Paul Newman in *The Long, Hot Summer* (1958).

Courtesy of JC Archives

Promises! Promises!

According to *The Long, Hot Summer*:

Lines to Use on That Special Woman

- "I'm goin' to show you how simple [lovemaking] is. You please me and I'll please you."

- "I'll tell you one thing. You're goin' to wake up in the morning smiling."

Responses to That Special Man

- "I'm a human being. . . . I set a price on myself . . . a high, high price."

- "I've got quite a lot to give. I've got things I've been saving up my whole life. Things like love, understanding, and jokes and good times and good cooking. I'm prepared to be the Queen of Sheba for some lucky man and the best wife any man could hope for."

apologizes to Joanne for his unremitting cockiness, she drops all her barriers, and the couple plans to marry.

Newman had already made several movies, but this extremely popular picture so well showcased his handsome looks and sexy demeanor that it made him a major screen star. For a rare change in the transient-come-to-town genre, the antihero meets his intellectual match in the no-nonsense heroine. However, she has two vulnerabilities: (1) her sexual attraction to the newcomer and (2) her need to please her father and society by eventually (even though she has stalled for several years) giving in to the convention that a woman's place is in the home—married and with children. As such, it makes the film's finale—in which a docile Woodward traipses into the family house in pursuit of Newman who is heading upstairs to the bedroom—pat and upbeat, as well as more acceptable to the mores of more conservative filmgoers.

High Plains Drifter

Universal, 1973, color, 105 minutes
Director: Clint Eastwood
Cast: Clint Eastwood, Verna Bloom, Marianna Hill, Mitchell Ryan, and Jack Ging

*W*esterns had long presented sagebrush tales of the taciturn loner showing up in town to settle grudges, to right wrongs, or, perhaps, just to eke out a living. Usually in the process he wins the attention of the intrigued heroine. Here, in his genre directorial debut, the star effectively plays upon his past screen image of the Man with No Name (the character from his 1960s Italian-made Westerns) as he strides his way through this symbol-laden, brutal tale.

A mystery man (Eastwood) arises from nowhere out of the desert vapor. He rides into the town of Lagos in the American Southwest, where he quickly proves himself a deadly marksman in a shootout with three

Clint Eastwood as the enigmatic stranger in *High Plains Drifter* (1973). Courtesy of JC Archives

gunmen. Before long, the townsfolk beg him to defend them against a gang of escaped convicts who are en route to destroy Lagos. In preparing for the showdown, cigar-chomping Clint coaches the locals while making peculiar demands on them (including having them paint the town red). When the adversaries arrive, Eastwood is nowhere to be seen, and the villains plunder the town. Their victory turns to ashes when Clint suddenly reappears and murders them one by one. Before the stranger disappears again into the desert heat, the surviving citizens are convinced that this benefactor is the spirit of the local sheriff once whipped to death by these same criminals. Along the way, the sexy, mysterious newcomer arouses the sexual interest of local women, including Bloom and Hill.

In this heavily stylistic revenge tale, the outsider is again the catalyst for all the violent action. Here is a case where to match the degree of charisma and accomplishments of the squinty-eyed hero, Mr. Joe Average would not have to stoop down to the moral level of the lead figure. Instead, to step into the hero's celluloid shoes, he'd have to ride a horse well, be expert with firearms, be handy with a bullwhip, and have great courage and fortitude, not to mention getting just the right tilt to his cowboy hat.

The Hot Spot

Orion, 1990, color, 130 minutes
Director: Dennis Hopper
Cast: Don Johnson, Virginia Madsen, Jennifer Connelly, Charles Martin Smith, and William Sadler

*S*cam artist Johnson rides into a hot, grimy Texas burg sure that somehow he'll come up with a scheme to make a quick buck even in this run-down town. Voluptuous sexpot Madsen quickly takes note of the studly new arrival and taunts him with, "There's only two things to do in this town. You got a

Real-Life Hot Shot

At the age of twelve, **Don Johnson (b. 1949)** had his first sexual relationship (with his five-year-older baby-sitter), and it was the start of his lady-killer status. He was twenty-four when he married a San Francisco dancer for a brief spell in 1973. Next he wed teenage actress Melanie Griffith in 1976. They divorced in 1977, remarried in 1989, but parted (again) in the mid-1990s. In between the Melanie unions Don had a fling with, among many others, country music star Tanya Tucker, and he had a four-year relationship with actress Patti D'Arbanville (with whom he had a son). In 1988 Johnson made even jaded show business observers do double takes when he began a liaison with Barbra Streisand. (They later recorded a duet together, the romantic ballad, "Till I Loved You.") Following a romance with eighteen-year-old Jodi Lyn O'Keefe who played his daughter on TV's *Nash Bridges* (1996–2001), he wed a San Francisco socialite (Kelly Phleger) in 1999. Go, Don, go!

TV?" He says no, which leads her to say, "Well then, you're down to one thing. Lotsa luck!" With his blood boiling, Don goes to work for her much older husband who owns a used car lot. There he not only pursues the sluttish Virginia but also goes after the lot's sad, virginal-looking bookkeeper (Connelly). If that's not enough to keep him busy, the energetic grifter is scheming to rob the local bank. A strong hint to how this gritty narrative ends is provided by the title (*Hell Hath No Fury*) of the 1952 Charles Williams's novel on which the picture is based.

In everyday *real* life, dealing with the heat and humidity of this Lone Star town would be more than sufficient activity for any sane individual. However, this being the movies and the glib lead figure being such a killer ladies' man, he goes at it hot and heavy with both leading women. In between the tough talk and the inevitable showdowns, the screenplay allows for several sweaty love scenes that one hopes were more fun to film than they are for viewers to watch. As for well-tanned, well-fed Johnson, his performance had too much self-satisfaction and too little grist to make it very satisfactory for moviegoers.

Don Johnson plays a stranger stirring up passion and trouble in a Texas town in *The Hot Spot* (1990). Photo by Albert L. Ortega

Caught

Sony Pictures Classics, 1996, color,
109 minutes
Director: Robert M. Young
Cast: Edward James Olmos, Maria Conchita Alonso, Arie Verveen, Steven Schub, and Bitty Schram

A Jersey City, New Jersey, fish market is the backdrop of this love triangle involving a married couple and—yup—a drifter. Low-key and, at times, too pretentious in its film noir attitudes, the acting pulls the film up by its bootstraps.

On the lam from the police, an Irish grifter (Verveen) walks into a small fish market owned by Olmos and his unhappy wife (Alonso). In a flash, Maria Conchita sizes up this young drifter as someone she wants to know better. She offers him not only a job at the store but a place in her home. Before long, whenever hard-working Edward falls asleep for the night, the reckless lovers are coupling sexually (in every available room of the house and in every conceivable position). The good times are threatened when Olmos and Alonso's son (Schub), a would-be comic, and his wife (Schram) show up unannounced.

The Hollywood Book of Love

The prodigal offspring, who has a bad cocaine habit, catches on to what is going on in the household. Jealous of the interloper, he sets into motion the climax in which two of the main characters die.

For a "refreshing" change, the loner anti-hero gets perhaps more than he deserves in this film's dour finale. Ironically, by then the viewer has found him to be dangerously engaging, despite (or because of) the many downsides to his personality and his past.

There are two primary lessons to be learned from this downbeat, sturdy feature: (1) if you *must* hire a new shop worker, use an employment agent, and (2) be thoughtful and give your spouse a good pair of earplugs and eyeshades before you engage in adultery on the home front.

The Locusts

Orion, 1997, color, 124 minutes
Director: John Patrick Kelley
Cast: Kate Capshaw, Jeremy Davies, Vince Vaughn, Ashley Judd, and Paul Rudd

*D*ear reader: fill in the blanks. In the 1960s, a _____ drifter (Vaughn), with a _____ past, turns up in a _____ Kansas town where he finds employment with a _____ widow (Capshaw) who has an insatiable appetite for her farm workers. Complicating the story—almost to the point of bizarreness—is the presence of Capshaw's twenty-one-year-old son (Davies), recently released from a mental

asylum. Perhaps the sanest character in sight is friendly Judd, a local who is irresistibly drawn to this virile stranger. Before Vince and Ashley wise up and burn rubber leaving town, Kate and Jeremy—who share sick family secrets—have met pathetic fates.

Who said joining the 4-H Club and working in the outdoors was a sure cure for what ails you?

All the Pretty Horses

Miramax/Columbia, 2000, color,
117 minutes
Director: Billy Bob Thornton
Cast: Matt Damon, Henry Thomas, Penelope Cruz, Lucas Black, and Rubén Blades

*T*here was much viewer anticipation about this arty production shot in Texas and New Mexico, but the truncated results did not please the director, the distributor, or the filmgoing public. That aside, this expensively produced ($45 million) western, set in 1949 Texas and Mexico, is a sprawling rite-of-passage saga focusing on the clashes and misunderstandings of two cultures. For a change, the vagrant male lead (Damon) is not facing his (mis)adventures alone but is accompanied by a pal (Thomas). After heading across the Rio Grande into Mexico, they team up with a young misfit runaway (Black) for a while. Later, the duo finds work at a ranch, but soon Matt earns the owner's (Blades) anger when he engages in an affair with the possessive

In *All the Pretty Horses* (2000), Matt Damon plays a young drifter who has the adventures of a lifetime south of the border.   Photo by Albert L. Ortega

man's sheltered daughter (Cruz). Thereafter, the two Americans end up in a Mexican jail where they are brutalized. Eventually they are released on the rancher's say-so, on condition that Damon never sees Penelope again. However, while Thomas heads back to the United States, Damon has a final, unsatisfying meeting with Cruz. Eventually, a weary Matt returns to Texas, weighed down by his overwhelming adventures. He is buoyed by a later reunion with the much-tamed Henry, who now works on a desolate farm.

Adding up the pros and cons of a mysterious, charismatic drifter with no past or future versus a levelheaded guy who has a game plan for life, has resided in the same city for more than a few years, and cries when his favorite ball team loses the pennant, it becomes obvious that the latter type of man is statistically a much better dating/marriage bet. With this in mind, if a woman still feels the need to spice up her existence with unpredictability and adrenaline rushes, she can get that at any time of the week by connecting to her Internet provider and, perhaps, hooking up with an online stranger—though this may prove to be unsatisfying in the end. Ah, decisions . . . decisions!!

9

The Lure of Bad Guys

In today's world, the most culpable law-breakers are often not part of underworld mobs. Instead, they are seemingly refined entrepreneurs operating from high-rise office building suites ruthlessly manipulating the stock market with crooked deals that adversely affect millions of people. Similarly on the contemporary screen, it is often hard to separate the good guys from the bad guys in action films, such as *XXX* (2002), where the ethics and demeanor of the supposed hero (Vin Diesel) are hard to distinguish from that of the story's villains.

This blurring of the lines between hero and villain is not new to the twenty-first century. Real life, literature, and theater have long found the urge to celebrate rogues (think Don Juan, Billy the Kid, or Bonnie and Clyde) as hearty individuals who boldly take their fate into their own hands. (The fact that, in the process, many innocent bystanders usually become their victims seems inconsequential in the overall glorification of these "good" baddies.)

By the time talkies took over Hollywood in the late 1920s, Tinseltown itself had an established tradition of elevating crook characters—such as the Lone Wolf and Arsene Lupin—into gentlemen thieves/heroes. As the social and economic order underwent upheaval thanks to the Great Depression that marked the thirties, it was not long before moviemakers followed the popular press in romanticizing gangsters. These self-made men appealed to the imagination of the masses who felt downtrodden in the face of the overwhelming capitalistic system. (Frequently regarded by the average person as the Robin Hoods of the new era, these mobsters, however, generally forgot to complete the rule of Sherwood Forest: steal from the rich *and* give to the poor. But the public did not seem to mind that oversight.)

There was another undercurrent at work in this continuous big-screen presentation of lawbreakers as exciting, often appealing individuals. It was the novelty of wrongdoers who dared to buck the norm, grab what they wanted, and not allow themselves to be oppressed by legal restrictions. Another element of this presentation was the sexual allure and vicarious adrenaline rush that women moviegoers felt watching exciting men of action become kings of their special worlds, which included having females at their beck and call. In subsequent decades, this celluloid theme of the lure of bad guys—which became more or less blatant oncamera depending on the strength of industry self-censorship at any given time—hardly diminished and is still present in today's Hollywood products.

A Free Soul

Metro-Goldwyn-Mayer, 1931, black-and-white, 91 minutes
Director: Clarence Brown
Cast: Norma Shearer, Leslie Howard, Lionel Barrymore, Clark Gable, and James Gleason

*I*n San Francisco, the swank daughter (Shearer) of a famous attorney (Barrymore) meets a handsome gangster (Gable) whom her father has been defending on a murder charge. Once Clark is acquitted, she invites him to their home, but her snobbish relatives are offended by this "lowlife." Spurred on by their rejection of her new friend, Norma bolts out of the house with him. En route to Gable's digs, rival gangsters

Just Wearing the Essentials

On the MGM lot or away from the studio, Shearer was the very proper wife of Metro's high executive Irving Thalberg, and she carefully avoided any hint of romantic disloyalty to her VIP spouse. But on the soundstage it was a far different matter. There, in the safety of role playing, she could be as provocative as she wished both in wardrobe and in behavior. Favoring very sophisticated, sexy ensembles, Norma thought wearing bras was inhibiting to her desired oncamera look and performance. She also had another habit, as costar Gable told friends: "Damn, the dame doesn't wear any underwear in her scenes. Is she doing that in the interests of realism or what?" In addition, Clark discovered that once the cameras started rolling, coy Norma was a hot tomato in their love scenes, capable of stimulating great expectations in her colead. However, once the scene concluded, she promptly returned to her dressing suite and, once again, became the demure Mrs. Thalberg.

fire on their car. The two escape unharmed, with Shearer exhilarated by the excitement. Before long she and Gable are lovers, which disgusts her father. His reaction to the affair is so strong that Norma makes a pact with heavy-drinking Lionel: if he gives up alcohol, she will abandon her gangster boyfriend. Later, when Barrymore returns to drinking, she gives in also and reunites with Gable. However, by now the novelty has worn off the affair and she attempts to break up with him. Angered by her rejection, he shoves her around. Her aristocratic ex-fiancé (Howard) arrives on the scene and shoots the mobster dead. After successfully defending Leslie in court, Lionel drops dead of a heart attack. Norma heads to New York to begin a new life with Leslie following her.

That a refined movie queen of Shearer's stature could play such an adventuresome socialite, one who sought only excitement and sex from her newfound lover, was both shocking and thrilling to her millions of fans.

In this picture she explains to Gable that he is, "just a new kind of man in a new kind of world." Filmgoers thought if such rationalization and daring behavior was OK for ritzy Norma, then perhaps it was more acceptable than everyday social standards of the time decreed.

This meshing of opposite types works magically on the screen, but in real life such a heroine would be lucky to escape with her life from this excursion into the danger zone. Even if the gangster or his rivals didn't eventually rub her out, it's highly likely that she

Chic Norma Shearer is intrigued by slick gangster Clark Gable in *A Free Soul* (1931). Courtesy of JC Archives

would have been arrested for criminal hobnobbing and not reporting the mobsters' activities to the police. That, in turn, might have led to a jail sentence, and there's nothing glamorous about a stretch in prison, what with its restricted dining menu, limited clothing options, and so forth.

Johnny Eager

Metro-Goldwyn-Mayer, 1942, black-and-white, 107 minutes
Director: Mervyn LeRoy
Cast: Robert Taylor, Lana Turner, Edward Arnold, Van Heflin, and Robert Sterling

*A*merica was on the verge of entering World War II when this slick gangster yarn was released. Before the country became totally engrossed in the patriotic spirit of wartime living, this feature exploited the attraction of a pretty rich girl for the forceful attentions of a dynamic, handsome mobster.

On parole from prison, Taylor pretends to be a law-abiding taxi driver. In reality he is still Mr. Big running all the crooked operations in town. Sociology student Turner comes into close contact with the hoodlum and soon gets to witness firsthand that he is still an unreformed gangster. However, by then she's fallen in love with this dangerous man. He stages the phony murder of a crony (Paul Stewart) in which Lana is duped into thinking she killed the underling to save her beloved. Robert uses the situation to black-

mail her father (Arnold), the district attorney who sent him to prison, into allowing him to open his dog track operation. The lawyer is forced to oblige. As time passes, Lana becomes sick with grief and guilt at her impossible situation, but she cannot control her love for Taylor, the man who is now ignoring her. Several associates of the kingpin persuade him to come clean to the deathly ill girl who is so under his spell. Having explained the truth to her, Taylor is involved in a deadly shootout with his archrivals. Badly wounded, he is shortly thereafter gunned down by a cop.

Look, if you are really drawn to the study of criminology, there are plenty of good textbooks available. Stick to reading them rather than experimenting with casework in the field. It's a lot safer in the long run.

A Place in the Sun

Paramount, 1951, black-and-white, 122 minutes
Director: George Stevens
Cast: Montgomery Clift, Elizabeth Taylor, Shelley Winters, Anne Revere, and Raymond Burr

*P*romoted with the tag line: "Young people asking so much of life . . . taking so much of love!" this much Oscar-awarded feature pivots on a weak-willed "hero," one who seesaws between two romances with fatal results. It is based on a real-life case in New

A glum Montgomery Clift contemplates his loveless future with pregnant Shelley Winters in *A Place in the Sun* (1951).   Courtesy of JC Archives

The Next Best Thing

During the making of *A Place in the Sun* **Elizabeth Taylor (b. 1932)**, who was in the midst of her short-lasting, stormy first marriage (to playboy Nicky Hilton), developed a huge crush on **Montgomery Clift (1920–1966)**, a situation sparked by their oncamera love scenes together. However, off the set, the handsome bachelor star was too overwhelmed by dealing with and/or avoiding his insecurities, homosexuality, alcoholism, and hatred of being in the limelight to respond to Elizabeth's many romantic overtures. Reluctantly, she settled for being his lifelong friend and confidant, and they made two additional features together: *Raintree County* (1957) and *Suddenly, Last Summer* (1959). As her career fortunes rose and his fell, she remained a true pal and great career booster.

York State and a famous novel (Theodore Dreiser's *An American Tragedy*, 1925). As the exceptionally good-looking and sensitive Clift was cast in the key male assignment, audiences were (and are) immediately predisposed to be more sympathetic to this success-hungry young man who wants his place in the sun and doesn't mind contemplating murder to ensure his upscale future.

Clift, the son of a religious mission worker (Revere), obtains a job in his uncle's bathing suit factory. Although against the rules, Montgomery secretly fraternizes with one of the workers (Winters), and they begin an affair. Meanwhile, he is drawn to wealthy Taylor, a carefree socialite who returns his romantic interest. He wants to break with Shelley, but she informs him that she is pregnant and he

must marry her. Clift procrastinates about wedding her, and Winters, who has learned of his rich girlfriend, arrives at the lake resort where he is visiting Taylor. She threatens to expose him to his new circle. Montgomery takes Shelley out on a deserted lake in a rowboat. He plans to kill her, but the boat accidentally capsizes and she drowns. He is arrested and tried for murder, despite his protestation that her death was accidental. Before he is to die in the electric chair, he is visited by Elizabeth who reaffirms her love for him.

Repeat after me, "I will take swimming lessons. I will take swimming lessons."

Pal Joey

Columbia, 1957, color, 111 minutes
Director: George Sidney
Cast: Rita Hayworth, Frank Sinatra, Kim Novak, Barbara Nichols, and Bobby Sherwood

The dictionary definition for *heel* is "a contemptibly dishonorable or irresponsible person." During his lifetime (1915–1998), crooner, actor, and bon vivant Sinatra lived up to that description on many occasions. Because he generally enjoyed playing up to his bad-boy, tough-guy reputation, he obviously found it amusing to take on the role of a prime jerk who is redeemed by the love of two very different types of women. With several alterations from the 1940 Broadway musical that had featured Gene Kelly as the hoofer heel, Frank starred as the crooner heel in this musical comedy vehicle that was severely sanitized for its screen presentation. Between well-choreographed production numbers and intimate crooning interludes, *Pal Joey* proved that a self-centered opportunist—not a very appetizing basis for a movie hero—can have irresistible charm for women of all walks of life.

Tossed out of a Northern California city for playing around with the mayor's daughter, Sinatra arrives unemployed and broke in San Francisco. A bandleader friend (Sherwood) lands him a gig as singer/master of ceremonies at a small local club. There the chorines—all except for frosty Novak—fall for his wiles. Undaunted, Frank pursues Kim. Meanwhile, during an entertainment gig at a posh charity event, he recognizes a local socialite (Hay-worth) as a former stripper friend. Their hot-and-cold relationship instantly revives, bolstered by her forthcoming promise to finance a fancy nightclub for him to operate. By the time the new venue is ready to open, Rita is aware of her lover's strong interest in Novak. Hayworth makes him pick: the club or Kim. Sinatra goes noble and chooses to leave town alone. However, at the last minute Novak joins him, suggesting they face the future together.

Picture a decent dude in the same dilemma as Frankie. He'd be taking a one-way Greyhound bus ride out of town and there would be no gorgeous lady at his side. Ah, the magic of movies!

Bonnie and Clyde

Warner Bros., 1967, color, 111 minutes
Director: Arthur Penn
Cast: Warren Beatty, Faye Dunaway, Michael J. Pollard, Gene Hackman, and Estelle Parsons

Several Hollywood films before and many thereafter would also seek to elevate the criminal into an engaging folk hero, but none succeeded better than did *Bonnie and Clyde*. Made on a $2.5 million budget, it earned $22.8 million in domestic theatrical rentals, won two Oscars (and eight other Academy Award nominations), and cemented the star status of both Beatty and Dunaway. With its glamorous rearrangement of the brutal actual facts, its allegorical theme about outsiders banding together to brave the world, and its crafty blend of action, comedic moments, and violence, this crime drama further popularized the gangster's image with moviegoers.

The movie's promotional ad line says it all: "They're young . . . they're in love . . . and they kill people." In the early 1930s, Beatty meets bored waitress Dunaway and they form a partnership based on the prospect of such exciting activities as robbing banks together. (Their romantic relationship fumbles along because he is sexually dysfunctional.) Soon, a simpleminded garage mechanic (Pollard) as well as Warren's brother (Hackman) and the latter's whiney wife (Parsons) join the gang. Robbing banks and killing those in their way, the group develops near legendary status among the lower classes who find their audacity thrilling and distracting from the woes of the Depression. Months pass, and only Beatty and Dunaway remain in the bank robbing business. At the end, they fall into a police trap and their bodies are riddled with rounds of bullets.

Before you and your girlfriend buy those firearms and shine up that dusty getaway car, take time to do a little public polling. How many surveyed think you bear any resemblance whatsoever to Beatty? How many agree your mate would look just great in 1930s costumes and a beret?

Faye Dunaway consoles co–bank robber Warren Beatty in *Bonnie and Clyde* (1967).

Courtesy of JC Archives

The Thomas Crown Affair

United Artists, 1968, color, 102 minutes
Director: Norman Jewison
Cast: Steve McQueen, Faye Dunaway, Paul Burke, Jack Weston, and Biff McGuire

At the time box-office draw McQueen was best noted for starring in an assortment of blue-collar antihero roles onscreen. While he plays a college-educated, dapperly dressed entrepreneur in this outing, his feisty character is still very antiestablishment. Everything in this project is geared to make the cultured lead character as likable, refined, and sexy as possible and to ignore his basic immorality.

The story is self-made rich man decides to bite the hand that feeds him. He concocts a bold scheme to rob a Boston bank in broad daylight utilizing five collaborators in crime who have never met him face-to-face and who don't even know each other. The job completed, he gives his associates their share of the loot and deposits the balance in a Swiss bank account. By now the insurance company, who has recompensed the bank for its loss, has sent in its lead investigator—stylish Dunaway—to handle the case. Before long, she is convinced that Steve is the culprit. In an elaborate game of cat and mouse, the two opponents square off, but, in the process, they fall in love with one another. Because neither one completely trusts the other, McQueen decides to test Faye's loyalty. He informs her he is robbing another bank and that he'll meet her after the caper is accomplished. Fighting her instincts to protect her lover, she brings a

police escort with her. However, crafty Steve has anticipated the end results of her torn loyalties and is already making his escape aboard a South American–bound plane. Dunaway is stunned.

The lesson of this morality tale? Enroll in charm school, purchase a good leather briefcase, and don't forget the most crucial element: the trouser cuffs of your snappy new designer suit should break just at the shoe line. With such solid credentials you can get away with murder.

Badlands

Warner Bros., 1973, color, 95 minutes
Director: Terrence Malick
Cast: Martin Sheen, Sissy Spacek, Warren Oates, Ramon Bieri, and Alan Vint

Based on the Charles Starkweather–Carol Fugate killing rampage through

Nebraska and other states in 1958, this low-budget feature has reached minor cult status over the years. Despite the graphic depiction of the downsides of the reign of terror of a misfit young garbageman and his lovesick fifteen-year-old accomplice in which several victims die, many viewers have embraced this picture as a sterling examination of tragic alienated youth. (Not by chance, the lead character has a Jimmy Dean complex and thrives on posturing as such, much to the approval of his empty-headed young companion.)

After meeting up with simplistic teenage Spacek in South Dakota, detached blue-collar worker Sheen quits his job to pursue their

Martin Sheen as the brooding sociopath in *Badlands* (1973). Courtesy of JC Archives

relationship. When her concerned father (Oates) refuses to let her leave town with him, Martin shoots him without a second thought. The two go into hiding for a spell, but pursuing bounty hunters confront Sheen and he kills them. As the couple runs from the law, there is more senseless killing as Sheen dispassionately destroys anything and everybody in his way. In Montana, Sissy refuses to stay with Martin, and she is soon in police custody. After a car chase, the cops apprehend Sheen who is eventually executed. As for Spacek, she later weds her defense attorney.

Few Hollywood features have so artistically depicted the short, senseless, murderous careers of two lost souls. Sheen is a standout as the James Dean–like figure who is so elated to find a gathering of cheering "fans" as the police lead him away in custody at the airport. But are these characters worthy of being role models? Wash your mouth out with soap if you are even thinking of saying "uh-huh."

Broadcast News

Twentieth Century-Fox, 1987, color,
132 minutes
Director: James L. Brooks
Cast: William Hurt, Albert Brooks, Holly Hunter, Jack Nicholson, and Robert Prosky

*O*ne does not always have to be viciously cruel to qualify for bad-guy status. Being self-centered and manipulative and, worst of all, mishandling a public trust certainly make an individual eligible for such a booby prize. In *Broadcast News*—produced in an era before media journalism had sunk so far in public expectations and opinion as it has today—the scoundrel is a smiling doofus. He is too dim-witted (and intellectually lazy) to be a real journalist and settles for being a handsome mouthpiece for whatever words are fed him to parrot to home viewers. That's sad enough, but, even worse, he has no compunction about manipulating his and others' emotions to make an effective (but phony) impression on air about a news story, thus diminishing further any semblance of integrity he has as a focus of credible information for the often gullible public. Adding insult to injury, this good-looking, charming airhead ends up getting ahead in his profession and "gets all the great women."

Obsessive Hunter is a news producer at the Washington, D.C., bureau of a major television network where her earnest friend Albert is an on-air news reporter. One day Holly meets appealing Hurt, a somewhat shy local newscaster, who is almost boastful about his lack of credentials even for such a post and admits that he survives merely on charisma and salesmanship. To Hunter's annoyance, this inadequate journalist is hired to do news at her network, and, to her further amazement, he is impressively successful with viewers and rises in favor with the big bosses. Later, when William proudly shows her a program he has put together on "date rape," she gains sudden respect for him, especially because he has

allowed his sensitivity to show on air. Only later does she learn from Brooks, who finally realizes he can never turn their friendship into a romance, that Hurt had molded his rape piece to reflect his supposed spontaneous concern. Seven years thereafter, at a national press gathering, the three meet again. By now Hurt has risen to be a prestigious network anchorman, while Brooks (who has a family) works at a local Oregon station. As for workaholic Hunter, she is still single and is about to be promoted to managing editor at the TV news network.

This biting satire can be taken as light-hearted romantic comedy, or, if one has serious concerns about the dumbing down of American culture and ethics, it may be seen as making solid points about our willingness to be swayed more by good looks and facile charm than by any display of internal substance (especially regarding that gray matter in the noggin).

I Love BOTH of You

Ever find yourself falling in love with your best pal but don't know what to do next? Here's how a self-effacing character (Brooks) handles the delicate situation in *Broadcast News*. He tells his clueless woman buddy (Hunter): "I would give anything if you were two people, so that I could call up the one who's my friend and tell her about the one that I like *so much!*"

Internal Affairs

Paramount, 1990, color, 115 minutes
Director: Mike Figgis
Cast: Richard Gere, Andy Garcia,
Nancy Travis, Laurie Metcalf, and
Richard Bradford

In *Internal Affairs* (1990) Richard Gere plays a murderous cop.   Photo by Albert L. Ortega

*B*lending film noir style with the police thriller genre has been popular with Hollywood filmmakers for decades (e.g., 1951's *The Racket* and 1967's *Warning Shot*). However, few such pieces have been as gritty as this well-assembled, R-rated feature in which usually enigmatic Gere gives one of his most focused, energetic performances. The picture's ironic ad teaser, "Trust him . . . he's a cop" has many layers of meaning, especially in an era when police corruption and misguided on-duty action have so shaken people's faith in these defenders of the public peace. But *Internal Affairs* goes several degrees further. It paints a sharp portrait of a sick soul (Gere) corrupted by power in his position of public trust. This lead villain is caught up in the clout afforded by his personal magnetism, which allows him to run roughshod over coworkers, the public, his wife, assorted mistresses, and even the crooked elements he so cockily deals with for his own benefit.

In Los Angeles, a new internal affairs investigator (Garcia) is paired with an experienced partner (Metcalf). Their assignment is follow through on a case involving a young police officer (William Baldwin) accused of corruption. The trail leads to respected law enforcer Gere. As the net closes in on Richard, he toys with Andy's psyche, suggesting that Garcia's wife (Travis) may be two-timing him. To protect himself, Gere, who is having an affair with Baldwin's wife, has the lawman killed so he can't squeal further, and then he arranges for the murderers to be liquidated. By now Garcia is so paranoid about his wife's fidelity and her possible romantic involvement with Gere that he is ready to kill this bad cop. Eventually there is a showdown at Andy's house, where Richard holds Travis hostage. In the final face-off Gere is shot dead resisting arrest.

OK, so some women have a fantasy about men in uniform who exude power and control. But if you're into role playing and need a role model, keep in mind that Gere is a plainclothes detective here. Oops.

The Talented Mr. Ripley

Paramount/Miramax, 1999, color,
139 minutes
Director: Anthony Minghella
Cast: Matt Damon, Gwyneth Paltrow,
Jude Law, Cate Blanchett, and Philip
Seymour Hoffman

The familiar maxim, "The grass is always greener . . ." about the enviable beauty of a neighbor's yard certainly applies to this visually sumptuous thriller. Here a needy nobody is so attracted by the lifestyle of a rich playboy that he literally kills to be part of that special world. But once he has murdered his prey and taken on a new identity, life becomes a constant struggle to maintain his phony status. However, for this sociopath, it's worth it. As he reasons, no matter the cost, "It's better to be a fake somebody than a real nobody."

In 1958 Damon is hired—because of a misconception on his wealthy employer's part—to travel to Italy to convince the man's son (Law) to give up his dissolute life and return home. On his way to Europe Matt meets an heiress (Blanchett) and passes himself off as the wealthy Jude. Once on the Continent, the seemingly docile Matt worms his way into the good graces of the hedonistic Jude. As he joins in Law's self-indulgent lifestyle among the rich set he becomes sexually infatuated with his new "friend." This unspoken feeling is not shared by Jude, who has two current girlfriends, including an American writer (Paltrow) and a pregnant Italian girl (Stefania Rocca). Later, when Law grows bored with Damon and starts to cut him out of his social circle, the frustrated Matt kills his benefactor. Further on, Matt murders again to keep his past actions secret and/or to make himself free of entanglements so he can romance the rich heiress who has suddenly come back into his bizarre life.

What the film suggests—but is made far clearer in Patricia Highsmith's 1955 novel on which the picture is based—is the ironic message that envy may get you what you covet, but it may not be worth the effort. In short, both lead males in this picture are shams—one immoral, one without gumption and goals. Each uses his ability and charm to pull the wool over the eyes of some people all the time. But there will always be people who see through the sham. So forget the business about sheep and wool and visit a good oculist. Clear vision is everything.

Certainly if Tinseltown products are to be taken on faith, the more bastardly a person is in a bold and stylish way, the easier it is for him to draw the attention and support of the opposite sex. With that rule in mind, Richard M. Nixon should have been a real winner with desirable ladies. But we did add the qualifier "stylish."

10

The Lure of Femme Fatales

From time immemorial men have generally married one type of woman (the proverbial wholesome type they could safely bring home to their mothers) but have been intrigued by (and/or played around with) another far different type of female. The latter are usually sinfully sexy—and sometimes dangerously predatory. The allure of dealing with a wanton—a person not confined by society's norms—is the thrill of participating in a hazardous relationship. Such risky situations are born out of many men's desire to break out of a rut of the expected, the safe, and the conventional.

History and fiction have been full of grasping females who would employ any available wile on the opposite sex to get their way (think Bathsheba, Delilah, Cleopatra, Lady Macbeth, Lucretia Borgia, and Mata Hari).

Movies were quick to pick up on the use of morally loose gals in screenplays as an intriguing and pretty (sometimes verging on the exotic) variation on the standard villain of traditional stage melodramas. By the 1910s the industry had begun exploiting a new variant of this socially amoral dame who was so often dangerous (and sometimes so deadly) to her male prey. She was known as a vamp (short for "vampire") and had her greatest practitioner oncamera in Theda Bara, who burst into movie prominence with 1915's *A Fool There Was*. Through conniving and granting sexual favors, Bara's celluloid alter ego worked her evil spell over a host of leading men, all of whom quickly fell prey to her rapacious ways.

As social mores changed over the decades, vamps per se went out of style, but their sisters under the skin were still rampant in the Hollywood movie product, ranging from the calculating flapper to the scheming whore (whose heart was *not* made of gold). Also to be considered are the sinister gals of 1940s and 1950s film noir movies as well as the cold-hearted, corrupt dames of later screen fare (e.g., Theresa Russell in 1987's *Black Widow*, Linda Fiorentino in 1994's *The Last Seduction*). You'd think after all these years that real-life and reel-life men would wise up and stop being fools just for the promise of alluring companionship and the hope of some memorable, lascivious sex. Oh well!

♥   ♥   ♥   ♥   ♥

She Done Him Wrong

Paramount, 1933, black-and-white,
66 minutes
Director: Lowell Sherman
Cast: Mae West, Cary Grant, Owen Moore, Gilbert Roland, and Noah Beery Sr.

*N*either tall nor slim nor young, West was nearly forty years old when she made this, her first starring vehicle. Long famous onstage for her saucy performances, she parlayed her originality, talent, and supreme self-confidence into a sensational movie career. Rules didn't apply to Mae. She broke them—especially those dealing with censorship. Moviegoers were agog at her risqué dialogue, tantalizing sex scenes (which made sex a joke but always at the expense of men and/or the morally pretentious), and audacious hourglass figure.

Based on her Broadway hit *Diamond Lil* (1928), *She Done Him Wrong* is set in New York's Bowery of the 1890s where West is the headline singer at gruff Beery Sr.'s fancy saloon. She is unaware that the bar is a cover for Noah's lucrative white slave trade and counterfeiting racket. Everyone is on the make for Mae, including suave gigolo Roland and a dastardly crook (David Landau). How-

Witty West

The one-of-a-kind **Mae West (1893–1980)** devoted many hours to creating pithy sayings for her movies on the subjects of men, sex, and the battle of the sexes. Her remarks are just as apt today as when they were created many decades ago. These gems are from *She Done Him Wrong*:

- "I was once so poor I didn't know where my next husband was coming from."

- "Men's all alike, married or single. It's their game. I happen to be smart enough to play it their way."

- "When women go wrong, men go right after 'em."

- When asked if she'd ever met a man who could make her happy, West's character snaps back with, "Sure. Lots of times."

ever, it is Grant, who operates a Salvation Army mission next door, who draws West's undivided attention and leads her to suggest, "Why don't you come up sometime, see me?" Later, Mae realizes what is really happening at the saloon, which gets her into a fracas with Noah's cohort (Rafaela Ottiano), whom West accidentally stabs. Before long, Mae is dealing with tough thug Moore, her ex-lover who has escaped from jail just to get even with her. Still later, Grant reveals he is a police undercover agent. After arresting Beery, he reluc-

Rafaela Ottiano (far left), Gilbert Roland (left), and Noah Beery Sr. (far right) have different motives for paying close attention to Mae West in *She Done Him Wrong* (1933).   Courtesy of JC Archives

tantly takes Mae into custody and cuffs her. "Are those absolutely necessary?" she wonders. "You know, I wasn't born with them." "No," he says. "A lot of men would have been safer if you had." Unfazed, she zings, "I don't know. Hands ain't everything."

Few movie bad girls were as impudent or amusing as West, but, as with other celluloid bad dames, no man oncamera was safe from her clutches once she'd hatched a scheme involving him as a victim. But what a way to go!

The Maltese Falcon

Warner Bros., 1941, black-and-white, 100 minutes
Director: John Huston
Cast: Humphrey Bogart, Mary Astor, Gladys George, Peter Lorre, and Sydney Greenstreet

This is the ultimate screen detective yarn: hard-boiled, fast-paced, full of double-crossing characters and snappy dia-

Humphrey Bogart threatens to use force on femme fatale Mary Astor in *The Maltese Falcon* (1941).
Courtesy of JC Archives

logue, and including a femme fatale with water in her veins and who can make men's blood boil.

Soon after Astor hires two San Francisco private detectives (Bogart and his partner Jerome Cowan) to follow a man who has allegedly run off with her younger sister, Cowan is murdered. As the corpses begin to pile up, cynical Humphrey is convinced Mary is at the heart of the mayhem. By then, however, he is in love with the striking woman and is going along for the bumpy ride. Before long, it develops that a valuable black falcon statue is the prize being sought by the two-faced Astor and several other despicable characters, including a fancy-talking fat man (Greenstreet) and a short foreigner (Lorre). Just when everyone believes the hunt for the sculpted Maltese bird is successfully concluded, they discover the bird in hand is a fake. By now the police have been summoned, and despite Astor's efforts to charm, beg, or wheedle her sucker detective boyfriend into saving her from arrest, Bogart reluctantly turns her over to the law.

Keep *The Maltese Falcon* in mind when you fill out that next career aptitude exam. If your answers point to a professional life as a private investigator, think twice, unless you're really ready to bite the bullet.

Double Indemnity

Paramount, 1944, black-and-white,
106 minutes
Director: Billy Wilder
Cast: Fred MacMurray, Barbara Stanwyck, Edward G. Robinson, Porter Hall, and Jean Heather

*F*orget the awful blond wig that Stanwyck wears in this sizzling film noir feature. Her Phyllis Dietrichson is one of the most calculating, coldhearted, evil women to ever populate a screenplay. What makes her character so intriguing is the blatant way in which she manipulates those around her. Unlike her intended prey, the moviegoer can see the wheels turning inside her mind as she computes the options for turning a situation or a ready victim to her advantage—no matter who gets hurt (or killed!) in the process. (When the villainess of this piece says, "We're both rotten," her partner-in-crime lover snarls back, "Yeah. Only you're a little more rotten.")

A Los Angeles insurance salesman (MacMurray) quickly finds himself lusting after a devious married woman (Stanwyck). Before long she hatches a plan to murder her husband (Tom Powers) and collect on his $50,000 policy, which contains a double indemnity clause for accidental death. With Barbara guiding their activities, the illicit duo commits the "perfect" murder of her spouse. The police accept Powers's death as a mishap. However, Robinson, an insurance claims adjuster and Fred's boss, is soon convinced that Barbara is the culprit. The investigator is certain if he can locate the widow's accomplice, he can break the case. When an increasingly panicky MacMurray discovers that Stanwyck plans to frame the murder on the fiancé of her step-daughter (Heather), Fred tries to break free of Barbara. But she wants the money and doesn't mind shooting her latest boyfriend to get the funds. But she gets her just rewards: the wounded MacMurray crawls back to the home office to dictate his account of the caper before dying from his wound.

If you're dating a new love interest, it wouldn't hurt to be somewhat observant. Is there something askew about her hairline? Does she wear a tawdry ankle bracelet? How about when you meet at a supermarket to shop—does she insist on rendezvousing in a deserted aisle and chatting with you only from the side of her mouth? By any chance

---

A Killer Movie

Promotional advertising for *Double Indemnity* included the following:

- "You can't kiss away a murder!"

- "From the moment they met it was murder!"

- "Paramount's terrific story of an unholy love, and an almost perfect crime!"

did her current husband's prior wife die under mysterious circumstances? Have you noticed your new lady recently exchanging knowing glances with her stepdaughter's boyfriend?

If the answer to any of the above is yes, run!

Leave Her to Heaven

Twentieth Century-Fox, 1945, color,
110 minutes
Director: John M. Stahl
Cast: Gene Tierney, Cornel Wilde, Jeanne Crain, Vincent Price, and Mary Phillips

When this thriller was released, the entertainment trade publication *Harrison's Reports* warned, "Extremely sensitive persons may find some of the situations highly distasteful and even sickening; but audiences that seek originality in story, tastefulness in production values, and perfection in direction and acting, will find it fascinating." This was said even at a time when the world had just gone through the horrors of World War II. It was assumed that there was very little left about human behavior that could shock the average citizen/filmgoer. One such exception, obviously, was a murderous soul hiding beneath a lovely feminine figure and her seemingly gentle personality. Her victim was that screen staple: a nice guy who becomes putty in her vicious hands.

Rejecting her lawyer boyfriend (Price), Tierney rushes into marriage with the new man (Wilde) in her life. Before long Gene's possessiveness has spiraled out of control and she causes Cornel's crippled brother (Darryl Hickman) to drown, so he will be out of their lives. Later, she gets pregnant thinking a child will draw her despondent spouse back to her. However, she suddenly realizes that an infant would claim some of her husband's time, so she throws herself down a flight of stairs, killing the unborn baby. Wilde eventually realizes his wife's true nature and prods a confession out of her. In disgust, he leaves her. Determined that no one else—especially her adopted sister (Crain) should have him, Tierney kills herself. Craftily she has left circumstantial evidence that will implicate Cornel and Jeanne in the homicide. At the trial, Wilde confesses the full story: he is given a two-year sentence for concealing evidence, while Crain goes free (and waits for him to be released from prison).

This movie certainly provides fresh meaning to the saying "Beauty is only skin deep."

Out of the Past

RKO, 1947, black-and-white, 97 minutes
Director: Jacques Tourneur
Cast: Robert Mitchum, Jane Greer, Kirk Douglas, Rhonda Fleming, and Richard Webb

This masterful entry deserves its sterling reputation as, perhaps, the best example of American film noir. It's a hard-hitting, uncompromising tale in which the fatalistic characters—good and evil—are destiny's fools, ensnared in a barrage of snowballing crimes and deceits. At the heart of the moral chaos is *not* the criminal mastermind and his thugs but a deadly dame who'd as soon kill the men in her life as make love to them.

The drama unfolds in California, New York, Nevada, and Mexico as former private eye Mitchum recalls how he was ensnared by Greer, the moll who put a near-fatal bullet into big-time gambler Douglas and absconded with his money. It's not long before Robert is Jane's pawn and lies to his client (Douglas) about her whereabouts. Further on, Greer shoots Mitchum's gumshoe partner (Steve Brodie) when he demands a cut of her ill-gotten cash. By now Robert realizes he has been played for a chump and soon leaves Greer to go back to a normal life. Back in the present, Mitchum is framed for murder by the vengeful Douglas, who has reunited with the lethal Greer. Before the fade-out most of the principals have paid with their lives.

It seems on the Hollywood screen—and in everyday life—males often cannot accept the idea that females are the weaker sex in men's minds only because men say they are, not because they really are.

Gilda

Columbia, 1946, black-and-white,
110 minutes
Director: Charles Vidor
Cast: Rita Hayworth, Glenn Ford, George Macready, Joseph Calleia, and Steven Geray

*I*f ever a role was tailor-made to a star's sultry image, it was that of the lead part in *Gilda* for Hayworth. Marlene Dietrich and Greta Garbo may have shone as exotic temptresses in past decades of screen fare, but the 1940s belonged to gorgeous, sensuous Rita. She was the perfect embodiment of a post–World War II femme fatale, one who could easily lead men to ruin with them going to the slaughter willingly, with a smile on their face!

A sarcastic American (Ford), an itinerant gambler, finds himself in Buenos Aires, where he is hired by the owner (Macready) of a

gambling casino to be his personal assistant. Later George (who is secretly involved in a tungsten cartel that had been supported by the Nazis) departs on a business trip. He returns with a new bride (Hayworth), not appreciating that this woman of the world formerly was involved romantically with Glenn. When George later must flee Argentina and is apparently killed in a plane crash, Ford takes over his operation and weds Rita. Glenn pays her back for having taunted him in past months by making her his virtual captive. Macready reappears on the scene but promptly meets a grisly end. Because Ford has cooperated with law enforcers, he and Hayworth—whose love-hate relationship has taken a turn for the better—are allowed to leave the country to start life afresh.

The moral of the story: if you're an American citizen committed to the world of gambling and dames with dubious reputations, stick to Las Vegas and Atlantic City. They're a heck of a lot closer.

Queen Bee

Columbia, 1955, black-and-white,
95 minutes
Director: Ranald MacDougall
Cast: Joan Crawford, Barry Sullivan, Betsy Palmer, John Ireland, and Lucy Marlow

*I*n transition from playing screen bitches (e.g., 1951's *Harriet Craig*) to portraying screen witches (e.g., 1962's *What Ever Hap-*

pened to Baby Jane?) movie veteran Crawford stampeded her way through this "refined" soap opera. On the plus side, she models an array of chic Jean Louis fashions.

Young and innocent Marlow arrives in Atlanta, Georgia, to visit her cousin (Palmer). Others on hand are Betsy's alcoholic brother (Sullivan), her sweetheart (Ireland), and Fay Wray, the sister of the manager of Barry's cotton mills (and Sullivan's jilted love from years ago). Into this mix sweeps Crawford, Sullivan's overly charming, controlling wife. Marlow initially thinks Joan to be a paragon of virtues—contrary to the local gossip—until she happens upon Crawford attempting to persuade John to resume a past affair with her. When Palmer learns of her fiancé's sordid past, she commits suicide. By now a disgusted Barry has determined to exterminate his viper of a wife and himself in a deliberate car

mishap. Meanwhile Ireland, having learned the true cause of Betsy's death, convinces Joan to take a ride with him—over a steep cliff.

While *Queen Bee* is not an artistic masterpiece, it is definitely a master lesson in how to be a deadly snake in the grass. And no one could be more intensely sinister on or off the screen than La Crawford. Don't even think for a minute that you might be able to reach her impeccable high standards.

Body Heat

Warner Bros., 1981, color, 113 minutes
Director: Lawrence Kasdan
Cast: William Hurt, Kathleen Turner, Richard Crenna, Ted Danson, and Mickey Rourke

*T*his picture has rightly been called *Double Indemnity* for the 1980s. Both films revolve around a venal wife plotting with her duped lover to kill her bothersome husband. The eighties being a far hipper age than the forties, the sex scenes onscreen here are far more overt and steamy, and the dialogue is far saltier (for example, one character says to the sex-hungry antihero, "Someday your d★★k is going to lead you into a very big hassle"). The picture was promoted with the tag line: "She taught him everything she knew—about passion and murder."

Florida attorney Hurt is maneuvered into an affair by Turner, the spouse of a wealthy, dishonest businessman (Crenna). She convinces William to help her murder Richard so

---

Romance in the Hollywood Mode

Usually predatory **Joan Crawford (1904–1977)** made a habit of having a love affair with her current film director, firmly believing that was the best way to have real control over the shape of the movie. During this production, however, the divorced actress turned her amorous attention to costar **John Ireland (1914–1992)**, who was then still married to actress Joanne Dru. By the time *Queen Bee* was released, Joan had already wed husband number five, Alfred N. Steele, the president of the Pepsi-Cola Company.

William Hurt finds himself entangled in Kathleen Turner's deadly scheme in *Body Heat* (1981).
Courtesy of JC Archives

Basic Instinct

TriStar, 1992, color, 128 minutes
Director: Paul Verhoeven
Cast: Michael Douglas, Sharon Stone, George Dzundza, Jeanne Tripplehorn, and Denis Arndt

The "highlight" of this R-rated thriller is the infamous police precinct interlude in which the pretty chief suspect (Stone) is undergoing questioning. In a ploy bound to distract the row of law enforcers seated opposite her, the detained woman casually sprawls in her chair and spreads her legs wide. Her posture reveals to her agog interrogators that she is not wearing panties. For added titillation, *Basic Instinct* contains lesbian love scenes, an athletic sexual coupling between Douglas and Stone, and messy liquidations of assorted characters.

she can inherit much of his assets and gain her freedom. The deed is done. However, greedy Kathleen wants all of her late husband's money and produces evidence that suggests that William is the culprit responsible for her spouse's death. As the law closes in on Hurt, he ascertains the circumstances that led to his being set up by the widow. By the finale, it seems Turner has met an explosive finish, but Hurt insists the situation is not what it seems to be.

Sharon Stone made her cinematic mark as the murderous heroine in *Basic Instinct* (1992).

Photo by Albert L. Ortega

When a retired rock star is murdered, his current girlfriend (Stone) is a chief suspect. A San Francisco police detective (Douglas), coping with an overdose of job stress, is assigned the high-profile case. The cat-and-mouse game continues as Michael uncovers various elements of Sharon's mysterious past, suggesting that many people who got too close to her are now deceased. By the time Douglas's partner (Dzundza) is stabbed to death with an ice pick and Michael has been tricked into shooting down the wrong suspect, Stone has completed her latest novel. Its

Tough Babe or Meek Mouse?

Thanks to *Basic Instinct* there is now a ready-made test for women to judge whether they have the aptitude to compete with the best of celluloid femme fatales. Answer the following questions with a yes or no.

1. A police investigator inquires, "Were you ever engaged in any sadomasochistic activity?" Would you respond, "Exactly what did you have in mind?"

2. If a lawman gets personal with his interrogation and demands to know if you ever did drugs with a murder victim, could you admit, "Cocaine," and then turn the tables with a cool comeback such as: "Have you ever f**ked on cocaine? . . . It's nice."

3. When a cop, drawn to your smoldering sex appeal, starts getting frisky and smirks, "You like playing games, don't you?" Should your immediate reply be, "I have a degree in psychology, it goes with the turf. . . . Games are fun"?

4. Are you the type to burst forth with witty observations like, "Killing isn't like smoking—you can stop."

If you answered yes to one or more of these questions, you're ready to sign up for the new reality show *Sociopaths 'R Us*.

subject matter concerns a law enforcer who tumbles romantically for a suspect who, in turn, murders him.

Going on the theory that a sexy dame would have to use every trick in the book to grab and keep the attention of a burned-out cop who has seen too much of life's seamier side, *Basic Instinct* leaves no rock unturned in making Douglas's law enforcer an emotionally and sexually pliable pawn in the grasp of quick-thinking, fast-reacting Stone. The sleazy gambits employed annoyed many critics but piqued the public's curiosity. Made on a budget of $49 million, the movie enjoyed a $352.7 million worldwide gross. It proved again that crime (of all sorts) definitely paid.

Cruel Intentions

Columbia, 1999, color, 95 minutes
Director: Roger Kumble
Cast: Sarah Michelle Gellar, Ryan Phillippe, Reese Witherspoon, Selma Blair, and Louise Fletcher

*U*pdating the premise of Choderlos de Laclos's 1782 novel *Les Liaisons Dangereuses*, which had been previously made into films several times, *Cruel Intentions* brings the Hollywood vixen up to date. Portrayed as a manipulative and spiteful wenchette by Gellar, she proves to be as scheming and calculating as her more mature celluloid forebears. Following the guidelines of prior genre pieces, the men (here boy toys) in her path are child's play to her artillery of devious and nasty games.

During a school holiday, blue-blooded Gellar hopes to convince her snobbish stepbrother (Phillippe) to seduce Blair because she had had the nerve to date Sarah Michelle's ex-boyfriend. Self-willed Ryan agrees to the sinister game but instead chooses to pursue Witherspoon. Gellar bets Phillippe that he can't deflower Witherspoon before school

Ryan Phillippe and Reese Witherspoon costar as aggressor and victim in *Cruel Intentions* (1999).
Photo by Albert L. Ortega

of Phillippe when he saves Witherspoon from being run down by a passing car. At Ryan's funeral, Selma exacts her revenge by distributing copies of the deceased's diary, which expose Sarah Michelle's evil ways to the whole crowd.

Who said high school was supposed to be the innocent years?

resumes again. (If Sarah Michelle wins, she gets Ryan's new car; if he is the victor, he gets to bed Gellar.) The plans go awry when Ryan falls in love with Reese. When other parties seek to break the couple apart, the result leads to further seductions, betrayals, and the death

The case histories of all these enticing cinema femme fatales should be a sufficient tutorial for even the most naïve man to get the message: don't bat out of your league. But if you insist on playing with the pros, remember, three strikes and you are out.

11

I've Got You Babe, or
Codependency Is the Name of the Game

"Why does she stay with that louse?" "What's that bad-news woman's great hold over him?" These are key questions family and friends ask when a wrongly matched couple bonds in a love relationship of sorts and—can you believe?—stays together after each knows the naked truth about the other's personality. Examples of this type of situation include the wife who remains with her alcoholic and physically abusive spouse for many punishing years and the meek man who lingers for a long stretch with a domineering, controlling mate (who figuratively castrates him daily). These are psychologically sick connections, which, in more recent decades, have been branded codependent relationships.

Remaining bound in such an unhealthy state of affairs is obviously bad for both parties. Ironically, it is usually the physically or psychologically addicted persons who first subconsciously realize the true nature of the situation with their domestic partners who have become emotional doormats. However, because these abusers are so self-absorbed in

their dependencies, rarely do they force the issue, which would remove the comforting enabler from their clutches. The latter, who seem at first blush to be innocent victims of their loved ones' mistreatment, are, in their own ways, as hooked as other people obsessed with drugs, alcohol, food, sex, and so forth. Breaking the chain of such codependency through the enablers' self-realizations, the use of tough love, or some other cure is an extremely rocky road. Some enablers, like the addicted, seek individual therapy or gain strength from support and twelve-step programs. Others, sadly, remain stuck in their tortuous situations for too long.

Hollywood likes nothing better than an offbeat domestic circumstance to sharpen the impact of a movie love story. Such twists to the usual situations of boy meets girl and boy gets girl allow the screenplay to veer off in unexpected directions. The dynamic of this damaging tie between the addicted and the enabler create fascinating voyeuristic situations for moviegoers who may never have been exposed—or were not aware that they had been—to such negative types of love companionships.

Blonde Venus

Paramount, 1932, black-and-white,
93 minutes
Director: Josef von Sternberg
Cast: Marlene Dietrich, Herbert Marshall, Cary Grant, Dickie Moore, and Sidney Toler

*T*he ads for this feature read, "What could she do but flee from love? She loved two men at once!" Such is the dilemma for the celluloid heroine to handle, but viewers are not to worry.

Blonde Venus was part of a then-popular movie cycle in which the heroine is forced by tough circumstances to drop her moral standards and survive the only way she knows—by selling her sexual favors to willing men. This genre also contains a subset in which not only is a virtuous young soul turned into a fallen woman but somewhere along the line in her descent into immorality (keep in mind this was still the era of politically incorrect double standards and the inequality of the sexes), she becomes a mother. This plot twist was almost guaranteed to win the sympathy of most women moviegoers. Oh, the contrived pain of it all!

Blonde Venus goes a step further than the usual such offering. In this saga, the alluring Dietrich is married to a handsome wimp (Marshall) who seems to relish his domestic despair and perpetuates the unhealthy situation at every opportunity. He's a bright, civilized, and sensitive soul, so how come he is so naïvely drawn to a worldly cabaret singer (Marlene) whom he meets during a visit to Germany? Did he learn nothing about the ways of the world when he attended college as a chemistry major? After the two marry and he brings Marlene to the United States, they settle into modest digs and parent a baby boy.

As grist for the plot, he develops radium poisoning from his research work and needs expensive medical treatment for it that is available only in Europe. What to do? She returns in a flash to cabaret performing and instantly meets an attractive playboy (Grant) who kindly gives her the money to pay for hubby's medical needs. Blinding himself to reality, Herbert accepts the money and then sails for Europe. This leaves Marlene free to romance Cary. A cured Marshall later returns to Amer-

It Takes One to Know One

During the moral rise, fall, and rise of Dietrich's chanteuse in *Blonde Venus*, she cracks to a cheap-looking club coworker nicknamed Taxi, "How much do you charge for the first mile?" It's a case of a hooker recognizing a sister in the trade.

ica and—shock, shock—learns of his wife's infidelity. Now he throws her out and demands that their boy (Moore) remain with him. "No," says Dietrich, who flees with the boy—moving from town to town, one step ahead of the law. Grant comes back into her life, but now Marlene is a changed woman, having grown bitter since finally losing custody of her son to her husband. She has a reunion with her son and, in the process, urbane Marshall forgives (!!!) her and takes her back into his household. Get a clue, Herbert.

A Star Is Born

Warner Bros., 1954, color, 176 minutes
Director: George Cukor
Cast: Judy Garland, James Mason, Jack Carson, Charles Bickford, and Tommy Noonan

*I*n the second of four versions (to date) of this tragic Hollywood love tale, Garland performs full throttle vocally. With her edgy, vulnerable, and energetic performance, she creates a sensational showcase for herself, leaving no raw nerve ending untouched. With its painful account of a show business couple whose careers go in different directions (hers from nobody to stardom, his from acclaim to has-been), it is a biting indictment of self-destructive love—on both parts.

When they first meet, Mason is a major film star, while Judy is a struggling singer

> ### Step Aside, Dr. Phil
>
> According to **Judy Garland (1922–1969)**, who roller-coasted through five marriages and many affairs in her emotionally bumpy life: "Most of the girls in Hollywood overdo their eagerness to please by resorting to a prop smile. How men hate that! There is nothing more annoying or discouraging to a man in the process of unloading his thoughts than the sight of an on-again–off-again artificial smile. A girl who can't smile naturally, pleasantly, and sometimes fondly should find other means to convey her reactions."

who wants to break into film. She is so bedazzled by his fame that it doesn't dawn on her what type of man she is becoming involved with. At their first meeting, the urbane movie legend is drunk, and she saves him from making a fool of himself at an industry benefit performance. Does she catch the warning signs: he's an alcoholic; I'm his self-appointed savior? Sadly, no. So for many more minutes viewers are treated to watching a train wreck in the making, waiting for the antihero's big crack-up when he finally stops the cycle of dragging his rising-star wife into his hell. Does he seek therapeutic help? Do any of their mutual friends try an intervention? Sure, this is the mid-1950s when such positive steps generally were not part of the American culture. But certainly taking a one-way walk

James Mason lashes out at the world while his too-obliging loved one (Judy Garland) tries to calm him in *A Star Is Born* (1954).   Courtesy of JC Archives

into the Pacific Ocean is not bound to leave your widow with a guilt-free chance at a fresh start.

The scripters fully appreciate that this great screen romance is not merely a love story gone wrong because of one party's faulty behavior. The finale finds the grieving Judy making her first public appearance some time after her hubby's suicide. At the film colony events, she walks front and center to the microphone and, with a choke in her voice, a wan smile, and her eyes searching for love from the audience-within-the-film, ventures to say, "Hello, everybody. This is Mrs. Norman Maine." Is this being brave by reminding the crowd of her late mate, or rather is it the act of a four-star codependent who refuses to come out of the other's shadow to find acceptance on her own terms. Oh, Judy . . . Judy . . . Judy.

Love Me or Leave Me

Metro-Goldwyn-Mayer, 1955, color,
122 minutes
Director: Charles Vidor
Cast: Doris Day, James Cagney, Cameron
Mitchell, Robert Keith, and Tom Tully

The often-saccharine Doris Day gives a resourceful performance as 1920s and 1930s torch singer Ruth Etting, a soulful vocalist of stage, screen, and recordings who had the misfortune to come under the influence of a crude, tough gangster Moe "the Gimp" Snyder (Cagney). He took control of her life (they married in 1922, divorced in 1937) and, in his passion for her, barged his way into confrontations with show business power brokers—which soon hurt as much as it initially helped her professional standing. Why such an extremely talented, pleasant-looking performer stays with a physically and emotionally abusive spouse is a subtext of this impressive musical, which won an Academy Award for Best Motion Picture Story. The movie contained such musical gems as "Ten Cents a Dance," "Never Look Back," the title tune, and what could be termed an enabler's anthem, "I'll Never Stop Loving You."

In the course of her addictive subservience to the hoodlum, Day's entertainer becomes a punching bag for his cruelty. At one early point in their "love" fest, as he is about to sock her, the thug rants, "Now look here, you stupid little broad. Do you know who I am? Do you think I let dames talk that way to me?" But Day's heroine is a game victim, that is until she finds "real" love with her pianist accompanist (Mitchell), for whom she finally leaves Cagney. Amen.

The Hustler

Twentieth Century-Fox, 1961, black-and-white, 133 minutes
Director: Robert Rossen
Cast: Paul Newman, Jackie Gleason, Piper Laurie, George C. Scott, and Myron McCormick

What are the odds of a weak-willed pool hall con artist (Newman) and a heavy-drinking, shy prostitute (Laurie) having a happy, trouble-free relationship? Not on planet Earth. But such characters' growing reliance on one another—and the eventual shattering of their ties—form the heart of this gripping entry. Add into the quotient a dramatic turn by TV prankster Gleason as cue stick wizard Minnesota Fats, and you've pushed up the entertainment level of this bleak love story several notches.

Actually, it is the casting of the coleads that stacks the deck so much against reality. When's the last time you saw a real-life pool shark who looked like Newman? Or when you last (if ever) passed through a bus terminal, did you glimpse, perhaps, a hooker worthy of your sympathy vote because she is crippled, wistful, and well educated? Well, relax. Courtesy of Twentieth Century-Fox, we meet such fictional folk.

Jackie Gleason and Paul Newman squaring off for the big pool game in *The Hustler* (1961).
Courtesy of JC Archives

Adding grit to the plot is the introduction of a coldhearted gambler (Scott) who manipulates Newman into being his client. When George fears that Piper's ongoing relationship with Paul will lessen his control of the pool player, he pushes her out of her lover's life and she commits suicide. Later, Newman wins the big playoff against Gleason, grabs the winnings, and walks out on a shocked Scott.

Anyone for a quick game of pool?

Loser to Loser

Great ways to deal with a codependent, courtesy of *The Hustler*:

- Pickup line: "Two ships that pass in the night should always buy each other breakfast."

- Being blind to reality: "You're not a loser. . . . You're a winner. . . . I love you. . . ."

- The big kiss-off: "I got no idea of love. Neither have you. Neither one of us would know what it was if we saw it coming down the street."

- The revelation of reality: "I made you up, didn't I? You weren't real. I made you up like everything else. . . . But . . . I wanted you to be real."

Days of Wine and Roses

Warner Bros., 1962, black-and-white,
117 minutes
Director: Blake Edwards
Cast: Jack Lemmon, Lee Remick, Charles
Bickford, Jack Klugman, and Alan Hewitt

*B*esides learning that chocolate lovers will
go ape over brandy alexanders, this
chronicle of two alcoholics' near destruction
of one another is an unrelenting drama of a
marriage gone whiskey sour. In this grim
domestic excursion, love takes a backseat to
scotch, beer, and any other available high-
proof beverage.

Lee Remick convinces husband Jack Lemmon to fall
off the sobriety wagon in *Days of Wine and Roses*
(1962).   Courtesy of JC Archives

Lemmon, a San Francisco public relations
man, drinks as hard as he works. He encounters secretary Remick, a nondrinker with a
heavy-duty sweet tooth. Before long the two
lovers marry, and soon Lee is downing booze
as fast as Jack is. After he loses several jobs
because of his addiction, he has a wake-up
call. They move in with her father (Bickford),
who runs a nursery, and plan to live a sober,
hard-working life. But both are lured back to
drink, and Lemmon ends up being hospitalized. After further slipups, he joins AA and
becomes a recovering alcoholic, able to care
for his daughter and himself. Meanwhile,
Remick is living on her own, existing on
drink and the kindness of men. She begs Jack
to take her back, but when she refuses to give
up alcohol, he asks her to leave once and
for all.

Lemmon and Remick are both pluses and
minuses in their film parts. They both turn in
superior performances. However, he is so
associated with smart-alecky comedic roles,

one waits for a wisecrack to pop out of his mouth. As for his costar, she is so luminous and innately intelligent a person, that her characterization as a low-esteem, low-ambition miss seems to ring hollow. But let's not knock small flaws. Warner Bros. could have just as easily cast its own Troy Donahue and Connie Stevens (the darlings of 1961's *Parrish* and other pictures) in these parts, and then what would this picture have become?

Lady Sings the Blues

Paramount, 1972, color, 144 minutes
Director: Sidney Furie
Cast: Diana Ross, Billy Dee Williams, Richard Pryor, James Callahan, and Paul Hampton

Billy Dee Williams and Diana Ross share a doomed romance in *Lady Sings the Blues* (1972).
Courtesy of Echo Book Shop

*J*azz vocalist Billie Holiday died in 1959 when only in her midforties, leaving great recordings, a few film appearances, and a legend. As a screen vehicle to showcase Ross (who had left the hit singing group The Supremes), this musical plays fast and loose with the facts. Nevertheless, it allows Diana, as Lady Day, to sing memorably such tunes as "Them There Eyes," "God Bless the Child," and "Good Morning Heartache." It teams her with handsome and charming Williams as her handsome and charming lover, husband, and enabler.

But as any sharp-eyed filmgoer could quickly figure out, the union of career-pressured, drug-addicted Diana and her free-spirited, playboy spouse is doomed from the start. When her addictions get to be too much for his freewheeling lifestyle, he throws her out. But every time she is about to hit rock bottom—something she really needs to do in order to start her recovery—he rescues her and starts the love-hate-dependency cycle all over again.

The moral of the tale? Rags-to-riches singers with golden voices should steer clear of good-looking, smooth lady-charmers whose smiles could easily light up Times Square during a total eclipse.

St. Elmo's Fire

Columbia, 1985, color, 110 minutes
Director: Joel Schumacher
Cast: Emilio Estevez, Rob Lowe, Andrew McCarthy, Demi Moore, and Judd Nelson

This is the ultra tribute to the yuppies of the 1980s me generation. Who better to star in this shallow, glitzy vehicle than Hollywood's own Brat Pack, a gaggle of mostly self-absorbed personalities who, like their onscreen characters, have had a most difficult time getting it all together.

Following their graduation from Georgetown University, several classmates/friends find their lives taking strange romantic and career turns over the years. Saxophonist Lowe has split from his wife and child and is temporarily involved with Mare Winningham, who has finally ditched a dreary mate of her parents' choice. Moore, in international banking, is obsessed with her ailing stepmother; later she faces a crisis when she loses her all-important job. Estevez, a lawyer in the making, becomes entranced with a doctor in training (Andie MacDowell). Nelson, who can't resist playing the field, thinks Ally Sheedy should be flattered he decides to marry her. Instead, they split up and she discovers happiness with her writer pal (McCarthy), who's long had a crush on her.

How Times Have Changed

At the time of *St. Elmo's Fire*, Hollywood's Brat Pack was the new "in" thing, long before their lives and careers grew complex and full of tabloid-caliber misbehaving.

How young and innocent were the costars of this vehicle at the time? Let's see . . .

- **Rob Lowe (b. 1964)** was still dating actress Melissa Gilbert and had no clue that he'd be making his own version of *sex, lies and videotape* (1989) in the years to come. To him, then, the phrase "west wing" meant a part of a turkey, not a career-salvaging TV series in his late-1990s future.

- **Demi Moore (b. 1962),** who had been fired from *St. Elmo's Fire* for substance abuse but then rehired when she promised to clean up her act, hadn't much of a clue at the time about actor Bruce Willis. The latter became her husband in 1987 and, before they divorced in 2000, they had three daughters. Ten-million-dollar paychecks for a film project were still in Demi's future, just as at present they seem to be far in her past.

- **Emilio Estevez (b. 1962)** began a relationship with Moore during the making of this picture, which resulted in their engagement before they split and she wed Bruce Willis. Emilio, who already had two offspring by his one-time significant other, model Carey Salley, would later (1992–1994) be wed to singer Paula Abdul. His most recent acting assignment was in the low-profile entry *Sand* (2000).

Need to know more? See the picture. But even from this brief snapshot cross-section it's obvious that this intertwining circle of friends and lovers mostly need to go their separate ways and, somehow, learn to stand on their own. Anyone caught helping them to remain vertical will be penalized five points.

When a Man Loves a Woman

Buena Vista, 1994, color, 125 minutes
Director: Luis Mandoki
Cast: Andy Garcia, Meg Ryan, Ellen Burstyn, Tina Majorino, and Philip Seymour Hoffman

*A*irline pilot Garcia and school guidance counselor Ryan are a seemingly happily married San Francisco couple who have two young daughters and a pleasant home. He remains oblivious to her increasing reliance on drinking to get through the day. Finally her secret is brought out into the open when she comes home drunk one day, smacks her daughter, and then passes out. After this crisis, she enters a recovery clinic to dry out and reposition her life. Meanwhile, competent, ever-patient Andy holds down the fort at home as best he can.

Visiting Meg at the facility, Andy feels like an outsider to her new life and friends, something that becomes a big problem when she returns home. He keeps wanting to fix matters that only she can deal with, and her refus-

ing to let him "make things better" makes him angry, frustrated, and resentful, which in turn distances her further. The foundering couple seeks marriage counseling, but it still ends with his moving out of their house and, later, relocating to Denver, Colorado, in order to keep his airline position.

Time passes. With six months of sobriety, Ryan stands before her AA group reciting her case history and receiving the listeners' earnest support. To her surprise, a remorseful Garcia appears at the gathering to offer his congratulations. His months with a codependency support group have obviously paid off.

This picture, which is full of feel-good preachy moments, seems far deeper than it really is. However, keep in mind this is a big-budgeted Hollywood movie geared for view-

Danger Signals

Have you heard your love partner say any of the following?

- "It was so much more fun in the old days. I'd get drunk, I'd pass out, and you'd put me back together again."

- "Stop making it better. It's not making it better."

- "You make me feel like a worthless, stupid weak animal."

- "We are supposed to try to be real."

  If these words sound familiar, oops!

ers to adore sweet, tousle-haired, pert Meg. So if Burstyn's crucial role as Ryan's cold-hearted, nagging mother barely survives in the final release print and Ryan's character constantly says she's not sure why her life has taken so many wrong turns, don't complain too loudly. As for Garcia, his character remains clueless for far too much of the picture, except during the tacked-on ending. In this finale full of breakthrough wisdom, he concedes, "I tried everything but listening . . . really listening, and that's how I left her [Ryan] alone." Wunderbar. The couple hears those magical love bells ringing once again, and as the movie concludes, the two of them are sharing a tender, private moment in the midst of the support group festivities.

Of course, I do worry about the health of Meg's Alice Green. Since giving up alcohol, she has been smoking up a storm and drinking far too much caffeinated coffee. Anyone want to join me in staging an intervention for misinformed Alice?

Meg Ryan has a strong role as a recovering alcoholic in *When a Man Loves a Woman* (1994).

Courtesy of Echo Book Shop

Casino

Universal, 1995, color, 182 minutes
Director: Martin Scorsese
Cast: Robert De Niro, Sharon Stone, Joe Pesci, James Woods, and Don Rickles

*I*n this well-regarded feature, Scorsese gives his proficient take on the mob's involvement in the growth of Las Vegas and how such participation over the years affects several characters. There's not much that is fresh in the narrative regarding the underworld's ties to the gambling capital, but there is a good deal to absorb in the tangled love relationship of the De Niro and Stone characters.

The story is told in flashback. In 1973, De Niro, a top-level bookie, is dispatched to Las Vegas by the mob to take over operation of a big casino (the Tangiers). His task is to ensure that a huge cash flow is skimmed from the daily take and laundered back to the mob's headquarters in Kansas City. Giving Robert backup is his old pal Pesci, a violent gangster. When De Niro encounters Stone, a hooker, he falls in love with the beautiful blonde, even though she insists her heart still belongs to her lover and pimp (Woods).

Despite, or because of, the challenge, Robert pursues Sharon with great determination and finally wins her consent to marriage when he promises to give her a rich life. As time passes, they have a child, he becomes more absorbed in his mob activities, and she renews her relationship with James and turns to heavy drinking to cope with her bad situation. Finally, determined to break free of De Niro—but keep his loot—she forces a showdown and takes off for Los Angeles with several million dollars in hand. Meanwhile, the FBI closes in on the mob, shutting down the Tangiers. To protect themselves from further investigation, the underworld leaders order a series of hits, which include having Stone and

Sharon Speak

With an IQ of 154, words of wisdom from **Sharon Stone (b. 1958)** should be worth heeding. So here goes:

- "It's my experience that you really can't lose when you try the truth."

- "Be willing to say yes, no matter who says no, and to say no, regardless of who says yes."

- "Never play cards with a guy named Doc. Never eat at a place called Mom's. And never have sex with anybody who has more problems than you do."

Woods killed. As for De Niro, he nearly dies in a car bomb blast but survives. He relocates to San Diego, where he returns to the bookie game. As for Las Vegas, times and influences have changed, and the city is now controlled by international conglomerates.

Broken Pact

As their world falls apart in *Casino*, Stone and De Niro's characters finally reach the end of their mutually self-destructive road. The parting is anything but peaceable, but hey, who promised whom a rose garden?

She: "We had a deal remember? You said if things didn't work out between us, I could get my stuff and I could leave."
He: "Look at my eyes. Do you see anything in the eyes that makes you think I'm going to let you take my child away from me? . . ."

Leaving Las Vegas

United Artists, 1995, color, 112 minutes
Director: Mike Figgis
Cast: Nicolas Cage, Elisabeth Shue, Julian Sands, Richard Lewis, and Valeria Golino

*I*f you ever think your romantic life couldn't be any worse or that your life has temporarily bottomed out, rush out and rent this film. After watching it, by comparison, your existence will seem a fragrant bed of roses.

Here we have two desperate characters—the type who are destined for one another. Because the script can't wait for fate to come along (wasted screen time is costly), Cage is seen driving drunkenly along the Las Vegas strip, where he almost runs down a pedestrian who just happens to be an unhappy hooker (Shue). He immediately puts the make on her, and the spiraling self-destructive romance moves into high gear.

What a pair! Nicolas is a Hollywood film production executive recently fired from his job for excessive alcoholism. (He admits, "I don't know if I started drinking because my wife left me or my wife left me because I started drinking." Also lost to him in the process is any association with his son.) Elisabeth, a prostitute who has run out on her Los Angeles pimp (Sands) and moved to Las Vegas, is bright and sensitive but suffers low self-esteem. (Nevertheless, she insists vainly, "I bring out the best in the men who f**k me.")

Cage is on a self-annihilating mission—he has come to the gaming capital to drink himself to death. As he careens from one massive drinking marathon to the next, with serious bouts of delirium tremens in between, he warns the increasingly caring and needy Shue, "You can never, never ask me to stop drinking. Do you understand?" However, she becomes so caught in her crusade to rescue him and indenture herself to him that she suggests, "Maybe you shouldn't drink so much." His answer: "Maybe I shouldn't breathe so much either." OK.

In this loopy entanglement of two lost souls, he quickly stakes out their mutual terrain: "We both know that I'm a drunk. And I know you are a hooker. I hope you understand I'm a person who is totally at ease with that. Which is not to say that I'm indifferent or I don't care; I do. It simply means that I trust and accept your judgment."

Before his four-week binge results in his death (as the two pathetically try to have affirming sex together), Elisabeth tells her therapist that Cage has been the first man she ever felt comfortable with and that she truly loves him. . . . She really does.

Another side effect of this eccentrically constructed, very well-acted (Cage won an Oscar) feature is that after viewing *Leaving Las Vegas*, it will have to be a hot day in hell before you can force anything stronger than ginger ale down your throat.

For the record, Shue's character has a distinctive name that only seems to pop up in movies. Her name is not Sara with an *a* but Sera with an *e*.

A Love Ode for Codependents

In a highly inebriated state, Cage embarrasses, confuses, and intrigues Shue when he asks her, "Are you desirable? Are you irresistible? Maybe if you drank bourbon with me, it would help. Maybe if you kissed me and I could taste the sting in your mouth it would help. If you drank bourbon with me naked. If you smelled of bourbon as you f**ked me, it would help. It would increase my esteem for you."

Having shared in these movies with so many unhappy souls caught in addiction, codependency, and self-eradication, do you still believe that togetherness is best? Have you really considered the virtues of the single life? It could be your personal salvation. Think of all the free time you'll have once you don't have to obsess about, second-guess, make excuses for, and worry about that reckless other person who has been part of your life.

12

Love for Sale, or Booty Calls for Pay

While many Americans are vocally opposed to the world's oldest profession on moral and/or religious grounds, others disdain prostitution because of pride ("I'd never pay for sex!") or for increasingly life-threatening health reasons (e.g., the fear of contracting AIDS). However, there has always been a segment of the public that is either openly or privately intrigued by the netherworld of prostitution. What appeals to them is not just the expectation of easy access to accommodating sex but also the allure of these enticing sex objects who are providing such forbidden pleasures. Then too, even though the (would-be) customer is paying for the services rendered, it is the prostitute (and/or the pimp or madam) who is really in control of the situation. This creates another element of attraction for the client, who is titillated by the notion of participating in such guilty (and/or illegal) role-playing games.

Knowing that box-office profits will be forthcoming from such provocative film fare, Hollywood has long pandered to the public's prurient interest in prostitution by presenting such characters onscreen (e.g., 1914's *The House of Bondage*, 1924's *The Fast Set*, 1930's *Lady of Leisure*). Sometimes Tinseltown has offered the controversial subject in the form of an edifying tract (e.g., 1914's *The Inside of the White Slave Traffic*, 1936's *The Cocaine Fiends*). Often, when the film industry and state morality codes have been at a particularly strict level, screenwriters have made their presentation of the topic more subtle. Thus, tarts are portrayed as club entertainers (1937's *Marked Women*, 1953's *From Here to Eternity*) or as plying other such seemingly harmless trades, leaving it for the more sophisticated filmgoers to catch on as to what the characters are *really* doing for a living.

Not only do some movie audiences thrive on watching racy story lines about sex for sale, but performers have always been attracted to portraying these sexual wantons. Such showy roles are guaranteed to grab audience attention and sometimes an Academy Award (e.g., Helen Hayes in 1931's *The Sin of Madelon Claudet*, Shirley Jones in 1960's *Elmer Gantry*, and Jane Fonda in 1971's *Klute*).

Thus, for all of these reasons—and more—prostitutes on the screen have become synonymous with glamorous, tantalizing figures, ones that the average person, in a flight of fantasy or actuality, might really envy. But, even given the proper outfits, makeup, and lighting, let alone the requisite special dialogue and careful direction, how many women could match the enthralling visual look and sexual magnetism of, say, Gloria Swanson in *Rain* (1928), Barbara Stanwyck in *Baby Face* (1932), Jean Harlow in *China Seas* (1935), Elizabeth Taylor in *Butterfield 8* (1960), or Julia Roberts in *Pretty Woman* (1990)? It is a competition that most women could never win. Nevertheless, the challenge doesn't stop couples in the confines of their bedrooms from playing such pretend games in which one is the tart and the other is the pliant, spellbound customer. But come on, who is really kidding whom? They do it so much better onscreen!

Susan Lenox—Her Fall and Rise

Metro-Goldwyn-Mayer, 1931, black-and-white, 74 minutes
Director: Robert Z. Leonard
Cast: Greta Garbo, Clark Gable, Jean Hersholt, John Miljan, and Alan Hale

The previous year—in her successful sound film debut—Garbo had played a prostitute in *Anna Christie*, as she would again in *Camille* (1936) and other such entries. Here, in this rather trashy narrative, she had ample opportunity to play the type of provocative yet sympathetic screen role that most every Hollywood beauty of the early 1930s would attempt. Namely, the part was that of the virtuous good girl gone "bad," thanks to a streak of bad luck, dastardly villains, and, of course, the demands of the obligingly titillating movie plot. As such her wardrobe, makeup, and style ranged from that worn by a wholesome farm girl to a city sophisticate to, eventually, a tawdry whore.

Running away from a pending arranged marriage to a brute (Hale), a Midwestern young woman (Garbo) encounters a handsome engineer (Gable) who offers her shelter. There is an immediate attraction, but fate soon separates them. When they next meet, he misconstrues her relationship with an older, wealthy man (Miljan). She is so embittered by his cruel snap judgment that she vows to become the immoral individual he has envisioned her to be. Her revenge works well, throwing him into an emotional tailspin. His career quickly goes on the skids, and he becomes a wandering drunk. Still intoxicated by her love for Clark, Greta follows him from city to city, finally tracking him to an obscure port city in Java, only to learn he has gone into the deep jungle on a work assignment. While waiting for him to return, and as punishment for ruining the man she adores, she degrades herself further by working as a hooker in a sleazy café/bordello. When they finally reencounter, their strong mutual love brings about their moral redemption, and they joyfully plan their future together.

Words That Hurt

He

- "Marry? That's funny! I should have paid you off. Left a few dollars on the bureau. That's the kind of language you understand."

- "I'll tell you what will become of you. You'll go from one man to another just like every other woman of the gutter."

She

- "I think the most amusing thing about men is that they mistake cruelty for character. They can't forgive. They have no . . . no tolerance."

- "I always hated men till I met you. Hated them! But from now on, it will be different."

All this story takes place in a scant seventy-four minutes of running time! Lesson to be learned: when you find your man, hold on to him at the start.

Red Dust

Metro-Goldwyn-Mayer, 1932, black-and-white, 83 minutes
Director: Victor Fleming
Cast: Clark Gable, Jean Harlow, Gene Raymond, Mary Astor, and Donald Crisp

*B*efore the stricter movie industry self-regulatory code took force in 1934, the Hollywood film fare of the early thirties was filled with "heroines" who were women of the street, luck-challenged individuals who were the victims of life's bad jokes. But in

Red Dust the leading lady is of a far different emotional fiber. She may be used by men for their sexual pleasure, but she is a sassy dame who is at the top of her game and has relatively little guilt either about her choice of profession or how she is regarded morally by those sanctimonious souls around her. As played by beautiful, sexy Harlow, Vantine is a plucky woman who defies conventions (and the law!) to obtain what she wants. In many ways, and despite her moral transgressions, the blond bombshell's brassy screen character here provides audiences with an emotional role model of a spirited, self-sufficient woman who refuses to let life get her down. Her resiliency is an asset that can still be appreciated (and even emulated) today.

In the remote interior of Indochina, Gable is in charge of a rubber plantation. He is visited by Harlow, a prostitute (she describes herself as "Pollyanna, the glad girl") who was

Jean Harlow finds Clark Gable to be a willing lover in *Red Dust* (1932).   Courtesy of JC Archives

ventional but one who is on the verge of committing adultery.) The hero concludes that this jungle situation is no place for Astor and rejects her, leading the rebuffed lady to wound him with a gunshot. Covering over the situation for the sake of naïve Raymond, Gable sends the couple on its way. By now he realizes that Jean is the right romantic choice for him. Amen!

Of Human Bondage

RKO, 1934, black-and-white, 83 minutes
Director: John Cromwell
Cast: Leslie Howard, Bette Davis, Frances Dee, Reginald Owen, and Reginald Denny

This is the first of three screen adaptations of W. Somerset Maugham's semi-autobiographical novel (1915). The powerful role of Mildred Rogers, the cockney tea shop waitress turned diseased streetwalker is one of those high-visibility parts meant for the likes of a gutsy, iconoclastic actress like Davis. Bette dared to eschew glamour onscreen to delve into her dimensional celluloid characterization with all the force at her command. More important for the viewer, her bravura performance (which set her on the road to industry stardom) is a wonderfully etched personification of every nasty thing people have ever thought about tarts: financially manipulative, emotionally heartless, socially crude, morally degenerate, and the type of person to vengefully attack her besotted

based in Saigon but is now on the run from the police. She asks for shelter until the next boat arrives to carry her to safety. Clark agrees, and the two quickly begin a sex relationship. Later, an idealistic mining engineer (Raymond) and his bride (Astor) arrive at the outpost. Before long, Clark is romantically intrigued with the married Mary, much to Jean's annoyance. (Harlow also finds it ironic that Gable should be drawn to the well-bred Astor, a woman supposedly so morally con-

benefactor when he is most vulnerable. And most satisfying (especially to sanctimonious moviegoers), the viper ends in the gutter and dies a painful death from a contracted disease. Nothing like watching a movie like this to make the less charitable viewer feel smugly superior and morally vindicated by the woman's fate.

In late-nineteenth-century England, the hero (Howard) suffers from a clubfoot and an overwhelming sense of inadequacy. He fails to become a great artist and resigns himself to a more practical career as a doctor. The student meets a tea shop waitress (Davis), and he quickly becomes overwhelmed by this crude, self-absorbed young woman. She realizes his weaknesses and plays on them, soon having him at her total beck and call. After she runs off with a boisterous German, he makes an emotional recovery, but Bette keeps cropping up in his life. Each time he succumbs to her wiles, always to his great emotional and finan-

cial detriment. Eventually she ends a bedraggled streetwalker who dies in a charity ward. Only then is Howard released from his bondage.

Mildred Rogers is a characterization that sticks with the moviegoer for a long time. If truth be told, there must be a bit of subconscious envy when one realizes how much power, attraction, and control this figure has over the hero. On another level, the story is an intriguing example of a sadomasochistic relationship in which each party is essentially getting exactly what his psyche craves, no matter how self-punishing it might be to the individual. The dynamics of this perverse love couple set a new low standard for any like-minded couple to meet, even in their wildest fantasies.

Top This Cruel Putdown

One of the most vicious dirty digs ever uttered in a Hollywood movie by a whore to her John—or by any type of character to another—is savagely spit out by Davis in *Of Human Bondage*:

> I never cared for you. Not once. . . . You bored me sick. I hated ya. It made me sick when I had to let you kiss me. I only did it because you begged me . . . and, after you kissed me, I always used to wipe my mouth.

Waterloo Bridge

Metro-Goldwyn-Mayer, 1940, black-and-white, 103 minutes
Director: Mervyn LeRoy
Cast: Vivien Leigh, Robert Taylor, Lucile Watson, C. Aubrey Smith, and Maria Ouspenskaya

This well-polished entry asks the weighty question: can a former ballet dancer (Leigh) in World War I London, whose fiancé dies on the battlefront and who turns to prostitution to survive, have a chance at redemption and happiness with an upper-crust British officer (Taylor)? For this movie,

Robert Taylor offers a drink to Vivien Leigh (cast as a streetwalker) as C. Aubrey Smith looks on in *Waterloo Bridge* (1940).   Courtesy of JC Archives

released in morally conservative 1940 and boasting a tale set in even more prim 1910s England, the answer is a resounding "No!" on two levels. First, there is that nasty thing of class difference—she comes from the lower classes, and he is a blue-blooded aristocrat, the type whose country place is a lavish ancestral home in Scotland. Second, there is that unforgiving double standard: men are willing to pay for her sexual favors, yet they despise her (but not themselves, of course) for being so immoral.

Waterloo Bridge being a Hollywood movie and Leigh—the recent winner of an Academy Award for her Scarlett O'Hara in 1939's *Gone with the Wind*—being a prized leading lady, her role was geared to generate audience appeal on a wide level. As a result, her character is conceived as one of fortune's fools, who pays for her moral breech of society's code by throwing herself in front of a speeding vehicle. In such a plot premise, Vivien has an actress's delight: she can play a vulnerable tart (sure to arouse interest from male filmgoers), yet she can be sympathetic (because fate has led to her moral downfall and because she sacrifices herself rather than taint the future of her aristocratic beau). How does anyone in real life—of whatever moral fiber—compete with such a stacked deck?

Dr. Jekyll and Mr. Hyde

Metro-Goldwyn-Mayer, 1941, black-and-white, 127 minutes
Director: Victor Fleming
Cast: Spencer Tracy, Ingrid Bergman, Lana Turner, Donald Crisp, and Barton MacLane

*B*ergman had not yet reached the zenith of her 1940s fame with American film-goers, but this radiant Swedish import was already a great favorite with the public. They perceived her to be in real life a reflection of her generally sympathetic, wholesome screen parts. When Ingrid agreed to play the trollop in this cinema thriller, audiences were intrigued that this popular personality could take on such a contrasting oncamera role. Many viewers could not separate the image of the offscreen actress from her film alter ego. As such, it created a duality to her performance as schizoid as that handed to Tracy in the highly contrasting roles of the genteel, good Dr. Jekyll and the fiendish killer Mr. Hyde.

In Victorian England, Dr. Henry Jekyll (Tracy) must delay an early marriage to a well-bred young lady (Turner) because of her stodgy nobleman father (Crisp). In his frustration he turns to his lab experiments with an elixir that radically changes both human nature and physiognomy. The drink turns him into the ugly and base Hyde, who finds solace with an immoral wench (Bergman). As time passes, Jekyll cannot control his transformations from the goodly physician into the

bestial Hyde. Eventually, having turned into a murderer, he is himself killed.

In this narrative, based on Robert Louis Stevenson's classic 1887 tale, audiences got a lot of food for thought. Besides the well-known tale of the beast that lies within all men, there is the dual nature of the seemingly heartless onscreen prostitute played by Ingrid. Is she as cruel and morally unscrupulous as the dialogue/plot suggests, or are there elements of an enticing heart-of-gold (drawn from the real-life image of the actress) thing present. This speculation gives the picture added dimension. It also poses provocative thoughts to more introspective moviegoers. What is the validity of the public face we put forth to the world, and does anyone—even our intimates—know the real person beneath the surface? For many of us, the questions remain open, for we feel inadequate or unwilling to deal with the possible answers. If only we had someone to write dialogue to illuminate *our* thoughts on the subject and to direct *our* reactions to such potentially unsettling revelations! But we're not as fortunate as screen characters.

Miss Sadie Thompson

Columbia, 1953, color, 91 minutes
Director: Curtis Bernhardt
Cast: Rita Hayworth, José Ferrer, Aldo Ray, Russell Collins, and Diosa Costello

What could seemingly be better for film-goers (especially men) than sultry Hayworth playing that tramp among tramps, Sadie Thompson (based on a 1921 short story and a 1922 play), on the big screen? Not only did she dance and sing (albeit her voice was dubbed) in this latest version of the well-known melodrama, but the musical picture was in color and 3-D. What's not to like?

Well, for one thing the much-filmed narrative had lost lots of its shock value to post–World War II audiences. Then too, the

hard-living sex symbol star was starting to look worn at age thirty-five. With the rare exception of her tantalizing movements in the "Blue Pacific Blues" song-and-dance number, her heart didn't seem much into the project, and, too frequently, she appeared detached from the lurid proceedings.

The updated chronicle presents Rita as a Waikiki-based prostitute forced to leave Hawaii and finding herself stranded on a tropic isle in the Pacific, one occupied by a detachment of marines. She immediately draws the attention of the girl-hungry soldiers, especially Ray. Another local is far less pleased by her arrival. That is a wealthy plantation owner (Ferrer) who happens to be a fanatical reformer, bent on keeping "evil" from the territory. His efforts to reform her have partial success, but his growing lust for Hayworth leads him to attack her one night. Distraught by his weakness, he commits suicide. As for Rita, having shucked her new demure demeanor, she departs for New Caledonia, agreeing to wait for Aldo.

A Sure Line for Dating Success

In *Miss Sadie Thompson*, Ray's character says to Sadie: "Honey, maybe knowing the worst about each other isn't such a bad way to begin."

American Gigolo

Paramount, 1980, color, 117 minutes
Director: Paul Schrader
Cast: Richard Gere, Lauren Hutton,
Hector Elizondo, Nina Van Pallandt, and
Bill Duke

*W*ith Hollywood so long an old boys' club, the power managers in the film capital were rarely comfortable (even when the industry self-censorship code was greatly revamped in the late 1960s) dealing onscreen with heterosexual and (especially) homosexual males involved in the prostitution game. The pathfinding *American Gigolo* broke these taboos in a big way with its high-profile, controversial subject matter and relatively frank presentation.

In Los Angeles, a well-groomed male prostitute has a lucrative clientele of wealthy women of varying ages. Being an entrepreneur, he attempts to cut out the middle person—an elegant pimp (Van Pallandt). He also turns his back on a gay black pimp (Duke) with whom he was once associated. In revenge, the latter sets up Richard as the fall guy in a homicide. Coming to his rescue is a beautiful married client (Hutton) who wants to prove her love for him.

Women watching *American Gigolo* are generally awed by handsome Gere (seen in one scene in frontal nudity). They also approve of his character's designer suits and high-fashion abode and are impressed by his character's knowing ways with women in and out of

I Dig My Work

In *American Gigolo*, Gere's male prostitute says with a flourish of satisfaction: "I was with a woman. . . . Her husband didn't care about her anymore. This woman hadn't had an orgasm in eighteen years. It took me three hours to get her off. . . . When it was over, it felt like I had done something, something worthwhile. Who else would have taken the time, cared enough to do it right?"

Nothing like having strong professional pride.

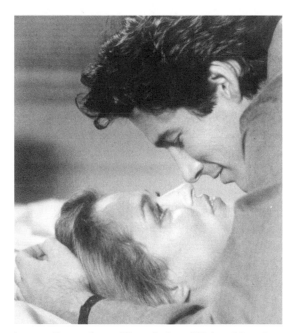

Lauren Hutton is a willing victim of Richard Gere's charms in *American Gigolo* (1980).
Courtesy of JC Archives

bed, his facility with languages, and his recurring efforts to better himself. Of course, this lead figure has a checkered past, might be considered a social parasite by most people, and is not very noble for dabbling in illegal activities. However, the overall package—especially when one does not have to deal with it in real life—is enticing to many viewers. With so many (consequential or not) pluses to Gere's character, his actions set a standard in and out of the bedroom that not many mere mortal men can meet.

Risky Business

Warner Bros., 1983, color, 98 minutes
Director: Paul Brickman
Cast: Tom Cruise, Rebecca De Mornay, Joe Pantoliano, Richard Masur, and Bronson Pinchot

*C*ruise has come a long way professionally since this breakthrough entry that helped to establish him as Hollywood's newest heartthrob, he of the 1,000-kilowatt smile and the killer sunshades. The film itself is a crafty wish-fulfillment excursion, riffing off that cherished fantasy of so many young (and old) men: to meet a beautiful call girl who wants to be with you emotionally and sexually not for money and favors but because she truly adores you. Wow!

High-achieving Chicago high schooler Cruise dreams of being admitted to Princeton University. When his upper-middle-class parents embark on a vacation, his academic conscientiousness takes a backseat to his adolescent hormones. He orders a prostitute by phone and meets an attractive hooker (De Mornay). The deed done, she soon takes up residence in his home to avoid her vicious pimp (Pantoliano). Later on, the enterprising Rebecca convinces Tom to host an orgy at his home, matching her circle of hookers with his group of affluent teen pals. The evening is a financial success, although he barely restores order to the house before his parents return. Now accepted to Princeton, Cruise discusses with De Mornay the potential of continuing their joint venture on the college campus.

Anyone who thinks he can fill Cruise's shoes for a remake or real-life rendition of this story, applications are available online.

High school student Tom Cruise becomes the manager of two enterprising women (Rebecca De Mornay, center, and Shera Danese, right) in *Risky Business* (1983). Courtesy of Echo Book Shop

Pretty Woman

Buena Vista, 1990, color, 117 minutes
Director: Garry Marshall
Cast: Richard Gere, Julia Roberts,
Ralph Bellamy, Jason Alexander, Laura
San Giacomo, and Hector Elizondo

Julia Roberts rose to screen fame playing a
prostitute in *Pretty Woman* (1990).
Photo by Albert L. Ortega

*O*n many levels this is a wonderful Cinderella story. On the screen it slickly tells
of a Hollywood Boulevard hooker (Roberts)
who meets her Prince Charming—a stuffy
multimillionaire corporate raider (Gere) from
back East. For pay they share sex, several days,
and his Beverly Hills penthouse hotel suite.
On one score, says Julia's character, the couple
has much in common: "We both screw people for a living." However, in most everything
else they are total opposites. Nevertheless,
their growing fondness turns to love, but they
separate because of a foolish misunderstand-
ing. Later, he arrives at Julia's apartment in his
chauffeur-driven limousine and declares his
great love for her. At the box office, this $14
million R-rated fantasy grossed more than
$178 million in domestic distribution, and the
film earned Roberts an Oscar nomination.

Dating Chatter That Works!

Within *Pretty Woman*, the two lead characters
toss off entertaining banter worthy of remembering for the right social situation:

He: "What's your name?"
She: "What do you want it to be?"

Or:

She: "You're late!"
He: "You're stunning."
She: "You're forgiven."

Kiss of the Dragon

Twentieth Century-Fox, 2001, color,
97 minutes
Director: Chris Nahon
Cast: Jet Li, Bridget Fonda, Tchéky Karyo,
Ric Young, and Burt Kwouk

*C*hinese-born action star Li made a strong
impact with filmgoers with this wham-
bang graphic action flick, an American-

French coproduction. The picture neatly plays off the martial art legend's oncamera reticence to participate in heavy-duty romantic scenes. As such, Jet is cast as a no-nonsense government official from mainland China who arrives in Paris to assist local authorities in catching a major heroin smuggler. Before long, the newcomer has been set up by a corrupt French police official (Tchéky) as the fall guy in the murder of the hunted dealer. To prove his innocence, Li must join forces with an American prostitute (Fonda) who witnessed the actual murder for which Jet is blamed. Meanwhile, Bridget, has her own agenda with the crooked Gallic lawman, for he is holding her young daughter hostage.

By the bone-crunching, butt-kicking finale, taciturn Jet has neatly dispatched not only his archenemy but the latter's array of deadly, muscular henchmen. As for Bridget, she and her offspring are happily reunited. Left unresolved at the picture's finale is the growing emotional/sexual bond between the lawman hero and his hooker confederate. Their occupations have made each extremely wary of trusting other people. Nevertheless, she is drawn by the handsome Asian's self-sufficiency and reliability, while he is attracted by her beauty, self-reliance, and vulnerability. They play cat and mouse with one another, as when she chides, "I'm not your type, huh?" and he responds ambiguously, "I don't have a type." On another occasion, he informs her—as if to explain away his seeming inability to have a meaningful personal life—"I'm a cop," to which chipper Fonda answers, "I am Santa Claus." Completing this playful interchange, the deliberately naïve Li asks her, "Who is Santa Claus?"

The moral of this international confection: where matters of the heart are concerned, there are no right or wrong sides of the law.

As Hollywood has so aptly illustrated with screen genre pieces about prostitutes and their dear hearts, a person in love/lust is generally willing to forgive his beloved any prior walk on the wild side—in some cases, that is what made the individual so enticing to the other in the first place. Now would be an apt time to hum a few stanzas of that popular old tune "Love for Sale."

13

Say It Better with Song and Dance

Raves and rock concerts to one side, music is a well-regarded remedy for "soothing the savage beast" in most of us. Similarly, melodic songs can be an aphrodisiac for a budding romance, helping to shape the proper mood for tender moments in a love relationship. Sometimes a certain song becomes "our" song for a couple, forever tied to special moments in their courtship such as the actual proposal of marriage. Or, how often have we relied on a catchy, popular song lyric to express an emotion we find far too difficult to say ourselves to the person of our dreams?

Taking up where the stage, records, and radio left off, Hollywood began using musical numbers in movies in the later 1920s as the industry converted from silents to talkies. Al Jolson made film history with his speaking, singing, and prancing in *The Jazz Singer* (1927). *The Broadway Melody* (1929), which seems extremely primitive, clichéd, and trite when seen today, was so innovative in its era that it won an Academy Award as Best Pic-

ture. Thereafter there was no stopping Tinseltown as it churned out all-talking, all-singing, all-dancing pictures, until the trend wore out moviegoers' enthusiasm a few years later. But the genre reemerged with gusto with *42nd Street* and *Dancing Lady* (both 1933).

Next came the rash of 1930s song-and-dance fests (e.g., 1934's *The Gay Divorcee*) starring Fred Astaire and Ginger Rogers. These elegant entries convinced moviegoers that with a little (or a lot of!) extra practice they might be as graceful on the ballroom floor as this praised screen love team who punctuated their delightful choreographed interludes with harmonious songs. Sixty years later in such excursions as Woody Allen's *Everyone Says I Love You* (1996), our onscreen alter egos were still expressing their romantic feelings in song and dance, this time relying on several marvelous old tunes. Ah, the magic of music!

♥   ♥   ♥   ♥   ♥

Dames

Warner Bros., 1934, black-and-white,
90 minutes
Director: Ray Enright
Cast: Joan Blondell, Dick Powell, Ruby
Keeler, ZaSu Pitts, and Hugh Herbert

*T*his was the fourth of seven popular
screen teamings of Keeler and Powell
and, once again, offered an array of intricate
dance numbers staged by Busby Berkeley in
his mind-boggling kaleidoscopic fashion,
which never fails to magnetize audiences. The
plot is shear nonsense: an eccentric million-
aire (Herbert), a do-gooder, promises his
cousin (Guy Kibbee) $100,000 because he
seems to be a very moral man. Before he can
collect the bounty, the married Kibbee finds
himself in an embarrassing moral scrape
caused by his being accidentally caught in a
compromising position with a frisky chorine
(Blondell). The latter, to help her stagestruck
boyfriend (Powell)—a distant relation of
Kibbee—blackmails Guy into backing Dick's
Broadway offering. By the wrap-up Hugh
decides to let others reform the world; he
now intends to have fun in life. So, the big
show goes on after all.

Within *Dames*, there are a variety of contrasting songs to show off Powell's crooning,
Keeler's tap dancing, and Berkeley's genius at
creating precision routines for his oncamera
chorus line. The numbers range from "The
Girl at the Ironing Board" (which is filled
with sexual images of a laundress pawing over
men's pajamas and long underwear) to the
snappy "Dames." However, the picture's high-

The Family Who Works Together Stays Together— Sometimes

After costarring in several features, including
Dames, **Joan Blondell (1909–1979)** and team-
mate **Dick Powell (1904–1963)** wed in 1936. It
was the second marriage for each and, as a
couple, they had one child together. By 1944,
their marriage was over, he having fallen in love
with rising star June Allyson. When writing her
novel *Center Door Fancy* (1972), a thinly veiled
autobiography, Joan included an unflattering
portrayal of her late second spouse.

light is the Al Dubin–Harry Warren item, "I
Only Have Eyes for You." Its visual shows
lovesick Dick and Ruby taking a long subway
ride during which they fall asleep. As Powell
dreams, a horde of girls appears, all wearing
masks of Ruby. Later, the girls bend over,
revealing they each have a board strapped to
their back. When they move into assigned
positions and the boards are fitted together, it
reveals a huge jigsaw picture of Keeler's face.
Fantastic visuals aside, this love melody has
remained popular to this present day, having
often shown up as background music in films
or in new recordings by contemporary pop
artists.

So, if you really want to impress your significant other that your romantic intentions
are serious, cut down on that wasteful couch
potato activity. Instead, allow for longer showers to provide for uninterrupted practice of

your vocalizing. Also, the next time you're mall shopping, drop in at Payless Shoes and purchase footwear with dance taps on the heels and toes. With such practical steps, you'll be prepared to say it with music.

Top Hat

RKO, 1935, black-and-white, 101 minutes
Director: Mark Sandrich
Cast: Fred Astaire, Ginger Rogers, Edward Everett Horton, Helen Broderick, and Erik Rhodes

For some moviegoers in the 1930s there was no finer musical love team than MGM's Singing Sweethearts, Jeanette Mac-Donald and Nelson Eddy, who paraded through several celluloid operettas (e.g., 1935's *Naughty Marietta*). On the other hand, for others, there was no beating the film chemistry of perky and pretty Rogers in tandem with debonair and graceful Astaire. First united oncamera in *Flying Down to Rio* (1933), the duo had, by now, perfected its teamwork, and this entry found the twosome at the top of their stylish form.

American entertainer Astaire is employed on the London stage. One day he encounters another American (Rogers) and is immediately attracted to her. She rebuffs his advances because she mistakenly believes he is wed to her pal (Broderick). (Actually, Helen is wed to the very fey Horton.) Meanwhile, Ginger is pursued by a hyperactive Italian dress designer (Rhodes), and the couple soon announces its

Ginger Rogers, Fred Astaire, and Erik Rhodes make an awkward love triangle in *Top Hat* (1935).
Courtesy of JC Archives

Kelly and Sinatra, the costars of 1945's *Anchors Aweigh*. This time, joined by Munshin, they are a trio of gobs on a day's shore leave in Manhattan who enjoy romantic adventures with three engaging women.

As the exuberant sailors sing and dance their way through New York City—depicted as a paradise of impressive landmarks, quaint byways, and no violence—the men encounter a fledgling ballerina (Vera-Ellen), a tap-dancing anthropologist (Miller), and a playful cab driver (Garrett). The sextet frantically crowd a lot of sightseeing and romancing into their brief time on land. Once their shore leave concludes, the men return to their ship, while their respective women promise to wait for them. With that, this sparkling musical comes to its finale.

Is it true that every member of Uncle Sam's navy can sing, dance, and crack jokes like this boisterous screen trio? Could Miller's dinosaur-studying character be somehow related to paleontologist Ross Geller of *Friends* fame? And when's the last time a New York cabbie invited you in a song to "Come Up to My Place"?

A Musical Tongue Twister

The ads for *On the Town* boasted, "Skirts, skyscrapers and scamperings as these three skittering scamps take highways and byways of the big city!"

Singin' in the Rain

Metro-Goldwyn-Mayer, 1952, color,
103 minutes
Directors: Gene Kelly and Stanley Donen
Cast: Gene Kelly, Donald O'Connor, Debbie Reynolds, Jean Hagen, and Cyd Charisse

*B*e honest. Every time you walk down a city street in the rain and pass a streetlight post, don't you have an irresistible urge—even for a moment—to break into a time step and shuffle, swing on the light poll, and stomp in a curbside water puddle as Kelly did in this picture? No? Then you're not the agile romantic I thought you were.

In the 1920s, Hollywood screen lovers Kelly and Hagen pretend to be as involved romantically offcamera as they are onscreen. Actually, Gene has no respect for untalented Jean, while she is so self-absorbed, it's doubtful she even knows he exists. Before long, Kelly has met aspiring singing star Reynolds, who has no interest in the movies. The two fall in love. Meanwhile, the talkie craze takes over Hollywood, which requires retakes on the latest Kelly-Hagen epic. Because Jean has such a screechy, high-pitched voice, studio musician O'Connor hits on the notion of having Debbie dub in Hagen's dialogue and singing. The costumed picture is premiered and is a big hit. In the process it is revealed to the audience that Reynolds is the dubber who saved the production. The swell-headed Jean is now washed up in pictures, while Debbie is on the verge of becoming a big star.

This revered, most satisfying musical proves the expression, "They don't make 'em like that anymore." It also instructs us that every ventriloquist gets her day in the limelight.

High Society

Metro-Goldwyn-Mayer, 1956, color,
107 minutes
Director: Charles Walters
Cast: Bing Crosby, Grace Kelly, Frank Sinatra, Celeste Holm, and John Lund

Sixteen years after Katharine Hepburn, Cary Grant, and James Stewart costarred in the admirable *The Philadelphia Story* (1940), the property was turned into a gilt-edged screen musical with a Cole Porter score. This movie matched the great crooner of the 1930s (Crosby) with his 1940s successor (Sinatra). As the project's leading lady, the studio cast

Bing Crosby flirts with Grace Kelly as a bemused Louis Calhern looks on in *High Society* (1956).
Courtesy of JC Archives

Explain Them to Me

At the time of making *High Society*, **Frank Sinatra (1915–1998)** was in the throes of ending his marriage to tempestuous movie star **Ava Gardner (1922–1990)**. Such marital misfires led the great ladies' man to admit later in life: "I'm supposed to have a Ph.D. on the subject of women. Truth is, I've flunked more often than not. I'm very fond of women. I admire them. But, like all men, I don't understand them."

twenty-eight-year-old Kelly. She numbered Bing among her former real-life boyfriends, but, by the time *High Society* was released in August 1956, she had become real-life royalty. Four months earlier she'd wed Prince Rainier III of Monaco.

Newport, Rhode Island, socialite Kelly is about to wed dreary Lund. To her surprise, her ex-husband (Crosby), a songwriter-promoter, arrives on the scene and insists that she will be wretched if she proceeds with this marital mismatch. Meanwhile, Sinatra and Holm, reporters for *Spy* magazine, show up, planning to both cover the city's annual jazz festival and get the dirt on the society marriage of the year. Grace is having doubts about her nuptials to John and flirts with womanizing Frank. However, it is Bing who holds the key to her heart, and the two eventually reunite.

The vehicle allows for Sinatra and Crosby to croon individually and in duet and for the irrepressible Louis Armstrong to cut loose on a few numbers. The highlight of the melodic, classy proceedings is the harmonizing of mellow Bing and radiant Grace (in a quavering voice) on the romantic ballad "True Love." The song became so popular with moviegoers and from radio airplays of the soundtrack album cut that it quickly developed into a standard sung at weddings for years to come.

My Fair Lady

Warner Bros., 1964, color, 170 minutes
Director: George Cukor
Cast: Audrey Hepburn, Rex Harrison, Stanley Holloway, Wilfred Hyde-White, and Gladys Cooper

Following an enormously successful Broadway and London stage run, *My Fair Lady* finally made it to the screen, eight years after its New York debut. In what created a storm of protest, the original cast's leading lady (Julie Andrews) was passed over for the movie colead in favor of box-office magnet Hepburn. The Belgian-born Audrey was game for the challenge of portraying a cockney, but her singing had to be dubbed (by Marni Nixon). As for Rex, he had talk-sung his way admirably through the stage rendition and did the same oncamera. The end cine-

matic results were tasteful if not innovative. A commercial success, the picture won eight Oscars (including Best Picture) as well as three additional Academy Award nominations.

In the years before World War I, phonetic teacher Harrison happens upon a crude but exuberant flower girl (Hepburn). Rex brags to his friend (Hyde-White) that in a matter of three months he can have this cockney miss

That Woman Should Look Familiar

Both in the long-running stage version and the hit movie adaptation of *My Fair Lady*, **Rex Harrison (1908–1990)** performed "I've Grown Accustomed to Her Face," a number that became closely associated with him. In real life, Sir Rex hardly had the opportunity to really get to know the women in his superactive life. He was married six times, including unions to actresses Lilli Palmer, Kay Kendall, and Rachel Roberts. Along the way, "Sexy Rexy," as he was dubbed by the press, had several affairs, including one with 1940s movie actress Carole Landis at a time when each was still wed to another. When Harrison attempted to break off his increasingly public and scandalous love connection, Landis became despondent and committed suicide. After the racy facts became public knowledge, the Britisher had to flee Hollywood (with his loyal spouse Palmer in tow) and return to stage acting until the ill winds eventually blew over.

A nervous Audrey Hepburn dances with perfectionist Rex Harrison in *My Fair Lady* (1964).
Courtesy of JC Archives

speaking faultless English and, he adds, be able to pass her off as royalty. The wager is accepted, and Audrey begins elocution lessons at Rex's home. In the appointed time, Harrison and Hyde-White succeed in making over the flower seller into a refined young woman. As the ultimate test of the transformation, they escort Audrey to the social event of the season where she is a smashing success. That accomplished, both Harrison and Hepburn realize that, in the process, they have fallen in love with one another.

If you have that irresistible urge to make over your loved one into that extra-special person of your dreams, you're treading in dangerous waters. Unlike the happy resolution to this pretty screen story, in real life a pupil often outgrows the teacher, and then where are you? Maybe you should start boning up on your own diction. For starters, think of a sentence that includes such rhyming words as *rain*, *plain*, and *Spain*, and shout it repeatedly until you have it tripping on your tongue.

Saturday Night Fever

Paramount, 1977, color, 119 minutes
Director: John Badham
Cast: John Travolta, Karen Lynn Gorney, Barry Miller, Joseph Cali, and Paul Pape

*T*here's such vitality and likability to Travolta's Tony Manero that this dated entry about the long-gone disco era (and all the fads that entailed) still has great appeal today. With his killer smile, simian stride, and flashy clothes, John's performance as the dance-happy Brooklynite defined a period of pop culture and set its own fashion trend. But God help us, didn't he deserve a better leading lady than Gorney to put through the paces at the 2001 Odyssey disco?

Not yet twenty, lower-middle-class Brooklyn youth Travolta wants more out of life than his menial job as a paint store clerk provides. He finds distraction and satisfaction hanging out with his buddies at the local disco, where the promiscuous Donna Pescow pursues him relentlessly. However, ambitious John sets his sights on the uppity Karen Lynn, who proudly boasts that she is soon moving to Manhattan

John Travolta shows Karen Lynn Gorney his disco moves in *Saturday Night Fever* (1977).
Courtesy of JC Archives

to be closer to her new secretarial job at a public relations agency. While his friends endure assorted traumas, Travolta's horizons are expanding beyond the dance floor. As he tells Gorney, he intends to follow her example by getting out of Brooklyn and making something of his own life.

With a trio of hit songs (including "How Deep Is Your Love") by the high-pitched Bee Gees, the film, its soundtrack, and Travolta were enormous successes. (To be noted, this is a rare musical in which the lead players do *not* sing but only dance to the music on the soundtrack.)

Words from on High

According to **John Travolta (b. 1954)** who, since 1991, has been married to actress Kelly Preston: "Sex with love is about the most beautiful thing there is—but sex without love isn't so bad, either."

Grease

Paramount, 1978, color, 110 minutes
Director: Randal Kleiser
Cast: John Travolta, Olivia Newton-John, Stockard Channing, Jeff Conaway, and Didi Conn

*I*f Fonzie with the greased-down hair and the Tuscadero babe of TV's *Happy Days* (1974–1984) didn't satisfy your thirst for a spoof of leather-clad motorcycle riders, there's always *Grease*. Based on the long-running Broadway play (1972), this calculated screen musical perpetuates the fictional world of Rydell High, where tough dudes are meek meat compared to those in the real world and the coeds are more into pajama party sleepovers with their pals than sleepouts with their sex-crazed boyfriends.

In the late 1950s in California, high school senior Travolta becomes intrigued with a new student (Newton-John) whom he'd met that past summer on the beach. Being a braggart, John tells his cronies that he'll soon bed the pretty blonde. This upsets the aggressive Channing, who foists her immoral self on Travolta's pal, Conaway. By now, John will do anything to impress Olivia, even trying to excel in sports. Failing in that approach, he is at a loss how to win her heart. She solves the problem by ditching her goody-goody image and becoming a groovy chick. Now the two are just perfect for one another. Meanwhile, Stockard and Jeff plan to wed.

If your high school days were anything like this, you belong in Ripley's "Believe It or

---

Did You Know?

- Five years after their *Grease* megahit, **John Travolta (b. 1954)** and **Olivia Newton-John (b. 1948)** reunited for the romantic comedy *Two of a Kind*, which proved to be a big flop.

- *Grease 2* (1982), the unsuccessful sequel to *Grease*, costarred Maxwell Caulfield and Michelle Pfeiffer.

Not." Otherwise, forget your fantasies to be today's answer to Marlon Brando from *The Wild One* (1951). After all, how big a fool do you want to be at your next high school class reunion? What would that *Grease* trio of Sandy, Betty, and Frenchy think of you then?

Moulin Rouge

Twentieth Century-Fox, 2001, color, 127 minutes
Director: Baz Luhrmann
Cast: Nicole Kidman, Ewan McGregor, John Leguizamo, Jim Broadbent, and Richard Roxburgh

*W*inning two Oscars (art direction/set decoration, and costumes) and nominated for six other Academy Awards, this rare contemporary excursion into the movie musical genre boasts some of the flashiest and most creative film editing this side of a Bruce Willis

The Magic "L" Word

The promotional ad campaign for *Moulin Rouge* revolved around the word *love*. Here are some of the production's assorted teaser lines:

- "Believe in truth, beauty, freedom, and above all things, love."

- "This is a story about *love*, music is the food of *love*, nothing matters but *love*."

- "The greatest thing you'll ever learn is just to love, and be loved in return."

action flick. Then too, its array of songs drawn from decades of popular favorites smartly showcases several well-known numbers in creative settings and situations that give fresh meaning to the lyrics.

At the end of the nineteenth century, Englishman McGregor relocates to Paris, hoping the bohemian atmosphere of Montmartre will inspire him to become a successful writer. He soon meets a colorful group of creative types, including a highly talented painter (Leguizamo). They convince Ewan to write a stage show for them. Next, they appoint him to approach the manager (Broadbent) of the Moulin Rouge club for backing. This leads to the financial support of the Duke (Roxburgh), who lusts after chosen lead performer Kidman. The production is

soon put into rehearsal. Because the eager nobleman has already asked Nicole to marry him, she keeps her growing love for Ewan a secret. When Kidman learns she has tuberculosis, she halts her romance with McGregor. However, the lovesick man persists in his courtship of her. On the show's opening night, he comes onto the stage and sings of his love for the leading lady. She returns the compliment. The jealous Duke, after failing to have his rival shot, stalks out of the theater. Meanwhile, Kidman succumbs to her disease and dies. As for McGregor, he is inspired to capture the many events of the past months as the basis for a grand love story.

Because *Moulin Rouge* takes place in 1899, don't hold any wild expectations that the actual Paris of today will be as raunchy, raucous, and wicked as presented in this film. Instead, save the price of air passage and settle in at home with a good bottle of French wine and a bubbling soufflé, and, if you must, dream on.

With so many examples to study and learn from, perhaps the next time you come to a tender emotional moment with your beloved, instead of reaching for a drink or a cigarette as a prop, how about white tie, tux, and walking stick. And if he's not getting the message of how much you love him, why not say it with music and belt out a song that says it all.

14

Revenge Fantasies, or Hell Has No Fury Like a Lover Scorned

For most people, the topic of romance is associated with positive and upbeat thoughts. For them, being in love suggests a delightful state of emotional bliss in which the heart beats faster and the pulse races furiously. For a majority of such love-struck individuals, a long-term involvement—whether as lovers or as husband and wife—is a logical possibility thereafter. The assumption is that once two people are committed to each other, the relationship will grow even stronger and deeper. Certainly, the heightened passion between the couple may diminish over time, but, by then, the bonds between the two will, one hopes, have grown stronger and the duo can continue its comfortable situation "forever."

But human beings are fickle. For an assortment of reasons they often fall out of love or lust with their significant other. When that happens, they do their best to break off the relationship as painlessly (usually for themselves) as possible. It might be as simple as calling it quits with one or both parties moving out of the shared living quarters. If the twosome is married, then a divorce—and all that entails—is in order.

This splitting apart of a love connection may make the initiator relieved and/or happy, but it often leaves the other party (i.e., the one being ditched) feeling betrayed. "How can they do that to me?", "What did I do to deserve such shabby treatment?", and "What am I going to do now?" are typical emotional responses to being cut out of a loved one's life.

Most victims of breakups pass through the normal stages of bewilderment, anger, and adjustment. In the end, they resign themselves to the situation and, eventually, move on with their lives. Others may pine for their lost love and try to woo him or her back. If that fails, they may never recover from their emotional loss. A much smaller portion of those deserted can think only of getting even with the "culprit" by making the other party suffer in one way or another. "I'll show him he can't make a fool of me!" Their emotional makeup is such that their wounded pride can be salved only by a dramatic response to the unwanted separation. They become consumed with plotting and executing revenge against the initiator of their current emotional unhappiness.

These acts of revenge between past lovers or former spouses have long intrigued Hollywood, for they allow one more variety of exciting, offbeat situations to be played out onscreen. As such, moviegoers can vicariously experience the payback they themselves may have thought of dishing out to the initiator but, being moral and levelheaded souls, would never dream of undertaking in real life. For still other viewers, these domestic retribution scenarios may serve as a basic how-to seminar in getting even with that dirty "rat" who abandoned the love boat.

Gaslight

Metro-Goldwyn-Mayer, 1944, black-and-white, 114 minutes
Director: George Cukor
Cast: Charles Boyer, Ingrid Bergman, Joseph Cotten, Dame May Whitty, and Angela Lansbury

*S*ometimes falling out of love with one's wife is not the issue at stake for a man wanting to get rid of his wife—especially if he was *never* in love with her in the first place. What if his motive for wedding her is to gain control of her wealth—one way or another?

Turnabout Is Fair Play

Having at last discovered that the cause of her self-doubts about her sanity were engineered by her calculating spouse, Bergman's love for Boyer vanishes in a flash. Relishing that she has cut her emotional ties to this fiend, she says, "Without a shred of pity, without a shred of regret, I watch you go with glory in my heart."

That's one (flowery) way of kissing off the sadistic brute who nearly destroyed her life.

Such is the diabolical scheme in this thriller set in England of the Victorian era.

After a whirlwind romance, young, pretty, and well-to-do Bergman is charmed into marrying debonair Boyer. To please her husband, she agrees to reopen the London house bequeathed to her by her aunt, a noted singer who was murdered twenty years earlier. Ingrid's initial bliss soon turns into dismay as she discovers Charles is a nagging, stern disciplinarian. What is worse, he constantly accuses her of doing things that she cannot remember having done. Before long, she wonders if she is losing her sanity. Things reach a nasty turn when Boyer humiliates her publicly, insisting loudly that she has stolen his valuable watch. Unnerved by this latest outburst, Bergman becomes hysterical. An observer to this interplay is Cotten, a Scotland Yard detective.

It turns out that Joseph, once a devotee of Ingrid's talented aunt, is determined to solve that previous homicide. In the process he

Duplicitous Charles Boyer takes advantage of his vulnerable wife (Ingrid Bergman) in *Gaslight* (1944).   Courtesy of JC Archives

investigates the situation at Ingrid's Thornton Square home and comes to the conclusion that the sadistic Boyer is trying to drive her crazy. (The villain wants to have her committed to an institution so he can search for her aunt's long-hidden jewelry—of which Bergman knows nothing—and destroy telltale evidence remaining from that decades-old crime.) Having gathered sufficient evidence, Joseph explains the diabolic situation to Ingrid. In a climactic showdown, the Scotland Yard man traps Charles in the attic, where he maneuvers him into confessing the truth.

A few thoughts for anyone prone to being swept off his or her feet by a slick, mysterious suitor: (1) sign a prenuptial agreement, (2) never live in a house that has an attic, and (3) beware of a cheeky young domestic who is putty in the hands of your "better" half.

What You See Is Not What You Get

Polished French actor **Charles Boyer (1899–1978)** was considered by many to be the ultimate in screen lovers: that dapper, handsome look . . . that accent. However, Bette Davis, who costarred with Charles in *All This, and Heaven Too* (1940), had different impressions of her leading man. "Terribly serious about his looks . . . a wig, a corset, lifts in his shoes, and so on. When he took all that off, he must have looked like the Pillsbury Doughboy."

Unfaithfully Yours

Twentieth Century-Fox, 1948, black-and-white, 105 minutes
Director: Preston Sturges
Cast: Rex Harrison, Linda Darnell, Barbara Lawrence, Rudy Vallee, and Kurt Kreuger

This brilliant excursion is a gem, unlike the middling 1984 remake, which teamed Dudley Moore with Nastassja Kinski and Armand Assante. The original version has style, wit, polish, and a wonderfully adept cast.

An unsuspecting Linda Darnell must cope with her highly jealous spouse (Rex Harrison) in *Unfaithfully Yours* (1948). Courtesy of JC Archives

Sir Rex

British **Rex Harrison (1908–1990)** may have been knighted by the English monarchy, but his supreme self-centeredness did not always endear him to others. (Actor Cesar Romero called Rex, "A pompous cad and an ambitious creep.") In turn, the dapper star had a very chauvinistic attitude toward the women in his life:

- "I vowed never to fit into the life of some woman. She has to fit into mine."

- "The happiest married men I know have a wife to go home to, not to go home with."

Returning to America from engagements abroad, famous concert conductor Harrison is led to believe by his snooty brother-in-law (Vallee) that Rex's beautiful young bride (Darnell) has been unfaithful (with Harrison's secretary Kreuger) during the maestro's absence. At first, Rex, a supreme egotist, refuses to believe the accusation. But his suspicious nature gets the best of him, and he quarrels with his loyal spouse.

That evening as he conducts the symphony orchestra, Harrison's imagination goes into high drive and he hatches three "perfect" schemes to get rid of his errant wife. (One plan is to murder her, another is to pay her off with a settlement, and the third is to force her

Did She or Didn't She?

Unfaithfully Yours offers a beginner's manual for a man suspecting his mate of infidelity. Of course, if the challenged wife happens to be innocent and witty, where does that leave him?

He: "You didn't do anything you shouldn't do while I was away, did you? I mean, like falling in love with anyone else or anything like that?"

She: "How could I fall in love with anyone else . . . when you took my heart with you?"

He: "No man ever had a better answer than that."

and Kurt to join him in a round of Russian roulette.) With the performance over, Rex rushes home and attempts to put his plans into operation, but everything goes wrong.

Meanwhile, without knowing the causes for her husband acting so strangely, Linda explains why she happened to be seen by Vallee coming out of Kreuger's room wearing a negligee. In actuality, she'd gone there to warn her sister (Lawrence), who was having an affair with Kurt, that her husband (Rudy) was on his way over there. His wild suspicions evaporated, Harrison begs Darnell to forgive him, but she is to never ask him to explain his bizarre behavior that night.

The moral of this slick tale is that reality can never, and should never, match one's fantasies.

Sudden Fear

RKO, 1952, black-and-white, 110 minutes
Director: David Miller
Cast: Joan Crawford, Jack Palance, Gloria Grahame, Bruce Bennett, and Virginia Huston

*E*ver meet someone new and have an instant gut feeling that this person isn't right for you? Later, you change your mind about the individual and, boy, do you let yourself in for a lot of needless trouble.

Highly successful playwright Crawford is in New York auditioning actors to play the leading man in her new Broadway work. One of the candidates is Palance, whom she vetoes for the key role. Later, when returning to San Francisco by train, the heiress is surprised to find that Jack is aboard. By the time the couple reaches the Golden Gate City they are in love and rush into a hasty marriage. She introduces the groom to all her friends. Only Bennett, her lawyer, is openly suspicious of the newcomer, but Crawford discounts this because he has long been in love with her.

To her dismay, Crawford discovers—thanks to a recording machine she forgot to switch off—that Palance deliberately lured her into marriage. He and his woman friend (Grahame) are plotting to kill her so all of her wealth will go to Jack. Self-reliant Joan determines to get her own revenge rather than turn the evidence over to the police. She concocts an elaborate scheme in which she will murder her husband in Grahame's apartment and leave enough circumstantial evidence to incriminate Gloria as the culprit.

Everything works as planned, but, at the last minute, she cannot go through with the crime. Now aware of her murderous design, a furious Jack chases after Joan in his car, planning to eliminate her. She eludes him. At this juncture, Grahame appears on the hilly San Francisco street where Joan was last seen. Because she is wearing a coat and scarf similar to Crawford's, the enraged Palance thinks she is his wife. He runs her down with his car. The impact kills not only Gloria but Jack as well. Regaining her calm, Joan returns home.

If anyone gets any murderous revenge notion from this suspense melodrama, keep in mind that even Miss Joan's feisty character backs off from her macabre plan. Then too, what are the odds that someone wearing the same outfit as you will be walking down the right street at the correct moment so everything ends neatly as in this picture?

Fatal Attraction

Paramount, 1987, color, 119 minutes
Director: Adrian Lyne
Cast: Michael Douglas, Glenn Close, Anne Archer, Ellen Hamilton Latzen, and Stuart Pankin

One-night stands never seemed the same after this psychological screen thriller was released. This highly successful movie prompted countless articles, talk show discussions, and so forth about the situations presented in this graphic, suspenseful film. With a woman as the "bad guy," *Fatal Attraction* chisels out a screen type in which a jilted female becomes the quickie sex partner from hell.

Douglas is a successful Manhattan attorney with an attractive wife (Archer) and a cute child (Latzen). At a publishing party he meets bright associate editor (Close) who is appealing to him, but he reminds himself that he is a happily married man. On a later occasion, Michael and Glenn find themselves together while his wife and child are out of town to visit relatives, and Douglas succumbs to an extramarital fling with the very willing Close. After athletic sex with her, he is ready to return home, but Glenn convinces him to spend the next day with her. When he attempts to break free that evening, she slashes

Danger Signals

Should your latest romantic/sexual fling say any of the following, take instant heed:

- "What happened? I woke up, you weren't here. I hate that."

- "I don't think I like this. The way you run away every time after we make love."

- "What am I supposed to do? You won't answer my calls, you change your number. I mean, I'm not gonna be ignored! . . ."

- "If you told me to get lost, I'd have more respect for you."

her wrists, and he nurses her through the night. Thereafter, he does everything possible to elude her clutches, but he is no match for the increasingly irrational Glenn. Meanwhile, Douglas hopes that once he and his loved ones are resettled in suburbia, she will be out of his life for good. No such luck!

In the ongoing battle of wills, Glenn terrorizes Michael and his family, from killing the daughter's pet rabbit to temporarily kidnapping the girl. By now Douglas has confessed his infidelity to Anne, who, in disgust, wants him out of her life. But, because of escalating harassment from Close, the couple remains together. Later, the combat shifts to Glenn's apartment and then back again to Michael's home as he resorts to increasingly dangerous means to rid himself of her once and for all. However, she seems unstoppable until Archer steps in and resolves the hellish situation once and for all.

As moralists are quick to point out, there's usually a price to pay for everything, including great, illicit sex. (Remember Douglas and Close making it together in her building's elevator and in the kitchen of her apartment?) But how many truly psycho monsters like Close's character is one likely to meet outside of slasher thrillers? Nevertheless, when sexy strangers come on to you—beware. If they seem to have a fascination with knives, especially watch out. Do they ask you a lot of intimate questions but turn moodily silent when you tell them things they obviously don't want to hear (e.g., I'm not leaving my marriage)? Most of all, are you really careful about unwanted individuals gaining access to your bathroom? They do say, you know, that more fatalities occur there than in any other room in one's house.

I Love You to Death

TriStar, 1990, color, 96 minutes
Director: Lawrence Kasdan
Cast: Kevin Kline, Tracey Ullman, Joan Plowright, River Phoenix, William Hurt, and Keanu Reeves

This wild tale plays like something a spaced-out scriptwriter might concoct. In actuality, it is based on real-life events. The array of talent involved and the offbeat casting compensate, to a degree, for this essentially one-joke sitcom that eventually wears very thin.

Kline operates a pizzeria with his wife (Ullman) and also manages their nearby apartment building. Between his two jobs, the randy Kevin finds time for quick sexual escapades. Both Tracey's European-born mother (Plowright) and Phoenix, a devoted

On Having Murderous Thoughts About a Loved One

In *I Love You to Death*, when the Yugoslavian-born mother hires a hit man to eliminate her unfaithful son-in-law, she explains to her perplexed daughter: "In America people kill each other left and right. It's like a national pastime."

worker at the pizza shop, become aware of Kline's adulterous adventures. However, Tracey is slow to accept the truth. Her first impulse is to kill herself. But then, egged on by Joan, she decides to do away with her errant husband.

Various schemes that involve a hit man, River, and Ullman fail to accomplish the deed. Kevin seems to be unstoppable. Finally, Phoenix contacts two drugged-out acquaintances (Hurt and Reeves) who manage eventually to wound their target, but still Kline does not die. By now the police are investigating the strange happenings and arrest this bizarre group of suspects. However, Kline comes to their rescue, bailing them out of jail. His reason: if Tracey loves him enough to do what she has done, then this must be his wake-up call. He promises his wife that he'll be a good husband from now on.

Just our luck, if we tried some of the murderous schemes undertaken in this flick, we'd end up succeeding all too well. Enough said.

Sleeping with the Enemy

Twentieth Century-Fox, 1991, color, 99 minutes
Director: Joseph Ruben
Cast: Julia Roberts, Patrick Bergin, Kevin Anderson, Elizabeth Lawrence, and Kyle Secor

*A*ppearances can be quite deceiving. For example, we think we want to be with someone so much, only to discover after we

have entered a relationship with that person that it is not at all what we anticipated. Then what to do, especially after discovering that the other person is a deeply disturbed individual who won't let go?

On the surface, Roberts and her financial consultant husband Bergin appear to have an ideal marriage. But after four years of togetherness, she knows all too well his evil private side: he is an obsessive and frighteningly possessive man. Because she was always too insecure and shy, she feared taking action to end the nightmare. However, now she plans her escape. She fakes being drowned in a storm and scurries away from Cape Cod with a new identity. Her destination is Cedar Falls, Iowa, where she can be close to her blind, ailing mother. As she settles into her new life, she lets down her guard enough to begin a romantic relationship with Anderson, a young drama instructor at the college in town. Then all hell breaks loose.

A series of events leads Bergin to conclude that his prized possession is not dead, and he craftily tracks Julia to the Midwest. Determined to punish his wife for daring to leave him—and make him feel like a fool—he eventually sneaks into Roberts's home and awaits her return. After Patrick confronts her,

Kevin arrives on the scene and is injured in a scuffle with the intruder. When the insane Patrick comes after Julia, the two struggle and she grabs his gun. After phoning for police help, she is forced to shoot Bergin.

Talk about movies where the heroine does dumb things when covering her trail as she vanishes into a new life. Is she secretly hoping the abusive creep will track her down so she can polish him off and have the last word in revenge? Where were her gut instincts when she first dated this twisted bastard? Aren't leading ladies supposed to have any brains?

Fear

Universal, 1996, color, 97 minutes
Director: James Foley
Cast: Mark Wahlberg, Reese Witherspoon, William Petersen, Amy Brenneman, and Alyssa Milano

*P*romoted with the ad line "Together forever. Or else," *Fear* is one of those *Fatal Attraction* (1987) rip-offs but with a decided edge—thanks to Wahlberg's disturbing performance and the R-rated violence.

In Seattle, Washington, pretty sixteen-year-old Witherspoon attends a rave where she meets hunky slacker Mark. Reese is quickly entranced by this handsome ne'er-do-well. When she excitedly brings her new boyfriend home to meet the family—which includes her architect father (Petersen), her stepmother (Brenneman), and the latter's young son (Christopher Gray)—he is

Singer Mark Wahlberg proved his acting mettle in such films as *Fear* (1996), in which he played the vengeful lover.   Photo by Albert L. Ortega

extremely polite and controlled. Nevertheless, William sees through the subterfuge and observes that the newcomer has a dark nature, but his daughter won't heed his warnings. Later, when Mark beats up a boy from school just because the boy hugs her, she begins to change her opinion of Wahlberg.

Things escalate further out of hand when William pays a visit to Mark's pad and discovers just how obsessed Wahlberg has become with his daughter. As a warning to stay away from her, Petersen wrecks the place. In revenge, Mark and his pals lay siege to Petersen's home. The escalating violence climaxes in a fierce struggle between William and Mark, with the latter tumbling out of a window to his death.

It is true that the three young leads (including Milano) in *Fear* are attractive and the plot formula is serviceable (whether you take the film seriously or for laughs). However, did you catch the onscreen dynamics between dad and daughter as he seeks to control, protect, and share too much space with his blossoming offspring? It should be enough to make anyone glad they don't have to live this heroine's life for real.

The First Wives Club

Paramount, 1996, color, 102 minutes
Director: Hugh Wilson
Cast: Goldie Hawn, Bette Midler, Diane Keaton, Maggie Smith, and Sarah Jessica Parker

*W*hen one of their college friends commits suicide after being dumped by her husband for a younger woman, her three pals (Hawn, Midler, and Keaton) examine their own domestic situations. They discover that they are very much in the same boat. Determined not to be victims in the domestic wars, they take matters into their own hands. Through shrewd manipulations they each manage to put their husbands behind the

proverbial eight ball, whether regarding careers, their financial holdings, or their new girl toys. Admitting defeat, the three husbands agree to fund the opening of a women's crisis center. By the finale, only Midler and her mate (Dan Hedaya) have patched up their romantic differences; the other two women have moved on with their lives.

Told with verve—that often lunges into out-and-out slapstick—*The First Wives Club* is based to a degree on a real-life group in Los Angeles. While the movie is a humorous tribute to women discarded by mates wanting new, young companions by their side, this threesome of pampered matrons leads too plush a life for us to feel really sorry for them. With their knack at delivering a song (e.g., "You Don't Own Me") in the picture, maybe they should spend their free time more productively—like auditioning for TV's *American Idol*.

An Anthem to Regrets

One (Keaton) of the trio of jilted spouses in *The First Wives Club* tells her ungrateful spouse (Stephen Collins): "I'm very sorry I ever met you. And I'm sorry that I allowed myself to love you for all those years. I'm sorry that I did nothing but be there for you every minute of every hour and support you in your every move. I'm sorry!"

By the end of this screen comedy, he's the very sorry one, indeed.

A Perfect Murder

Warner Bros., 1998, color, 107 minutes
Director: Andrew Davis
Cast: Michael Douglas, Gwyneth Paltrow,
Viggo Mortensen, David Suchet, and
Sarita Choudhury

Sometimes a movie's ad campaign (let alone the film's title) tells you far more than it should. For example, regarding *A Perfect Murder*, the teaser lines read: "A powerful husband. An unfaithful wife. A jealous lover. All of them have a motive. Each of them has a plan." Perhaps the moviemakers thought that because the picture was already promoted as a remake of Alfred Hitchcock's *Dial M for Murder* (1954)—the classy screen thriller starring Ray Milland and Grace Kelly—there was no need to keep silent about the new edition's basic plot.

In this updated version, Douglas is an apparently prosperous Wall Street bond dealer married to a much younger woman (Paltrow), an interpreter at the United Nations. Michael discovers that she is having an affair with a young painter (Mortensen) but does not confront her. Instead, he offers the flustered Viggo an alternative: murder Gwyneth for a $500,000 fee or have his unresolved criminal background brought to the fore. But, on the scheduled night of the killing, Viggo sends an associate to do the deed, and Paltrow kills the intruder.

Not to worry. A game Douglas swings with the plot punches. He meets again with Mortensen, only to be blackmailed with a recording of him explaining to Viggo how to enter the apartment and commit the murder. The painter, who is really indifferent to Paltrow, thinks he has pulled a fast one on Douglas, but the joke is on him. Viggo is soon dead. By now, Gwyneth finally is figuring out the situation: her husband is actually deeply in debt, she has a large estate that would pass to him on her demise, and she's discovered the apartment key that Michael had left for the killer to use. Not profiting from the knowl-

Gwyneth Paltrow plays a woman who must deal with a homicidal husband in *A Perfect Murder* (1998). Photo by Albert L. Ortega

Get a Clue

It doesn't take a genius to figure out that the focal couple in *A Perfect Murder* needs more help than a marriage counselor can provide:

Paltrow: "We'll work it out? Let me tell you something, you work it out on your f**king own! This is over!"
Douglas: "You're not leaving me; the only way you leave me is dead!"

Or:

Douglas: "When you wake up tomorrow, all this will seem like a bad dream."
Paltrow: "What if there is no tomorrow?"

great showcase. Ignore that the picture's title leaves itself wide open for puns, or that the film's ad line ("Everyone has their limit") prodded some critics to detail their own cinematic thresholds. What's of interest here is that Lopez functions as a Charles Bronson–like vengeance machine. It suggests that in the new millennium there are more options for battered women than shelters and the court system.

Waitress Jennifer marries rich, handsome Campbell and they have a child (Allen). All

Jennifer Lopez plays a woman who studies martial arts to survive her murderous mate in *Enough* (2002). Photo by Albert L. Ortega

edge that his wife killed the last trespasser who threatened her harm, Douglas attempts to do her in. Who loses this final tug-of-war is easy to guess.

Enough

Columbia, 2002, color, 114 minutes
Director: Michael Apted
Cast: Jennifer Lopez, Bill Campbell, Tessa Allen, Juliette Lewis, and Dan Futterman

*F*orget for the moment that the scripting and directing of this action revenge feature leave a great deal to be desired, or that as a star vehicle for personable Lopez it's not a

seems blissful, despite hubby's strange mood swings (which should have immediately sent the heroine and child packing). She discovers eventually that he is having a series of affairs. When confronted, his response is to physically abuse Lopez. In quick succession she finds ways to protect herself and discovers (thanks to plot manipulations, loopholes, and so forth) that her only real chance is to take her daughter and run. Being an intuitive super sleuth, clean-cut Bill pursues her relentlessly, tracking her down wherever she goes. What he doesn't know before the showdown occurs is that the once-meek Lopez has been studying self-defense and is now a tough crackerjack at the sport. Woe to Campbell when he as the proverbial bad penny turns up one time too many. All of which leads the story line to

the movie's other ad line: "Self-defense isn't murder." You figure it out from there.

Domestic abuse is no laughing matter in real life, but, at times, it comes close to such here.

Hey, here's an idea for you to consider. Instead of getting involved romantically/sexually with a jerk that everyone warns you is ultra-bad news, how about saying no to the temptation right from the start. It would certainly eliminate potential later grief with Mr. or Miss Bad News. Don't worry, you can still play out your revenge fantasies vicariously through Hollywood's ongoing crop of sweet revenge entries.

15

Love Affairs to Remember

When used together, the relatively simple words *love* and *affair* take on a variety of meanings. The phrase might mean a rapturous romance between two young lovers, each of whom is single and not committed to another. Or it could suggest, at the opposite extreme, a couple, one or both of whom are wed to others, being involved intimately.

Reactions to this two-word expression have greatly altered over the years. For example, in the twentieth century, society's laws on domestic relationships, moral standards, and customs changed, usually moving from the strict to the much more liberal. The newly accepted notions of what was acceptable romantic (and/or sexual) behavior between a man and a woman affected how the public at large regarded the term *love affair*.

It is hard for today's young generation to appreciate that, just several decades ago, chastity was expected (if not always maintained) by both men and (especially) women until they married. For a couple to have premarital sex—let alone live together without

benefit of clergy—was considered shocking. For an individual to enjoy a sexual relationship with a married person was, according to society, committing adultery, one of the activities vetoed in the Bible's Ten Commandments.

In contrast, nowadays consenting sex between adults (even teenagers), whether they are wed or not, fails to raise many scornful eyebrows. Paralleling this change in what is considered proper—even legal—behavior has been the community's attitudes toward marriage. Not so many generations ago, it used to be that if a couple wed they were expected—and contemplated the same themselves—to stay wed for their lifetime. Currently, if one studies statistics on the history of the divorce rate in the United States and elsewhere, such a notion is given, at best, lip service by most people. Brides and grooms today often have hardly unpacked their wedding gifts before they are filing for separation and/or splitting for good. Then too, having a failed first marriage, apparently, has little impact on a person before he or she jumps into the next domestic situation. These days nothing is forever. The only thing that apparently counts is "living for the moment."

Hollywood has taken all of this into consideration as, over the twentieth century and into the new millennium, it produced its feature film output dealing with love affairs.

Back Street

Universal, 1932, black-and-white,
86 minutes
Director: John M. Stahl
Cast: Irene Dunne, John Boles, George Meeker, ZaSu Pitts, and June Clyde

*B*ased on Fannie Hurst's popular, if old-fashioned, 1932 novel, this woman's picture helped to consolidate Dunne's reputation as a queen of the screen weepers. The movie itself (remade in both 1941 and 1961) became a benchmark of the Hollywood tearjerker par excellence. As the genre required—and filmgoers (especially female) demanded—the heroine is long-suffering but generally a good sport about the love relationship that has thrust her into social disgrace and loneliness. Regarding the man in the situation, in that era of strong double standards, his responsibility in creating compromised moral circumstances was regarded far less critically by observers. In turn, this wink-and-a-smile attitude—especially by other men—about the male in the immoral caper resulted in far less damage to his reputation or community status.

Near the turn of the twentieth century, a few months before he is to wed another woman, the young banker Boles meets Cincinnati-based Dunne. The two fall deeply in love. He arranges for her to meet his mother in the park. But on the important date, Irene is helping her sister out of an emotional scrape. As a result, the still-single Irene doesn't see John for another five years until they chance upon one another in New York City. By then he is married and has two children. However, he swears he still loves her desperately, and he installs her in an apartment. Because of his professional and social prominence, they must never be seen together publicly. Her life revolves around those few times when he can break away to be with her.

When Boles learns that one of Irene's past suitors has resuggested marriage, John ends that possibility by stressing to his mistress that he cannot live without her. As such, their affair continues for twenty-five years. Eventually, Boles's children learn of their father's affair, but the wife never discovers the deception. While on a trip to Paris, John dies, with his last thoughts being of Dunne. His son (Richard Bakewell) visits Irene, promising that he will take care of her financially because she was not mentioned in her lover's will. After Bakewell departs, Irene fantasizes how different her life would have been if she had not missed that fateful park meeting years ago. Lost in her memories, she dies.

In today's moral climate, such hypocrisy and noble suffering would never wash. However, at least onscreen, and especially in bygone times, such emotional martyrdom seemed the height of delicious romance. Try sitting home night after night, week after week, waiting for your loved one to spend a few stolen moments with you. The idea doesn't seem very promising, does it?

Anna Karenina

Metro-Goldwyn-Mayer, 1935, black-and-white, 95 minutes
Director: Clarence Brown
Cast: Greta Garbo, Fredric March, Freddie Bartholomew, Maureen O'Sullivan, and Basil Rathbone

Leo Tolstoy's novel (1876) of an aristocratic Russian woman who flouts convention for the sake of a grand affair had been filmed previously by Garbo as the silent movie *Love* (1927) with screen idol John Gilbert as her costar. At that time, she was at

I Have That Certain Feeling

Anna Karenina is filled with ominous premonitions of what is to befall the lead characters. For example, early in the feature, as Garbo and her brother (Reginald Owen) depart the railroad station, they witness the accidental death of a worker who is sucked under the wheels of a moving train. The soulful Greta notes—quite correctly—that this is an "evil omen." Later, as Garbo and March scamper off to Italy for an illicit holiday, the heroine has a strong feeling that they'll be "punished for being so happy." Still further in the proceedings, the leading lady predicts (quite correctly), "One day I shall find myself alone."

the height of her heavily promoted romance with Gilbert, and the movie adaptation was another showcase to exploit their situation. To make the silent picture entry more appealing to filmgoers, the story line was made contemporary and the plot had the tragic heroine survive (!) at the finale. Addressing those artistic differences from Tolstoy's book, the 1935 film rendition strives to more faithfully adhere to the emotional and social repercussions the heroine suffers for her indiscretions. (To be noted, in typical chauvinistic fashion, the hero makes few long-term sacrifices himself for defying conventions and for leading Anna Karenina into living in sin with him.)

In late-nineteenth-century Russia, Garbo is wed to an important government official (Rathbone), and together they have a child

(Bartholomew). On a visit to Moscow from St. Petersburg, Greta meets dashing March, a young officer of the royal guard. There is immediate chemistry between the two, both of them ignoring the fact that she is already wed and a mother. When Garbo returns home, she is taken aback that the smitten Fredric has followed her and is insistent on furthering their relationship. Unable to control their passion, the two enter into an affair.

Soon Rathbone as well as March's superior officers are aware of the scandalous situation. Fredric pressures his mistress to make a com

plete break with her husband. Meanwhile, the arrogant Basil insists his wife choose between her lover and the respectability of marriage. If she picks dishonor, she will be banished from their home and be prohibited from seeing their son ever again. Ruled by her heart, she goes with March on a "honeymoon" to Venice. When they return to Russia, he is angered at his banishment from the army. He abandons Greta to join his regiment in fighting a war. Hoping to see him one last time, Garbo rushes to the railroad station only to find him bidding farewell to a new sweet-

A married woman (Greta Garbo) sacrifices her family and social position to be with her soldier lover (Fredric March) in *Anna Karenina* (1935). Courtesy of JC Archives

heart. In despondency she throws herself under a passing train.

Some might say that the heroine's lack of self-control brought all her problems crashing down on her. Other more dreamy souls see her suicide as a grand romantic gesture. But keep in mind that if you wanted to attempt such a final act today, you'd have to deal with the unreliability of Amtrak. If Anna had to do that, the poor dear might still be stuck at the station waiting for any train finally to pass her way.

Intermezzo, A Love Story

Selznick International/United Artists, 1939, black-and-white, 70 minutes
Director: Gregory Ratoff
Cast: Leslie Howard, Ingrid Bergman, Edna Best, John Halliday, and Cecil Kellaway

*I*n the course of this film about "immoral" love in the world of music, the heroine assesses her torrid affair with a married man: "Let's say I have been an intermezzo in his life." This speech is what gives the drama its title and taught the average moviegoer a new word: *intermezzo* (i.e., a short dramatic or musical diversion between entertainments or situations). With its famous love theme by Heinz Provost, this feature introduced the Swedish-born Ingrid Bergman to American moviegoers.

World-famous concert violinist Howard is contentedly married to Best with whom he has two children. After he returns home from

A radiant Ingrid Bergman shares an illicit romance with married Leslie Howard in *Intermezzo, A Love Story* (1939).   Courtesy of JC Archives

a lengthy tour, Leslie falls in love with Bergman, the tutor of his young daughter (Ann Todd). For her part, Ingrid, a pianist with great promise, has long professionally admired Leslie and easily slips into a romantic intrigue with him. Her conscience soon gets the better of her, and she attempts to leave him. He is unable to let her go and instead leaves his family. He and his paramour

Unable to Enjoy the Moment

If you insist on chancing an illicit love affair, keep your ears alert for any of the following statements from your beloved. It could signal highly dangerous romantic waters ahead.

- "Oh, I am ashamed, and I hate being ashamed. . . . We can't go on lying to people who trust us. It's impossible. It's unbearable!"

- "I tried to pretend there was no past."

- "What am I, your shadow? I don't exist without you. . . . But it is enough. Let me be with you like this, always."

- "I wonder if anyone has ever built happiness on the unhappiness of others."

go on a long holiday to the Continent. Their happiness is marred by their guilt over having made his family innocent victims. When her mentor (Halliday) advises Ingrid she has won a long-hoped-for music scholarship, he uses the situation to convince Bergman to release her hold on Howard. She returns home, as does Leslie. The latter must endure his daughter's near death in an auto accident before he and his wife reconcile.

If you ever find yourself embroiled in a sticky romantic situation like the one depicted in *Intermezzo*, please take a cue from Bergman's Anna Hoffman. Try sending your loved one an E-mail saying, "We know in our hearts that love like ours is wrong—that it drags itself down with remorse and fears and

the unhappiness of others." It may just work and get you out of a no-win situation.

Also keep in mind that the love match depicted so tenderly in *Intermezzo* was filled with problems. Howard is an egocentric lost in the glory of celebrity; how long would he have put up with Bergman as she undoubtedly rose in the musical world and perhaps stole away some of his limelight? Then too, he was nearly twice her age and a bit of a wimp who seemingly couldn't get along without his faithful, practical spouse (Best) who kept his life and home in immaculate order. Was Ingrid's heroine ready—or even able—to take on such heavy domestic responsibilities?

At least, now having seen this picture, you know where that wonderfully haunting love theme ("Intermezzo") comes from.

The Letter

Warner Bros., 1940, black-and-white, 95 minutes
Director: William Wyler
Cast: Bette Davis, Herbert Marshall, James Stephenson, Frieda Inescort, and Gale Sondergaard

Few screen dramas from Hollywood's golden age—or later—have been so atmospheric (especially considering the bulk of it was shot on studio sets) or given their leading ladies such great, dramatic entries. The setting is a rubber plantation some distance from Singapore in Malaysia. Beneath a full moon gunshots are heard as a man staggers out onto the veranda. He is soon followed by Davis (clad in a dressing gown) who calmly fires the rest of the revolver load into the victim. Later, when confronted by her husband (Marshall), who had been away on business, and family friend/attorney Stephenson, Bette insists, "He tried to make love to me and I shot him."

We viewers guess, and the houseboys lurking in the shadows already know, that calculating Davis is lying. Soon even her extremely proper barrister is suspicious of her and sneers, "I don't want you to tell me anything but what is needed to save your neck." Only her poor sap of a husband, still totally in love with her after ten years, doesn't see the truth. Bette had been carrying on a long-term affair with a local white man, a relationship that terminated when he had the temerity to marry—worst of all—a Eurasian woman (Sondergaard). In a jealous snit Bette had written him to come see her that fateful night or she wouldn't "answer for the consequences." He complies and is murdered. The lawyer reluctantly helps his client retrieve the

vital letter from the widow. There are conditions attached: the vengeful woman demands $10,000 and Bette must deliver the money in person.

With the damaging evidence now out of the way, the defendant is freed. However, Herbert belatedly discovers the contents of the document, and it leads to his wife's confession with the all-crushing line: "With all my heart, I still love the man I killed." (To appease the industry's self-censorship administration, the finale has Bette paying the supreme price for her adultery and murder.)

The movie is dated because of its colonialist attitudes and its bigotry against mixed-blooded people, but it is a gripping study of a very civilized man who makes a gut-wrenching admission to his erring wife, "If you love a person you can forgive anything." Talk about blind love! It is also a picture of a very controlled woman who becomes a victim of her obsession with her lover. (She admits, "I was like a person with some loathsome disease who doesn't want to get well.")

A Letter to Three Wives

Twentieth Century-Fox, 1949, black-and-white, 103 minutes
Director: Joseph L. Mankiewicz
Cast: Jeanne Crain, Linda Darnell, Ann Sothern, Kirk Douglas, and Paul Douglas

Writer/director Mankiewicz won two Oscars for this scintillating study of marriage, adultery, and the ties that bind people in

Ann Sothern, Linda Darnell, and Jeanne Crain each suspect that their husband is the man who has run off with an ex-friend of theirs in *A Letter to Three Wives* (1949).   Courtesy of JC Archives

romantic relationships. In a suburban New York community, as three married women (Crain, Darnell, and Sothern) embark on an excursion boat, they receive a note from a mutually disliked girlfriend (the voice of Celeste Holm) saying that she has left town and taken a "sort of memento" with her— i.e., one of their husbands. Because they are stuck on the Hudson River pleasure craft, the trio must pretend nothing is wrong to the others, all the while wondering if they are the victim of the man-grabbing ex-friend. By the finale, the ladies—including both Jeanne and Linda, whose husbands (Jeffrey Lynn and Paul Douglas, respectively) were "missing" when they returned from the boating trip— discover that they still have ample opportunities to repair their marriages.

Offcamera Shenanigans

During the making of *A Letter to Three Wives*, beauteous **Linda Darnell (1921–1965),** then still wed to cinematographer **Peverell Marley (1899–1964),** began a love affair with director Mankiewicz, who was twelve years her senior. Linda and the filmmaker also worked together in *No Way Out* (1950). Their romance ended soon thereafter. She always claimed that she was the inspiration for his 1954 feature *The Barefoot Contessa*.

The fateful day trip depicted in *A Letter to Three Wives* might have been a test drive for the TV series *The Love Boat* (1977–1986). These three contrasting types certainly could have used the wisdom of a Captain Stubing or bartender Isaac Washington.

Strangers When We Meet

Columbia, 1960, color, 117 minutes
Director: Richard Quine
Cast: Kirk Douglas, Kim Novak, Ernie Kovacs, Barbara Rush, and Walter Matthau

Visually stunning and often emotionally empty, this glorified soap opera thrusts Douglas and Novak—each married to another—into romantic proximity. Before long they are in breathless pursuit of one another and so engulfed by the heat of passion that they contemplate starting life over together. But can architect Kirk tear himself away from his loyal wife (Rush) and their two offspring? No way! Can Kim leave her mate, undemonstrative though he may be? Nope! So Douglas and Novak separate for good when he departs with his family to undertake a huge building commission in Hawaii. The two ex-lovebirds know that, in the future, they will be strangers when they next meet.

Besides the presence of two such healthy specimens as Novak and Douglas and the distraction of Kovacs in a dramatic assignment as an oddball, successful writer, there is Matthau as a slimy lech. Although married, his character doesn't hesitate to make a play for Rush when he discovers that Kirk is fooling around with Kim. Not only does Barbara reject his unwanted advances, but he is the beneficiary of a sock in the nose from Douglas. This prompts Matthau to respond philosophically, "How are we any different from each other?" Kirk has no ready answer for that, but it sets him on the moral path for the movie's righteous finale.

So folks, if you don't want to (further) jeopardize your marriage, when you decide on major upgrades to your home, rather than hiring an architect, stick to Home Depot and do the repairs yourself. It could be a lot cheaper than divorce court.

The Sandpiper

Metro-Goldwyn-Mayer, 1965, color, 116 minutes
Director: Vincente Minnelli
Cast: Elizabeth Taylor, Richard Burton, Eva Marie Saint, Charles Bronson, and Robert Webber

There's nothing like a real-life scandal to bolster the proceeds of a movie. Having begun their love affair during the making of *Cleopatra* (1963) in Rome while each was married to another, the superstar couple did not wed until the spring of 1964. By then they'd costarred in *The V.I.P.s* (1963). Eager for a quick, fresh cash influx to support their extravagant lifestyle, the high-profile duo contracted to make this piece of junk for which Taylor was paid $1 million and Burton received $750,000. The producers got their money's worth because the trashy feature grossed $7 million in domestic distribution. The claptrap project even won an Oscar—for the film's theme song, "The Shadow of Your Smile," by Paul Francis Webster and Johnny Mandel.

Painter Taylor, a free soul, and her illegitimate boy (Morgan Mason) reside in a plush ocean-view cabin in Monterey, California. A bohemian, Elizabeth only reluctantly sends her maladjusted offspring to private school when pushed to do so by a local judge. The institution of choice is run by an Episcopalian minister (Burton). As the youngster settles into his new environment, Taylor and the married Burton become romantically involved, with Liz rhapsodizing, "I never knew what love was before." Before long, he

Once Is Good, Twice Is Better

To date, **Richard Burton (1925–1984)** has been the only mate that **Elizabeth Taylor (b. 1932)** has married twice. Their first nuptials took place in 1964 in Montreal, Canada, while he was in a pre-Broadway tour of *Hamlet*. Divorced in June 1974, the couple rewed in October 1975. This time the site of choice was a mud hut village on the Botswana game preserve in Africa. Less than a year later, the twosome divorced again.

A Deed So Despicable

At one juncture in the overly melodramatic *The Sandpiper*, a self-reproaching Burton tells Saint of his gross misconduct with Taylor: "We made love—even in motels. God help me!"

Richard Burton and Elizabeth Taylor conduct an oncamera adulterous relationship in *The Sandpiper* (1965).
Courtesy of JC Archives

is embarrassed—no, make that ashamed—by the weakness of his flesh. (At one point, he scowls, "Oh, God, grant me some small remembrance of honor!") When their fling becomes common knowledge, the school officials demand his departure. Before obliging, he lectures these duplicitous types on their self-serving ways and then marches off into the sunset. However, he's not accompanied by either Taylor or by his wife (Saint). Why? He's hoping to rediscover the ideals that had inspired him in youthful days.

A Guide for the Married Man

Twentieth Century-Fox, 1967, color, 89 minutes
Director: Gene Kelly
Cast: Walter Matthau, Robert Morse, Inger Stevens, Sue Ane Langdon, and Claire Kelly

*E*xpert lech Morse decides it's his divine duty to instruct a basically contented mar-

Fit for a Sampler

Perhaps the boisterous theme of this cinema sex romp is best summed up by the Oscar Wilde quote used as one of the movie's story line captions: "The one charm of marriage is that it makes a life of deception absolutely necessary for both parties."

ried suburbanite (Matthau) on the ways and means of committing adultery and how *not* to get caught in the process. Says smug Robert, "Basic principle number one: never, *never* say you'll be where you can be found not to be."

With such a mentor, Walter is quickly on the road to ruin. Morse peppers his seminars with pertinent examples of sex-chasing people he knows (which allows for a series of vignettes featuring cameos by such diverse personalities as Jack Benny, Lucille Ball, Art Carney, and Jayne Mansfield). Because this breezy feature was unleashed in the relatively still moralistic 1960s, there has to be just desserts for all parties. Philandering Morse gets caught with his pants down while pursuing Langdon. As for Matthau, he quickly decides that such extracurricular activities are better left as fantasies. He rushes home to his adoring wife (Stevens), announcing with a sigh of relief, "There's no place like home!"

Sneaky Robert Morse is the center of attention in *A Guide for the Married Man* (1967) as (left to right) Sue Ane Langdon, Jackie Russell, Inger Stevens, and Walter Matthau pivot in his devious orbit.
Courtesy of JC Archives

Hannah and Her Sisters

Orion, 1986, color, 106 minutes
Director: Woody Allen
Cast: Woody Allen, Michael Caine, Mia Farrow, Barbara Hershey, and Dianne Wiest

*B*oasting a great complexity of interrelationships among its characters, this superior Allen entry is a sophisticated blend of drama and wry comedy. In focusing on a Manhattan theatrical family (aged parents Maureen O'Sullivan and Lloyd Nolan and their four daughters: Farrow, Hershey, Wiest, and Carrie Fisher), the subjects of love, fidelity, and adultery are effectively explored.

The story momentum builds at a family dinner where Caine, married to Farrow, realizes he has a yen for his sister-in-law (Barbara). Pursuing the matter, he suggests to wanna-be actress Hershey that he accompany her to an AA meeting, to which she responds, "You'd have a good time. I know you would." While their mismatched togetherness is running its fruitless course, hypochondriac Allen,

Mia's ex-spouse, when not convinced that he has a fatal brain tumor, courts one of his ex-sisters-in-law (Wiest). Their mutual disdain turns into admiration and love. At the next family Thanksgiving dinner, arch cynic Woody is surprised and overjoyed to learn that Dianne, his new wife, is pregnant. He has

How to Protect Your Low Self-Esteem on a Date

- If your new love interest happens to be a would-be writer who wants to read you her latest effort, explain, as did Allen to Wiest in *Hannah and Her Sisters*, "I've been doing all my own reading since I was forty."

- When your companion explains her taste in music, shoot her a disdainful look and scoff, "You don't deserve Cole Porter. You should stay with those guys that look like they're going to stab their mother."

Woody's Special World

The diminutive, bespectacled **Woody Allen (b. 1935)** has had a series of romantic alliances ranging from comedian/actress Louise Lasser (wife number two) to actresses Diane Keaton and Jessica Harper. His long-time significant other was frequent costar **Mia Farrow (b. 1945)**. When that union fell apart in a scandal involving his special relationship to Mia's Korean adopted daughter, Soon-Yi, Farrow was replaced in Allen's next picture, *Manhattan Murder Mystery* (1993), by still-pal, Keaton. Woody and Soon-Yi wed in 1996.

rediscovered that real life is more refreshing than a Marx Brothers movie.

Unfaithful

Twentieth Century-Fox, 2002, color, 123 minutes
Director: Adrian Lyne
Cast: Richard Gere, Diane Lane, Olivier Martinez, Chad Lowe, and Kate Burton

Lyne, who gave us *Fatal Attraction* (1987), turns again to the sexual thriller genre in this remake of Claude Chabrol's *La Femme Infidele* (1969). The film's theme of sexual hungering is centered on a foundation of "Be happy for this moment, for this moment is your life."

A seemingly content suburban New York housewife (Lane) doesn't realize how much her comfortable marriage to successful Gere—with whom she has a nine-year-old son—is lacking in sexual passion and fulfillment. That discovery comes one day in Manhattan when, during a windstorm, she is literally thrown into contact with a handsome stranger (Martinez). He's a hunk with a sexy foreign accent who invites her upstairs to his loft to repair her scrapes. She quickly discovers that this rare-book dealer has a graduate degree in pleasing a woman. He always knows just the flattering thing to say, "Your eyes are amazing, do you know that? You should never shut them, not even at night." Before long

Don'ts for a Married Woman Having an Affair

- If a seductive Calvin Klein model–type invites you up to his place to see his book collection, say no. Inform him you belong to the Book-of-the-Month Club.

- Never leave your name and/or phone number on your lover's answering machine. Give the affair some mystery. Besides, it makes it too easy for someone checking up on you.

- Avoid such adolescent whims as following your boyfriend into the coffee shop rest room and taking forever to return to your girlfriends left at the table. They can, after all, eat a muffin *and* be quite observant at the same time.

- When that new special man provides you with exciting, arduous sex, don't say, "Thank you." Remind him that you have a back condition and that you receive a sufficient workout at the chiropractor.

Gere becomes suspicious and hires a private detective, and his wife's heavy-duty affair is uncovered. This leads to a deadly encounter between Richard and Olivier. What remains is how the once mutually satisfied couple cope with each other's secrets, especially when the police become involved. That the ambiguous finale seems a pat cop-out is one of the picture's weak points.

The believable characterizations provided by Gere and Lane are what give *Unfaithful* its strength. As the story develops, they are each surprised by how extended togetherness can breed indifference and how a sudden crisis can reignite their mutual emotional ties. However, wouldn't a marriage counselor be a far safer way of rediscovering the path back to a loving marriage situation?

In summation, I defer to movie star Richard Dreyfuss who explained once, "People who commit adultery must die. Everyone knows that. Any movie tells you that!"

16

Till Death Do Us Part

When couples are young and in the midst of a great romance, their optimism is often boundless and the promise of eternal togetherness (as in "I'll love you forever") seems more a realistic assessment of what lies ahead than a mere flight of passionate fancy. At this young age and caught up in an emotional high, one foresees the future—and the joys of sharing daily life with a loved one—as stretching on endlessly. How tragic, then, when such devotion is cut short by one of the partner's dying—long before his or her expected time to pass away. While such dying is tragic for the soon-to-be deceased, it is a crushing, weighty blow to the survivor who now has only memories of what once was for comfort.

Yet, the prospect of eventual death should not be a total surprise to any rational individual—it is, after all, the end of the life cycle. However, some of us refuse to deal with this inevitability and deliberately turn our thoughts elsewhere. But society keeps reminding us that the future for any individual on Earth has its time limits. For example, in many marriage ceremonies—a point of great celebration and hope for what lies ahead—custom has dictated that such nuptials frequently contain a somber reference for the couple to reflect on: "till death do us part."

Hollywood knows that many moviegoers enjoy a good cry as much as a hearty laugh—each being a form of distracting and satisfying entertainment. With this in mind, filmmakers have long provided audiences with such vicarious emotional releases in their pictures. Over the decades, they have produced many tearjerkers involving romantic relationships suddenly ended by the demise of a love partner. If one or both of the characters know that death (e.g., from a terminal disease or punishment from the legal system) lies ahead, it makes the story all the more satisfyingly bittersweet and weepy for the viewer. Add into the mix the situation where the soon-to-die figure is in the bloom of youth, and the sad tale becomes that much more emotionally involving.

♥   ♥   ♥   ♥   ♥

Camille

Metro-Goldwyn-Mayer, 1937, black-and-white, 105 minutes
Director: George Cukor
Cast: Greta Garbo, Robert Taylor, Lionel Barrymore, Elizabeth Allan, and Jessie Ralph

*I*n book, stage, and film form, this celebrated tale of the sophisticated prostitute living in 1840s France has long been a favorite with the public. When the divine Garbo starred in her rendition of this Alexandre Dumas work, audiences flocked to see her portray the infamous Lady of the Camellias who finds the first great love of her life, only to have fate deal her a nasty blow.

Having come to Paris six years earlier, a former farm girl (Garbo) has turned into a beautiful courtesan, one noted for her extravagances. Urged by friends to seriously plan for the future, she has taken a wealthy, middle-aged baron (Henry Daniell) as her new lover. But Greta is soon distracted by a sincere young man (Taylor) of the middle class who showers her with expressions of his devoted love. Choosing passion over money, she follows Robert's advice to move to the country and gain a fresh approach to life. More important, he hopes the country air will help her recover from her recurring tuberculosis. One day, Taylor's father (Barrymore) visits her and begs the worldly woman to give up his son

Did You Catch the Warning Signs?

Love can be blind, but you owe it to yourself to shake loose from your romantic trance to really listen to and observe your date. There may be telltale warnings that the relationship is doomed to end abruptly:

- Does she frequently spit up blood into her handkerchief?

- Is your girlfriend subject to fainting spells and periods of no energy?

- When you gave her a novel (an Oprah book selection, no less), did she say offhandedly, "I don't like sad stories. But we all die . . . so perhaps this will be sold at my auction."

- After you bared your soul and expressed eternal love for her, did she casually counter with, "You will never love me for thirty years. No one will."

- Following your reconciliation after that last big argument, did she suggest, "Perhaps it's better if I live in your heart where the world can't see me. If I am dead there will be no staying of our love."

because associating with her will ruin his potential career in the diplomatic service. As a result, she tells her lover she no longer loves him and sends him away. Next, she returns to Paris and continues her reckless life with the baron. Before long, Garbo's ailment resurfaces

A devastated Robert Taylor holds his dying lover (Greta Garbo) in *Camille* (1937).   Courtesy of JC Archives

and she becomes gravely ill. Learning of her plight and the truth of why she had rejected him, Robert visits her. After gaining forgiveness from him, she dies in his arms.

Sumptuously photographed and showcasing Garbo at her most beautiful and most assured, the film earned an Oscar nomination for Greta, but she failed to win the Academy Award. That disappointment aside, the role established a benchmark for actresses portraying such ill-fated characters. But who in real life could match up to this Swedish celebrity in her professional and physical prime? Most women today could scarcely carry off wear-

The Divine Garbo

The Swedish-born star **Greta Garbo (1905–1990)**, known as a love goddess onscreen, never married in real life. While she had highly publicized romances with actor John Gilbert (whom she almost wed on a few occasions), film director Rouben Mamoulian, renowned music conductor Leopold Stokowski, and dietitian/lecturer Gaylord Hauser, one of her more intriguing romances—and greatest passions—was with socialite Mercedes de Acosta.

ing such frilly, bouffant costumes, let alone conveying the complex emotions of this tragic heroine who has seen too much of the world but not enough of life.

Dark Victory

Warner Bros., 1939, black-and-white,
105 minutes
Director: Edmund Goulding
Cast: Bette Davis, George Brent, Humphrey Bogart, Geraldine Fitzgerald, and Ronald Reagan

*T*his romantic, morbid tale (promoted as "The love story no woman will ever forget") is the cream of the crop when it comes to tragic screen love stories. Then at the peak of her box-office powers, Davis milks the celluloid narrative for every possible audience tear—and she succeeds admirably. She is cast as one of the Long Island horse set, the spoiled, rich twenty-three-year-old who insists, "I'm young and strong and nothing can touch me." She confides to her good friend (Fitzgerald), "I shall probably marry one day . . . no hurry for that." But there is, for she has been having bizarre physical symptoms throughout the past six months, including blurred vision, loss of short-term memory, numbness in her right hand, and severe headaches that won't quit.

Bette is referred to a Manhattan brain surgeon (Brent) who promptly diagnoses that she has a deadly growth in her head that requires immediate surgery. He operates, and

Handy Platitudes

If fate deals you a raw hand and, God forbid, your life expectancy is dangerously low, it helps to have a few ready-made words of comfort available to ease the pain of those around you. Here are a few bits of wisdom (from *Dark Victory*) to commit to memory should the situation warrant:

- "You know, I'm not afraid anymore."

- "When death comes, it comes as an old friend."

- "Nothing can hurt us now. What we have, can't be destroyed. That's our victory, our victory over the dark."

- "I'm the lucky one. All I'll miss is growing old and getting worn out."

- "I must show him I can do it [die] alone. Perhaps it will help him get over some bad moments."

Davis soon feels quite herself again. However, George is keeping from her the latest medical verdict in her case. The prognosis is negative—she will be dead within ten months, but she will go peacefully. She learns the horrifying truth, goes into denial and anger, and then, during acceptance, reconciles with patient Brent who has fallen in love with her. They marry and move to his Vermont farm where he conducts lab experiments that one day might save people with such medical problems as his wife. Just as he rushes off to

New York City to a medical conference to discuss his pathfinding lab results, she gets the physical warning signs that the end is upon her. She nobly sends him off as she goes upstairs to her bedroom where she peacefully awaits her finale.

At one time or another, many of us have morosely envisioned our sudden, tragic death, a passing—we tell ourselves—bound to make those in our inner circle weep with regret. Making the fantasy even more satisfying, we imagine dying in a brave, noble way. No sad songs for us, we say. We'll expire courageously and gallantly. If we could only be there to see how our loved ones and friends would weep at our death, that would make the maudlin dream complete. That would prove we'd made our mark on the world.

This is hogwash! Do some good, unselfish deeds now for others, while you are healthy and able. Substitute a glow of satisfaction for positive actions well done instead of that childish melancholy wish to make the world miss you and prove your importance.

A pensive Bette Davis ponders her bleak future while a concerned Humphrey Bogart tries to comfort her in *Dark Victory* (1939). Courtesy of JC Archives

Goodbye, Mr. Chips

Metro-Goldwyn-Mayer, 1939, black-and-white, 114 minutes
Director: Sam Wood
Cast: Robert Donat, Greer Garson, Terry Kilburn, John Mills, and Paul Henreid

This well-polished feature was shot at MGM's British studios and introduced redheaded Garson to American filmgoers. She has a relatively short role in this entry, seen as the radiant woman who renews the spark of life and happiness into a forty-year-old British schoolteacher (Donat).

As the new term begins in the 1930s at Brookfield School in England, the scene flashes back to 1870, when Robert, a new instructor, arrives at the venerable institution. His adjustment is slow, and he develops a protective shell as a strict disciplinarian, which hardens further over the years. While a dedicated teacher, he becomes unpopular with students and forgotten by those in charge. On a rare vacation, he travels to Austria where he encounters Greer. They fall in love and marry. With her warmth and verve he becomes a new man, now appreciated by faculty and students alike. However, during childbirth, Garson and their baby die. He overcomes his great grief by cherishing her memory and treating each new crop of students with great humanity. After he retires from Brookfield he lives nearby so he can watch over the incoming classes of students. On his deathbed, the eighty-something overhears his doctor saying what a misfortune it is that Donat never had children. The aged teacher corrects the physician: "You're wrong, I have. Thousands of them, thousands of them. And, all my boys."

This is a far cry from the schools depicted in such films as *Blackboard Jungle* (1955), *Stand and Deliver* (1988), or *American Pie* (1999). Such polite students. . . . Such immaculate classrooms. . . . Such sensitive coworkers. . . . Such sentiment!

Wuthering Heights

United Artists, 1939, black-and-white, 103 minutes
Director: William Wyler
Cast: Merle Oberon, Laurence Olivier, David Niven, Donald Crisp, and Geraldine Fitzgerald

Sometimes tragic love in a movie has a "happy" resolution, especially if one believes in the great hereafter and the film has a lush Alfred Newman background music score.

In England at the turn of the nineteenth century, a young orphan boy from the streets of Liverpool is taken by an aristocrat into a fancy estate on the coastal moors. At Wuthering Heights, the youth grows up to be a stable hand. Mistreated by the late aristocrat's cruel son (Hugh Williams), the worker (Olivier) remains because of his love for the offspring's beautiful sister (Oberon). However, Merle, anxious to escape the gloom of her brother's household, allows herself to fall in love with a wealthy, cheerful neighbor (Niven), and she marries him. This romantic betrayal sends the embittered Laurence away from Wuthering Heights. Years later he returns a wealthy man and buys control of Wuthering Heights. To exact further revenge on Merle, he weds her sister-in-law (Fitzgerald), treating Geraldine miserably. Later, when he learns that Oberon is very ill, he rushes to her bedside where she dies in his arms. His grief is immense and he becomes more brooding and cruel over the coming years. Long haunted by the sound of her crying out his name in the wind, one night, during a storm, he follows her voice to their secret meeting place. There, he is later found dead, and (in a vision) viewers witness the reunited couple strolling into eternity and to the peace of their childhood castle.

All right. Let's practice together: "Heathcliff! Heathcliff!"

The Eddy Duchin Story

Columbia, 1956, color, 123 minutes
Director: George Sidney
Cast: Tyrone Power, Kim Novak, Victoria Shaw, James Whitmore, and Rex Thompson

*M*any film watchers today may not be familiar with New York café society pianist/bandleader Eddy Duchin who held sway in the 1930s and 1940s before dying of leukemia in 1951. On the other hand, this gilt-edged musical admirably blends real-life biography with fiction and a great music score (with Carmen Cavallaro at the keyboard) to present a teary story of great love cut short. It's bound to strike responsive chords with most viewers.

Arriving in Manhattan from Boston, enthusiastic young musician Power works his way up in the entertainment world as a charming pianist. He romances socialite Novak and, despite their very different backgrounds, they wed. Shortly after giving birth to their child, she dies, leaving him bereft. He seeks escape in work, military duty during World War II, and so forth. Having abandoned his baby boy a decade earlier to the care of relatives, he now reestablishes a rapport with the youth—aided by an understanding British lady (Shaw) whom he weds. Once again, his happiness is cut short, this time by his own fatal disease.

So many tearful peaks pile up in this lushly emotional screen outing that the sheer number might make even easily pleased viewers jaded. However, because the courtship between ambitious Tyrone and self-confident, beautiful Kim is so effectively staged, viewers are won over. In the end, the musician's battle to win back his child's confidence and to find happiness in a new marriage has one rooting for the unlucky hero.

A word of advice: if you devote endless hours to practicing the piano to win the heart of your intended sweetheart with a private concert, plan your presentation carefully to make that romantic impression low-key and effective. Candelabras and sequin-studded ermine capes are a no-no. Really!

Love Story

Paramount, 1970, color, 100 minutes
Director: Arthur Hiller
Cast: Ali MacGraw, Ryan O'Neal, John Marley, Ray Milland, and Russell Nype

To this day no one is quite sure what this film's most quoted line ("Being in love means never having to say you're sorry") truly means. However, this oversweet movie confection made a box-office killing (more than $106 million in domestic distribution) and has gone down in pop culture as one of Tinseltown's greatest love stories.

Prelaw Harvard student O'Neal meets Radcliffe undergrad MacGraw. Their differ-

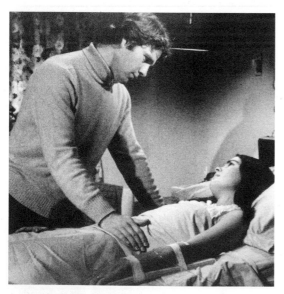

A gravely ill Ali MacGraw is watched over by her onscreen husband (Ryan O'Neal) in *Love Story* (1970). Courtesy of JC Archives

Pickup Lines— Cambridge Style

Most of us have never trod the Massachusetts campus of Harvard University, but there's nothing wrong with learning from the example of these Ivy Leaguers:

He: "You know . . . you're not that great looking."
She: "I know. But, can I help it if you think so?"

Or:

He: "What makes you so smart?"
She: "I wouldn't go out for coffee with you. That's what."
He: "Well, what if I wasn't even gonna ask you to go out for coffee with me?"
She: "Well, that's what makes you stupid."

ences (e.g., backgrounds, religions, points of view) are many, but their attraction to each other is immediate. Ali's father (Marley), a pastry chef, is thrilled when the couple weds, but Ryan's blue-blooded dad (Milland) is furious that the couple refuses to wed in a church. Ryan and his family stop speaking, and Ali becomes his whole life. She sacrifices her career to support him through law school. They relocate to Manhattan, where he has an excellent law firm post. Later he learns from her physician that she is dying and tries to hide the prognosis from her but soon realizes she already knows. Eventually she must be hospitalized, and he borrows the necessary funds from Milland without explaining the cause. As Ali dies she urges Ryan not to regret their unhappy twist of fate, as she has no regrets. Thereafter, when he leaves the hospital he encounters his dad who, having learned the full situation, now attempts to make amends.

As you sniffle through this feature, bear in mind that these characters give shallowness new meaning. For example, our clean-cut hero asks over the soundtrack mournfully, "What can you say about a twenty-five-year-old girl who died?" His brilliant reply includes that she was beautiful (certainly a matter of personal taste) and that "she loved Mozart and Bach . . . and the Beatles." That's the best he can come up with? Oh, brother!

Terms of Endearment

Paramount, 1983, color, 129 minutes
Director: James L. Brooks
Cast: Debra Winger, Shirley MacLaine, Jack Nicholson, Danny DeVito, and Jeff Daniels

*I*n this multi-Oscar winner, the intertwining lives of an eccentric Houston, Texas, widow (MacLaine) and her strong-willed daughter (Winger) are traced over several years. While Shirley deals with various suitors and begins dating her next-door neighbor,

a dissolute ex-astronaut (Nicholson), Debra is having a difficult marriage in the Midwest with her college professor husband (Daniels). The latter is having affairs with his students. In retaliation, Winger has a fling with a local bank worker (John Lithgow). Later, having reunited with Jeff, Debra discovers she has cancer, and medical treatments do not stop its spread. Daniels becomes emotionally frozen while attempting to cope with his wife's tragic end, while MacLaine proves to be a tower of strength. After Winger's passing, Daniels gives in to Shirley's wish that the grandchildren live with her. Thereafter, the

Bedroom Talk

Who says movies can't be informative? How about the following interchanges as MacLaine and Nicholson jockey for control in their complex courtship?

She: "Would you like to come in?"
He: "I'd rather stick needles in my eyes."

Or:

She: "Do you have any reaction at all to my telling you I love you?"
He: "I was just inches from a clean getaway."

As to the act of lovemaking:

He: "I like the lights on."
She: "Then go home and turn them on."

The ill-fated Debra Winger shares a tender moment with her cheating mate (Jeff Daniels) in *Terms of Endearment* (1983). Courtesy of JC Archives

oldest child proves to be a handful until Jack steps into the situation to help out.

Promoted with the catchphrase, "Come to laugh, come to cry, come to care, come to terms," this feature became a must-see picture for many Americans. The female characters certainly come off best in this offbeat entry, which mixes anguish and humor in an intriguing blend. As for Daniels's Flap Horton (how's that for a name?), he is far from anyone's role model. He might just qualify as poster boy for Dysfunctional, Cheating Dads Anonymous. And how overly forgiving is Winger's Emma Greenway Horton? What real-life person with her credentials would have put up with the creep for so long?

Steel Magnolias

TriStar, 1989, color, 118 minutes
Director: Herbert Ross
Cast: Sally Field, Dolly Parton, Shirley MacLaine, Daryl Hannah, and Julia Roberts

"Sometimes laughter is a matter of life and death," insists this cry-or-else feature set in small-town Louisiana. Largely focused on the local beauty shop operated by Parton, the townsfolk include eccentric MacLaine, wealthy Olympia Dukakis, and proud mama Field. The latter's daughter (Roberts) is about to wed. Julia, a severe diabetic, ponders with the beauty shop crowd the fairness of wedding her fiancé (Dylan McDermott) because her illness makes childbearing hazardous to her survival. Not long after she marries, however, Roberts becomes pregnant, determined to live life to the fullest. Her father (Tom

Skerritt) is delighted with the news, but overly protective Sally is frightened of the possible consequences. After Julia gives birth to a healthy baby, it proves the birth has put a severe strain on her kidneys. Later, with Field as an organ donor, Roberts undergoes a transplant that initially seems successful. Soon thereafter, she falls into a coma and dies. At the funeral, Sally's friends rally round and help her through the crisis.

Filled with tart one-liners and several offbeat female characters, the picture's young bride and groom could easily have gotten lost in the plotline shuffle (as do most of the picture's male characters). However, with radiant Roberts as the beaming, ever-optimistic bride who wants to be a complete wife to her husband, this story arc remains the thread holding together the feature.

Some of the plot points in *Steel Magnolias* could happen only in a movie. For example, Julia's character reasons she must risk having a baby herself because her medical records make a legal adoption unlikely. If single parents can adopt in most jurisdictions, certainly a household with two parents (albeit one seriously ill) should pass muster. Yes?

Dying Young

Twentieth Century-Fox, 1991, color, 106 minutes
Director: Joel Schumacher
Cast: Julia Roberts, Campbell Scott, Vincent D'Onofrio, Colleen Dewhurst, and Ellen Burstyn

*W*ith such a solid cast, this maudlin offering aimed to be equal to that ultimate tearjerker, *Dark Victory* (1939), or even the romantic weeper, *Love Story* (1970). (The ad slogan for *Dying Young* reads, "She's giving him something nobody else could. A reason to live.")

Instead, *Dying Young* remains far too detached for its own good and is much too tentative with its manipulative plot premise. (Originally the film had the male lead dying, but test audiences thought that finale to be too grim, and a more ambiguous ending was substituted.)

At loose ends since breaking up with her boyfriend, San Franciscan Roberts answers an ad for a caregiver. Despite her lack of any nursing background, she is hired by twenty-eight-year-old leukemia sufferer (Scott), the son of a wealthy businessman (David Selby). She quickly moves into his basement apartment and helps him through the ongoing

---

Almost Honeymooners

During the filming of *Steel Magnolias* in Natchitoches, Louisiana, costars **Julia Roberts (b. 1967)** and **Dylan McDermott (b. 1962)** began an offcamera romance that led to their engagement but was later terminated. Each went on to wed others.

ordeal of chemotherapy. Friendship turns to romance and, while on vacation up the California coast, they become lovers. Campbell soon insists that his disease is in full remission, but he is secretly shooting up with morphine to deaden the pain of his disease. When Roberts discovers the reality, she convinces him to restart his hospital treatments. As inducement, she promises him her continued love and companionship through whatever may come.

If you buy into this claptrap, you are one easily pleased person who has no clue that life isn't so tidy, doesn't allow for so many coincidences, and rarely, if ever, brings together such a number of people whose swift mood changes seem contrived in order to fit the plot requirements.

Here on Earth

Twentieth Century-Fox, 2000, color,
96 minutes
Director: Mark Piznarski
Cast: Chris Klein, Leelee Sobieski, Josh Hartnett, Michael Rooker, and Annette O'Toole

*B*ringing the romantic tearjerker into the new millennium, *Here on Earth* hopes to make the viewer really care about its paperthin characters. Among their number is Klein's snotty and rich (but handsome and bright) preppie, who learns a major life lesson when he gets into a drag race with a townie (Hartnett), which leads to the destruction of the diner in the next town where young Sobieski is a waitress. The wise judge orders both young men to spend the summer rebuilding the restaurant. In the process, hayseed Josh can only stand back in amazement and disappointment that his girlfriend, Leelee, has become attracted to Chris.

But every movie wanting to be a heartwrencher must include a sudden onscreen announcement that all is not right with one of its lead characters. Sobieski is the person of choice here. As such, it's revealed that the cancer that has formed on her knee has now spread to her liver. Angry and numbed by the news of her hopeless condition, she decides, despite the protests of those who love her (which includes Chris up close, Josh from afar, plus family and friends), to let nature take its course and get the chaos over with. She reasons, "So I live another year or two. It's not worth it."

The feel-good ending to this entry doesn't do much to make viewers' tear ducts swell for long, unfortunately.

Actually, if any young woman in the real world had the chance to date and then choose romantically between heartthrobs Klein and Hartnett, their response would undoubtedly be, "It's to die for." Which, of course, would give them the proper state of mind to properly take on the role of a stricken heroine such as in *Here on Earth*.

No one should have to endure the physical and emotional pains of a fatal ailment that the tragic figures suffer in these Hollywood-made tearjerker movies. Such agony can't be outweighed by the excitement of suddenly becoming a sympathetic center of attention or the object of so much later grief. So stop practicing how to best faint onto a nearby couch or to utter that feeble final good-bye to everyone in your circle. After all, will your insurance plan pay for a great wardrobe, flattering lighting, and a string orchestra working overtime playing a sappy love melody? I think not.

17

High Spirits, or Love Is Eternal

How often have we heard (or spoken ourselves) the expression, "Our love will never die," or "I will love you forever"? For some people these are not just extravagant, idle words but a firm belief that strong romantic devotion transcends either one or both love partners' stay on Earth. This notion that death cannot separate love couples from their great bond with one another may seem the height of foolishness to some mortals. But to other less pragmatic souls, where love and faith are at all involved, *nothing* is impossible, and scoffers on the topic are to be ignored totally.

Just as literature and theater did before them, Hollywood movies have often explored the theme of ghosts onscreen. Sometimes the spirits are vengeful (e.g., 1981's *Ghost Story*) or horrific (e.g., 1988's *Ghost Town*) or merely giddy (e.g., the various versions of *The Canterville Ghost*). But of interest to us here are those American-made feature films dealing with one or both members of a romantic duo whose ghost spirit "materializes" on Earth for certain people to see.

Sometimes the assumed mission of a ghost is to comfort loved ones left behind, urge them to go on with their mortal lives, and assure them that, later, the couple will be reunited in an afterlife of one form or another. Other times, the specter is purported to appear to a loved one left behind in order to urge the survivor to undertake a special task—to put things right with a particular situation on Earth. In these cases, there is supposedly nothing frightening about these benevolent apparitions who make their presence known to fulfill missions of good intentions on behalf of still-mortal loved ones.

For the record, a ghost (i.e., the soul of a dead person . . . a wandering apparition) should *not* be confused with angels (i.e., heavenly attendants of God) *nor*, most certainly, with devils (i.e., great spirits of evil).

Maytime

Metro-Goldwyn-Mayer, 1937, black and
white, 132 minutes
Director: Robert Z. Leonard
Cast: Jeanette MacDonald, Nelson Eddy,
John Barrymore, Herman Bing, and
Tom Brown

*I*n their third and most elaborate screen
teaming, the singing lovebirds of Hollywood movie operetta fame are featured in a
sumptuously mounted tale of enduring love
that magically transcends the death of one
romantic partner. The production is so rich in
detail, contains such a wealth of contrasting
songs, and provides such intense romanticism
that it is hard not to be drawn into the vortex
of its all-enveloping schmaltz.

At a May Day celebration in a small American town in the early 1900s, an elderly
recluse (MacDonald) recalls events in her
tragic life that occurred forty years before in
the France of Emperor Louis Napoleon.
There she is a famous opera singer who feels
indebted to her mentor/instructor, the much
older Barrymore. Life becomes complicated
when she falls in love with an impetuous
young American singer (Eddy). No matter
how much it hurts, she refuses to go back on
her vows to wed Barrymore. Therefore, she
and Eddy must part company.

Years later in New York City, Jeanette and
Nelson find themselves assigned to star in the
same opera at the Metropolitan. Working
together convinces the couple they must

Jeanette MacDonald and Nelson Eddy rehearse an
aria for their lavish screen operetta *Maytime*
(1937).   Courtesy of JC Archives

never be parted again. The insanely jealous
Barrymore, who is witnessing this unbearable
train of events, cannot deal with the possibility of losing his beloved. In a rage, he rushes
to Eddy's apartment where he shoots the
singer. The latter dies in MacDonald's arms.

Back in the present, the aged Jeanette sits
in her garden absorbed in thoughts of her
unfulfilled past love. Slowly, life ebbs from
her fragile body. As she dies, her spirit arises
and is met at the garden gate by that of Nelson's. Together they stroll off into eternity
singing "Sweetheart," the love song they first
sang together on a glorious May Day picnic

decades ago at the beautiful park in St. Cloud, France.

Depriving oneself of romance for decades because one still pines for a deceased loved one is a fine notion for the movies. There, on the big screen, it can seem brave, dreamy, and spiritual to moviegoers. But keep in mind that the actors playing these highly charged roles go home at the end of the workday to their significant others. And, hey, we in the audience aren't participating in much abstinence ourselves. After all, who's hand are you clasping so tightly as you watch this picture?

Topper

Metro-Goldwyn-Mayer, 1937, black-and-white, 98 minutes
Director: Norman Z. McLeod
Cast: Constance Bennett, Cary Grant, Roland Young, Billie Burke, and Alan Mowbray

One side effect of the Depression in the 1930s was that the collapse of America's economy prompted Hollywood to offer filmgoers an unending stream of screen comedies hoping that laughter would lure problem-plagued moviegoers into the cinema. One of the most delightful of these escapist offerings was this screwball comedy.

A wealthy, young, and carefree married couple (Grant and Bennett) enjoys a fun, but unproductive, lifestyle. Following a night of extensive club hopping in New York City, they are driving recklessly through the coun-

tryside when their car smashes into a tree and the two are killed. Almost immediately their spirits rise from their bodies. Soon they sense that before they can enter heaven, they must accomplish at least one good deed on Earth. They target their rich banker friend (Young) as the individual in greatest need of help. Currently, he leads a stuffy existence, henpecked by his conformist socialite wife (Burke). Cary and Constance vow to teach Roland how to really live . . . how to have fun. To accomplish their task they must make their presence known to Young, which causes more than enough complications. However, when the married pranksters instigate their

A Very Earthy Movie Star

The always very glamorous, fashionable **Constance Bennett (1904–1965)** was a movie star in the fullest sense. Everything about her lifestyle was oversized, including the number of her husbands—she had five spouses over the decades.

Bennett was also noted for her quick wit, which sometimes included wry remarks about herself. One evening while out gambling in Hollywood with actor Gilbert Roland (her husband number four), Constance became annoyed with his too-easy spending of her funds. She turned to her studio mogul pal Darryl F. Zanuck and commented, "The f**king I'm getting is not worth the f**king I'm getting." The witticism made the Tinseltown rounds and became a much-employed remark thereafter because it aptly fit so many movie colony situations.

shenanigans on others (who can't see or hear them as the banker can), things take an even more wild and humorous turn. Eventually, the vaporous couple succeeds in salvaging Roland's sense of fun and converting his straitlaced spouse into a much more compassionate, flexible person. With that accomplished, the ghost duo says good-bye to their pal and departs from Earth.

Mischief, pratfalls, and witty dialogue aside, *Topper* suggests that ectoplasms—especially when they are the stars of a major picture—demand earthly nice touches from their studio bosses, including frequent costume changes, good hair days, and flattering cinematography.

A Guy Named Joe

Metro-Goldwyn-Mayer, 1943, black-and-white, 120 minutes
Director: Victor Fleming
Cast: Spencer Tracy, Irene Dunne, Van Johnson, Lionel Barrymore, and Esther Williams

*H*oping to boost the morale of war-weary filmgoers, many of whom had suffered (or would suffer) the loss of loved ones on the battlefront, this feature was perfectly in tune with World War II movie audiences (and has its application in today's climate of terrorism and instant wars). At such troublesome times, what better message to put forth than that when a beloved dies in battle, his or her mortal remains transform into a heavenly spirit

Comforting Thoughts

A Guy Named Joe provides a sterling message a spirit can convey to a dear one about her departed love:

If the memory of that love is going to make you unhappy all the rest of your life, there must have been something wrong with it. It should have been the kind that filled your heart so full of love that you just had to go out to find someone to give it to. . . . That's the only kind that lives.

who can return to Earth to help those in special need of guidance. One such category of recipients is grieving loved ones who must be nurtured into getting on with their lives, including finding new special people to fill their emotional needs.

Promoted with the tag line, "A guy—a gal—a pal—it's swell!" this inspirational film concerns ace U.S. pilot Tracy who is killed in action over the Atlantic Ocean not far from England. Spencer is amazed to find himself in the Great Above and to be assigned to return to Earth where his presence must guide a novice army flyer (Johnson) who is not making the grade. Under Tracy's tutelage, Van succeeds in his training and is shipped to an Allied base in New Guinea. The invisible Spencer, who tags along, is taken aback to discover that his girlfriend (Dunne), a Ferry Command pilot, is stationed there too and that she and Johnson are quickly developing a special rapport. Although confused and hurt, Tracy is sure of what he must do. First, he guides Irene through a very dangerous mission—one originally assigned to Johnson before she snuck into his plane and grabbed the task—to bomb a Japanese munitions dump. That feat accomplished, Spencer must tackle the hardest job ever. As Irene and her spirit passenger return to base, he must convince Irene (through making her feel his thoughts) that no matter how great her love is for him, her obligation is to the living, in this case the eager and loving Johnson. Landing on the field, the phantom speaks his unheard but heartfelt farewell, "Good-bye, good-bye, darling." Released from her love ties to the past, Dunne rushes into the arms of the waiting Johnson.

The Ghost and Mrs. Muir

Twentieth Century-Fox, 1947, black-and-white, 104 minutes
Director: Joseph L. Mankiewicz
Cast: Gene Tierney, Rex Harrison, George Sanders, Edna Best, and Vanessa Brown

*T*alk about opposites who attract! This highly romantic fabrication set in turn-of-the-twentieth-century England matches a high-spirited widow with the ghost of a crusty, chauvinistic sea captain. As the graceful narrative unfolds, the warmhearted film proves again that Hollywood is a master at

Gene Tierney as the earthly widow and Rex Harrison as the ghostly ship's captain in *The Ghost and Mrs. Muir* (1947). Courtesy of JC Archives

engineering a great screen love story even when one of the principal characters has already gone to the Great Beyond.

British widow Tierney and her young daughter (played by child actress Natalie Wood) relocate to the English seaside town of Whitecliff where they occupy a cottage with a spectacular ocean view. Before long she discovers that what the real estate agent had warned her about is true: the house is haunted by the spirit of the sea captain (Harrison) who had owned Gull Cottage at the time of his passing four years earlier. Soon the bearded apparition materializes for Gene, and, in the coming months, the swashbuckling seaman and the spunky widow develop a great kinship that turns into love. Later, when Tierney has an opportunity for an earthly romance, Harrison steps aside. However, her romance with the mortal Sanders is aborted when she

Dialogue Gems

The sparkling screenplay to *The Ghost and Mrs. Muir* contains insightful dialogue jewels:

Heroine: "He took me unawares!"
Ghost: "My dear. Since Eve picked the apple, *no* woman has ever been taken entirely unawares."

And:

Heroine: "It's no crime to be alive!"
Ghost: "No, my dear. Sometimes it's a great inconvenience. The living can be hurt."

A Life-or-Death Choice

To stay faithful to the memory of a loved one, or to get on with the business of life and love? That dilemma is addressed in *The Ghost and Mrs. Muir* when Harrison informs Tierney regarding her developing romance with a London-based writer (Sanders):

You've made your choice. The only choice you could make. You've chosen life. And that's as it should be, whatever the reckoning. . . . You must make your own life amongst the living and whether you meet fair winds or foul, find your own way to harbor.

accidentally discovers he is already a married man. She returns to her beloved cottage, always hoping that Rex's spirit will one day reappear. Years pass, and as she dies her ghost rises from her body and is greeted by that of Harrison's. Together they vanish into the fog and the clouds.

Portrait of Jennie

Selznick Releasing, 1948, black-and-white, and a color sequence, 86 minutes
Director: William Dieterle
Cast: Jennifer Jones, Joseph Cotten, Ethel Barrymore, Cecil Kellaway, David Wayne, and Lillian Gish

*F*illed with Academy Award–winning special effects (including a massive hurricane sequence) and the then novelty of color footage (with the finale shot of Jennie's portrait in multiple hues), this lush but preposterous production got a split vote of confidence from critics and the public at the time of release and even today. With its over-the-top romanticism and plot loopholes, it can't really withstand the tough scrutiny of jaded viewers. However, for those who, as in *Peter Pan*, want to believe, this is an intimate, ethereal love story told on a big scale.

In the mid-1930s, a struggling young artist (Cotten) crosses Central Park on his way home. He encounters a strange young girl (Jones) who makes references to events and places from the past. Before leaving him, the girl begs the stiff-lipped painter to wait for her until she grows up one day. She explains that she knows he is lonely and that they are meant to be together in the future. Thereafter, he meets Jennifer on several occasions, and each time she has magically matured by a few years. Beguiled by this mystery woman, Joseph tracks down her background and discovers that the real-life girl who once attended a convent school had died many years ago during a fierce New England hurricane.

On the anniversary of her death, Cotten is on hand at Jones's favorite sailing spot—near a lighthouse at Cape Cod. During a terrible storm he hears his loved one summoning him. Although he tries to save her, she insists that she must die. However, she insists, they will never be truly separated. With that, she

Sage Advice

Portrait of Jennie offers intriguing points of view about a mortal dealing with a loved one already in the spirit world:

- "I know we were meant to be together. The strands of our lives are woven together and neither the world nor time can tear them apart."

- "As you grow older, you'll learn to believe in lots of things you can't see."

is pulled away by a huge wave and disappears. Slowly the artist makes peace with the world, convinced that he hasn't really lost her but that they will be reunited in the hereafter. Meanwhile, an acclaimed painting he has done of the elusive heroine is hanging in a fine New York art museum.

This is one of those plots that should carry a special warning: "Do not try to duplicate the feats in this movie on your own. The stunts performed in this film were accomplished by professionals under controlled circumstances." Just to be really safe, heed those TV weather forecasts very carefully indeed if you and your sweetheart should be planning a romantic vacation to Old Cape Cod during the stormy season. Just be sure to stick to clam chowder and lobster stew, and leave conquering the high seas for another time.

Brigadoon

Metro-Goldwyn-Mayer, 1954, color,
108 minutes
Director: Vincente Minnelli
Cast: Gene Kelly, Van Johnson,
Cyd Charisse, Elaine Stewart, and
Barry Jones

Adapted from the hit 1947 Broadway musical by Alan Jay Lerner and Frederick Loewe, this film boasts wonderful dancing, a great score, and an attractive cast. (On the downside, the film was entirely lensed on studio soundstages, which gives the visuals a very artificial, constricted look.)

Of key interest here is the plot's fable about a mystical Scottish village that only "resurfaces" every hundred years. It is a town where no one grows older and love can be eternal. The only dampening agent—according to the premise—is the locals' fear that one day a townsperson will leave the confines of Brigadoon. If that occurs, it will break the magical spell and cause this special community to vanish forever. (The story may seem quaint to some viewers, but it has analogies to contemporary life where urbanization has not only damaged the balance of nature but pulled many country dwellers into city living, resulting in many such individuals losing sight of life's simpler pleasures.)

While hunting in the Scottish Highlands, Americans Kelly and Johnson stumble across a village not marked on their map. Gene soon

The Dreamer vs. the Realist

In *Brigadoon* the two lead male characters debate the age-old argument of the optimist versus the pessimist: is that mug of coffee in front of me half full or half empty?

Kelly: "You don't believe in anything, do you?"
Johnson: "Of course I do. Well practically anything I can understand. Anything that's real to me . . . like things I can touch, taste, hear, swallow."
Kelly: "What about the things you don't understand?"
Johnson: "I dismiss them."

Which type of person has better odds in making a love connection with a future mate?

encounters pretty Charisse, while footloose Van keeps dodging an amorous sheepherder (Dody Heath). Cyd has the village schoolmaster (Jones) explain the town's strange history to Kelly. Because he is already in love with Cyd and dissatisfied with his life back in the United States, Gene is easily convinced of the truth of the miracle of Brigadoon. On the other hand, cynical Van is eager to return home and eventually convinces his pal to go with him. Once back in New York, Johnson convinces himself the bizarre experiences

Cyd Charisse and Gene Kelly share a magical moment on a heather-filled Scottish hill in *Brigadoon* (1954).
Courtesy of JC Archives

abroad never happened. In contrast, Kelly broods about his lost love. As such, he breaks his engagement to his Manhattan girlfriend and returns to Scotland to the outskirts of Brigadoon. Because of his strong love and need for Charisse, the town springs to life again, and he rushes across the bridge to his lady love who waits with outstretched arms. Kelly is now part of the miracle of Brigadoon.

According to *Brigadoon*'s premise, Kelly and Charisse's characters literally live happily ever after. Of course, it may take them many millenniums to pass through a full life cycle, but hey, they can always pass the time watching "The Heather on the Hill" or checking out the goings on "Down on MacConnachy Square." And a great time killer is "Waitin' for My Dearie."

The Gift of Love

Twentieth Century Fox, 1958, color,
105 minutes
Director: Jean Negulesco
Cast: Lauren Bacall, Robert Stack, Evelyn
Rudie, Lorne Greene, and Anne Seymour

A certain famous greeting card company
suggests that when you care enough to
give the very best, you should send one of
their products to a loved one. However, this
entry, a remake of 1946's *Sentimental Journey*
(starring Maureen O'Hara, John Payne, and
Connie Marshall), has a much nobler idea.
Provide your loved one with an adopted child
to keep the warmth of family love in his heart
after you have gone to meet your maker.

Bacall and her physicist husband (Stack) of
five years have a happy domestic life on the
Northern California coast. One day she suffers a heart attack but refuses to let her work-
occupied spouse know. When she learns that
she has only a short time to live, she decides
that adopting an orphan girl (Rudie) might
give her beloved a reason to keep on living
after she passes on. Without explaining the
reason to him, she follows through on her
plan. After Lauren dies, Robert has a hard
period of adjustment. Meanwhile, the
deceased woman materializes to the youngster to help guide her in comforting Stack.
One night when the still-distraught widower
scolds young Evelyn, she runs off to the cliff
where she and Lauren first met. There she
slips and tumbles unconscious onto the beach
below as the tide starts coming in. Back at the
house, Stack has a strong premonition that
something is wrong. He calls the police and
institutes a search. He finds Rudie on the
beach just in time. Later, with Evelyn's prodding, he admits that it was the spirit of his late
wife who sent him out to search for her.

The screenwriters certainly contrived to
make this tearjerker play out its highly emotional plot. Today, scripters would have had a
far easier time of it. For example, the soon-
to-be deceased could have thoughtfully left a
series of videotaped messages of love and
guidance for her surviving mate.

It's the Thought That Counts

The advertising tag line for *The Gift of Love* pro-
claims, "No woman can give more than the gift
of love . . . no picture will be closer to your heart
than *The Gift of Love*."

Kiss Me Goodbye

Twentieth Century-Fox, 1982, color,
101 minutes
Director: Robert Mulligan
Cast: Sally Field, James Caan, Jeff Bridges,
Paul Dooley, and Claire Trevor

U nlike the Brazilian-made original (1978's
Dona Flor and Her Two Husbands) starring
Sonia Braga, José Wilker, and Mauro Men-
doca, this Hollywood remake is strained and

slight. Nevertheless, it offers an appealing cast and a premise rich for further cinematic exploration.

Three years after the death of her Broadway choreographer husband (Caan), Field is considering marrying well-intentioned Egyptologist Bridges. To prepare for her new life, she reopens her Manhattan townhouse only to discover that it is inhabited by the materialized specter of her late spouse. (In true ghost story fashion, only she can see and hear him.) This forces the perplexed Sally to balance her ongoing love for the deceased with the virtues of her pleasant but essentially cloddish beau.

Domestic matters aren't helped when James constantly reemerges at the most inopportune moments, such as when she is making love with Jeff in her bedroom. Once she convinces Bridges that Caan has come back into her life, he accepts the spirit's existence and the two men enjoy repeated banter with one another. Eventually, the ghost admits his true purpose for appearing to her: he must help Sally drive out her constant memories of him so she can exist contently in the present.

Jeff Bridges snuggles up to his fiancée (Sally Field) unaware that the ghost of her late husband is lurking around her life in *Kiss Me Goodbye* (1982). Courtesy of JC Archives

(The process is helped when she suddenly discovers that her spouse had cheated on her throughout their marriage.) Ready to move forward with life, Field marries Bridges, while a jovial Caan does a fast dance step and bids his loved one good-bye. He then vanishes.

Promoted as "a hauntingly romantic comedy" and (vainly) urging moviegoers: "If you want to laugh and have a good time, this is the movie," *Kiss Me Goodbye* lit no box-office fires.

Suggestion of the day: if you insist on a threesome to spice up your bedroom athletics, consider checking that each participant has his or her feet firmly planted on terra firma. Don't try to give new meaning to the term "high-spirited romance."

Ghost

Paramount, 1990, color, 127 minutes
Director: Jerry Zucker
Cast: Patrick Swayze, Demi Moore, Tony Goldwyn, Whoopi Goldberg, and Vincent Schiavelli

A huge money earner ($217.5 million in domestic distribution) in its day, *Ghost* is a phenomenal wish-fulfillment fantasy saturated with grandstand theatrical gestures and enough special effects to give the spectral doings a ring of plausibility. (The film's ad slogan was "You Will Believe!") This box-office hit also boasts its share of near slapstick moments. They were provided by Goldberg, who, as the fake medium, was rewarded with an Academy Award. To prompt the desired tearful responses of audiences, the picture showcases repeatedly a lush rendition of the old song "Unchained Melody," which swells on the soundtrack at appropriate story points.

A successful young New York banker (Swayze) shares a spacious loft apartment in New York City with his artist lover (Moore). The two are passionate about each other but afraid to commit to marriage, especially Patrick who has a sense of foreboding. One night he is mugged on the way home and dies. Swayze is amazed to discover that his spirit is still on Earth. His essence hovers around his loved one, although she can't see or hear him. Later, in Brooklyn, he happens across a spiritual adviser (Goldberg) who for some reason can hear him. He pressures her into acting as his interpreter for Demi, hoping to warn Moore in time that their supposed good friend (Goldwyn) is actually behind the murder.

With Whoopi's reluctant assistance, Patrick protects Demi from Tony, the latter being killed in a final confrontation with the ghost and dispatched to a hellish resting place. After reaffirming their great love, Swayze zooms off to the hereafter in a blinding glow of light. As he vanishes to the Great Above, he excitedly tells tearful Demi, "It's amazing . . . the love inside. You take it with you. . . ."

To quote the villain of this celluloid piece, "You're talking ghosts here for Christ sake!" And indeed *Ghost* is just about that. So if you're skeptical about the film's context, you'll find this maudlin romance yarn hard to accept and certainly not something to keep in mind should a loved one suddenly expire. However, just to play it safe, heed the practical observation of one character in this film: "OK, according to this psychic lady there are ghosts and spirits all over the place watching us all the time. Hell, I'm never going to get undressed again."

To Gillian on Her 37th Birthday

Triumph, 1997, color, 93 minutes
Director: Michael Pressman
Cast: Peter Gallagher, Michelle Pfeiffer, Claire Danes, Laurie Fortier, and Freddie Prinze Jr.

The advertising campaign for this feature, based on a 1984 off-Broadway play, touted, "Some love lasts a lifetime. Real love lasts forever." Well, not quite.

Two years after his wife (Pfeiffer) died in a boating accident, a college professor (Gallagher) discovers that his in-laws have invited a pretty divorcée (Rachel Seidman-Lockamy) to his Nantucket home for the weekend, hoping she will distract him from his unresolved loss. But the invitee has a tough job ahead of her because distraught Peter is still so attached to his dead spouse that he sees visions of her and carries on long discussions with the specter. This "craziness" bothers his literal sister-in-law (Kathy Baker), who is insistent that Gallagher's teenage daughter (Danes) come live with her and her husband and have a normal life with people who aren't so overly involved with a dead loved one. Resistant at first, Peter has a change of heart when his overwhelmed offspring expresses how much she needs "to let my mother be dead." Shocked into action, Gallagher bids a touching farewell to luminous Pfeiffer on the beach. He explains, "I can't let you be real anymore. . . . I can't. . . . I've got to be real for [our daughter] Rachel." With that, Michelle, sad at breaking this last connection with earthly beings, walks along the water and disappears into the mist.

After watching this film, I wished that this well-intentioned, sentimental weeper (written for the screen by Pfeiffer's husband, David E. Kelley) had been crafted more substantially. At the same time I had the nagging feeling that I was falling short as a sensitive human being because I'd never experienced that kind of great love that can make a dead beloved materialize. "What's wrong with me?" I wondered. Then it hit me. This movie had succeeded with its premise far more than

Compliant Ghosts

In *To Gillian on Her 37th Birthday*, the specter of his late wife (Pfeiffer) informs her mortal spouse (Gallagher) of a few basic facts about friendly phantoms: "What I say I want is what you really want. I'm only here because you want me here."

even a borderline romantic like me cared to admit. These days I'm thinking of relocating to an ocean-view property. Maybe Michelle's spirit is still hovering around the salty ether and is in need of a good chat.

As demonstrated in Hollywood's treatment of romantic spirits on the screen, none of the mortals in such ghost tales is rushing to call 1-800-Ghostbusters. On the other hand, in real (versus reel) life, your friends and relatives, let alone business associates, are not going to deal too well with your spending quality time conversing animatedly with the dearly departed. They might start to think they've slipped to the bottom of the list in your priorities. So, be understanding if this leads them to gently hint that, perhaps, you should attend a meeting or two of Ghost Enablers Anonymous.

18

Relationships on a Pedestal

Over its long history, Hollywood has often been accused by censorship groups of corrupting the public's morals by depicting far too much sex and violence in its onscreen products. For some, especially those with conservative viewpoints, this may well be true. On the other hand, Tinseltown has also created its share of positive film entertainment, filled with—if you will—wholesome values.

Such uplifting movie fare often involves inspiring family-oriented entries (e.g., 1948's *The Secret Garden*, 1960's *Pollyanna*, and 2002's *Tuck Everlasting*) in which the point of view is geared primarily for the young and the very young at heart. Then there are other pictures—with a mature focus on adults—that have set standards for filmgoers about great, enriching love relationships. Such movies may be about people in the first blushes of love or couples who have been married for years. In either case, they establish (fantasy) guidelines for moviegoers who

aspire subconsciously to reach those heightened levels of depicted sharing, caring, selflessness, and joy at being together in a loving situation.

While we may tell ourselves that these "perfect" oncamera love relationships are merely fabricated models that have little to do with reality, they, nevertheless—like so much else in the movies—have a tremendous impact on audiences. They not only help in formulating relationship goals but also provide a measure for comparison. People can stack up their own real-life love partnerships against what they see detailed so gloriously on the screen.

Striving to reach such depicted goals may result in frustration, but we can at least experience vicariously a beautiful, righteous love that fate has yet to allow us to experience fully on a firsthand basis.

The Thin Man

Metro-Goldwyn-Mayer, 1934, black-and-white, 91 minutes
Director: W. S. Van Dyke II
Cast: William Powell, Myrna Loy, Maureen O'Sullivan, Nat Pendleton, and Minna Gombell

*T*his was only the second of fourteen pictures these two sterling performers (Powell and Loy) made together, but it estab-lished a mold that became tremendously popular with the public. Based on a 1932 Dashiell Hammett novel, the resultant film was the start of a highly successful movie detective series in which the thriller genre was blended with screwball comedy. Most impor-tant, it presented a husband-and-wife team who was chic, bright, very much in love, and tremendously enjoying each other's company. They each had their "flaws": he had an over-fondness for cocktails and could be a bit lazy; she had a taste for mayhem and was always

William Powell, Myrna Loy, and their cute terrier, Asta, in *The Thin Man* (1934).　Courtesy of JC Archives

eager to rush into a dangerous situation for the thrill of the experience. Nonetheless, this new love team showed moviegoers that being married was not the end of romantic adventure but could be filled with domestic bliss in which neither individual took the other for granted. Could one ask for more than that?

When her inventor father disappears, O'Sullivan begs dapper Powell to help find him. While he and his chic wife (Loy) insist he has given up the detective business, circumstances force him to take on the caper while they are in New York. Often accompanied by their white wirehaired terrier, Asta, the sleuthing duo follows the clues as the murders pile up. To resolve the case, William has the police round up all the suspects and

Banter Makes the Heart Grow Fonder

One of the key ingredients for a Thin Man movie entry is the witty repartee between Powell and Loy. Their interchanges are often tinged with light sarcasm but remain bright and witty, and each knows that the other speaks with love and frivolity in his or her heart. For example:

Loy: "I think it's a dirty trick to bring me all the way to New York just to make a widow out of me."
Powell: "You wouldn't be a widow long."
Loy: "You bet I wouldn't."
Powell: "Not with all your money."

A Dapper Star

William Powell (1892–1984), the king of screen sophistication, was married three times (including to movie star Carole Lombard). At the time of Jean Harlow's death in June 1937, he was engaged to wed this platinum blond sex symbol. Over the years, a trio of his costars had quite different points of view about this matinee idol:

Myrna Loy: "He was a brilliant actor, a delightful companion, a great friend, and above all, a true gentleman."
Bette Davis: "He had a big mouth and quite a sexual appetite."
Carole Lombard: "The son of a bitch is acting even when he takes his pajamas off."

make them attend a dinner party he and Myrna will host. Using a series of questions and allegations, the actual culprit is unmasked. With the adventure over, Powell and Loy can return home to California.

As a result of the box-office success of *The Thin Man*, Powell and Loy made six additional entries in the series, ending with 1947's *The Song of the Thin Man*. The enduring popularity of this property led to a later TV series and even a Broadway musical based on the detective duo. However, neither follow-up creative venture was successful in re-creating the magic that existed between these two stars. So let that be a lesson: enjoy watching the Thin Man movies, and don't frustrate yourself trying to match the costars' superior sparkle with your significant other.

A British household puts on a happy face for a family reunion in the World War II drama *Mrs. Miniver* (1942) with Christopher Severn, Greer Garson, Clare Sandars, Walter Pidgeon, and Richard Ney.
Courtesy of JC Archives

Mrs. Miniver

Metro-Goldwyn-Mayer, 1942, black-and-white, 134 minutes
Director: William Wyler
Cast: Greer Garson, Walter Pidgeon, Teresa Wright, Dame May Whitty, and Henry Travers

With the United States' entry into World War II, moviegoers were especially partial to films that depicted the strength of a family bound by great love and selflessness. Because many Americans then looked to England not only as a wartime ally but also as the leader in refined (and noble) taste, the British-set *Mrs. Miniver* could not have been released at a more appropriate time. The movie was a tribute to a brave mother who not only keeps up her family's morale on the home front but even deals face-to-face with the dastardly enemy.

Despite growing world tensions in the summer of 1939, the British family headed by Pidgeon and Garson carry on. The household, which includes their two youngest children, welcomes home the oldest child (Richard Ney) from college. Richard soon becomes romantically involved with Wright, the granddaughter of a local noblewoman (Whitty). Later, the couple becomes engaged on the night he ships out to war.

When not keeping the house going, tending to the children, and making the best of evenings spent in a bunker to avoid the German bombing raids, Greer and Walter help their neighbors and country. While Pidgeon is away assisting with the mass evacuation of Dunkirk, Garson deals with an injured but vicious German pilot (Helmut Dantine) who has survived a crash and shows up at Greer's doorstep. The man is turned over to the police. Later, Teresa is killed during a German raid on the town. Despite the calamities to themselves and the country, Greer and Walter join the surviving townsfolk for a service at the badly bombed local church. There the vicar reaffirms his congregation's faith in England's future.

The Minivers may seem to some viewers to be a cloyingly sweet and impossibly decent married couple, but for many, then and now, they were the epitome of everything a husband and wife should be—especially in such a perilous period. To make the duo seem a bit more human, the screenplay reveals them indulging in occasional extravagant whims (e.g., her buying a smart hat at a London shop in the film's opening scenes) and not always agreeing on every decision in life. Most important, it shows each of them bolstered by the other's love and courage, allowing them to present a solid front against a wide range of adversities. The picture won several Oscars including a Best Actress Academy Award for Garson. This was the second of nine pictures the duo made together, including a sequel titled *The Miniver Story* (1950).

In your wildest imagination you probably could not create a list of hardships or brave situations to match those facing Garson and Pidgeon in *Mrs. Miniver*. Keep in mind it required four credited writers to come up with the array of obstacles depicted in this emotional excursion.

It's a Wonderful Life

RKO, 1946, black-and-white, 129 minutes
Director: Frank Capra
Cast: James Stewart, Donna Reed, Lionel Barrymore, Thomas Mitchell, and Henry Travers

*Y*uletide TV showings of *It's a Wonderful Life* have become such a tradition in America and elsewhere that the holiday season would seem far less complete without watching this beloved classic.

In this fable of small-town life, an upstanding citizen (Stewart) and loving family man experiences a series of financial reverses and domestic crises through no fault of his own. The highly agitated family man decides that the only way out of his scrapes is to commit suicide so that his $15,000 life insurance policy will clean up the money mess. At this traumatic junction, the heavenly hierarchy answers James's desperate pleas for help. Being short-staffed, they dispatch an aged apprentice angel (Travers) to assist the foundering man. Travers leads Stewart through his past in Bedford Falls and shows him what would have happened if he had not been around to do his good deeds that touched the lives of so many others. Near the finale, the angel tells James: "You see . . . you really had a wonderful life. Don't you see what a mistake it would be to throw it away?" With that, Stewart rushes home to find that everything has worked out for the better and that there is really much to rejoice about. Surrounded by his loving wife (Reed), family, and friends, he shares in heartfelt holiday toasts.

The warmth and rapport that exist between Stewart and Reed's characters oncamera became an instant part of Americana, something that people wanted to aspire to in their own lives. It might be overly cynical to remind ourselves that it takes an extremely noble constitution—not to mention a great many plot contrivances—to put up with all the sacrifices that this hero does over his lifetime or to exhibit the tremendous patience and love his wife provides her mate.

Nonetheless, it is probably likely that most of us, with or without a benevolent guardian angel, would abandon the good fight long before this lead character does.

Adam's Rib

Metro-Goldwyn-Mayer, 1949, black-and-white, 101 minutes
Director: George Cukor
Cast: Spencer Tracy, Katharine Hepburn, Judy Holliday, Tom Ewell, and David Wayne

"*I*t's the Hilarious Answers to Who Wears the Pants . . . MGM's Rib Roarious Battle of the Sexes." So boasted the ads for this,

---

Domestic Banter

Having lost to his wife in the courtroom in *Adam's Rib*, Tracy is not about to admit defeat to his strong-willed feminist wife. This leads to a choice battle of words and will between the deeply in-love couple:

Hepburn: "No difference between the sexes. None. Men, women. The same."
Tracy: "They are, huh?"
Hepburn: "Well, maybe there *is* a difference. But it's a *little* difference."
Tracy: "Vive la difference!"
Hepburn: "Which means?"
Tracy: "Which means: hurray for that little difference!"

A married lawyer couple (Spencer Tracy and Katharine Hepburn) juggles professional and domestic issues in *Adam's Rib* (1949).   Courtesy of JC Archives

the sixth screen teaming of Tracy and Hepburn. In the atmosphere of post–World War II, the social structure was slowly changing in the United States regarding male dominance in the workplace and at home. Who better to play out this ongoing battle for supremacy between men and women than Tracy and Hepburn, who had shown in *Woman of the Year* (1942) how, through love and growing respect, opposites attract and can compromise with one another?

When a daffy blonde (Holliday) with a bad aim shoots and wounds her spouse (Ewell) who is having an affair, Katharine, an attorney who believes in equal rights for women, takes the defense. As luck has it, her husband, a New York assistant district attorney, is assigned to prosecute the case. Now he must deal with her theories of female equality in the courtroom as well as at home. As the trial proceeds, Hepburn wryly promotes the theory that what is good for the goose is good for the gander. Her tactics win an acquittal for the defendant.

This popular entry was a primer course on how to conduct a marriage on a more even footing. Of course, it helped mightily that the lead characters had the benefit of a sharp script by the husband-and-wife team of Garson Kanin and Ruth Gordon. Unfortunately, these scripters have both passed on, so they can't help you smooth out your own real-life scenario.

Roman Holiday

Paramount, 1953, black-and-white,
119 minutes
Director: William Wyler
Cast: Gregory Peck, Audrey Hepburn, Eddie Albert, Hartley Power, and Laura Solari

*I*n her first Hollywood-produced picture, strikingly beautiful Hepburn won an Academy Award and stole the hearts of moviegoers. She created a new mold of an elegant but down-to-earth heroine who, with great charm and vulnerability, reaches out for love. In the process, she causes the object of her affection to be that much better a person for the experience.

This Cinderella tale concerns the heir (Audrey) to the throne of a European country who is in Rome, Italy, on a goodwill tour. Overwhelmed by the pressures of her schedule and the demands of her position, she rebels. She slips out of the embassy and embarks on a brief lark in the Eternal City. Her chance companion is a correspondent (Peck) for an American news service. While he soon discovers her real identity, he allows her to pretend to him and to others that she is merely a student. Together they caper about the city seeing the sights and enjoying each other's company. By day's end, the couple has fallen in love. However, they realize that their futures cannot be together. Tenderly bidding each other farewell, they part. The next day when the princess conducts a media conference, Peck and his photographer pal (Albert) are among those in attendance. From a distance Audrey and Gregory exchange warm glances before parting permanently.

Warning: forget the 1987 TV movie remake of *Roman Holiday* starring Catherine Oxenberg and Tom Conti. Like most mere mortals, the new cast lacks the spark and finesse to bring magic to the fairy-tale plot—which I'm afraid is what would happen to most of us if we tried to duplicate a similar bittersweet romantic situation.

Breakfast at Tiffany's

Paramount, 1961, color, 115 minutes
Director: Blake Edwards
Cast: Audrey Hepburn, George Peppard, Patricia Neal, Buddy Ebsen, and Mickey Rooney

*C*leaning up the morality of its hero and heroine as originally presented in Truman Capote's 1958 novella, this box-office bonanza showcases Hepburn as a madcap young lady who lives in a partially furnished brownstone apartment on Manhattan's fashionable East Side. She "earns" her income from the $50 her gentlemen escorts provide her when she needs powder room change and from the $100 weekly she is paid to visit a gangster convict at Sing Sing Prison. Her routine is shaken up when she encounters a young writer (Peppard), the paid companion to an older woman (Neal), who has an apartment in Audrey's building.

As George falls in love with the unpredictable, whimsical Hepburn, he briefly meets an older Texan (Ebsen) who was once wed to Hepburn when she was fifteen (the union had been annulled). After sending the lovelorn but understanding Buddy back home, Audrey continues her romance with George. However, she plans to wed a rich, snobbish South American, but the latter breaks with her when she is innocently involved in a drug-smuggling operation. At a low ebb, she is about to leave town, but Peppard convinces her of his love and their chance for a happy future together.

The film's theme song ("Moon River") won an Oscar, and the picture itself helped to establish a new breed of strong and self-sufficient heroines who are not dependent on the opposite sex, but who, nevertheless, are susceptible to having the blues (referred to in the film as the "mean reds") and to needing comfort from a loving man.

For Hepburn's zany Holly Golightly, whenever she gets depressed, she hastens to Tiffany's elegant Fifth Avenue store where merely looking at the splendid jewelry, elegant gifts, and so forth, picks up her spirits tremendously.

Is there a branch of that upscale emporium at your local mall?

Personal Property

In the romantic *Breakfast at Tiffany's*, two self-sufficient but needy people find their soul mate in one another. An underlying question for them is how much love each must give up to be with the other.

Peppard: "I love you. You belong to me."
Hepburn: "No. People don't belong to people."
Peppard: "Of course they do."

Barefoot in the Park

Paramount, 1967, color, 104 minutes
Director: Gene Saks
Cast: Robert Redford, Jane Fonda, Charles Boyer, Mildred Natwick, and Herbert Edelman

When a film is based on a Neil Simon Broadway comedy (1963) such as this lighthearted entry is, moviegoers don't expect the characters to be especially true to life. They are looking for the amusing one-liners and sight gags for which the playwright is famous. In the case of this screen excursion, however, the two coleads (Fonda and Redford) are so attractive playing the pleasantly quirky lovebirds that viewers easily succumb

Jane Fonda and Robert Redford are blissful young marrieds at the start of *Barefoot in the Park* (1967). Courtesy of JC Archives

Adventurous Fonda thinks their bohemian abode is a lark, but Redford is quickly irritated by the lack of amenities in their drab new surroundings. As each of the newlyweds tries to adapt to the other, they suffer pangs of fear, regret, and frustration about being tied to one another. During this trying period of adjustment each makes changes: Jane realizes that marriage cannot be a full-time lark, while Robert appreciates that his stuffy viewpoint on life needs to be greatly modified. Approaching the future on a much better footing, the couple happily reconciles.

If you think you can match Fonda and Redford in this tribute to young lovers, then rush out to the nearest library and check out a copy of the play for you and your significant other to perform.

to wishing they were one or the other of these characters. (For older viewers, there are Natwick as Fonda's mother and Boyer as the congenial roué neighbor to provide a more mature version of opposites attracting one another and softening their hard edges through a budding friendship/romance.)

After a wonderful honeymoon at New York's Plaza Hotel, Jane and Robert, he being a conservative young attorney, move into their Greenwich Village walk-up apartment.

He Says, She Says

In the course of this film, the hero and heroine discover they have opposing approaches to life. Not only does the following exchange represent the essence of the couple's differences, but it efficiently works in the comedy's title:

Fonda: "You have absolutely no sense of the ridiculous. Like last Thursday night. You wouldn't walk barefoot with me in Washington Square Park. Why not?"

Redford: "Simple answer. It was seventeen degrees."

Fonda: "Exactly. It's very logical. It's very sensible, but it's no fun."

Claudine

Twentieth Century-Fox, 1974, color,
92 minutes
Director: John Berry
Cast: Diahann Carroll, James Earl Jones,
Lawrence Hilton-Jacobs, Tamu, and
David Kruger

*H*aving furthered the cause of integration by starring in the groundbreaking TV sit-com *Julia* (1968–1971), its pathfinding African American star (Carroll) headlined this whole-some yet gritty romance between a single mother in Harlem and a jovial garbage collec-tor (Jones). Made during Hollywood's explo-sion of black-themed movies in the early 1970s, this film differed greatly from the usual action-and-violence entry (e.g., 1971's *Shaft*, 1973's *Cleopatra Jones*). *Claudine* offers an intriguing (if not always successful) blend of Disney-type family fare spliced with moments of tough street life in New York's uptown ghetto.

A jovial garbage collector (James Earl Jones) and a self-sufficient single parent (Diahann Carroll) find happiness together in *Claudine* (1974).   Courtesy of JC Archives

Having six children and two ex-husbands, Diahann struggles to make ends meet. Her bleak life changes when she meets the cheerful sanitation engineer. Although her children are resentful at first of this intruder in their household, they come to respect him and appreciate what he has brought into their mother's and their lives. Meanwhile, her eldest son (Hilton-Jacobs) has joined a black militant group and proves a thorn in everyone's side. By the finale, Carroll and Jones have wed and her offspring accept him as one of the family.

With this movie, Carroll and Jones presented full-bodied characterizations that gave ethnic minority filmgoers role models. It was a step in the right direction, even if the script made every situation work out too patly and symmetrically.

When Harry Met Sally . . .

Columbia, 1989, color, 95 minutes
Director: Rob Reiner
Cast: Billy Crystal, Meg Ryan, Carrie Fisher, Bruno Kirby, and Steven Ford

One of the most successful and enduring date movies of recent decades, this slickly constructed entry has much to say on how opposites can attract one another romantically even as they fight that magnetism.

In 1977 Crystal and Ryan graduate from the University of Chicago and become acquainted when she gives him a ride to New

Men vs. Women

In their lengthy courtship, the lead characters of *When Harry Met Sally . . .* devote a good deal of thought to how they differ and why they shouldn't have a relationship—romantic or otherwise. Crystal's cynical observations are worthy of note:

- "No man can be friends with a woman that he finds attractive. He always wants to have sex with her."

- "There are two kinds of women: high maintenance and low maintenance. You're the worst kind. You're high maintenance, but you think you're low maintenance."

York City. This first encounter ends badly as Meg despises his overriding pessimism plus his awkward attempt at making a pass at her. Five years later they meet again. By now each is involved with another. Another five years thereafter the two encounter each other yet again. She has broken up with her boyfriend, and he is in the process of getting a divorce. They finally see beyond their surface differences and develop a close platonic relationship.

When their rapport takes a romantic turn, they introduce each other to their best friends (Fisher and Kirby), hoping they will make a love connection. However, it is Carrie and Bruno who hit it off, and the two eventually marry. Many months later, with Crystal and Ryan alternating between feuding and commiserating about each one's miserable love life, they reconnect on New Year's Eve. Billy admits his love for Meg. Finally, after twelve years and three months of knowing each other, the twosome marries.

Perhaps the best-known scene from this R-rated comedy hit is the coffee shop sequence in which Ryan insists to Crystal that men never know when a woman is faking an orgasm. To prove her point, she simulates the situation (heavy breathing, sighs of ecstasy, and so forth) to his embarrassment and amazement. After Meg's riveting performance, a customer (Estelle Reiner) seated nearby says to her waiter, "I'll have what she's having." Would such a laugh-provoking (yet serious) scene happen in real life? Doubtful! How many of us are as liberated, cute, and intense as Meg's quirky character?

Let Me Count the Ways

A much-appreciated sequence in the highly romantic *When Sally Met Harry* . . . occurs when Crystal enumerates the reasons he knows he truly loves Ryan:

> I love that you get cold when it's seventy-one degrees out. . . . I love that you get a little crinkle above your nose when you're looking at me like I'm nuts. . . . And I love that you are the last person I want to talk to before I go to sleep at night.

Sleepless in Seattle

TriStar, 1993, color, 104 minutes
Director: Nora Ephron
Cast: Tom Hanks, Meg Ryan, Bill Pullman, Ross Malinger, and Rosie O'Donnell

"*M*arriage is hard enough without bringing such low expectations into it," Ryan's fiancé (Pullman) tells her. By now Meg, a Baltimore, Maryland, journalist, is beginning to realize that as nice and rich as he is, hyperallergic Bill is not the man for her. One night she listens to a national call-in radio talk show and hears the host talking with a phone-in (Hanks) she labels "Sleepless in Seattle." It develops that Tom's beloved wife has died and he has relocated from the Midwest to Washington, hoping to make a new life for his eight-year-old son (Malinger) and himself. Ryan uses her media resources (and a private detective) at work to find this voice that has struck such a joyful chord in her heart. She becomes so obsessed with meeting this possible true love that she flies to Seattle. However, she barely manages to say "hi" to this love object before she loses her courage and flies back East.

By now Hanks's son is so eager for his dad to find a new love and to have a happy home again that he communicates with Meg (pretending to be his father). He sets up a meeting with her in New York City, and she agrees to keep the appointment. Because Tom won't follow through on this wild matchmaking, the boy flies to Manhattan on his

Dating—Contemporary Style

Forced back into the dating game after many years, widower Hanks is given advice on what to expect by his pal (Rob Reiner): "Things are a little different now. First, you have to be friends. You have to like each other. Then you neck. This could go on for years. Then you have tests, and then you get to do it with a condom. The good news is you split the check."

own. As such, his dad is forced to follow after him. There, atop the Empire State Building, Ryan meets Hanks and his boy face-to-face. There is magic in the air as the threesome happily takes the elevator down to ground level and starts on the pathway to a new life together.

Craftily, this feel-good love story utilizes both plot line and footage from *An Affair to Remember* (1957) in order to create the ingre-

dients necessary to make a romance as wonderfully idealistic as depicted in the movies.

If your expectations run high that you can duplicate the great perfect loves as shown on the Hollywood screen, take this little test. Check out the following speech by Tom Hanks's character in *Sleepless in Seattle* (1993) in which he enumerates why he loved his late wife so much. If you can match—and please be honest—its romanticism and passion in your own words and emotions, you're ready for the cinema big leagues.

> It was a million tiny little things that when you add them all up, it just meant that we were supposed to be together. . . . I knew the very first time I touched her. It was like coming home. Only to no home I'd ever known. I was just taking her hand, to help her out of a car, and I knew it. It was like magic.

19

Walking Down the Wedding Aisle

For many—especially brides—getting married is the most memorable day of their lives. It is something they have often dreamed about, and even planned for, since they were small children. For others— especially grooms—becoming a husband sometimes is colored by thoughts that the ceremony represents the end of personal freedom and the start of great financial and emotional responsibilities. For a smaller

The Second Time Around

Some Tinseltown celebrities believe in the old saying that "love is better the second time around." The following are among those entertainers who have married the same partner twice. Listings include those couples who divorced and rewed, *not* those notables who chose to renew their vows to their current spouse.

Desi Arnaz—Lucille Ball
Jean-Pierre Aumont—Marisa Pavan
Milton Berle—Joyce Mathews
Richard Burton—Elizabeth Taylor
Art Carney—Jean Myers
David Carradine—Gail Jensen
Stephen Crane—Lana Turner
José Ferrer—Rosemary Clooney
Elliott Gould—Jennifer Bogart
Jon Hall—Raquel Torres

Don Johnson—Melanie Griffith
John Kappas—Florence Henderson
Freddie Karger—Jane Wyman
Alfred Maxwell—June Allyson
Carroll O'Connor—Nancy Fields
Richard Pryor—Flynn BeLaine
George C. Scott—Colleen Dewhurst
Jean-Claude Van Damme—Gladys Portugues
Robert Wagner—Natalie Wood

Who's Keeping Score?

The following list is a selection of those Hollywood notables over the decades who have made the trip to the wedding altar the most number of times. To qualify, the personality must have tied the matrimonial knot at least five times.

Lash LaRue	10	Richard Burton	5	Rita Hayworth	5
Jennifer O'Neill	9	Joan Collins	5	Betty Hutton	5
Zsa Zsa Gabor	8	Joan Crawford	5	Herb Jeffries	5
Stan Laurel	8	Linda Cristal	5	Boris Karloff	5
Mickey Rooney	8	Robert Cummings	5	Barbara La Marr	5
Elizabeth Taylor	8	Tony Curtis	5	Fernando Lamas	5
Lana Turner	8	Arlene Dahl	5	Carole Landis	5
Richard Pryor	7	Vic Damone	5	Bela Lugosi	5
George Brent	6	Paul Douglas	5	Herbert Marshall	5
Rex Harrison	6	Mel Ferrer	5	Victor Mature	5
Dick Haymes	6	Eddie Fisher	5	Barbara Payton	5
Hedy Lamarr	6	Rhonda Fleming	5	Ginger Rogers	5
Claude Rains	6	Henry Fonda	5	George C. Scott	5
Martha Raye	6	Clark Gable	5	Billy Bob Thornton	5
Gloria Swanson	6	Eva Gabor	5	Ruth Warrick	5
Lex Barker	5	Judy Garland	5	Johnny Weissmuller	5
Constance Bennett	5	Leo Gorcey	5	Gig Young	5
Ernest Borgnine	5	Cary Grant	5		

group, the day is highly traumatic because they are taking wedding vows largely because the bride-to-be is pregnant and the couple's conscience—or perhaps a persuasive relative (remember the shotgun weddings of bygone eras?)—is pressuring the duo into tying the marital knot . . . now!

Whatever the emotions and expectations of the "happy" couple on its wedding day, it is generally an occasion that brings together the duo's relatives and friends to celebrate. Now

the decision makers must cope with the minutia of the big event. Whom to include in the festivities? Will there be a problem seating Aunt Millie next to Uncle Joe at the rehearsal dinner? Should the reception hall motif be traditional or contemporary? What color will the bridesmaids' bouquets be? The details seem (deliciously or painfully) endless and the cost exorbitant.

Because planning and undertaking a wedding is such a major occurrence for most couples-to-be, the details of the event are deeply embedded in their memories and don't require a wedding album of photos to prompt a flood of joyful (or not) reminiscences. Also because preparing for and experiencing a wedding is such a common experience, Hollywood has long found fertile ground for screenplays revolving around the big lifestyle event and using the wedding ceremony to dazzle moviegoers with elaborate gowns, settings, and situations. This has led to such classic comedies as Buster Keaton's *Seven Chances* (1925), Claudette Colbert's *The Palm Beach Story* (1942), and the recent *My Big Fat Greek Wedding* (2002). Then too, there have been a host of serious Tinseltown pictures involving nuptials: Joan Crawford's *Forsaking All Others* (1934), Barbara Stanwyck's *Stella Dallas* (1937), Marlon Brando's *The Godfather* (1972), Robert De Niro's *The Deer Hunter* (1978), and Omar Epps's *The Wood* (1999).

The Old Maid

Warner Bros., 1939, black-and-white,
95 minutes
Director: Edmund Goulding
Cast: Bette Davis, Miriam Hopkins,
George Brent, Jane Bryan, and Donald
Crisp

This tearjerker is a woman's picture in the ultragrand Davis manner. It features not one but two weddings. Unfortunately for Bette's character, neither of the nuptials is hers. In this elaborately produced saga of self-sacrifice, she ages from her late teens until well into middle age, suffering (not always so nobly) throughout the many decades.

In 1861 in Philadelphia, Hopkins marries James Stephenson, even though her former fiancé (Brent) shows up that day to reclaim her. Because Miriam's cousin, Bette, has long had a crush on George, she follows him when he leaves Hopkins's, and they spend the night together. The next day Brent departs for Civil War service and later dies in action. Meanwhile, Davis travels out West where she gives birth to George's love child. Returning home, she opens a nursery for war orphans in order to disguise the fact that she is caring for her illegitimate daughter.

Time passes and Bette is set to wed Jerome Cowan, Miriam's brother-in-law. That day, Davis confesses the truth about her baby to Hopkins, who insists she morally cannot marry Cowan. The groom-to-be is told Bette is suffering from tuberculosis, and the ceremony is called off. Later, after Hopkins's husband dies, Davis and her daughter come to live with well-to-do Miriam. Thereafter, to give the growing girl (Bryan) a name and an inheritance, Hopkins adopts her. In the process, Bette is shoved into the background, reduced to being the strict spinster watchdog. As Jane's own wedding approaches, the long-suffering Bette insists on telling her offspring the truth, but Miriam convinces her otherwise. As a conciliatory gesture, Miriam has Bryan, before departing with the groom on their honeymoon, give Davis the final goodbye kiss. This meaningful moment brings a glow of happiness to Bette's face.

Miriam Hopkins (right) consoles Bette Davis on the latter's ill-fated wedding day in *The Old Maid* (1939). Courtesy of JC Archives

And you think you had problems on your wedding day. Give us a break! What can equate to the pain and suffering this "heroine" endures in nineteenth-century Pennsylvania?

The Philadelphia Story

Metro-Goldwyn-Mayer, 1940, black-and-white, 112 minutes
Director: George Cukor
Cast: Cary Grant, Katharine Hepburn, James Stewart, Ruth Hussey, and John Howard

*F*or many baby boomers and others, this romantic comedy remains a perennial favorite. It's a love story of a mismatched couple who discovers, the second time around, that they are really meant for each other.

Sparkling dialogue, smooth acting, and gilt-edged production values make this a most memorable movie. (This classic would later be transformed into the 1956 screen musical *High Society*, with Bing Crosby, Grace Kelly, and Frank Sinatra.)

After spending much of the 1930s playing eccentric, strong-minded women, Hepburn returned to the screen with a softer movie image. In *The Philadelphia Story* she is much more openly feminine, congenial, vulnerable, and romantic. Not that her Tracy Lord is any walk in the park. She is bright and earnest but unforgiving of anyone who breaks the moral strictures she holds so dear. Unwilling to deal with her playboy husband's (Grant) frailties—drinking too much, not settling down to "important" work—that marriage fell apart. Now this Philadelphia socialite is to wed a stuffy, self-made man (Howard). Cary shows up at her family's expensive suburban home bent on preventing her from making this error of judgment. Meanwhile, reporters from a national gossip magazine have wormed their way into Hepburn's home to cover the pending high-society nuptials and to uncover the dirt concerning the father's indiscretions.

At first repulsed by the media intruders (Stewart and Hussey), Katharine becomes entranced with James when she learns he is a fine book writer. As for Ruth, she has long been in love with her coworker, but the situation has never been ripe for their romance to develop openly. Stewart (who won an Oscar for his performance) makes a play for Katharine but soon realizes that if they pursue a romance, her money would stand between them. By then, pompous John has

Words to the Wise

In assessing his indiscretions in middle age, the heroine's father (John Halliday) observes, "What most wives fail to realize is that their husbands' philandering has nothing whatsoever to do with them."

Meanwhile, Halliday's society matron wife, who has taken his romantic dabbling most personally, sighs, "Now I have my self-respect but *no* husband."

broken his wedding plans with Katharine. But that's no problem. Cary has been waiting for this opportunity and tells Hepburn the marriage ceremony will go on as planned, but he will be the groom.

This delightful story could happen to any of us—that is *if* we were wealthy and to the manor born, had a house full of colorful relatives, and had a love partner smart enough not to give up on us. We can dream, can't we?

Father of the Bride

Metro-Goldwyn-Mayer, 1950, black-and-white, 92 minutes
Director: Vincente Minnelli
Cast: Spencer Tracy, Joan Bennett, Elizabeth Taylor, Don Taylor, and Billie Burke

*I*f any movie should be required viewing for a wedding couple, this is it. Despite the exaggeration of situations for comic effect, it captures the nuances of the escalating hysteria so often involved in planning and executing the nuptials, during which the real purpose of the wedding (i.e., the future husband and wife being joined in matrimony) gets lost among the many details and petty squabbles. This picture is also a telling essay on how the bond between father and daughter is altered—yet, one hopes, strengthened—by her becoming an adult and part of another man's household.

One evening, Elizabeth Taylor, the daughter of attorney Tracy and his wife Bennett, announces that she intends to marry Don Taylor. Joan is thrilled, but Spencer has his doubts about the man's family. However, after meeting his perspective in-laws he allows that they are "regular" people. As the wedding plans take shape, Tracy is aghast as what started out to be a small, intimate occasion blossoms into a huge church wedding with a large reception to follow at Spencer's home. One crisis after another is resolved, including a spat between the newlyweds-to-be as to where they should honeymoon. By now, the father of the bride is terribly concerned that every last detail be perfect, and by the big day, he is frazzled. To his amazement—and everyone else's pleasure—the wedding proceeds successfully. After the young couple has rushed off for the honeymoon and the last guests have departed, an exhausted but happy Tracy and Bennett can finally sit down and relax.

This exceedingly popular film led to a sequel (1951's *Father's Little Dividend*). Forty years later, Steve Martin, Diane Keaton, and

In *Father of the Bride* (1950), Elizabeth Taylor excitedly opens wedding gifts while her household looks on: (left to right) Marietta Canty, Spencer Tracy, Tom Irish, Rusty Tamblyn, and Joan Bennett.   Courtesy of JC Archives

Kimberly Williams starred in the remake of *Father of the Bride*. The three reprised their roles for *Father of the Bride Part II* (1995).

Father Knows Best

By the finale of *Father of the Bride*, Tracy's Stanley T. Banks has survived the traumas of his daughter's marriage festivities. Contentedly, he tells the viewer: "Nothing's really changed, has it? You know what they say: my son's my son till he gets him a wife, but my daughter's my daughter all of her life. All of our life."

The Catered Affair

Metro-Goldwyn-Mayer, 1956, black-and-white, 93 minutes
Director: Richard Brooks
Cast: Bette Davis, Ernest Borgnine, Debbie Reynolds, Barry Fitzgerald, and Rod Taylor

With Gore Vidal adapting Paddy Chayefsky's 1955 teleplay for the screen, *The Catered Affair* boasts a most literate script. There is novelty in seeing Davis in such an unglamorous role as a frumpy, Irish, middle-aged woman and in watching Reynolds, usually confined to musicals, providing a solid dramatic performance. On the other hand, the drab setting is a constant downer. Most of the action takes place in the cramped Bronx apartment of Bette and her cab driver husband (Borgnine), which they share with their two children (Reynolds and Ray Stricklyn) plus Davis's cranky old uncle (Fitzgerald).

The movie traces the financial and emotional repercussions involved as the groom's family insist on expanding the size and quality of the wedding festivities and a perplexed Borgnine wonders how he will pay for the big day. Tempers flare as Debbie and Rod feel pressured by the situation, especially by Bette who has invested so much emotionally in making this day a very important event for her only daughter. Eventually, the two assert themselves and demand that the major plans be canceled and that, instead, they have a simple church wedding and a tiny wedding dinner thereafter. As Davis and Borgnine head to the church, their relationship has been renewed. The various crises and arguments

Wedding Advice

In *The Catered Affair*, hardworking housewife Davis counsels her no-nonsense but bubbly daughter (Reynolds) on the meaning and expectations of getting married:

- "Don't get married thinking it's only a good time. It's not a bad time, but it's not a good time—living all your life with one man and struggling to bring up the children decent."

- "One day you'll find out a lot of time has gone by and you'll wake up knowing this is the way it's always going to be—just like this, day after day, year after year. Just the same. And that's why being married is such a big thing."

Real-Life Honeymooners

Before starting *The Catered Affair*, costar **Debbie Reynolds (b. 1932)** married singer **Eddie Fisher (b. 1928)** at Grossingers, a Catskills resort, in September 1955. At the time of the highly publicized event, they were America's sweethearts, each of them being enormously popular with the public.

brought about by Debbie's wedding plans have prompted them to air many personal grievances, and they feel better prepared to face the future together.

As the flip side to *Father of the Bride* (1950), *The Catered Affair* is somber, sometimes slow going. A hard life has weathered both Davis and Borgnine, and they, in turn, weigh us down emotionally with their solemn overreactions to the wedding and their efforts to resolve domestic problems. It makes one thankful for the presence here of pert and optimistic Reynolds. But are we sure she's really this couple's offspring? I didn't catch any family resemblance in looks or spirit, but hey, that's Hollywood.

Debbie Reynolds models her wedding gown for her mother (Bette Davis) in *The Catered Affair* (1956).

Courtesy of JC Archives

The Pleasure of His Company

Paramount, 1961, color, 115 minutes
Director: George Seaton
Cast: Fred Astaire, Debbie Reynolds, Lilli Palmer, Tab Hunter, and Gary Merrill

*S*ophisticated screen fare like this has unfortunately virtually disappeared from our landscape. Few families could hope to be (or want to be) as theatrically eccentric, loving, and convivial as this frothy clan, but a movie is allowed some liberties.

Learning that his daughter (Reynolds) is planning to marry, globe-trotting playboy Astaire returns to San Francisco after a fifteen-year absence. Debonair, charming, and self-indulgent, he quickly turns his ex-wife's (Palmer) household upside down to suit his whims. Soon he has agitated Lilli and aggravated her wealthy second husband (Merrill) but beguiled twenty-something Debbie. Suave Fred is more bemused than approving of her marriage choice—a rather dull, unsophisticated rancher (Hunter). His reaction to Tab rubs off on Reynolds, who is so captivated by her carefree dad that she announces that the wedding is called off and she plans to accompany her parent around the world and care for him in his senior years. Proud, vain Astaire is alarmed by her pigeonholing him as on the threshold of "old age." He insists the nuptials go forward as intended. As for him, he takes off on another adventure, accompanied by the household's manservant (Harold Fong).

As Astaire departs for glamorous destinations unknown, one can easily imagine his Pogo Poole someday encountering Rosalind Russell's zany character from 1958's *Auntie Mame* in some exotic port of call with these two unique figures making sweet music together. Between cocktails they might well discuss the folly of self-centered individuals who interfere so recklessly with their offspring's domestic situation.

The Graduate

Embassy, 1967, color, 105 minutes
Director: Mike Nichols
Cast: Anne Bancroft, Dustin Hoffman,
Katharine Ross, William Daniels, and
Murray Hamilton

*M*any people remember this very successful black comedy because of its
generational-gap love affair between a recent
college graduate (Hoffman) and the married
Bancroft. (She is one of his parents' friends

and of their age.) Other fans best recall the
film's wry line delivered by a character (Walter Brooke) as he gives Dustin a hot career
tip: "I just want to say one word to you—just
one word. . . . *Plastics.*" Also emblazoned on
people's memories is the story line's bizarre
church wedding sequence.

Returning to Los Angeles after graduating
from a noted Eastern college, Hoffman is
given a big celebratory party by his pleased
parents. One of the guests (Anne) asks Dustin
to drive her home. Once there she attempts to
seduce him, but they are interrupted by the

Dustin Hoffman and Katharine Ross have an emotional setback in *The Graduate* (1967).   Courtesy of JC Archives

Once a Player

In his earlier years, **Dustin Hoffman (b. 1937)**, who has been twice married, was quite girl crazy and reportedly enjoyed many flings. Speaking of his past romantic inclinations, the Oscar-winning star has said:

- "There used to be a time when it was impossible for me to have a woman friend if we weren't lovers."

- "I've [always] been attracted to women who were working behind counters—salesgirls, working girls, waitresses—rather than rich women who go shopping every day."

Dustin and together they escape aboard a passing bus.

A word of caution: if you envision duplicating Hoffman's last-minute rescue of your girlfriend/bride-to-be, you need to be prepared. Be sure that the ceremony is taking place at a church with an accessible crucifix positioned nearby so you can jam it into the church's door and stop the wedding party from pursuing you and the "kidnapped" bride. Also, check with the local public transit company. You want to time your escape with the passing by of a bus that you and your girlfriend can quickly board. Oops. Don't forget to have exact change handy as well.

sounds of her husband's car pulling into the driveway. Before long, Hoffman is involved in an affair with predatory Bancroft, but the novelty soon wears thin for him. Meanwhile, his parents set him up on a date with Anne's daughter (Ross), and he soon comes to care for her greatly. A vengeful Anne spills the beans, and a disgusted Katharine returns to college at Berkeley. Thereafter, her parents push their daughter into wedding a conventional student (Brian Avery) she's been dating. Increasingly hysterical, Dustin finally discovers where the wedding is to take place. He reaches the Santa Barbara church just as the final vows are being said. He screams out his beloved's name, much to the shock of the wedding party and guests. Despite her parents' best effort to stop her, Ross rushes to

A Wedding

Twentieth Century-Fox, 1978, color, 125 minutes
Director: Robert Altman
Cast: Carol Burnett, Desi Arnaz Jr., Amy Stryker, Vittorio Gassman, and Geraldine Chaplin

Trying to replicate the success of *Nashville* (1975), filmmaker Altman assembled here an impressive cast (which also includes silent screen veteran Lillian Gish and such movie personalities as Lauren Hutton, Nina Van Pallandt, and Dina Merrill). This potpourri concerns the intermingling and clashing of two families as they gather for the nuptials of Arnaz Jr. and Stryker. Anal retentive wedding planner Chaplin is aghast when

Desi Arnaz Jr. and Amy Stryker are the focal couple in the ensemble drama *A Wedding* (1978).

Courtesy of JC Archives

forth reveal the true nature of the diverse wedding guests. Late that evening the bride's parents (Burnett and Paul Dooley) discover their girl is pregnant by Desi and depart in disgust. When they encounter a fatal traffic accident seemingly involving the newlyweds, they rush back to the groom's family home. There, amidst recriminations, arguments, and compromise, the two factions are relieved to discover that the fatalities were "only" two wedding guests and not the bride and groom. With family differences adjusted and accepted, life goes on for everyone.

Pray real hard that you never have such a collection of troublesome, self-centered relatives as those who are depicted in this celluloid exercise.

My Best Friend's Wedding

TriStar, 1997, color, 105 minutes
Director: P. J. Hogan
Cast: Julia Roberts, Dermot Mulroney, Cameron Diaz, Rupert Everett, and Philip Bosco

*W*hat should you do if you discover your best friend and former lover is about to marry another? If you are Roberts, you rush to Mulroney's side in Chicago when he begs you to attend the celebration and help him through his nervousness about the event. By the time she arrives on the scene, Julia is convinced she still loves Dermot and is determined to break up the pending nuptials. But

nothing goes according to schedule. Besides all the guests being extremely late for the reception because of delays during the church service, Gish, the matriarch of the groom's family, dies upstairs. (Her passing is kept a secret for a time so the festivities will not be spoiled.)

As the crowded reception proceeds, chaos reigns as romantic intrigues, snobbism, and so

she has not counted on his wealthy fiancée (Diaz) being such a nice (as well as flinty) person. Every creative scheme that Roberts undertakes to split up the couple only backfires. In desperation, she summons her gay friend (Everett), whom she introduces to everyone as her fiancé. Charming as Rupert is—and he steals the movie—his presence doesn't make Mulroney sufficiently jealous. Damn! After additional stabs at turning Dermot against Cameron, Julia's manipulation works. But by now, Roberts regrets her machinations and explains the truth to the couple. She urges them to marry as planned, and she is on hand at the reception, dancing happily with Everett.

No matter how hard this pleasant but contrived outing tries to make our Julia seem like her usual lovable onscreen self, her character's dirty deeds do not suggest that she is really, at

heart, a trustworthy, honorable soul. My suggestion: when planning your wedding, do *not* add her to the guest list, and in your own real life, be wary of former steady dates.

The Best Man

Universal, 1999, color, 120 minutes
Director: Malcolm D. Lee
Cast: Taye Diggs, Nia Long, Morris Chestnut, Harold Perrineau Jr., and Terrence Howard

*M*ade by filmmaker Spike Lee's cousin, this ensemble piece is a smooth dissection of what happens to the principals and guests during the hectic weekend of a wedding. Established author Diggs arrives in New York to serve as best man for Chestnut's marriage to Monica Calhoun. Unbeknownst to him, Long, a TV producer, has already circulated proofs of his new book, a semiautobiographical work that has thinly veiled accounts about several of those attending the festivities. Even more disturbing to Morris is his realization that the book discloses that Taye and Monica once hooked up sexually. All of this leads to endless friction before Diggs convinces Chestnut to go through with the planned ceremony. By now, Taye realizes it is his girlfriend (Sanaa Lathan) whom he loves —and not feisty Nia—so he proposes to Lathan.

Although several of the African American characters presented border on stereotypes

A Tiny Little Favor

There's scarcely a wedding in history that has run entirely smoothly. In *My Best Friend's Wedding*, the groom (Mulroney) gets a surprising request from a past love (Roberts):

Michael, I love you. I've loved you for nine years. I've just been too arrogant and scared to realize it, and . . . well now I'm just scared. So, I realize this comes at a very inopportune time, but I really have this gigantic favor to ask of you. Choose me. Marry me. Let me make you happy. Oh, that sounds like three favors, doesn't it?

(but not enough to be politically incorrect) and handsome Diggs isn't that credible as a writer, the dialogue is sufficiently tart to compensate for these failings. But why does the script leave pretty, ambitious Long alone at the finale? In real life, she would be high on the priority list for any available (single) male.

My Big Fat Greek Wedding

Lions Gate, 2002, color, 96 minutes
Director: Joel Zwick
Cast: Nia Vardalos, John Corbett, Michael Constantine, Lainie Kazan, and Andrea Martin

"*Y*ou better get married soon. You're starting to look old." This is the unvarnished advice Greek restaurant owner Constantine tosses at his frumpy thirty-year-old daughter (Vardalos). She accepts his practical advice with bitter resignation, wondering when the right man will ever come along. But things pick up for her when she escapes from her job as a "seating hostess" at the family eatery and goes to work for her aunt (Martin) who operates a travel agency. Motivated by her new independence, Nia revamps her outfits and look (e.g., getting rid of her ugly glasses in favor of contact lenses; restyling her straggly, matted hair; using makeup). She emerges a radiant youngish woman. As if by divine intervention, one of her customers is handsome, congenial high school teacher Corbett

It's All Greek to Me

In the course of *My Big Fat Greek Wedding*, we are presented a minitutorial on Greek culture and, in particular, on marriage:

- "The men may be the head of the house, but the women are the neck, and they can turn the head any way they want."

- "Greek women, we may be lambs in the kitchen, but we are tigers in the bedroom."

Not to be forgotten is a cardinal rule enunciated by the lead character early on in the narrative. She relates that Greek woman have three purposes in life: to marry a Greek, to have Greek children, and to feed everyone till the day she dies.

(who happens to be a vegetarian, which makes her family think he is a Martian). Before long, the shy couple falls in love. They announce their plans to wed, which launches tremendous rejoicing from her large array of immigrant relatives but meets with mild disdain from his straight-laced WASP parents. Following a prenuptial party in which the two contrasting families must coexist and eat, and eat, and dance (urged on by Kazan as the Greek earth mother), the much-heralded wedding occurs. The heroine's dreams have finally come true as she and Corbett bring up their children sharing the ethnic cultures of both sides of the family.

Promoted with the catchphrase, "Love is here to stay . . . so is her family," *My Big Fat Greek Wedding* is based on the play and screenplay by Vardalos, a former member of Chicago's Second City improvisational troupe. Made for $5 million, this feel-good sleeper gained tremendous word of mouth and went on to gross well over $240 million in domestic distribution.

With her miraculous transformation, I wondered why this picture's heroine didn't choose to open an Image Transformation franchise. Rarely has a film character since Bette Davis in *Now, Voyager* (1942) gone through such a physical change as Toula Portokalos. There must be something in baklava that produces such changes for very special, worthy people.

With all of this in mind, if you still have the fortitude to go the route of a fancy wedding rather than eloping, you are a brave soul willing to test the good graces of the fates. On second thought, maybe, maybe, you just might want to reconsider the virtues of the single life. That way you'll never have to share the TV remote control. (Or, if you do go the marriage route, be a big spender and invest in two TVs and/or two fully loaded remote controls.)

20

Marriages on the Rocks

*I*t used to be in the United States that when a couple married it was "forever." However, that tradition has long gone the way of the nickel candy bar. Poof! Concepts on the sanctity (and necessity) of matrimony became much looser in twentieth-century America. In turn, attitudes (and laws) regarding divorce become much more liberal as to requirements for when a husband and wife sever their once-binding relationship, make custody provisions if children are involved, divide their assets, and so forth. By the early

Hello—Good-Bye

Hollywood's fast-paced lifestyle has long been ahead of the national curve in America, and that includes celebrities walking down the marriage aisle and then having a near-immediate change of heart. Here are some of the shortest marriages on record in the history of Tinseltown.

Rudolph Valentino—Jean Acker	1 day	Wallace Beery—Gloria Swanson	3 weeks
Felipe de Alba—Zsa Zsa Gabor	8 days	Ludlow Ogden Smith—	
Dennis Hopper—Michelle Phillips	8 days	Katharine Hepburn	3 weeks
Dennis Rodman—Carmen Electra	9 days	Gig Young—Kim Schmidt	3 weeks
Gregg Allman—Cher	10 days	Burt Lancaster—June Ernst	1 month
Robert Evans—		Jeremy Thomas—Drew Barrymore	1 month
Catherine Oxenberg	12 days	Ernest Borgnine—Ethel Merman	38 days
Michael Tell—Patty Duke	13 days	Sammy Davis Jr.—Loray White	2 months

twenty-first century, with an increasing number of couples choosing to live together without bothering to get married officially, the idea of divorce no longer seems so unthinkable to the public at large.

That's not to say that splitting apart a domestic union of whatever length isn't often painful to one or both of the parties involved. However, the moral stigma that used to be attached to divorce is long gone. The increasing frequency of divorces in the United States has spawned industries ranging from lawyers specializing in divorce to such TV shows as *Divorce Court.* (I'm also sure that out there somewhere a greeting card company has created a special line of merchandise devoted to acknowledging that specific change of lifestyle.)

Over the decades, Hollywood has reflected—and to a degree even shaped—moviegoers' thoughts on the holy bonds of matrimony and the process involved in a divorce. Films dealing with the splitting up of a once-"happy" couple provide great opportunities for scripters to write poignant, throat-choking scenes as the realities of a divorce hit the principal characters. On the other hand, for some couples, a divorce comes as a great relief and allows the characters to engage in new emotional/sexual relationships (if they haven't already). This can provide the grist for amusing situations as the once couple vie merrily (or viciously) with one another to be the first to find a new mate and/or ensure that their former love partner has a hell of a time making a new romantic connection.

♥ ♥ ♥ ♥ ♥

A Bill of Divorcement

RKO, 1932, black-and-white, 70 minutes
Director: George Cukor
Cast: John Barrymore, Billie Burke, Katharine Hepburn, David Manners, and Henry Stephenson

*I*n her screen debut Hepburn has a whopper of a dramatic challenge with her complex characterization. She is a young British adult who, on Christmas Day, suddenly comes face-to-face with the father (Barrymore) she has never known. (He has spent the past twenty years in a mental asylum.) Not only must they deal with the awkwardness of getting to know one another, but Katharine is in for a further jolt. She'd been told for years by her mother (Burke) that her dad was institutionalized because he had suffered shell shock

The Great Lover

Known as "the Great Profile," **John Barrymore (1882–1942)** also was prodigious in his love of booze and women. Between many brief affairs—or vice versa—he wed four times. His last trip down the wedding aisle was to his very young actress protégé Elaine (Jacobs) Barrie. Their union lasted four stormy years before she divorced him in late 1940 on grounds of cruelty.

Father (John Barrymore) and daughter (Katharine Hepburn) have a traumatic reunion in *A Bill of Divorcement* (1932).   Courtesy of JC Archives

informs her fiancé (Manners) that they must not marry because she dares not risk having children who could inherit the family strain of insanity. What is then to be Hepburn's fate? She nobly agrees to become her father's caregiver, an assignment that will end only with his eventual death.

Modern science and psychiatric specialists might dispute the genetic theories put forth in this second of three movie versions of Clemence Dane's play (1921). However, the dramatic impact of the story premise can't be beat for teary film fare. Martyrdom permeates the screen as Hepburn gallantly informs her perplexed mother, "I'm very like father. . . . Father is my job, not yours." Just as the bill of divorce has freed the matron of her legal obligations to her past husband, so this legal split up of a family creates a new one for the loving offspring now committed to a life of selfless giving. (Of course, left unsaid is what this character will be like decades later after her father's passing. Poor lady!)

on the front lines during World War I. Now she learns the bitter truth: insanity runs in his side of the family.

In a whirlwind of emotional repercussions, resilient Hepburn suddenly understands her new obligations in life. First of all, there is the matter of her mother. Billie has just finalized her divorce from John and now plans to wed her suitor (Paul Cavanagh). By now Burke's feelings toward her ex-husband are ones of pity rather than love. With Katharine's blessing, the mother follows through on her plans to wed her lawyer beau. As for Katharine, she

The Awful Truth

Columbia, 1937, black-and-white,
90 minutes
Director: Leo McCarey
Cast: Irene Dunne, Cary Grant,
Ralph Bellamy, Alexander D'Arcy, and
Cecil Cunningham

*L*ong before American television's continuously diluting sitcom mentality dribbled

In their divorce hearing, Irene Dunne and Cary Grant (right) fight for custody of their beloved dog, while the stern judge (Paul Stanton) attempts to keep order in the courtroom in *The Awful Truth* (1937).
Courtesy of JC Archives

over into feature films, screen comedies were bright, witty, memorable, and filled with often daffy but very urbane types. At the height of Hollywood's golden age of comedy—the 1930s—came this wacky screwball excursion devoted to a civilized divorce that neither party really wants.

When Grant misunderstands his wife's relationship with her French music teacher (D'Arcy), the wheels of matrimonial breakup grind into motion. Meanwhile, she is suspicious of her dapper husband's mysterious disappearance for the past two weeks. He claims he was in Florida, but there's no evidence to prove it. Before long, they are in divorce court, with the only major ground for contention being who will gain custody of their cute little dog, Mr. Smith. In short order, pert

Irene sails out of the proceedings with Mr. Smith and several congratulatory baskets of fruits from her friends in tow. Soon she has a new beau, a homegrown Texan (Bellamy) whom Grant ridicules at every occasion. (By now Cary's not so sure that the divorce was a good idea.) Not to be outdone in the getting-even sweepstakes, when Grant becomes engaged to an heiress (Molly Lamont), Dunne shows up at Molly's swanky home pretending to be Cary's sister from down South. She acts as vulgarly as possible hoping to destroy her ex's pending nuptials. It works. Before long, the duo, whose divorce has yet to come final, is traipsing off to a mountain cabin where, thanks to fate and a few script contrivances, they are happily reunited.

Few of us possess the breeziness and charm of Grant and Dunne, and we certainly don't have a battery of scriptwriters to feed us amusing and clever dialogue. Therefore, it's pretty clear that it would be unlikely for you to duplicate *The Awful Truth* in your own life should your love relationship break up.

The Women

Metro-Goldwyn-Mayer, 1939, black-and-white, and color, 132 minutes
Director: George Cukor
Cast: Norma Shearer, Joan Crawford, Rosalind Russell, Mary Boland, and Paulette Goddard

At the start of this urbane comedy involving several females whose lives intertwine, Shearer learns that her spouse is playing around with another woman. While she considers the options for herself and her young daughter (Virginia Weidler), her society matron mother (Lucile Watson) warns, "Don't confide in your girlfriends. . . . If you let them advise you, they'll see to it in the name of friendship that you lose your husband and your home."

The loss of husband and home almost occurs for several established and rising stars in this stellar showcase. (One of the film's gimmicks is to have no males in the cast of characters.) It is learned that Norma's successful businessman spouse is going through a midlife crisis, which has led him to hook up with mercenary department store clerk Crawford. Reflecting on the repercussions from male menopause, Watson, a bastion of tart information, sighs, "We women are so much more sensible. When we tire of ourselves, we change the way we do our hair or hire a new cook or—or decorate the house. I suppose a man could do over his office, but he never thinks of anything so simple."

Several catfights later, battle-weary Joan admits defeat in combating Shearer and her pack of friends, telling them, "There's a name for you ladies, but it isn't used in high society—outside of a kennel." At the wrap-up, Norma enthusiastically returns to her errant but remorseful husband. She admits freely that in forgiving his transgressions, she is showing "No pride at all. That's a luxury a woman in love can't afford."

The wonderful performances and its smart film style aside, feminists should hate this picture, which is structured around the outmoded premise that a man is king and his wife thrives only by the grace of His Majesty.

Penny Serenade

Columbia, 1941, black-and-white,
125 minutes
Director: George Stevens
Cast: Irene Dunne, Cary Grant,
Beulah Bondi, Edgar Buchanan, and
Eva Lee Kuney

*I*n the era before artificial insemination and other scientific methods of helping to

When the Fat Lady Has Sung

In one of the more emotional peaks of *Penny Serenade*, a woeful Dunne says to her husband (Grant): "But we don't need each other any more. When that happens to two people, there's nothing left." Summing up that their marriage appears to be over, she analyzes, "When something came along that hit us hard enough, we couldn't face it together."

What a vibrant commentary on a domestic union gone flat.

create babies, if a woman was barren, she felt life had cheated her and that she was failing to fulfill her part of the marriage bargain. By the early 1940s when this picture was made, the relatively new idea that a couple could adopt with no stigma attached to the process or to the youngster was gaining currency with the general public. *Penny Serenade* is an ode to a marriage derailed by tragedies involving offspring. A drama with comedic interludes, it is the third and final screen teaming of the magical Dunne and Grant.

Told in flashback as a saddened wife (Irene) plays recordings of songs that were important during her courtship and marriage to Cary, she relives the chapters of their relationship. It all began when she was a music store clerk and met her husband-to-be, a journalist. The couple soon wed and then, months later, she joins him in Japan where he is on assignment as a news correspondent. Previously uninterested in children, he is jubilant that she is now pregnant. However, during an earthquake she suffers a miscarriage and, thereafter, is unable to have children.

Grant and Dunne relocate to Rosalia, California, where Grant operates a small newspaper. Struggling to survive financially, they finally agree to adopt a child (Kuney). However, after a few years of joy, the girl dies from a sudden ailment. Distraught, the two become strangers to one another and, finally, Irene decides to leave Grant. While Cary makes a fresh effort to patch up their marriage, the orphanage phones with news that they have a new youngster for the couple to adopt. Anticipating a fulfilling future, the couple abandons all plans to separate.

This tear-inducing entry is what used to be called a four-hankie weeper. Watching it anew, one can only wonder what wild directions this tender tale would have taken if the songs Dunne reminisces over were not sentimental love ballads of the 1920s and 1930s but, rather, the hip-hop and rock material of today. It boggles the mind.

Payment on Demand

RKO, 1951, black-and-white, 90 minutes
Director: Curtis Bernhardt
Cast: Bette Davis, Barry Sullivan, Jane Cowl, Kent Taylor, and Betty Lynn

*M*ade after Davis's glory days at Warner Bros. were over and before her sensa-

I Should Have Tried Harder

In a memorable moment within *Payment on Demand*, divorced Davis tells her marriage-bound daughter (Lynn): "Don't try too hard to make him something else. If you love a man and lose him you might think it would make you an individual again. You might think that being alone again would make you a person. It doesn't. You're nobody."

tional comeback in *All About Eve* (1950 but not released until after *Payment on Demand*), this feature suffers from being more ambitious than its script or settings allow. Nevertheless, it is a riveting examination of how well-to-do women cope with loneliness after divorce in a world that they perceive has no place for an unmarried matron.

After helping her lawyer husband (Sullivan) become successful in his career and raising their two daughters, Bette discovers that her disgruntled spouse wants a divorce and to end this "whole meaningless mess." In flashback she recalls the struggle they had to make a go of life and the aggressiveness with which she tackled any problem confronting them. Davis moves from shock to anger when she learns that Barry has been seeing another woman (Frances Dee) and threatens to use evidence of his affair to ruin him in court. Anxious to cut his losses, he agrees to her excessive demands regarding the divorce settlement.

Later, having tasted the empty life offered (then) to a single, middle-aged woman with too much time and money on her hands, Bette would give anything to have another chance at her dissolved marriage. Breaking down into tears, she confesses to her ex-spouse: "I'm finding out how miserable it is to be alone. I'm finding out how much a part of you I was."

Being tough but vulnerable was Davis's stock-in-trade oncamera, and no one could suffer as nobly (or dramatically) as this movie queen. However, wouldn't it have been nice if, between her hard-nosed approach to her marriage and her social climbing, this blemished screen heroine could have done meaningful charity work, gone back to school, or even—heaven help us—take a job as a sensible solution to her loneliness.

Who's Afraid of Virginia Woolf?

Warner Bros., 1966, black-and-white, 132 minutes
Director: Mike Nichols
Cast: Elizabeth Taylor, Richard Burton, George Segal, and Sandy Dennis

*I*t was major news when real-life marrieds Taylor and Burton were signed to costar in the screen adaptation of Edward Albee's remarkable Broadway play (1962). At thirty-four, Elizabeth was a decade or so too young for her role as the foulmouthed yet seductive

> *Top This*
>
> In a moment of pique, the inebriated Taylor zings at her sloshed spouse (Burton), "I swear if you existed, I'd divorce you."

wife, and Richard was obviously British in a part constructed for a middle-aged American. Nevertheless, they successfully managed the assignment. In the process, Taylor won her second Oscar. The picture itself is a grueling depiction of a twenty-year union corroded by smashed dreams, cruel habits, and the frustrations of being caught in an intensifying stalemate with life.

On the campus of New Carthage College in New England, middle-aged Richard—an associate professor of history—and his shrewish wife (Elizabeth)—the daughter of the college's president—are embroiled in another late-night squabble. By now their battle ritual includes being drunk and being, by turn, maudlin, vicious, and lewd. Breaking into this latest skirmish are Segal, an ambitious newcomer to the chemistry department, and his whiny, overly obliging wife (Dennis). The latter could easily be a poster child for passive-aggressive behavior.

During the early hours of the morning, Taylor and Burton treat their perplexed, increasingly drunk guests to cruel parlor games ("Humiliate the Host," "Hump the Hostess," and "Get the Guests"). Each of these pastimes is a sadistic exercise in psychological torment that leads the participants to

Elizabeth Taylor and Richard Burton play out another round in their ongoing domestic war in *Who's Afraid of Virginia Woolf?* (1966).   Courtesy of JC Archives

dredge up their darkest fears and dankest character traits. In the most brutal emotional assault of all, Richard, the perpetual weakling, gets revenge on Elizabeth (for having fornicated upstairs with Segal). He destroys the myth of their imaginary child. This fictitious offspring had provided the couple with a common meeting ground, scapegoat, and means of emotional self-protection in coping with one another. By "burying" their nonexistent son, Richard is forcing the twosome to face each other squarely and honestly. It puts Elizabeth, exhausted from the night's warfare,

into a deeply vulnerable mood. Thus, when he sings the title line of "Who's Afraid of Virginia Woolf," a parody of the children's song about the big bad wolf, she weakly replies, "I am."

There are more (emotional) punches delivered in this drama than in a heavyweight boxing championship match. One wonders if the Hollywood love team playing these roles appreciated how much their real life would come to resemble the fussin', feudin', and fightin' George and Martha of this screen drama.

Divorce, American Style

Columbia, 1967, color, 109 minutes
Director: Bud Yorkin
Cast: Dick Van Dyke, Debbie Reynolds, Jason Robards Jr., Jean Simmons, and Van Johnson

*N*ominated for an Oscar in the Best Original Screenplay category, this wry commentary on the mod, mad 1960s was coscripted by Norman Lear (*All in the Family, Maude*). Rambunctious and brazen, this sly comedy examines marriage and divorce from both romantic and economic points of view.

Reynolds thinks that her married life has become stale—that she and Van Dyke don't communicate enough. With the prodding of a marriage counselor and "helpful" friends, the two find themselves in divorce court. Later, Dick's divorced friend (Robards Jr.) suggests that if Van Dyke were to wed Jason's ex (Simmons) and Debbie, in turn, was matched with a new man, that would end troublesome alimony payments for him and Dick. Reynolds is soon paired off with a wealthy used car dealer (Johnson), and Dick and Jean hit it off. One night, however, they visit a nightclub to see Pat Collins, the Hip Hypnotist perform. While in a trance, Deb-

Dick Van Dyke and Debbie Reynolds are the discontented central figures in *Divorce, American Style* (1967).
Courtesy of JC Archives

bie is asked to kiss the one man in the audience she really loves. She picks Dick, which paves the way for a reconciliation. Now Robards Jr., who has a pregnant girlfriend to deal with, tries to team Simmons with Johnson. The games continue.

If only real-life marriages and divorces worked so smoothly and symmetrically, in which every harsh statement is a one-liner joke and everyone ends up happy. Hey, that would be just like the movies.

terrible as a mother to their young son (Henry) and in the most crushing blow tells a stunned Dustin, "I don't love you anymore." Insisting she needs to find herself, she abandons her family. Overnight, a perplexed Hoffman is forced to become a real father, caring for his emotionally wounded offspring, barely keeping his overflowing feelings in check, and trying to cope with a demanding job that he is too distracted to handle.

Fifteen months after she has left them, Meryl contacts Hoffman and says she now wants custody of their son. Dustin retaliates by hiring an expensive divorce attorney (Duff) and enduring an emotionally grueling court hearing in which every aspect of his life is put under scrutiny. Because of the court's traditional partiality to mothers in such cases and because Hoffman has had employment problems trying to be a Mr. Mom, Streep is given custody of their boy. However, in a turnabout, she acknowledges ("I came to take my son home, but I realize he is home") that their child will be better off with the father and bows out of the situation.

Kramer vs. Kramer

Columbia, 1979, color, 105 minutes
Director: Robert Benton
Cast: Dustin Hoffman, Meryl Streep, Jane Alexander, Justin Henry, and Howard Duff

"*Y*ou married the wrong person," Streep tells her husband (Hoffman), a New York ad agency art director. She insists that she's

Dustin Hoffman begs his wife (Meryl Streep) not to leave their marriage and son in *Kramer vs. Kramer* (1979).
Courtesy of JC Archives

Let's forgive the seemingly tacked-on "happy" ending of *Kramer vs. Kramer,* for Hollywood is only providing what most moviegoers demand—an upbeat finale. But what was Meryl honey doing all those months away from New York City? We know that somewhere along the line she acquired a new boyfriend (not seen in the picture), but she doesn't seem to have found herself yet. Couldn't she have enrolled in a few psychology courses at the New School (a bus ride away from the high-rise apartment she shared with Dustin) and maybe tried group therapy and/or a support group? At least Hoffman's character learned something useful from the long ordeal—how to make French toast in a cramped kitchen. Could he possibly have a career on cable TV's Food Network?

Six Degrees of Devastation

It is difficult to say who is enduring more inner pain when the vanished Streep writes a letter to her little boy. It is a painful message that a devastated Hoffman reads aloud to the bewildered child: "I will always be your mommy and I will always love you. But I just won't be your mommy in the house, but your mommy of the heart."

The War of the Roses

Twentieth Century-Fox, 1989, color,
116 minutes
Director: Danny DeVito
Cast: Michael Douglas, Kathleen Turner,
Danny DeVito, Märianne Sagebrecht, and
Sean Astin

The moral of this wild black comedy about an ugly divorce is that materialism can spoil the spirituality of a marriage. After seventeen years wed to a successful attorney (Douglas), Turner, a fledgling caterer, wants out of her marriage. No, she tells her aggrieved spouse, there's not another man— nor a woman—in the picture. She says she knew the relationship was over when he was rushed to the hospital recently with a serious

Michael Douglas plays a vindictive husband engaged in a battle to the finish with his vengeful wife in *The War of the Roses* (1989).

Photo by Albert L. Ortega

Words from the Bar

The War of the Roses is peppered with cynical observations from divorce attorney DeVito:

- "If love is blind, marriage is like having a stroke."

- "When a couple starts keeping score . . . there isn't any winning, there's just degrees of losing."

- "A civilized divorce is a contradiction in terms."

medical emergency (a suspected heart attack), because she felt elated that fate would be giving her a new chance at life on her own.

Thanks to a crafty divorce lawyer (DeVito), Turner gains custody of the couple's prized house, but through a legal technicality, Douglas wins the right to live there as well. The battle lines are drawn as they split the living quarters, each determined to be the aggressor. Friends, household pets, wardrobes, and even

Grounds for Divorce

In *The War of the Roses*, Turner explains her reasons for wanting to divorce Douglas: "When I watch you eat, when I see you asleep, whenever I look at you lately, I just want to smash your face in."

We rest our case.

the furniture all become targets for the deadly combat between the ex-spouses. The finale finds the feuding couple dangling from a chandelier that comes crashing to the ground and ends their escalating warfare. The Roses are no more.

Could this no-holds-barred domestic romp really have been based on the true-life adventures of Roseanne and Tom Arnold?

The Story of Us

Universal, 1999, color, 94 minutes
Director: Rob Reiner
Cast: Michelle Pfeiffer, Bruce Willis, Rita Wilson, Julie Hagerty, and Paul Reiser

*M*uch is artistically wrong with this dissection of a disintegrating marriage, but its creative failures don't overshadow the picture's key theme: the little things in a domestic situation can lead to its breakdown.

After fifteen years together, Los Angeles writer Willis and his wife (Pfeiffer), a crossword puzzle compiler, realize that their life (which includes their two children and a nice home) has become an empty facade. They discuss the problem with their friends (some sympathetic, some wisecracking, all a bit smarmy) and soulfully examine their early years together. While the offspring are at summer camp, the couple tries a trial separation. However, it only proves how unequipped they are to change their lifestyle. By the time the kids return from vacation, Michelle and Bruce have reunited.

A Domestic Rule to Live By

According to Rob Reiner's sardonic character in *The Story of Us*, "Love is just lust in disguise, and lust fades, so you damn well better be with someone who can stand you."

This meandering movie has great parallels to a lackluster domestic relationship: it has two personable leads and starts promisingly, but it then bogs down into stale sameness. There is one cogent remark in the film. Early on, one of the focal characters says, "Fighting became the language of the relationship."

If Hollywood movies on marriages teach us anything, it is to *not* enter into matrimony without a good reserve of witticisms, smart shtick, and hip wardrobe. You must have best friends to confide in (but who never burden you with their own problems). It also helps if you happen to have an available chalet condo in Aspen, Colorado, so that when you decide to rekindle the marriage, you have a great spot for the makeup sex. Oh yes, be sure there is a well-lit mirror in the bathroom. You'll be spending a lot of time staring into it, recollecting moments of first love with your spouse and those years when the storm clouds of disharmony crept into your daily life. But never fear, because, as in most films, everything will end happily ever after for you.

Bibliography

Books

Armstrong, Richard B., and Mary Willems Armstrong. *Encyclopedia of Film Themes, Settings and Series.* Jefferson, N.C.: McFarland, 2001.

Barbour, Alan G., ed. *Screen Ads Monthly.* Kew Gardens, N.Y.: Screen Facts, 1967.

Berlin, Joey, ed. *Toxic Fame: Celebrities Speak on Stardom.* Detroit: Visible Ink, 1996.

Bernard, Jami. *Chick Flicks: A Movie Lover's Guide to the Movies Women Love.* Secaucus, N.J.: Citadel, 1997.

Bernstein, Jonathan. *Pretty in Pink: The Golden Age of Teenage Movies.* New York: St. Martin's, 1997.

Boller, Paul F., Jr., and Ronald L. Davis. *Hollywood Anecdotes.* New York: Ballantine, 1987.

Borsting, Elizabeth. *Celebrity Weddings & Honeymoon Getaways.* Cold Spring Harbor, N.Y.: Open Road, 1998.

Brooks, Tim, and Earle Marsh. *The Complete Directory to Prime Time Network and Cable TV Shows: 1946–Present.* 20th anniversary ed. New York: Ballantine, 1999.

Carabillo, Toni, Judith Melui, and June Bundy Csida. *Feminist Chronicles: 1953–1993.* Los Angeles: Women's Graphics, 1993.

Corey, Melinda, and George Ochoa. *The Dictionary of Film Quotations.* New York: Crown, 1995.

Cott, Nancy F. *Public Vows: A History of Marriage and the Nation.* Cambridge, Mass.: Harvard University Press, 2000.

Craddock, Jim, ed. *VideoHound's Golden Movie Retriever, 2003.* Detroit: Visible Ink, 2002.

Crawley, Tony, compiler/ed. *The Wordsworth Dictionary of Film Quotations.* Ware, Hertfordshire, England: Wordsworth, 1994.

Drop, Mark. *Dateline: Hollywood: Sins and Scandals of Yesterday and Today.* New York: Friedman/Fairfax, 1994.

Editors of Consumer Guide. *Movie Trivia Mania.* New York: Beekman House, 1984.

Gatlin, Rochelle. *American Women Since 1945.* Jackson, Miss.: University Press of Mississippi, 1987.

Geller, Jaclyn. *Here Comes the Bride: Women, Weddings, and the Marriage Mystique.* New York: Four Walls Eight Windows, 2001.

Hadleigh, Boze. *Hollywood Babble On: Stars Gossip About Other Stars.* New York: Perigee, 1995.

Halliwell, Leslie. *Mountains of Dreams: The Golden Years of Paramount Pictures.* New York: Stonehill, 1975.

Hartog, Hendrik. *Man and Wife in America: A History.* Cambridge, Mass.: Harvard University Press, 2000.

Harvey, James. *Romantic Comedy in Hollywood: From Lubitsch to Sturges.* New York: Knopf, 1987.

Haun, Harry. *Movie Quote Book.* New York: Harper, 1983.

Houseman, Victoria. *Made in Heaven.* Chicago: Bonus, 1991.

Hyatt, Wesley. *The Encyclopedia of Daytime Television.* New York: Billboard, 1997.

Jasper, Margaret C. *Marriage and Divorce.* Dobbs Ferry, N.Y.: Oceana, 1994.

Kirkendall, Lester A., and Arthur E. Gravatt, eds. *Marriage and the Family in the Year 2020.* Buffalo, N.Y.: Prometheus, 1984.

Langman, Larry, and Paul Gold. *Comedy Quotes from the Movies.* Jefferson, N.C.: McFarland, 1994.

Lucaire, Ed. *The Celebrity Almanac.* New York: Prentice Hall, 1991.

McClelland, Doug. *Hollywood on Hollywood: Tinseltown Talks.* Boston: Faber & Faber, 1985.

———. *Hollywood Talks Turkey: The Screen's Greatest Flops.* Boston: Faber & Faber, 1990.

———. *Star Speak: Hollywood on Everything.* Boston: Faber & Faber, 1987.

McCoid, Sheridan, ed. *Hollywood Lovers.* London, England: Orion, 1997.

Miller, Frank. *MGM Posters: The Golden Years.* Atlanta: Turner, 1994.

Mingo, Jack, and John Javna. *Primetime Proverbs: The Book of TV Quotes.* New York: Harmony, 1989.

Nowlan, Robert A., and Gwendolyn W. Nowlan. *Film Quotations.* Jefferson, N.C.: McFarland, 1994.

Parish, James Robert. *The Fox Girls.* New Rochelle, N.Y.: Arlington House, 1971.

———. *Hollywood Bad Boys.* Chicago: Contemporary, 2002.

———. *The Hollywood Book of Death.* Chicago: Contemporary, 2001.

———. *Hollywood's Great Love Teams.* New Rochelle, N.Y.: Arlington House, 1974.

————. *The Paramount Pretties*. New Rochelle, N.Y.: Arlington House, 1972.

————. *The RKO Gals*. New Rochelle, N.Y.: Arlington House, 1973.

————. *Today's Black Hollywood*. New York: Kensington, 1995.

Parish, James Robert, and Don E. Stanke. *Hollywood Baby Boomers*. New York: Garland, 1992.

Parish, James Robert, and Gregory Mank. *The Best of MGM: The Golden Years: 1928–1959*. New York: Arlington House/Crown, 1981.

Parish, James Robert, and Lennard DeCarl. *Hollywood Players: The Forties*. New Rochelle, N.Y.: Arlington House, 1976.

Parish, James Robert, and Michael R. Pitts. *The Great Hollywood Musical Pictures*. Metuchen, N.J.: Scarecrow, 1992.

————. *Hollywood Songsters* (2nd ed.). New York: Routledge, 2002.

Parish, James Robert, and Ronald L. Bowers. *The MGM Stock Company: The Golden Era*. New Rochelle, N.Y.: Arlington House, 1973.

Parish, James Robert, and William T. Leonard. *The Funsters*. New Rochelle, N.Y.: Arlington House, 1979.

————. *Hollywood Players: The Thirties*. New Rochelle, N.Y.: Arlington House, 1976.

Petersen, James R. *The Century of Sex: Playboy's History of the Sexual Revolution: 1900–1999*. New York: Grove, 1999.

Quirk, Lawrence J. *The Great Romantic Films*. Secaucus, N.J.: Citadel, 1974.

Rees, Nigel. *Cassell's Movie Quotations*. London, England: Cassell, 2000.

Rich, B. Ruby. *Chick Flicks*. Durham, N.C.: Duke University, 1997.

Robertson, Patrick. *Film Facts*. New York: Billboard, 2001.

Rockport Publishers, ed. *Great Movie Graphics*. Rockport, Mass.: Rockport, 1995.

Rothman, Ellen K. *Hands and Hearts: A History of Courtship in America*. New York: Basic, 1984.

Schreiber, Sandy. *Hollywood Gets Married*. New York: Clarkson Potter, 2002.

Sennett, Ted. *Lunatics and Lovers*. New York: Limelight, 1985.

Shipman, David. *Movie Talk: Who Said What About Whom in the Movies*. New York: St. Martin's, 1989.

Staggs, Sam. *All About "All About Eve."* New York: St. Martin's, 2001.

Stallings, Penny. *Flesh & Fantasy*. New York: Harper & Row, 1989.

Steinberg, Cobbett. *Reel Facts: The Movie Book of Records*, updated ed. New York: Vintage, 1982.

Tropiano, Stephen. *TV Towns*. New York: TV Books, 2000.

Vance, Malcolm. *The Movie Ad Book.* Minneapolis: Control Data, 1981.

Walker, John, ed. *Halliwell's 2002 Film and Video Guide.* London, England: HarperCollins Entertainment, 2001.

Periodicals

Biography
Bridal Guide
Classic Film Collector
Classic Image
Current Biography
Daily Variety
Ebony
Empire
Entertainment Weekly
Film Threat
Filmfax
Films in Review
Films of the Golden Age
Globe
Hollywood Reporter
InStyle
Jet
L.A. Weekly
Los Angeles Daily News
Los Angeles Times
Movie Collectors World

Movieline
National Enquirer
New Times—Los Angeles
New York Daily News
New York Observer
New York Post
New York Times
Newsweek
Parade
People
Playboy
Premiere
Sight & Sound
Star
Time
Total Film
Us Weekly
Vanity Fair
Wedding Pages
Wedding Super Guide
Weddingbells

Internet Websites

All Movie Guide: www.allmovie.com
All Music Guide: www.allmusic.com
E! Entertainment TV Online: www.eonline.com
Internet Movie Database: www.imdb.com

Index

Note: Numbers in bold refer to pages with photographs.

About the Author

James Robert Parish, a former entertainment reporter, publicist, and book series editor, is the author of many published major biographies and reference books of the entertainment industry. These include *Hollywood Divas*, *Jet Li*, *Hollywood Bad Boys*, *The Encyclopedia of Ethnic Groups in Hollywood*, *The Hollywood Book of Death*, *Gus Van Sant*, *Jason Biggs*, *Whoopi Goldberg*, *Rosie O'Donnell's Story*, *The Unofficial "Murder, She Wrote" Casebook*, *Let's Talk! America's Favorite TV Talk Show Hosts*, *The Great Cop Pictures*, *Ghosts and Angels in Hollywood Films*, *Prison Pictures from Hollywood*, *Hollywood's Great Love Teams*, and *The RKO Gals*. Mr. Parish is a frequent oncamera interviewee on cable and network TV for documentaries on the performing arts. He resides in Studio City, California.

James Robert Parish   Photo by Levon

If you have enjoyed *The Hollywood Book of Love*, you will want to read other books by Hollywood chronicler James Robert Parish. You will find out all the juicy details of your favorite celebrities, from their devilish doings, scandalous acts, and their sometimes-sensational final exits.

The Hollywood Book of Death
The Bizarre, Often Sordid, Passings of More than 125 American Movie and TV Idols

The death of a celebrity is often as fascinating as—and sometimes *more* intriguing than—a star's actual life. From the grisly end of Sharon Tate at the hands of the Manson family and the mysterious demise of Bob Crane to the peaceful passings of Lucille Ball and George Burns, *The Hollywood Book of Death* is a captivating and appealingly packaged volume of more than 125 television and movie stars' final curtain calls.

Paperback • 0-8092-2227-2 • $16.95

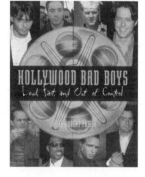

Hollywood Bad Boys
Loud, Fast, and Out of Control

Which legendary rebel was known as "the human ashtray" throughout L.A.'s S&M clubs? Can you count (not on one hand) the number of times Robert Downey Jr. has been sent to the slammer? It's tough to keep track of the many escapades and misadventures of Tinseltown's baddest boys, but with *Hollywood Bad Boys*, celebrity watchers can easily follow the fascinating and detailed accounts of the screen's most infamous rascals and rogues over many scandalous decades.

Paperback • 0-07-138137-6 • $14.95

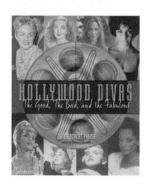

Hollywood Divas
The Good, the Bad, and the Fabulous

From Marilyn Monroe to Madonna, Zsa Zsa Gabor to J. Lo, Drew Barrymore to Elizabeth Taylor, bestselling author James Robert Parish reveals the high jinks of Hollywood's favorite "It Girls," whose overdrives to personal and career excess have earned them the rank of diva. This photo-filled volume delivers an eye-popping, backstage peek into the wild private lives and cutthroat careers of 70 rampaging bad girls of Hollywood.

Paperback • 0-07-140819-3 • $14.95

Find all the dish on your favorite stars in these scintillating titles, available at a bookstore near you.